Information Technology Governance and Service Management:
Frameworks and Adaptations

Aileen Cater-Steel
University of Southern Queensland, Australia

INFORMATION SCIENCE REFERENCE

Hershey · New York

Director of Editorial Content: Kristin Klinger
Senior Managing Editor: Jennifer Neidig
Managing Editor: Jamie Snavely
Assistant Managing Editor: Carole Coulson
Typesetter: Jeff Ash
Cover Design: Lisa Tosheff
Printed at: Yurchak Printing Inc.

Published in the United States of America by
        Information Science Reference (an imprint of IGI Global)
        701 E. Chocolate Avenue, Suite 200
        Hershey PA 17033
        Tel: 717-533-8845
        Fax: 717-533-8661
        E-mail: cust@igi-global.com
        Web site: http://www.igi-global.com

and in the United Kingdom by
        Information Science Reference (an imprint of IGI Global)
        3 Henrietta Street
        Covent Garden
        London WC2E 8LU
        Tel: 44 20 7240 0856
        Fax: 44 20 7379 0609
        Web site: http://www.eurospanbookstore.com

Library of Congress Cataloging-in-Publication Data

Information technology governance and service management : frameworks and adaptations / Aileen Cater-Steel, editor.

p. cm.

Summary: "This book provides an in-depth view into the critical contribution of IT service management to IT governance, and the strategic and tactical value provided by effective service management"--Provided by publisher.

Includes bibliographical references and index.

ISBN 978-1-60566-008-0 (hbk.) -- ISBN 978-1-60566-009-7 (ebook)

1. Information technology--Management. I. Cater-Steel, Aileen, 1954-

HD30.2.I5287 2009

004.068--dc22

                    2008009102

British Cataloguing in Publication Data
A Cataloguing in Publication record for this book is available from the British Library.

All work contributed to this book set is original material. The views expressed in this book are those of the authors, but not necessarily of the publisher.

Table of Contents

Section I
Reviews of IT Governance Research

Chapter I

Sherrena Buckby, Queensland University of Technology, Australia
Peter Best, University of Southern Queensland, Australia
Jenny Stewart, Griffith Business School, Australia

Chapter II

Junghoon Lee, Yonsei University, Korea
Changjin Lee, Yonsei University, Korea

Chapter III

David Musson, Macquarie Graduate School of Management, Sydney, Australia

Section II
IT Governance Case Studies

Chapter IV

Jyotirmoyee Bhattacharjya , The University of Sydney, Australia
Vanessa Chang, Curtin University of Technology, Australia

Section III
IT Governance:
Its Relationship to Business and Other Frameworks

Section IV
IT Service Management Frameworks

Detailed Table of Contents

Section I
Reviews of IT Governance Research

Chapter I

> *Sherrena Buckby, Queensland University of Technology, Australia*
> *Peter Best, University of Southern Queensland, Australia*
> *Jenny Stewart, Griffith Business School, Australia*

Buckby, Best, and Stewart provide a comprehensive understanding of the current state of IT governance literature across five key focus areas: strategic alignment of business and IT systems; delivery of value from IT systems; risk management of IT systems; management of IT resources; and measurement of the performance of IT systems. The objectives are to present a detailed overview of research across the key focus areas of ITG, identify important gaps in ITG research, and to guide future thinking and research on ITG.

Chapter II

> *Junghoon Lee, Yonsei University, Korea*
> *Changjin Lee, Yonsei University, Korea*

This chapter aims to clarify the concept of ITG through conducting a literature review, suggesting some implications of this work for practitioners and indicating directions for the future study of ITG. Most managers acknowledge the importance of managing IT assets within a framework of IT governance (ITG), but only a small number of academic treatments deal with ITG, meaning that businesses often find themselves making their governance decisions in a vacuum.

Chapter III

David Musson, Macquarie Graduate School of Management, Sydney, Australia

This chapter proposes that there are three different concepts that are grouped together as IT governance: IT governance as a framework or audit process; IT governance as IT decision-making; and IT governance as a branch of corporate governance. Through a review of the literature, Musson brings together the disparate views of IT governance so as to permit a broader view of this important subject.

Section II
IT Governance Case Studies

Chapter IV

Jyotirmoyee Bhattacharjya , The University of Sydney, Australia
Vanessa Chang, Curtin University of Technology, Australia

This chapter introduces key IT governance concepts and industry standards and explores their adoption and implementation in the higher education environment. It provides a valuable example to practitioners by demonstrating that IT governance processes, structures, and relational mechanisms adopted by these institutions generate value through improvements in a number of key focus areas for IT management.

Chapter V

Lynne Gerke, University of Tasmania, School of Accounting & Corporate Governance,
Australia
Gail Ridley, University of Tasmania, School of Accounting & Corporate Governance,
Australia

Using a public sector audit office in an Australian state, Gerke and Ridley examine the potential to use an audit program based on the Control Objectives for Information and Related Technologies (CobiT) framework. The results suggest that the CobiT-derived instrument was effective for IT audit, and was able to be tailored to the needs of the organisation, when evaluated against a number of criteria.

Chapter VI

Tony C. Shan, Bank of America, USA
Winnie W. Hua, CTS. Inc, USA

Shan and Hua consider the challenges in managing the complexity in architecture design. They define a methodical approach to effectively manage the complexity in architecture design and rationalize the architectural assets of IT application portfolios in a service-oriented paradigm. The holistic framework provides a multidisciplinary approach of portfolio analysis and service-oriented architecture planning. A case study in the finance industry illustrates the use of this framework in real-world scenarios.

This study compares the IT Governance setups of three large service sector firms in Korea. It seeks to identify the activities, types, and determinants of firms' ITG decision- making processes, and to suggest the basis on which forms of ITG may represent rational selections for given service companies. The proposed and partially validated ITG framework should be useful for further research and practice of ITG.

Chapter VIII

The Australian Standard for the Corporate Governance of Information and Communication Technology (ICT) AS8015 (Standards Australia, 2005) is used as the focus of this chapter. Recommendations are provided to enhance the effective implementation of this Standard's principles within an organisation. These recommendations concern such factors as identifying and addressing issues surrounding the implementation of this Standard and the actions that could be undertaken to improve the effectiveness of ICT governance by sharply focusing upon the governance aspects of ICT within business, as opposed to the management aspect of ICT.

Chapter IX

This case study reports on a major restructure incorporating both CobiT and ITIL principles. As well as describing the new reporting and internal structures of the Division, the alignment of the goals of the Division to the corporate goals is discussed. Care was taken to ensure that the new ICT structure was logical and conducive to operational effectiveness, efficiency and sound ICT governance, and could provide pathways and opportunities for career progression, client-focus, and role delineation and functional accountability.

Section III
IT Governance:
Its Relationship to Business and Other Frameworks

The control frameworks of CobiT and ITIL provide a mapping of organizational roles from the capital interest at the highest level, through to the implementation level in an enterprise system. Security affects all processes within an organization structure and both control frameworks provide varying capability for control at different levels in an organization. In this chapter the security process is mapped from two control frameworks at the strategic layer and the issue of effective management tactics discussed from the theoretical structures within the problem area.

This chapter focuses on the importance of both corporate and IT governance, and demonstrates that IT governance is a very important sub-component of corporate governance. The authors present a framework which should facilitate a strong understanding of the different factors and mechanisms that impact firm governance. A number of interesting empirical results relating to these governance mechanisms are presented with examples that link corporate and IT governance.

The I-Fit research project commenced as a joint activity of a regional ICT consultancy with a university research center. The main goal of the project is to help the consultants to improve alignment between business and IT in the client organizations. The I-Fit project takes the perspective of the business manager: how a business manager can influence and increase the value of the IT services received. The I-Fit model was developed based on the literature on strategic alignment and Information Quality. The model assumes causal relationships between "IT Governance," "Strategic Alignment," "Information Quality," and "Business Performance" in an organization.

This chapter focuses on young Internet-based firms and articulates the knowledge and skills required by IT professionals. Building on the general IT governance principle of aligning business and IT, it introduces an adequate competence model, outlines its dimensions, and suggests a framework for modeling the effects of factors internal and external to the firm on the value propositions of the different dimensions. The authors hope that a comprehensive understanding of the role of IT-related competence will assist founders not only in finding suitable partners, but also in aligning e-business strategy and information technology in Internet-based ventures.

Rogers assesses the role maturity models can play in enterprise IT governance. Frameworks such as the Capability Maturity Model make it possible to assess maturity in key areas. The author describes additional maturity models that have no formal association with a comprehensive framework, the application of which represent significantly less overhead than the larger frameworks that include a maturity model component. The author seeks to present a broad perspective on maturity models that enterprises can use as a preliminary means of evaluating available tools. This overview of maturity models can facilitate the selection of a model to bring about improved IT governance in one or more focus areas.

This chapter aims to bridge the gap between high-level IT governance and software development governance. A model for governance in general is presented and then used to describe IT and software development domain-specific governance. The model is built based on a review of the literature and a set of scenarios. The process of transition to agile software development is used to demonstrate the domain-specific governance schemes.

The aim of this chapter is to alert decision makers to the fact that outsourcing IT incorporates residual risks even when widely recommended operational controls are implemented. After briefly reviewing existing formal governance frameworks and their treatment of IT outsourcing, an analytical model for considering outsourcing benefits and risks is introduced. Some strategic IT governance issues that become critical once a firm outsources a significant proportion of its IT services are highlighted. Effective control processes are necessary, but not sufficient for good corporate governance and those responsible for corporate governance should ensure that both operational and strategic governance issues are considered when IT is substantially outsourced.

Portfolio Management principles are the foundation of building effective governance. This chapter is intended primarily for managers who are preparing to implement portfolio management concepts in an organisation and students of IT Project Management, who wish to understand the difference between Project and Portfolio Management. While there is literature available discussing portfolio management at the conceptual level, there is not enough available which translates these concepts into tactical implementation. Practitioners can benefit from discussing implementation approaches that can be tailored to suit individual needs. This chapter shows one of the many ways to implement a portfolio management framework.

The purpose of this chapter is to help business and information managers to adapt IT management arrangements to suit the organisational context by examining the issues associated with alignment of IT governance and service management, identifying contingencies, and developing a framework. After examining the requirements for IT governance, the organization is considered as a system and competing needs for integration and differentiation within the organisation are examined. The emerging concept of information systems as a contributor of value is also discussed and a framework developed.

Section IV
IT Service Management Frameworks

Chapter XIX

Jon Iden, Norwegian School of Economics and Business Administration, Norway

A real life ITIL project is presented and analysed based on a longitudinal case study. The purpose is to illustrate how the ITIL process reference model for some processes may be used almost as a blueprint, while ITIL for other processes may be profoundly adapted to suit the context and the needs of the implementer. Furthermore, the success factors and the impediments for successful implementation are discussed. This chapter will especially inform practitioners about how ITIL may be utilized and how an implementation project might be organized.

Chapter XX

Neil McBride, De Montfort University, UK

This chapter describes a suggested model for developing a service strategy within IT services. It discusses the content and process of developing an IT service strategy. The example of hospital information systems is used to illustrate the strategic process. In order to set the scene for the strategic process, the state of information systems strategy research is discussed and set in the context of the developing service management research literature. A case is made for a migration from an IT strategy based primarily on the development of a portfolio of IT systems to a service-strategy based on the development of a portfolio of business services.

Chapter XXI

Manuel Mora, Autonomous University of Aguascalientes, Mexico
Ovsei Gelman, Universidad Nacional Autónoma de México, Mexico
Rory O'Connor, Dublin City University, Ireland
Francisco Alvarez, Autonomous University of Aguascalientes, Mexico
Jorge Macias-Luevano, Autonomous University of Aguascalientes, Mexico

A descriptive-conceptual overview of the main models and standards of processes formulated in the Systems Engineering (SE), Software Engineering (SwE) and Information Systems (IS) disciplines is provided. Given the myriad of models and standards reported, the convergence suggested for the SE and SwE models and standards, and the increasing complexity of information systems, the authors argue that these standards become relevant to the IS discipline. Based on the aims and principles identified, the authors report and posit the concepts of process, system and service as conceptual building blocks for describing such models and standards. Initial theoretical and practical implications for the Information Systems discipline of such models and standards are discussed.

Chapter XXII

Perspectives of IT-Service Quality Management: A Concept for Life Cycle Based
Claus-Peter Praeg, University of Stuttgart, Germany
Dieter Spath, University of Stuttgart, Germany

Based on the IT-industrialization and an increased customer orientation in IT-Service management, the aspect of quality becomes increasingly important. This chapter introduces an IT-Service management framework for the use of quality management concepts in the context of the life cycle phases of IT-Services. It argues that IT-Service management, combined with quality management and a life cycle approach for IT-Services provides a new perspective for organizations to provide high quality IT-Services. The aim is to support organizations in the effective use of quality management concepts depending on IT-Service life cycles.

Chapter XXIII

Chee Ing Tiong, HD Digital Solutions, Australia
Aileen Cater-Steel, University of Southern Queensland, Australia
Wui-Gee Tan, University of Southern Queensland, Australia

This study explores financial metrics that organisations could use in measuring the return on investment from their adoption of the IT Infrastructure Library (ITIL) framework. ITIL outlines an extensive set of best practices for IT service management in organizations but as yet there is limited academic research on measuring the return on investment from ITIL adoption. This literature review discusses the importance of measuring return on investment in ITIL and some of the available measurement metrics for IT investment that could be adapted. A measurement model for measuring investment return on ITIL service management is proposed.

Chapter XXIV

Dirk Malzahn, OrgaTech GmbH, Germany

Malzahn describes how models for software development and service delivery can be integrated into a common approach to reach an integrated product life cycle for software. The models include SEI's Capability Maturity Model Integration (CMMI), SPICE (Software Process Improvement and Capability Determination, ISO 15504) and ISO 20000 (Service Management). Whilst the CMMI constellation approach delivers an integration perspective defined in three models (development, acquisition and services), SPICE and ISO 20000 need additional alignment to be usable in an integrated approach.

Foreword

IT governance is one of these concepts that suddenly emerged and became an important issue in the information technology (IT) era. I am not sure as to when the concept surfaced. Gartner introduced the idea of "improving IT governance" for the first time in their Top 10 CIO Priorities for 2003; it was then ranked third. In 1998, the IT Governance Institute[1] was founded to generate awareness of the IT governance concept. In academic and professional literature articles titled with IT governance began to emerge in the late 1990's. In the context of the 2002 Hawaii International Conference of System Sciences (HICSS), I defined IT governance as "*the organisational capacity exercised by the board, executive management and IT management to control the formulation and implementation of IT strategy and in this way ensuring the fusion (alignment) of business and IT*"[2]. During the last six years that I have been involved with this issue, I witnessed that many organizations started with the implementation of IT governance in order to achieve a better alignment between business and IT. Today, because of the pervasive use of technology and in many cases the critical dependency on information technology, IT governance is high on the agenda and many organizations are implementing IT governance practices.

From my practical experience, I have seen that these IT governance implementations are often driven by IT, while one would expect that the business would take a leading role here as well. This leading role of IT appears to be a paradox, but the same thing happened in the era of business process reengineering, where also in many cases IT took a leading role in reinventing the business processes. After many years of work in this field, I have come to the point to acknowledge that IT is likely (or should be) a very good "change agent" in the organization to get these business challenges realised.

IT governance can be deployed using a mixture of various structures, processes, and relational mechanisms. IT governance structures include mechanisms for connecting and enabling contacts between business and IT such as business/IT steering committees. IT governance processes refer to the formalization of business/IT decision making and monitoring such as portfolio management. The relational mechanisms finally are about the collaborative relationship among business and IT such as joint training. Recent PhD studies[3] have studied in detail these IT governance mechanisms and explored their relationship with business/IT alignment, which should ultimately lead to higher business outcomes. Various chapters in this book also contain further research on the relevance of the IT governance practices.

For many years, I have been involved in the development of two leading IT governance frameworks, COBIT and VALIT[4]. Both best practices frameworks are developed by practitioners and originate respectively from the mid-1990's and from 2006. They describe a set of best practices for management, control and security of information technology with COBIT focusing on the IT processes itself and VALIT on the IT related business processes. The growing importance of the COBIT and VALIT frameworks is also acknowledged in this book by several chapters discussing specific issues about these frameworks. As there is still little academic research available around these frameworks, so hopefully this book will initiate further research in this domain.

The important message from both COBIT and VALIT is that IT has to deliver and run applications efficiently and that business value from these applications can only be reached through business change management projects by the business. It is therefore that *business or corporate governance of IT* is probably a better term for IT governance indicating more clearly that IT governance is a joint operation of business and IT and that both have to develop and implement specific processes for this. It is worthwhile to note here that currently an ISO Standard *Corporate Governance of IT* focusing on the business audience is under development.

After all, the crucial question about IT Governance or better Business Governance of IT remains whether IT governance practices can help in generating business value from investments in IT. As already indicated in this foreword, this is a rather complex relationship. Currently, I am conducting within my IT Alignment and Governance (ITAG) Research Institute[5], practice-oriented research on this issue by investigating the relationship between the use of COBIT/VALIT practices and business/IT alignment and ultimately how this impacts business outcome.

I hope that this book may help business and IT practitioners in implementing the right IT governance practices and that it may motivate academics to further research the IT governance implementations and to explore the relationship with business and IT alignment and business outcome.

ENDNOTES

[1]   see www.itgi.org

[2]   Van Grembergen, W. (2002). Introduction to the minitrack: IT governance and its mechanisms. In *Proceedings of the 35th Hawaii International Conference on System Sciences.*

[3]   De Haes, S. (2007). *The impact of IT governance practices on business/IT alignment in the Belgian financial services sector.* University of Antwerp. Bjorn, C. (2007). *Business-ICT alignment. Practices and determinants.* Katholieke Universiteit Leuven.

[4]   see www.isaca.org

[5]   see www.uams.be/itag

Wim Van Grembergen
University of Antwerp (UA)
University of Antwerp Management School (UAMS)

Wim Van Grembergen *is professor at the Business Faculty of UFSIA (University of Antwerp) and is a guest professor at the University of Leuven (KUL). He teaches information systems at the undergraduate and executive level, and researches in business transformations through information technology, audit of information systems, and IT evaluation. Van Grembergen presented at the European Conference on Information Systems (ECIS) in 1997 and 1998 and at the Information Resources Management Association (IRMA) Conferences in 1998, 1999, and 2000. He was Track Chair of "IT Evaluation Methods and Management" for the 2000 and 2001 IRMA-conference. He published articles in journals such as Journal of Strategic Information Systems, Journal of Corporate Transformation, Journal of Information on Technology Cases and Applications, IS Audit & Control Journal and EDP Auditing (Auerbach). He also has several publications in leading Belgian and Dutch journals and published in 1997 a book on business process reengineering in Belgian organizations and in 1998 a book on the IT Balanced Scorecard. Currently, he is editing a book on IT evaluation. He is engaged in the development of CobiT 3rd Edition. Until recently he was academic director of the MBA program of UFSIA and presently he is coordinator of a master program on IT-audit. Professor Van Grembergen has consulted with a number of organizations and is a member of the board of directors of an IT company servicing a Belgian financial group.*

Preface

Recent corporate scandals such as HIH and OneTel in Australia, and Enron and Worldcom in the United States have raised the importance of corporate governance and prompted governments to provide guidelines to reduce risks to shareholders, employees, and consumers. In the United States, the Sarbanes-Oxley Act 2002 introduced stringent corporate governance requirements and organizations around the world are following the lead of the US and focusing on corporate governance. For example, in Australia, the AS 8000 Good Governance Principles was released in 2003 making Standards Australia the first standards body in the world to publish national guidelines on corporate governance. The Australian standard AS 8015 *Corporate Governance of Information & Communications Technology* is being considered by an International Standards working group as a candidate for adoption as an international standard.

Increasingly, IT governance is considered an integral part of corporate governance. There has been rapid increase in awareness and adoption of IT governance. As well as seeking to conform to national governance requirements (such as the Sarbanes-Oxley Act), organizations are establishing IT governance to ensure that IT is aligned with the objectives of the organization. IT governance includes leadership, organizational structures, and processes to ensure that the organization's IT sustains and extends the organization's strategy. To ensure that IT is aligned with the objectives of the organizations, and sustains and extends the organization's strategy, senior managers are implementing IT governance frameworks. Organizations are under pressure to improve their IT governance and service quality and are investing in training, consultants, hardware, and software to implement frameworks such as Control objectives for information and related Technology (CobiT) and the IT Infrastructure Library (ITIL).

Associated with IT governance is the management of IT services provided. Organizations are grappling with the challenges of improving availability and capacity of business-critical applications while improving service levels, reducing support costs and lowering incident and problem resolution times. The increasing use of outsourcing contracts to multiple service providers raises challenges for IT governance and service management. Apart from articles in the practitioner press, there is very little research published in this important area. The frameworks available are continually evolving. Many organizations have already adopted the IT Infrastructure Library (ITIL) framework. This framework has recently been revised from Version 2 to Version 3. As well as investing in the new editions of the ITIL books, organizations are considering how to transition from Version 2 to 3 and the implications in terms of conversion training and tool sets. An international standard on IT Service Management has been released – ISO/IEC 20000. Many organizations are seeking to gain certification to this standard for competitive advantage in tendering for outsourced service provision and also by internal IT groups as a defence against outsourcing threats. To further complicate the IT Service Management environment, the Software Engineering Institute is developing two complimentary 'constellations' to accompany the Capability Maturity Model Integration (CMMI). These constellations focus on acquisition and service management. As these additional frameworks share common processes with the CMMI, it is expected that organizations that have invested in the CMMI framework will be interested in the two new constellations.

The objective of this book is to examine current popular IT governance and IT service management frameworks and standards. It strives to present a variety of views from many countries and perspectives about how these standards are used by organizations. As these frameworks are increasingly widely adopted, they are revised and improved. Consequently, organizations need to keep up-to-date with the revisions to the frameworks. This book provides an in-depth view of challenges and benefits experienced by organizations in their initial adoption of the frameworks and then incorporating the subsequent revisions. Furthermore, this book highlights the critical contribution of IT service management to IT governance, and the strategic and tactical value provided by effective service management.

In my own research on IT Governance or IT Service Management, I found there was little published research on these topics and felt that there was a need for a collection of recent research. The motivation for this book came from my attendance at various conferences such as the International Conference on IT Governance, the European Conference on Information Systems and the Australasian Conference on Information Systems. I contacted authors I had met at these conferences and encouraged them to extend their research as a contribution to this collection. The call for multiple chapters was also promoted through the ISWorld and IRMA mailing lists and this approach resulted in contributions from an international cohort of authors.

This book makes its mark by providing a collection of recent research outcomes covering most of the popular frameworks used for IT governance and service management. It contributes to the subject matter by providing up-to-date reviews of the extant literature. The case studies provide empirical evidence of the experience of many organizations from various countries.

STRUCTURE OF THE BOOK

This book is divided into four sections.

Section I sets the scene by providing literature reviews of previous research to date on IT governance. It is essential in any new area of study to establish a cumulative research tradition. Researchers will find this literature review valuable and it will facilitate building on previous studies and identifying gaps in the research effort to date.

The opening chapter by Buckby, Best, and Stewart provide a comprehensive understanding of the current state of IT governance literature across five key focus areas: strategic alignment of business and IT systems; delivery of value from IT systems; risk management of IT systems; management of IT resources; and measurement of the performance of IT systems. The authors present a detailed overview of research across the key focus areas of IT Governance (ITG), and by identifying important gaps in ITG research guide future thinking and research on ITG.

The second chapter by Lee and Lee aims to clarify the concept of ITG through conducting a literature review, suggesting some implications of this work for practitioners and indicating directions for the future study of ITG. Most managers acknowledge the importance of managing IT assets within a framework of ITG, but only a small number of academic treatments deal with ITG, meaning that businesses often find themselves making their governance decisions in a vacuum.

David Musson proposes that there are three different concepts that are grouped together as IT governance: IT governance as a framework or audit process; IT governance as IT decision-making; and IT governance as a branch of corporate governance. Through a review of the literature, Musson brings together the disparate views of IT governance so as to permit a broader view of this important subject.

Section II provides six case studies of IT Governance in countries as geographically diverse as Australia, Korea, and the United States of America. These case studies will be of practical use to managers who are embarking upon IT Governance initiatives.

Bhattacharjya and Chang introduce key IT governance concepts and industry standards and explore their adoption and implementation in the higher education environment. This chapter provides a valuable example to practitioners by demonstrating that IT governance processes, structures, and relational mechanisms adopted by these institutions generate value through improvements in a number of key focus areas for IT management.

Using a public sector audit office in an Australian state, Gerke and Ridley examine the potential to use an audit program based on the Control Objectives for Information and Related Technologies (CobiT) framework. The results suggest that the CobiT-derived instrument was effective for IT audit, and was able to be tailored to the needs of the organization, when evaluated against a number of criteria.

Shan and Hua consider the challenges in managing the complexity in architecture design. They define a methodical approach to effectively manage the complexity in architecture design and rationalize the architectural assets of IT application portfolios in a service-oriented paradigm. The holistic framework provides a multidisciplinary approach of portfolio analysis and service-oriented architecture planning. A case study in the US finance industry illustrates the use of this framework in real-world scenarios.

The next chapter, by Lee and colleagues compares the IT Governance setups of three large service sector firms in Korea. It seeks to identify the activities, types, and determinants of firms' IT governance decision making processes, and to suggest the basis on which forms of IT governance may represent rational selections for given service companies. The proposed and partially validated IT governance framework should be useful for further research and practice of IT governance.

The Australian Standard for the Corporate Governance of Information and Communication Technology (ICT) AS8015 is used by O'Donohue, Pye, and Warren as the focus of their chapter. Recommendations are provided to enhance the effective implementation of this standard's principles within an organization. These recommendations concern such factors as identifying and addressing issues surrounding the implementation of this standard and the actions that could be undertaken to improve the effectiveness of ICT governance by sharply focusing upon the governance aspects of ICT within business, as opposed to the management aspect of ICT.

Academics and practitioners collaborated Mark Toleman on the case study in Chapter IX. It reports on a major restructure incorporating both CobiT and ITIL principles at an Australian University. As well as describing the new reporting and internal structures of the Division, the alignment of the goals of the Division to the corporate goals is discussed. Care was taken to ensure that the new ICT structure was logical and conducive to operational effectiveness, efficiency and sound ICT governance, and could provide pathways and opportunities for career progression, client-focus, and role delineation and functional accountability.

Section III is the largest section in the book and provides many and varied perspectives on the relationship of IT Governance with business, corporate governance, and IT security. This section also considers governance as it relates to IT portfolio management, outsourcing, and software development.

Brian Cusack uses the control frameworks of CobiT and ITIL to provide a mapping of organizational roles from the capital interest at the highest level, through to the implementation level in an enterprise system. Security affects all processes within an organization structure and both control frameworks provide varying capability for control at different levels in an organization. In this chapter the security process is mapped from two control frameworks at the strategic layer and the issue of effective management tactics discussed from the theoretical structures within the problem area.

Chapter XI focuses on the importance of both corporate and IT governance, and demonstrates that IT governance is a very important subcomponent of corporate governance. Borth and Bradley present a framework which should facilitate a strong understanding of the different factors and mechanisms that impact firm governance. A number of interesting empirical results relating to these governance mechanisms are presented with examples that link corporate and IT governance.

Alea Fairchild and colleagues report on the I-Fit research project which commenced as a joint activity of a regional ICT consultancy with a university research center. The main goal of the project is to help the consultants to improve alignment between business and IT in the client organizations. The I-Fit project takes the perspective of the business manager: how a business manager can influence and increase the value of the IT services received. The I-Fit model was developed based on the literature on strategic alignment and Information Quality. The model assumes causal relationships between "IT governance," "Strategic Alignment," "Information Quality," and "Business Performance" in an organization.

This chapter by Kollmann and Hasel focuses on young Internet-based firms and articulates the knowledge and skills required by IT professionals. Building on the general IT governance principle of aligning business and IT, it introduces an adequate competence model, outlines its dimensions, and suggests a framework for modeling the effects of factors internal and external to the firm on the value propositions of the different dimensions. The authors hope that a comprehensive understanding of the role of IT-related competence will assist founders not only in finding suitable partners, but also in aligning e-business strategy and information technology in Internet-based ventures.

Rogers assesses the role maturity models can play in enterprise IT governance. Frameworks such as the Capability Maturity Model make it possible to assess maturity in key areas. The author describes additional maturity models that have no formal association with a comprehensive framework, the application of which represent significantly less overhead than the larger frameworks that include a maturity model component. Rogers seeks to present a broad perspective on maturity models that enterprises can use as a preliminary means of evaluating available tools. This overview of maturity models can facilitate the selection of a model to bring about improved IT governance in one or more focus areas.

The next chapter by Yael Dubinsky and colleagues aims to bridge the gap between high-level IT governance and software development governance. A model for governance in general is presented and then used to describe IT and software development domain-specific governance. The model is built based on a review of the literature and a set of scenarios. The process of transition to agile software development is used to demonstrate the domain-specific governance schemes.

The aim of the chapter by Ann Rouse is to alert decision makers to the fact that outsourcing IT incorporates residual risks even when widely recommended operational controls are implemented. After briefly reviewing existing formal governance frameworks and their treatment of IT outsourcing, an analytical model for considering outsourcing benefits and risks is introduced. Some strategic IT governance issues that become critical once a firm outsources a significant proportion of its IT services are highlighted. Effective control processes are necessary, but not sufficient for good corporate governance and those responsible for corporate governance should ensure that both operational and strategic governance issues are considered when IT is substantially outsourced.

Portfolio Management principles are the foundation of building effective governance. Murali Ramakrishnan's chapter is intended primarily for managers who are preparing to implement portfolio management concepts in an organization and students of IT Project Management, who wish to understand the difference between Project and Portfolio Management. While there is literature available discussing portfolio management at the conceptual level, there is not enough available which translates these concepts into tactical implementation. Practitioners can benefit from discussing implementation approaches that can be tailored to suit individual needs. This chapter shows one of the many ways to implement a portfolio management framework.

The purpose of the chapter by Dowse and Lewis is to help business and information managers to adapt IT management arrangements to suit the organizational context by examining the issues associated with alignment of IT governance and service management, identifying contingencies and developing a framework. After examining the requirements for IT governance, the organization is considered as a system and competing needs for integration and differentiation within the organization are examined. The emerging concept of information systems as a contributor of value is also discussed and a framework developed.

The focus in **Section IV** is IT Service Management. Models such as ITIL and ISO/IEC 20000 are described and extended and illustrated with a case study. This section considers the importance of quality, strategy and return on investment issues in relation to IT Service Management.

Jon Iden presents and analyses a real life ITIL project based on a longitudinal case study. The purpose is to illustrate how the ITIL process reference model for some processes may be used almost as a blueprint, while ITIL for other processes may be profoundly adapted to suit the context and the needs of the implementer. Furthermore, the success factors and the impediments for successful implementation are discussed. This chapter will especially inform practitioners about how ITIL may be utilized and how an implementation project might be organized.

The chapter by Neil McBride describes a suggested model for developing a service strategy within IT services. It discusses the content and process of developing an IT service strategy. The example of hospital information systems is used to illustrate the strategic process. In order to set the scene for the strategic process, the state of information systems strategy research is discussed and set in the context of the developing service management research literature. A case is made for a migration from an IT strategy based primarily on the development of a portfolio of IT systems to a service-strategy based on the development of a portfolio of business services.

A descriptive-conceptual overview of the main models and standards of processes formulated in the systems engineering (SE), software engineering (SwE) and information systems (IS) disciplines is provided by Manual Mora and colleagues. Given the myriad of models and standards reported, the convergence suggested for the SE and SwE models and standards, and the increasing complexity of information systems, the authors argue that these standards become relevant to the IS discipline. Based on the aims and principles identified, the authors report and posit the concepts of process, system and service as conceptual building blocks for describing such models and standards. Initial theoretical and practical implications for the Information Systems discipline of such models and standards are discussed.

Based on the IT-industrialisation and an increased customer orientation in IT-Service management, the aspect of quality becomes increasingly important. This chapter by Claus-Peter Praeg and Dieter Spath introduces an IT-Service management framework for the use of quality management concepts in the context of the life cycle phases of IT-Services. It argues that IT-Service management, combined with quality management and a life cycle approach for IT-Services provides a new perspective for organizations to provide high quality IT-Services. The aim is to support organizations in the effective use of quality management concepts depending on IT-Service life cycles.

Chee Ing Tiong and colleagues explore financial metrics that organizations could use in measuring the return on investment from their adoption of the IT Infrastructure Library (ITIL) framework. ITIL outlines an extensive set of best practices for IT service management in organizations but as yet there is limited academic research on measuring the return on investment from ITIL adoption. This literature review discusses the importance of measuring return on investment in ITIL and some of the available measurement metrics for IT investment that could be adapted. A measurement model for measuring investment return on ITIL service management is proposed.

Malzahn describes how models for software development and service delivery can be integrated into a common approach to reach an integrated product life cycle for software. The models include SEI's Capability Maturity Model Integration (CMMI), SPICE (Software Process Improvement and Capability Determination, ISO 15504) and ISO/IEC 20000 (Service Management). Whilst the CMMI constellation approach delivers an integration perspective defined in three models (development, acquisition and services), SPICE and ISO/IEC 20000 need additional alignment to be usable in an integrated approach.

BOOK DEVELOPMENT PROCESS

A double-blind review process was used for all chapters submitted to the editor. Authors of selected chapters were invited to act on the reviewers' comments and resubmit their chapters to the editor. Chapters were checked and final revisions applied.

I have enjoyed the process of compiling this book and in particular working with the contributors who provided such wide-ranging research on the topic of IT governance and service management. It is up to you, the readers to decide if the perspectives offered here are relevant to your research or to the practical application of the concepts in your organizations. I would be delighted to hear your feedback on the usefulness of this collection.

DISCLAIMERS

No product or service mentioned in this book is endorsed, nor are any claims made about the capabilities of such product or service.

All trademarks are copyrighted to their respective owners.

Aileen Cater-Steel
Editor

Acknowledgment

The authors who contributed to this book deserve my heartfelt thanks for their contribution, patience and cooperation throughout the long and complex process of compiling this book. All the contributors are listed with biographical sketches in a section near the end of the book.

The reviewers also played an essential role, and I know the authors were very appreciative of the valuable comments provided by the reviewers. I sincerely thank the reviewers for taking the time to read and comment on the original submissions. Their contribution was an essential ingredient necessary to improve the content and presentation of the chapters.

Thanks also to Professor Wim Van Grembergen, for providing the Foreword and for his outstanding contribution to the filed of ICT goverance. A special note of thanks to the staff at IGI Global; they provided the necessary process, templates, reminders, and project management of the entire process from my first proposal to this final publication.

Finally, I wish to thank my husband, Michael Steel, for his continued support, patience, and love.

Aileen Cater-Steel
Editor

Section I
Reviews of IT Governance Research

Chapter I
The Current State of Information Technology Governance Literature

Sherrena Buckby
Queensland University of Technology, Australia

Peter Best
University of Southern Queensland, Australia

Jenny Stewart
Griffith Business School, Australia

ABSTRACT

This chapter introduces current and prior IT governance literature across five key focus areas being strategic alignment of business and IT systems, delivery of value from IT systems, risk management of IT systems, management of IT resources and measurement of the performance of IT systems. The chapter focuses on synthesising the current literature on ITG to achieve three primary objectives. First, the review presents a detailed overview of research across the key focus areas of ITG. Second, the synthesis of the literature identifies important gaps in ITG research. Third, the review aims to guide future thinking and research on ITG in each of the focus areas. This chapter will provide a comprehensive understanding of the current state of IT governance literature.

INTRODUCTION

The research literature on information technology governance (ITG) is diverse and expansive, emanating from business, organizational, and information technology research paradigms. This chapter focuses on synthesising the current literature on ITG to achieve three primary objectives. First, the review presents a detailed overview of research on the key focus areas of ITG. Second, the synthesis of the literature identifies important gaps in ITG research. Third, the review aims to guide future thinking and research on ITG.

The review of ITG literature has been organized using the five key components (focus areas) identified by the IT Governance Institute (ITGI). The focus areas are strategic alignment of business and IT systems, delivery of value from IT systems, risk management of IT systems, management of IT resources and measurement of the performance of IT systems (ITGI, 2003).

Our motivation for this review of the ITG literature stems from the growing dependency of organizations on IT resources (ITGI, 2006c) and their increasing need to better manage/govern these significant IT investments (ITGI, 2007). There is an increasing call worldwide for boards of directors and governing bodies to take responsibility for the governance of IT assets (ITGI, 2003; Trites, 2003) in much the same way as they govern an organization's financial and reporting processes. ITG has become more prominent worldwide in the past few years as organizations in the United States must now monitor ITG as part of their compliance with the provisions of the Sarbanes-Oxley Act (2002).

IT GOVERNANCE DEFINITION

IT governance is recognized as an integral part of enterprise governance. It "consists of the leadership and organizational structures and processes that ensure that the organization's IT sustains and extends the organization's strategies and objectives" (ITGI, 2003, p.10). The ITGI further defines ITG as "the management process which ensures delivery of the expected benefits of IT in a controlled way to enhance the long-term success of the enterprise" (ITGI, 2000, p.27). Broadbent (2003c, p.1) considers that "IT governance is about who is entitled to make major decisions, who has input and who is accountable for implementing those decisions. It is not synonymous with IT

management. IT governance is about decision rights, whereas IT management is about making and implementing specific IT decisions". Weill (2004, p.3) defines ITG as "specifying the framework for decision rights and accountabilities to encourage desirable behaviour in the use of IT". These definitions indicate that ITG is intended to ensure that the organization and its board of directors or governing body are conscious of managing its IT investment responsibly, efficiently, and effectively.

IT GOVERNANCE STANDARDS

The release of a voluntary Australian Standard AS8015-2005 "Corporate Governance of Information and Communication Technology" by Standards Australia (2005) has emphazised the importance of ITG for Australian organizations. Further, there are a number of international standards which are relevant to ITG. The International Organization for Standardization (ISO) and International Electrotechnical Commission (IEC) released ISO/IEC 27001 and 27002 on information security in 2005 (ISO/IEC, 2005a; ISO/IEC 2005b). These standards aim to provide clear guidelines of best practice on information security management across 12 key sections and replace prior standards on this issue. Standard ISO/IEC 12207 on the software life cycle processes, which was amended in December 2004, is also relevant to ITG of organizations. This standard establishes processes and activities applicable to the acquisition and configuration of software services (ISO/IEC, 2004a). The international standard on Software Process Improvement and Capability Determination (SPICE) ISO/IEC 15504 assists organizations to assess their overall capabilities for delivering software (ISO/IEC, 2004b).

There are several frameworks designed to provide guidance on the implementation and management of ITG. The Information Technology Infrastructure Library (ITIL) is a framework which aims to assist in the delivery of high quality IT services through the dissemination of best practice approaches. The framework incorporates extensive management procedures that should support organizations in achieving quality and value from IT operations. ITIL is an integrated set of process oriented best practices for managing IT services (United Kingdom Office of Government Commerce and IT Service Management Forum, 2005). Another tool which employs ITIL best practices and extends the ITIL framework into enhanced processes and additional value added functionality is the IT Service Management Framework (ITSM). This framework enables better assessment, planning, and implementation of ITIL processes (ITSM, 2007).

The Capability Maturity Model Integration (CMMI) process improvement approach has also been used to assess the effectiveness of organizational ITG processes (Software Engineering Institute, 2007). The CobiT framework Version 4.1 presents good ITG practices which represent the consensus of experts and aims to assist organizations to implement a detailed program of IT governance structures including ITG control objectives, management guidelines, and maturity models (ITGI, 2007).

These frameworks, standards and guidelines form an important part of the performance measurement focus area of ITG. In addition, they also provide resources which assist organizations to implement aspects of the other four focus areas. Literature relating to the implementation of these frameworks, in particular the CobiT framework, will be discussed in a later section.

FIVE KEY FOCUS AREAS OF IT GOVERNANCE

The ITGI has identified that IT governance consists of five key focus areas (ITGI, 2003). In this section, each of these areas will be defined and briefly discussed in order to develop your

understanding of the key components of ITG. In the next section, a detailed review of the research in each of these focus areas will be provided.

Strategic Alignment of Business and IT

Strategic alignment of business and IT is defined as "whether an enterprise's investment in IT is in harmony with its strategic objectives (intent, current strategy, and enterprise goals) and thus building the capabilities necessary to deliver business value" (ITGI, 2003, p.22). Strategic alignment between business and IT processes is also often referred to as business-IT alignment and aims to ensure that IT assets are being used efficiently to assist the entire organization. Strategic alignment has become an important issue for organizations with considerable IT assets as synergism of IT resources with the goals and objectives of the organization has been linked to improved performance (Bergeron, Raymond & Rivard, 2004).

Delivery of Value from IT Systems

Delivery of value from IT systems has been defined as "the on-time and within-budget delivery of appropriate quality, which achieves the benefits that were promised" (ITGI, 2003, p.24). This critical component of ITG processes aims to confirm that IT resources deliver maximum business value. This issue has become important, as organizations have invested in large IT systems over the last decade. Boards of directors and other stakeholders are seeking to determine that value has been delivered from these significant investments as part of their governance processes.

Risk Management of IT Systems

Risk management of IT systems has become a critical element, as almost all organizations are now dependent on IT resources to conduct their day-to-day operations. Risk management of IT systems has been defined as "the extent to which IT assets are protected and the level of assurance required" (ITGI, 2003, p.27). Business organizations have traditionally focused on financial risk, but have recently become more concerned with operational and systematic risk due to pressure from regulators and other governance bodies. Technology risk and information security issues form a prominent part of operational and systematic risk considerations (ITGI, 2001).

Management of IT Resources

IT resource management is concerned with the management of IT resources and the organization of IT infrastructures within an organization. Management of IT resources has been defined as "the optimal investment, use and allocation of IT resources (people, applications, technology, facilities, data) in servicing the needs of the enterprise" (ITGI, 2003, p.28). This key dimension of ITG processes focuses on board level monitoring of IT resources and expenditures with the aim of ensuring the suitability of IT assets to meet the day-to-day operational needs of the enterprise.

Measurement of the Performance of IT Systems

IT performance measurement is concerned with "tracking project delivery and monitoring IT services" (ITGI, 2003, p.29) and determining whether IT systems have achieved the goals set for them by the board and senior management. Performance measures should be linked to and measure results of strategies focused on strategic alignment, value delivery, risk management, and IT resource management. Performance measurement allows assessment of achievements against plans and appropriate corrective action.

THE CURRENT STATE OF ITG LITERATURE

This section provides a detailed review of research literature over the past two decades on the five key focus areas of ITG. Tables summarising the research studies relevant to each focus area are provided together with a discussion of the key outcomes of the research in each area.

Strategic Alignment of Business and IT Research

Table 1 provides a detailed review of research literature on the issue of strategic alignment of business and IT (Buckby, 2008). This Table provides details of the methods used, organizations/subjects studied, issues examined, and results obtained in forty-one studies.

Research on strategic alignment of business and IT has involved the development of a large number of models and frameworks. The Strategic Alignment Model (SAM) of Henderson and Venkatraman (1991) was one of the first research models developed in this focus area. The SAM proposed that strategic alignment consists of two key dimensions: strategic fit and functional integration. Strategic fit consists of business strategy (the need to make choices that position the organization externally in the market) and organization infrastructure and processes (the need to determine the internal structures necessary to achieve this market position). Functional integration assists the organization to align its functional processes with internal and external variables (Henderson & Venkatraman, 1991). The SAM has formed the basis for a series of other papers which extend the model by applying it to a specific organization or by revising the components of each domain (Henderson & Venkatraman, 1993, 1999; Henderson & Thomas, 1992). Luftman, Lewis, and Oldach (1993) further developed the SAM to form the Strategic Alignment Framework

(SAF) while Papp (1999) extended the model by identifying seven financial measures which could be linked to improvements in strategic alignment within organizations. Some studies such as Burn and Szeto (1999) and Avison, Jones, Powell, and Wilson (2004) have found empirical support for the SAM model and its structures. However, a recent study by Bricknall, Darrell, Nilsson, and Pessi (2007) did not find strong support for the principles of the SAM.

The development of new models associated with strategic alignment continued with alternative models being proposed by Smaczny (2001), Kearns and Lederer (2003), Bergeron et al. (2004) and Strnadl (2006). Smaczny (2001) developed a practical alternative model to SAM by indicating that an alignment model should have continuous synchronisation among business strategy, IT strategy, business operational plan and IT operational plans. He suggested that synchronization between business units and the enterprise and fusion between business and IT leaders would ensure that alignment was more efficient and effective. Kearns and Lederer (2003) tested their alternative model and found that information intensive firms are more likely to knowledge share and thus have stronger strategic alignment. This has practical implications for organizations in terms of how they disseminate organizational information. Bergeron et al. (2004) proposed a model which adopted a definition of fit as gestalt, and examined the impact of co-alignment between business strategy, business structure, IT strategy and IT structure on business performance using a mail survey across 110 small and medium sized businesses. Strandl (2006) presented a four-layer model of processes, information, services, and technology integration as the tool necessary to bridge the gap between business and IT.

Luftman (2003) developed an important strategic alignment measurement tool by designing detailed maturity models for six key strategic alignment criteria. These criteria are communications, competence/value measurements, gover-

nance, partnership, technology scope, and skills maturity. The Luftman maturity models were tested in Silvius (2007) on a number of international and Dutch firms. Silvius (2007) found that the assessed scores of business-IT alignment (BIA) maturity were higher than expected and there was a difference in perception of BIA maturity between business and IT professionals. Avison et al. (2004) developed a practical framework that assists management to determine current alignment levels. Both of these frameworks provide important guidance to ITG practitioners on the detailed issues which enable business and IT alignment. Martin, Gregor, and Hart (2005) also found support for the categorization of the alignment enablers of Luftman & Brier (1999).

D'Souza and Mukherjee (2004) presented four critical tasks that managers must undertake to improve business-IT alignment and outlined three key constraints that must be recognized by an organization if business-IT alignment is to be successful. More recently, Sledgianowski and Luftman (2005) have developed the strategic alignment maturity assessment (SAMA) framework to measure the level of strategic alignment across six key criteria, extending the prior work of Luftman (2003). A study considering strategic alignment from a communication perspective was Couglan, Lycett, and Macredie (2005) which found that business and IT divisions need to implement better mechanisms of communication to improve strategic alignment. Some of the other key outcomes relating to strategic alignment of business and IT include (1) the development of an integrated architecture framework (Maes, Rijsenbrij, Truijens & Goedvolk, 2000), (2) the identification of the key enablers and inhibitors of strategic alignment (Luftman & Brier, 1999), (3) the introduction of fusion (i.e., where IT is one of the business functions thus removing the need for IT-business alignment) as a key element impacting on strategic alignment (Smaczny, 2001), (4) the discovery of organizational processes that enhance strategic alignment, and (5) the discussion of the relationship between short-term and long-term alignment (Reich & Benbasat, 2000).

A number of research studies have also attempted to extend the perception of strategic alignment processes and to identify practical implications by conducting case studies and interviews with a variety of organizations. Cumps, Viaene, Dedene, and Vandenbulcke (2006) found that good governance of IT investments has an important impact on business-IT alignment. This is especially so where IT is a real business enabler and the impact of IT investments on different aspects of the business is considered in new project business cases/proposals. Silvius (2007) conducted focus groups with IT managers to explore differences in BIA in theory and practice. This study identified some key BIA practices including information quality, having a clear strategic vision, and developing IT awareness in senior business management. Beimborn, Wagner, Franke, and Weitzel (2007) identified the most important practical aspect of operational alignment to be the mutual understanding between business and IT.

All the models developed and identified in the strategic alignment focus area have the potential to assist organizations to better structure their business and IT processes and to improve ITG. Hence, the previous discussion, together with the summary provided in Table 1, should assist both academics and practitioners to better understand strategic alignment of ITG.

Delivery of Value from IT Systems Research

Research on delivering value from IT systems is shown in Table 2 for 22 research studies (Buckby, 2008). Research on IT value delivery has not been as prolific as the research on strategic alignment of business and IT processes. However, model and framework development have been important aspects of research work in both these focus areas. The early work of Chan (2000), which presented a review of value delivery literature, identified that IT value research has tended to focus on theory generation and development of new methods and measures. Davern and Kuffmann (2000) developed a model which presents the theoretical elements of the IT value creation process. This model was one of the first to examine the relationships between IT project value, IT management and IT impacts. The main argument of their theoretical framework was distinguishing between potential value of IT systems and the realized value and return from these systems. Davern and Kauffman (2000) felt that distinguishing between the two types of value was crucial to obtaining a proper measure of value from IT systems. This framework was a key contributor to the early knowledge on IT value delivery.

Sircar, Turnbow, and Bordoloi (2000) also made an important contribution to value delivery research by developing a framework which examined the links between firm performance and IT investments. McKay, Marshall, and Smith (2003) broadened the examination of the value of IT by proposing a model linking planning/alignment, evaluation and benefits to delivery of value of IT investments. They found broad support for their model and identified five key phases which assist in value delivery through a series of case studies. Lee and Menon (2000) considered that IT value consists of links between overall, technical and allocative efficiency and that organizations needed to learn to take advantage of technology to achieve value. A further study by Tallon, Kraemer, and Gurbaxani (2000) developed a process oriented model to assess the impact of IT on critical business activities. This research study found that strategic alignment and IT investment evaluation are important contributors to firm performance and value. Ryan and Harrison (2000) investigated the hidden costs and benefits associated with the value of IT investments and found that social subsystem costs and benefits must be incorporated in IT investment decisions if value is to be realized from these investments,

Table 1. Current status of research on strategic alignment of business and IT

Study	Method (s)	Organizations/Subjects	Issues Examined/Domain	Results
Van Lier and Dohmen (2007)	• Model development • Case study	• 6 organizations	• Discusses the links between benefits management and strategic alignment and their influence on IT outsourcing • Discusses models for each of the issues • Uses maturity models of Luftman (2000) to assess strategic alignment	• Found that case studies with higher strategic alignment and benefits management are linked to IT outsourcing success
Silvius (2007)	• Model development • Focus groups • Hypothesis development and testing • Pilot study participants	• 23 Chief Information Officers and IT managers from trade, manufacturing and financial companies in the Netherlands • 12 Dutch firms participated in pilot study	• Discusses importance of strategic alignment for organizations • Presents a series of theoretical models identifying different aspects of strategic alignment • Develops four hypothesis for testing by pilot study participants	• Presents practical strategic alignment issues identified in focus group discussions • Identifies strategic alignment maturity levels for pilot study participants • Discusses the difficulties with strategic alignment in practice
Beimborn, Wagner, Franke and Weitzel (2007)	• Case studies • Interviews	• 4 branches of a retail bank • Bank management	• Testing for links to recent alignment literature • Assessing the impact of strategic alignment on system usage and success of business processes • Draws on knowledge from SAM model	• Found that IS usage is directly linked to strategic alignment between business and IT units and internal alignment between organizational units • Found that IT staff did understand business needs
Van Grembergen, De Haes and Van Brempt (2007)	• Delphi method	• Financial industry participants	• Examines links between business goals, IT goals and IT processes • Considers validation of business and IT goals identified in pilot study • Considers balanced scorecard perspectives to break up goals • Considers how IT goals contribute to business goals	• Produces a reviewed and prioritized list of IT goals and business goals • Three important IT goals were part of the corporate contribution perspective • Business goals under the financial perspective were included
Bricknall, Darrell, Nilsson and Pessi (2007)	• Case study	• Astra Zenaca (AZ)	• Compares the balanced scorecard of this organizations to SAM model and the traditional balanced scorecard model (Kaplan and Norton 1992) • Analyses alignment in the case study organization in considerable detail	• Found a weak match to balanced scorecard • Found stronger links between business and IT strategies • Did not find a strong match to principles of SAM model
Strnadl (2006)	• Framework development	• No data	• Development of a process-driven architecture model (PDA) • Provides detail of each layer of the PDA process	• Developed PDA model which includes four layer concept of process, information, services and technology integration • Identified future issues
Wagner, Beimborn, Franke, Weitzel (2006)	• Case studies	• Three branches of a retail bank employing identical information systems • Credit co-operative banks	• Examines usage, alignment and experience constructs • Tests a number of indicators of these constructs	• Supports alignment literature findings • Provides insights into the importance of alignment in operations • Provides evidence of positive impacts between alignment and IT usage

continued on following page

Table 1. continued

Study	Method (s)	Organizations/Subjects	Issues Examined/Domain	Results
Cumps, Vianene, Dedence and Vanden-bulcke (2006)	• Survey • Score development	• Organizations in Belgium, France, Germany, The Netherlands, Italy, Spain and the United Kingdom	• Analyses business/ICT alignment in order to deduce practical guidelines for managers • Development of an alignment score measure consisting of 6 groups of alignment competences	• Demonstrates the influence of different ICT strategies on business/ICT alignment performance • Describes how organizations obtain on average better alignment performance scores by establishing specific ICT management routines.
Martin, Gregor and Hart (2005)	• Case studies • Qualitative research	• Case studies of six government agencies • 20 executives and 48 middle and junior managers	• Assesses the social dimension of the strategic alignment and what mechanisms enable this alignment	• Supports the categorization by Luftman et al. (1999) of alignment enablers
Coughlan, Lycett and Macredie (2005)	• Framework development • Interviews • Case study	• Major UK bank/top-level management from retail and IT departments	• Considers communication element of alignment • Concerned with organizational infrastructure • Examines perceptions of the business-IT relationship	• Develops a practical and structured methodology for categorizing communication issues in organizations • Identifies nine (9) key themes from interviews which relate to communication in the strategic alignment domain. • Found that organizations needed to implement better mechanisms of communication to improve strategic alignment.
De Haes and Van Grembergen (2005)	• Framework Development • Interviews • Case Study	• Belgian financial organization	• ITG implementation framework developed • Considers relationship between the ITG framework and strategic alignment	• Provides guidance for practitioners on practical application of IT Governance processes • Analysis of organizational ITG structures, processes and relational mechanisms provided
IT Governance Institute (2005e)	• Framework development • Survey	• Respondents to PWC (2003) and Lighthouse Global Surveys (2004) of IT professionals	• Identified importance of strategic alignment • Considered ability of organization to achieve business and IT alignment • Discussed role of CEO, Board and CIO in achieving strategic alignment	• Results of studies indicate business-IT alignment to be very important • Half of survey respondents did not have a formalized governance process to ensure effective business and IT alignment
Sledgianowski and Luftman (2005)	• Case study • Measurement tool development	• International specialty chemicals manufacturer	• Strategic Alignment Maturity Assessment (SAMA) framework applied to case study organization to measure level of strategic alignment across six criteria	• Compared initial strategic alignment assessments with follow up assessments • Cash flow, debt levels and employee numbers all showed improvements due to measurement tool being applied to organization
Avison, Jones, Powell and Wilson (2004)	• Model testing • Framework development • Case study	• Financial services firm in Australia	• Tested Strategic Alignment Model (SAM) (Henderson & Venkatraman 1993) by applying data from completed projects to determine the usefulness of this model	• SAM model found to have conceptual and practical value • Proposes a practical framework that allows management to determine current alignment levels

continued on following page

Table 1. continued

Study	Method (s)	Organizations/Subjects	Issues Examined/Domain	Results
Bergeron, Raymond and Rivard (2004)	• Theory testing • Mail survey • Model development	• 110 small firms	• Examines the impact of fit between all four alignment domains on firm performance • Cluster analysis used to test the research propositions • Empirically validates model through survey with small firms	• Proposes a new model of strategic alignment with 6 key constructs • Develops new measures of IT strategy and IT structure • Identifies three ideal patterns of alignment • Identifies the impact of patterns of alignment on organizational performance
D'Souza and Mukherjee (2004)	• Conceptual	• No data	• Considers practical challenges associated with achieving successful Business-IT alignment • Identifies four macro trends which will impact on adoption of IT over next decade	Highlights four critical tasks that managers should undertake to achieve successful BIT alignment ie take measured steps, identify critical factors that affect your organization's IT-business alignment, employ a phased process of implementing IT-business alignment processes and be prepared to make structural changes to the organization
Luftman (2003)	• Assessment methodology development	• Tested on 50 global 2000 companies	• Identifies 6 IT-business alignment criteria or maturity categories – Communications, competency/value measurement, governance, partnership, technology scope and skills	• Developed maturity models for sub-items under each of the 6 key criteria. • Develops strategic alignment assessment score for each organization
Kearns and Lederer (2003)	• Model development • Survey • Development of hypotheses	• Field survey of 161 Chief Information-tion Officers of companies with annual revenue of $75million or more	• Assessed the influence of information intensity on strategic alignment • Examined how six model constructs linked to IT being used for competitive advantage • Identified that successful IT alignment is dependent on CEO and CIO participation and appropriate business and IT planning processes	• Developed a model of six constructs and hypothesized relationships • Found that model and constructs accounted for variation in organizational performance • Study results indicate that information intensive firms are more likely to knowledge share and thus have stronger strategic alignment
Peak and Guynes (2003)	• Model development • Model testing	• Medium sized mid western power company • 75 Senior Managers and upper middle managers from five business units	• Identified Strategic alignment planning critical success factors • Collected data to test model developed.	• Identified four dimensions of IT alignment to assess information • Developed a series of models to aid in IT strategic alignment
Gold (2002)	• Model development	• No data	• Critical success factor methodology • Developed a strategic data model for the firm	• Identified link between Critical Success Factors for IS systems and Business strategy

continued on following page

Table 1. continued

Study	Method (s)	Organizations/Subjects	Issues Examined/Domain	Results
Croteau and Bergeron (2001)	• Model development • Hypothesis development • Surveys	• Top Managers from 223 Organizations	• Examined the fit between business strategy, technological deployment and organizational performance • Developed a research model and three hypotheses • Used survey data to test the model	• Identified profiles of technological deployment associated with Business strategy • Increased the knowledge on the impact of IS on organizational performance
Hirschheim and Sabherwal (2001)	• Profile development • Case studies	• Case studies of 3 large Australian organizations	• Proposed strategic IS alignment model with four components being business strategy, IS role, IS sourcing and IS structure • Identified three strategic alignment profiles being Infusion, Alliance and Utility • Examined profiles and tested model using case study data	• Identified factors which affect strategic alignment synchronization • Reported the profiles and components of three case study organizations
Smaczny (2001)	• Model development	• No data	• Considered whether Henderson (1990) Strategic Alignment Model (SAM) still applicable • Detailed literature review of strategic alignment models • Proposed new strategic alignment model	• Proposed that fusion be considered the future method of aligning business-IT • Considered SAM model out of date as sequential in orientation.
Reich and Benbasat (2000)	• Model development • Model testing	• 10 business units in the Canadian Life Insurance Industry • 57 semi-structured interviews with 45 participants	• Examined the influence of several factors on the social dimension of alignment • Tested both short term and long term alignment aspects within the business units • Measured communications between business and IT executives • Measures connections between IT and Business Planning • Measured shared domain knowledge and IT implementation success	• Found three business units had a high level of short term alignment and three had low short term alignment and three business units had high long term alignment and three had low long term alignment • Research model corroborated for short term alignment but not long term alignment • Identified the most predictor of alignment was a high level of communication between IT and business executives and creating an environment in which shared domain knowledge can grow.
Maes, Rijsenbrij, Truijens and Goedvolk (2000)	• Model development	• No data	• Extended work of Maes (1999) • Developed a generic framework for the business-IT relationship • Developed an Integrated Architecture Framework • Final model developed was the Unified Framework for Alignment	• Identified 6 key constructs of business-IT alignment being strategy, structure, operations, business, information and communication and technology • Developed new model from existing models and literature on strategic alignment

continued on following page

Table 1. continued

Study	Method (s)	Organizations/Subjects	Issues Examined/Domain	Results
Burn & Szeto (1999)	• Survey • Model testing	• Survey over a range of industries	• Factors that contribute to successful strategic alignment using the SAM model as its framework • Stage 1 factors that impacted on CEO's and CIO's during strategic alignment process. • Stage 2 interviews in a selected industry group that had been successful at strategic alignment. • 12 hypotheses tested and results produced	• Business and IT managers had no significant difference with regard to strategic alignment. Slight difference in the area of problems of alignment. • 3 Key success factors identified
Luftman & Brier (1999)	• Surveys	• Executives attending classes at IBM's Advanced Business Institute	• Identifies 6 most important enablers and inhibitors of strategic alignment • Identifies 12 components of alignment	• Identifies the factors that successfully aligned organizations concentrate upon • Identifies Steering Committee critical success factors
Luftman, Papp & Brier (1999)	• Interviews	• Interviews with business and IT executives at IBM's Advanced Business Institute	• Identifies 12 components of alignment • Identifies areas that help or hinder business/ IT alignment • Analyses results of a multi-year study of strategic alignment • Applied SAM model	• Found that strong executive support for IT, IT involved in strategy development, IT understands the business, business-IT partnership, well prioritized IT projects, IT demonstrates leadership as key enablers • IT/business lack close relationships, IT does not prioritize well, IT fails to meet its commitments, IT does not understand business, senior executives do not support IT
Maes (1999)	• Model development	• No data	• Development of a generic framework for information management • Extends vertical and horizontal dimensions of SAM model to include operations and information /communication	• Developed generic framework for information management and explained the key components of this new framework
Papp (1999)	• Model development • Model testing	• 500 firms over five years	• Further develops the strategic alignment model (SAM) of Henderson & Venkatraman (1991) • Studies 18 financial measurements and firm's reputation for the effect on firm's alignment perspective	• 7 measures identified as linked to strategic alignment within organizations being anticipated performance, liquidity, income, growth, net profitability, earnings and debt-to-equity • Identified a series of steps organizations should take to better align their strategies
Van Der Zee and De Jong (1999)	• Framework development • Measurement tool developed • Case studies	• 2 case studies – small bank and national food retailer	• Presents a new framework for IT and business alignment based on integration • Used the concepts of balanced business scorecard in two case studies	• Business balanced scorecard could be a valuable contributor to implementation of an integrated business and IT planning and evaluation process

continued on following page

Table 1. continued

Study	Method (s)	Organizations/Subjects	Issues Examined/Domain	Results
Bruce (1998)	• Conceptual • Scorecard development	• No data	• Develops a scorecard for evaluating business and IT alignment • How much IT investment is contributing to business values • Identified business and IT alignment as a necessity not a luxury	• Identifies ways companies use IT to achieve positive impact on shareholder value • Consequences of not aligning are missed opportunities (strategic and tactical) • Identifies culture, decision making processes, customers, investments, organization, performance measures, strategy as keys for operationalising alignment
Broadbent and Weill (1993)	• Case studies • Model development	• Case studies of 4 Banks in the Australian Banking Industry	• Developed a strategic alignment model for strategic alignment in the finance industry (related to prior models) • Used case study research design involving multiple sources of data collected in a structured manner	• Found that the firm wide strategy formation processes of the banks, rather than there IT methodologies were central to the alignment of business and information strategies. • Identified 6 propositions relating to firm wide strategy processes which facilitated alignment of IT and business strategy
Luftman, Lewis and Oldach (1993)	• Framework development • Case study	• Case study of IBM	• Further expanded the elements of business strategy, IT strategy, organizational infrastructure and processes and IT infrastructure and processes • ITG identified as part of IT strategy quadrant of IT strategy	• Identified IT governance as the extent of ownership of technology or the possibility of technology alliances or both • Provides further explanation and elements of IT strategy, IT infrastructure and processes, strategic fit and functional integration • Considers the four domains to be interrelated • Develops the Strategic Alignment Framework (SAF) based on SAM model
Henderson & Venkatraman (1993) (1999)	• Model development	• No data	• Model Development – refined SAM model • Identified organizations inability to realise value from IT due to lack of alignment between business and IT	• Identified the same four domains as prior model but revised the components of these domains. • Identifies the same two dimensions as prior model
Henderson and Thomas (1992)	• Model testing • Case study	• Case study of Hospital	• Case study applying SAM model to hospital situation • Considered role of strategy in general theory of organizations • Suggested that alignment means more than just linking Business and IT strategies	• Development of a strategic alignment model which determined the level of alignment (business and IT) by measuring alignment across 2 dimensions and 4 domains. Applicable to hospitals. • 2 dimensions (strategic fit and strategic integration) • 4 domains (hospital business strategy, hospital IT strategy, hospital infrastructure, IT infrastructure)

continued on following page

Table 1. continued

Study	Method (s)	Organizations/Subjects	Issues Examined/Domain	Results
Henderson & Venkatraman (1991)	• Model development	• No data	• Model Development - Strategic Alignment model (SAM)	• Development of Strategic Alignment Model (SAM) • Identified 2 dimensions (Strategic Fit and Functional Integration) • Identified 4 domains (Business strategy, IT strategy, Organizational infrastructure & processes and IT infrastructure and processes)
Erikson, Magee, Roussel and Saad (1990)	• Conceptual • Case study	• Discussed goals of strategic technology management	• Case study approach	• Identified five questions to use in systematically examining the relationship between technology management and business strategy • Identified categories of technological strength and classification of technologies by competitive impact.
Henderson (1990)	• Conceptual • Model development	• Interviews with senior line executives (28 interviews conducted)	• Critical need to build effective working relationships between line managers and IS managers	• Provided a descriptive model of concept of partnership between business and IS managers • Provided a general of Business- IS partnership
Henderson & Sifonis (1988)	• Conceptual • Model development	• No data	• Used diagrams and case studies to discuss key strategic planning issues • Three key issues associated with strategic planning (levels of abstraction, decomposition, validity) • Considered the relationship between critical success factors and strategic planning levels	• Found commonalities between strategic IS planning and strategic business planning • Diagram of the links between strategic business planning and strategic IS planning • Identified how strategic goals can be linked between IS and Business plans
Henderson, Rockart & Sifonis (1987)	• Conceptual • Construct development	• No data	• Used a critical success methodology • Strategic planning in IS systems • Critical success factors • Strategic planning frameworks	• Developed a strategic data model using CSF methodology

for example, productivity, quality of work, and change management.

Dedrick, Gurbaxani, and Kraemer (2003) presented a detailed review of the literature between 1985 and 2002 which examined the relationship between IT investment and economic performance. The paper traced the issue of the "productivity paradox" surrounding IT investments. The review of over fifty papers in this area

provides important insight into the impact on IT investments and organizational economic performance. The analysis found that at "both firm and country level, greater investment in IT is associated with greater productivity growth" (Dedrick et al. 2003, p. 1). In an associated stream of research concerning value of IT investments, Melville, Kraemer, and Gurbaxani (2004) reviewed over 200 IT business value articles which examined the association between IT and organizational performance and found that IT does generate a wide range of benefits. They developed a model of IT business value using a resource based view of the organization and used this model together with five research questions to group the research and discuss its implications. Weill (2004) and, Weill and Ross (2004) both reported details of an extensive study of 250 enterprises across 23 countries and identify the five major IT decisions and six governance archetypes that assist organizations to effectively govern their IT. The study develops an ITG framework (a matrix of governance archetypes and decision domains) and tests this model using a case study of the State Street Corporation. Weill and Ross (2004) identified key characteristics of top governance performers including leadership involvement, engagement, clear business objectives, differentiated business strategies, more formally approved exceptions and fewer changes in governance. Weill (2004) identified five main factors that relate to variations in governance patterns, namely strategic and performance goals, organizational structure, governance experience, size and diversity, industry and regional differences. He further noted that top performers design ITG to support their performance goals and govern IT as they would any other key enterprise asset.

The important impact of the research in this focus area has been the improved understanding of what drives IT value and the concepts that are linked to value as identified in Dedrick et al. (2003); Melville et al. (2004); Weill (2004); Kwon and Watts (2006); and Tallon (2007). The recent study of Ward, De Hertogh, and Viaene (2007) found that, whilst most organizations focus on benefits management processes early in projects, they are less likely to focus on benefits management at the end of the project. This finding has important practical implications because benefits management in the longer term is what most organizations are likely to be seeking. It is interesting to note that the ITGI (2005a) found

that the most effective methods of value delivery measurement are in-house methods whilst Gregor, Fernandez, Holtham, Martin, Stern, and Vitale (2005) proposed that achieving business value from IT was within the organization's control and was not dependent on industry type or size.

The value delivery research has also extended knowledge on the methods used to value IT projects and investments (ITGI, 2005g; ITGI, 2006a). The Val IT framework (ITGI, 2006a) has provided considerable advice to organizations on the key principles and processes which will assist with achieving value from IT resources. This framework has been developed from best practice and ITG specialist knowledge worldwide and has been examined by Thorp (2006).

Risk Management of IT Systems Research

28 studies focusing on research associated with risk management of IT systems are presented in Table 3 (Buckby, 2008). Research in this focus area has gathered momentum over the last five years and has been much broader in depth than the other focus areas. It has, however, helped develop an understanding of IT risk issues within organizations. The key focus in this area of ITG research has been the development of conceptual thoughts and models on the factors associated with IT risk. Models in this area have focused on identifying risks, risk management, and risk assessment or measurement processes.

The research concerned with identifying risks has focused predominantly on outsourcing, IT projects and security risks. Gewald and Helbig (2006) developed a governance model for mitigating outsourcing risks, and Benvenuto and Brand (2005) identified the drivers of outsourcing and developed a generic risk assessment model. Bahli and Rivard (2005) have been instrumental in developing measures of risk factors associated with outsourcing IT operations. They developed measures and tested the reliability of these mea-

Table 2. Current status of research on delivery of value from IT systems

Study	Method (s)	Organizations/Subjects	Issues Examined/Domain	Results
Thatcher and Pingry (2007)	• Model development	• Firms that produce digital products or traditional products	• Develops a series of duopoly models of quality-price competition and series of monopoly models of quality-price choice to determine the impact of IT investments on organizational profit, productivity and consumer value	• Found that IT investments may not result in improvements in business value measures (ie generating profits by reducing production costs, improving product quality, improving firm productivity and increasing consumer value). • This study views IT investment as a commodity where IT investment does not create a market advantage for the organization
Heier, Borgman and Maistry (2007)	• Case studies	• 4 international implementation sites	• Considers impact of ITG software on value delivery from IT systems • Examines relationship between ITG applications, ITG processes and value delivery from IT	• Business value from IT appears to be assisted by implementation of ITG software from 4 cases • Organizations need to work on ITG processes as well as software to see value delivery from IT systems.
Ward, De Hertogh and Viaene (2007)	• Web survey	• Benulux and UK participants	• Builds on Ward et al. (1996) study on benefits management of IT investments • Investigating the state of current practice across the benefits management process	• Presents empirical evidence on benefits management processes • Small percentage of organizations have adopted benefits management processes for IT investments • Most organizations focus on benefits management in early stages of investment • Fewer organizations focus on benefits management at end of project • Adoption of methodologies for management of investments has improved
Tallon (2007)	• Matched survey • Hypothesis development • Hypothesis testing	• Executives in 241 firms from 1600 randomly drawn from S&P compustat firms in range $100M to $3B	• Examines issues about the impact of IT business value on firm performance • Uses resource based view of the firm as a theoretical driver for this research	• Found associations between high IT business value and organizations with multi-focused business strategies
Kwon and Watts (2006)	• Survey	• IT managers	• Investigates the impact on firm performance of two types of IT value practices – efficiency and knowledge management and looks at the relationship to dynamism and hostility • Develops 10 hypotheses	• Found that hostility and dynamism are significantly associated with IT value • Found associations between IT value and organizational performance
Thorp (2006)	• Conceptual	• No data	• Discussion on value management framework • Identifies the importance of value management of IT systems to organizations	• Develops key principles associated with management of value of IT systems including discussion of the Val IT framework from the IT Governance Institute (2006)
ITGI (2006a)	• Conceptual • Framework development	• No data	• Develops Val IT Framework • Assists organizations to achieve optimal value from IT investments	• Develops key principles and processes to assist organizations to achieve value from IT resources.

continued on following page

Table 2. continued

Study	Method (s)	Organizations/Subjects	Issues Examined/Domain	Results
Gregor, Fernandez, Holtham, Martin, Stern, Vitale and Pratt (2005)	• Telephone survey	• 1050 organizations of varying sizes from 15 of the 17 Australian and NZ standard industry classification codes • 50 structured interviews with organizations	• Addresses six research questions • Assesses issues associated with the circumstances and settings of ICT implementation, ICT contribution, factors which influence the value, what management practices relate to ICT benefit	• Results of study suggest that achieving business value from ICT is within the organization's control • This value is not significantly dependent on the organization's industry or size
ITGI (2005f)	• Conceptual • Survey data	• 2004 ITGI survey with Lighthouse Global of 200 IT professionals from 14 countries	• Discusses current performance management governance approaches	• Most effective method of value delivery measurement was in-house developed methods. • Most organizations in the survey used Return on Investment to measure the value of IT projects and investments • IT department performance was generally measured for value by an in-house method or balanced scorecard approach
ITGI(2005g)	• Conceptual	• No data	• Defines value delivery • Develops ideas about how to measure value returns from IT assets	• Discussion on measurement processes to assess value delivery from IT projects and assets
Rau (2004a)	• Measurement tool development • Case studies	• CEO of large HMO • Large international bank • Large financial institution	• Uses balanced scorecard approach and applied to development of conceptual framework of the CIO Dashboard Performance Management Program • Develops CIO Dashboard which is the final output of the program presents a concise graphical image of KPI's for IT. • Incorporates the IT Balanced Scorecard	• Develops CIO Dashboard which makes the key performance indicators of the organization available to stakeholders • Presents an important approach to better informing stakeholders/governing bodies of value of IT.
Weill (2004), Weill and Ross (2004)	• Framework development	• 250 enterprises across 23 countries	• Identifies 5 major IT decision that large enterprises make and 6 governance archetypes organizations use for making decisions which lead to obtaining value from IT • Studies top performing organizations and identifies what makes them different from others • Identifies seven characteristics of top governance performers	• Identifies five main factors that relate to variations in governance patterns being strategic and performance goals, organizational structure, governance experience, size and diversity, industry and regional differences • Develops ITG arrangements matrix which demonstrates the interactions between governance archetypes and decision domains and uses the matrix to analyses a case of State Street Corporation • Identifies two types of top performers being top ITG performers and top financial performers • Identifies the three most effective arrangements related to ITG performance • Presents 8 ITG critical success factors

continued on following page

Table 2. continued

Study	Method (s)	Organizations/Subjects	Issues Examined/Domain	Results
Kohli and Devaraj (2004)	• Framework development	•	• Considers three central themes associated with business value • IT payoffs are organization responsibility • Management of IT payoffs begins prior to investment and continues after implementation • IT payoffs are contingent on creating and exploiting complementary assets •	• Presents AIAC framework which includes four phases related to IT investment payoffs being alignment, involvement, analysis and communication • Provides detailed analysis of components of model and how they can be successfully implemented
Melville, Kraemer and Gurbaxani (2004)	• Model Development • Literature Review	• No data	• Identifies that IT value depends on a variety of factors • Applies resource based theory to the mode	• Identified that associations between IT and organizational performance define key concepts • Develops a model of IT business value and uses it to identify what is known about this issue • Identifies areas of future research
Dedrick, Gurbaxani and Kraemer (2003)	• Framework Development • Literature Review	• No data	• Presents a detailed review of the published literature from 1990-2001 which discussed the links between IT investment and productivity in the US economy. • Develops a general framework for classifying the research • Provides detailed tables analysing the research studies	• Considers the research at country, industry and firm levels to present limitations and existing research and areas of future research. • The study found that IT investment was associated with productivity growth at both the firm and country level • Presented areas of future research
McKay, Marshall and Smith (2003)	• Model development • Case studies	• Interviews with CIO of six of Australia's Top 50 companies	• Establishes a model of the value of IT • Proposed that this model was central to good ITG • Tested the veracity or validity of this model • Used interpretative case studies- empirical data to test support for the model	• Planning/alignment, evaluation and benefits are linked to delivery of value from IT investments. • Case studies found that these three factors can be categorized into 5 main phases (building the business case, Alignment and prioritization. Evaluation, system acquisition and implementation) • Only weak links to ITG processes
Tallon, Kraemer and Gurbaxani (2000)	• Model development • Survey	• 304 business executives worldwide	• Developed a process oriented model to assess the impacts of IT on critical business activities	• Found that corporate goals for IT can be classified into four types – unfocused, operations focus, market focus and dual focus • Found that strategic alignment and IT investment evaluation contributes to higher perceived levels of IT value
Sircar, Turnbow and Bordoloi (2000)	• Framework development	• 2000 observations of 624 firms	• Examined the relationship between firm performance and IT/Corporate Investments	• Develops IT Investment Framework • Found from analysis that results indicated that IT investment is an important contributor to a firm's performance

continued on following page

Table 2. continued

Study	Method (s)	Organizations/Subjects	Issues Examined/Domain	Results
Lee and Menon (2000)	• Model development	• Washington State Department of Health Hospital Database	• IT value is assessed by considering overall efficiency, technical efficiency and allocative efficiency	• Found that organization was still learning to take advantage of technology and had not reached a mature stage of IT use.
Ryan and Harrison (2000)	• Theoretical development • Interviews	• 50 IT decision makers from a variety of industries	• Considered whether traditional valuation analyses are incomplete and whether there are hidden costs or benefits to identified • Extends theory by describing systematic patterns of whether costs and benefits should be included or not	• Found that social costs and benefits accrue when IT resources are acquired • These benefits are pivotal in determining IT's effectiveness
Davern and Kauffman (2000)	• Model development	• No data	• Developed a model identifying links between potential value and realized value and differentiating between them	• Analyses differences between potential and realizable value
Chan (2000)	• Literature analysis	• No data	• Analysed research on IT value measures from 1993 to 1998. • Aimed to investigate trends in IT value measurement	• Found from analyses that IT value research has focused on theory generation and development of new methods and measures • Most research addresses the question what value do IT investments provide

sures for factors that had been identified in prior research i.e. transaction risks, client risks and supplier risks as impacting on IT outsourcing risks. Du, Keil, Lars, Shen, and Tiwana (2006) together with Johnstone, Huff, and Hope (2006) have developed models which consider the issue of risk in IT projects and in particular the conflict resolution processes associated with projects. A number of studies have focused on security risks such as Broadbent (2003); Von Solms and Von Solms (2004); Van Solms (2005); ITGI (2005d); ITGI (2005c); Chapin and Akridge (2005); ITGI (2006b); Pironti (2006); and Ross (2006). These studies identified that properly governed information security is important to organization and, that security is linked to business continuity. The also explored reasons why information security processes are not successful, and developed a program for assessing the maturity of organizational IT security processes.

IT risk management research has focused on a variety of issues. Development of preliminary

measures of risk and the identification of key risk factors have been important contributions to the research in this focus area. Young and Jordan (2002) developed an integrated approach to risk management which aimed to ensure risk management was considered from the lowest level of decision making through to the board level. Levine (2004) concludes that risk management spending is increasing as boards realize that understanding and mitigating IT risks is an important part of enterprise risk management processes.

Research on IT risk assessment includes the development of a risk assessment model by Du et al. (2006) which focuses on how individuals assess risks in IT projects and what affects their perception of IT risk. The findings of this study highlight that perceived control over the project affects an individual's perception of IT risk within projects. This could highlight to organizations that IT risk assessments may need to be conducted by staff within and in control of the project and then compared in an attempt to remove individual risk perception bias. Hinz and Malinowski (2006) also focused on risk assessment processes and developed a model which includes problem solving in personal networks as part of the risk assessment process. These models are some of the first to focus on the role of individuals in making IT risk assessments and give organizations a key insight into how IT risk assessments may be performed and the potential issues associated with these assessments.

Another study which made an important contribution to understanding of risk management processes is Broadbent, Kitzis, and Hunter (2004), which identified four ways of coping with risk namely mitigation, transfer, acceptance, and

avoidance. These risk responses also form part of globally accepted enterprise risk management models established by the Committee of Sponsoring Organization of the Treadway Commission (COSO) (COSO 2004) and Standards Australia and Standards New Zealand (2004).

IT risk management research is still developing and to date only a few key issues have been addressed. The models in this area as still evolving as are the risk assessment processes. IT risk is often seen as forming part of enterprise risk management processes and as such is evaluated by models including the COSO framework.

Table 3. Current status of research on risk management of IT systems

Study	Method (s)	Organizations/Subjects	Issues Examined/Domain	Results
Du, Keil, Mathiassen, Shen and Tiwana (2006)	• Model development • Hypothesis development and testing	• 102 practitioners with high IT projects expertise • 105 university students with low IT projects expertise	• Assesses risks in IT development projects under different conditions • Focuses on three conditions: the perceived control over the IT project, use of an attention shaping tool and the expertise of the individual conducting the assessment • Model considered that perceived control, risk analysis tool and expertise are linked to risk perception and continuation decisions	• Develops a research model of risk perception • Found that perceived control influences risk perception but not behaviour • High expertise participants identified higher levels of risk in IT projects • Provides important assistance for both novice and experienced practitioners
Hinz and Malinowski (2006)	• Model development	• Interviews with experts	• Considers the issue of personal networks as an addition to existing risk assessment models of end user IT.	• Develops a model which integrates personal network characteristics into a model of risk assessment • Combines social network analysis and IT risk management theory to better understand social networks and their links to corporate risk management
Johnstone, Huff and Hope (2006)	• Framework development • Case study	• Case study of medium public entity NZ government funded entity • Interviews with six major stakeholders using a critical incident method of data collection	• Use system concepts to develop a overall research framework focusing on the conflict resolution processes associated with projects • Identified governance as consisting of authority structures, mechanisms and policies	• Develops a framework to examine conflicts in IT projects by developing a model of the conflict resolution process • Case study used to validate the use of the framework for usefulness • Model found to be useful and valid for assessing project conflict.

continued on following page

Table 3. continued

Study	Method (s)	Organizations/Subjects	Issues Examined/Domain	Results
Gewald and Helbig (2006)	• Conceptual • Case study	• Case study of large outsourcing service provider	• Outsourcing governance models • Model is based on extensive experience of one of the largest outsourcing providers worldwide	• Develops a governance model for mitigating outsourcing risks • Model consists of strategic direction, governance principles and organizational structures.
IT Governance Institute (2006b)	• Conceptual	• No data	• IS governance is responsibility of board of directors and senior executives and consists of leadership, organizational structures and processes that safeguard information	• Outlines the benefits of information security governance and the role of boards and management in monitoring Information security governance • Presents a guide for self assessment of Information security governance practice
Jogani (2006)	• Conceptual	• No data	• Examined the development of a mobile technology governance framework	• Establishes policy on mobile technology governance
Pareek (2006)	• Conceptual	• No data	• Discussion of the risk and reward correlation graph • Identified key types of risk ie market, credit, exogenous and operational • Discussed effective risk management strategies and risk mitigation tools and enablers	• Proposes organizations establish a business case for risk management • Risk management should be important for every manager and organizational culture should focus on risk identification and management across the organization • Establishes of a database of organizational risks is important
Pironti (2006)	• Survey	• 148 Certified Information Security Managers	• Develops an effective governance process for information security • Outlines 5 basic outcomes which can result from an effective governance approach to information security	• Results of the study support the notion that properly governed information security is important to organizations
Ross (2006)	• Conceptual	• No data	• Examines the issues associated with the relationship between information security and business continuity management (BCM) • Identifies BCM and security as two points on a spectrum of risk management • Indicates that BCM is the loss caused by a physical event and security is a loss caused by a logical event	• Found a link between business continuity and security • Business continuity plans should include outages of all sorts, not just disasters (ie planning to improve recoverability from logical events)
Bahli and Rivard (2005)	• Risk measurement development • Survey	• 132 IT executives	• Aims to validate measures of risk factors associated with outsourcing IT operations • Identifies three major sources of risk factors for IT outsourcing – the transaction, the client and the supplier.	• Develops preliminary measures of IT outsourcing risk factors and an overall risk score for each outsourcing project • Demonstrates that organizations need to pay attention to risk factors as a source of risk in IT outsourcing situations • Project risk assessment helps to determine which outsourcing project to undertake
Benvenuto and Brand (2005)	• Conceptual	• No data	• Outlines the drivers of outsourcing and identifies risk analysis process and elements of risk management	• Develops a generic risk management model

continued on following page

Table 3. continued

Study	Method (s)	Organizations/Subjects	Issues Examined/Domain	Results
Chapin & Akridge (2005)	• Model development	• No data	• Develops of a security program maturity model • Relates security to risk assessment processes	• Develops a program of assessing the maturity of organizational IT security processes to enable improvements in the security processes over time.
Gerber and Von Solms (2005)	• Model development	• No data	• Identifies a growing need for protecting information from risks faced globally	• Develops a model of risk management and links to three research paradigms ie natural science, theoretical science and social science
IT Governance Institute (2005c)	• Conceptual	• No data	• Presents a number of considerations for security managers on Information security governance • Aims to develop a holistic view of risk	• Develops an important resource for security managers which outlines key issues for consideration, the information sources relevant to these issues, the evaluation and performance criteria related to each issues and security program initiatives related to each issue
IT Governance Institute (2005d}	• Conceptual	• No data	• Defines and discusses information risk management • Identifies a number of key risks facing organizations and discusses survey results from a global IT survey	• Identifies that to enable effective governance IT risks should be identified as strategic, program, project or operational risks • Suggests a plan for dealing with IT risks
Van Solms (2005)	• Theoretical development	• No data	• Discusses the relationship between information security operational management and information security compliance management • Defines and identified key components of the two separate dimensions of Information Security governance	• Identified Information Security governance as an integral part of good IT and corporate governance • Recommends that Information security operational management and information security compliance management be recognized as two separate dimensions of Information Security Governance • Recommends the establishment of a separate information security compliance management department
Broadbent, Kitzis and Hunter (2004)	• Conceptual	• No data	• Identifies new IT risks which CIO's must take responsibility for: Business interconnections, regulatory compliance, consumer demand for privacy protection and rising costs of IT failures • Discusses the need for CIO's to consider IT and enterprise risks holistically	• Identifies 4 ways of coping with risk: mitigation, transfer, acceptance and avoidance • CIO's need to establish a good risk management process which identifies targets & threats, and calculates associated risk and potential loss
Stewart (2004)	• Conceptual	• No data	• Highlights the complexities of risk assessment in relation to IT information security • Risk compensation theory and risk management is discussed	• Identifies some new directions in terms of risk management for security professionals, companies and the security industry

continued on following page

Table 3. continued

Study	Method (s)	Organizations/Subjects	Issues Examined/Domain	Results
Von Solms and Von Solms (2004)	• Conceptual	• No data	• Discussed the issues associated with implementing a successful information security plan	• Identified the 10 deadly sins of information security which prevent companies implementing a successful comprehensive information security plan • Developed a tick list to evaluate the company's security plan
Kliem (2004)	• Conceptual	• No data	• Identified Offshore development risks by risk category ie financial, managerial, behavioural and legal risks • Discussed risk analysis and how to perform risk controls	• Developed a risk and goals matrix based on project objectives
Levine (2004)	• Conceptual	• No data	• Discusses the drivers for risk management solutions, outlines the technology issues associated with risk management solutions	• Presents an argument for the use of risk assessment processes and solutions
COSO (2004)	• Model development	• No data	• Establishes a methodology for risk management	• Develops a methodology for risk management using a quantitative risk assessment process
Standards Australia and Standards New Zealand (2004)	• Standard Setting	• No data	• Establishes a methodology for risk management	• Develops a methodology for risk management using qualitative risk assessment process
SAS Ltd (2004)	• Survey	• International Benchmark survey June 2004	• Reported International benchmark survey into operational risk management in the financial services industry	• Found that 20% of respondents do not have an operational risk program • Found that IT and systems failure is the biggest source of operational risk • Identified key IT risk factors
Ataya (2003)	• Interviews	• 50 senior IT executives at Fortune 1000 companies	• Considered the impact of risk on decision making on new IT investments	• Found that IT plans should IT and enterprise risk assessments
Hadden, DeZoort and Hermanson (2003)	• Survey	• Audit committee members	• Considered who has the technical expertise to address IT risks, who is addressing IT risks and is there a good match between these parties • Survey was developed to assess audit committee members perceptions of their oversight of 34 specific IT risks	• Suggested that audit committees could be involved in IT risk oversight • Audit committee members perceived their personal qualifications to oversee IT risks as moderate • Audit committee oversight role was assessed to be below moderate • Audit committee involvement in IT risk oversight to date has been reduced by the committee's reliance on top management to address IT risks • Raises the question of whether some audit committees have relied too heavily on management reporting of IT risks
Wiederkehr (2003)	• Conceptual	• No data	• Discussion of IT security awareness program	• Develops an IT security awareness program

continued on following page

Table 3. continued

Study	Method (s)	Organizations/Subjects	Issues Examined/Domain	Results
Young and Jordan (2002)	• Framework Development • Case study	• Case study of project failure	• Establishes the theoretical groundwork to develop an integrated approach to risk management and IT governance • Developed an IT governance framework to communicate risk from an operational to strategic level within organizations	• Development of an integrated multi-stakeholder risk management framework • Applied the IMS risk management framework to a case of IT failure • Identified IT governance weaknesses from case study

Management of IT Resources Research

Management of IT resources research has been extensive over the last 20 years. See Table 4 (Buckby, 2008). 31 studies in this focus area have examined IT architecture/structure models, ITG models, IT steering committees, IT project management and ITG models. Early studies in this area have been concerned with the structure and IT decision making processes of organizations, such as Sambamurthy and Zmud (1999) and Peterson, O'Callaghan, and Ribbers (2000). These studies considered the impact of IT structure models, that is, centralized, decentralized, federal and hybrid. Peterson et al. (2000) and Peterson (2001) found that no matter how the structure of IT divisions was organized, one of the most important issues for good IT governance was good coordination of IT resources. Schwarz and Hirschheim (2003) extended the knowledge of prior studies on IT structures. They argued that organizations need to manage IT resources optimally in order to achieve good ITG. Bushel (2007) contributed valuable discussion to the key advantages and disadvantages between federated and central IT structure models. This conceptual study proposed that the federated model cannot be an effective structure unless governance is handled correctly.

Hamaker (2000) proposed that taking a regular inventory of IT resources would assist with IT resource management processes. Ribbers, Peterson, and Parker (2002) examined the procedural and social mechanisms of ITG which was a new approach to resource management research. Broadbent (2003) also adopted a novel approach by focusing on IT resource management from an assignment of decision rights perspective. This study developed key domains, governance styles and a combination matrix in its examination of ITG. Weill and Ross (2004) and Weill (2004) extended the knowledge on ITG resource management and how top performing organizations manage their ITG structures and processes. Kohli and Devaraj (2004) developed an organizational process for managing IT investments and measuring the associated IT pay-offs. Their AIAC framework included four phases related to IT investment payoffs, these being alignment, involvement, analysis and communication. The research provided detailed analysis of the components of their model and how they can be successfully implemented. It further tested them on the Holy Cross Health System. Kohli and Devaraj (2004) made three key recommendations on IT investment pay-offs as a result of their findings namely (1) IT payoffs are the responsibility of the entire organization, not just the IT department, (2) management of IT payoffs begins prior to the investment and continues through post implementation and (3) IT payoffs are contingent upon creating and exploiting complementary assets. This study makes a significant contribution to the understanding of value delivery from IT investments.

Later studies on IT resource management have focused on broader models of ITG such as the ITGAP model which posits that ITG consists of IT value drivers, ITG capabilities, ITG complexity and IT value (Peterson, 2004). Powell and Yager (2004) examined the differences between two IT groups in the same company including their IT structures and coordination mechanisms. This study found that IT structures and coordination mechanisms could not fully explain the differences between the two groups. Culture, structure, internal economy, methods and tools, and metrics and rewards were considered to be important ITG mechanisms. De Haes and Van Grembergen (2006) found that organizations were applying

a mix of IT resource structures, practices and mechanisms to build an ITG framework. The research in this area has assisted academics and practitioners to better understand how organizations are structuring their IT processes and thus gives clearer insight into how they should be governing their IT investments.

Measurement of the Performance of IT Systems

Table 5 presents a detailed review of the IT performance measurement literature, summarising the results of 21 studies (Buckby, 2008). The research in this focus area has examined measurement

Table 4. Current status of research on management of IT resources

Study	Method (s)	Organizations/Subjects	Issues Examined/Domain	Results
Robinson (2007)	• Model development	• No data	• Examines the development of a ITG reference model	• Development of an ITG reference model • Identification of three factors which influence an organization's business profile • Developed a customised ITG reference model to architecture
Bushell (2007)	• Conceptual	• Data from industry surveys	• Discussion of central vs federated models of IT organizational structures	• Identifed that 77% of organizations surveyed by CIO magazine used a centralized model of IT organizational structure. • Federated model can not be an effective structure unless governance is right
De Haes and Van Grembergen (2006)	• Framework development • Research proposition development • Proposition testing	• Pilot case studies in Belgian Organizations	• Develops a research question which focused on the link between IT governance and fusion between business and IT • Extends the prior work of De Haes and Van Grembergen (2004).	• From pilot cases, tentative conclusion was that organizations are applying a mix of structures, practices and relational mechanisms to build an IT governance framework • Identifies three levels of operation of IT governance ie strategic, management level and operational level
Milis, Viaene and Ribbers (2006)	• Case studies	• 12 Large ICT projects in Banking and insurance industry • 45 stakeholders interviewed	• Examines the role of the ICT project evaluation process especially the feasibility evaluation • Aims to establish a link between the main trigger for a project and the thoroughness of the feasibility process • Uses the Butler Cox classification to classify the main triggers of each project	• Found that an ICT project's main trigger functions as a moderating variable in the feasibility process • Found that despite feasibility evaluations being important were often not done thoroughly. • Recommended that this be an issue which could improve ICT governance

continued on following page

Table 4. continued

Study	Method (s)	Organizations/Subjects	Issues Examined/Domain	Results
Wilcocks, Feeny and Olson (2006)	• Framework development • Case studies	• Longitudinal case studies of a medium-sized organization beginning to outsource and a multi-national and a national bank with international interests who were involved in large scale outsourcing arrangements who had adopted the Feeny – Wilcocks framework	• Extension and revision of core IS capability framework of Feeny and Wilcocks (1998) to identify 9 capabilities • 9 capabilities included ITG, business system thinking, relationship building, designing technical architecture, making technology work, informed buying, contract facilitation, contract monitoring and vendor development • Case study analysis of 2000-2005 data about IT sourcing arrangements	• Organizations need to develop long-term strategic focus by applying all 9 capabilities • Framework emerged as a good evolutionary tool rather than an instant fix option • Core IS capabilities are related to governance mechanisms in place
Wilcoxson and Chatham (2006)	• Psychometric testing	• 130 Senior IT and General Managers	• Investigates the personal and behavioural characteristics of IT and general managers and compared these to reported leadership behaviour research	• IT managers were found to have a preference for decision making based on logic and objectivity rather than on emotions and feelings. • The managers were also found to focus equally on big picture and detailed concrete information • Found a strong contrast between leadership styles for IT and general managers which suggested a different approach to managerial roles • This indicates a greater task orientation on the part of IT managers.
Van Grembergen, De Haes and Moons (2005)	• Case studies	• 8 industries	• Discusses the relationship between business goals, IT goals and IT processes • Gathers preliminary evidence of the relationships	• Develops an initial view of ITG relationships by gathering evidence on the links between business goals, IT goals and IT processes
Brown and Grant (2005)	• Literature review • Framework development	• No data	• Presents a literature review of ITG research • Develops a Conceptual Framework for IT Governance Research to provide a logical structure for ITG research	• ITG research classified into two separate streams of research being ITG forms and ITG contingency analysis • Draws attention to the key papers which have developed contemporary ITG frameworks
De Haes and Van Grembergen (2004)	• Framework development	• No data	• Defines ITG and explains its relationship to enterprise governance • Posits that effective governance is determined by way IT function is organized and where the IT decision making authority is located within the organization • Discusses the role of the IT strategy/steering committee • Discusses the practical use of the IT Balanced scorecard	• Develops an IT governance framework which includes supporting structures, processes and relational mechanisms • Identifies that the key to effective IT governance is the relational mechanisms between business and IT staff and ongoing knowledge sharing between departments
Meyer (2004)	• Conceptual	• No Data	• Identifies 5 organizational systems of governance that can be applied to IT governance • Posits a role for oversight and audit of IT governance mechanisms	• Found that culture, structure, internal economy, methods and tools, and metrics and rewards are all important aspects of systemic IT governance mechanisms

continued on following page

Table 4. continued

Study	Method (s)	Organizations/Subjects	Issues Examined/Domain	Results
Peterson (2004)	• Theoretical development • Case study	• Case Study of Johnson & Johnson	• Presents a holistic view of IT governance • Considered that structural, process and relational capabilities are all important aspects of effective ITG	• Developed ITGAP model for use in assessing the effectiveness of organization's ITG architecture • ITGAP model posits that ITG consists of IT value drivers, ITG capability, ITG complexity and IT value
Powell and Yager (2004)	• Theoretical development) • Case Study • Interviews	• Mid sized US insurance company with 1,000 employees • Interviews with Vice Presidents of each IS group	• Examines the differences between two IS groups in the same company and compares to IS governance theory (centralized, decentralized or hybrid IS structures) and IS coordination theories (formal vs informal coordination) • Develops three research propositions	• Found that IS governance and IS coordination theories could not fully explain the differences between the groups
Rau (2004b)	• Conceptual • Model development	• No data	• Presents ideas and concepts on the way to govern IT • Presents an IT governance design structure that encourages participation from all stakeholders	• Develops a best practice IT organization governance design • Effective IT governance takes considerable time to achieve
Sherer (2004)	• Model development	• No data	• Prioritization of IS projects should be part of the strategic vision of the organization • Considers that reporting structure of IS organization and the involvement of a steering committee for investment prioritization are key influences on final IS project selection	• Develops a model of IT selection process based on strategic vision • Found that strategic vision affects IT governance decisions
Weill (2004) Weill and Ross (2004)	• Framework development	• 250 enterprises across 23 countries	• Identifies 5 major IT decision that large enterprises make and 6 governance archetypes organizations use for making decisions • Studies top performing organizations and identifies what makes them different from others • Identifies 7 characteristics of top governance performers	• Presents broad patterns of ITG • Identifies that five main factors that relate to variations in governance patterns • Develops ITG arrangements matrix which demonstrates the interactions between governance archetypes and decision domains • Develops 8 ITG critical success factors
Schwarz and Hischheim (2003)	• Model development • Case studies	• 6 Case Studies in Oil and Gas Industry	• Develops a model of IT governance • Explores difference in perceptions toward IT and the organization of IT activities • Uses an extended platform logic perspective which included a success metric and operationalised ITG using the platform logic perspective	• Found differences and similarities between firms with respect to IT capabilities, relational and integration mechanisms, measures of success and relationships with business units • Results indicate that organizations are now focused on two way relationship oriented approach to management of IT structure • Moves discussion on ITG away from structures to relationships

continued on following page

Table 4. continued

Study	Method (s)	Organizations/Subjects	Issues Examined/Domain	Results
Young and Jordan (2003)	• Conceptual	• No data	• Develops understanding of how senior management influenced IS project success • Significant component of the analysis related to IT governance issues • Postulates that mature IT governance is characterized by accountability to transparently resolve conflicts of interest between multiple stakeholders	• Senior managers influence success by committing time to be made aware of issues and actively participating to resolve conflict • Board should take a monitoring role to ensure benefits are delivered and failing projects terminated • Passion of stakeholders is the key indicator of success and governance
Broadbent (2003b)	• Conceptual	• No data	• Conceptualises that good IT governance effectively combines what decisions need to be made, who makes them and how they are enacted.	• Identifies 5 key domains about IT decisions, six IT governance styles and a matrix to determine what IT governance looks like
Kim (2003)	• Hypothesis development • Hypothesis testing	• 334 firms using B2B Supply Chain Planning Solutions 1990-1998	• Examines the effects of IT on the governance of firms that are using IT for competitive advantage	• Found that increased use of firm specific IT is found to be associated with decreases in outsourcing and increases in number of employees • Also found that the use of relation specific IT is negatively related to the degree of vertical integration
Ribbers, Peterson and Parker (2002)	• Framework development • Case studies • Interviews • Document analysis	• 9 Large complex organizations within different industries across Europe and North America • Interviews with business and IT executives • Analysis of Company documents	• Examines the procedural and social mechanisms of IT governance • Develops 2 research propositions • Posits that environmental contingencies moderate the relationship between IT governance processes and IT governance outcomes	• Found that effective IT governance processes across the cases were associated with methodological and social issues. Neither fully explains effective IT governance processes. • Highlights the gap between theory, empirical research and practice on effective IT governance processes.
Sohal and Fitzpatrick (2002)	• Survey	• Senior IT Officers in 59 Large Australian organizations	• Compares IT usage levels between three levels of intensity	• Companies categorized into three groups based on intensity of IT use in organization • Data revealed that the more involved senior management was in IT decision making, the more likely management will accept the role of IT in the success of their organization • Compares results to International study on same issue
Keyes-Pearce (2002)	• Theoretical development	• No data	• Presents a view of CIO's about IT governance • Compares this with perceptions of CIO's and e-business managers of large organizations migrating to e-business	• Found a disparity of focus between academics and industry consultants as to the importance of IT governance • Found that ITG practice varies widely and view of organizations about IT governance varies widely • Little research on maturity of IT governance

continued on following page

Table 4. continued

Study	Method (s)	Organizations/Subjects	Issues Examined/Domain	Results
Mukherji (2001)	• Theoretical development	• No data	• Considers the impact of IT on organizations. • Examines how changes in organization structures are lined to changes in IS architecture • Examines the impact of the internet	• Found that the impact of IT on organizations has been considerable • Traces the evolution of changing information systems architectures and their impact on organizations • Found that changes in organizations structure, strategy and decision making processes may be linked to changes in computer technology and design • The internet is becoming a great leveller across organizations
Peterson (2001)	• Exploratory study • Framework development • Case studies	• 3 Large European Based Financial Services Organizations	• Extends the theoretical model of Petersen et al. (2000) • Develops 4 research propositions to test the model	• Found support from case studies for 3 research propositions and that ITG coordination needs to be actively managed in a transnational organisation • Effective hybrid configurations require complex structural, functional and social mechanisms for coordination
Karimi, Bhattacherjee, Gupta and Somers (2000)	• Hypothesis testing	• 213 IT managers in financial services industry	• Hypothesizes relationships between level of sophistication of IT steering committees and level of sophistication of IT management within organizations • Examines impact of IT steering committees on the management of IT functions • Sophistication of IT management involved management awareness of organization's long term IT strategic plans • More sophisticated management of IT leads to better value delivery from IT and forms part of the IT governance process	• Presence and role of IT steering committees were found to be significantly related to the level of IT management sophistication within the organizations in the study • Firms wanting to benefit from steering committees would determine the steering committees role to coincide with the level of IT management sophistication desired
(Doughty, 2000)	• Measurement development	• No Data	• Develops a method of determining the effectiveness of IT steering committees • Attempts to develop an audit report on steering committee functions	• Identified IT steering committee effectiveness measures
Hamaker (2000)	• Conceptual	• No Data	• Proposes that an inventory of organizational IT resources would assist with IT governance processes • Identifies three components of IT governance (IT hardware and software infrastructure, firm's strategic vision and decision making processes)	• Considered linking each division's mission critical functions along with IT systems used to perform these functions would assist with assessing extent of organizational IT functions and their role

continued on following page

Table 4. continued

Study	Method (s)	Organizations/Subjects	Issues Examined/Domain	Results
Peterson, Callaghan and Ribbers (2000)	• Theoretical development • Case studies	• 6 Case Studies of Dutch Financial Services Organizations	• Develops 5 theoretical propositions • Develops a conceptual framework for conducting multiple comparative case study research • Expands conceptualization of ITG and focuses on IT decision making processes. • Anticipated a hybrid configuration for complex organizations	• Found that ITG was not solely concerned with the formal allocation of IT decision making authority. • Irrespective of locus on control, mechanisms for co-ordination needed to be included for governance of IT. • In competitive environments, effective ITG is more likely to resemble a network of relationships than classical hierarchical structures.
Sambamurthy and Zmud (1999)	• Theory development • Hypothesis development • Survey • Case studies	• Survey of 35 firms • 8 Case studies of Governance arrangements selected from 35 firms	• Identifies that three primary modes of ITG over last 20 years (centralized, decentralized and federal)- IT decision making processes • This study examined multiple contingency forces influence on the mode of IT governance used in an enterprise • Develops theory that contingency forces interact with each other and either amplify, dampen or override their mutual influences on IT governance.	• Found that multiple contingencies provide a useful framework for understanding how contingency forces operate together in influencing the location of IT decision rights
Broadbent and Weill (1997)	• Framework development • Case studies	• Case studies of large organizations	• Examines the relationship between IT infrastructure and organizational business and IT maxims • Develops framework "management by Maxim" • Examines how successful firms create business driven IT infrastructures and their infrastructure decision making processes	• Identifies categories of Business and IT maxim • Business and IT should set strategic objectives together to assist alignment of strategy and a business driven IT infrastructure • Identifies four views of IT firm infrastructure ie none, utility, dependent and enabling • Maxims assist an organization to better view infrastructure and thus
Karake (1992)	• Hypothesis development • Hypothesis testing	• 72 Large Publicly-held American organizations (36 companies in each category of centralized vs decentralized IT structure)	• Examines relationships between IT structure, control and corporate governance using publicly available data about ownership	• Found that IT structure (centralized vs decentralized) is strongly related to ownership and control (ie shareholdings) • Higher the management ownership the more centralized the IT structure, the lower the management ownership the more decentralized the IT structure is likely to be

Table 5. Current status of research on measurement of performance of IT systems

Study	Method (s)	Organizations/Subjects	Issues Examined/Domain	Results
Dahlberg and Lahdelma (2007)	• Surveys	• 109 senior executives from 20 enterprises	• Examines the role of ITG maturity evaluations by senior executives and their links to outsourcing.	• Found links between ITG and outsourcing • Survey instrument found to have consistent results
Lambeth (2007)	• Conceptual	• No data	• Encouraging organizations to consider ITGI resources to assist with ITG	• Recommending the virtues of ITGI resources for assistance with ITG
Dahlberg and Kivijarvi (2006)	• Framework development • Measurement tool	• 27 public/private sector organizations	• Discusses measurement of ITG effectiveness	• Develops a new integrative IT governance framework and an assessment tool to measure ITG effectiveness
Blumenberg and Hinz (2006)	• Conceptual	• No data	• Discusses links between IT-BSC and bayesian belief network	• Discusses how bayesian belief network can be used to improve the ITBSC
Van Grembergen and De Haes (2005a)	• Model development	• No data	• Discusses relational mechanisms and their role in ITG	• Examines ITG and links to relevant structures, processes and relational mechanisms.
Van Grembergen and De Haes (2005c)	• Measurement development	• No data	• Development of an IT governance balanced scorecard including corporate contribution, stakeholders, future orientation and operational excellence as drivers	• Developed detailed IT governance balance scorecard including detailed breakdown of the key components
Van Grembergen and De Haes (2005b)	• Conceptual	• No data	• Discusses CobiT's management guidelines and extends the understanding of these guidelines.	• Provides advice on CobiT management guidelines • Discusses Key performance indicators and key goal indicators
Warland and Ridley (2005)	• Interviews	• Semi-structured interviews with 9 participants from three Tasmanian Government Agencies	• Discusses the awareness and understanding of IT Control frameworks ie CobiT, ITIL etc	• Found that their was little adoption of formal or informal IT control frameworks in the Tasmanian State Government
Hardy and Guldentops (2005)	• Conceptual	• No data	• Provides advice on CobiT 4.0 framework . • Identifies the main changes in this new CobiT framework	• Identifies benefits users will achieve from new framework
Murray (2004)	• Framework development	• No data	• Discusses IT department performance	• Development of a framework for assessing and managing the review of IT project performance
Fairchild (2004)	• Model Testing	• Case studies	• Tests the outsourcing maturity model an established framework	• Found support from the cases for the outsourcing maturity model
Pederiva (2003)	• Conceptual	• No data	• Discusses main issues and lessons learned re CobIT maturity models • Discusses benchmarking	• Discusses how organizations can apply the CobIT maturity model process in a practical sense
Van Grembergen, Saull and De Haes (2003)	• Case study	• Case study of Insurance company	• Identified a firm specific IT BSC • Discussed Balanced scorecard method, IT BSC and its elements	• Concluded that development and application of firm specific IT BSC would assist with establishing IT governance best practice in the organization • Identified that strategic ITBSC should be cascaded into operational services, governance services and development services scorecards

continued on following page

Table 5. continued

Study	Method (s)	Organizations/Subjects	Issues Examined/Domain	Results
Van Grembergen, De Haes and Amelinckx (2003)	• Measurement development	• No data	• Develops a ITBSC for service level management • Establishes links between IT BSC and CobiT	• CobiT and ITBSC can ensure better measurement of whether organization getting value from service level agreements
Guldentops (2003)	• Conceptual	• No data	• Discusses maturity measurement processes	• Develops maturity model – rising star chart which assists with measurement of maturity model attributes
Gold (2003)	• Measurement development	• No data	• Establishs a BSC strategy model	• Establishs an ITBSC model and discusses the ITBSC processes
Guldentops, Van Grembergen and De Haes (2002)	• Measurement development	• Survey of CobiT users	• Reports findings of maturity models across industries, size, geography, driving forces, inhibiting forces	• Discusses the maturity model process and the results of a survey of CobiT users
Van Grembergen and Amelinckx (2002)	• Measurement development	• No data	• Develops an ITBSC for e-business projects • Establishes links between ITBSC and e-business processes	• Generic e-business balanced scorecard developed
Van Grembergen (2000)	• Case study	• Case study of a bank	• Discussed how the IT balanced scorecard (ITBSC) can be linked to the business balanced scorecard (BBSC) to support IT/business governance and alignment processes	• If use a cascade of scorecards linking Business BSC to IT BSC and then to IT strategic, IT development and IT operational scorecards, IT governance measures and concerns will be identified to top management • Identifies key components of development and strategic IT BSC for a bank
Saull (2000)	• Measurement development	• No data	• Discusses ITBSC processes	• Develops extended ITBSC based on prior research
Van Grembergen and Van Bruggen (1997)	• Model development •	• No data	• Discusses application of balanced scorecard approach to IT division contribution to organization	• Develops IT balanced scorecard based on original balanced scorecard approach of Kaplan and Norton (1992)

methods of ITG including the development of the IT balanced scorecard (ITBSC) and maturity model assessments for strategic alignment processes. The ITBSC, which can be used to measure the performance of IT systems, was adapted from the balanced scorecard (BSC) model of Kaplan & Norton (1992). Van Grembergen and Van Bruggen (1997) were one of the first to explore how the BSC could be adapted to measure the IT department's contribution to the business. Saull (2000) used both of these sources to establish a new BSC framework that described the contributions of the IT department in more detail.

Van Grembergen (2000) examined the links between the ITBSC and the business balanced scorecard (BBSC) to support IT/business governance and alignment processes. They extended the ITBSC to an e-business, service level management and firm specific context (Van Grembergen & Amelinckx, 2002; Van Grembergen, De Haes & Amelinckx, 2003; Van Grembergen, Saull & De Haes, 2003). Van Grembergen and De Haes (2005c) build on the ITBSC to develop an ITG balanced scorecard. Their research has since been extended to examine the relationship between structures, process and relational mechanisms (Van Grembergen, De Haes, and Van Brempt

(2007). The work by these researchers has made an important contribution to the understanding of ITG measurement and has presented many issues for consideration by practitioners.

This research focus area also is concerned with the development of measurement models such as "The Control Objectives for Information and Related Technology Framework (CobiT)". This comprehensive model aims to provide good practice guidelines and measurement techniques for control over information, IT and related risks. The processes identified by CobiT 3.0 and 4.0 and more recently CobiT 4.1 and Val IT include operational level measures of ITG processes and are grouped under planning and organization, delivery and support, acquisition and implementation and monitoring (ISACF, 2000; ITGI, 2005, ITGI, 2006a, ITGI, 2007). Other key measurement models are ITIL and ITSM which were briefly discussed earlier. The measurement of quality and value from IT services, which forms part of these frameworks, has been adopted by a large number of organizations either in isolation or together with other frameworks such as CobiT, CMMI and the ISO/IEC standards (ITGI, 2007; Software Engineering Institute, 2007, ISO/IEC, 2004a; ISO/IEC, 2004b; ISO/IEC, 2005a; ISO/IEC, 2005b). Comparison of measurement models has also made an important contribution to this research focus area.

The issues associated with the implementation of the CobiT framework have been studied by Tyler (2000) and Weiderkehr (2000). The use of the CobiT maturity model to assess the level of ITG processes being used in a corporation has also received attention (Guldentops, 2003; Guldentops, Van Grembergen & Haes, 2002; Pederiva, 2003). A further area of research has focused on the acceptance of CobiT as a management tool for use with ITG (Guldentops et al., 2003; Legrenzi, 2003).

POSSIBLE FUTURE DIRECTIONS IN IT GOVERNANCE RESEARCH

In the prior section, research across the five focus areas was presented. The research in these focus areas has been performed in relative isolation and whilst this research contributes to the overall understanding of the key components of ITG, it has not adopted a holistic view point.

For ITG to become an accepted part of organizational governance processes in the same way that corporate governance has been accepted, ITG research needs to develop models which encompass all focus areas of ITG. The models would also need to incorporate measurement methods which could be based on prior research in performance measurement. A number of researchers including Dahlberg and Kivijarvi, (2006); De Haes and Van Grembergen, (2005); Peterson (2004) have attempted to develop holistic ITG models but there is still much room for improvement in fusing ITG into one process. A recent study by Bowen, Cheung, and Rohde (2007) explores the factors influencing IT governance structures, processes and outcome metrics and builds a model which relates these factors to ITG effectiveness.

Strategic Alignment of Business and IT Research

Research focusing on the strategic alignment of business and IT processes has been proactive in the development of models and frameworks to assist the understanding of the relationships between business and IT within an organization. There have been many models developed, but there has been a paucity of research which has tested existing models to determine their appropriateness in describing and measuring strategic alignment within organizations. To further develop the research in this area, studies could focus on the development of extended models of business-IT alignment that take into account the important prior work of Henderson and Venkatraman, (1993); Luftman, (2003); Strnadl, (2006); Sledgianowski and Luftman, (2005); and De Haes and Van Grembergen, (2005). Testing of existing models could also assist with development of future research in this area.

Possible research questions which could be considered in the future in this focus area are as follows:

- Do effective strategic alignment processes lead to more effective ITG?
- Are strategic alignment processes linked to improved organizational performance?
- Which of the existing strategic alignment models best explain the relationship between business and IT within an organization?
- What are the similarities and differences between the existing strategic alignment models?
- What are some practical recommendations organizations could use to improve their strategic alignment processes?
- How does assessing maturity of strategic alignment processes assist an organization to improve their ITG processes?

Delivery of Value from IT Systems

Research on the delivery of value from IT systems has had a similar focus to strategic alignment research with a number of models and frameworks developed. There have been two key issues studied within this focus area: (1) distinguishing between the potential value and realizable value of IT systems and (2) the link between organizational performance and delivery of value from IT systems. As with strategic alignment research, there has been little focus on the testing of these models. Development of practical methods for organizations to improve their understanding of value delivery and their ability to measure it effectively would make an important contribu-

tion to research in this area. Whilst the prior research of Davern and Kauffman, (2000); Sircar et al. (2000); Dedrick et al. (2003); Melville et al. (2004); Tallon (2007); and Ward et al. (2007) has provided a greater understanding of value delivery processes, further work is needed to extend knowledge on this issue.

Possible research questions which could be considered in the future in this focus area are as follows:

- Does the establishment of ITG processes in an organization lead to improved value delivery from IT systems?
- What are some practical recommendations to assist organizations to improve their value delivery processes?
- Does measurement of value delivery from IT systems (post implementation) lead to improved organizational performance?
- What are the most effective methods of measuring value delivery from IT systems?
- How regularly should value delivery be assessed for organizational IT systems?

Risk Management of IT Systems

Risk management of IT systems research has focused on three main areas. These are identification of IT risks, risk management models and frameworks and risk assessment processes. The identification of risks research has provided important understanding of outsourcing, IT projects and security risks. The development of an integrated model of risk management by Young and Jordan (2002) has made an important contribution to this focus area. Development of models/frameworks extending this work would broaden the knowledge of IT risk management processes. Studies that identify practical methods that organizations could use to improve their IT risk management processes and better assess IT risks would also be beneficial. Globally accepted enterprise risk management processes could play an important role in future research by assisting with the definition of IT risk in enterprise risk management processes.

Possible research questions which could be considered in the future in this focus area are as follows:

- What are practical methods that organizations could use to better manage and assess IT risks?
- Does assessment of IT risks lead to better mitigation of IT risks?
- Does the development of risk management processes within an organization lead to more effective ITG?
- Does the assessment of outsourcing and IT project risks lead to better organizational risk management processes?

Management of IT Resources

Management of IT resources has been an extensive area of ITG research. Much of the research has focused on the best type of IT resource structure for an organization. Other key outcomes of the research in this focus area have been the development of broader models of ITG (De Haes & Van Grembergen, 2006; Peterson, 2004). Despite the research on IT resource structures, the debate on the advantages and disadvantages of these structural models continues with the recent research of Bushell (2007). Further research on the issue of IT structural models would assist in giving organizations more practical knowledge of which structure to choose and why. The continued development of broader holistic models of ITG will also make a key contribution to future research on this issue.

Possible research questions which could be considered in the future in this focus area are as follows:

- What are the key differences between the IT resource structural models?

- Does a particular IT resource model lead to improved ITG?
- What are some practical methods organizations could use to better manage their IT resources?
- How can an organization assess the maturity of their IT resource management processes?

Measurement of the Performance of IT Systems

Research on the measurement of the performance of IT systems has predominantly focused on measurement processes including maturity models and IT balanced scorecard methods (Van Grembergen, 2000; Van Grembergen & Amelinckx, 2002; Van Grembergen, De Haes & Amelinckx, 2003; Van Grembergen, Saull & De Haes, 2003; Van Grembergen et al., 2007). This focus area has also encompassed ITG measurement models such as CobiT. Future research in this area should focus on improving measurement techniques. Performance measurement processes must support and assess all areas of ITG for a holistic model of ITG to be successfully developed. Practical methods that organizations could use to better measure all ITG focus areas would make an important contribution to ITG research. Some of the models and assessment techniques to date, including maturity models, the ITBSC, the ITIL framework and others, provide methods that could be further developed to assist practitioners to achieve better measurements of ITG and its effectiveness.

Possible research questions which could be considered in the future in this focus area are as follows:

- What practical methods could organizations use to better measure ITG focus areas?
- How can maturity models be developed for all ITG focus areas and how can an overall ITG maturity be successfully measured?

• Would the development of an ITG strategic informational dashboard assist organizations to improve their ITG processes?

CONCLUSION

Despite extensive research in each of the focus areas, considerable work is needed to further the understanding of ITG and to develop a successful holistic measure of ITG. To enable ITG to become an accepted part of organizational strategic and operational governance processes, it is important that researchers develop more practical methods for organizations to use in establishing and assessing ITG. The conduct of future research addressing the issues raised in the prior sections should lead to improved ITG within each focus area and the establishment of holistic models and frameworks of ITG.

REFERENCES

Ataya, G. (2003). Risk-aware decision making for new IT investments. *Information Systems Control Journal, 2*, 12-14.

Avison, D., Jones, J., Powell, P., & Wilson, D. (2004). Using and validating the strategic alignment model. *Journal of Strategic Information Systems, 13*(3), 223-246.

Bahli, B. & Rivard, S. (2005). Validating measures of information technology outsourcing risk factors. *Omega, 33*(doi:10.1016/jomega.2004.04.003), 175-187.

Beimborn, D., Wagner, H.-T., Franke, J., & Weitzel, T. (2007). The influence of alignment on the post-implementation success of a core banking information system: An embedded case study. *Paper presented at the 40th Hawaii International Conference on System Sciences*, Hawaii.

Benvenuto, N. A. & Brand, D. (2005). Outsourcing - A risk management perspective. *Information Systems Control Journal, 5*, 35.

Bergeron, F., Raymond, L., & Rivard, S. (2004). Ideal patterns of strategic alignment and business performance. *Information & Management, 41*, 1003-1020.

Blumenberg, S. A. & Hinz, D. J. (2006). Enhancing the prognostic power of IT balanced scorecards with Bayesian belief networks. *Paper presented at the 39th Hawaii International Conference on System Sciences*, Hawaii.

Bowen, P. L., Cheung, M. Y. D., & Rohde, F. H. (2007). Enhancing IT governance practices: A model and case study of an organization's efforts. *International Journal of Accounting Information Systems, 8*(3), 191-221.

Bricnall, R., Darrell, G., Nilsson, H., & Pessi, K. (2007). Aligning IT strategy with business strategy through the balanced scorecard in a multinational pharmaceutical company. *Paper presented at the 40th Hawaii International Conference on System Sciences*, Hawaii.

Broadbent, M. (2003a). Keys to effective security. *CIO, 11*(7).

Broadbent, M. (2003b). The right combination. *CIO Canada, 11*(4), 13-14.

Broadbent, M. (2003c). Understanding IT governance. *CIO Canada, 11*(4).

Broadbent, M., Kitzis, E., & Hunter, R. (2004). Armed against risk. *Optimize, 44*.

Broadbent, M. & Weill, P. (1993). Improving business and information strategy alignment: Learning from the banking industry. *IBM Systems Journal, 32*(1), 162.

Broadbent, M. & Weill, P. (1997). Management by Maxim: How business and IT managers can create IT infrastructures. *Sloan Management Review, 38*(3), 77.

Brown, A. E. & Grant, G. G. (2005). Framing the frameworks: A review of IT governance research. *Communication of the Association for Information Systems, 15*, 696-712.

Bruce, K. (1998). Can you align IT with business strategy? *Strategy and Leadership, 26*(5), 16-21.

Buckby, S. (2008). *Board review of IT governance in Australian universities.* Unpublished doctoral dissertation, Queensland University of Technology, Australia.

Burn, J. M. & Szeto, C. (1999). A comparison of the views of business and IT management on success factors for strategic alignment. *Information & Management, 37*, 197-216.

Bushell, S. (2007). When egos dare. *CIO, June,* 37-44.

Chan, Y. E. (2000). IT value: The great divide between qualitative and quantitative and individual and organizational measures. *Journal of Management Information Systems, 16*(4), 225.

Chapin, D. A. & Akridge, S. (2005). How can security be measured? *Information Systems Control Journal, 2*, 43.

Committee of Sponsoring Organizations of the Treadway Commission (COSO) (2004). *Enterprise risk management - Integrated framework.* Retrieved April 29, 2008, from http://www.coso.org/publications.htm

Coughlan, J., Lycett, M., & Macredie, R. D. (2005). Understanding the business-IT relationship. *International Journal of Information Management, 25*(4), 303-319.

Croteau, A.-M. & Bergeron, F. (2001). An information technology trilogy: Business strategy, technological deployment and organizational performance. *Journal of Strategic Information Systems, 10*, 77-99.

Cumps, B., Viaene, S., Dedene, G., & Vandenbulcke, J. (2006). An empirical study on business/ICT alignment in European organizations. *Paper presented at the 39th Hawaii International Conference on System Sciences*, Hawaii.

Dahlberg, T. & Kivijarvi, H. (2006). An integrated framework of IT governance and the development and validation of an assessment instrument. *Paper presented at the 39th Hawaii International Conference on System Sciences*, Hawaii.

Dahlberg, T. & Lahdelma, P. (2007). IT governance maturity and IT outsourcing degree: An exploratory study. *Paper presented at the Hawaii International Conference on System Sciences*, Hawaii.

Davern, M. J. & Kauffman, R. J. (2000). Discovering potential and realizing value from information technology investments. *Journal of Management Information Systems, 16*(4), 121.

De Haes, S. & Van Grembergen, W. (2004). IT governance and its mechanisms. *Information Systems Control Journal, 1*, 27.

De Haes, S. & Van Grembergen, W. (2005). IT governance structures, processes and relational mechanisms: Achieving IT/business alignment in a major Belgian financial group. *Paper presented at the 38th International Conference on Systems Sciences*, Hawaii.

De Haes, S. & Van Grembergen, W. (2006). Information technology governance best practices in Belgian organizations. *Paper presented at the 39th Hawaii International Conferences on System Sciences*, Hawaii.

Dedrick, J., Gurbaxani, V., & Kraemer, K. L. (2003). Information technology and economic performance: A critical review of the empirical evidence. *ACM Computing Surveys, 35*(1), 1-28.

Doughty, K. (2000). *The myth or reality of information technology steering committees.* Retrieved April 29, 2008, from www.isaca.org/art3a.htm

D'Souza, D. & Mukherjee, D. (2004). Overcoming the challenges of aligning IT with business. *The Executive's Journal*, Winter, 23-31.

Du, S., Keil, M., Lars, M., Shen, Y., & Tiwana, A. (2006). The role of perceived control, attention-shaping, and expertise in IT project risk assessment. *Paper presented at the 39th Hawaii International Conference on System Sciences*, Hawaii.

Erickson, T. J., Magee, J. F., Roussel, P. A., & Saad, K. N. (1990). Managing technology as a business strategy. *Sloan Management Review, 31*(3), 73.

Fairchild, A. M. (2004). Information technology outsourcing (ITO) governance: An examination of the outsourcing management maturity model. *Paper presented at the 37th International Conference on System Sciences*, Hawaii.

Gerber, M. & Von Solms, R. (2005). Management of risk in the information age. *Computers & Security, 24*(1), 16-30.

Gewald, H. & Helbig, K. (2006). A goverance model for managing outsourcing partnerships. *Paper presented at the 39th Hawaii International Conference on System Sciences*, Hawaii.

Gold, R. S. (2002). Enabling the strategy-focused IT organization. *Information Systems Control Journal, 4*, 21.

Gold, R. S. (2003). Building the IT organization balanced scorecard. *Information Systems Control Journal, 5*, 46.

Gregor, S., Fernandez, W., Holtham, D., Martin, M., Stern, S., Vitale, M., et al. (2005). *Achieving value from ICT: Key management strategies*. Canberra: Department of Communications, Information Technology and the Arts, ICT Research Study.

Guldentops, E. (2003). Maturity measurement - First the purpose, then the method. *Information Systems Control Journal, 4*, 15.

Guldentops, E., Van Grembergen, W., & Haes, S. (2002). Control and maturity survey: Establishing a reference benchmark and a self-assessment tool. *Information Systems Control Journal, 6*, 32-35.

Hadden, L. B., DeZoort, F. T., & Hermanson, D. (2003). IT risk oversight: The role of audit committees, internal auditors and external auditors. *Internal Auditing, 18*(6).

Hamaker, S. (2000). Your IT applications inventory is all in your head - An observation related to IT governance tools. *Information Systems Control Journal, 5*, 21.

Hardy, G. & Guldentops, E. (2005). CobiT 4.0: The new face of CobiT. *Information Systems Control Journal, 6*.

Heier, H., Borgman, H. P., & Maistry, M. G. (2007). Examining the relationship between IT governance software and business value of IT: Evidence from four case studies. *Paper presented at the 40th Hawaii International Conference on System Sciences*, Hawaii.

Henderson, J. C., Rockart, J. F., & Sifonis, J. G. (1987). Integrating management support systems into strategic information systems planning. *Journal of Management Information Systems, 4*(1), 5-24.

Henderson, J. C. & Sifinos, J. G. (1988). The value of strategic IS planning: Understanding consistency, validity, and IS markets. *MIS Quarterly, 12*(2), 187-200.

Henderson, J. C. (1990). Plugging into strategic partnerships: The critical IS connection. *Sloan Management Review, 31*(3), 7.

Henderson, J. C. & Thomas, J. B. (1992). Aligning business and information technology domains: Strategic planning in hospitals. *Hospital & Health Services Administration, 37*(1), 71.

Henderson, J. C. & Venkatraman, N. (1991). Understanding strategic alignment. *Business Quarterly, 55*(3), 72.

Henderson, J. C. & Venkatraman, N. (1993). Strategic alignment: Leveraging information technology for transforming organizations. *IBM Systems Journal, 32*(1), 4.

Henderson, J. C. & Venkatraman, N. (1999). Strategic alignment: Leveraging information technology for transforming organizations. *IBM Systems Journal, 38*(2/3), 472-484.

Hinz, D. J. & Malinowski, J. (2006). Assessing the risks of IT infrastructure - A personal network perspective. *Paper presented at the 39th Hawaii International Conference on System Sciences*, Hawaii.

Hirschheim, R. & Sabherwal, R. (2001). Detour in the path toward strategic information systems alignment. *California Management Review, 44*, 1(87-108).

Information Systems and Control Foundation. (2000). *CobiT* (3rd ed.). USA: Information Systems Control Foundation.

International Organization for Standardization (ISO) & International Electrotechnical Commission (IEC). (2004a). *ISO/IEC 12207 - Software lifecycle processes Amd 2*. Retrieved April 29, 2008, from www.iso.org

International Organization for Standardization (ISO) & International Electrotechnical Commission (IEC). (2004b*). ISO 15504-4:2004 - Process assessment - Part 4: Guidance on use for process improvement and process capability determination*. Retrieved April 28, 2008, from www.iso.org

International Organization for Standardization (ISO) & International Electrotechnical Commission (IEC) (2005a). *ISO/IEC 27001 information technology - Security techniques- Information security management systems requirements*. Retrieved April 29, 2008, from www.iso.org

International Organization for Standardization (ISO) & International Electrotechnical Com-

mission (IEC) (2005b). *ISO/IEC 27002 standard - Information technology – Security techniques - Code of practice for information security management*. Retrieved April 29, 2008, from www.iso.org

IT Governance Institute (ITGI) (2000). IT governance roundtable - Sponsored by the IT governance institute. *Information Systems Control Journal, 4*, 27-28.

IT Governance Institute (ITGI) (2001). *Board briefing on IT governance*. Retrieved April 29, 2008, from www.itgi.org

IT Governance Institute (ITGI) (2003). *Board briefing on IT governance* (2nd ed.) Retrieved April 29, 2008, from www.itgi.org

IT Governance Institute (ITGI) (2004). *IT governance status report*. Retrieved April 29, 2008, from www.itgi.org

IT Governance Institute (ITGI) (2005a). *CobiT 4.0.* Rolling Meadows, IL: IT Governance Institute.

IT Governance Institute (ITGI) (2005b). *Governance of outsourcing*. Retrieved April 29, 2008, from www.itgi.org

IT Governance Institute (ITGI) (2005c). *Information risks: Whose business are they?* Retrieved April 29, 2008, from www.itgi.org

IT Governance Institute (ITGI) (2005d). *Information security governance - Top action for security managers*. Retrieved April 29, 2008, from www.itgi.org

IT Governance Institute (ITGI) (2005e). *IT alignment: Who is in charge?* Retrieved April 29, 2008,, from www.itgi.org

IT Governance Institute (ITGI) (2005f). *Measuring and demonstrating the value of IT*. Retrieved April 29, 2008, from www.itgi.org

IT Governance Institute (ITGI) (2005g). *Optimising value creation from IT investments*. Retrieved April 29, 2008, from www.itgi.org

IT Governance Institute (ITGI) (2006a). *Enterprise value: Governance of IT investments, The Val IT framework*. Retrieved April 29, 2008, from www.itgi.org

IT Governance Institute (ITGI) (2006b). *Information security governance: Guidance for boards of directors and executive management*. Retrieved April 29, 2008, from www.itgi.org

IT Governance Institute (ITGI) (2006c). *IT governance global status report 2006*. Retrieved April 29, 2008, from www.itgi.org

IT Governance Institute (ITGI) (2007). *CobiT 4.1*. Rolling Meadows, IL: IT Governance Institute.

IT Service Management (ITSM) (2007). *Overview of ITSM*. Retrieved April 29, 2008, from www.itsm.info/ITSM.htm

Jogani, A. (2006). Governance of mobile technology in enterprises. *Information Systems Control Journal, 4*, 25-27.

Johnstone, D., Huff, S., & Hope, B. (2006). IT projects: Conflict, governance and systems thinking. *Paper presented at the 39th Hawaii International Conference on System Sciences*, Hawaii.

Kaplan, R. & Norton, D. (1992). The balanced scorecard-measures that drive performance. *Harvard Business Review*, January-February, 71-79.

Karake, Z. A. (1992). An empirical investigation of information technology structure, control and corporate governance. *Journal of Strategic Information Systems, 1*(5), 258-265.

Karimi, J., Bhattacherjee, A., Gupta, Y. P., & Somers, T. M. (2000). The effects of MIS steering committees on information technology management sophistication. *Journal of Management Information Systems, 17*(2), 207.

Kearns, G. S. & Lederer, A. L. (2003). A resource-based view of strategic IT alignment: How knowledge sharing ceates competitive advantage. *Decision Sciences, 34*(1), 1-27.

Keyes-Pearce, S. V. (2002). Rethinking the importance of IT governance in the e-world. *Paper presented at the 6th Pacific Asia Conference on Information Systems*, Tokyo, Japan.

Kim, S. M. (2003). *Information technology and governance: Substitution and complementary*. University of Illinois at Urbana-Champaign, Illinois.

Kliem, R. (2004). Managing the risks of offshore IT development projects. *Information Systems Management, 21*(3), 22.

Kohli, R. & Devaraj, S. (2004). Realizing the business value of information technology investments: An organizational process. *MIS Quarterly Executive, 3*(1), 53-68.

Kwon, D. & Watts, S. (2006). IT valuation in turbulent times. *Journal of Strategic Information Systems, 15*, 327-354.

Lambeth, J. (2007). Using CobiT as a tool to lead enterprise IT organizations. *Information Systems Control Journal, 1*(28-29).

Lee, B. & Menon, N. M. (2000). Information technology value through different normative lenses. *Journal of Management Information Systems, 16*(4), 99.

Legrenzi, C. (2003). The second edition of the European survey on the economic value of information technology: Inventory of practices concerning IT governance. *Information Systems Control Journal, 3*, 50.

Levine, R. (2004). Risk management systems: Understanding the need. *Information Systems Management, 21*(2), 31.

Luftman, J. N. (2000). Addressing business-IT alignment maturity. *Communications of the Association for Information Systems, 4*(14), 1-50.

Luftman, J. N. (2003). Assessing IT/business alignment. *Information Systems Management*, Fall, 9-15.

Luftman, J. N. & Brier, T. (1999). Achieving and sustaining business-IT alignment. *California Management Review, 42*(1), 109-121.

Luftman, J. N., Lewis, P. R., & Oldach, S. H. (1993). Transforming the enterprise: The alignment of business and information technology strategies. *IBM Systems Journal, 32*(1), 198.

Luftman, J. N., Papp, R., & Brier, T. (1999). Enablers and inhibitors of business-IT alignment. *Communications of the Association for Information Systems, 1*, 1-32.

Maes, R. (1999). *A generic framework for information management.* Retrieved April 29, 2008, from http://primavera.fee.uva.nl/html/working_papers.cfm

Maes, R., Rijsenbrij, D., Truijens, O., & Goedvolk, H. (2000). *Redefining business-IT alignment through a unified framework.* PrimaVera Working Paper Series - University of Amsterdam.

Martin, N., Gregor, S., & Hart, D. (2005). The social dimension of business and IS/IT alignment: Case studies of six public-sector organizations. *Australian Accounting Review, 15*(3), 28-38.

McKay, J., Marshall, P., & Smith, L. (2003). Steps towards effective IT governance: Strategic IT planning, evaluation and benefits management. *Paper presented at the 7th Pacific Asia Conference on Information Systems*, Adelaide, South Australia.

Melville, N., Kraemer, K. L., & Gurbaxani, V. (2004). Review: Information technology and organizational performance: An integrative model of IT business value. *MIS Quarterly, 28*(2), 283-322.

Meyer, N. D. (2004). Systemic IS governance: An introduction. *Information Systems Management, 21*(4), 23.

Milis, K., Viaene, S., & Ribbers, P. (2006). *On how the feasibility study is influenced by an ICT project's main trigger. Paper presented at the 39th Hawaii International Conference on System Sciences,* Hawaii.

Mukherji, A. (2001). The evolution of information systems: Their impact on organizations and structures. *Management Decision, 40*(5/6), 497-507.

Murray, J. P. (2004). Judging IT department performance. *Information Systems Management,* Spring.

Papp, R. (1999). Business-IT alignment: Productivity paradox payoff? *Industrial Management & Data Systems, 99*(8), 367.

Pareek, M. (2006). Living with risk. *Information Systems Control Journal, 6,* 35-38.

Peak, D. & Guynes, C. S. (2003). Improving information quality through IT alignment planning: A case study. *Information Systems Management,* Fall, 22-28.

Pederiva, A. (2003). The CobiT maturity model in a vendor evaluation case. *Information Systems Control Journal, 3,* 26.

Peterson, R. (2001). Configurations and coordination for global information technology governance: Complex designs in a transnational European context. *Paper presented at the 34th International Conference on Systems Sciences,* Hawaii.

Peterson, R. (2004). Crafting information technology governance. *Information Systems Management, 21*(4), 7.

Peterson, R. R., O'Callaghan, R., & Ribbers, P. M. A. (2000). Information technology governance by design: Investigating hybrid configurations and integration mechanisms. *Paper presented at the International Conference of Information Systems,* Brisbane, Queensland, Australia.

Pironti, J. P. (2006). Information security governance: Motivations, benefits and outcomes. *Information Systems Control Journal, 4,* 45-48.

Powell, A. & Yager, S. E. (2004). Exploring reputation differences in information systems groups. *Journal of Information Technology Cases and Applications, 6*(2), 5-26.

Rau, K. G. (2004a). The CIO dashboard performance management program: Measuring and managing the value of IT. *The Executive's Journal*, Winter.

Rau, K. G. (2004b). Effective governance of IT: Design objectives, roles, and relationships. *Information Systems Management, 21*(4), 35.

Reich, B. H. & Benbasat, I. (2000). Factors that influence the social dimension of alignment between business and information technology objectives. *MIS Quarterly, 24*(1), 81-113.

Ribbers, P. M. A., Peterson, R. R., & Parker, M. M. (2002). Designing information technology governance processes: Diagnosing contemporary practices and competing theories. *Paper presented at the 35th International Conference on Systems Sciences*, Hawaii.

Robinson, N. (2007). The many faces of IT governance: Crafting an IT governance architecture. *Information Systems Control Journal, 1*, 14-16.

Ross, S. J. (2006). IS security matters: Converging need, diverging response. *Information Systems Control Journal, 2*, 8-9.

Ryan, S. D. & Harrison, D. A. (2000). Considering social subsystem costs and benefits in information technology investment decisions: A view from the field on anticipated payoffs. *Journal of Management Information Systems, 16*(4), 11.

Sambamurthy, V. & Zmud, R. W. (1999). Arrangements for information technology governance: A theory of multiple contingencies. *MIS Quarterly, 23*(2), 261-290.

SAS Ltd. (2004). *Operational risk management in the financial services industry.* April 30, 2008, from http://www.sas.com/industry/banking/oprisk/index.html

Saull, R. (2000). The IT Balanced Scorecard- A Roadmap to Effective Governance of a Shared Services IT Organization. *Information Systems Control Journal, 2*, 31-38.

Schwarz, A. & Hirschheim, R. (2003). An extended platform logic perspective of IT governance: managing perceptions and activities of IT. *The Journal of Strategic Information Systems, 12*(2), 129-166.

Sherer, S. A. (2004). IS project selection: The role of strategic vision and IT governance. *Paper presented at the 37th Hawaii International Conference on System Sciences*, Hawaii.

Silvius, A. J. G. (2007). Business and IT alignment in theory and practice. *Paper presented at the 40th Hawaii International Conference on System Sciences*, Hawaii.

Sircar, S., Turnbow, J. L., & Bordoloi, B. (2000). A framework for assessing the relationship between information technolgy investments and firm performance. *Journal of Management Information Systems, 16*(4), 69.

Sledgianowski, D. & Luftman, J. (2005). IT-business strategic alignment maturity- A case study. *Journal of Cases of Information Technology, 7*(2), 102.

Smaczny, T. (2001). Is an alignment between business and information technology the appropriate paradigm to manage IT in today's organizations? *Management Decisions, 39*(10), 797-802.

Software Engineering Institute (2007). *What is CMMI?* Retrieved April 30, 2008, from www.sei.cmu.edu/cmmi/general/index.html

Sohal, A. S. & Fitzpatrick, P. (2002). IT governance and management in large Australian organizations. *International Journal of Production Economics, 75*(1-2), 97.

Standards Australia (2005). *Corporate governance of information & communication technology- AS8015-2005*: Standards Australia.

Standards Australia & Standards New Zealand (2004). *Risk management AS/NZS 4360:2004:* Standards Australia/Standards New Zealand.

Stewart, A. (2004). On risk: Perception and direction. *Computers & Security, 23*(5), 362-370.

Strnadl, C. F. (2006). Aligning business and IT: The process-driven architecture model. *Information Systems Management, 23*(4), 67-77.

Tallon, P. P. (2007). Does IT pay to focus? An analysis of IT business value under single and multi-focused business strategies. *Journal of Strategic Information Systems, 16*(3), 278-300.

Tallon, P. P., Kraemer, K. L., & Gurbaxani, V. (2000). Executives' perceptions of the business value of information technology: A process-oriented approach. *Journal of Management Information Systems, 16*(4), 145.

Thatcher, M. E. & Pingry, D. E. (2007). Modeling the IT value paradox. *Communications of the ACM, 50*(8), 41-45.

Thorp, J. (2006). Value management-responding to the challenge of value. *Information Systems Control Journal, 5*, 21-22.

Trites, G. (2003). Director responsibility for IT governance. *Paper presented at the University of Waterloo IS Assurance Symposium*, University of Waterloo Canada.

Tyler, R. (2000). Implementing CobiT in New South Wales Health. *Information Systems Control Journal, 3*, 30-32.

United Kingdom Office of Government Commerce & IT Service Management Forum (2005). *The information technology infrastructure library (ITIL) - Version 3*. Retrieved April 30, 2008, from www.itil.uk.com, www.itsm.info/ITIL.htm

Van Der Zee, J. T. M. & De Jong, B. (1999). Alignment is not enough: Integrating business and information technology management with the balanced business scorecard. *Journal of Management Information Systems, 16*(2), 137-156.

Van Grembergen, W. (2000). The balanced scorecard and IT governance. *Information Systems Control Journal, 2*, 40-43.

Van Grembergen, W. & Amelinckx, L. (2002). Measuring and managing e-business projects through the balanced scorecard. *Paper presented at the 35th Hawaii International Conference on System Sciences*, Hawaii.

Van Grembergen, W. & De Haes, S. (2005a). CobiT's management guidelines revisited: The KGIs/KPIs cascade. *Information Systems Control Journal, 6*, 54.

Van Grembergen, W. & De Haes, S. (2005b). *IT governance and its mechanisms*. Retrieved April 30, 2008, from www.uam.be

Van Grembergen, W. & De Haes, S. (2005c). Measuring and improving IT governance through the balanced scorecard. *Information Systems Control Journal, 2*, 35.

Van Grembergen, W., De Haes, S., & Amelinckx, I. (2003). Using CobiT and the balanced scorecard as instruments for service level management. *Information Systems Control Journal, 4*, 56.

Van Grembergen, W., De Haes, S., & Moons, J. (2005). Linking business goals to IT goals and CobiT processes. *Information Systems Control Journal, 4*, 18-22.

Van Grembergen, W., De Haes, S., & Van Brempt, H. (2007). Prioritising and linking business and IT goals in the financial sector. *Paper presented at the 40th Hawaii International Conference on System Sciences*, Hawaii.

Van Grembergen, W., Saull, R., & De Haes, S. (2003). Linking the IT balanced scorecard to the business objectives at a major Canadian financial group. *Journal of Information Technology Cases and Applications, 5*(1), 23-45.

Van Grembergen, W. & Van Bruggen, R. (1997). Measuring and improving corporate information technology through the balanced scorecard technique. *Paper presented at the Fourth European Conference on the Evaluation of Information Technology*, Delft, (pp.163-171).

Van Lier, J. & Dohmen, T. (2007). Benefits management and strategic alignment in an IT outsourcing context. *Paper presented at the 40th Hawaii International Conference on System Sciences*, Hawaii.

Von Solms, B. & Von Solms, R. (2004). The 10 deadly sins of information security management. *Computers & Security, 23*(5), 371-376.

Von Solms, S. H. (2005). Information security governance - Compliance management vs. operational management. *Computers & Security, 24*(6), 443-447.

Wagner, H.-T., Beimborn, D., Franke, J., & Weitzel, T. (2006). IT business alignment and IT usage in operational processes: A retail banking case. *Paper presented at the 39th Hawaii International Conference on System Sciences*, Hawaii.

Ward, J., De Hertogh, S., & Viaene, S. (2007). Managing benefits from IS/IT investments: An empirical investigation into current practice. *Paper presented at the 40th Hawaii International Conference on System Sciences*, Hawaii.

Warland, C. & Ridley, G. (2005). Awareness of IT control frameworks in an Australian state government: A qualitative case study. *Paper presented at the 38th Hawaii International Conference on System Sciences*, Hawaii.

Weill, P. (2004). Don't just lead, govern: How top-performing firms govern IT. *MIS Quarterly Executive, 3*(1), 1-17.

Weill, P. & Ross, J. W. (2004). *IT governance-How top performers manage IT decision rights for superior results*. Boston, Massachusetts: Harvard Business School Press.

Wiederkehr, B. J. (2000). Group wide implementation of CobiT framework. *Information Systems Control Journal, 5*, 27-29.

Wiederkehr, B. J. (2003). IT security awareness program. *Information Systems Control Journal, 3*, 30-32.

Willcocks, L., Feeny, D., & Olson, N. (2006). Implementing core IS capabilities: Feeny-Willcocks IT governance and management framework revisited. *European Management Journal, 24*(1), 28-37.

Willcoxson, L. & Chatham, R. (2006). Testing the accuracy of the IT stereotype: Profiling IT managers' personality and behavioural characteristics. *Information & Management, 43*, 697-705.

Young, R. C. & Jordan, E. (2002). IT governance and risk management: An integrated multistakeholder framework. *Paper presented at the Asia Pacific Decision Sciences Institute*, Bangkok, Thialand.

Young, R. C. & Jordan, E. (2003, 10-13 July). Passion & IT governance. *Paper presented at the 7th Pacific Asia Conference on Information Systems*, Adelaide South Australia.

Chapter II
IT Governance–Based IT Strategy and Management:
Literature Review and Future Research Directions

Junghoon Lee
Yonsei University, Korea

Changjin Lee
Yonsei University, Korea

ABSTRACT

Domestic and global companies are increasingly using information and communication technologies as a means of delivering their strategic visions and thus maintaining a competitive advantage. The value of information assets has increased as firms' asset base shifts from tangible to intangible properties, placing a premium on firms' capacity to develop, manage and utilize their information assets. In this environment, companies aim to strengthen their business control over IT resources, maximizing performance through defining the responsibilities of all staff involved in IT resource management and processes. However, while most managers acknowledge the importance of managing IT assets within a framework of IT governance (ITG), only a small number of academic treatments deal with ITG, meaning that businesses often find themselves making their governance decisions in a vacuum. This chapter therefore aims to clarify the concept of ITG through conducting a literature review, suggesting some implications of this work for practitioners, and indicating directions for the future study of ITG.

INTRODUCTION

As information and communication technology develops, an increasing number of companies are recognizing the potential value of IT resources in delivering their firm's strategic vision. IT is no longer a supporting tool for business, but a fundamental component of company strategy in such roles as operations, internal audit, compliance and decision support. A recent survey conducted by the IT Governance Institute (ITGI) with CEO/CIOs drawn from 22 countries shows that 87% of respondents agree that IT plays an important role in achieving company goals in the broadest sense (ITGI, 2006).

In recent years, leading international organizations have focused attention on effective corporate governance as means of improving the performance of firms' IT assets. These efforts have intensified in the wake of large-scale frauds such as Enron and WorldCom in the United States and shareholders ensuing dissatisfaction with companies. Multinationals and others have devised corporate governance structures to clarify and monitor the respective roles and responsibilities of shareholders, management, and employees (OECD, 2004). These structures have laid greater emphasis on the importance of IT assets and ITG structure, aiming to minimize financial risks on IT investment by providing transparency, accountability, and manageable processes. These criteria entail the effective allocation of IT resources in terms of clear structures and decision-making procedures for IT management. In this juncture, it has become imperative to redefine effective ITG, seeking to understand governance's role in aligning organizations' information assets with their strategic goals (Webb, Pollard & Ridley, 2006). This alignment contributes to the creation of value in companies, through suggesting optimal amounts of risk for companies to take both in designing their management structures and in proactively responding to new business circumstances.

Despite the importance of ITG, however, little informed academic research has been carried out on the subject. While business's level of awareness for the need for good ITG is rising in practice, current research has yet to address the potential use of ITG as a soft-side of IT infrastructure (e.g., of decision-making bodies and policies) in improving organizational competency. The purpose of this chapter is, therefore, to examine the current literature and to suggest a future direction for research on ITG. This chapter attempts to examine various definitions and frameworks of ITG through conducting a literature review, classified into six different taxonomies: (1) the origin of ITG, (2) ITG definitions; (3) research topics related to ITG; (4) the timeline of ITG research; (5) levels of ITG analysis; and (6) methodology. Lastly, we analyze existing ITG frameworks, concluding by suggesting the necessity for the development of an integrated ITG framework

RESEARCH METHODOLOGY

In reviewing the existing ITG research relating to ITG, we surveyed a wide range of recent research in academic and industrial fields. While most review articles take account only of articles in the top academic journals in their areas, we found it desirable to take in as many references as possible covering IT-related practitioner articles and the industrial presentations given by consulting firms (Webster & Watson, 2002). This is because research in ITG is led by industry as much as by academics. The source materials surveyed for this chapter include: first, the leading journals n the MIS field, such as *MIS Quarterly, Information System Research, Journal of Management Information Systems, Communications of the ACM,* the *Harvard Business Review,* and the *Sloan Management Review,* and second, related articles found through academic search engines such as Business Source Premier, Science Direct and the AIS e-library. In addition, we reviewed articles arising out of some important conferences such as *ICIS, ECIS, ACIS, PAICS, AMCIS, HICCS, ITG International Conference* and Korean journals and conferences. The range of articles studied thus spanned publications in academic journals, working papers, the technical reports of major institutions, and books. Our searches were governed by the keyword(s) 'IT/IS governance'. We found a total initial sample of 144 articles, 30 of which were removed from the review process due to only treating ITG tangentially. As a result, a total of 114 articles were obtained and carefully reviewed.

LITERATURE REVIEW

The Origin of ITG

ITG focuses on the transparent and efficient management of firm IT resources, aiming to ensure that the enterprise's IT sustains and extends the organization's strategies and objectives (ITGI, 2005). ITG can be characterized by attributes such as transparency, control, effectiveness, and efficiency. These attributes are described from the perspective of two research streams: corporate governance and IT management, as shown in Figure 1.

Firstly, most research on corporate governance has been concerned to resolve conflicts of interest between various corporate stakeholders (Becht et al., 2002; Shleifer & Vishny, 1997). In corporate governance, researchers have suggested that transparency can be accomplished by a proper distribution of authorities and responsibilities among stakeholders, whose activities are then monitored on shareholders' behalf. Following the "OECD Principles of Corporate Governance," which were originally developed to provide a set of corporate governance standards and guidelines, corporate governance provides a structure through which company objectives may be set, as well as the means of attaining those objectives and monitoring governance performance (OECD, 2004). ITG inherits characteristics from corporate governance, seeking to ensure the transparent management and control of IT assets through forms of committee. This stream of research on ITG emphasizes the structure of an organization. In other words, the research classifies the structure of IT organizations into the three categories, "centralized," "decentralized," and "hybrid (federal)" according to their modes of distributing authorities and responsibilities for decision-making. This line of research has also determined the factors affecting the selection of organizational modes for different types

Figure 1. The origin of ITG research

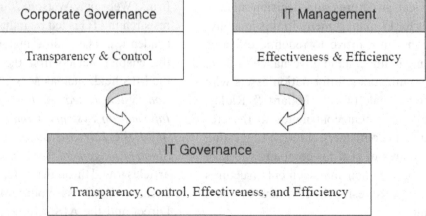

of firm (Brown & Grant, 2005; Heier, Borgman & Maistry, 2007; Sambamurthy & Zmud, 1999). However, although many researchers insist that ITG represents an integral part of corporate governance, most research looks more narrowly at IT assets, without any connected consideration of corporate governance.

Meanwhile, traditional research on the IS field has proposed efficient IT management as potentially one of the solutions to the so-called "IT productivity paradox problem" (Brynjolfsson, 1993; Hoogeveen & Oppelland, 2002; Soh & Markus, 1995). This stream of research is more concerned with the processes of IT management than with the structure of IT organizations (Heier et al., 2007). Soh and Markus (1995) analyze the effects of IT expenditure on organizational performance using process theory, stressing the importance of effective IT management. The particular strand of research stresses the need to improve IT processes in order to manage IT more effectively. Recently, further research works have suggested the value of introducing standardized IT methodologies such as ITSM (IT Service Management)/ITIL (IT Infrastructure Library), CMM, and EA (Enterprise Architecture) and the establishment of IT processes as a mode of the effective management of IT resources (Bhattacharjya & Chang, 2006; Getter, 2007; Sallé, 2004; Wagner, 2006)

IT Governance Definitions

Despite ITG's importance and the currency of the term since the late 1990's, academics working in the area continue to define the term in a number of ways (Webb et al., 2006). This lack of a comprehensive definition has possibly impeded in-depth research, further limiting the validity of cross-study comparisons of results (Keyes-Pearce, 2002; Simonsson & Johnson, 2006; Webb et al., 2006). It is thus necessary to clarify the concept of ITG through systematically classifying and drawing together various definitions of ITG in the

hope of supporting active research. A variety of definitions of ITG are summarized in Table 1.

These diverse definitions may be classified into three perspectives. Firstly, researchers seek to understand ITG as the location of decision-making rights and accountabilities within organizations (ITGI, 2003; Peterson, 2004; Simonson & Johnson, 2006; Weill & Woodham, 2002). Weill and Woodham (2002), Peterson (2004), and Simonson and Johnson (2006) define ITG as basically decision-making in the IT domain, focusing on the distribution of decision rights and accountabilities (or responsibilities) for the effective use of IT resources.

Secondly, researchers understand ITG as involving the strategic alignment between IT and business in order to achieve enterprises' full business value (Grembergen, 2004; Webb et al., 2006). Grembergen (2004) and Webb et al. (2006) define ITG as those activities maximizing business value through bringing about this strategic alignment. In achieving this goal, they emphasize the effective control of resources, performance management, and risk management.

Lastly, ITG may be defined as those IT organization structures and processes seeking to achieve organizations' strategy (Korac-Kakabadse & Kakabadse, 2001; ITGI, 2003). Korac-Kakabadse and Kakabadse (2001) describe IS/ITG as dealing with the structure of relationships and processes aiming to develop, direct and control IS/IT resources such that IT adds value to the firm's pursuit of its strategic objectives. The ITGI (2003) define ITG as the responsibility of company executives and the board of directors, referring inclusively to the leadership, organizational structures and processes ensuring that enterprises' IT sustains organizations strategies and objectives. The Australian Standards provide guiding principles for the directors of organizations on the effective, efficient, and acceptable use of ICT, setting out six principles in the context of a model of good corporate governance (AS 8015-2005, 2005).

Table 1. IT Governance definitions

Researcher	Definition of IT Governance
Korac-Kakabadse and Kakabadse (2001)	IS/ITG concentrates on the structure of company relationships and processes in seeking to develop, direct and control IS/IT resources. These arrangements add value to organizations as they pursue enterprise goals. ITG aims to balance risk and return for IS/IT resources and their processes.
Weill and Woodham (2002)	ITG specifies decision rights and accountability frameworks encouraging the best use within firms of IT.
ITGI (2003)	ITG is the responsibility of the board of directors and executive management. It forms an integral part of enterprise governance and consists of the leadership and organizational structures and processes which ensure that organizations keep to and extend their strategy.
Peterson (2004)	ITG describes the distribution of IT decision-making rights and responsibilities among different enterprise stakeholders, defining the procedures and mechanisms for making and monitoring strategic IT decisions.
Grembergen (2004)	ITG refers to the organizational capacity exercised by the board, executive management and IT management in formulating and implementing IT strategy, as this brings together business and IT.
AS 8015-2005 (2005)	The reference denotes an ITG system for the direction of Communication Technology (ICT) assets. The system involves evaluating, directing and monitoring ICT plans as these support business, and deals inclusively with ICT strategies and policies.
Simonson and Johnson (2006)	ITG concerns IT decision-making, that is, preparation for, making and implementing decisions regarding goals, processes, people and technology on a tactical and strategic level.
Webb et al. (2006)	ITG refers to the strategic alignment of IT with business, aiming to release maximum business value through the development and maintenance of effective IT accountability and performance and risk management.

In short, ITG can be commonly defined as the clarification of decision-making rights and responsibilities as companies seek to leverage IT assets to business goals. This alignment is designed to allow organizations to achieve their goals through putting in place a systematic series of activities establishing structures and processes. Research suggests that organizations work on three levels in developing IT governance frameworks, designing "structures", "processes", and "communication protocols or approaches" (Grembergen, 2004; Weill & Ross, 2004). Structures refer to organizational units and roles responsible for making IT decisions, such as committees, executive teams, and business/IT relationship managers. Processes involve the arrangement of formal decision-making and the design of forms of monitoring checking that daily behaviors are consistent with

firm IT policy. Monitoring also provides input to decision-making as regards investment proposals and evaluation processes, architecture exception processes, service-level agreements, chargeback, and certain metrics. Communication approaches include announcements, advocates, channels, and education efforts disseminating IT governance principles and policies. These may also inform workers of the outcomes of IT decision-making processes (Grembergen, 2004; Weill & Ross, 2004).

Research Topics Addressed

This work classifies a variety of ITG research topics into categories as shown in Figure 2. About 39% of the existing literature relates to ITG frameworks, with other work addressing issues such as risk management, ITG implementation, ITG measurement, governing IT outsourcing, aligning business activities and IT, IT project governance, ITG awareness, ITG impact on business performance, ITG effectiveness, ITG awareness, ITG modeling, and ITG software products.

Most previous research on ITG frameworks can be categorized into two main streams, one dealing with ITG forms (centralized, decentralized, hybrid, or federal) for the effective management of IT resources, and the other dealing with contingent influences on such forms (Brown & Grant, 2005). Sambamurthy and Zmud (1999) note the way in which organizations select ITG forms based on how they locate decision-making authority for principal IT activities, that is, the use of IT assets, project management, and the design of specific IT infrastructures. The authors categorize these contingency factors into three areas, corporate governance, economies of scope, and organizations' absorptive capacity, examining these factors influences on ITG forms according to the theory of multiple contingency. Chin, Brown, and Hu (2004) identify five contingency factors—the structure of corporate governance, government regulations and policies, global and local market competition, organizational culture,

and organizational IT competence. The last two factors are related to how companies' ITG structures develop in the course of mergers and acquisitions. They also perform an exploratory case study of an international telecommunications company validating these factors as shaping the development of ITG.

While the early stages of research on ITG mostly focused on the design of ITG frameworks for IT decision-making, since 2004 research has diversified into various topics including risk management, ITG implementation, ITG measurement IT outsourcing governance, business-IT strategic alignment, IT project governance, ITG impacts on firm performance, ITG effectiveness and so on. Figure 3 illustrates the explosion of analyses of ITG in the form of timeline, indicating the need to classify and synthesis current approaches.

In particular, Figure 3 shows the diversification of research on ITG in the past three years. For example, as practitioners' awareness of the importance of ITG has grown, research has begun to tackle the question of how effectively to implement ITG within organizations (Bhattacharjya & Chang, 2006; Cater-Steel, Mark Toleman, & Chown, 2006; Getter, 2007; Heier et al. 2007; Letsoalo Brown, & Njenga, 2006). Companies

Figure 2. Diversity of research topics in ITG

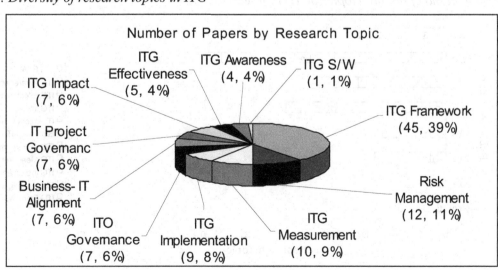

have begun to develop ITG mechanisms to control risks in response to new compliance requirements. In the wake of corporate scandals like Enron, risk management has rapidly become one of the most discussed subfields of ITG research (Debreceny, 2006; Hoappa & Wiander, 2006; Njenga & Brown, 2006). In addition, more recently researchers have addressed the measurement of firms' ITG maturity level. In this respect, Simonsson, Johnson, and Wijkström (2007) develop an ITG maturity assessment model, which comprises a modeling language for ITG based on Cobit, and a transparent analysis framework which enables the aggregation of single metrics into comprehensive maturity scores. This type of work is considerably more sophisticated than research on ITG in its early stage, which dealt mainly with ITG-related frameworks in terms of structures and processes (Brown, 1997; Peppard, Edwards, & Lambert, 1999; Sambamurthy & Zmud, 1999). More up-to-date work rather develops integral frameworks for assessing and verifying the impacts of ITG on business value (Csaszar & Clemons, 2006; Huang, Zmud, & Price, 2006; Sääksjärvi, 2006; Tanriverdi, 2006; Wagner, 2006).

In summary, further studies will be required to deal with relationships between ITG activities and business performance in such parameters as improved transparency and strengthened competitiveness; moreover, research will have to formulate more thoroughly the indicators evaluating ITG activities' efficiency. It is also possible that future ITG research could propose practical measures for strengthening company competitiveness by through the alignment of IT assets and business. Systematic frameworks would then govern the relationship between IT and other functions of corporate operations.

Timeline Research

The historical development of ITG research can be illustrated through the use of a timeline. The number of research papers published by year is shown in Figure 4.

The analysis points to a dramatic increase in the number of articles published over the past four years, implying a recent pickup of interest on ITG. 89 articles, about 78% of the 114 articles in total, have been published since 2004. This explosion of interest coincides with the collapse of WorldCom, suggesting that increasingly ITG is being envisioned as an integral element of effective corporate governance, helping deliver an international standard of corporate transparency. In line with such trends, industry and practi-

Figure 3. Trend of research topics on ITG by year

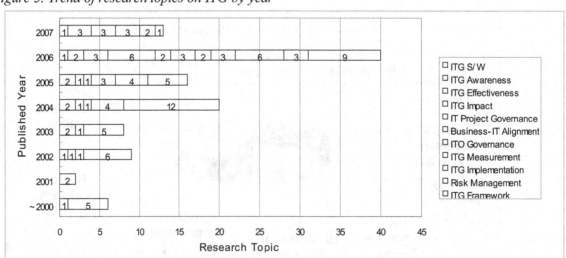

Figure 4. Number of papers published by year

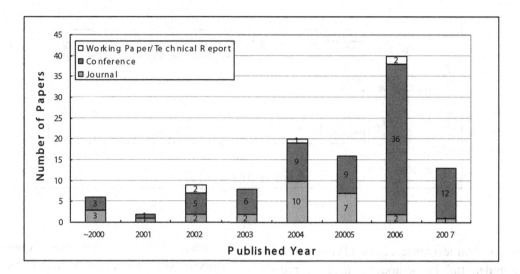

tioners have convened conferences such as the ITG International Conference, which especially focuses on ITG issues, and an ITG session has been part of the *Hawaii International Conference on System Sciences (HICSS)* since 2005. These papers, however, while increasing in number, have yet to reach a stage of consensus among researchers and practitioners. This absence seems to be closely related to the lack of a unified ITG definition, and the concomitant lack of a theoretical framework accommodating systematic attempts to describe ITG.

Unit of Analysis

Classifying articles by unit of analysis indicates that most research works to date have addressed ITG issues (either explicitly or implicitly) at a firm level; see Figure 5. Generally, the nature of ITG itself facilitates this level of analysis. ITG almost necessarily comprises questions of organizational structure, processes, and leadership for decision-making, as firms seek to support their strategic outcomes through their IT assets deployment. Further, the centrality of IT in transparency means that in rationalizing decision structures,

ITG is typically conceived at firm level (ITGI, 2003; Weill & Ross, 2004). Most research has then followed through these concepts in seeking to examine ITG as the relationship between business units (typically management or other firm functional units in relation to ITG), illuminating the connection between ITG design and maximal corporate performance.

Although most companies have by now managed a large number of IT system projects, very little research is devoted to ITG at the project level, concerning such issues as effective IT project control (or IT project governance). Among 114 articles, only seven mention the importance of IT project governance as a framework for resolving conflicts among stakeholders in the execution of IT projects (Dekkers, 2004; Henry, Kirsch, & Sambamurthy 2003; Johnstone, Huff, & Hope, 2006; Mähring, 2002; Sherer, 2004; Young, 2006; Young & Jordan, 2003). Meanwhile, though mergers and acquisitions are now considered one of the most effective strategies for enhancing corporate competitiveness in rapidly changing market environments, only one paper considers ITG in cases of mergers and acquisitions (Chin et al., 2004). The suggestion here is

Figure 5. Unit of analysis

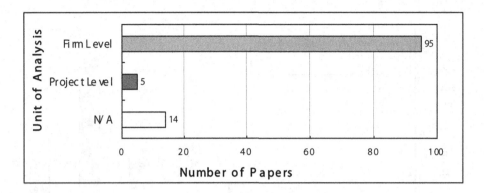

that interfirm level research on ITG may also be required in studying or modeling the convergence of different industries (e.g., the converged service of mobile phone banking with different parties). Firm, business and service convergence in this way creates another dimension of IT complexity, meaning that analytical frameworks may need to consider the coordination of multiple IT resources in describing the way forward for industry.

Research Methodology

Scientific papers' research methodology can be mainly divided into three different categories by purpose, exploratory study, descriptive study, and causal study. Exploratory studies are useful when researchers lack a clear idea of the problems that their research may encounter. These studies aid researchers to formulate concepts more clearly, to establish priorities, to develop operational definitions, and improve final research designs. In contrast to exploratory studies, descriptive studies aim only to characterize phenomena associated with a subject population, breaking this down among accounts or descriptors, or discovering associations among different variables. In a causal study, researchers seek to explain relationships among variables. Descriptive and causal studies centrally differ in their objectives, with descriptive studies concerned to answer "who," "what,"

"where," "when," or "how much" questions, and causal "why" (Cooper & Shindler, 2002).

The publications classified by these categories are summarized in Figure 6. It shows that the bulk of research undertaken in the ITG area remains exploratory except only ten articles. This result seems mainly due to the immaturity of ITG research, which lacks established theoretical frameworks in its early stages. Most of the exploratory research was conducted using case studies, undertaken through document analysis, survey, Delphi methods, and so forth. Case studies have proved to date one of the most popular research methods in the ITG field as shown in Figure 6; these have usually involved, as generally, the analysis of a phenomenon in its natural environment, by means of data collection using such methods as direct observation, interviews, document analysis (Gonzalez, Gasco, & Llopis, 2006).

In addition to case studies, document analysis is widely used dealing with themes of ITG frameworks, IT project governance, risk management, and ITG measurement. Surveys are also used to evaluate firms' and managements' awareness level of issues in ITG (Ahn, Yang, & Han, 2006; Na, Lee, Lee, & Lim, 2005), as well as in analyzing problems related with ITG frameworks, risk management and the outsourcing of ITG. Grembdergen, Haes, and Brempt (2007) use a Delphi method to build up a generic cascade from

Figure 6. Number of papers published by research methodology

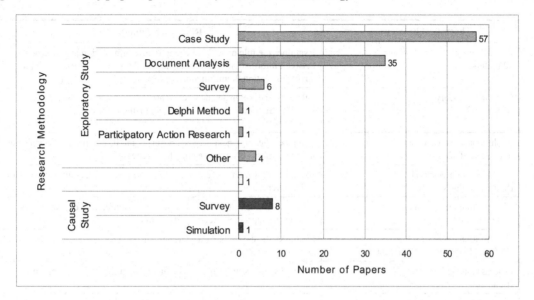

business goals to IT goals and IT processes in order to better understand their inter-relationship. While many exploratory studies are interesting, it remains difficult to generalize their findings.

Most causal research in ITG is performed based on survey methods, although exceptionally Csaszar and Clemons' (2006) study uses simulation. Causal research works attempt to investigate relations between ITG and business performance usually through survey methods (Tanriverdi, 2006) and simulation (Csaszar & Clemons, 2006). Cumps, Viaene, Dedene, and Vandenbulcke (2006) apply a resource-based view in analyzing the effects of business-ICT (Information and Communication Technology) alignment for firms seeking to sustain their competitive advantage. Jeong, Kang, and Lee (2007), meanwhile, develop a measurement instrument for ITG in three domains: IT resource and performance management, IT project management, and IT service management. Sääksjärvi (2006) investigates the impacts of strategic alignment and ITG on IT outsourcing success. Green and Ali (2006) study the roles of ITG mechanisms and their impact on the overall effectiveness of

ITG. Henry (2003) develops a project-level conceptualization of ITG and tests how IT project governance arrangements are influenced by the distribution of business and IT knowledge. He also tests their impact on project performance.

There is currently a dearth of descriptive research in the field seeking to offer a broader understanding of ITG. We can find only one descriptive study, which focuses on strategic alignment as a key objective of ITG, developing a benchmark for this value which is then tested against a sample (Musson & Jordan, 2006).

In this field, theoretical frameworks both provide a basis for in-depth investigations, such as causal research, and represent a basic scheme organizing further characterizations of individual instances. Classifying the existing research, only 16 articles, making up about 14% of all research examined in Table 2, drew substantially on theoretical frameworks, while the rest mainly remained at a conceptual level without adducing theoretical backgrounds.

There is a need for future research on ITG to present itself in the context of a cumulative tradition. New work could then specify its theoretical

Table 2. Theoretical framework for ITG research

Theoretical Framework	Research Summary
Agent Theory (Wu, 2006)	Examines the role of ITG in helping reduce information asymmetry between information security functions and top management and, in turn, adverse selection in information security
Cybernetic Theory (Peppard, 2005)	Attempts to develop an approach to assessing an organization's existing ITG structure as well as developing methods for constructing ITG structures
Evolutionary-Based Views (Cumps et al., 2006)	Examines the alignment between business and ICT as positively contributing to business performance and effectiveness
Multiple Contingency Theory (Sambamurthy & Zmud, 1999)	Examines how multiple and interacting contingent forces influence modes of IT governance
Organization Design Theory (Peterson, 2004)	Presents a holistic view of ITG, in which structural, process, and relational capabilities represent integral parts of an effective ITG architecture
Organization Theory (Ribbers, Peterson & Parker, 2002)	Examines the design and effectiveness of ITG processes from both rational and social perspectives
Process Change Theory (Leih, 2007)	Evaluates how certain types of regulatory changes are impacting on ITG
Project Theory, organizational Control Theory, Professions Theory (Mähring, 2002)	Addresses the organizational control of IT projects, specifically how control evolves over time and how executives engage in control tasks
Resource-Based Views (Cumps et al., 2006; Janssen & Joha, 2006; Tanriverdi, 2006; Wagner, 2006; Willcocks, Feeny, & Olson, 2006)	Examines the sources of cross-unit IT synergy and the conditions under which cross-unit IT synergies improve the performance of multibusiness firms (Tanriverdi, 2006), Examines the challenges of implementing a core IS capabilities framework (Willcocks et al., 2006), Examines the alignment between business and ICT as improving business performance and effectiveness (Cumps et al., 2006), Aims to link RBV with information management modes such as the IT infrastructure library (ITIL) to explain the impact of IT on firm success (Wagner, 2006) Aims to develop a better understanding of the ITG necessary to share services in public administration (Janssen & Joha, 2006)
Rational-analytical Theory, Social-Political Theory (Peterson, Parket, & Ribbers, 2002)	Examines the design and effectiveness of ITG processes from both rational-analytical and social-learning perspectives
Situational Leadership Theory (Peterson & Fairchild, 2003)	Examines tasks, relationships, and change orientations in e-business leadership
Social Systems Theory (Ask, Bjornsson, Johansson, Magnusson, & Nilsson, 2007)	Uses Niclas Luhmann's concepts of paradox and deparadoxization as a starting point for looking at ITG within large, Swedish organizations
Strategic Alignment Model (Sääksjärvi, 2006)	Analyses IS outsourcing in the strategic context of IT management, dealing with both organizational and IT infrastructures

framework and begin to offer operative guidelines to industrial practitioners, for example, through suggesting some of the practical implications of different ITG designs.

IT Governance Framework

Some researchers have sought to develop a more comprehensive ITG framework by combining a variety of existing definitions and approaches. In general, frameworks designate the structure of a set of objects within a given domain, besides describing the relationships among those objects (Dibbern, Goles, Hirschheim, & Jayatilaka, 2004). The organizing effect of frameworks is especially useful during the early stages of research in a domain in delineating a research area, providing a foundation for the description of knowledge, and uncovering or highlighting opportunities for more specific theory development and testing within the domain in question (Dibbern et al., 2004).

One of the most frequently referenced frameworks in ITG is the Control Objectives for Information and related Technology (COBIT) framework as proposed by ITGI. ITGI, established in 1998 to advance international thinking and standards

in directing and controlling enterprises' information technology, offers the COBIT framework as a tool for integrating and institutionalizing good practices, ensuring individual enterprises' IT supports their business objectives.

In the COBIT framework, the ITG focus area is divided into five subareas as shown in Table 3: strategic alignment, value delivery, resource management, risk management, and performance management. These five areas consist of topics which executive management needs to address in governing IT within their enterprises (ITGI, 2005).

The Australian Standard for the Corporate Governance of ICT (AS 8015-2005, 2005) represents one of the most important efforts to date to provide a framework for practical use by company directors in evaluating, directing and monitoring their organizations' ICT portfolio. As shown in Table 4, this standard sets out six principles for the good corporate governance of ICT, applicable to most organizations including public and private companies, government entities, and not-for-profit organizations.

The standard also proposes an ICT governance model in the form of a cycle with phases known

Table 3. IT governance focus areas in COBIT

ITG Focus Area	Definition
Strategic Alignment	Focuses on ensuring strong connections between business and IT plans; defining, maintaining and validating IT value propositions; and aligning IT with enterprise operations
Value Delivery	Executes value propositions throughout the delivery cycle, ensuring that IT delivers promised benefits against business strategies, optimizing costs and proving the intrinsic value of IT
Resource Management	Specifies the optimal investment in, and the proper management of, critical IT resources, including applications, information, infrastructure and people. Key issues relate to the optimization of knowledge and infrastructure
Risk Management	Defines risk awareness among senior corporate officers, stressing the need to understand enterprises' risk appetite, compliance requirements, and transparency; embeds risk management responsibilities within the organization
Performance Management	Tracks and monitors strategy implementation, project completion, resource usage, process performance and service delivery, using, for example, balanced scorecards translating strategy into action to achieve goals not captured by conventional accounting methods

Table 4. The six principles of AS 8015-2005

Principles	Explanation
Principle 1	Establish clearly understood responsibilities for ICT
Principle 2	Plan ICT to best support organisations
Principle 3	Acquire ICT validly
Principle 4	Ensure that ICT performs well, whenever required
Principle 5	Ensure ICT conforms with formal rules
Principle 6	Ensure ICT use respects human factors

as Evaluate-Direct-Monitor, as shown in Figure 7. In this model, directors govern ICT through three main tasks; (1) evaluating the use of ICT, (2) directly preparing and implementing plans and policies, and (3) monitoring performance against policies and plans.

More generally within this research stream, Simonsson and Johnson (2006) define ITG as the IT-related decision making concerning such assets as hardware, software, information processes, staff, and company strategic goals, proposing a comprehensive framework in which ITG is separated among three dimensions; its domain, decision-making processes, and scope. Peterson's (2004) definition of ITG is of a situation of dispersed authority and responsibility for IT decisions among different interested parties; his research is concerned to suggest mechanisms and processes for the control and monitoring of effective IT decision making. Grembergen (2004) extends Peterson's original ITG framework into a more diversified mixture of structures, processes and relational mechanisms of use in optimizing ITG resource allocations to ensure responsible decision-making. Brown and Grant (2005) review existing papers on ITG, proposing a conceptual framework synthesizing current research and representing a logical underpinning for future work. The authors classify enterprises ITG structures into centralized or decentralized based on the organizational placement of decision-making

authorities and the organizational structuring of IT activities. They conclude the best ITG form for a given firm is contingent on a variety of factors such as its organizational structure, decision-making structure, organizational environment, industry, firm size.

Conversely, Korac-Kakabadse and Kakabadse (2001) extend Peterson's work in the direction of generating a new controlled method for measuring the effect of IT, rationally evaluating IT according to its characteristics, and offering a basis for IS/IT technology-based development. Webb et al. (2006) claim that the function of ITG lies in strategically relating IT and business, aiming to release maximal business value through effective IT control, incorporating the assignment of responsibilities and management of performance, risks and IT development. For this approach, the crucial components of ITG are the strategic relationships between business units, IT's role in value delivery, performance management, control, and responsibility.

Finally, Weill and Ross's ITG framework (2004) offers some scope for the amalgamation of the above two perspectives. This framework is especially concerned to devise appropriate mechanisms governing corporate IT decisions. The authors categorize the scope of IT decision making into five areas pertaining to decision-making and responsibility: IT principles, IT architecture, IT infrastructure strategies, business applica-

Figure 7. Model for corporate governance of ICT in AS 8015-2005

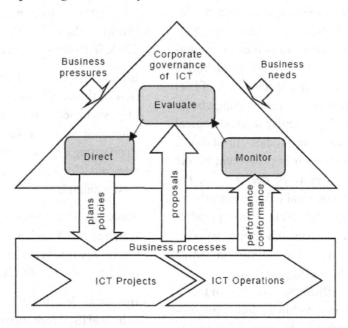

tion needs, and IT investment and prioritization. Weill and Ross's aim is to examine the types of ITG decision activities suitable for the business environment of given companies by sorting firms among six archetypes of ITG structure: business monarchies, IT monarchies, feudal arrangements, federal arrangements, IT duopolies, and anarchy. These arrangements differ according to the location and scope of decision activities. They also suggest a governance mechanism composed of structural elements, committees, and policy as an effective means of driving ITG performance (Weill & Ross, 2004).

In summary, some researchers have tried to arrange various notions of ITG and to propose a comprehensive framework for ITG. However, the frameworks that they proposed cover only some parts of ITG and most frameworks do not consider the importance of corporate governance. Thus, it is essential to develop more comprehensive ITG framework to facilitate further research on ITG (Keyes-Pearce, 2002; Simonsson & Johnson, 2006; Webb et al., 2006).

CONCLUSION

This chapter has attempted to lay down guidelines for future research on the basis of a classification and analysis of the current literature on ITG. It drew on a broader range of literature than is customary in some reviews, generating the following conclusions.

Firstly, ITG research is confronted with a need to develop a comprehensive ITG framework building systematically on the various definitions of ITG so far offered. This study would encourage forthcoming works to seek to develop, or to rely on some form of, an integrated ITG framework; this would both guide case-study and other characterizations of specific instances, and contribute towards a continuously developing tradition of academic analysis. Further, the ITG frameworks suggested by research needs to take account of enterprises' requirements in terms of transparency, as both will facilitate internal auditing and compliance on a strategic level with international standards, and foster company competitiveness.

Secondly, this study analyzed existing works from various perspectives, taking note of, for example, the origin of their problem areas, their definition, research themes, timelines, methodology and theoretical frameworks. Establishing a chronological picture of the development of ITG research in this way is helpful in providing a baseline for future study. In particular, methodological analysis revealed existing studies' limitations, suggesting a basis for their improvement. Some problems with existing work derive from the lack of an agreed theoretical basis in classifying research issues. In categorizing existing studies according to different research topics, we also suggested possible future directions in which ongoing work might usefully be taken.

This study, nevertheless, is limited in that it only considers research within the following subcategories of ITG, that is, business/IT strategic relationships, IT outsourcing, and ITSM/ITIL. Most of all, this study points to the pressing need for research to develop a systematic, inclusive framework according to which further studies of ITG can proceed.

REFERENCES

Ahn, J., Yang, J., & Han, S. (2006). A study on recognition and implementation of IT governance in Korean public institutions. In B. Cusack (Ed.), In *Proceedings of the 2006 IT Governance International Conference* (pp.107-120), Auckland, New Zealand.

Ask, U., Bjornsson, H., Johansson, M., Magnusson, J., & Nilsson, A. (2007). IT governance in the light of paradox: A social systems theory perspective. In *Proceedings of the 40th Hawaii International Conference on System Sciences*, Hawaii.

AS 8015-2005 (2005). *Australian standard: Corporate governance of information and communication technology*. Standards Australia: Sydney, Australia.

Becht, M., Bolton, P., & Röell, A. (2002). *Corporate governance and control*. ECGI - Finance Working Paper No. 02/2002. Retrieved May 1, 2008, from http://ssrn.com/abstract =343461

Bhattacharjya, J. & Chang, V. (2006). An exploration of the implementation and effectiveness of IT governance processes in institutions of higher education in Australia. In B. Cusack (Ed.), In *Proceedings of the 2006 IT Governance International Conference* (pp. 153-164), Auckland, New Zealand.

Brown, A. E. & Grant, G. G. (2005). Framing the frameworks: A review of IT governance research. *Communications of the Association for Information Systems, 15*, 696-712.

Brown, C. V. (1997). Examining the emergence of hybrid IS governance solutions: Evidence from a single case site. *Information Systems Research, 8*(1), 69-94.

Brynjolfsson, E. (1993). The productivity paradox of information technology. *Communications of the ACM, 36*(12), 66-77.

Butler, M. (2004). Cover story: IT governance - Who is the godfather of governance? *Information Economics Journal*, 7-9.

Chin, P. O., Brown, G. A., & Hu, Q. (2004). The impacts of mergers & acquisitions on IT governance structures: A case study. *Journal of Global Information Management, 12*(4), 50-74.

Cooper, D. R. & Schindler, P. S. (2002). *Business research methods* (8th ed.). McGraw-Hill/Irwin.

Csaszar, F. & Clemons, E. (2006). Governance of the IT function: Valuing agility and quality of training, cooperation and communications. In *Proceedings of the 39th Hawaii International Conference on System Sciences*, Hawaii.

Cumps, B., Viaene, S., Dedene, G., & Vandenbulcke, J. (2006). An empirical study on business/ICT alignment in European organisations.

In *Proceedings of the 39th Hawaii International Conference on System Sciences*, Hawaii.

Debreceny, R. S. (2006). Re-engineering IT internal controls: Applying capability maturity models to the evaluation of IT controls. In *Proceedings of the 39th Hawaii International Conference on System Sciences*, Hawaii.

Dekkers, T. (2004). IT governance requires quantitative (Project) management. *IWSM/MetriKon*. Retrieved May 1, 2008, from http://www.sogeti. nl/images /ACFftCN2J_tcm6-1776.pdf

Dibbern, J., Goles, T., Hirschheim, R., & Jayatilaka, B. (2004). Information systems outsourcing: A survey and analysis of the literature. *ACM SIGMIS Database, 35*(4), 6-102.

Getter, J. R. (2007). Enterprise architecture and IT governance: A risk-based approach. In *Proceedings of the 40th Hawaii International Conference on System Sciences*, Hawaii.

Gonzalez, R., Gasco, J., & Llopis, J. (2006). Information system outsourcing: A literature analysis. *Information & Management, 43*(7), 821-834.

Green, P. & Ali, S. (2006). Effective information technology governance mechanisms in public sectors: An australian case. In *Proceedings of the 10th Pacific Asia Conference on Information Systems* (pp. 1070-1089), Kuala Lumpur, Malaysia.

Grembergen, W. V. (Ed.) (2004). *Strategies for information technology governance*. Hershey, PA: Idea Group Publishing Inc.

Grembergen, W. V., Haes, S. D., & Brempt, H. V. (2007). Prioritising and linking business and IT goals in the financial sector. In *Proceedings of the 40th Hawaii International Conference on System Sciences*, Hawaii.

Heier, H., Borgman, H. P., & Maistry, M. G. (2007). Examining the relationship between IT governance software and business value of IT: Evidence from four case studies. In *Proceedings*

of the 40th Hawaii International Conference on System Sciences, Hawaii.

Henry, R. M., Kirsch, L. J., & Sambamurthy, V. (2003). The role of knowledge in information technology project governance. In S. T. March, A. Massey & J. I. DeGross (Eds.), In *Proceedings of the 24th International Conference on Information Systems* (pp. 751-758), Seattle, Washington.

Hoappa, J. M. & Wiander, T. J. (2006). Implementation experiences of the information security management system - Case study. In B. Cusack (Ed.), In *Proceedings of the 2006 IT Governance International Conference* (pp. 79-85), Auckland, New Zealand.

Hoogeveen, D. & Oppelland, H. J. (2002). A socio political model of the relationship between IT investments and business performance. In *Proceedings of the 35th Hawaii International Conference on System Sciences*, Hawaii.

Huang, R., Zmud, R. W., & Price, R. L. (2006). Evaluating the effects of IT governance structures in small and medium-sized enterprises. In *Proceedings of the 12th Americas Conference on Information Systems*, Acapulco, México.

ITGI (2003). *Board briefing on IT governance* (2nd ed.). IT Governance Institute. Retrieved May 1, 2008, from http://www.isaca.org/Content/ ContentGroups/ITGI3/Resources1 /Board_Briefing_on_IT_Governance/26904_Board_Briefing_final.pdf

ITGI (2005). *COBIT 4.0*. IT Governance Institute. Retrieved May 1, 2008, from http://www.itgi.org/ template_ITGI.cfm?template=/ContentManagement/ContentDisplay.cfm&ContentID=27263

ITGI (2006). *IT governance global status Report – 2006*. IT Governance Institute. Retrieved May 1, 2008, from http://www.itgi.org/template_ITGI. cfm?template=/Content Management/ContentDisplay.cfm&ContentID=24226

Janssen, M. & Joha, A. (2006). Governance of shared services in public administration. In *Proceedings of the 12th Americas Conference on Information Systems*, Acapulco, México.

Jeong, S. R., Kang, J., & Lee, B. G. (2007). The conceptual definition and the measurement development for IT governance. *Journal of Korea Information Processing Society, 14-D*(2), 225-234.

Johnstone, D., Huff, S., & Hope, B. (2006). IT projects: Conflict, governance, and systems thinking. In *Proceedings of the 39th Hawaii International Conference on System Sciences*, Hawaii.

Keyes-Pearce, S. V. (2002). Rethinking the importance of IT governance in the e-world. In *Proceedings of the 6th Pacific Asia Conference on Information Systems* (pp. 256-272), Tokyo, Japan.

Korac-Kakabadse, N. & Kakabadse, A. (2001). IS/IT governance: Need for an integrated model. *Corporate Governance, 1*(4), 9-11.

Leih, M. (2007). Regulatory impact on IT governance: A multiple case study on the Sarbanes-Oxley Act. In *Proceedings of the 13th Americas Conference on Information Systems*, Keystone, Colorado.

Letsoalo, K., Brown, I., & Njenga, K. N. (2006). An investigation of enablers and inhibitors of IT governance implementation: A case study of a South African enterprise. In B. Cusack (Ed.), In *Proceedings of the 2006 IT Governance International Conference* (pp.27-35), Auckland, New Zealand.

Mähring, M. (2002). *IT project governance: A process-oriented study of organisational control and executive involvement*. SSE/EFI Working Paper Series in Business Administration, No 2002:15. Retrieved May 1, 2008, from http://swoba.hhs.se /hastba /papers/hastba2002_015.pdf

Mähring, M. (2006). The role of the board of directors in IT governance: A review and agenda for research. In *Proceedings of the 12th Americas Conference on Information Systems*, Acapulco, México.

Na, J., Lee, J., Lee, J., & Lim, G. (2005). A study of CIO's perception and execution level of ITG in Korean companies. In *Proceedings of the Korea Society of Management Information Systems Conference*, Seoul, Korea.

Njenga, K. N. & Brown, I. (2006). On improvisation: Framework for the soft approach to managing security risk in South African. In B. Cusack (Ed.), In *Proceedings of the 2006 IT Governance International Conference* (pp. 97-106), Auckland, New Zealand.

OECD (2004). *OECD principles of corporate governance*. Retrieved May 1, 2008, from http://www.oecd.org/dataoecd/32/18/31557724.pdf

Peppard, J. (2005). The application of the viable systems model to information technology governance. In D. Avison, D. Galletta & J. I. DeGross (Eds.), In *Proceedings of the 26th International Conference on Information Systems* (pp. 45-58), Las Vegas, Nevada.

Peppard, J., Edwards, C., & Lambert, R. (1999). *A governance framework for information management in the global enterprise*. School of Management Working Papers;9/99. Retrieved May 1, 2008, from https://dspace.lib.cranfield. ac.uk/bitstream/1826 /459/2/SWP0999.pdf

Peterson, R. R. (2004). Configurations and coordination for global information technology governance designs in a transnational European context. In *Proceedings of the 34th Hawaii International Conference on System Sciences*, Hawaii.

Peterson, R. R. & Fairchild, A. M. (2003). Exploring the impact of electronic business readiness on leadership capabilities in information technology governance. In *Proceedings of the*

36th Hawaii International Conference on System Sciences, Hawaii.

Peterson, R. R., Parket M. M., & Ribbers, P. M. A. (2002). Information technology governance processes under environmental dynamism: Investigating competing theories of decision making and knowledge sharing. In L. Applegate, R. Galliers & J. I. DeGross (Eds.), In *Proceedings of the 26th International Conference on Information Systems* (pp. 563-576), Barcelona, Spain.

Ribbers, P. M. A., Peterson, R. R., & Parker, M. M. (2002). Designing information technology governance processes: Diagnosing contemporary practices and competing theories. In *Proceedings of the 35th Hawaii International Conference on System Sciences*, Hawaii.

Sallé, M. (2004). IT service management and IT governance: Review, comparative analysis and their impact on utility computing. *HP Labs* (Tech. Rep. HPL-2004-98). Retrieved May 7, 2008, from http://www.hpl.hp.com/techreports/2004/HPL-2004-98.pdf

Sambamurthy, V. & Zmud, R. W. (1999). Arrangements for information technology governance: A theory of multiple contingencies. *MIS Quarterly, 23*(2), 261-290.

Schwarz, A. & Hirschheim, R. (2003). An extended platform logic perspective of IT governance: Managing perceptions and activities of IT. *Journal of Strategic Information Systems, 12*(2), 129-166.

Sherer, S. A. (2004). IS project selection: The role of strategic vision and IT governance. In *Proceedings of the 37th Hawaii International Conference on System Sciences*, Hawaii.

Shleifer, A. & Vishny, R. W. (1997). A survey of corporate governance. *The Journal of Finance, 52*(2), 737-783.

Simonsson, M. & Johnson, P. (2006). Defining IT governance—A consolidation of literature.

Submitted to the 18th Conference on Advanced Information Systems Engineering. Retrieved May 7, 2008, from http://www.ics.kth.se/Publikationer/Working%20Papers/EARP-WP-2005-MS-04.pdf

Simonsson, M., Johnson, P., & Wijkström, H. (2007). Model-based IT governance maturity assessments with Cobit. In H. Österle, J. Schelp & R. Winter, R. (Eds.), In *Proceedings of the 15th European Conference on Information Systems* (pp. 1276-1287), University of St. Gallen, St. Gallen, Swiss.

Soh, C. & Markus, M. L. (1995). How IT creates business value: A process theory synthesis: A process theory synthesis. In G. Ariav, C. Beath, J. I. DeGross, R. Hoyer & C. F. Kemerer (Eds.), In *Proceedings of the 16th International Conference on Information Systems* (pp. 29-41), Amsterdam, The Netherlands.

Sääksjärvi, M. (2006). Success of IS outsourcing as a predictor of IS effectiveness: Does IT governance matter? In R. Hirschheim, A. Heinzl & J. Dibbern (Eds.), *Information systems outsourcing, enduring themes, new perspectives and global challenges* (2nd ed.) (pp. 283-302), Springer, Berlin Heidelberg.

Tanriverdi, H. (2006). Performance effect of information technology synergies in multibusiness firms. *MIS Quarterly, 30*(1), 57-77.

Wagner, H. -T. (2006). Managing the impact of IT on firm success: The link between the resource-based view and the IT infrastructure library. In *Proceedings of the 39th Hawaii International Conference on System Sciences*, Hawaii.

Webb, P., Pollard, C., & Ridley, G. (2006). Attempting to define IT governance: Wisdom or folly? In *Proceedings of the 39th Hawaii International Conference on System Sciences*, Hawaii.

Webster, J. & Watson, R. T. (2002). Analyzing the past to prepare for the future: Writing a literature review. *MIS Quarterly, 26*(2), xiii-xxiii.

Weill, P. & Ross, J. W. (2004). *IT governance - How top performers manage IT decision rights for superior results*. Cambridge, MA: Harvard Business School Press.

Weill, P. & Ross, J. W. (2005). A matrixed approach to designing IT governance. *Sloan Management Review, 46*(2), 26-34.

Weill, P. & Woodham, R. (2002). Don't just lead, govern: Implementing effective IT governance. *CISR working paper* (No. 326). Retrieved May 7, 2008, from http://dspace.mit.edu/bitstream/1721.1/1846/2/4237-02.pdf

Willcocks, L., Feeny, D., & Olson, N. (2006). Implementing core IS capabilities: Feeny-Willcocks IT governance and management framework revisited. *European Management Journal, 24*(1), 28-37.

Wu, Y. (2006). Controlling adverse selection in information security budgeting: An IT governance approach. In *Proceedings of the 12th Americas Conference on Information Systems*, Acapulco, México.

Young, R. C. & Jordan, E. (2003). Passion & IT governance. In *Proceedings of the 7th Pacific Asia Conference on Information Systems* (pp. 941-955), Adelaide, Australia.

Young, R. C. (2006). What is the ROI for IT project governance? Establishing a benchmark. In B. Cusack (Ed.), In *Proceedings of the 2006 IT Governance International Conference* (pp. 59-68), Auckland, New Zealand.

Chapter III
IT Governance:
A Critical Review of the Literature

David Musson
Macquarie Graduate School of Management, Sydney, Australia

ABSTRACT

This chapter reviews the IT governance literature. It proposes that there are three different concepts that are grouped together as IT governance. These concepts are IT governance as a framework or audit process, IT governance as IT decision-making and IT governance as a branch of corporate governance. It argues that the first of these concepts is not a senior management issue, but an aid to a business process and that the remaining two concepts are complementary. The chapter recommends that the term IT governance is seen as a crucial part of the board's wider corporate governance task, and suggests that is concerning that the view of IT governance as IT decision-making rarely pays any attention to the role of the board in a crucial decision-making process. The chapter is intended to bring together the disparate views of IT governance so as to permit a broader view of this important subject.

INTRODUCTION

IT governance is a much-used term, but it has a confusing literature, with the term being used with several different meanings. This may partly be because different target audiences each seek information focussed on their requirements. So, for example, CIOs are pressed to adopt "best practice" in their IT service management; risk managers need to manage IT risk; senior managers wish to ensure that their staff manage their

IT projects efficiently; board members want to discharge their corporate governance obligations towards IT. These different activities are lumped together under the heading of IT governance. Perhaps this is because IT governance sounds grander than service management or risk management; whatever the reason, IT governance has a diverse literature. This chapter examines the literature on IT governance, and proposes a three-way division of the broad field covered by the term.

BACKGROUND

Most organizations rely on their information technology, and, it is widely claimed, expenditure on IT is a large proportion of company budgets (e.g., Weill & Olsen, 1989). It is not surprising then that a global survey by KPMG in 2004 found that 77.4% of respondent companies were vitally dependent on IT for their continuing operation (KPMG, 2004). In most companies, the top-level management of IT is seen as a matter of corporate governance; the literature shows that poorly performing IT systems can jeopardize the entire organization (see, for example, the role of IT in the collapse of One.Tel (Avison, 2003; Avison, Wilson & Hunt, 2003)). The corporate governance of IT, which is referred to as IT governance in the literature, is a significant part of the total corporate governance task for a board. However, unlike corporate governance, there are no standards for IT governance (Nolan & McFarlan, 2005), and "Because there has been no comparable body of knowledge and best practice, IT governance doesn't exist per se" (Nolan & McFarlan, 2005, p. 98). The literature on IT governance is largely concentrated on the operational management of IT and there is little on the requirements for the corporate governance of IT. Weill and Ross (2004) suggest that IT governance is normally delegated to the CIO, although the board retains overall responsibility for governance. Perhaps this delegation is explained by Jordan (2001) and Jordan and Musson (2003), who offer evidence that many Australian board members have "at best only survival skills in IT"; however, no clear picture arose from their research on how a board's IT governance responsibilities were discharged. A survey by PricewaterhouseCoopers (PwC, 2004) found that, whilst more than 91% of CEOs understood that IT was central to the continuing success of their companies, more than two-thirds of them were unable or unwilling to answer questions on their system of IT governance. In fact, 42% of them worldwide and 44% in the Asia-Pacific region said that they did not intend to implement a system of IT governance (PwC, 2004). However, two studies have found that board members have little interest in IT. One study, Jordan and Musson (2003), investigated Australian board members' attitudes to the governance of e-commerce, and noted that, "...boards do not appear to carry out their corporate governance duties, at least in respect of electronic commerce risk" *(Section 5)*.

The second study, of 17 medium to large Canadian companies, noted that "The risks and opportunities IT presents .... may require a level of technical insight that is often absent from the boardroom. .... The net effect is that many boards are reluctant to deal with IT governance issues" (Huff, Maher & Munro, 2004, p. 1), and that "...most boards seem to be passive receivers of information about IT as opposed to aggressive, proactive questioners. We saw little board-level concern about the company's return on its IT investment, for example, or the appropriate level of IT expenditures" (Huff, Maher & Munro, 2004, p. 3).

A review of the literature suggests that directors may not be the only people confused about IT governance; it shows that there are at least three different meanings applied to the term. This chapter reviews the use of the term IT governance in the literature.

LITERATURE REVIEW

There is an extensive literature on IT governance, but much of it is theoretical, and there is little on the actual processes involved with IT governance; a gap exists between theoretical frameworks and contemporary practice (Ribbers, Peterson & Parker, 2002). Analysis shows that there are three principal schools of thought on IT governance in the literature. These are:

- IT governance as a framework or an audit process.

- IT governance as IT decision-making, and
- IT governance as a branch of corporate governance.

These three schools are discussed in the following sections.

IT Governance as a Framework or an Audit Process

A number of writers suggest frameworks that are detailed and intended for implementation by middle managers, and which the writers call IT governance "frameworks." These frameworks facilitate the processes of IT management and of internal IT control. This view of IT governance may have been reinforced by the introduction in the US of the Sarbanes-Oxley Act (SOX, 2002). This was enacted on 30th July 2002, following the collapse of a number of large US companies, including Enron and Worldcom. The Sarbanes-Oxley Act (SOX, 2002) moves the emphasis of US corporate governance away from voluntary disclosure, and towards the regulation of disclosure and, more generally, corporate conduct. The Sarbanes-Oxley Act (the Act) explicitly addresses the responsibilities of the CEO, the CFO and the external auditor, in the areas of transparency, integrity and accountability in financial reporting and the system of internal control. As both financial reporting and the system of internal control are heavily dependent on IT, the Act also has a profound effect on systems of IT governance. However, the Act deals with a small part of the total IT governance obligations of a director, essentially those that can be audited.

Some of the frequently cited frameworks are:

- CoBIT
- ITIL
- ISO/IEC 27001 (2005a), ISO/IEC 17799 (2005b), BS 7799 (2000).

These frameworks are not alternative treatments of the same issues; indeed, there is little overlap between them. Most of the literature concerned with these frameworks is practical in nature; there is little discussion of them in the academic literature. They are briefly discussed in the next section.

CoBIT (Control objectives for Information Technology), from the US-based Information Systems Audit and Control Association (ISACA), an IT auditing body, is a proprietary approach to implementing and evaluating controls in the IT environment (ITGI, 2002). It is a normative framework of 34 overall control objectives. These are divided into a hierarchy of auditable processes intended to support a total of 318 detailed control objectives. CoBIT provides a number of tools to assist in managing IT, including performance measures and critical success factors (CSFs) for the management processes, and maturity models to help organizations to benchmark their performance in managing their IT. The CoBIT view of IT governance is concerned with two issues (ITGI, 2002):

- Ensuring that IT delivers value to the business
- Ensuring that IT risks are mitigated

CoBIT is useful as an aid to operational managers implementing an IT project, and more particularly as a tool for auditing the alignment of business and IT objectives (Sallé, 2004).

ITIL (Information Technology Infrastructure Library) is from the UK government, which was originally devised in the 1980's by CCTA (now OGC) for auditing the IT activities of government agencies (Sallé, 2004). A list of these publications is given in OGC (2004). The ITIL library is set of "best practice" standards for IT service management. ITIL is concerned with the critical business processes needed to provide high quality IT services; it does not concern itself with strategic issues (Sallé, 2004). In addition to the library documents, there is a veritable industry in software tools, accreditation, audit, training and consulting on ITIL

ISO/IEC 27001 (2005a), ISO/IEC 17799 (2005b) and BS7799-2 (2000). These are concerned with the specialised subject of Information Security Management. They are intended for technical staff that are responsible for initiating, implementing, and maintaining information security within their organizations. ISO/IEC 27001:2005 (ISO 2005a) is a specification for an information security management system, and ISO/IEC 17799:2005 (ISO, 2005b) is a code of practice for implementing an information security management system. ISO/IEC 27001 is a certifiable standard, that is to say that organizations can have their information security measures certified by independent assessor against the requirements of the Standard. References in the literature may also be found to BS7799-2:2000; this was replaced by ISO/IEC 27001 in October 2005 (ISO, 2005a).

Spafford (2003) noted that *"COBIT, ISO 17799 and ITIL all serve as excellent frameworks by which to improve IT governance" but only COBIT deals with an overall system of control for IT.* These frameworks are not alternative treatments; indeed, there is little overlap between the three. Most of the writers promoting these frameworks as IT governance frameworks "…do not take into account the broad view of IT governance, but instead simply describe one aspect or other of the concept" (Webb, Pollard & Ridley, 2006, p.5).

One other document that is frequently cited is the Australian Standard on IT Governance, AS 8015 – 2005 (AS, 2005). Although described as a Standard, this document is actually intended to "…provide a framework of principles" (p.2) to guide directors on "…the areas of risk associated with the implementation and use of ICT" (p.5). It provides a useful but very high-level overview of the processes needed to be put in place to provide corporate governance of IT. However, the term "risk" here appears to be used to describe unwanted outcomes, and the Standard does not

seem to consider the strategic opportunities that IT could afford an organization. This is perhaps surprising; most of the authorities quoted in the following sections of this chapter are concerned to ensure that the rewards as well as the risks of IT are properly managed. Unlike the other frameworks considered in this section, AS 8015 is aimed at top management.

IT Governance as IT Decision-Making

This, the dominant view of IT governance (Peterson, Parker & Ribbers, 2002), narrowly defines the term as the allocation of decision rights and accountability so to encourage desirable behaviour in the use of IT (e.g., Weill & Broadbent, 1998). This view sees IT governance as a structure concerned with the management and supply of IT services (Peterson, 2003), and concentrates on the locus of the IT decision-making authority within an organization (Brown, 1997; Sambamurthy & Zmud, 1999; Weill, 2004; Weill & Woodham, 2002). Early work argued that the governance structure for a company depended on a number of factors (see, for example Brown, 1997) but this contingency approach was complex and difficult to apply in practice. The interaction of the factors was a particular sticking point; many writers assumed that the factors would not interact (notably Henderson & Venkatraman, 1992). Those writers who did assume interaction produced frameworks of especial complexity (e.g., Sambamurthy & Zmud, 1999). In this early view, IT governance is concerned with three issues (Sambamurthy & Zmud, 1999, p. 262):

- IT infrastructure management, which refers to decisions concerning the "… nature of hardware and software platforms, annual enhancements to these platforms, the nature of network and data architectures and the corporate standards for procurement and deployment of IT assets" (Sambamurthy & Zmud, 1999, p. 262).

- IT use management, which refers to decisions concerning "... applications prioritisation and (short and long-term) planning and the day-to-day delivery of operations and services" (Sambamurthy & Zmud, 1999, p. 262).
- Project management, which requires the "...blending (of) knowledge of IT infrastructure capabilities and capacities with knowledge associated with the conceptualisation, acquisition, development and deployment of information systems applications" (Sambamurthy & Zmud, 1999, p. 262).

This literature identifies three modes of IT governance (Sambamurthy & Zmud, 1999, Brown & McGill, 1994). These are:

- **Centralized**, where corporate management have the crossorganizational IT decision-making authority.
- **Decentralized**, where divisional management have IT decision-making authority for their systems, and
- **Hybrid or Federal**, where corporate management has IT infrastructure decision-making authority for the entire organization, and divisional management has authority for their applications and system development.

The literature suggests that the hybrid mode is dominant (Hodgkinson, 1996; Sambamurthy & Zmud, 1999; Weill & Broadbent, 2003).

This view of IT governance is similar to the earlier debates on the organizational structure of the IT function (see for example King, 1983; Olsen & Chervany, 1980; Tavakolian, 1989). Part of this debate concerns whether the IT function should be centralised, controlling organization-wide IT services from a single unit, or decentralised, with each business unit having its own IT function (Dearden, 1987). Neither choice is applicable in every case (Boynton, Jacobs & Zmud, 1992).

The literature makes a link between this form of IT governance and corporate governance. A number of writers have suggested that the form of corporate governance used by an organization is reflected in their IT governance (Applegate, McFarlan and McKenney, 1999; Brown & McGill, 1994; Sambamurthy & Zmud, 1999). Thus, for example, centralized organizations also centralise their IT, and decentralized organizations also decentralize their IT.

Later work is more concerned with the architecture, rather than the modes, of IT governance. The work of Weill and Ross (2004, 2005) proposes six styles or archetypes of IT governance, which shows the location of the decision rights for IT governance. These are:

- The Business Monarchy, where decisions are made by C level managers.
- The IT monarchy, where decisions are made by IT managers.
- Federal, where decisions are made by C-level managers together with the managers of at least one of the business operating groups.
- Feudal, where decisions are made by the C Level managers of a business unit.
- Duopoly, where decisions are jointly made by IT managers and by the managers of at least one business unit, and
- Anarchy, where each user can make their own decisions.

These have some resemblance to the modes of IT governance noted previously (Brown & McGill, 1994; Sambamurthy & Zmud, 1999). The Business and IT Monarchies are similar to the Centralized form, and the Federal form is common to both frameworks.

Based on their IT governance work, Weill and Ross (2005) propose that there are five decision domains. These are:

- IT principles, which decides such questions as the role of IT and the basis of funding of IT projects

- IT architecture, which discusses the way in which the core business processes are implemented in IT
- IT infrastructure strategies, which decides the set of IT infrastructure services needed to support the company's strategic objectives
- Business application requirements, which determines the set of business applications needed to support the company's business objectives, and
- IT investment and priorities, which ensures that the IT investment continues to support the company's changing needs.

These issues are also discussed in the IT practitioner-focussed Strategic Information Systems Planning (SISP) discipline. The IT principles questions are addressed by many writers, especially Martino (1983) and Galliers (1987). The technical aspects of the IT architecture questions (but not the business processes ones) are addressed by Galliers (1987) and later by Lederer and Sethi (1996). The technical aspects of IT infrastructure are addressed by Galliers (1987) and the management issues of IT infrastructure are also discussed by Wilson (1989). Business application needs are addressed by Martino (1983) and Galliers (1987), and IT investment and prioritization by Martino (1983). The significant matter here is that Weill and Ross (2005) are addressing a business audience, not a technical one, and that they have brought these issues together and successfully brought them to the attention of business managers. Weill and Ross (2005) also argue strongly for transparency in the IT governance process. They say that "A huge barrier to effective IT governance is lack of understanding how decisions are made, what processes are being implemented and what the desired outcomes are.....more communications generally means more effective governance" (p. 28).

This sensible advice is equally applicable to the wider subject of the corporate governance of

IT. Whilst the detailed issues discussed by Weill and Ross (2005) are usually dealt with by senior managers, the board has a larger task in guiding the organization's direction and priorities. This larger task is discussed in the following section.

IT Governance as a Branch of Corporate Governance

Tricker (1984) noted, "The governance role is not concerned with running the business per se, but with giving overall direction to the enterprise..." (p. 6). Thus, IT governance is concerned with the control and strategic direction of IT at board level (AS, 2005; ITGI, 2003). Richard Hogg, the President of the Australian Computer Society, used this meaning of IT governance in his keynote address to the CIO 2002 conference. "There is (in Australia) an over reliance (by boards) on consultants to report on ICT governance issues... Corporate boards must learn what questions to ask about ICT governance. ... It is poor corporate governance to push ICT governance down to the ICT manager level. ICT is an integral part of their business and ICT governance is an integral part of corporate governance. Just awareness is no longer enough—true understanding of ICT is now required" (Hogg, 2002, my additions in parentheses).

According to the literature, IT governance is concerned with the board's responsibility to ensure that the company's IT meets the present and future demands of the business and of the business's customers (AS, 2005; Peterson, 2003) and that the risks arising from IT are mitigated (AS, 2005; Cilli, 2003). It does this by assessing, directing and monitoring the company's IT to ensure that the required benefits and business outcomes are being achieved (AS, 2005; KPMG, 2005b). Jordan and Silcock (2005) suggest that an organization that is able to do this is "IT-capable" and summarise this capability in the following terms: "The board must be assured that the organization is able to identify needs and opportunities to exploit IT, and is then able to satisfy them" (Jordan & Silcock, 2005, p. 22).

The Board is assisted in these tasks by the company's executive management and its IT management (Van Grembergen, 2002). According to De Haes and Van Grembergen (2006) IT governance is practised at three levels within the organization. These are:

- The strategic level, which they take to be the company board.
- The senior management level, and
- The operational management level.

All of these levels thus need to be addressed by any explanation of IT governance.

Johnstone, Huff, and Hope (2006) propose that there are three components to IT governance. These are:

- An authority structure.
- A set of board policies, and
- A set of mechanisms or processes.

They note that the authority structure is that set up by the board to manage IT, which includes both appointments such as the IT manager and (often) an oversight committee. The board policies are those "decision guidelines and restraints" (Johnstone, Huff & Hope, 2006, p. 4) devised by the board to control the use of IT in the company, including the business and IT strategies. The mechanisms of IT governance are discussed in the following paragraphs.

The link between the managers responsible for managing an IT function and the board of their organization, according to the literature, is three-fold.

Firstly, the actions of IT management are guided by a stable, formal, agreed business strategy (Hirschheim, Klein & Lyytinen, 1995; Lederer & Sethi, 1996) and corporate objectives (O'Connor, 1993). The development of business

strategy and the oversight of its implementation, as earlier noted, are board responsibilities.

Secondly, IT is a substantial part of a company's capital investment. It is generally said to be one of the largest investments made by a company (Weill & Broadbent, 1998). Without proper control, this investment can be dissipated. Lord Blythe, the chairman of Diageo, quoting Gartner research, said that "on average, 20% of the corporate IT budget is spent on initiatives that don't achieve their objectives" (Blythe, 2005). Blythe noted that companies were "wasting enormous amounts of money and effort on IT investments" and that most companies "fail to derive value from them" (Blythe, 2005). The oversight of this investment and the task of ensuring that the investment is appropriately targeted are board responsibilities.

Thirdly, IT carries risks (Markus, 2000). Given the centrality of IT to the operation of most companies and the companies' heavy capital investments in IT, the risk of, for example, failure, underperformance or overspend on IT needs to be understood and managed at board level (Jordan & Silcock, 2005).

In order to control the overall implementation of the aligned business/IT strategy, companies often have an oversight or steering committee (Earl, 1989; Hoffman, 2004; Nolan, 1982). According to the literature, in some cases this committee includes board members (Hoffman, 2004; Nolan & McFarlan, 2005a) but it is generally comprised of senior business managers plus the IT manager (ITGI, 2003). This committee handles the alignment of IT and business strategies, sets the standards for IT (Van den Heijden, 2001), determines the level of investment for the chosen IT projects (Bacon, 1992) and sets the priorities and allocates resources for these projects (Earl, 1989; Nolan, 1982). It does not meet frequently; Ward and Peppard (2002) say four to six times a year (p. 376).

Board Control of IT Projects

According to the literature, the aligned strategy is implemented as a series of prioritised IT projects (Luftman, Lewis & Oldach, 1993) that have roles in the implementation of the business strategy (Luftman, Papp & Brier, 1999). How these projects are controlled and monitored is not usually covered by the governance literature (Johnstone, Huff & Hope, 2006) Papers on governance (e.g., Hoffmann & Weill, 2004; Peterson, 2004; Weill & Ross, 2005) are concerned with the setting of strategy and priorities, and stop before the implementation of the strategy. However, the board has a responsibility to monitor the implementation of strategy, and generally delegates this responsibility to management (Van den Berge & Baelden, 2005), whilst retaining the accountability for strategy implementation.

The literature proposes that the board controls the conception, authorisation and implementation of these IT projects through a high-level committee (Weil & Ross, 2004, 2005). The management of complex IT projects has been a key issue for IT practitioners for more than thirty years (Ackoff, 1967; Keider, 1984; Sauer, 1993). According to the literature, control of the authorization and implementation of an IT project must be disciplined. One observer has noted that the causes of IT project failure are typically "...unclear objectives and requirements, lack of business commitment, change of business requirements, and poor communication" (Hyde, 2002).

In a similar vein, KPMG (2005b) notes that board members are often involved in the early stages of a project, especially the budget setting, but their interest and thus the level of IT governance "tends to fall away" as the project progresses (KPMG, 2005b, p. 4).

The literature suggests that there are three key processes that, as part of their IT governance responsibilities, boards must put in place and closely monitor, to manage IT projects and to maintain the strategic alignment of business and IT strategies. These are:

- The preparation, by senior management, of a business case which sets out the specification, expected strategic or operational benefits and costs of the project (Ballantine & Stray, 1998), the organizational changes required by the project (Weill & Ross, 2004) and the known or foreseeable risks of the project (Markus, 2000) and the necessary organizational and process changes associated with the project (Wiegers, 1998; Wilcocks & Griffiths, 1994). Using this business case, a board, or a member of senior management acting under the board's authority, can evaluate the proposal and compare its costs and benefits to other IT proposals competing for company funds (Weill & Ross, 2004). This consideration of the business case is an important part of the board's IT governance responsibilities (Weill & Ross, 2004). The business case is not discarded when the project is initiated, but forms the project baseline, against which the project is measured for its complete lifecycle (KPMG, 2005b).

- The use of project management disciplines (Lyytinen & Hirschheim, 1987; Parr, Shanks & Darke, 1999), to ensure that implementation cost and time budgets set out in the business case are adhered to, and unforeseen risks dealt with as they arise, and

- The use of a post-implementation review of each IT project, to evaluate the success of the project against its business case (Nelson, 2005), so as to ensure that the project is still appropriate to the company's needs (Sohal & Ng, 1998), that the benefits promised in the business case have been realized (Sohal & Ng, 1998) and to learn any lessons to be applied on future projects (Nelson 2005).

Each IT project is controlled by a committee, which has at least three members. These are (Beath, 1991; McKenney, Copeland & Mason, 1995; Rockart & DeLong, 1988):

- A member of the top management team, who acts as the "owner" of the project.
- The responsible line manager acting as the project sponsor, and
- A project manager who is responsible for the management of the project

The project committee reports to the executive-level IT committee (Renkema, 1998). The processes are discussed in the next section.

The Business Case

A new IT project is initiated by the senior management of the business unit or department concerned in the following way: A business case is produced for the project by the business unit manager who is accountable to the board for the project; this includes the technology to be used and details any associated organizational and/or business process changes (De Haes & Van Grembergen, 2005). The advantages of using a business case are illustrated by the 18 case studies in NOIE (2003). This report notes that, "There is clear merit in documenting a business case outlining the scope and objectives of the ICT project and the benefits that are being sought throughout its implementation... (and) to establish a basis for subsequent review of performance and assessment of the results achieved. The business case process is therefore seen as important for the shaping and alignment of expectations within the organization, and of important external stakeholders, such as key customers and suppliers" (NOIE, 2003, p. 124, my addition in brackets).

The business case for a project requests the budget for a proposed project (Brigham & Houston, 2004), justifying the budget by the benefits of the project. According to the literature, the business case sets out the project benefits (Remenyi, Sherwood-Smith & White, 1997), both in terms of:

- Tangible benefits, that is benefits for which management can both identify and provide a value (Milis & Mercken, 2004), using financial measures such as the Return on Investment (Radcliffe, 1982), which measures the effectiveness of management in producing returns with its assets. It is a percentage return, calculated by dividing the net income that is attributable to the project by the value of investment in the project, and
- Intangible benefits of the proposed system, which are understood by management (Milis & Mercken, 2004), but more difficult to estimate, as they cannot be directly measured (Remenyi, Money & Sherwood-Smith, 2000). Techniques suggested in the literature include Information Economics (Parker & Benson, 1988), on which IBM based their IT consulting procedures (Strassman, 1990), and Balanced Scorecard (Kaplan & Norton, 1992, 1993, 1996), where a set of measures is selected under four categories, financial, customer, internal operations and innovation and learning. However, Serafeimidis and Smithson (2000), using a case study, suggest that in practice, these intangible benefits may be discounted by operational management.

The business case should discuss the foreseeable risks (Wiegers, 1998; Wilcocks & Griffiths, 1994). These risks can arise in many areas of operation. For this reason, the company's risk management system is connected to the project through the project committee (NOIE, 2003). The business case should also discuss the changes to business processes and the associated training caused by the project (Luftman, 2003), including these costs in the total budgeted cost of the project.

The business case is often a complex document, requiring careful attention (Gunasekaran, Love, Rahimi & Miele, 2001). Many boards, however, do not appear to comprehend what they read: KPMG (2005b) found that 51% of respondents said that their boards had a limited awareness of the benefits and risks of proposed IT projects, and that 20% of senior management had a similarly limited understanding (p. 14). This reflects the findings of Jordan and Musson (2003) that most boards were neither interested nor curious about IT issues.

Project Management Methodologies

For senior management, one of the most significant IT governance challenges is the risk that projects that are strategically necessary (or even critical) may fail, under perform or over-run their cost and time budgets (EQuest, 2004; Jordan & Silcock, 2005). The risks related to IT projects are considerable (Markus, 2000). Poor project management may cause complete project failure (Whittaker, 1999); as noted earlier, the management of IT projects has been a major problem for IT managers since the 1960's (Ackoff, 1967; Cole, 1995; Keider, 1984; Sauer, 1993) and the need to improve IT project management is widely documented (e.g., Lin & Pervan, 2001; Schwalbe, 2002; Standish, 2003). Formal project management methodologies are regarded by the literature as essential to the management of IT projects (Sommerville, 2004), Top management support is considered to be essential; KPMG (1997), in a survey of 1,400 organizations, found that the key factor in failed IT projects was the lack of top management commitment to the project management disciplines.

Post-Implementation Reviews

Post-implementation reviews (PIRs), which are processes that audit recently completed IT projects, are either recommended or included in most software development methodologies (e.g., SSADM, DDSM – see Ward and Peppard (2002), p. 438). A post-implementation review is essential "….to ensure that systems are still appropriate to

meet the business needs and that benefits have been obtained" (Sohal & Ng, 1998, p. 213).

The PIR ensures that the original investment case and justification for the project are compared to the actual benefits of the project (Sohal & Ng, 1998); in addition, it allows for both organizational learning on the specification and management of IT projects and a method of continuous improvement to IT systems (Doll, Deng & Scazzero, 2003).

In terms of the benefits of a new IT system, Seddon, Graeser, and Willcocks (2002) suggest that there are two types of benefit, namely the intangible "soft" user benefits and the tangible financial benefits. However, a report on a survey of IT project management, KPMG (2005b) notes that the survey found that there was a "…continued lack of ability of most organizations to accurately measure the achievement of benefits derived from their projects" (KPMG, 2005b, p. 8).

The report notes that only 2% of respondents achieved the targeted benefits of IT projects all of the time. Ezingeard, Irani, and Race (1999) suggest that post-implementation reviews are, in practice, rarely carried out. Kumar (1990) concluded that most PIRs were carried out in order to formalize the completion of the project, and that many PIRs were carried out too close to the completion of the project to be of any assistance in evaluating the project.

CONCLUSION

To summarize the foregoing sections, the literature proposes that IT governance is dependent on six factors. These are:

- The appointment of a high-level committee to oversee the implementation of IT strategy on behalf of the board.
- Alignment of the business and IT strategies by the high-level committee.

For each IT project:

- A business case is prepared by senior management.
- Once the business case is approved, a project committee is appointed.
- A project manager is appointed to oversee the project using project management methodologies.
- A post-implementation review is undertaken, to examine the project and to learn any lessons which can be applied to future projects.

This chapter has identified the three principal schools of IT governance and given examples of the literature associated with each school. The first view, the frameworks, do not form part of the senior management task of IT governance. Rather they are tools to audit the process (as in CoBIT) or much more detailed views of one aspect of governance (service management, in the case of ITIL).

The other two views are directly concerned with the corporate governance of IT. The second view is concerned with one key aspect of IT governance, the management and supply of IT services. The third school is concerned with the board's management of a company's IT so as to maintain the alignment of business and IT strategies and to implement IT projects in a controlled way, according to the priorities set by the board. The second and third views have a number of principles in common, notably the need for the alignment of business and IT strategies. For practical purposes, these two views are complementary, in that the second view provides a detailed examination of part of the IT governance task of boards.

The study of the topic of IT governance is not well served by use of the term to describe part of the task. It is recommended that the term IT governance is seen as a crucial part of the board's wider corporate governance task. It is concerning that the view of IT governance as IT decision-making rarely pays any attention to the role of the board in the decision-making process.

Given that, for most companies, IT is essential to the operation of the company, the corporate governance of IT deserves a more prominent place in the literature than it is currently afforded.

THE OUTLOOK FOR IT GOVERNANCE

For smaller companies with no IT departments, improvements in IT governance, if any, may be slow in coming. Despite evidence that the use of consultants for short-term projects is very beneficial (Nevo, Wade & Cook, 2007), there is evidence that consultant use amongst smaller companies is limited (van Akkeren & Cavaye, 1999). Musson (2007) reports a number of case studies of smaller Australian companies. One company, which had grown rapidly and which sought to improve its efficiency, started to look at new warehousing software, of a scale and cost that the company had not previously experienced. The software salesman was honest and direct with the company, but the company had no IT department, and the company's senior management, without a background in IT, may have been unable to understand what they were committing to. The result was a large overspend, a delayed implementation date, and a lack of exploitation of the functionality of the software that the company purchased. This case study reinforces the essential role of IT expertise and skills in good IT governance.

The outlook for IT governance in larger companies is, I suggest, mixed. On the positive side, the PricewaterhouseCoopers 2006 IT governance survey noted that, "for 87 percent of the participants, IT is quite to very important to the delivery of the corporate strategy and vision. For 63 percent of the respondents, IT is regularly or always on the board's agenda" (PwC, 2006).

On the negative side, a survey by CSC in 2006 found that just 15% of UK CIOs reported to the CEO; most of the rest were in the extended management team, often reporting to the CFO (IT Leader, 2006). Even if they reported to the CEO, it is possible that their ability to implement systems that closely fitted their company's IT strategy may be limited. In general, the literature assumes that boards and their senior management are free to devise their strategic IT requirements and implement them. In practice, the growth of complex systems such as ERP with its "one size fits all" "best practices" (Wagner & Newell, 2004) and the tendency to change the company to fit the IT rather than the other way round suggests that the requirements of IT governance are here sacrificed to cost considerations. The systems are generally inflexible, so "they tend to lock companies into rigid business processes" (Hegel and Brown 2001). This rigidity is directly opposed to the flexibility that is proposed that companies adopt, in the literature (see, for example Sambamurthy & Zmud, 1999; Sambamurthy, Venkatraman & DeSanctis, 1993).

In general, then, the prospects for IT governance are, surprisingly, not consistent with the importance of IT to business. The need for IT expertise in smaller companies, in order to evaluate proposed systems, will be partly alleviated by the increasing familiarity with IT by new generations of business managers. The popularity of very large integrated systems in larger companies is unlikely to wane, however, and it is here that mismatches between strategy and IT are likely to continue to occur.

REFERENCES

Ackoff, R. L. (1967). Management misinformation systems. *Management Science, 14*(4), 147–156.

AS (2005). *Corporate governance of information and communication technology, AS 8015 - 2005.* Sydney: Standards Australia.

Avison, D. E. & Fitzgerald, G. (2003). *Information systems development: Methodologies, techniques and tools* (3rd ed.). Maidenhead: McGraw-Hill.

Avison, D. E., Wilson, D., & Hunt, S. (2003, May). An IT failure and a company failure: A case study in telecommunications. *Paper presented at the 8th Congress of Association for Information Management*, Grenoble, France.

Bacon, C. (1992). The use of decision criteria in selecting information systems/technology investments. *MIS Quarterly, 16*(3), 335 – 342.

Ballantine, J. & Stray, S. (1998). Financial appraisal and the IS/IT investment decision-making process. *Journal of Information Technology, 13*(3), 3 – 14.

Beath, C. M. (1991). Supporting the information technology champion. *MIS Quarterly, 15*(3), 355 – 372.

Blythe, J. (2005). *Management challenges of technology; Speech to Wharton Global Alumni Forum: The Wharton School.* Retrieved May 8, 2008, from http://knowledge.wharton.upenn.edu/index.cfm?fa=viewfeature&id=1228

Boynton, A. C., Jacobs, G. C., & Zmud, R. W. (1992). Whose responsibility is IT management? *Sloan Management Review, 33*(4), 32 – 38.

Brigham, E. & Houston, J. (2004). *Fundamentals of financial management* (10th ed.). London: Harcourt/Thomson.

Brown, C. (1997). Examining the emergence of hybrid governance solutions: Evidence from a single case site. *Information Systems Research, 8*(1), 69 – 94.

Brown, C. V. & Magill, S. L. (1994). Alignment of the IS function with the enterprise: Toward a model of antecedents. *MIS Quarterly, 18*(4), 371 – 403.

Cilli, C. (2003). IT governance: Why a guideline? *Information Systems Control, 3*. Retrieved May

8, 2008, from http://www.isaca.org/Template.cf m?Section=Home&Template=/ContentManagement/ContentDisplay.cfm&ContentID=15933

Cole, A. (1995). Runaway projects—Cause and effects. *Software World, 26*(3), 3 – 5.

De Haes, S. & Van Grembergen, W. (2006). Information technology governance best practices in Belgian organisations. *Paper presented at the 39th Hawaii International Conference on System Sciences*, Hawaii.

Dearden, J. (1987). The withering away of the IS organisation. *Sloan Management Review, 28*(4), 87 – 91.

Doll, W. J., Deng, X., & Scazzero, J. A. (2003). A process for post-implementation IT benchmarking. *Information and Management, 41*(2), 199 – 212.

Earl, M. J. (1989). *Management srategies for information technology.* Hemel Hempstead: Prentice-Hall.

EQuest (2004). *The Australian IT project landscape.* Sydney: EQuest Consulting and iGATE Global Solutions. Retrieved May 8, 2008, from http://www.eqc.com.au/EQuest%20iGate%20P roject%20Management%20Survey%20May%2 02004.pdf

Ezingeard, J.-N., Irani, Z., & Race, P. (1999). Assessing the value and cost implications of manufacturing information and data systems: An empirical study. *European Journal of Information systems, 7*(4), 252 – 260.

Fama, E. & Jensen, M. (1983). Separation of ownership and control. *Journal of Law and Economics, 26*, 301 – 325.

Galliers, R. D. W. (1987). Information systems planning in the UK and Australia - A comparison of current practice. *Oxford Surveys in IT, 4*, 223 – 255.

Gunasekaran, A., Love, P. E. D., Rahimi, F., & Miele, R. (2001). A model for investment justification in information technology projects. *International Journal of Information Management, 21*, 349 – 364.

Hegel, J. & Brown, J. S. Your next IT strategy. *Harvard Business Review, 9*(79), 105 – 113.

Henderson, J. C. & Venkatraman, N. (1992). Strategic alignment: A model for organizational transformation through information technology. In T. A. Kochan & M. Useem (Eds.), *Transforming organizations.* Oxford: Oxford University Press.

Hirschheim, R., Klein, H. K., & Lyytinen, K. (1995). *Information systems development and data modelling – Conceptual and philosophical foundations.* Cambridge: Cambridge University Press.

Hodgkinson, S. T. (1996). The role of the corporate IT function in the federal IT organization. In M. J. Earl (Ed.), *Information management: The organizational dimension.* Oxford: Oxford University Press.

Hoffman, T. (2004, May 17). IT oversight gets attention at board level. *Computerworld*

Hoffmann, F. G.-M. & Weill, P. (2004). *Banknorth: Designing IT governance for a growth-oriented business environment.* Cambridge: Center for Information Research, Sloan School of Management.

Hogg, R. (2002). Keynote address. *Paper presented at the CIO 2002*, Sydney. Retrieved May 8, 2008, from http://www.acs.org.au/news/050302. htm.

Huff, S. L., Maher, M. P., & Munro, M. C. (2004). What boards don't do - but must do - about information technology. *Ivey Business Journal On-Line* (September/October), 1 - 4. Retrieved May 8, 2008, from http://www.iveybusinessjournal. com/view_article.asp?intArticle_ID=511

Hyde, A. (2002). Defining IT project success and failure. In B. Runciman (Ed.), *BCS review 2002*. Swindon: British Computer Society.

ISO (2005a). *ISO/IEC 27001 - Information technology - Security techniques - Information security management systems - Requirements.* Geneva: International Standards Organisation

ISO (2005b). *ISO/IEC 17799 Information technology — Code of practice for information security management.* Geneva: International Standards Organisation. Retrieved May 8, 2008, from http://www.iso.org/iso/en/StandardsQueryFormHandler.StandardsQueryFormHandler?scope=CATALOGUE&sortOrder=ISO&committee=ALL&isoDocType=ALL&title=true&keyword=17799

ITGI (2002). *CoBIT: Control objectives for information and related technology* (3rd Ed.). Rolling Meadow, IL: IT Governance Institute. Retrieved May 8, 2008, from http://www.isaca.org/AMTemplate.cfm?Section=Downloads&Template=/MembersOnly.cfm&ContentID=15988

ITGI (2003). *Board briefing on IT governance* (2nd ed.). Rolling Meadows, IL: IT Governance Institute. Retrieved May 8, 2008, from http://www.itgi.org/Template_ITGI.cfm?Section=ITGI&Template=/ContentManagement/ContentDisplay.cfm&ContentID=6606

IT Leader (2006). Time for CIOs to get on board. *IT leader.* Retrieved May 8, 2008, from http://www.the-itleader.com/features/feature434/

Johnstone, D., Huff, S. L., & Hope, B. (2006). IT projects: Conflict, governance and systems thinking. *Paper presented at the 39th Hawaii International Conference on System Sciences,* Hawaii

Jordan, E. & Musson, D. J. (2003, June 9 - 11). The board view of electronic business risk. *Paper presented at the 16th Bled eCommerce Conference,* Bled, Slovenia

Jordan, E. & Silcock, L. (2005). *Beating IT risks.* Milton, Qld: Wiley.

Kaplan, R. B. & Norton, D. P. (1992). The balanced scorecard - Measures that drive performance. *Harvard Business Review, 70*(1, Jan/Feb), 71 – 79.

Kaplan, R. B. & Norton, D. P. (1993). Putting the balanced scorecard to work. *Harvard Business Review, 71*(5), 134 – 142.

Kaplan, R. B. & Norton, D. P. (1996). Using the balanced scorecard as a strategic management system. *Harvard Business Review, 74*(1), 75 – 85.

Keider, S. P. (1984). Why information systems development projects fail. *Journal of Information Systems Management, 1*(3), 33 – 38.

King, J. L. (1983). Centralised versus decentralised computing: Organisational considerations and management options. *Computing Surveys, 15*(4), 320 – 349.

KPMG (1997). *What went wrong? Unsuccessful information technology projects.* San Francisco: KPMG. Retrieved May 8, 2008, from www.audit.kpmg.ca/vl/surveys/it_wrong.htm

KPMG (2004). *Creating stakeholder value in the information age: The case for information systems governance.* Sydney: KPMG.

KPMG (2005a). *Strategic risk management survey.* Sydney: KPMG. Retrieved May 8, 2008, from http://www.kpmg.com.au/Portals/0/ias_whitepaper-str-risk-mgt-survey200502_071441.pdf

KPMG (2005b). *Global IT project management survey.* Sydney: KPMG. Retrieved May 8, 2008, from http://www.kpmg.com.au/Portals/0/irm-prm-global-it-pm-survey2005.pdf

Kumar, K. (1990). Post implementation evaluation of computer-based information systems: Current practice. *Communications of the ACM, 33*(2), 203 – 212.

Lederer, A. L. & Sethi, V. (1996). Key prescriptions for strategic information systems planning. *Journal of Management Information Systems, 13*(1), 35 – 62.

Lin, C. & Pervan, G. (2001). IS/IT investment evaluation and benefits realisation issues in a government organization. *Paper presented at the The Twelfth Australasian Conference on Information Systems*, Coffs Harbour.

Luftman, J. N. (2003). *Competing in the information age: Align in the sand.* Oxford: Oxford University Press.

Luftman, J. N., Lewis, P. R., & Oldach, S. H. (1993). Transforming the enterprise: The alignment of business and information technology strategies. *IBM Systems Journal, 32*(1), 198 – 221.

Luftman, J. N., Papp, R., & Brier, T. (1999). Enablers and inhibitors of business - IT alignment. *Communications of the Association for Information Systems, 1*. Retrieved May 8, 2008, from http://is.lse.ac.uk/support/ICIS/2000/pdf-files/AIS/0111CAIS.pdf

Lyytinen, K. & Hirschheim, R. (1987). Information system failures - A survey and classification of the empirical literature. *Oxford Surveys in Information Technology, (4)*, 257 – 309.

Markus, M. L. (2000). Toward an integrative theory of risk control. In R. Baskerville, J. Stage & J. I. DeGross (Eds.), *Social perspectives on information technology* (pp. 167 - 178). Boston: Kluwer Academic Publishers.

Martino, C. L. (1983). *Information systems planning to meet business objectives: A survey of practices.* New York: North Holland.

McKenney, J. L., Copeland, D. G., & Mason, R. O. (1995). *Waves of change: Business evolution through information technology.* Boston: Harvard Business School Press.

Meredith, J. R. & Mantel, S. J. (1995). *Project management: A managerial approach.* Chichester: John Wiley.

Milis, K. & Mercken, R. (2004). The use of balanced scorecard for the evaluation of Information and communication technology projects. *International Journal of Project Management, 22*(2), 87 – 97.

Nelson, R. R. (2005). Project retrospectives: Evaluating success, failure and everything in between. *MIS Quarterly Executive, 4*(3). Retrieved May 8, 2008, from http://www.misqe.org/jsp/showpaper.jsp?ob1=67&ob2=92&ob3=false

Nevo, S., Wade, M. R., & Cook, W. D. (2007). An examination of the trade-off between internal and external IT capabilities. *Journal of Strategic Information Systems, (16)1*, 5 – 23.

NOIE (2003). *Productivity and organisational transformation: Optimising investment in ICT.* Canberra: National Office of the Information Economy. Retrieved May 8, 2008, from http://www2.dcita.gov.au/ie/publications/2003/03/ovum_report

Nolan, R. L. (1982). Managing information systems by committee. *Harvard Business Review, 60*(4), 72 – 79.

Nolan, R. L. & McFarlan, F. W. (2005). Information technology and the board of directors. *Harvard Business Review, 83*(10), 96 – 106.

O'Connor, A. D. (1993). Successful strategic information systems planning. *Journal of Information Systems, 3*(2), 71 – 83.

OGC (2004). ITIL publications. Retrieved May 8, 2008, from http://www.ogc.gov.uk/index.asp?docid=1000364

Olsen, M. H. & Chervany, N. L. (1980). The relationship between organisational characteristics and the structure of the information services function. *MIS Quarterly, 4*(2), 57 – 68.

Parker, M. M. & Benson, R. J. W. (1988). *Information economics: Linking business performance to information technology.* Englewood Cliffs, NJ: Prentice Hall.

Parr, A., Shanks, G., & Darke, P. (1999). The identification of necessary factors for successful implementation of ERP systems. In N. Ojelanki, L. Introna, M. D. Myers & J. I. DeGross (Eds.), In *Proceedings of IFIP Working Group 8.2 Conference on New Information Technologies in Organizational Processes: Field Studies and Theoretical Reflections on the Future of Work.* Boston: Kluwer Academic Publishers.

Peterson, R. (2003). Integration strategies and tactics for information technology governance. In W. Van Grembergen (Ed.), *Strategies for information technology governance.* Hershey, PA: Idea Group Publishing.

Peterson, R. K. (2004). Crafting information technology governance. *Information Systems Management,* (Fall), 7 - 22. Retrieved May 8, 2008, from http://www.itknowledgebase.net/dynamic_data/3619_2288_governance.pdf

Peterson, R. K., Parker, M. M., & Ribbers, P. M. A. (2002, December 15 - 18). Information technology governance processes under environmental dynamism: Investigating competing theories of decision making and knowledge sharing. *Paper presented at the 23rd Annual International Conference on Information Systems,* Barcelona

PwC (2004). *IT governance global status report.* Rolling Meadows: IT Governance Institute.

PwC (2006). *IT governance survey.* Rolling Meadows: IT Governance Institute.

Radcliffe, R. C. (1982). *Investment: Concepts, analysis, strategy.* Glenview, IL: Scott, Foreman and Co.

Remenyi, D., Sherwood-Smith, M., & White, T. (1997). *Achieving maximum value from informa-tion systems: A process approach.* Chichester: John Wiley & Sons.

Renkema, T. J. W. (1998). The four P's revisited: Business value assessment of the infrastructure impact of IT investments. *Journal of Information Technology, 13*(3), 181 – 190.

Ribbers, P. M. A., Peterson, R. R., & Parker, M. M. (2002). Designing information technology governance processes: Diagnosing contemporary practices and competing theories. *Paper presented at the Proceedings of the 35th Hawaii International Conference on System Sciences - 2002,* Hawaii. Retrieved May 8, 2008, from http://csdl.computer.org/comp/proceedings/hicss/2002/1435/08/14350241b.pdf

Rockart, J. F. & De Long, D. W. (1988). *Executive support systems: The emergence of top management computer use.* Homewood, IL: Dow Jones-Irwin.

Salle, M. (2004). *IT service management and IT governance: Review, comparative analysis and their impact on utility computing.* Palo Alto: Hewlett-Packard Laboratories. Retrieved May 8, 2008, from http://www.hpl.hp.com/techreports/2004/HPL-2004-98.pdf

Sambamurthy, V., Venkatraman, S., & DeSanctis, G. (1993). The design of information technology planning systems for varying organizational contexts. *European Journal of Information Systems, 2*(1), 23-35.

Sambamurthy, V. & Zmud, R. W. (1999). Arrangements for information technology governance: A theory of multiple contingencies. *MIS Quarterly, 23*(2), 261 – 290.

Sauer, C. (1993). *Why information systems fail: A case study approach.* Henley-on-Thames: Waller.

Schwalbe, K. (2002). *Information technology project management* (2nd ed.). Boston: Course Technology.

Seddon, P. B., Graeser, V., & Willcocks, L. P. (2002). Measuring organizational IS effectiveness: An overview and update of senior management perspective. *The Data Base for Advances in Information Systems, 33*(2), 11 – 28.

Serafeimidis, V. & Smithson, S. (2000). Information systems evaluation in practice: A case study of organizational change. *Journal of Information Technology, 15*(2), 93 – 105.

Sohal, A. S. & Ng, L. (1998). The role and impact of information technology in Australian business. *Journal of Information Technology, 13*(3), 201 – 217.

Sommerville, I. (2004). *Software engineering* (7th ed.). Harlow: Pearson Education.

SOX (2002) Sarbanes-Oxley Act (Public Company Accounting Reform and Investor Protection Act of 2002), No. 107-204, 116 Stat. 745 C.F.R.

Spafford, G. (2003, April 22). The benefits of standard IT governance frameworks. *Datamation on-line*.

Standish (2003). *CHAOS Chronicles v3.0*. West Yarmouth, MA: The Standish Group International, Inc.

Strassman, P. A. (1990). *The business value of computers*. New Canaan, CT: The Information Economics Press.

Tavakolian, H. (1989). Linking the information technology structure with organisational competitive strategy: A survey. *MIS Quarterly, 13*(3), 309 – 317.

Tricker, R. I. (1984). *Corporate governance: Practices, procedures and powers in British companies and their boards of directors*. Aldershot: Gower.

van Akkeren, J. & Cavaye, A. L. M. (1999). Factors affecting entry-level internet technology adoption by small business in Australia – Evidence from three cases. *Journal of Systems and Information Technology, 3*(2), 33-48.

Van den Berghe, L. A. A. & Baelden, T. (2005). The monitoring role of the board: One approach does not fit all. *Corporate Governance, 13*(5), 680 – 690.

Van den Heijden, H. (2001). Measuring IT core capabilities for electronic commerce. *Journal of Information Technology, 16*(1), 13 – 22.

Van Grembergen, W. (2002). Introduction to the minitrack on IT Governance and its Mechanisms. *Paper presented at the The 35th Hawaii International Conference on System Sciences (HICSS)*, Hawaii.

Wagner, E. L. & Newell, S. (2004). Best for whom?: The tension between "Best practice" ERP packages and diverse epistemic cultures in a university context. *Journal of Strategic Information Systems, 13*(4), 305 – 328.

Ward, J. & Peppard, J. (2002). *Strategic planning for information systems*. Chichester: John Wiley & Sons Ltd.

Ward, J. & Peppard, J. (2002). *Strategic planning for information systems*. Chichester: John Wiley & Sons Ltd.

Webb, P., Pollard, C., & Ridley, G. (2006). Attempting to define IT governance: Wisdom or folly? *Paper presented at the the 39th Annual Hawaii International Conference on Systems Science*, Hawaii.

Weill, P. (2004). Don't just lead, govern: How top-performing firms govern IT. *MIS Quarterly Executive, 3*(1), 1 – 17.

Weill, P. & Broadbent, M. (1998). *Leveraging the new infrastructure: How market leaders capitalize on information technology*. Boston: Harvard Business School Press.

Weill, P. & Broadbent, M. (2003). *Creating effective IT governance, A Gartner EXP premier research report*. Stamford, CT: Gartner.

Weill, P. & Olson, M. (1989). Managing investment in information technology. *MIS Quarterly, 13*(1), 2 – 17.

Weill, P. & Ross, J. W. (2004). *IT governance: How top performers manage IT decision rights for superior results*. Boston: Harvard Business School Press.

Weill, P. & Ross, J. W. (2005). A matrixed approach to designing IT governance. *MIT Sloan Management Review, 46*(2), 26 – 34.

Weill, P. & Woodham, R. (2002). *Don't just lead, govern: Implementing effective IT governance* (Working Paper No. 4237-02). Boston: MIT Sloan School of Management. Retrieved May 8, 2008, from http://papers.ssrn.com/sol3/Delivery.cfm/SSRN_ID317319_code020724590.pdf?abstractid=317319&mirid=1

Whittaker, B. (1999). What went wrong? Unsuccessful information technology projects. *Information Management and Computer Security, 7*(1), 23 – 29.

Wiegers, K. (1998). Know your enemy: Software risk management. *Software Development*, October. Retrieved May 8, 2008, from http://www.processimpact.com/articles/risk_mgmt.html

Willcocks, L. & Griffiths, C. (1994). Predicting risk of failure in large-scale information technology projects. *Technological Forecasting and Social Change*, (47), 205 – 228.

Wilson, T. D. (1989). The implementation of information systems strategies in UK companies: Aims and barriers to success. *International Journal of Information Management, 9*, 245 – 258.

ENDNOTE

[1] There is a document from Standards Australia, AS8015, Corporate governance of information and communications technology (AS 2005), but this gives a statement of principles and a high-level model.

Section II
IT Governance Case Studies

Chapter IV
Adoption and Implementation of IT Governance:
Cases from Australian Higher Education

Jyotirmoyee Bhattacharjya
The University of Sydney, Australia

Vanessa Chang
Curtin University of Technology, Australia

ABSTRACT

This chapter introduces key IT governance concepts and industry standards and explores their adoption and implementation in the higher education environment. It shows that IT governance processes, structures and relational mechanisms adopted by these institutions generate value through improvements in a number of key focus areas for IT management. It is hoped that the study will inform both practitioners and researchers and lead to a better understanding of the relationship between IT governance structures, processes and relational mechanisms and business benefits.

INTRODUCTION

Over the past decade, IS/IT governance has become a key issue of concern for senior IT decision makers around the world. The underlying goals for adopting formal IT governance practices are improvement of business performance and conformance with regulations. This exploratory study examines how IT governance is implemented in two Australian institutions through a number of structures, processes, and relational mechanisms and how industry best practice frameworks such as CobiT, ITIL, ISO17799 and ISO/IEC20000 have been utilized in the implementation. The study reveals a number of important findings in the context of the implementation of IT governance in the higher education environment. The relationship between IT governance adoption and implementation and business benefit issues will also be discussed in the chapter. The next few sections of this chapter contains a detailed literature review regarding IT governance, and the important IT related issues in the Australian higher education sector. This is followed by a discussion of the research questions and methodology and then the case study institutions are described. Finally, the findings from the study are presented and the conclusions and directions for future work are discussed.

BACKGROUND

Corporate and IT Governance

Corporate governance has become increasingly important worldwide, especially in the wake of the Enron and MCI WorldCom incidents in the US. The Australian Stock Exchange Corporate Governance Council defines corporate governance as *"... the system by which companies are directed and managed. It influences how the objectives of the company are set and achieved, how risk is monitored and assessed, and how performance is optimised"* (ASX, 2003). IT governance has increasingly become a key area of concern under the umbrella of corporate governance because of the pervasive influence of information systems and the associated technology infrastructure in every area of an organization's activities. The IT Governance Institute describes IT governance as being an integral part of the corporate governance which consists of "the leadership and organizational structures and processes that ensure an organization's IT sustains and extends the organization's strategy and objectives" (ITGI, 2003).

Previous Research in IT Governance Implementation

The term IT governance, started to appear in the research literature towards the late 1990's, with its main proponent being the IT Governance Research Institute (De Haes & Van Grembergen, 2005). Recent surveys suggest that the need to implement and improve IT governance has been receiving growing recognition amongst senior IT management across the world. A survey of top 10 priorities for senior IT management by Gartner Inc. in 2003, found the need for improving IT governance to be included in the list for the first time (De Haes & Van Grembergen, 2004). Surveys of members of the Society of Information Management (SIM) in 2003, 2004 and 2005 also revealed that IT governance was amongst the top ten concerns of IT executives (Luftman, 2005; Luftman, Kempaiah & Nash, 2006). However, implementing IT governance can be an extremely complex undertaking (Brown, 1997; De Haes & Van Grembergen, 2004; Duffy, 2002; Marshall & McKay, 2003; Sambamurthy & Zmud, 1999; Weill & Ross, 2005). In 2003, a survey conducted by the IT Governance Institute through PricewaterhouseCoopers of 335 CEO/CIO level executives around the world showed a lag in practice (ITGI, 2004). The survey found that while 75% executives recognized the requirement for implementing IT governance only 40% were taking any action in this direction. This may be explained by the complexities of implementing IT governance.

While previous research on IT governance implementation focussed on IT governance structures and associated contingency factors (e.g., Brown, 1997; Sambamurthy & Zmud, 1999), later work has identified a number of different mechanisms for implementing IT governance (De Haes & Van Grembergen, 2004; Weill & Ross, 2005). This chapter adapts the framework presented by De Haes & Van Grembergen (2004) to explore IT governance implementations in the higher education sector. Based on the work of Peterson (2004), De Haes and Van Grembergen (2004) propose that IT governance can be implemented through a framework of structures, processes, and relational mechanisms. Structures include the existence of well defined roles and responsibilities and IT steering committees. Processes involve strategic decision making and the use of various IT governance frameworks and standards (e.g., CobiT and ITIL) which can provide the IS organisation with the means of examining its activities and its value to business. Relational mechanisms include shared learning and strategic dialogue between business and IT, and ensuring proper communications at all times.

The structures, processes and relational mechanisms are also divided into tactics or roles and mechanisms or means to implement IT governance (De Haes & Van Grembergen, 2004). For example, the tactics for structures are to form IT executives, committees and councils. The mechanisms are to ensure that there is an IT organisation structure; roles and responsibilities are assigned, a CIO appointed, and the formation of an IT strategy or steering committee. As for processes, the tactics are to ensure that strategic IT decision making and monitoring are formed. This may be accomplished by setting mechanisms such as strategic information systems planning, balanced IT scorecards, service level agreement, COBIT, ITIL and IT alignment of governance maturity models, that would enhanced the processes of implementing IT governance. Finally, relational mechanisms are required to ensure participation from stakeholders, businesses and IT. This is required to ensure an on-going dialogue with the main players. The mechanisms to ensure a smooth running of this include a shared understanding of business/IT objectives, nonavoidance conflict resolution, crossfunctional business/IT training, and crossfunctional business/IT job rotation.

International Standards and Commercially Available Frameworks for IT Governance and Management

A number of IT best practice frameworks and standards such as Control Objectives for Information and Related Technology (CobiT), ISO/IEC 17799, IT Infrastructure Library (ITIL) and Capability Maturity Model (CMM) are available to IT organizations to help them improve their accountability, governance, and management. CobiT is designed by the IT Governance Institute as a high-level "umbrella" framework for IT governance and it works very well with other frameworks like ITIL and ISO/IEC 17799 which focus on specific aspects of IT management. The framework identifies 34 IT processes over 300 control objectives across four IT domains: (1) planning and organization, (2) acquisition and implementation, (3) delivery and support, and (4) monitoring (ITGI, 2000; 2005). The planning and organization domain addresses strategic and tactical issues and how IT can optimally contribute to achieving business goals. The acquisition and implementation domain deals with the development or acquisition of IT solutions, as well as their implementation and integration with business processes. This domain also covers the maintenance of existing systems. The delivery and support domain covers the actual delivery of services ranging from security and continuity related operations to training. Support processes are required to ensure the delivery of services. The monitoring domain addresses the issue of management oversight of the organization's control processes and the need for independent audits. The IT Governance Institute has recently published the fourth edition of CobiT, the first update since 2000. It is described as an incremental improvement on CobiT 3.0 and provides a number of useful additions to the older version (Bodner, 2006; Symons, 2006).

The IT Infrastructure Library (ITIL) is a comprehensive documentation providing guidance regarding best practices for IT service management (ITIL, 2007a; 2007b). The Central Computer and Telecommunication Agency (CCTA) in the UK established the Information Technology Infrastructure Library (ITIL) in 1989 (Sallé, 2004) in order to improve its IT organization. At present the UK's Office of Government Commerce (OGC) is responsible for managing ITIL. ITIL is also supported by the IT Service Management Forum (itSMF). In 2000 the OGC, in collaboration with the British Standards Institution (BSI) and itSMF, revised ITIL in order to integrate it with the BSI Management Overview, the BSI specification for service management (BS 15000-1) and the BSI code of practice for service management (BS150000-1) (ITIL, 2007a). The BSI Management Overview provides a high level introduction to ITIL, while the ITIL books expand on the information and provide guidance regarding the subjects addressed within BS150000. BS15000 has now been replaced by ISO/IEC 20000:2005. Like its predecessor, ISO/IEC 20000 is a two part standard (1SO, 2005a). The first part specifies requirements for IT service management while the second part provides a code of practice. The ITIL documentation, now available in version three, takes a lifecycle approach to guidance (ITIL, 2007b). It is organized around five core titles: (1) Service Strategy which provides a view of ITIL that ensures that all elements of the Service Lifecycle is focused on customer outcomes, (2) Service Design which provides guidance for producing and maintaining IT architectures and policies and documents for designing appropriate IT infrastructure service processes and solutions (3) Service Transition which provides guidance for the transition of services in the business environment, (4) Service Operation which details control and delivery activities for achieving excellence in daily operations, and (5) Continual Service Improvement which focuses on the process of identifying and introducing improvements to service managements.

Another standard that can be implemented alongside CoBiT and ITIL is ISO/IEC 17799:2005 (expected to be renamed ISO/IEC 27002 in 2007/08). The standard was originally developed from BS 7799 which provides a code of practice for developing information security standards in an organization (ISO, 2000). However, unlike CoBiT and ITIL, it was not designed to be a certification standard. It has recently released a companion standard, ISO/IEC 27001 that can be used for the purpose of certification instead of the older and superseded BS 7799-2 on which it is based (ISO, 2005b). A new risk management standard BS 7799-3:2006 is also presently available from the British Standards Institute. This standard provides support and guidance for the risk management aspect of ISO/IEC 27001:2005.

In addition to these frameworks and international standards, Australian organizations have three local standards available to guide their IT governance and management practices. These are AS 8015-2005 (ICT governance standard), AS ISO/IEC 20000.1-2007 (specification for ICT service management) and AS ISO/IEC 20000.2-2007 (code of practice for ICT service management).

The ICT governance standard, AS 8015-2005, provides a set of guiding principles for senior business decision makers regarding the effective and efficient use of information and communication technology (ICT) within their organizations, irrespective of the industry sector. The standard addresses the governance of ICT resources for the provision of information and communication services within the enterprise (Standards Australia, 2005). The standard is currently in the process of being developed into an international standard. It has been accepted as a Draft International Standard (ISO/IEC DIS 29382) by the ISO in early 2007 (ISO, 2007).

Standards Australia (2007a; 2007b) provides a two part service management standard AS ISO/IEC 20000-2007. The first part (AS 20000.1-2007) outlines the requirements that a service provider needs to fulfil in order to deliver an acceptable quality of managed service to customers, while the second part (AS 20000.2-2007) recommends a common terminology for IT service providers, so that effective processes may be established. AS 20000.1-2007 is identical to ISO/IEC 20000.1-2005 and AS 20000.2-2007 is identical to ISO/IEC 20000.2-2005. They supersede AS 8018.1-2004 and AS 8018.2-2004.

Implementation of these frameworks may vary from one region to another. A recent Forrester Research survey of 135 IT managers in North America revealed that about 20% rely on CoBiT while another 20% use ITIL (Dubie, 2005). A survey of 110 respondents by Cater-Steel and Tan (2005) at a recent Australian itSMF conference showed that while all respondents were at different stages of implementing ITIL, less than a third are also implementing CoBiT. These frameworks are not necessarily mutually exclusive and increasing the value of IT from a business perspective requires an understanding of their strengths, weaknesses and focus (Symons, 2005). IT governance frameworks are being increasingly adopted around the world because they not only assure conformance with regulations but also help in ensuring performance (Liew, 2006). Organizations may benefit from adopting what they find useful from each framework rather than just adopting a single one (Chickowski, 2004).

There are, however, very few academic publications examining the issues and problems with the adoption and implementation of these frameworks and standards. Ridley, Young, and Carroll (2004) found that this to be particularly true in the case of publications related the CoBiT framework, a majority of which tend to be practitioner publications. Cater-Steel and Tan (2005) make a similar observation regarding the available publications on ITIL.

Emergent Framework of IT Governance Mechanisms and Focus Areas

The IT Governance Institute has identified five focus areas of IT governance (ITGI, 2005): (1) strategic alignment, (2) value delivery, (3) resource management, (4) risk management, and (5) performance measurement.

According to ITGI (2005, p. 6): Strategic alignment is about ensuring the linkage of business and IT plans; on defining, maintaining and validating the IT value proposition; and on aligning IT operations with enterprise operations. Value delivery is about executing the value proposition throughout the delivery cycle, ensuring that IT delivers the promised benefits against the strategy, concentrating on optimising costs and proving the intrinsic value of IT. Resource management is described as the optimal investment in, and the proper management of, critical IT resources in applications, information, infrastructure and people. Key issues of resource management relate to the optimisation of knowledge and infrastructure. Risk management is concerned with risk awareness by senior corporate officers, understanding of compliance requirements, transparency about the significant risks to the enterprise, and embedding of risk management responsibilities into the organisation. Performance measurement is about tracking and monitoring strategy implementation, project completion, resource usage, process performance and service delivery, using, for example, balanced scorecards that translate strategy into action to achieve goals measurable beyond conventional accounting.

The two primary concerns of IT governance, value delivery and risk management, are driven by strategic alignment and accountability concerns respectively. Both require adequate resources and need to be measured against the objectives of the business.

The emergent framework as illustrated in Figure 1 combines the framework of De Haes and

Van Grembergen and the IT governance focus areas. In order for a business to be effective, the framework indicates that an organization's IT governance structures, processes and relational mechanisms must be set in place.

As mentioned previously, IT governance structures identify various roles and responsibilities in the context of IT governance in an organization (De Haes & Van Grembergen, 2004). Processes describe how those with appropriate responsibilities are involved in the governance rather than the day-to-day operational management of IT. Relational mechanisms ensure the success of structures and processes by addressing ways of improving the relationship between business and IT (De Haes & Van Grembergen, 2005). This suggests a dynamic relationship between these three components of IT governance as shown in Figure 1. Optimizing the balance between structures, processes and relational mechanisms could lead to substantial benefits for business through improvements in the five focus areas of IT governance identified by the IT Governance Institute (ITGI, 2005).

This study uses the framework presented in Figure 1 to explore the IT governance implementations in two institutions of higher education.

IT Governance in Australian Institutions of Higher Education

Higher education is a multibillion dollar industry in Australia, and as such, it is of vital importance to the country's economy (Higher Education IT Consultative Forum, 2000; Nelson, 2002). It is both a major consumer of IT products and services as well as a major provider of services using ICT. IT has helped the improvement of a range of activities including research, teaching, learning and administration in the higher education environment. Significant developments have been made by these institutions in the area of online teaching and learning. The demand for IT based products and services, has also increased as a result of the rapid increase in student population in the last 15 years.

There is much work that needs to be done by university governing bodies and policy makers

Figure 1. The emerging IT governance and business benefits framework

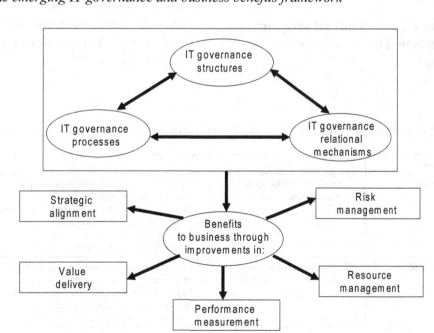

in order for these universities to continue tapping emerging information technologies in order to maintain their competitive positions internationally (Higher Education IT Consultative Forum, 2000). The issues range from infrastructure, applications, delivery and services to staffing and appropriate regulatory frameworks. IT applications have also not yet penetrated all aspects of university teaching and more effort is required to bring about improvements in this area. However, despite the wide range of concerns facing IT governing bodies in Australian universities in the information economy, there has been very little research regarding how IT governance may be suitably implemented in these institutions in order for them to provide optimal benefits to higher education.

RESEARCH QUESTION AND METHODOLOGY

The chapter investigates the adoption and implementation of IT governance in two Australian institutions for higher education. The research question is:

How is formal IT governance adopted and implemented within the higher education environment in Australia?

As suggested by Benbasat, Goldstein, and Mead (1987), the case research method is useful for addressing the *"how"* questions, that is, in the exploratory stage of knowledge building. This is particularly useful for a study on IT governance in the context of institutions of higher education in Australia, where the knowledge of researchers regarding new methods, techniques, problems and prospects lags that of practitioners. A case research strategy is expected to provide rich insight in this context.

Two leading institutions of higher education in Australia in different stages of adopting and implementing formal IT governance practices were selected for the study based on the availability of senior IT and business decision makers in these institutions for participating in this research. The study was undertaken in 2006. In keeping with participants' requests for anonymity, the institutions will be referred to as Institution A and Institution B in this chapter. The data collected was primarily qualitative in nature. The data was gathered from semi-structured interviews with senior IT and business decision makers in both institutions as well as from relevant documents obtained from interviewees and the websites of the institutions. The interviews were recorded and later transcribed and analysed. The data sources from the institutions are summarized in Table 1.

Table 1. Data sources from the two case study institutions

Institution	Interviewees	Documents
Institution A	- 2 senior IT decision makers - 2 senior business decision makers	- Overall strategic plan and strategic IS plan - Disaster recovery plan - Organizational chart and committee structures - Security policies and procedures - Personnel statistics - Student satisfaction surveys
Institution B	- 2 senior IT decision makers - 1 senior business decision maker	- Overall strategic plan and strategic IS plan - Proposed IT governance model - Organizational chart and committee structures - Security policies and procedures - Personnel statistics

THE CASE STUDY INSTITUTIONS

Institution A was established in the 1960's. The institution has over 3,000 academic and administrative staff members and over 30,000 students. Its primary goals are to achieve excellence in teaching, learning, research and development. Its present priorities include providing flexible learning opportunities, developing facilities and technological infrastructure to support research priorities, forming partnerships with industry and government and improving its revenue generation. The institution has an overall strategic plan as well as a number of divisional plans and maintains a balanced scorecard. It has six academic divisions which are subdivided into several schools, centres and departments, as well as a number of support areas including central IT services, finance, and student and staff services. The institution is publicly funded, with annual revenue of around A$400 million, 10% of which is spent on IT. The institution's IT history began in the 1960's, with the acquisition of a computer for the mathematics department. In the early 1970's, a computer system was installed primarily for teaching purposes. This was followed by the in-house development of an accounting package, signalling the first move towards corporate applications. The institution decided on continued development of both teaching and administrative applications, although these were to be handled separately. Since the various teaching and administrative divisions had specific application needs, the decisions regarding the procurement or development of applications lie with the divisions. In the late 1980s the institution received its first Australian Academic and Research Network (AARNET) connection and the use of email followed soon after.

Institution B was established in the early 1900's. It has over 2000 academic and administrative staff members and over 16,000 students. Like Institution A, it aims to advance teaching, learning and research. It has nine academic divisions and a number of support areas. The institution has an overall strategic plan and a number of divisional plans. The publicly funded institution's annual revenue is around A$500 million about 1.5% of which is spent on central IT and about 4.5% across the divisions. Divisional IT services and the library have separate IT budgets. Historically IT has been devolved to central administration, the academic divisions and the library.

In 1999 Institution A had an ICT review conducted by an external consulting firm. The review identified a devolved IT structure. A number of key issues including the negative impact of divergent IT directions in the divisions on overall corporate effectiveness, inadequate strategic planning and coordination related to ICT across the institution, inadequate ICT resources and lack of leadership at the senior level of senior management were reported in the review. As a direct result of the 1999 review, they adopted CoBiT in the year 2000 to evaluate the current IT processes within the institution.

Institution B has recently adopted a formal IT governance model. In early 2006 they commissioned a new Strategy Manager and Director of IT to set up their IT governance model with an aim to centralize their IT governance structure. The next three sections explore the adoption and implementation of IT governance through a mixture of structures, processes and relational mechanisms in these two institutions.

As proposed in Figure 1, the institutions implement IT governance through a combination of structures, processes and relational mechanisms in different focus areas.

IT GOVERNANCE STRUCTURES

IT governance structures include clearly defined roles and responsibility of IT executives to manage the IT structure within the organization (De Haes & Van Grembergen, 2004). This may include setting up of IT committees to oversee various IT strategies and functions of IT within the organization.

Institution A

Currently, Institution A has about 200 staff members employed in the IT area. Of the 200 staff members, 100 are located in the central IT services and the other 100 within the divisions. Despite the observations made in the 1999 review it has not been possible to integrate the ICT across the institution into a single unit due to lack of an institution wide support for such a change. However, some enterprise wide standards for ICT have been developed and the need for compliance by the divisions has been recognized. Duplication of some services across the divisions remains a cause of significant concern and it is believed that considerable cost savings could result from avoiding such duplication.

Institution A has a formal reporting channel whereby the Director of central IT services reports to the Pro-Vice Chancellor. The role of the Director is primarily that of a technology professional though there is a growing realization of the need for the role to be more business oriented. The Director of central IT oversees three Associate Directors who are responsible in the infrastructure, applications and services areas respectively. A recent development has been the formation of the IT strategy committee, which reports to and advises the institution's planning and management committee. The IT strategy committee in its present form was established in mid 2005. It currently includes the Director of central IT services, representatives of all divisional IT groups, the Director of Finance, representatives from R&D, the Pro-Vice Chancellor and key stakeholders. The committee makes recommendations regarding the alignment of ICT with the goals of the institution, monitors the activities of the central and divisional IT service providers and fosters effective communication amongst them.

The formation of the IT strategy committee in mid 2005 and the development of the enterprise wide standards reflect the recognition by senior business and IT decision makers of the need for a formal IT Governance model to support a centralized decision making structure. The shift from a devolved or decentralized IT structure to a centralized structure in Institution A is consistent with the results of a survey by Mendez (2005) of IT executives in Europe which showed a significant shift in the IT organization structure from decentralized or federated models to centralized ones.

Telecommunication and network related decision making in the institution has been centralized since the beginning. However, this has not been the case with desktop computers and servers because of the IT revolution in the 1980's. This has continued to this day, resulting in the institution's federated IT organization structure. There are six divisional IT groups which manage their own servers and desktop PCs independently of central IT. The divisional IT groups have independent funding and decision-making structures from central IT. Although they provide the same kind of services as the central IT group, their standards and practices may vary from those of central IT. Over the past year central IT has moved towards developing good relationships with divisional IT managers. This has helped in the achievement of some alignment between the central and divisional IT groups.

Institution B

In Institution B, there are about 70 IT staff in central IT and a similar number spread over the nine divisions and the library. As in the case of Institution A, this structure has led to considerable duplication of IT staff efforts. IT has five major areas – administration including budget and staffing, strategy and governance, client services including desktop and student Internet support, systems services including database support and systems development, and technical services looking after network and servers. The managers of these areas report to the Director of IT who reports to the Director of Finance.

Unlike Institution A, the role of the Director of IT in Institution B is that of a general business manager rather than a technology professional. This shift in the role for the Director of IT was decided in 2005 by the new Director of Finance based on his experience in the resources sector. It was believed that the position of the Director of IT required someone who clearly understood the business needs of the institution and has an overall technology focus.

A formal IT governance model specifying the various roles and responsibilities based on COBIT 4.0 was adopted at the beginning of 2006 when the new Strategy Manager was appointed. This model is now in the process of being implemented. The adoption of the model has led to a significant improvement in the involvement of business in IT decision making. The IT steering committee is expected to meet on a quarterly basis and provide an opportunity for communication on key IT issues amongst IT and business decision makers. The IT steering committee is advised by a technical advisory group which is comprised of all the central and divisional IT managers. Smaller working groups are also constituted from the divisional stakeholders and central IT staff as and when required for specific projects. The IT Director and Strategy Manager are responsible for decisions regarding standardization of IT infrastructure strategies and architecture. Decisions regarding business application needs are made by business decision makers with input from IT.

A summary of IT governance structures in Institution A and Institution B, based on the De Haes and Van Grembergen framework is shown in Table 2.

IT GOVERNANCE PROCESSES

IT governance processes involve strategic decision making and the use of various performance monitoring frameworks and tools such as Strategic Information Systems Planning, COBIT, ITIL, Balanced Scorecard, Information Economics and others (De Haes & Van Grembergen, 2004).

Institution A

The institution has an overall strategic plan and follows a balanced scorecard. ICT has an ICT enabling plan, which is regularly updated. An important issue in this regard is that this ICT enabling plan is not directly associated with a budget for strategic expenditures. The present budget allocation for ICT is for staff, software licenses, site licenses, and refreshing the IT infrastructure. Although the need for a new document management system has been recognized by both IT and business decision makers, in order for the institution to improve its record keeping, appropriate funds for such procurement are yet to be acquired.

IT management decision making within the institution is influenced by the guiding principles of the Australian ICT governance standard AS 8015-2005 and the service management standards AS 8018.1-2004 and AS 8018.2-2004. COBIT 3.0

Table 2. A summary of IT governance structures in the case study institutions

	Structures	Institution A	Institution B
Tactics	– IT executives and accounts	– Yes	– Yes
	– Committees and councils	– Yes	– Yes
Mechanisms	– Roles and responsibilities	– Yes (evolving)	– Yes (evolving)
	– IT organization structure	– Yes (evolving)	– Yes (evolving)
	– CIO on board	– No	– No
	– IT strategy committee	– Yes (recent)	– No
	– IT steering committee(s)	– No	– Yes (recent)

has been adopted since the year 2000 for assessing and improving the institution's IT governance processes. A direct effect of this has been the realization by senior IT decision makers that the effective utilization of CoBiT across the institution requires a more centralized IT governance environment. However, given the size of the CoBiT 3.0 framework, only a small number of processes and objectives are identified for review each year. The objectives were initially based on a large number of interviews conducted across the campus in 2000 by IT staff. In subsequent years, objectives have been identified based on the original interviews and results of an annual survey of student and staff satisfaction on IT issues.

ITIL is used as the standard for service management. A number of operational level staff members have ITIL Foundation level training. The current focus is on getting better at incident management, change management, problem management, IT strategic planning and managing the IT architecture. The progress made has also been assessed against CoBiT and ITIL. Consultative, Objective and Bi-functional Risk Analysis (COBRA), a software package, based on ISO17799 is being used for facilitating risk management.

Since CoBiT requires the use of a standard project management methodology, Project Management Body of Knowledge (PMBOK) has been selected as the guide in this regard. Based on the perceptions of business decision makers, in the last two years IT has shown considerable maturity in project management and delivery. This is the result of adopting a strong project management methodology.

People Capability Maturity Model (P-CMM) is used as the standard of IT staff management and development. However, a lot of work is required in the area of staff development.

The value to business from the implementation of best practice frameworks has been in terms of reducing the number of ad-hoc processes, bringing a lot of discipline to IT support activities and improving accountability. Whilst IT has

made significant strides since the year 2000, the IT management recognizes that there is a long journey ahead.

One problem that has been faced in implementing the best practice frameworks like CoBiT, which have high resource requirements, has been the shortage of adequate staff. The demand for staff time and services are also increasing. Most of the central IT teams find it difficult and at times challenging to achieve their operational objectives. Staffing in the server support area, for example, consists of about 10 people supporting 300 servers of various kinds, implementing changes to the infrastructure as well as managing large applications being used by thousands of people. Despite the staffing issue, however, process improvements continue to take place because of the continued commitment of senior IT management.

Another key area of difficulty has been that of finding appropriate performance metrics measurement. Currently, technical measures being used include percentage downtime, percentage access failure, the number of students accessing their email on a regular basis on the official communications channel and so on. One particular measure, the number of available desktops in the computer laboratories per student was found to be not particularly useful. It was found that when the number of desktops was doubled based on survey responses; the satisfaction level was actually lower than in the previous year. Management decision makers in the institution attribute this to the increasing expectations from ICT facilities with the rapid advances technology. The institution continues to work on developing balanced business-IT metrics.

Institution B

While Institution A has been using CoBiT 3.0 to evaluate and improve key IT processes, Institution B has utilized CoBiT 4.0 to develop its overall IT governance model and outline the various roles and responsibilities. The development of the IT governance model has resulted in substantial involvement of business decision makers in making decisions regarding IT investment, risk and priorities. This has made it easier for business decision makers to appreciate the value of key decisions regarding IT. The initial problem faced in the implementation of the model was the lack of IT governance concepts amongst business decision makers and the resistance to change. This is gradually being overcome and the need for accountability for IT related decision making across the institution is better accepted. This is achieved by communicating to business decision makers their roles and responsibilities in IT related decision making for the benefit of the business, without making it necessary for them to know any technical details regarding CobiT.

CobiT is also being used for risk assessment and management. While ISO17799 provides guidance on what needs to be done in the context of security, CobiT guides management on how these goals should be achieved. The IT security manager has been trained in ISO17799 and will additionally undertake the security management training program provided by the developers of CobiT.

The institution has an overall strategic plan and central IT undertakes strategic information systems planning under the supervision of the IT steering committee. Service level agreements are in place for hosting and managing applica-tion systems including the student system, the facilities management system, the HR and finance system.

At present there is a lack of enterprise-wide standards for infrastructure and applications. The key issues that IT intends to tackle over the next year include the lack of standards and controls and the existence of multiple help desks. As part of the central IT service desk project, it is planned to implement ITIL to handle change and incident management over the next few months. As part of the ITIL implementation service desk staff will be required to undertake ITIL Foundation level training. Capability is also being built up in the project management and business process analysis domain to reduce the current dependence on external consultants.

As in the case of Institution A there is difficulty in deciding on which metrics to measure. Current metrics being used include the number of service calls being answered to completion, the number of network and database administrators and the ratio of total IT cost to organizational cost. However, there is a realization that these metrics are not adequate for representing the value of IT to business.

A summary of IT governance processes in Institution A and Institution B, based on the De Haes and Van Grembergen framework is shown in Table 3.

Table 3. A summary of IT governance processes in the case study institutions

	Processes	Institution A	Institution B
Tactics	−Strategic IT decision making −Strategic IT monitoring	−Yes −Yes	−Yes −Yes

Mechanisms	−Strategic IS planning
	−Balanced IT scorecards
	−Information economics
	−Service level agreements
	−CobiT and ITIL
	
	−IT alignment/ governance
	  maturity models
		−Yes (improving)
		−No (some technical measures)
		−No
		−No
		−Yes along with other standards
		  since 2000
		−No (considered early days for
		  maturity models)
			−Yes (improving)
			−No (some technical measures)
			−No
			−Yes
			−CobiT with ISO17799 since early 2006
			−No (considered early days for maturity
			  models)

IT GOVERNANCE RELATIONAL MECHANISM

Relational mechanisms according to De Haes and Van Grembergen (2004) include shared learning and strategic dialogue between business and IT, and ensuring proper communications at all times.

Institution A

The key stakeholder groups for central IT include teaching staff, students, business process owners, research and development, and divisional IT management whilst those for divisional IT include teaching staff and students. There are efforts being made by central IT to improve the quality and frequency of communications with these groups.

Communications often take place at the tactical level. For instance, if a significant outage of services is being considered, divisional IT contacts and business process owners are informed and their responses are used to guide appropriate decision-making. In case of policy changes, e-mails are sent out by the particular group within IT that is responsible for that policy. The senior IT decision maker responsible for infrastructure also meets with the divisional IT management on a monthly basis. Over the last couple of years there has been emphasis on strategic level dialog. The monthly meetings of the newly formed ICT committee are also helping to improve communications between business and IT. This increased effort made by IT decision makers to liaise with business, has led to a growing perception of IT as a valued service provider rather than just a cost of doing business.

An area requiring further attention is staff development. Currently there is no staff retention program for IT staff and no opportunity for cross-training. There is also a need for increasing staff numbers in central IT. While an integration of IT services centrally might help solve the problem of staff shortage, opposition at the divisional level has yet to be overcome.

Institution B

Communication with key stakeholders is being considered to be of vital importance over the coming months in order to successfully implement the new IT governance model. The principal stakeholder groups for IT include the teaching staff, students, research and development, university administration, and the library. Communication with these groups is carried out through informal discussions, working groups and committee meetings. Unlike in previous years, conflicts between central IT and divisional IT are now actively resolved through discussions at the steering committee meetings.

The understanding of IT by business and vice versa is improving gradually and IT is emerging as an asset and a valued service provider. There has been a recent policy shift geared towards more balanced business and technical hiring within central IT.

A summary of IT governance relational mechanisms in Institution A and Institution B, based on the De Haes and Van Grembergen framework is shown in Table 4.

FINDINGS

A Comparison Between Institutions A and B

The chapter addresses the question of how formal IT governance practices can be adopted within the higher education environment. The increased dependence of IT in the higher education environment has also led to the awareness of the need for adopting formal IT governance practices. As seen in the previous sections both institutions have been implementing IT governance through a mixture of structures, processes and relational mechanisms.

Table 4. A summary of IT governance relational mechanisms in the case study institutions

	Relational Mechanisms	Institution A	Institution B
Tactics	– Stakeholder participation – Business/IT partnerships – Strategic dialog – Shared learning	Improving on all counts	Improving on all counts
Mechanisms	– Active participation by principal stakeholders – Collaboration between principal stakeholders – Partnership rewards and incentives – Business/IT co-location – Shared understanding of business/IT objectives – Active conflict resolution (non-avoidance) – Cross-functional business/IT training – Cross-functional business/IT job rotation	– Improving – Improving – No – Improving – Improving – Recent attempts – No – No	– Improving – Improving – No – Improving – Improving – Recent attempts – No – No

Based on the experiences of Institutions A and B, the following findings emerge with regard to the implementation of IT governance:

1. Professionals in both institutions agree that while an institution of higher education has to deal with low staffing levels, this should not be a deterrent in adopting industry best practices. They also agree that instead of adopting any one best practice framework, it is important to evaluate the strengths and weaknesses of the business and selectively adopt a combination of the relevant elements of best practice frameworks and standards such as CoBiT, ITIL, ISO17799, AS 8015-2005, AS 8018.1-2004 or AS 8018.2-2004 that are necessary to support the business.

2. The two institutions vary in their approach in implementing CoBiT and in the version of CoBiT being implemented. The application of CoBiT 3.0 for improving individual processes was an important eye-opener for management in Institution A because it focused attention on the need for centralization of decision making, having well defined IT governance roles and responsibilities, and developing enterprise-wide standards. In Institution B the overall IT governance structure is being implemented based on the CoBiT 4.0 framework. It is believed that this approach would help in the utilization of CoBiT 4.0 for improving processes across the university rather than just at central IT.

3. Institutions of higher education may benefit from experiences gained in IT governance implementation in other industries. In the case of Institution B, the background of the Director of Finance in the resources sector helped in identifying the need for the role of the Director of IT to be more business oriented (a need also being gradually recognized in Institution A). The Strategy Manager's background in the finance sector helped in developing the governance model for the institution fairly quickly based on the CoBiT 4.0 framework.

4. CoBiT requires the use of a good project management methodology. Institution A's adoption of CoBiT has led to its adoption of PMBOK. This was particularly important as the institution's IT staff does a considerable amount of the project implementation and delivery work in-house.

5. A key difference between CoBiT and ITIL noted by professionals in both organizations is in the availability and cost of documentation. There is a considerable amount of CoBiT related documentation and research papers available free of cost from the Information Systems Audit and Control Association

(ISACA) Website and additional information is available through mailing lists. ITIL documentation, on the other hand, is considerably more expensive.

6. Both institutions have realized that although the use of multiple learning management systems and multiple email systems may be the existing norm in the divisions, this leads to duplication of ICT staff efforts without increasing the satisfaction of staff and students across the institution. A consolidation of systems could potentially help in the reduction of staff numbers (leading to reduced costs) while providing a better direction for staff efforts.

7. In both institutions, the disparity in ICT services across the institutions lead to difficulties in managing the perceptions of students and staff. In Institution A, student dissatisfaction with ICT services at the divisional level is reflected on their perception of ICT in general in the annual surveys. A consolidation of services (e.g. helpdesks, printing) could help in maintaining the same standards of services across the institution (in both cases) and make it easier to manage perceptions.

8. In both institutions improving communication between central IT and divisional IT groups are helping in the general acceptance of central IT standards.

9. In both institutions improving communication between IT and business has led to the gradual acceptance of IT as a valued service provider rather than just a cost of doing business, in an institution whose core business is not IT.

The Relationship Between Structures, Processes and Relational Mechanisms

As discussed previously, De Haes and Van Grembergen (2004) provide a broad framework for implementing IT governance through a mixture of structures, processes and relational mechanisms. However they do not explicitly discuss the relations between these three and how they relate to business benefits. The findings of the study support the emerging framework presented in Figure 1.

The study suggests that the development of IT governance structures (eg. IT strategy committee) leads to improved relational mechanisms and the adoption of IT governance processes (eg. the implementation of best practice frameworks such as ITIL) across the enterprise. The findings associated with Institution A suggests that there is a need to have a formal IT Governance structure with clearly defined roles and responsibilities in order to facilitate the adopted IT governance processes. As discussed in the findings, Institution A is shifting to a centralized IT governance structure. By adopting a formal IT Governance structure, Institution A strives to strengthen relational mechanisms. Improving relational mechanisms through formal and informal communications ensures broader support for improving IT governance structures and processes. The findings associated with Institution B affirms the framework as shown in Figure 1 in that they used COBIT to guide, develop and establish a formal IT Governance model including various structures, processes and relational mechanisms. Whilst Institution B presently lacks enterprise-wide standards (e.g., architectural, service management), they plan to implement ITIL as the service management standard with their IT staff requiring to undertake ITIL Foundation level training. Institution B has also considered key stakeholders to be vital and this has resulted in a policy geared towards a more balanced between business and IT hiring within central IT. While the institutions are in the early stages of experiencing business benefits from their evolving structures, processes and relational mechanisms, a longitudinal study would shed further light on the benefits of their IT governance practices.

The study also suggests that the range of structures, processes and relational mechanisms implemented by each organisation may differ from those presented in the De Haes and Van Grembergen (2004) framework.

The Five Focus Areas of IT Governance

The focus of IT governance implementation in the two institutions seems to be on five key areas as shown in Figure 1.

IT governance in the two institutions is implemented through a number of processes, structures and relational mechanisms in the context of these five areas. The focus area of strategic alignment in the four institutions appears to be addressed through processes such as strategic IS planning and the adoption and implementation of industry frameworks such as ITIL and COBIT that help in the attainment of business objectives. Structures like steering committees are used to involve business decision makers in strategic level IT decision-making. This growing interaction between business and IT is helping to build a shared understanding between business and IT on key issues. This is an important relational mechanism in the De Haes and Van Grembergen framework (2004).

With respect to value delivery (Figure 1), the adoption of standards such as PMBOK and ITIL for improving project management and service delivery was found to be an important process. While ITIL has been adopted by both institutions, PMBOK appears to have been adopted by institutions A only. Attention given by management to ensure staff training was found to be an important relational mechanism.

COBIT and ISO17799 were found to have been adopted by institutions A and B for risk management purposes. The adoption of P-CMM is guiding the management of human resources in institution A. It must be noted that although both institutions had reasonably well understood roles and responsibilities for the management of key

resources such as business applications and supporting infrastructure, the institutions are all yet to have a formal documented governance model in place clearly outlining these structures.

As in other industries measuring the performance of IT remains a big challenge for IT decision makers in institutions of higher education and suitable measures are gradually being developed. COBIT has been used for evaluating IT process maturity in Institution A.

While there has been progress in all five focus areas, the development of formal governance models with input from key business decision makers could help in continuing to generate value for business in the two institutions.

LIMITATIONS AND FUTURE WORK

The study focuses on the implementation of structures, processes and relational mechanisms in two institutions of higher education and the focus areas for these implementations. It does not seek to address specific educational market drivers influencing IT governance implementations or the operational management issues that a well designed IT governance model helps to facilitate. Future research in these directions as well as on the integration of IT and corporate governance in the higher education sector would help in strengthening the findings. Further longitudinal investigations of IT governance practices in the higher education sector would help in testing the IT governance-business benefits framework presented in Figure 1 and addressing the present limitations of the study.

CONCLUSION

The chapter highlights some key issues regarding the adoption of formal IT governance practices in the higher education sector for the benefit of practitioners, academics, and researchers. As discussed in the previous section, the findings of study provide support for the framework presented in Figure 1. Institutions A and B were found to have implemented IT governance through a combination of various structures, processes and relational mechanisms. Benefits to business in the two institutions were found to arise from improvements in strategic alignment, value delivery, performance measurement, resource and risk management as the various mechanisms of IT governance evolve in these institutions. However, it must be noted that as both institutions are in the process of developing their formal governance models and the extent of benefits from IT governance may become more clearly understood in the future. One of the institutions has already received feedback from the authors regarding the findings of the study and is in the process of implementing some of the recommendations.

REFERENCES

ASX (2003). *Principles of good corporate governance and best practice recommendations.* Retrieved May 10, 2008, from http://www.asx.com.au/about/pdf/ASXRecommendations.pdf

Benbasat, I., Goldstein, D., & Mead, M. (1987). The case research strategy in studies of information systems. *MIS Quarterly, 11*(3), 368-386.

Bodnar, G. H. (2006). What's new in CoBiT 4.0. *Internal Auditing, 21*(4), 37-44.

Brown, C. V. (1997). Examining the emergence of hybrid IS governance solutions: Evidence from a single case site. *Information Systems Research, 8*(1), 72-94.

Cater-Steel, A. & Tan, W. (2005). Implementation of IT infrastructure library in Australia: Progress and success factors. In *Proceedings of the IT Governance International Conference,* Auckland.

Chickowski, E. (2004). Taking models of IT governance – Is it time to evaluate your decision-making process? *Processor, 26*(15). Retrieved May 10, 2008, from http://www.processor.com/editorial/article.asp

De Haes, S., & Van Grembergen, W. (2004). IT governance and its mechanisms. *Information Systems Control Journal, 1.*

De Haes, S. D. & Van Grembergen, W. (2005). IT governance structures, processes and relational mechanisms: Achieving IT/Business alignment in a major Belgian financial group. In *Proceedings of the 38ᵗʰ Hawaii International Conference on System Sciences,* Hawaii.

Dubie, D. (2005). Taking on IT service management. *Network World, 2*(23), 8.

Duffy, J. (2003). *IT governance and business value part 1: IT governance – An issue of critical influence.* Retrieved May 10, 2008, from http://www.networkworld.com/research/ reports/IDC27291.html

Higher Education IT Consultative Forum (2000). *The way forward – Higher education action plan for the information economy department of education science and training.* Retrieved May 10, 2008, from http://www.backingaustralias future. gov.au/ fact_sheets.htm

ISO (2000). *Standards of 2000.* Retrieved May 10, 2008, from http://www.iso.org

ISO (2005a). *ISO/IEC 20000 benchmarks provision of IT service management.* Retrieved May 10, 2008, from http://www.iso.org

ISO (2005b). *ISO/IEC 27001 international information security standard published.* Retrieved May 10, 2008, from http://www.iso.org

ISO (2007). *Draft international standard ISO/IEC DIS 29382 corporate governance of information and communication technology.* Retrieved May 10, 2008, from http://www.iso.org

ITGI (2000). *CoBiT 3rd edition - Executive summary*. IT Governance Institute, USA.

ITGI (2005). *CoBiT 4.0 – Control objectives, management guidelines, maturity models*. Retrieved May 10, 2008 from http://www.itgi.org

ITGI (2003). *Board briefing on IT governance*. Retrieved May 10, 2005, from http://www.itgi.org

ITGI (2004). *IT governance global status report*. Retrieved May 10, 2008, from http://www.isaca.org

ITIL (2007a).*What is ITIL*. Retrieved May 10, 2008, from http://www.itil-officialsite.com/AboutITIL/WhatisITIL.asp

ITIL (2007b). *Service management – ITIL ® (IT Infrastructure Library) Version 3*. Retrieved May 10, 2008, from http://www.best-management-practice.com/ officialsite.asp?FO=1245494

IT Governance Ltd. (2006). *BS 7799-3:2006 – Risk management guidelines*. Retrieved May 10, 2008 from http://www.itgovernance.co.uk

Liew, K. (2006). Challenges of compliance – The CoBiT bridge. *Computerworld, 12*(15). Retrieved May 10, 2008, from http://www.computerworld.com.sg

Luftman, J. (2005). Key issues for IT executives 2004. *MIS Quarterly Executive, 4*(9), 269-285.

Luftman, J., Kempaiah, R., & Nash, E. (2006). Key issues for IT executives 2005. *MIS Quarterly Executive, 4*(2), 81-99.

Marshall, P. & McKay, J. (2003). Steps towards effective IT governance: Strategic IT planning, evaluation and benefits management. In *Proceedings of the 7th Pacific Asia Conference on Information Systems*, Adelaide.

Mendez, M. A. (2005). *The state of IT governance in Europe: Business technographics Europe*. Retrieved May 10, 2008, from http://www.forrester.com/Research/ Document/Excerpt/0,7211,37201,00.html

Nelson, B. (2002). *Higher education at the crossroads – An overview paper*. Retrieved May 10, 2008, from http://www.backingaustraliasfuture.gov.au/fact_sheets.htm

Peterson, R. R. (2004). Information strategies and tactics for information technology governance. In W. Van Grembergen (Ed.), *Strategies for information technology governance*. Hershey, PA: Idea Group Publishing.

Ridley, G., Young, J., & Carroll, P. (2004). CoBiT and its utilization: A framework from the literature. In *Proceedings of the 37th Hawaii International Conference on System Sciences*, Hawaii.

Sallé, M. (2004). *IT service management and IT governance: Review, comparative analysis and their impact on utility computing*. Retrieved May 10, 2008, from http://www.hpl.hp.com/techreports/2004/HPL-2004-98.pdf

Standards Australia (2007a). *AS ISO/IEC 20000.1-2007 information technology – Service management – Part 1: Specification*. Retrieved May 10, 2008, from http://www.standards.com.au

Standards Australia (2007b). *AS ISO/IEC 20000.2-2007 information technology – Service management – Part 2: Code of practice*. Retrieved May 10, 2208, from http://www.standards.com.au

Standards Australia (2005). *AS 8015-2005: Corporate governance of information and communication technology*. Retrieved May 10, 2008, from http://www.standards.com.au

Sambamurthy, V., & Zmud, R. W. (1999). Arrangements for information technology governance: A theory of multiple contingencies. *MIS Quarterly, 23*, 2, 261-290.

Symons, C. (2005). *IT governance survey results: More work to be done*. Retrieved May 10, 2008, from http://www.forrester.com/Research/Document/ Excerpt/0,7211,36804,00.html

Symons, C. (2006). *CoBiT 4.0 is a strong governance platform*. Retrieved http://www.forrester.com/Research/Document/Excerpt/0,7211,39122,00.html

Weill, P., & Ross, J. (2005). A matrixed approach to designing IT governance. *MIT Sloan Management Review, 46*(2), 26-34.

Chapter V
Tailoring CobiT for Public Sector IT Audit:
An Australian Case Study

Lynne Gerke
University of Tasmania, School of Accounting & Corporate Governance, Australia

Gail Ridley
University of Tasmania, School of Accounting & Corporate Governance, Australia

ABSTRACT

This chapter examines the potential to use an audit program based on the Control Objectives for Information and related Technologies (CobiT) framework for IT audit within a public sector audit office. It documents research that derives, implements and evaluates such a program with the cooperation of the public sector audit office in an Australian state. Additionally a comparison of the study results was undertaken with those of Guldentops, van Grembergen and de Haes (2002), Liu and Ridley (2005) and the European Organisation of Supreme Audit Institutions (EUROSAI) IT Working Group CobiT Self-assessment Project. The results suggest that the CobiT-derived instrument was effective for IT audit, and was able to be tailored to the needs of Tasmanian state public sector organization, when evaluated against a number of criteria.

INTRODUCTION

Information technology (IT) facilitates the actions of most organizations in both the public and private sectors. Its near ubiquitous status has lead to a significant change in the practice of auditors. Previously when computers were not as prevalent auditors generally chose to work "around" the technology. That is, activities and documents were scrutinised prior to entry into the computer system, and output from the system was also examined. Auditors chose not to involve themselves with the inner workings of information systems. Gradually, as computers become more prevalent auditors began to incorporate them into their daily practice, using computer aided audit techniques (CAATs). Finally, when the technology became an integral part of the way in which society functioned, auditors were forced to examine the ways in which the technology impacted on both the financial data, which had been their traditional focus, and the organization in a broader context. To guide the effective use of IT in organizations, practitioners and academics developed a comprehensive framework called the Control Objectives for Information and related Technologies (CobiT). The CobiT framework links IT and business objectives and provides guidance on how best to audit information systems.

The CobiT framework (now in Version 4.1) is widely used internationally for IT control and audit. Although a body of practitioner literature exists, the CobiT framework has been subject to little academic scrutiny, particularly regarding its usefulness for IT governance and audit. The framework is large, and has associated with it a comprehensive set of Audit Guidelines. However, the constraints of public sector audit offices make it difficult to implement these audit guidelines in full. Consequently, there has been interest in tailoring the framework to a size that is more appropriate for implementation. To do so requires decisions on which components of the control framework should be retained, and which to omit. Appropriate tailoring will retain the components of the framework that make IT audits more relevant and meaningful in the local context.

This chapter presents a case study of a CobiT implementation for IT audit, documenting a research project that built on the very small body of international academic research involving the CobiT framework. The study utilises the results of research conducted by Gerke and Ridley (2006) to develop an IT audit instrument that is subsequently tested within a state government audit office in Australia. The implementation is then

subject to evaluation and the results compared to those obtained in previous international and national CobiT assessment studies.

BACKGROUND

The background section considers IT-related frameworks, before reviewing relevant literature on the CobiT framework and examining the setting for the study.

IT-Related Frameworks Including CobiT

IT frameworks are used to "facilitate effective IT governance" (Warland & Ridley, 2005). The IT Governance Institute (ITGI) states the primary goal of IT frameworks to be the development of a set of best practices concerning IT processes and controls within an organization as well as a scale to rate them (ITGI, 2000c, p. 10). A number of IT-related frameworks has been referred to within the practitioner literature. The most common include CobiT, the Information Technology Infrastructure Library (ITIL), the Integrated Capability Maturity Model (CMMi), Six Sigma and the International Standards Organization (ISO) Standards number 17799 and 9000 (Anthes, 2004; Spafford, 2003; Violino, 2005). Each framework has been derived to meet a specific need, and the more commonly used ones continue to evolve to meet practitioner requirements. It is not the intention of this chapter to provide an in depth discussion of the strengths and weaknesses of IT frameworks. This has been done well in the practitioner literature, with articles by Anthes (2004) and Violino (2005; 2006) providing overviews of numerous frameworks.

The CobiT framework was selected for use in this research as it was derived specifically to guide the practice of IT audit and is used extensively throughout the public and private sectors for this purpose. The next section provides more information on the CobiT framework.

CobiT

The CobiT framework was developed by the Information Systems Audit and Control Association (ISACA) in response to a perceived need for a framework for the internal control of IT. Built on best practice, it has been maintained and upgraded to reflect changes in these processes.

CobiT 3.0 consists of 34 IT processes grouped into the four broad domains, *Planning and Organization, Acquisition and Implementation, Delivery and Support* and *Monitoring.* The research reported in this paper used CobiT Version 3.0; however, Version 4.1 has been released more recently. There are some differences between versions 3.0 and 4.1 including the number of IT processes, while the terms "IT process" and "control objective" had different names in Version 3. A control objective is defined in Version 3 as "a statement of the desired result or purpose to be achieved by implementing control procedures in a particular IT activity" (ITGI, 2000c). The most recent names for these elements will be used in this paper. Version 3 had between three and thirty control objectives associated with each IT process, giving a total of 318 control objectives. For ease of reference, each IT process is labelled with a prefix containing the initials of the domain in which it is grouped and a number, followed by a brief descriptive title. An example of this nomenclature is *DS5, Ensure Systems Security.* This IT process, the fifth in the *Delivery and Support* domain, is concerned with ensuring the overall security of systems.

The CobiT Management Guidelines (ITGI, 2000a) contain a set of Maturity Models which provide the practitioner with a means of scoring the organization's performance on a Likert-type scale ranging from 0 (non-existent) to 5 (optimized). The Maturity Models have been developed to be specific to each of the individual IT processes. In the Framework section of the Management Guidelines, a generic maturity model is presented; this model is not specific to any particular IT process. Maturity levels may be assessed by seeking evidences to evaluate the level of compliance with an individual IT process. Where maturity levels are used as a basis for audit, a minimum acceptable level is often set (see for example the Australian National Audit Office (ANAO), 2004, p. 33). This level represents a point at which the auditor considers that the IT control arrangements that are in place are adequate.

As an aid to IT auditors, the CobiT documentation also includes a comprehensive set of audit guidelines which may be useful in designing an audit program. The benefits of using the CobiT framework for IT audit derive from the framework's alignment between the IT function and the business goals of the organization. CobiT allows use of the entire framework or an abbreviated version of it, if constraints prohibit application of the full framework (ITGI, 2000b). Selection of key IT processes to tailor the IT audit is standard practice in some public sector audit offices (Johannesson, 2004). When using the COBIT framework for IT audit the auditor tests claims made by the organization about the way in which it met both the IT processes and IT control objectives. Evidence is sought in interviews with key personnel, through the examination of documents and systems, and through other processes.

The CobiT Executive Summary (ITGI, 2007a) gives a more comprehensive overview of the framework. The Executive Summary can be accessed via the reference list at the end of this chapter.

The next section reviews relevant publications about COBIT, and research that has examined its use in assessing the IT function.

Previous CobiT Studies

Much of the available literature about the CobiT framework has been written by practitioners, for practitioners (Ridley, Young & Carroll, 2004), including people linked to ISACA and the associated ITGI. The literature produced by ISACA and ITGI sources is not extensively referenced by academic authors (Brown & Nasuti, 2005). The worldwide adoption of the framework in both the public and private sectors, has led to the suggestion that CobiT should be the subject of rigorous academic research (Ridley et al., 2004). The limited relevant research that has been undertaken to date is considered next.

Guldentops, van Grembergen, and de Haes (2002) invited organizations to assess their own IT performance against a list of IT processes from CobiT identified by a panel of senior IT and audit experts as being the most important. Performance was measured using a generic maturity scale defined by the framework, similar to the specific maturity models provided by CobiT for each of the IT processes. Liu and Ridley (2005) used the same list of IT processes to examine self-assessed maturity within Australian federal and state public sector organizations.

The European Organisation of Supreme Audit Institutions is the peak body of national audit offices or Supreme Audit Institutions (SAIs) from the European continent (EUROSAI, undated). An ongoing project to design a CobiT-based self-assessment tool for SAIs has been undertaken by the EUROSAI IT Working Group (undated). Participants examined the IT aspects of their own organization in a workshop environment to determine the 10–15 key IT processes in achieving the goals of the SAI, and assess the maturity level of the IT processes considered to be the most important

Gerke and Ridley (2006) derived a list of 17 IT processes from CobiT that were perceived as the most important by 25 state and local government organizations within an Australian state. This list contained eight IT processes that were common to both the original list derived in Guldentops et al. (2002) and used by Liu and Ridley (2005), as well as the EUROSAI project. A further three IT processes were found to be common to either Guldentops et al. (2002) and Liu and Ridley (2005), or to the EUROSAI project.

It can be seen that none of the studies reviewed here has derived, tested or evaluated an abbreviated audit program based on the CobiT framework. The next section gives a brief description of the setting in which the study occurred and concludes with the aims of the research.

Study Aims and Setting

Australia is a federation of six states and two territories. Each of the states and territories has an independent government and public service, in addition to the national government and public service. Tasmania is an island, the only Australian state located south of the Australian continent. The island is small in both size and population with approximately half a million residents. The seat of the Tasmanian state public sector is in Hobart, the capital, which was founded in 1804, making it the second oldest city in Australia.

The Tasmanian Audit Office (TAO) is an independent authority charged, amongst other responsibilities, with upholding public integrity within Tasmania (TAO, 2004). Although some restructuring has since occurred at the TAO, at the time the study took place, the Electronic Data Processing (EDP) auditors also supported and assisted the financial audit team as required. The IT audit program used at the time was derived in-house. The focus of the program was on the IT function, without consideration of the integration of IT with the business function. As is usual in the public sector, the TAO operated under constraints of both time and other resources. Consequently, the implementation of full CobiT-based IT audits was not possible. While the TAO sought to use CobiT for IT audit to facilitate alignment between business and IT goals in Tasmanian Government organizations, it also wanted to reduce the size of CobiT by selecting the IT processes to audit that were most relevant.

Given the substantial public sector investment in IT infrastructure and the potential benefits of using CobiT for IT audit, there were three aims of this study.

1. To derive an abbreviated CoBiT-based audit instrument for use in IT audits of Tasmanian state government organizations.
2. To implement the audit program so developed by trialling it in a number of IT audits within the Tasmanian public sector.
3. To assess the effectiveness of the program in the examination of IT function performance for Tasmanian public sector organizations.

METHODOLOGY

This section examines the research methodology, looking at the research design and data collection, and the way in which the data were analyzed.

Research Design and Data Collection

An objective ontology, a positivist epistemology and quantitative methods were adopted for this research. The literature and research within the IT audit field is mostly positivist in nature, and utilises quantitative methods. Since the TAO practices under a predominantly objective and positivist philosophy, use of a similar approach for the development and use of an audit instrument was considered likely to enhance the credibility of the findings.

This study undertook the derivation of an instrument for IT audit that had been tailored to the needs of the Tasmanian state government organizations from the CoBiT framework, and its subsequent trial with selected clients of the TAO, as well as an evaluation of its effectiveness. The instrument used the ranked list of IT processes previously identified by Gerke and Ridley (2006) as being the most important for Tasmanian public sector organizations. The study builds on the work of Guldentops et al. (2002) and Liu and Ridley (2005) by extending international research within an Australian setting. A list of potential audit

measures were compiled, drawing upon three separate sources, before being subjected to a set of inclusion and exclusion criteria to produce the final instrument. This process is outlined in greater detail in the section entitled Deriving Audit Measures. After deriving the audit instrument as outlined, minor revisions were made based on feedback obtained from the TAO.

The IT audit instrument was implemented in nine state public sector organizations in Tasmania to collect empirical audit data, which were later used to evaluate the instrument. The organizations were selected by the TAO primarily by the size and complexity of their IT function, so that most organizations selected made considerable use of IT. The audits took the form of a semi-structured interview with either a senior manager or a person in charge of IT, and were conducted within the organizations' premises. During the course of the interview, relevant documentation from the organization was examined and/or collected to support interview notes. For example, where an organization indicated that a password policy existed, a copy was requested. In some cases such a policy was sighted only, while in others a copy was given to the researcher.

The interview notes were summarized and presented in tabular form. For each individual point of assessment (referred to as "audit measures", or simply "measures") the summary was compared to the text of the CoBiT Generic Maturity Model (ITGI, 2000a) to determine its maturity level. For each organization, the mean of the individual maturity levels for each audit measure within an IT process was then calculated to give an overall maturity level for that process. In this way the maturity level for each IT process was directly related to the organization's compliance with individual audit measures.

The maturity level was used as a tool to enable quantitative comparison of audit outcomes for individual measures and IT processes among the audited organizations. Additionally the resultant maturity levels also facilitated comparison against those of previous studies set in the Australian and international public sectors. However, the process used to assign maturity levels in the audit phase of this research varied from the self-assessment technique used by Guldentops et al. (2002) and Liu and Ridley (2005), as it was based on audit evidence.

Having examined the research design and data collection for the study, the next section examines data analysis.

Analysis

Gerke and Ridley (2006) produced three tiers of IT processes ranked in order of perceived importance to Tasmanian public sector organizations, with the first tier containing only *DS5 Ensure Systems Security*. Using a single IT process to conduct an IT audit would result in a superficial examination of the IT function in each of the audited organizations. However, to conduct audits of all the 17 IT processes on the abbreviated list derived by Gerke and Ridley (2006) using all the associated measures listed in the CobiT Audit Guidelines (ITGI, 2000b,) would have exceeded the resources available. Given that one IT process was insufficient for the audit program and the list of 17 was considered too many, the first two tiers of IT processes were used, with seven IT processes in all. The next section examines the way in which the audit measures were selected for inclusion in the audit instrument.

Deriving Audit Measures

Possible audit measures for each IT process were drawn from three sources: an internal document from the ANAO listing all the audit measures to be investigated while auditing operations in the IT environment (the audit program); a TAO document, similar to the ANAO document; and the CobiT Audit Guidelines (ITGI, 2000b). More than 180 possible audit measures were identified, associated with the seven IT processes to be used for the trial instrument.

Given that the aim of the research was to trial the abbreviated instrument in as many organizations as possible, while still providing meaningful results, it was decided to limit the number of audit measures to a number that could be reasonably examined in an interview of approximately two hours. As the three sources provided more audit measures than could be audited in such an interview, some needed to be eliminated. First the researcher looked for points of similarity between the two audit office documents. If a measure was considered to be important by both audit offices it was included in the final listing. The second method of developing the list of audit measures was though the application of the following exclusion criteria:

- Measures bearing a designation of "mandatory/in scope" from the ANAO document were considered for inclusion and subjected to the remaining exclusion criteria;
- Audit measures that required the researcher to seek evidence from outside the organization being audited were excluded due to the time this would take, and for ethical reasons;
- Measures relating to organizational types which were not found within the population were excluded. The ANAO document made reference to some Australian Government organizations which did not have Tasmanian equivalents, while the CobiT Audit Guidelines made reference to some organizational features that were only relevant to the private sector;
- Certain audit measures listed within the ANAO document were endorsed for examination "… where appropriate." These measures were omitted from the final audit program unless there was a high degree of certainty that they would be applicable; and
- Measures that were too broad to be directly related to any of the IT processes were ex-

cluded to avoid the potential of forming an incomplete or inaccurate audit opinion.

A full listing of all audit measures included in the final audit program can be found in Appendix A.

Once derived the audit instrument was then used to conduct a series of IT audits as outlined in the next section.

Audit Procedure

It was not possible to audit all organizations that participated in the study by Gerke and Ridley (2006) due to time constraints. However, eight of those 25 state and local government organizations accepted an invitation to participate in the IT audits, while another organization which had not taken part in the original study was also included. The organizations are listed in Table 1 with an indication of whether they were at a state or local government level, along with their formal organizational type. Each type of organization that participated in the previous study was also represented in this study. It should be noted that four government departments that participated in the audit phase are designated as government agencies. In the Tasmanian public sector the term agency is defined by the State Services Act (2000). It includes organizations directly controlled by the

government (departments) and other organizations specified by the legislation. Agencies are generally held to a higher standard of accountability, reporting directly to their responsible minister in the government.

In undertaking the audit procedure using semi-structured interviews, the interviewee was asked to provide evidence of the way in which the organization addressed the individual audit measures. All organizations participating in the audits had previously been supplied with text that explained each IT process used. The CobiT 4.1 document (ITGI, 2007b), containing the full text of all the IT processes, is available for free download.

All documentation made or acquired to support an audit opinion is known as audit working papers. An example of working papers are the notes made in the course of the audit interviews. These notes were designed to act both as a record of the interview and a memory aid for the researcher when evaluating the adequacy of the IT processes in the organizations audited.

When the data were assessed against the Generic Maturity Model from the CobiT Management Guidelines (ITGI, 2000a) a match was sought between the evidence and the key requirements of each maturity level, in order to assess development of the IT function. A maturity level was considered to be attained if all requirements of

Table 1. Organizations participating in audits

Organization	Level	Organization Type
A	State	Department (Agency)
B	State	Department (Agency)
C	State	Commission
D	State	Commission
E	State	Department (Agency)
F	State	Government Business Enterprise
G	State	Department (Agency)
H	State	Board
I	Local	Council

that particular level were considered to be met. A maturity level was then assigned to each measure according to the scale shown in Table 1.

0 (non-existent): no processes, the organization considered the audit measure was not relevant to their situation;
1 (initial): addressed indirectly or in an ad hoc manner;
2 (repeatable): informal or undocumented procedures exist;
3 (defined): addressed by documented policies and formalised training;
4 (managed): formal documentation and/or training, subject to continuous monitoring and improvement, and may involve a limited amount of automation;
5 (optimised): meets Maturity Level 4 and includes elements of automated workflow.

As explained, once each individual audit measure for a particular IT process had been assigned a maturity level, the mean of these values was determined. In one instance the mean maturity levels for organizations were compared using a Student's T-test to test for significant differences between means.

The process of implementing the audit instrument was also used in evaluating the utility of the CobiT framework for use in Tasmanian public sector IT audit.

Instrument Evaluation

The audit instrument was evaluated in a number of ways.

1. **Interview duration:** As a primary aim of the study was to develop an IT audit tool that was consistent with the time constraints of a public sector audit office, the duration of the audit interview was a key evaluation criterion.

2. **Expert validation:** Independent expert evaluation of the derived audit instrument was also used.
3. **Linkage of IT and business goals:** Because an important characteristic of CobiT is to align use of IT with organizational goals, the utility of the audit instrument to find linkages between the IT function and the broader business function was also considered in the evaluation.
4. **Relevance of the instrument:** Since a key aim of the study was to develop an IT audit tool that was relevant to the Tasmanian context, both for the public sector audit office and the organizations that participated in the study.
5. **Triangulation of sources:** The instrument was benchmarked against audit instruments from a limited number of Australian public sector audit organizations.

The results are reported and discussed next, along with a comparison with previous studies.

RESULTS AND DISCUSSION

Results and discussion appear in the next section on the audit procedure, the seven IT processes examined, comparisons against previous related studies and the evaluation of the audit instrument. The study's limitations are also discussed at the end of the section.

Conduct of Audits and Assigning Maturity Levels

The audit interviews ranged in duration from approximately 40 minutes for the smallest organization to 100 minutes for the organization with the most complex IT infrastructure.

The next six sections present the maturity ratings assigned for the audited organizations for each IT process. The IT processes are presented in the order of priority for Tasmanian government organizations, as determined by Gerke and Ridley (2006). Each section contains a table showing the maturity levels assigned for the participating organizations for each of the audit measures, associated with the particular IT process. The tables also display the means for the individual measures and organizations, as well as the overall mean for the IT process.

DS5 Ensure Systems Security

The most highly ranked IT process in the Tasmanian public sector, *DS5 Ensure Systems Security*, (Gerke & Ridley, 2006), is concerned with the business goal of "safeguarding information against unauthorised use, disclosure or modification, damage or loss" (ITGI, 2000a, p. 70). *Ensure Systems Security* is enabled by "logical access controls which ensure that access to the systems, data and programmes is restricted to authorised users" (ITGI, 2000a, p. 70).

The low means for some individual audit measures for DS5, as listed in Table 2, may in-

dicate a deficiency in the way that some aspects of this IT process were addressed within these organizations. Six organizations were assigned non-existent (0) or initial (1) maturity levels for the way in which they addressed Audit Measure 11, *daily or weekly reviews of audit trails of access or activity*. As a consequence, Measure 11 had the lowest mean assigned maturity level of all audit measures for this IT process. However, it would appear that reviewing audit trails is critical to the underlying principles of the IT process, *Ensure Systems Security*.

The Tasmanian Government, through the Information Security Charter 2003, required all public sector organizations designated as "Agencies" by legislation to have in place an information security policy. Of the four organizations audited that were required by the Charter to have an information security policy in place (Organizations A, B, E, and G), and marked by an asterisk in the tables, all had done so. Of the other organizations, three (Organizations F, H, and I) had security policies in place, Organization D was developing a security policy, while

Table 2. Maturities assigned for DS5 Ensure Systems Security

Organization	A	B	C	D	E	F	G	H	I	Mean
1	4	4	0	1	4	4	4	4	2	3.00
2	3	4	2	4	4	4	4	3	3	3.44
3	4	4	3	4	4	4	4	3	3	3.67
4	4	4	2	4	3	2	3	3	2	3.00
5	4	4	4	4	4	4	3	4	4	3.89
6	4	4	4	4	4	4	2	4	4	3.78
7	4	4	0	3	4	3	2	3	0	2.56
8	2	3	4	0	4	2	4	0	4	2.56
9	4	4	2	4	4	2	4	4	4	3.56
10	4	4	0	4	2	4	4	4	4	3.33
11	1	4	0	1	1	1	4	4	0	1.78
12	4	4	4	4	4	4	4	4	4	4.00
Mean	3.50	3.92	2.08	3.08	3.50	3.17	3.50	3.33	2.83	3.21

Note: Minimum mean values are in bold; maximum mean values are in italicized bold

Organization C did not have a security policy and had no plans to develop one.

For *DS5 Ensure Systems Security,* the organizations required by the Charter to have security policies had higher organizational mean maturities (ranging from 3.50 to 3.92) for DS5 than all the other organizations (ranging from 2.08 to 3.33). Using a Student's T-test all these former means were found to be significantly different ($p = 0.00097$, at $\alpha = 0.05$) than all the latter. Moreover, the organizations that had security policies in place although not required to do so under the charter also had higher organizational mean maturities. This was found to be the case regardless of whether the organization was currently developing a security policy. These results suggest that development of a security policy was beneficial for individual organizations' systems security. However, other factors such as organizational size may also have contributed to the higher means.

The approaches to Audit Measure 12, assessing the *need to formally indicate the user's acceptance of policies around Internet and e-mail usage,* varied from a need for formal sign off, to no requirement to indicate acceptance. The approach used did not appear to affect the maturity level assigned, since all the organizations had

such policies and communicated them. Several participants indicated that formal sign off on such policies was not used, on legal advice.

DS4 Ensure Continuous Service

IT process *DS4 Ensure Continuous Service,* is concerned with the business goal of "making sure IT services are available as required and ensuring a minimum business impact in the event of a major disruption" (ITGI, 2000a, p. 68). It was ranked second in the list derived by Gerke and Ridley (2006). *DS4 Ensure Continuous Service* is enabled by "having an operational and tested IT continuity plan which is in line with the overall business continuity plan and its related business requirements" (ITGI, 2000a, p. 68).

Of the 13 detailed IT processes associated with *DS4 Ensure Continuous Service,* six make reference to a continuity plan within their titles. One organization had no business continuity plan and no disaster recovery plan, as reflected by being assigned maturity level 0 for Audit Measure 1 (see Organization I in Table 3). However, its interviewee indicated that the formation of these plans was to be considered at an imminent meeting. Another organization considered its long and short range plans to be business continuity and disaster recovery plans.

Table 3. Maturities assigned for DS4 Ensure Continuous Service

Organization	A	B	C	D	E	F	G	H	I	Mean
1	3	3	3	4	4	4	4	4	0	3.22
2	4	4	5	4	4	4	4	4	3	4.00
3	4	4	3	3	3	4	4	3	3	3.44
4	3	3	4	4	2	4	4	3	2	3.22
5	4	4	3	4	4	4	4	4	4	3.89
6	4	4	4	4	4	4	4	4	4	4.00
7	3	3	3	3	3	3	3	3	3	3.00
Mean	3.57	3.57	3.57	3.71	3.43	3.86	3.86	3.57	2.71	3.54

Note: Minimum mean values are in bold; maximum mean values are in italicized bold

While many organizations stated that the organization's Internet publication policy was not the responsibility of the Information Technology department, most managers indicated that the relevant policies were in place and that the organization had strict controls over such publication. This finding is reflected in the high mean (4.00) for Measure 2.

PO1 Define the Strategic Information Technology Plan

Ranked third by Gerke and Ridley (2006), the IT process *PO1 Define a Strategic Information Technology Plan* is concerned with the business goal of "striking an optimum balance of information technology opportunities and IT business requirements as well as ensuring its further accomplishment" (ITGI, 2000a, p. 24). *PO1 Define a Strategic Information Technology Plan* is enabled by "a strategic planning process undertaken at regular intervals giving rise to long-term plans; the long-term plans should periodically be translated into operational plans setting clear and concrete short-term goals" (ITGI, 2000a, p. 24).

One organization did not have an IT planning or steering committee. This organization was consistently assigned lower maturity ratings. It was the only organization to be assigned level 0 (non-existent) for an audit measure for PO1 (see Organization I in Table 4). Not only did it have the lowest mean assigned maturity for both *DS4 Ensure Continuous Support*, and *PO1 Define a Strategic Information Technology Plan* (see Tables 3 and 4), it also had the second lowest mean assigned maturity level for *DS5 Ensure Systems Security*. This result may be linked to its organizational type, as the organization concerned was a local government body, the only one to be audited in this study.

Information obtained during the audit indicated that linkage of both long and short range IT plans to the organizational long and short-range plans was approached in different ways across the organizations. For example, in one organization the IT plans were an integral part of the business plans. In contrast, a second organization used an overarching departmental initiative to dictate the broad direction of the IT plans.

DS11 Manage Data

The IT process *D11 Manage Data* is concerned with the business goal of "ensuring that data remains complete, accurate and valid during its input, update and storage" (ITGI, 2000a, p.

Table 4. Maturities assigned for PO1 Define a Strategic Information Technology Plan

Organization	A	B	C	D	E	F	G	H	I	Mean
1	3	3	3	3	3	3	3	3	0	2.67
2	1	3	2	3	3	2	2	2	2	2.22
3	3	2	3	3	3	3	3	3	2	2.78
4	3	2	3	3	3	3	3	3	1	2.67
5	3	2	3	4	3	3	3	3	3	3.00
6	3	3	3	3	3	3	2	3	3	2.89
7	3	3	2	3	3	3	3	3	3	2.89
8	3	3	3	3	3	3	3	3	3	3.00
Mean	2.75	2.63	2.75	3.13	3.00	2.88	2.75	2.88	2.13	2.76

Note: Minimum mean values are in bold; maximum mean values are in italicized bold

Table 5. Maturities assigned for DS11 Manage Data

Organization	A	B	C	D	E	F	G	H	I	Mean
1	4	1	3	3	0	3	3	1	3	2.33
2	4	4	3	3	0	3	3	3	1	2.67
3	1	1	1	3	3	1	1	3	3	1.89
4	1	1	1	3	0	3	3	3	0	1.67
5	1	1	3	3	0	3	3	3	0	1.89
6	1	3	3	4	3	3	3	3	3	2.89
7	4	3	0	0	1	0	2	2	0	1.33
8	1	1	1	1	1	2	1	1	0	1.00
9	3	0	3	4	0	4	3	3	0	2.22
10	4	4	4	4	4	4	4	4	4	4.00
11	3	3	3	3	3	3	3	3	3	3.00
12	3	3	3	3	3	1	0	0	3	2.11
13	4	4	3	3	3	3	3	3	0	2.89
14	4	4	3	4	4	3	3	3	3	3.44
15	3	0	1	3	0	3	0	3	3	1.78
16	1	3	3	3	1	2	4	3	3	2.56
17	3	0	1	4	0	3	0	3	3	1.89
18	1	4	3	3	0	3	1	3	3	2.33
Mean	2.56	2.22	2.33	3.00	1.44	2.61	2.22	2.61	1.94	2.33

Note: Minimum mean values are in bold; maximum mean values are in italicized bold

82). It is enabled by "an effective combination of application and general controls over the IT operations" (ITGI, 2000a, p82). *DS11 Manage Data* was ranked fourth on the list compiled by Gerke and Ridley (2006).

Many of the audit measures for the *Manage Data* IT process were not considered by IT managers to be applicable in their organizations, as reflected in the low mean maturity levels for both organizations and measures seen in Table 5. However, the wide variation among assigned maturity ratings within *DS11 Manage Data* seen in Table 5 may indicate an inconsistent approach to the management of data within individual organizations. This conclusion is supported by the indication from some managers that many of the audit measures were addressed on a case-by-case basis by individual systems administrators or business units.

The audit measure, *integrity, confidentiality and non-repudiation of sensitive messages transmitted over public networks such as the Internet* was managed poorly by many organizations, as evidenced by the assignment of maturity ratings of either 0 (non-existent) or 1 (initial) in over half the organizations audited. One manager believed sending sensitive messages was not done within their organization, while another provided advice not to do it. The *risk of misaddressing messages by letter, fax or e-mail* was indicated by many as almost impossible to mitigate. Most organizations addressed the problem for e-mail by use of an all of government or global address book and the government directory where possible, but in most cases the responsibility was left to individual users.

DS12 Manage Facilities

The IT process *DS12 Manage Facilities* is concerned with the business goal of "providing a suitable physical surrounding which protects the IT equipment and people against man-made and natural hazards" (ITGI, 2000a, p. 84). Ranked fifth in importance to the public sector organizations surveyed by Gerke and Ridley (2006), it is enabled by "the installation of suitable environmental and physical controls which are regularly reviewed for their proper functioning" (ITGI, 2000a, p. 84).

Most organizations had well developed policies and procedures around the management of their physical premises. This is reflected in the mean maturity levels seen in Table 6. All organizations had means of at least Level 3. IT facilities were locked over night, with the exception of one organization, which was manned at all times. In most cases access to the IT department was through the reception, where it was necessary to sign in to the organization as a visitor. Security was provided either by security personnel or through the use of programmable devices, such as proxy cards or small electronic devices commonly called dongles. Such devices were used in most cases to access the premises after hours.

Table 6. Maturities assigned for DS12 Manage Facilities

Organization	A	B	C	D	E	F	G	H	I	Mean
1	5	5	5	5	5	5	5	5	5	5.00
2	5	5	5	5	5	5	5	5	5	5.00
3	5	3	1	5	5	5	5	5	5	4.33
4	4	4	4	4	4	4	4	4	4	4.00
5	5	5	4	4	5	1	1	4	4	3.67
6	4	4	3	3	3	3	3	3	3	3.22
7	5	5	3	3	3	4	4	4	3	3.78
8	4	3	3	3	3	3	3	3	3	3.11
9	4	2	2	0	0	0	0	0	0	0.89
10	3	3	0	3	3	1	0	3	1	1.89
11	3	3	3	4	3	0	4	3	1	2.67
12	3	4	4	4	4	3	4	4	4	3.78
13	4	4	4	3	4	3	3	3	3	3.44
14	3	4	3	4	3	4	4	4	4	3.67
15	4	3	2	2	3	3	4	3	3	3.00
16	4	4	4	4	4	4	4	4	4	4.00
17	3	3	3	3	3	3	3	3	3	3.00
18	4	5	3	3	3	3	3	3	3	3.33
19	4	0	4	3	1	3	3	3	3	2.67
20	4	1	3	3	4	3	4	3	4	3.22
Mean	4.00	3.50	3.15	3.40	3.40	3.00	3.30	3.45	3.25	3.38

Note: Minimum mean values are in bold; maximum mean values are in italicized bold

In all but one case the reception logs were not examined by the IT department to review departmental visitors. Consequently, as seen in Table 5, the related Audit Measure 9 had the lowest mean assigned maturity. Only one organization required visitors to the computer facilities to sign in to the IT department, in addition to the generic sign-in at reception. However, in all cases access to the server room was restricted to those who were accompanied by an authorized member of staff or those who had been issued with appropriate access privileges.

AI6 Manage Changes

The IT process *AI6 Manage Changes* is concerned with the business goal of "minimising the likelihood of disruption, unauthorised alterations and errors" (ITGI, 2000a, p. 58). It is enabled by "a management system which provides for the analysis, implementation and follow-up of all changes requested and made to the existing IT infrastructure" (ITGI, 2000a, p. 70).

Many of the audit measures examined for *AI6 Manage Changes* were based around making changes to program code. One manager considered that most of the change management audit measures were not applicable to their organization as no coding took place within it. The same manager had previously indicated that the organization sought to appoint a programmer. When such an appointment was made and internal development and change processes began, the organization should reconsider its position for related audit measures. It can be seen from Table 7 that Organization C was assigned a maturity level of 0 (non-existent) for four of the six audit measures and consequently gained a mean maturity level for AI6 of less than one. Several organizations indicated that code was kept by individual vendors or contractors and so they could not comment on the adequacy of such code libraries. However, most managers considered users to be aware of, and understand, the need for formal change control procedures.

PO8 Compliance with External Requirements

The IT process *PO8 Compliance with External Requirements* is concerned with the business goal of "meeting legal, regulatory and contractual obligations" (ITGI, 2000a, p. 38). It is enabled by "identifying and analysing external requirements for their IT impact, and taking appropriate measures to comply with them" (ITGI, 2000a, p. 38). *PO8 Compliance with External Requirements* was ranked seventh in the study by Gerke and Ridley (2006).

Table 7. Maturities assigned for AI6 Manage Changes

Organization	A	B	C	D	E	F	G	H	I	Mean
1	3	3	1	3	3	4	4	3	2	2.89
2	3	3	1	3	3	4	4	3	2	2.89
3	1	4	0	2	0	2	1	2	0	1.33
4	3	4	0	3	1	3	4	3	1	2.44
5	4	0	0	3	3	3	4	3	3	2.56
6	3	0	0	3	1	3	1	3	3	1.89
Mean	2.83	2.33	0.33	2.83	1.83	3.17	3.00	2.83	1.83	2.33

Note: Minimum mean values are in bold; maximum mean values are in italicized bold

Table 8. Maturities allocated for PO8 Compliance with External Requirements

Organization	A	B	C	D	E	F	G	H	I	Mean
1	2	3	3	3	3	4	4	3	0	2.78
2	4	4	4	4	4	4	4	4	4	4.00
3	3	3	2	3	3	3	3	3	3	2.89
4	4	3	0	3	3	4	3	0	3	2.56
5	3	0	0	3	1	0	3	0	3	1.44
6	3	0	0	0	0	4	3	0	0	1.11
Mean	3.17	2.17	1.50	2.67	2.33	3.17	3.33	1.67	2.17	2.46

Note: Minimum mean values are in bold; maximum mean values are in italicized bold

As can be seen in Table 8, Audit measures 5, *insurance contracts*, and 6, *EDI processes*, were considered by many of the managers not to be applicable to their organization, and so were assigned a maturity level of 0. Only four organizations indicated that organizational policies and insurance contracts were aligned, with a fifth indicating that little insurance was held for IT. Six of the nine organizations did not have EDI processes, reflecting greater use of replacement technologies in more recent years. These findings are reflected in the figures for the lowest means in Table 8. Both the lowest organizational mean and the lowest mean for a measure were at Level 1 (initial).

In the following section the results are compared against those for previous studies.

Comparison with Previous Studies

The methodologies employed by previous studies (Guldentops et al. (2002); Liu and Ridley, 2005) and in the EUROSAI Self Assessment Project required organizations to assess their own maturity against the COBIT maturity models. It may be anticipated that an independent evaluation would be more objective than a self-assessment and result in lower maturity levels being assigned. Of the seven most highly ranked IT processes considered in this research, five were included in both

the previous studies and the EUROSAI project, suggesting the broadly accepted importance of these processes.

Mean maturity levels were not available for the EUROSAI project and so no comparison can be made with the results of that investigation. The mean maturity levels of the IT processes from each of the other previous studies are displayed in Table 9, along with a comparison against those for the current research. Means only are given for the international study, as standard deviations were not available. Only the public sector results are presented for the international study.

It was expected that the mean assigned maturity level would correspond to the order of importance of the IT process to the organization, as seen in the Australian and international results. However Table 9 indicates that this is not the case for the results from the current study, set in Tasmania. When considering the mean assigned maturity levels, the Tasmanian public sector organizations audited were found to perform best in *DS4 Ensure Continuous Service* rather than in *DS5 Ensure Systems Security*. However, as the organizations that were required to have a security plan and policy in place were outnumbered by those not subject to such a requirement, this characteristic may have acted to reduce the mean assigned maturity level found for *Ensure Systems Security*.

Table 9. Maturity level means for common IT processes

IT process	Mean and Standard Deviation for Maturity Level				
	Tasmania		Australia (Liu & Ridley 2005)		International (Guldentops et al. 2002)
	Mean	Std Dev	Mean	Std Dev	Mean
DS5	3.21	1.25	3.40	0.96	2.66
DS4	3.54	0.74	3.24	1.06	2.32
PO1	2.76	0.59	2.91	1.26	2.17
DS11	2.33	1.34	3.06	1.02	2.48
AI6	2.33	1.33	3.18	1.05	2.40

The standard deviations of IT processes in this research were lower than those from Liu and Ridley (2005) for *DS4 Ensure Continuous Service*, and *PO1 Define a Strategic Information Technology Plan*, while they were higher than those noted by Liu and Ridley (2005) for *DS5 Ensure Systems Security, DS11 Manage Data* and *AI6 Manage Changes*. When comparing the two studies it is important to remember that the current study is based on results from only nine organizations, whereas Liu and Ridley (2005) obtained 102 responses and gathered data from all states in Australia. Furthermore, some data for the latter study were gathered from much larger organizations than those in the current study.

Evaluation of Audit Instrument

An evaluation of the audit instrument using the five criteria stated earlier appears below.

1. **Interview duration:** The longest audit interview conducted was approximately 100 minutes, which met the evaluation criterion set of a maximum of two hours per audit. Consequently, as the audit instrument could be used to complete an audit interview within the specified time frame, this characteristic

was seen as contributing to the validation of the instrument.

2. **Expert validation:** The IT audit instrument developed for this study was evaluated using expert review. Only minor changes to the IT audit instrument were suggested as a result of this review. All the changes were implemented before the audits were undertaken.

3. **Linkage of IT and business goals:** Use of the audit instrument resulted in a link being established between the IT processes audited and the business goals of the organizations, during the IT audit. This was evidenced by the requirement to produce organizational policy documents as well as through anecdotal evidence from the managers being interviewed. As much of the value of using CobiT for IT audit is derived from the alignment between the IT processes and the organizational goals, this result was interpreted as a further validation of the audit instrument.

4. **Relevance of the instrument:** The instrument contained the seven IT processes that were most highly ranked by Tasmanian state public sector organizations, as reported by Gerke and Ridley (2006). As a result, the

IT audit investigated IT processes that were relevant and important to Tasmanian state public sector organizations. Tailoring the instrument, and therefore the IT audits, to the most important IT processes enabled the size of the audit instrument to be reduced. This characteristic facilitated use of CobiT for IT audit in a way that was also consistent with the resources of the TAO. Therefore, the relevance of the IT audit instrument so developed was also considered to validate the instrument.

5. **Triangulation of sources:** The instrument included measures obtained from the TAO and the ANAO, as well as from the CobiT Audit Guidelines. The identification of some audit measures in multiple sources demonstrated the appropriateness of those measures, and provided further validation of the IT audit instrument.

Limitations

The maturity models used in the previous related studies (Guldentops et al., 2002; Liu & Ridley, 2005) were different to those used in this study. This study used a generic maturity model to assign maturity ratings to each of the audit measures. Although the generic model was the foundation of the maturity model specific to each IT process used by the other studies, it provided less guidance and so required more interpretation by the researcher when assigning the maturity levels. However, the researcher who undertook the audits for the Tasmanian study was likely to be more familiar with CobiT than the organizational respondents in the other two studies, and so required less guidance.

The assessment of maturity in the studies by Guldentops et al. (2002) and Liu and Ridley (2005) was by individuals employed within the organizations being assessed. In the Tasmanian research the researcher assessed maturity using evidences obtained through audit. It is expected that evidential assessment made by a trained independent third party may be more objective, potentially lowering the assigned maturities.

Due to the pace of organizational change the year in which the studies were undertaken may have also influenced the results. Everything else being equal, it would be expected that more recent studies would reveal more mature IT processes.

The use of a researcher rather than a practitioner to conduct the audits may have led to less exploratory questioning when assessing the way in which the audit measures were met within each organization. It is possible that this may have reduced the assigned maturity levels and the time taken to conduct the IT audits. However, the TAO has successfully used an amended form of the instrument for their IT audit program since the conclusion of the study.

The next section provides a conclusion to the study by reviewing the aims of the research and relating these to its outcomes.

CONCLUSION

This research set out to develop and trial an abbreviated IT audit instrument based on the CobiT framework within selected state public sector organizations in Tasmania. Additionally it sought to evaluate the derived instrument and to compare the audit results with those obtained in other studies.

The IT audit instrument derived contained five IT processes from CobiT that were also identified as being important by previous studies (Guldentops et al., 2002; Liu and Ridley, 2005). These were: *DS5 Ensure Systems Security, DS4 Ensure Continuous Support, PO1 Define a Strategic Information Technology Plan, DS11 Manage Data,* and *AI6 Manage Changes.* The remaining two IT processes, *DS12 Manage Facilities* and *PO8 Ensure Compliance with External Requirements* were not included in the studies by Guldentops et al. (2002) and Liu and Ridley (2005), and so reflect the particular needs of the Tasmanian State Government organizations that participated in the study by Gerke and Ridley (2006).

The IT audit instrument developed was evaluated as appropriate by a number of methods including expert validation, triangulation, interview duration and perceived relevance of the audit program. The quality of the instrument developed is further evidenced by the authority given by the Tasmanian Audit Office to the researcher to undertake the IT audits, and use of the outcomes of this research to inform future IT audits in the Tasmanian State public sector.

The trial audits showed that the instrument contained few audit measures that were not relevant to the Tasmanian public sector, which suggests that its development was appropriate. The audit results indicate that there was a wide variation in the approaches to IT governance within the organizations audited, which appears to be linked to the organizational size and type.

The research results suggest that the instrument derived from CobiT for this study was both effective for IT audit, and tailored to the needs of Tasmanian state public sector organizations, when evaluated against a number of criteria. Therefore this academic study adds credibility to practitioner reports that it is possible to implement CobiT to produce an effective IT audit instrument that reflects the needs of individual organizations. Further academic research is needed to assess the effectiveness of other elements of CobiT.

ACKNOWLEDGMENT

Includes excerpts from CobiT: Control Objectives for Information and Related Technology (3rd Edition). ©1996, 1998, 2000 IT Governance Institute (ITGI). All rights reserved. CobiT is a registered trademark of the Information Systems Audit and Control Association and the IT Governance Institute. Used by permission.

The authors would like to thank the Tasmanian Audit Office particularly Christina Buell and Kate Tamayo for their assistance in facilitating this research.

REFERENCES

ANAO (2004). Auditing in an evolving environment (A focus on auditing standards and framework). In *Proceedings of the Institute of Certified Public Accountants and CPA Australia, CPA forum.* Retrieved May 11, 2008, from www.anao.gov.au/uploads/documents/Auditing_in_an_Evolving_Environment.pdf

Anthes, G. H. (2004). Model mania. *Computerworld, 38*(10), 41–45.

Brown, W., & Nasuti, F. (2005). What ERP systems can tell us about Sarbanes-Oxley. *Information Management & Computer Security, 13*(4), 311.

EUROSAI (undated). *EUROSAI institutional information* Webpage. Retrieved May 11, 2008, from http://www.eurosai.org/Ingles/info_inst.htm

EUROSAI IT Working Group (undated). *IT self assessment flyer.* Retrieved May 11, 2008, from http://www.eurosai-it.org/9282000/d/flyer_it.pdf

Gerke, L. B., & Ridley, G. (2006). Towards an abbreviated CobiT framework for use in an Australian state public sector. In S. Spencer & A. Jenkins (Eds.), In *Proceedings of the 17th Australasian Conference on Information Systems,* Adelaide: Australasian Association for Information Systems.

Guldentops, E., van Grembergen, W., & de Haes, S., (2002). Control and governance maturity survey: Establishing a reference benchmark and a self-assessment tool. *Information Systems Control Journal,* 6. Retrieved May 11, 2008, from http://www.isaca.org/Template.cfm?Section=Archives

&CONTENTID=16122&TEMPLATE=/Content-Management/ContentDisplay.cfm

ITGI (2000a). *COBIT 3rd edition management guidelines*. Retrieved May 11, 2008, from http://www.isaca.org/Template.cfm?Section=Obtain_COBIT

ITGI (2000b). *COBIT 3rd edition audit guidelines*. Retrieved May 11, 2008, from http://www.isaca.org/Template.cfm?Section=Obtain_COBIT

ITGI (2000c). *COBIT 3rd edition control objectives*. Retrieved May 11, 2008, from http://www.isaca.org/Template.cfm?Section=Obtain_COBIT

ITGI (2007a). *COBIT 4.1 executive summary*. Retrieved May 11, 2008, from http://www.isaca.org/AMTemplate.cfm?Section=Downloads&Template=/ContentMannagement/ContentDisplay.cfm&ContentID=34172

ITGI (2007b). *COBIT 4.1: Framework control objectives, management guidelines, maturity models*. Retrieved May 11, 2008, from http://isaca.org/Content/NavigationMengu/Members_and_Leaders/COBIT6/Obtain_COBIT/Obtain_COBIT.htm

Johannessen, R. (2004). Risk-based sampling Using COBIT. *intoIT The INTOSAI IT Journal*, 19. Retrieved May 11, 2008, from http://www.nao.org.uk/intosai/edp/intoit_articles/19_09_COBIT.pdf

Liu, Q., & Ridley, G. (2005). IT control in the Australian public sector: An international comparison. In D. Bartmann, F. Rajola, J. Kallinikos, D. Avison, R. Winter, P. Ein-Dor, Becker, Jr, F. Bodendorf, C. Weinhardt (Eds.), In *Proceedings of 13th European Conference on Information Systems*, Regensburg: ECIS Standing Committee.

Ridley, G., Young, J., & Carroll, P. (2004). COBIT and its utilization: A framework from the literature. In R. H. Sprague, Jr. (Ed.), In *Proceedings of the 37th Hawaii International Conference on System Science (HICSS)*, Los Alamitos: IEEE Computer Society.

Spafford, G. (2003). *The benefits of standard IT governance frameworks*. Datamation Internet Website. Retrieved May 11, 2008, from http://itmanagement.earthweb.com/netsys/article.php/2195051

TAO (2004). Tasmanian Audit Office Webpage. *Who we are and what we do*. Retrieved May 12, 2008, from http://www.audit.tas.gov.au/aboutus/whowhat.html

Violino, B. (2005). IT frameworks demystified. *Network World, 22*(7), S18-20.

Violino, B. (2006). Sorting the standards. *Computerworld, 40*(16), 46-47.

Warland, C., & Ridley, G. (2005). Awareness of IT control frameworks in an Australian state government: A qualitative case study. In R. H. Sprague, Jr. (Ed.), In *Proceedings of the 38th Hawaii International Conference on System Science (HICSS)*, Los Alamitos: IEEE Computer Society.

APPENDIX A: AUDIT MEASURES INCLUDED IN THE AUDIT INSTRUMENT

DS5 Ensure Systems Security

1. Has the organization developed a security statement and policy?
   - Confirm the statement and/or policy exists, is endorsed and communicated.
   - Confirm that the policy/plans/procedures are current.
2. Determine whether remote access is used in the organization.
   - Identify policy and procedures over the granting, modifying and removal of remote access.
   - Determine how the organization controls this access.
   - Confirm that remote access is regularly reviewed.
3. Are there formalised procedures in place for the granting, modifying and removal of user access privileges?
   - Are requests for user access documented?
   - What is the approval process for granting access?
   - Is access removed for users that have left the organization?
   - How is IT staff made aware of staff leavers?
   - Is removal of system's access done in a timely manner?
   - What are the procedures for granting and removing emergency/ temporary access?
   - Are periodic reviews of user access conducted?
   - Are periodic reviews conducted of user profiles to ensure appropriate access rights?
4. Confirm that review of users have been undertaken on regular basis, and all exceptions actioned.
5. How are users uniquely identified to the each system components (ie unique user id and password)?
6. Does the agency have a password policy that incorporates the following:
   - Minimum and maximum length.
   - Special restrictions on the setting of passwords (ie at least one numeric character).
   - System forced change.
   - History preventing/limiting reuse.
   - Lockout after number of unsuccessful attempts.
   - System timeouts.
7. Review system configuration and confirm that password policy has been set and this is consistent with security policy and procedures
8. Identify whether multiple layers of passwords are required for sensitive functions application ie SU to root, firecall etc.
9. Are there network access logs?
10. Are these logs regularly reviewed by appropriate staff?
11. An audit trail of access/activity is reviewed daily or weekly.
12. Are there formal policies in regard to:
    - Internet use.
    - E-mail use.
    - File Sharing.

13. How are these disseminated amongst staff, particularly new users?
14. Do staff members have to agree with these policies?

DS4 Ensure Continuous Support

1. Verify the existence of a current and endorsed IT continuity plan.
2. Determine if the key business stakeholders have provided input to the continuity plan
3. Review publication policy, eg management required to approve all Internet content.
4. Evaluate how the agency ensures the backup/archiving has completed correctly (e.g., are tapes readable?)
5. Does the agency periodically check data maintained to ensure integrity and correctness?
6. Review and evaluate standard backup and archiving procedures
7. For each system, what types of backups are performed (consider frequency, cycle and rotation)?
8. Are these backups performed in accordance with the predetermined backup schedule?
9. Are the backups/archives stored in appropriately secure, on-site and off-site, locations?
10. Determine if media at off-site location are matched to appropriate media management system

DS11 Manage Data

1. For a selected sample of source documents consistency is evident with respect to stated procedures relating to authorisation, approval, accuracy, completeness and receipt by data entry, and data entry is timely.
2. Audit trails are provided to facilitate the tracing of transaction processing and the reconciliation of disrupted data.
3. Error handling procedures and actions comply with established policies and controls.
4. Output reports are secured awaiting distribution, as well as those already distributed to users in compliance with established procedures and controls.
5. Disposed sensitive information procedures and actions comply with established policies and controls.
6. Media storage sites are physically secure and inventory current.
7. Adequate protections ensure integrity, confidentiality and nonrepudiation of sensitive messages transmitted over the Internet or any other public network.
8. The risk of misaddressing messages (by letter, fax or e-mail) is mitigated by appropriate procedures.
9. Controls that are normally applied to a specific transaction or process, such as faxing or automatic telephone message answering, also apply to computer systems that support transaction or process (e.g., fax software on a personal computer).
10. Obtain a copy of backup and archiving policy and procedures.
11. Determine what training has been provided to operations staff with regard to backup/archiving and restore procedures.
12. Determine if the backup and restore procedures been documented sufficiently to allow someone other than the primary IT resource to perform the necessary tasks.
13. Is test data protected and controlled:
14. Minimize use of personal information for test purposes

15. If used the data should be depersonalized before use
16. Strict controls in place over access to a programs source library.
17. Data security function:
18. The function is staffed with sufficient personnel of appropriate expertise and experience.
19. User and group profiles should be defined to reflect CIS and user department organization ensuring that appropriate segregation of duties is maintained.
20. Profile attributes and special authorities should reflect users' business functions.
21. Access to online editors which have capabilities to replace/modify file contents, internal storage areas or programs is limited through access control software or security profiles to system administrator or other authorized personnel
22. Audit trail of all changes is kept.
23. Direct editing is approved and fully documented.
24. Audit trails of changes to transaction files and master files are kept.

DS12 Manage Facilities

1. The building is locked down overnight (outside of business hours).
2. Building visitors are monitored by reception and security.
3. Restriction beyond the reception area is restricted via locks (i.e., proxy cards).
4. Access outside of business hours requires appropriate privileges or proxy cards.
5. Video/sensor monitors in place throughout the building.
6. Adequate procedures are in place for providing and terminating staff members' physical access.
7. The server room is physically locked (i.e., proxy cards).
8. Access to the room is restricted to relevant staff (i.e., IT staff only).
9. Adequate procedures are in place for providing and terminating staff members' physical access
10. Video cameras monitor the entry points to the server room.
11. The room is within sight of IT staff.
12. No other access risks (windows, etc.).
13. Is there a signing in procedure for visitors entering the computer facilities?
14. Are reviews conducted of the visitor registration logbook?
15. Is there a long-term plan for the facilities required to support the agency's computing environment?
16. Are periodic reviews of access privileges and profiles conducted?
17. Adequate fire devices in place:
    ◦ Air conditioning unit.
    ◦ Humidity/temperature monitors.
    ◦ Fire/smoke alarms/sensors.
    ◦ Fire extinguishers.
18. Temperature and humidity is controlled and monitored (i.e., air conditioner unit, vesda system).
19. Is the server room adequately located? Consider:
    ◦ Other business operations nearby.
    ◦ Areas prone to natural disaster.
    ◦ The type of business conducted, that may pose risk of terrorism.
    ◦ Nearby water risks (i.e., running water pipes, etc.).

20. Appropriate floors - antistatic.
21. Boxes are all racked and raised.
22. All components of the communication network under the organization's control are physically secured.
23. Appropriate back-up or alternative routing for key elements in communication networks exist.
24. Access to terminals which may have network master terminal status is restricted.
25. All boxes feature uninterruptible power supply (UPS).
26. UPS are regularly tested.
27. Appropriate shutdown and battery time.

PO1 Define a Strategic Information Technology Plan

1. Minutes from IT planning/steering committee meetings reflect the planning process.
2. Relevant IT initiatives are included in the IT long- and short-range plans (i.e., hardware changes, capacity planning, information architecture, new system development or procurement, disaster recovery planning, installation of new processing platforms, etc.).
3. IT initiatives support the long- and short-range plans and consider requirements for research, training, staffing, facilities, hardware and software.
4. Consideration has been given to optimising current and future IT investments.
5. IT long- and short-range plans are consistent with the organization's long- and short-range plans and organizational requirements.
6. Plans have been changed to reflect changing conditions.
7. IT long-range plans are periodically translated into short-range plans.
8. Tasks exist to implement the plans.

PO8 Ensure Compliance with External Requirements

1. External requirements reviews are:
   ○ Current, complete and comprehensive with respect to legal, government, and regulatory issues.
   ○ Result in prompt corrective action.
2. Reviews of safety and health are undertaken within the IT function to ensure compliance with external requirements.
   ○ Problem areas which do not comply with the safety and health standards are rectified.
3. IT compliance with the documented privacy and security policies and procedures.
4. Existing contracts with electronic commerce trading partners adequately address the requirements specified in organizational policies and procedures.
5. Existing insurance contracts adequately address the requirements specified in organizational policies and procedures.
6. Actual electronic data interchange (EDI) processes being deployed by the organization ensure compliance with organizational policies and procedures, and compliance with the individual electronic commerce trading partner contracts (and the EDI vendor contract if applicable).

AI6 Manage Changes

1. For a sample of changes, the following have been approved by management:
   - Request for change.
   - Specification of change.
   - Access to source programme.
   - Programmer completion of change.
   - Request to move source into test environment.
   - Completion of acceptance testing.
   - Request for compilation and move into production.
   - Overall and specific security impact has been determined and accepted.
   - Distribution process has been developed.
2. Review of change control documentation for inclusion of:
   - Date of requested change.
   - Person(s) requesting.
   - Approved for change request.
   - Approval of change made — IT function.
   - Approval of change made — users.
   - Documentation update date.
   - Move date into production.
   - Quality assurance sign-off of change.
   - Acceptance by operations.
3. Analyze types of changes made to system for identification of trends.
4. Evaluate adequacy of IT libraries and determine the existence of base line code levels to prevent error regression.
5. Code check-in and check-out procedures for changes exist.
6. Change control log ensures all changes on log were resolved to user satisfaction and that there

Chapter VI
Comprehensive Architecture Rationalization and Engineering

Tony C. Shan
Bank of America, USA

Winnie W. Hua
CTS. Inc, USA

ABSTRACT

This chapter defines a methodical approach, named Comprehensive Architecture Rationalization and Engineering (CARE), to effectively manage the complexity in architecture design and rationalize the architectural assets of IT application portfolios in a service-oriented paradigm. This comprehensive model comprises a prescriptive method to perform a systematic assessment of information systems applications in an application/project portfolio. The process is broken down to 5 interrelated steps: Data Collection, Reverse Engineering, Technology Assessment, Technical Recommendations, and Action Plan for Rationalization. The details and key artifacts are specified for each step in the overarching process. The outcome of the comprehensive analysis consists of a range of technical recommendations and a course of action, which are characterized along three dimensions: refactoring, reengineering, and rearchitecting. The holistic framework provides a multidisciplinary approach of portfolio analysis and service-oriented architecture planning. Practice guidelines and future trends are also articulated in the context. A case study in the finance industry is presented, to illustrate the use of this framework in real-world scenarios.

INTRODCUTION

In today's on-demand business world, the electronic business models demand increasingly higher performance of information technology (IT) systems. We must provide a higher level of services at a lower cost, for the business to compete and succeed. This means that IT has to build more complex, flexible, scalable, extensible, and forward-thinking technical solutions, to meet the ever-growing business needs.

Many large organizations like worldwide financial institutions typically have very large portfolios consisting of a vast number of IT applications and systems built, acquired, or purchased in the past years to provide electronic services for external customers and internal employees, leveraging mixed technologies and platforms to meet diverse functional and nonfunctional requirements from distinct lines of business. In the finance industry, the business operations generally encompass different business divisions in consumer, commercial, small business, wealth management, capital markets, brokerage, and investment. Products and services are delivered via different channels such as Automated Teller Machines (ATMs), Web browsers, interactive voice response, live agents, emails, pervasive devices, and so forth. For the sake of effective management of architecture assets and rationalization of architecture designs in such a heterogeneous environment, an discipline-driven engineering approach is of critical importance to abstract concerns, divide duties, mitigate risks, simplify the complexity, reverse-engineer established systems, discover revamping opportunities, overhaul old systems, and measure technology maturity, which leads to well-contemplated program recommendations and action plans for rationalization.

BACKGROUND

Prior work on the IT architecture has strived to address the complexity issue in architecture design, which has grown exponentially as the computing paradigm has evolved from a monolithic structure to a service-oriented architecture. John Zachman (1987) pioneered a framework consisting of a logical structure for classifying and organizing the descriptive representations of an enterprise IT environment's artifacts that are significant to the management of the organization as well as to the development of the enterprise's information systems. Zachman Framework takes the form of a two-dimensional matrix, and has achieved a level of penetration in the business and information systems architecture domains. Its primary usage is for planning and problem solving, but it tends to implicitly gear towards the data-driven and process-decomposition approach. It operates above and across the level of individual projects. Likewise, Extended Enterprise Architecture Framework (E2AF) (IEAD, 2004) uses a similar a 2-D matrix structure. Its scope contains business, information, system, and infrastructure. E2AF is more technology-oriented than Zachman Framework.

To overcome the deficiencies in the preceding two methods, Rational Unified Process (RUP) (Kruchten, 2003) attempted a use-case driven, object-oriented and component-based approach by means of Unified Modeling Language (UML). In the concept of 4+1 views, the overall system structure is interpreted from multiple perspectives. RUP tends to be more process-oriented, originated in a waterfall-like approach. It pays little attention to either system operations or software maintenance, and lacks a broad coverage on runtime topology and testing capabilities. Its main focus is on the individual project level. RUP has recently been expanded to Enterprise Unified Process (EUP) (Nalbone, Vizdos &

Ambler, 2005), and part of it has been ported to the public domain in the initiative of OpenUP (OpenUP, 2007).

The Open Group Architectural Framework (TOGAF) (Open Group, 2007) is another heavyweight approach, with a set of supporting tools for developing enterprise architecture to meet the business and information technology needs in an organization. TOGAF has three core parts: Architecture Development Method (ADM), Enterprise Architecture Continuum, and TOGAF Resource Base. The scope of TOGAF covers Business Process Architecture, Applications Architecture, Data Architecture, and Technology Architecture. TOGAF is characterized by the concerns of enterprise architecture instead of individual application architecture.

All of the abovementioned approaches are heavyweight methodologies, so that the initial on-boarding activities can be time-consuming. On the other hand, Model-Driven Architecture (MDA) (OMG, 2007) takes an agile approach. The business/application logic is decoupled from the underlying platform technology in MDA. MDA constitutes the Platform-Independent Model (PIM) and Platform-Specific Model (PSM), resulting in greater portability and interoperability as well as increased productivity and eased maintenance thanks to the model independency. MDA is primarily employed for the system-modeling phase in the development lifecycle.

The Information Technology Infrastructure Library (ITIL) (ITIL, 2007) specifies the organizational structure and skillset requirements in an IT environment and a set of standard operational management procedures and practices for managing IT operations and associated infrastructure. The operational procedures and practices are vendor-agnostic and apply to prominent aspects within the IT Infrastructure. Version 3 comprises Service Strategy, Service Design, Service Transition, Service Operation, and Continual Service Improvement.

IEEE Standard 1003.0 (IEEE, 1995), also known as ISO/IEC 14252, is an architectural framework built on POSIX open systems standards. ANSI/IEEE 1471-2000 (IEEE, 2000) is recommended practice for architecture description of software-intensive systems. It provides definitions for the architecture description, asserts the multi-view nature of architecture descriptions, separates the notion of view from viewpoint, and captures rationale and inconsistencies. IEEE 1471 has been recently accepted by ISO JTC1 as ISO/IEC 42010:2007. The ISO Reference Model for Open Distributed Processing (RM-ODP) (Putman, 2001) is a coordinating framework for the standardization of distributed processing in heterogeneous environments. It creates a structure that integrates the support of distribution, interworking and portability, through five "viewpoints" and eight "transparencies". Scenario-based Architecture Analysis Method (SAAM) (SEI, 2007) was designed to analyze the changeability of information systems but is useful to test nonfunctional aspects. Architectures are examined by SAAM via scenarios in terms of quality attributes. The Solution Architecture of N-Tier Applications (Shan, 2006) presents a multilayer and multipillar model for web applications.

Other related studies on IT architecture frameworks are for the most part targeted towards particular domains. They can become useful references if a team plans to create their own model for their organization. The C4ISR Architecture Framework (DoD, 1997) provides comprehensive architectural guidance for the various Commands, Services, and Agencies within the U.S. Department of Defense, so that interoperability and cost-effectiveness are ensured in the military systems. The Treasury Enterprise Architecture Framework (TEAF) (Treasury Department, 2000) guides the planning and development of enterprise architecture in all bureaus and offices of the Treasury Department. The Federal Enterprise Architecture (FEA) framework (Federal Office of Management and Budget, 2007) defines direction and guidance to U.S. federal agencies for structuring enterprise architecture. The Purdue Enterprise Reference Architecture (PERA) (Purdue University, 2007) is tailored to the computer integrated manufacturing.

A plethora of today's real-world practices of information systems development are still manual, error-prone, and not well planned, which inevitably yields chaotic outcomes and failures in the execution. A Forrester report (Murphy, 2004) revealed that 73% of the IT spendings are allocated for existing applications. According to a recent survey (Standish Group, 2007), a vast majority of information systems projects are behind schedule, over budget, or canceled prior to completion. A lack of a systematic framework to objectively assess and rationalize the design artifacts is one of the major causes of this mishap.

A new model is proposed in the next section, with more detailed descriptions of the key characteristics and features of the constituents in the section that follows. Afterwards a case study of applying the new framework in a real-life scenario is presented, followed by the best practice recommendations and future trends. The conclusions are discussed in the last section.

COMPREHENSIVE MODEL

As discussed in the foregoing section, most of the previous methods reveal the architectural aspects of a software-intensive application to some extent from a single viewpoint or limited perspectives. A comprehensive approach to evaluating the end-to-end IT solution architectures is evidently necessary to establish a systematic disciplined process. A highly structured mechanism is thus designed in this article to satisfy this ever-growing need, and present a holistic assessment process for prominent architectural elements, components, knowledge, platforms, planning, and their dependencies. Governance procedures may be set up

accordingly in this approach as an overarching process to facilitate the creation, organization, management, and sunset of the architecture assets and solution platforms at different levels in a large organization.

Design Tenets

The development of the disciplined mechanism followed a set of key design principles, part of which were adapted from (Open Group, 2007) but significantly modified/expanded to be tailored to the services-oriented architecting process.

Business Principles

- **Primacy of principles:** These principles of solution architecting apply to all organizations within the enterprise.
- **Maximize benefit to the enterprise:** Architecting management decisions are made to provide maximum benefit to the Enterprise as a whole.
- **Architecting management is everybody's Business:** All organizations in the enterprise participate in architecting management decisions needed to accomplish business objectives.
- **Business continuity:** Enterprise operations are maintained in spite of system interruptions.
- **Common use applications:** Development of applications used across the enterprise is preferred over the development of similar or duplicative applications which are only provided to a particular organization.
- **Compliance with law:** Enterprise architecting management processes comply with all relevant laws, policies, and regulations.
- **IT Responsibility:** The IT organization is responsible for owning and implementing IT processes and infrastructure that enable solutions to meet user defined requirements for functionality, service levels, cost, and delivery timing.

- **Protection of intellectual property:** The enterprise's IP must be protected. This protection must be reflected in the IT Architecture, Implementation, and Governance processes.

Technical Principles

- **Control technical diversity:** Technological diversity is controlled to minimize the nontrivial cost of maintaining expertise in and connectivity between multiple processing environments.
- **Interoperability:** Software and hardware should conform to defined standards that promote interoperability for data, applications, services and technology.

Application Principles

- **Technology independence:** Applications are independent of specific technology choices and therefore can operate on a variety of technology platforms.
- **Ease of use:** Applications are easy to use. The underlying technology is transparent to users, so they can concentrate on tasks at hand.

Data Principles

- **Data asset:** Data is an asset that has value to the enterprise and is managed accordingly.
- **Data sharing:** Users have access to the data necessary to perform their duties; therefore, data is shared across enterprise functions and organizations.
- **Data accessibility:** Data is accessible for users to perform their functions.
- *Data Trustee*: Each data element has a trustee accountable for data quality.
- **Common vocabulary and data definitions:** Data is defined consistently throughout the enterprise, and the definitions are understandable and available to all users.
- **Data security:** Data is protected from unauthorized use and disclosure. In addition to the traditional aspects of national security classification, this includes, but is not limited to, protection of pre-decisional, sensitive, source selection sensitive, and proprietary information.

Change Management Principles

- **Requirements-based change:** Only in response to business needs are changes to applications and technology made.
- **Responsive change management:** Changes to the enterprise architecture/infrastructure environment are implemented in a timely manner.

Conceptual Model

The Comprehensive Architecture Rationalization and Engineering (CARE) framework is designed as a disciplined solution. It defines a comprehensive analysis method to objectively evaluate various aspects in information systems applications within a portfolio. The *CARE* model is a holistic framework to help analyze and optimize the strategies, thought processes, methods, tradeoffs, and patterns in the information systems design. The focus of *CARE* is on the cross-application technical assessment within a specific business domain.

As shown in Figure 1, the analysis process consists of 5 interrelated steps:

- Step 1 – Data collection of current state
- Step 2 – Reverse-engineering to recreate high-level models
- Step 3 – Technology assessment
- Step 4 – Technical recommendations
- Step 5 – Action plan for rationalization

Figure 1. Comprehensive architecture rationalization & engineering framework

CARE FRAMEWORK

Technology Grid for Data Collection

To start with, we need to fully comprehend the current state of an IT portfolio. A cross-application technology grid is therefore designed to capture the existing system data. The key aspects defined in the grid are scoped out in the categories of project, architecture, technology, integration, system management, quality of services and nonfunctional requirements. As illustrated in Table 1, the grid serves as a template to document the factual information consistently for each application and system in a portfolio. These aspects are further drilled down to define more granular details as

individual attributes that characterize the respective aspect categories. The definitions of these detailed attributes are provided in the table.

Reverse-Engineering

Due to historical reasons, a great many of existing applications are lack of sufficient documentation about the design and architecture model. In order to conduct apple-to-apple comparisons among applications in a portfolio, a consistent format is required to represent the architecture designs in a semi-standard fashion. The practice of reverse engineering is leveraged to recreate a series of architecture models that are absent in existing applications: conceptual, logical, physical, and

Table 1. Technology grid

Scope	Attribute	Description	App1	App2
Project	Business context	Business strategy, architecture, requirements and background, operations		
	Timeline	Project plan and status, roadmap		
	Resources	Point of contacts, roles and responsibilities		
Architecture	Conceptual	A set of design principles, function blocks		
	Logical	A blueprint of architectural layers, modules, components, and their interactions/relationships		
	Physical	Physical representation of logical architecture with platform selection, product mapping		
	Deployment	The topologic layout and infrastructure intended to support the deployment of applications		
	Data (Storage)	The structure of an organization's logical and physical data assets and the associated data management resources		
	Capacity	The amount work that a system is capable of completing in a given period of time		

continued on following page

Table 1. continued

Technology	Framework	Semi-complete support structure in which a solution can be organized and developed		
	Component	A system element offering a predefined service and able to communicate with other components		
	Utilities	Toolkits and packages for system development		
	Business rules	Rules for business logic processing		
	Workflow/ Process	Process orchestration and workflow collaborations		
	UI design	User interface specification and development		
	Navigation	Flow and system site map		
Integration	Integration points	System edges and boundary from an external viewpoint		
	Interfaces	Interaction contract		
	Protocol	Access methods		
	Communication mechanisms	Synchronous, asynchronous, batch, file transfer, email, etc		
	Dependency	Matrix for upstream and downstream impacts		
System Management	Configurations	System configurations		
	Monitoring	Operations health, system status		
	Reporting	User reports, system reports, notification		
	Backup	Data, system, environment backup		
	Technology recovery	Disaster recovery, failover, business continuity		
Quality of Services	Availability	The percentage of time when system is operational		
	Scalability	The ability to handle growing amount of work		
	Usability	The extent to which a product can be used by specified users to achieve specified goals		
	Inter-operability	The capability to communicate, execute programs, or transfer data among various functional units		
	Portability	The ability of a program to be ported from one platform to another		
	Reusability	The likelihood a segment of code or service can be used again to add new functionalities with slight or no modification		
	Maintainability	The ease with which a system or component can be modified to correct faults, improve performance, or other attributes, or adapt to a changed environment.		
Non-functional Requirements	SLA	Service-level agreement		
	Security	Authentication, authorization, audit		
	Regulation	Regulatory requirements and compliance		
	Standards	Industry and enterprise standards conformance		
	Policies	Governance policies and certification		

deployment architectures, as well as other component architecture artifacts. Furthermore, additional architecture models may be reconstructed to capture the design decisions and constraints in large-scale complex systems, such as the use case model and system context model. Through this exercise, the tradeoff justifications and compromises made during the original analysis and designs, if not previously documented, are also uncovered.

Technology Assessment

Based on the data collected in the technology grid and the architecture models established in the reverse engineering efforts, a thorough assessment is conducted to fully analyze the applications in a systematic manner. Techniques like Strength-Weakness-Opportunities-Threats (SWOT) may be utilized to facilitate evaluations. A checklist is built as a set of criteria metrics to assess architectural artifacts in a domain, as shown in Table 2.

Table 2. Technology assessment checklist

Area	Description
Business process	Analyze the process capabilities, efficiency, quality, and implementation in business process management and modeling
System	Assess the enterprise systems
Application	Evaluate the solution at the application level
Data	Examine the data, information, knowledge processing
Architecture	Investigate the architecture designs and models
Technology	Justify the technical options and decisions
Security	Identify security requirements and solution designs
Infrastructure	Appraise the fitness of the solutions in the infrastructure environment
Quality of services	Trace the QoS attributes and design implementations
Operations	Review the run-time execution of the solutions (Dev, Test, Prod)
Testing	Assess the testing coverage and requirement traceability
Integration	Examine the integration points and mechanisms
System management	Analyze the enterprise-wide administration of distributed computer systems
Build and deployment	Evaluate the software module packaging and installation
Configuration management	Inspect the version control and component repository management tools
Gap analysis	Conduct gap analysis to identify potential change areas
Tool selection	Determine the selection rationales for tools
Methodology selection	Justify the suitability and robustness of methodologies chosen
Process customization	Analyze the end-to-end IT development lifecycle
Defect tracking	Evaluate the bug handling procedure
Change control	Assess the governance process for change control management
Code quality metrics	Review the code quality control and metrics used

Technical Recommendations

An array of technical recommendations is generated as a result of the comprehensive technology assessment. To effectively manage the enhancement advice and justify necessary tradeoffs, the recommendations are categorized into three groups: refactoring, reengineering, and rearchitecting.

Refactoring

Refactoring is useful to improve an existing application without drastic structural changes. It also helps reverse-engineer an application to restore the technical model, if it was not created in the forward engineering process, which is not uncommon in old systems that lacked disciplines in development. Some common refactoring practices are:

- Reorganize internal structure
- Restructure source code
- Rename variables, methods, classes and interfaces
- Rearrange the class hierarchy
- Move code into a separate method
- Consolidate methods
- Decompose methods and classes
- Improve program design and structure
- Enhance maintainability
- Eliminate bad practices code
- Compose methods
- Move features between objects
- Reorganize data
- Simplify conditional expressions
- Make method calls simpler
- Deal with generalization
- Maximize reuse
- Use refactoring tools
- Enforce naming conventions
- Establish coding style
- Create and utilize reusable components
- Promote loose coupling

- Apply encapsulation, inheritance, and polymorphism
- Rationalize class hierarchy
- Refine service granularity (coarse, medium, fine)
- Adjust service interface (chunky vs. chatty)
- Leverage inversion of control
- Employ annotations

Reengineering

Reengineering is a viable solution to migrate an application to next-generation technologies with no major architectural restructuring. Reengineering is basically the examination and alteration of a system to reconstitute it in a new form. It is sometimes the most cost-effective way to remake legacy systems without having to throw away the investment spent in the past years. The following are recommended reengineering exercises:

- Revamp existing systems
- Exploit the most appropriate technologies
- Reengineer business process
- Alter software
- Reexamine data processing
- Modify application design
- Adjust methodology
- Plan transition
- Remodel system
- Define migration strategies
- Modernize access and integration
- Formulate transformation techniques
- Utilize wrapper technology
- Leverage service enabling techniques
- Consolidate systems
- Decompose applications and services
- Reverse-engineer key technical functions
- Ensure compatibility and interoperability
- Encapsulate legacy systems
- Rationalize integration mechanisms
- Revise security considerations

Rearchitecting

Rearchitecting is necessary if an application almost reaches the end of its lifecycle in terms of its technical model and architecture maturity. Rearchitecting involves a complete overhaul to redesign a system. Replatforming is usually a major renovation, which falls in between Reengineering and Rearchitecting. Key design considerations in rearchitecting include:

- Conduct business process analysis
- Devise conceptual model (service partitioning)
- Identify core services and aggregated services
- Design process workflow and access mechanism
- Develop process orchestration and business integration
- Specify logical architecture
- Define data architecture
- Plan physical architecture
- Formulate system topology
- Handle communications and integration
- Create service interface and definition
- Leverage application framework (MVC model)
- Reconsider component design
- Use design patterns
- Automate unit testing
- Manage build and deployment
- Align system management to SLA
- Exploit UI rendering techniques
- Unify data persistence mechanism
- Consider aspect-based specialized technology: data caching, session management, performance tuning, and entitlement.

Action Plan for Rationalization

With the technical recommendations generated, the action items are further rationalized and prioritized to create an action plan for execution.

An action plan is a time-ordered activity schedule with deliverables to apply the change recommendations. In this rationalization roadmap, milestones are defined, typically by quarter, and detailed working items are specified to progressively transit the systems in a portfolio to another maturity level. Furthermore, the resources are allocated in a Gantt chart and necessary trainings are planned to retool the skillsets. Governance and project management are also placed to steer the overall rationalization implementation. Risk impacts are investigated and the funding model is established.

Applying the Framework in Application Portfolio Management

To illustrate the use of this framework in real-world scenarios, we will present a case study in the financial industry. The Check Clearing for the 21st Century Act (or Check 21 Act) is a United States federal law (public Law 108-100) enacted into law October 28, 2003. The law allows the recipient of a paper check to create a digital version, thereby eliminating the need for further handling of the physical document. Despite the lack of a grand industry road map, there still has been some notable progress around check electronification since Check 21 was adopted. Nowhere is this progress more evident than in the area of remote capture, in which clients digitize checks on their end and send them to their banks electronically to clear. Remote capture offers some definite revenue opportunities, and obvious cost savings. A large financial institution in the US has built several lines of check remote capture systems for various channels to further digitize the check-clearing process. However, due to a lack of standards in the industry, these systems were developed in silos at different times through the past few years.

The CARE framework was called upon to help evaluate and rationalize this remote capture portfolio. The objectives of using the CARE model are to understand application interdependencies, discover duplications and crossovers in current applications, identify best options for application migrations or consolidations, and enable better technology decisions.

Current-State Data Collection

The technology grid was used to collect the data of the current portfolio state. We interviewed each individual project team and key stakeholders to gather very detailed information and clarify the critical design artifacts for different projects. Moreover, several brainstorming sessions were organized to holistically walk through the business process, check processing, storing and retrieving in an end-to-end fashion. Key data elements were captured and validated in this exercise.

Reverse-Engineering

High-level models were recreated in the reverse engineering efforts. Figure 2 is a conceptual model of the portfolio. We utilized the layering technique to document the functional blocks in the capture processing. There are five layers in the model – Client Layer, Transition Zone Layer, Landing Zone Layer, Distributed Image Processing Layer, and Mainframe Image Processing Layer. Additionally, the Work Control & Management module coordinates various tasks and deals with administration.

In the Client Layer, several types of clients are supported in this portfolio: exchange with Federal Reserve Bank, interbank exchange via SVP CO appliance, Fiserv server, Thick/Thin/Smart clients, and Brach Image Capture system.

Figure 2. Portfolio conceptual model

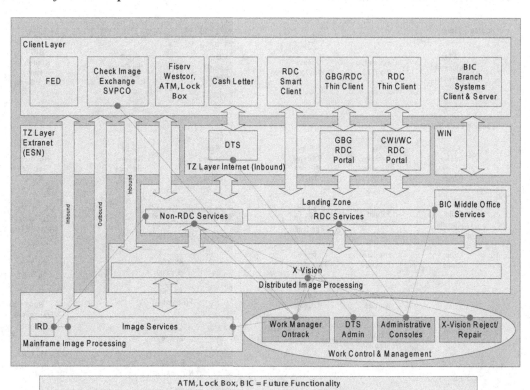

Figure 3. Transition zone layer details

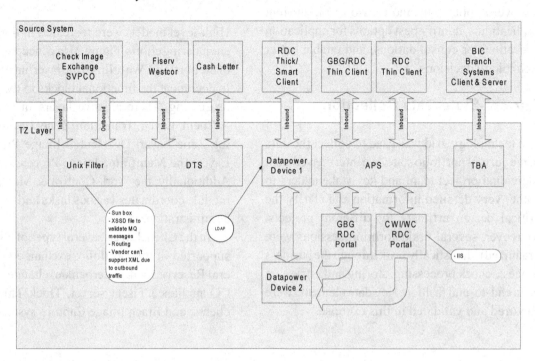

Figure 4. Landing zone layer details

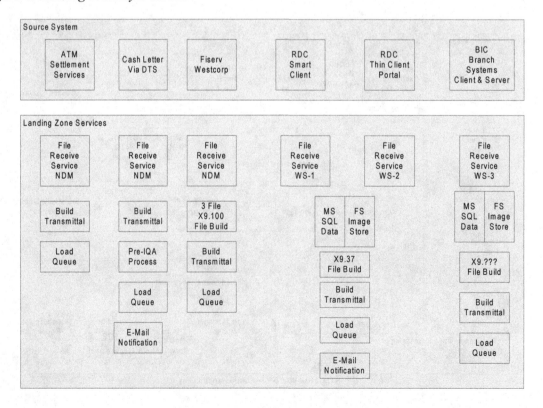

Figure 5. Image processing layer details

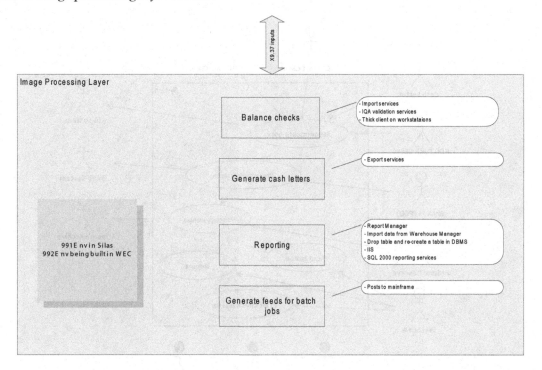

To analyze the artifacts in great detail, each layer is further drilled down to identify the processing modules and functional blocks. The details of the Transition Zone, Landing Zone, and Image Processing Zone layers are illustrated in Figure 3, 4, and 5, respectively.

Technology Assessment

Further in-depth investigation and evaluation were performed to objectively assess the design soundness and identify possible duplicated functions in the portfolio. The in-depth analysis reveals some interesting findings in the Landing Zone Layer. Consequently, UML is leveraged to document the functional requirements and processing flow. Figure 6 is the use case diagram created. A number of actors are identified and several use cases are specified. The actor figures on the left side represent the existing interfacing applications in the production environment. The actors on the top symbolize the new channels under development,

while the actors at the bottom stand for the future systems that are to be developed. Moreover, the pre-processing data logic is displayed in an activity diagram, depicted in Figure 7. Comparing Figure 7 against Figure 4, it turns out that the similar preprocessing logic was implemented individually in five different systems in the portfolio – a significant amount of overlapping and redundancy in silo channels.

A topology diagram, shown in Figure 8, is generated as well, which reveals that functional redundancy exists at the server level in the portfolio. The physical machines are dedicated to particular channels without resource sharing. The middleware for inter-server communications seems neither well planned nor optimized.

Technology Recommendations

Based on the assessment results, the following recommendations were made to improve the current portfolio.

Figure 6. Use case diagram

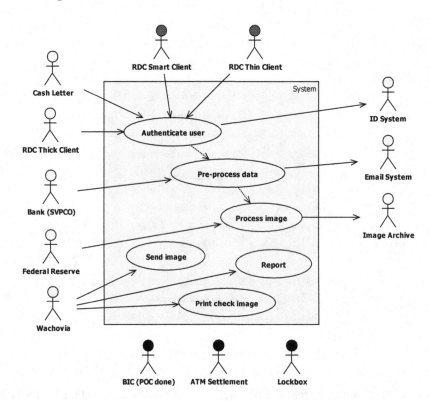

Figure 7. Pre-processing activity diagram

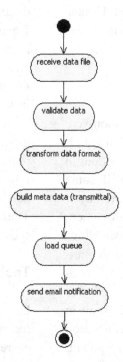

Figure 8. Topology diagram

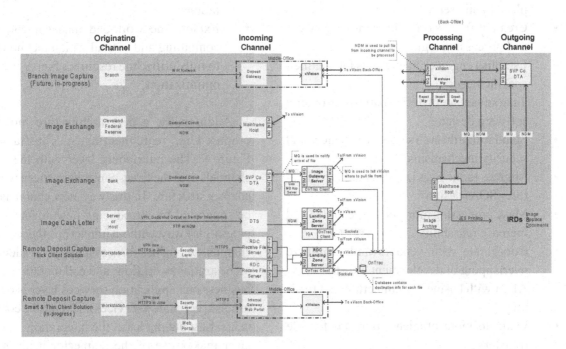

Refactoring

- Consolidate similar implementation codes/ logics into components
- Use a more efficient method for cross-site data replication, e.g. SRDF of AFS Report Manager data in the Image Processing Layer
- Enhance traffic load-balancing for the onTrac system
- Reuse the XML gateway appliance
- Clustering of MS SQL Servers in the Landing Zone Layer
- Plan for the additional data center for 991 and 992 environments
- Evaluate the roadmap of SVP CO for the support of XML web services at the TZ Layer

Reengineering

- Consolidate Web Services in Landing Zone Layer

- Build common services in Landing Zone Layer: channel support, format transformation, build transmittal, data validation, email notification, IQA
- Combine/Service-enable AFS and IBM products for IQA
- Define service interfaces in Landing Zone Layer (Design by Contract principle)
- Leverage XML appliance device for authentication and authorization as well as web services security beyond Smart Client
- Consolidate the similar functionality implemented in the Web Portal for Thin Client and the Unix Filter for SVP CO in the TZ Layer

Rearchitecting

- Focus on key technical areas: for example, WMQ upgrade, high availability, reliability, report services
- Identify future services and catalog common sharable services

- Plan for on-demand resource sharing in place of silo servers
- Create a framework with generic services and processing logic
- Establish engineering patterns for channel-specific needs
- Take advantage of design patterns in overall software design
- Standardize the web services interfaces and security mechanisms
- Migrate to the Service-Oriented Architecture (SOA) design
- Make processing more loosely-coupled and increase reusability
- Coordinate with vendors and minimize overlapping of development efforts
- Align with business architecture and roadmap
- Evaluate more efficient approach for file transfers
- Investigate end-to-end performance tuning points

- Consolidate redundant function implementations
- Explore the workload management, grid computing and virtualization technologies to fully utilize the resources for on-demand optimization

Additionally, a new architecture model is proposed for rearchitecting, as illustrated in Figure 9. The interfacing layer with the client channels uses the front-controller pattern with an adapter structure. In this way, new channels can be supported by introducing new adapters in a plug-n-play way, without impact on other existing channels. A business processing layer is added for orchestration, workflow, and collaborations. The business and application services layer is design to construct shared services and reusable components. Last but not least, the integration services layer makes use of the connector mechanism, providing flexibility and interoperability.

Figure 9. New architecture

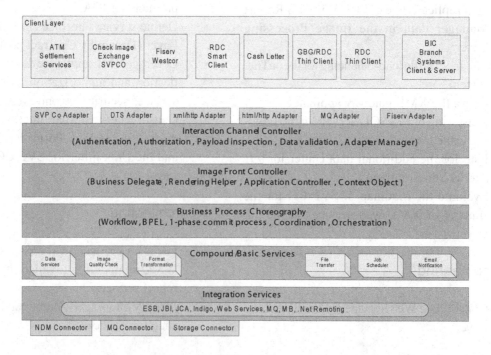

Table 3. Rationalization approach comparison

Approach	Pros	Cons
Unchanged	• No impact on existing schedules or timelines • No additional investment or resources needed	• Hard to maintain the existing silo channels • Increased TCO & complexity for new channels
Refactoring	• Small changes • Low risk • Address immediate needs • Fast to implement	• Minor fixes • Transient workarounds • Don't cover architecture-level challenges/concerns
Reengineering	• Incremental enhancements • Reasonable balance of cost, risk, impacts, and benefits • More stable, reliable env.	• Some fundamental architectural and infrastructural issues remain. • May impact current production operations
Rearchitecting	• Migrate the overall architecture to a SOA paradigm • Take advantage of the latest advanced technologies	• New investments • Extra resources needed to build new systems while maintaining the existing production environments

Action Plan for Rationalization

The strengths and weaknesses of different rationalization approaches are contrasted in Table 3. It provides head-to-head comparisons to assist decision-making as well as future project planning.

Each approach has its own pros and cons. Depending on the short-term tactical needs and long-term strategic goals, these approaches must be further justified and contemplated. The resources and budget availability also have a big influence on the tradeoff analysis. A hybrid approach in combination of multiple approaches may become a viable execution plan in reality. Additional recommendations for the action plan consist of:

- Justify different options to decide which approach to take next
- Consider a hybrid approach
- Allocate dedicated resources for future work
- Mitigate risks associated with changes

- Combine rationalization efforts with new-channel activities
- Align end-state architecture with business architecture roadmap
- Adjust project development process to incorporate cross-domain architecture reviews and best practices
- Plan necessary training for retooling

Figure 10 summarizes the rationalization process, key artifacts, activities, and outcome results.

RECOMMENDATIONS AND FUTURE TRENDS

Despite promising efforts in the past few years, application/project portfolio management is still an evolving and immature space. Some of the key challenges in this area are how to standardize the descriptions of architecture models, how to unify the notations, how to define a common

Figure 10. Rationalization activities in CARE framework

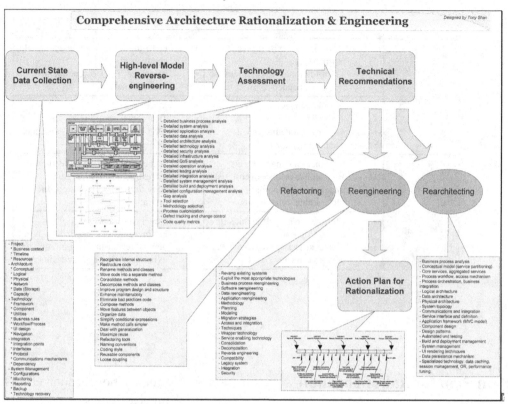

ontology with regard to the architectural attributes, how to objectively assess the robustness of a system architecture model, how to conduct apple-to-apple comparative investigations between heterogeneous architecture models, and how to quantify the maturity of a portfolio. Effective portfolio rationalization methods tend to evolve and mature through continuing research and practitioners' practices in the field. It can be foreseen that multiple disciplines will be incorporated and leveraged in the rationalization efforts, and various techniques will converge to formulate the integrated best practices in the future. The evolution in other related areas such as complex event processing and domain-specific modeling will accelerate the rate of consolidation and convergence. Furthermore, qualitative approaches are expected to be united with quantitative analysis

and formal methods, leveraging both scientific and engineering methodologies and processes.

CONCLUSION

A methodical approach, named Comprehensive Architecture Rationalization and Engineering (CARE), is defined to effectively manage the complexity in architecture design and rationalize the architectural assets of IT application portfolios in a service-oriented paradigm. This comprehensive model comprises a prescriptive method to conduct a systematic assessment of information systems applications in an application/project portfolio. The process is broken down to five interrelated steps: Data Collection, Reverse Engineering, Technology Assessment,

Technical Recommendations, and Action Plan for Rationalization. The details and key artifacts are specified for each step in the overarching process. The outcome of the thorough analysis comprises a range of technical recommendations and action plans, which are characterized along three dimensions: refactoring, reengineering, and rearchitecting. The holistic framework provides a multidisciplinary approach for portfolio rationalization and service-oriented architecture planning. Practice guidelines and future trends are also articulated in the context. This systematic model can be directly used or customized, if not applied in its entirety, to analyze and revamp various types of information systems in different industries. A case study in the financial services industry is presented, to illustrate the use of this framework in real-world scenarios.

REFERENCES

DoD C4ISR Architecture Working Group (1997). *C4ISR architecture framework* (Version 2). Retrieved May 11, 2008, from http://www.fas.org/irp/program/core/fw.pdf

Eclipse (2007). *Eclipse process framework*. Retrieved May 11, 2008, from http://www.eclipse.org/epf

Federal Office of Management and Budget (2007). *Federal enterprise architecture framework*. Retrieved May 11, 2008, from http://www.whitehouse.gov/omb/egov/a-2-EAModelsNEW2.html

IEAD (Institute for Enterprise Architecture Developments) (2004). *Extended enterprise architecture framework*. Retrieved May 11, 2008, from http://www.enterprise-architecture.info

IEEE Standard 1003.0-1995 (1995). *IEEE guide to the POSIX open system environment*. Retrieved May 11, 2008, from http://standards.ieee.org/reading/ieee/std_public/description/posix/1003.0-1995_desc.html

IEEE Standard 1471-2000 (2000). *IEEE recommended practice for architectural description of software-intensive systems*. Retrieved May 11, 2008, from http://standards.ieee.org/reading/ieee/std_public/description/se/1471-2000_desc.html

ITIL (2007). *Information technology infrastructure library*. Retrieved May 11, 2008, from http://www.itil.org.uk

Kruchten, P. (2003). *The rational unified process: An introduction* (3rd ed.). Massachusetts: Addison Wesley.

Murphy, P. (2004). *Forrester report: Application portfolio management tools*. Retrieved May 11, 2008, from http://www.forrester.com/Research/Document/Excerpt/0,7211,34229,00.html

Nalbone, J., Vizdos, M., & Ambler, S. (2005). *The enterprise unified process: Extending the rational unified process*. New Jersey: Prentice Hall PTR.

OMG (Object Management Group) (2007). *Model driven architecture*. Retrieved May 11, 2008, from http://www.omg.org/mda

OpenUP (2007). *OpenUP/Basic development process*. Retrieved May 11, 2008, from http://www.eclipse.org/epf/openup_component/openup_vision.php

Purdue University (1989). *The Purdue enterprise reference architecture*. Retrieved May 11, 2008, from http://pera.net

Putman, J. R. (2001). *Architecting with RM-ODP*. New Jersey: Prentice Hall PTR.

Shan, T .C., & Hua, W. W. (2006). Solution architecture of n-tier applications. In *Proceedings of 3rd IEEE International Conference on Services Computing* (pp. 349-356), California: IEEE Computer Society.

Software Engineering Institute (SEI) at CMU (2007). *Scenario-based architecture analysis method*. Retrieved on May 11, 2008, from http://www.sei.cmu.edu/architecture/scenario_paper

Standish Group (2007). The Standish group chaos report 2006. Retrieved May 11, 2007, from http://www.standishgroup.com

The Open Group (2007). *The open group architecture framework*. Retrieved May 11, 2008, from http://www.opengroup.org/togaf

Treasury Department CIO Council (2000). *Treasury enterprise architecture framework* (Version 1). Retrieved May 11, 2008, from http://www.eaframeworks.com/TEAF/teaf.doc

Zachman, J. A. (1987). A framework for information systems architecture. *IBM Systems Journal, 26*(3), 276-295.

Chapter VII
A Comparative Case Study of Three Korean Firms:
Applying an IT Governance Framework

Junghoon Lee
Yonsei University, Korea

Jungwoo Lee
Yonsei University, Korea

Ja Young Lee
Yonsei University, Korea

ABSTRACT

Research has recently begun to place greater emphasis on the strategic application of IT in seeking to integrate firms' IT infrastructures and business processes, thus boosting companies' business values. In this context, efforts have been made to formulate workable structures for companies' IT governance (ITG); however, little practical research has considered the effect of different forms of ITG in a range of domestic and multinational companies. This study undertakes a comparative case study analysis of the ITG setups of three large service sector firms in Korea. This research work sought to identify the activities, types, and determinants of firms' ITG decision making processes, and to suggest the basis on which forms of ITG may represent rational selections for given service companies. The study was based on in-depth interviews with representatives of three firms, analysis of in-house materials, and the application of multiple perspectives dealing with ITG domains. Case study analysis yielded a detailed picture of the characteristics of ITG related decision making within the firms, suggesting the validity of the proposed ITG framework. The proposed and partially validated ITG framework should be useful for further research and practice of ITG.

INTRODUCTION

In an increasingly competitive global environment, information systems are becoming more and more critical, forcing firms to turn their attention to decision processes relating to information systems and information technologies (IS/IT). Further, as managers and stakeholders become aware of the potential uses of IT, an increasing number of companies are attempting to use IT as an important strategic tool in maximizing the value of firms' resources and in delivering strategic goals (ACADYDA, 2002; ITGI, 2006; Patel, 2003). However, while firms have grasped the importance of IS/IT, many remain unsure which IT governance (ITG) structures and processes will enable them to get the most out of their considerable IT/IS expenditure (Posthumusa & Solms, 1995; Shleifer & Vishny, 1997; Van Grembergen, 2003). Companies face the challenge of having to proactively design structures and processes for the management of their information assets.

In this regard, ITG aims to strengthen firms' control over their IT resources. ITG deals with risk management in IT investment, with the design of control and performance management systems, and with the strategic management of interactions between IS/IT and other business processes and functions (ITGI, 2000). ITG has emerged as a defined and urgent business problem concerning the demarcation of clear lines of responsibility and accountability in IS/IT management (Weill & Woodham, 2002).

Despite firms' increasing awareness of ITG, however, very little academic literature addresses this emerging topic. Further, it is not simply possible to apply or cascade the characteristics of corporate governance onto ITG, as information resources have different features from other assets (Lee, Lee & Ahn, 2006). Studies found that, while acknowledging the importance of ITG, CIOs are still searching for a comprehensive and applicable ITG framework in which they can deliver ITG (Lim, Lee, Rah, Yoon & Lee, 2004).

The framework would link ITG to other processes and specify appropriate channels for information, reporting, decision-making and control.

In characterizing ITG activities systematically, this chapter develops a comprehensive ITG framework through which it undertakes three case studies of service firms in Korea. In other words, this chapter offers a comparative case study applying a preliminarily identified ITG framework, exploring the following research questions:

1. What are the major decision areas in ITG?
2. What are the key mechanisms for ITG?
3. How are ITG practices designed and implemented within firms?

The first two questions are partially answered by constructing an exploratory framework for ITG in Section 2 through a literature review and interviews with practitioners, and the third question is partially answered through a comparison of the three firms' internal governance structures and processes related to IS/IT.

THEORETICAL BACKGROUND

As research and practice in the area of corporate governance precedes that in IS/IT, this section provides a brief overview of the literature on CG (Corporate Governance) and extends the review into IT governance topics.

Corporate Governance

After the large-scale accounting frauds in the U.S. of Enron and WorldCom, many companies are making great efforts to improve their CG, seeking to monitor more effectively the rights and responsibilities of a range of stakeholders, including shareholders, management, and employees (Brown & Grant, 2005). According to the OECD Principles of Corporate Governance (2004), relationships between stakeholders, such as the management, board of directors, and investors, are critical in CG both in boosting firms' economic efficiency and in raising investor confidence. Literature revealed that the scope of CG after Enron is defined much more broadly. Current definitions of CG take in, for instance, decisions on how a corporation sets its goals, goes about achieving them, and monitors and directs action plans throughout the implementation process (Kose & Senbet, 1998). Vives (2000) asserts that corporations are run by professional managers not directly responsible to investors, meaning that companies' governance schemes must resolve issues of "adverse selection" and "moral hazard". Vives (2000) defines CG as a tool facilitating the alignment of interest between entrepreneurs/managers and external investors, overcoming these classical economics problems. Shleifer and Vishny (1997) offer a comparable definition of CG as a means for investors to secure a profit on their investment, adding that from an investor's point of view, the term denotes the company structure and system of supervision calculated to maximize management performance.

Good CG leads to the efficient distribution of resources and capital, maximizing profit and permitting shareholders to observe CEOs' corporate management (Black, Jang, H. & Kim, 2003; Brown & Caylor, 2004). In other words, when CG is effectively set up, nonexecutive shareholders should be able to review the critical decisions of management and to provide feedback. In this sense, one element of good CG will be the timely release of information relevant to a firm's future prospects. Vishwanath & Kaufmann (1999) define transparency as a timely flow of credible information pertaining to the economic, social and political aspects of a firm's future, while Bushman and Smith (2003) define CG as the widespread availability of relevant, reliable information vis-à-vis the periodic performance, financial position, investment opportunities, governance, value, and risks of publicly traded firms (OECD, 2004).

IT Governance

Although the term, "IT governance," was initially used in the early 1990's by Loh and Venkatraman (1992) and by Henderson and Venkatraman (1993) to describe a series of mechanisms enabling corporations' best use of their IT capabilities, the term has only recently begun to attract sustained academic attention. In recent years, ITG has been variously defined by a range of academics and practitioners, as pertaining to the locus of IT-related decision making (Brown & Magill, 1994); as the allocation of responsibilities between different authorities in IT-related decision making (Luftman, 1996), and as patterns of authority governing key IT activities (Sambamurthy & Zmud, 1999). The term ITG may also denote those organizational skills or capabilities developed jointly by IT teams and other business units in developing synergies (Van Grembergen, 2003), as well as those processes determining the sharing and monitoring of IT decision-making powers (Weill & Ross, 2004). The ITGI has expanded these definitions to refer to those organizational processes and structures supporting overarching systems for the fulfillment of broad corporate strategies (ITGI, 2001). In this regard, ITG includes such activities as creating value through bringing about strategic alignments between IT and business (ITGI, 2001); improving transparency and accountability in relation to IT activities (Weill & Vitale, 2002); increasing productivity through effective IT services and applications; devising decision-making systems for risk management, and setting up IT resources for accountability. These diverse definitions and perspectives naturally lead academics to propose integrated frameworks for ITG.

Analyzing the field further, Weill (2004) identifies a number of IT decision-making areas related to ITG: (1) IT principles, (2) IT architecture, (3) IT infrastructure strategies, (4) business application needs, and (5) IT investment and prioritization. Along with these areas, his work defines six different ITG archetypes: business monarchy, IT monarchy, feudal arrangements, federal arrangements, IT duopoly, and anarchy. Weill aims to understand which ITG archetypes best fit the specific context of different corporate environments for each decision area. Moreover, his proposed framework presents a range of governance mechanisms in the form of a choice for companies of organizational structures, procedures, and forms of committee and policy to organize and implement effective ITG. Simonsson and Johnson (2006) identifies three dimensions of ITG: decision domains (e.g., types of decision making related to goals, processes, people, and technology); decision scope (e.g., levels of decisions in terms of time-length and organization); and decision making processes (e.g., forms of conceptualizing, making decisions and monitoring decisions' effects in relation to firms' IT assets and their bearing on the real world). Webb, Pollard, and Ridley (2006) define ITG as the activities linking IT with business, such as (1) strategic alignment, (2) IT value transfers, (3) performance management, (4) risk management, (5) regulations, and (6) responsibility delegation. Peterson (2004) views ITG as the delegation of responsibilities and decision-making power to various stakeholders within a corporation, suggesting that governance may be understood as the set of mechanisms and procedures supervising strategic decision-making. Dahlberg and Kivijarvi (2006) view ITG as an integrated management system comprised of three different IT activities: planning, execution and evaluation, and feedback. COBIT (Control Objectives for Information Related Technology) has been recognized by the IT Governance Institute as a potential standard for such activities offering adaptable control guidelines for IT practitioners (ITGI, 2000). COBIT proposes 4 domains with 32 processes. However, COBIT is limited in that it is expressed almost entirely in terms of process, focusing on how to govern but not what to govern.

Previous ITG Case Studies

Alongside the theoretical development of frameworks, several studies introduce actual case analyses, applying exploratory frameworks as an analytical device. Park, Jung, Lee, and Jang (2006) list and analyze internal ITG activities related to IT standards-setting in a semi-conductor manufacturer. Their single case study describes how the company was able to leverage the productivity of its IT unit by generating and imposing standards and standardized outcomes, thereby optimizing the execution of related IT processes. They found standards setting provided by an internal audit process to be effective as a front-end activity of ITG. Jang and Lee (2005) examine a firm's decision-making structure in the light of Weill's ITG framework. Lee et al. (2006) examine the ITG of two Korean service companies in terms of the structures, processes and relational mechanisms proposed by Van Grembergen (2003). Similarly, Bhattacharjva and Chang (2006) conduct an exploratory study investigating Australian higher education institutions' utilization of international standards such as COBIT, ITIL and ISO17799. Letsoalo, Brown, and Njenga (2006) examine a large South African enterprise, identifying 12 key factors enabling and inhibiting IT implementation. The enablers are senior management support for investment/projects, a project champion and external support, while the key inhibitors of successful implementation are a lack of clear IT processes, inadequate human resources and inadequate stakeholder involvement. Park, Lee and Lee (2007) examine ITG practices in the Korean service industry from the perspective of complex adaptive systems (CAS). Through analyzing the key issues relating to ITG complexity, the authors identify several governance principles.

Linking ITG to CG

A number of scholars and practitioners have attempted to build on existing definitions and frameworks in presenting architectures for use by businesses for use in their own specific environments. However, most proposed frameworks are limited insofar as they suppose a certain conception of ITG in relation to its CG attributes; further, frameworks tend as yet not to be validated by empirical research. Given, however, IT's major impact on firms' formulation and execution of their business strategies, there is a clear need for ITG frameworks that capture appropriate relationships between ITG and wider CG, especially in terms of IT's contribution to the planning stages of company action plans (Van Grembergen & De Haes, 2005). As a number of researchers have emphasised, IT resources are not to be regarded as independent, separate assets but rather as key elements of corporate resources. The optimal deployment of IT assets has the potential to improve business processes maximising corporate return on investment (ROI). According to the ITGI (2001) and Weill and Ross (2004), in overseeing ITG, companies' board of directors need to possess a strong level of insight into the possible roles of IT in general, and should in specific instances clarify the strategic goals and financial benefits accruing through the best use of IT. A recent survey conducted by the ITGI and PWC (2007) has shown that half the participants felt that their current ITG practices focused more on issues of compliance, control and "operational IT", than on the delivery of strategy as overseen by (or necessarily involving) company boards. Yet the close relationship asserted by many authors between CG and ITG suggests that in designing ITG frameworks, it should be plausible to cascade general governance attributes to ITG, or otherwise to make IT processes and functions inherit such attributes. This chapter, through utilizing such inherited characteristics, will look to present an ITG framework that maximizes the benefits of a corporation's ITG practices, offering firms strengthened capabilities of coordination and control. In this way it aims to yield more effective mechanisms for the structured governance of an IT organization.

PROPOSED ITG FRAMEWORK

This study develops an ITG framework integrating currently available designs. Specifically, it seeks to characterize an IT decision-making and control system capable of fulfilling corporate strategies and aims through rational IT principles. Implementing such an ITG framework would allow a corporation to observe activities of efficiency, transparency and accountability in its corporate IT activities. Based on our literature review, this section presents a comprehensive treatment of a generic ITG scheme, aiming to remedy the insufficiencies of previous frameworks through incorporating all the essential elements of CG attributes, as shown in Figure 1.

The proposed framework is presented in terms of three different dimensions: "ITG decision areas", "IT activities", "IT control". Each of these areas is associated with the generic IT activities of a firm (planning, development, operation) specifying proposed governance structure and co-ordination and control mechanisms for governance in each domain. Combining these three dimensions, the framework enables users to pair firms' major ITG decision areas with appropriate key governance mechanisms and to determine an appropriate level of ITG practices incorporating CG attributes.

ITG Decision Areas

The framework presents five core decision-making areas of ITG described by earlier studies as forming the core of the ITG decision domain (ITGI, 2004; Peterson, 2004). The term "strategic alignment" indicates an attempt to make firms' IT strategy coincide with their corporate strategy, usually through communicating between IT and other business units, so increasing the firm's business value. IT resource management is concerned with the quality of firms' overall IT services through the effective management of IT resources such as information, infrastructure,

Figure 1. Proposed IT governance framework

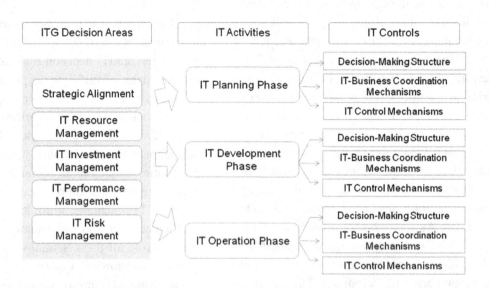

IT architectures, applications, and so forth. As an area, IT investment management designates businesses' efforts to improve the value of their IT assets through systemic and detailed evaluations and through monitoring the performance of their IT investments. Finally, IT risk management deals with the measures necessary to increase business consistency and security through establishing a risk-managing method and security system for IT resources. This area will include the production and maintenance of any firm information assets and comply with external regulations (ITGI, 2004; Peterson, 2004; Simonsson & Johnson, 2006).

IT Activities

Each ITG decision area may be broken down into three stages of activity: IT planning, IT development and IT operations. In view of the IT management process suggested by Boynton Zmud, and Jacobs (1994) in studying the work processes of a leading company, as well as the COBIT framework proposed by the ITGI (2000), this study attempts to highlight specific activities through which companies can operationalise ITG plans. During the IT planning stage, firms

will seek to understand all IT-related issues, including requests made by each area of business, and will accordingly establish plans for an IT strategy, generating a schedule or structure of IT activities. Firms' IT development stage will include all activities relating to these planned activities, carried out in terms of a development cycle stretching from planning to implementation, and integrally featuring project and change management. Lastly, the IT operational stage will concern various maintenance and IT support services, many of which will serve users (e.g., the help desk) as well as supporting continuous IT infraoperation processes, including monitoring and evaluation activities.

IT Control

Previous studies have also advanced influential definitions of ITG as the allocation of IT decision-making rights and responsibilities among IT-related stakeholders, and integrally as the procedures and mechanisms involved in making and monitoring strategic IT decisions. ITG pays specific attention to questions of who makes IT decisions and how (Peterson, 2004). The proposed framework classifies issues of the location and structure of IT control into three separate subfields: issues of organizational structure and activity, coordination mechanisms between business and IT, and control mechanisms. In the organisational domain, the proposed framework attempts to correlate decision-making and leadership structures with certain types of company needs, clarifying various stakeholders' rights and responsibilities. The next stage of our description designates channels through which IT and business units can exchange opinions, devising in this respect appropriate coordination mechanisms (De Haes & Van Grembergen, 2006; Peterson & Fairchild, 2003). In terms of firms' control mechanisms, the study attempts to analyse ITG efficiency, accountability and transparency as the ultimate goals of CG through applying four control measures as specified in the context of businesses' integral ITG frameworks (or overarching forms of organizational control). The activities included under such a remit include IT supervision and monitoring, evaluation and compensation on the one hand, and internal controls (e.g., IT internal audit/supervision, policy regulation and adherence to operational IT guidelines) on the other.

CASE STUDY METHODOLOGY

This work uses a comparative case study as a method for eliciting particular firms' ITG practices using the proposed framework. We selected three large enterprises in the Korean service industry of a similar firm size and business domains. Each firm understood their IT assets as competitive resources and operated in an industry which had invested comparatively heavily in IT. We chose three enterprises on the basis of the widely accepted thesis that the validity and reliability of quantitative studies increases when more than one case is placed under review (Benbasat, Goldstain & Mead, 1987; Yin, 1984). Further, case studies have a proven range of uses in helping researchers

to formulate theories, in verifying theories, and in proving certain conditions across a number of different studies (Benbasat, 1987). Data from the three companies under review was collected through trustworthy institutions and various media, and in-depth interviews held with firm CIOs, IT team leaders, and other senior managers of business units of each company. A team of five researchers conducted each interview using a semi-structured format in periods of about two hours. Each case company provided additional documentation concerning their ITG practices (e.g., ISP, EA practices, ITSM/ITIL practices, IT BSC practices, information security practices, IT compliances organizational charts for the company and IT departments, project management guidelines, IT management process diagrams, IT ROI, etc.). Due to confidentiality reasons, we are unable to make company names public. Our case study design took particular efforts to make clear to companies the research question, that is, what procedures and governance mechanisms companies used to manage their ITG structures. Rather than focusing on the board level in investigating ITG practices, we made the decision to observe overall IT-related decisions as they were arrived at between business and IT units. It emerged that IT units were solely responsible for some aspects of IT decision making, since other business units were unfamiliar with the technical side of IT. In summary, then, this study adopted as its unit of analysis "ITG practices in the Korean IT based service sector."

Table 1 provides background information on the case study companies. Company "A" is an IT-based service provider, with a market-dominant position in Korea. Company "B" occupies third position in the same market as Company A, and is currently aiming to strengthen its competitiveness by increasing market share. The final case Company C holds second position in this marketplace, and is looking to make up the gap by offering new emerging technology-based products and services to customers. All three companies deploy a range of 5 to 9 teams in an independent IT department of about 60 to 100 members, including an IT planning team, an IT technology team, and an IT risk management team. The Companies A and B also outsource system development and maintenance to a leading IT service companies in Korea, while Company C runs in-house IT development and maintenance, as shown in Table 1.

ANALYSIS: COMPARATIVE CASE STUDY

This section compares the ITG related activities in the three companies against each other using the proposed framework. We have organized subsections of this analysis into five domains (dealing with strategic alignment, IT resource management, IT investment management, IT performance management and IT risk management). In each of these five domains, the framework uses three phases of planning, development, and operation as structuring its analysis.

Strategic Alignment

This decision area relates to firms' strategic alignment activities, dealing with setting performance indicators for achieving firm's strategic objectives and formulating and executing IT strategy.

IT Planning Phase

In the planning stage for effecting strategic alignment between IT and business, firms take stock of their business direction, formulate goals and action plans and propose IT strategies optimally integrated with business strategies objectives. This process involves the identification and definition of all relevant IT-related activities and processes. In Company A, either a Relationship Manager (RM), IT manager, or the IT department typically propose IT strategies to an IT Investment Review Committee (IT IRC), which reviews and approves these. No separate control organizations exist for the auditing or supervision of the alignment process. However, an informal control structure links up between IT managers and other managers. IT manager consult extensively with

Table 1. Case backgrounds

	Company A	Company B	Company C
Annual Revenue (KRW, billion)	10,651	3,943	6,507
% of IT Investment (2006. 12)	1.88%	0.76%	1.23%
No. of IT Teams	1 IT Unit/4 Teams	1 IT Unit/9 Teams	2 IT units/8 Teams
No. of IT Staff (excluding outsourced)	64	62	108
IT Org. Types	Centralized	Centralized	Centralized
Outsourcing Types (No. of People)	Outsourcing to family company (150)	Outsourcing to family company (140)	In-sourcing
IT Management Tools	ITSM/ITIL, EA, ISO 17799, CMM/CCMi, SLA/SLM	ITSM/ITIL, EA, ISO 17799, CMM/CMMi. SLA/SLM, BSC	ITSM/ITIL, CMM/CMMi, ISO 17799, 6 Sigma. BSC

business managers before submitting a proposal to the IT IRC.

Company B maintains a regular Junior Committee (JC) staffed by IT and senior managers, which assesses and passes proposals up to an IT IRC through the mediation of the company CIO and relevant team leaders. The CIO and team leaders participate in the JC meeting. The JC oversees the overall business conduct of the IT department, as well as involving itself with other business units in terms of strategic decisions at the interface of technology and other operations. The company's IT IRC communicates strategic decisions and policy changes to corresponding business units and executives. This body also refers to Key Performance Indicators (KPIs) defined for IT strategy. Measurements of IT performance are reported to higher board-level bodies as feedback on management innovations. Both companies recognized ISP as an important tool for effecting strategic alignment and had implemented a formal ISP revision process. ISP outcomes are managed and revised on a regular basis by a team led by the IT department.

Company C runs a dedicated team for BRM (Business Relationship Management) tasked with improving IT-business strategic alignment. In addition, an "Executive Steering Committee (otherwise known as the Value Improvement Committee: VIC)" oversees these alignments, discussing and making decisions on any IT related issues. The company has also established a number of KPIs for its IT organization aiming to improve strategic alignment by propagating the BRM guidelines throughout the enterprise.

IT Operational Phase

The IT operation phase in strategic alignment includes all activities designed to satisfy both the strategic and operational requirements of running optimized IT services in the context of cooperative decisions between IT and business units. Actions, for example, may include defin-

ing IT service levels or in providing firm-wide education on IT capabilities.

In this regard, Company A has implemented an EA/ITA framework in order to encourage business/IT partnerships, though the framework has yet to be fully implemented across the company. The framework designates EA/ITA related activities and processes envisioning IT-business alignment. However, the firm restricts EA/ITA workshops to the context of exceptional change management.

In terms of building IT operations into a broader context of strategic alignment, Company B is also at an early stage, though it has put an IT Service Level Council in place. This council serves as a liaison between IT and business units. Both companies execute and operate a targeted service level under the responsibility of the IT technology team. However, existing alignment processes do not cover "over-the-horizon" issues but rather aim at improving operational efficiency. Company C, meanwhile, has set a number of KPIs for its IT service operations, without as yet defining any objectives related to strategic alignment in this process.

IT Resource Management

The decision area of IT resource management includes the management of corporate IT infrastructure, system applications, invisible information property and the implementation of EA/ITA and ITSM/ITIL.

IT Planning Phase

During the IT planning for resource management, companies define an IT architecture in accordance with company EA/ITA principles and standards. Companies then set an appropriate IT infrastrategy directing the efficient use of IT resources. In all three companies, the IT planning team and the IT technology team holds responsibility for IT resource planning. Companies' IT

IRC approve plans, and CIOs finalize decisions. Although companies are making efforts to align their IT resources through establishing EA/ITA and ITSM systems, these endeavors remain at an early stage. However, Company C has implemented a BPM (Business Process Management) system governing IT resource management with coordinates an "Information Practices Council" with an up-and-running ITSM system to retrieve real-time IT operations data.

IT Development Phase

This phase refers to all activities related to the processes of introducing and implementing new IT architectures, applications or infrastructures, as well as to maintenance performed during the development cycle. In Company A, RMs at the business units and/or IT planning teams gather suggestions from business units concerning the development of new systems. In other words, the RMs collaborate with IT teams to capture the system requirements for new systems or to justify IT investment decisions. They also write an investment proposal using cost and benefit analysis using given templates. The IT IRC then analyses all proposals making final investment decisions targeting optimized resource allocation.

In company B, operations send their business requirements for new IT application development and report any operational IT issues via a Service Request System (SRS) sent to the IT department. The IT department critically reviews each request, determining whether service levels can be maintained by in-house corrective actions or whether separate projects need to be funded and launched. Proposed projects are passed up to the company IT IRC for consideration and approval, before the CIO makes the final investment decision.

Company A and B have further developed and implemented an EA/ITA framework. Company 'A' primarily relies on a BA (Business Architecture) system in which the firm takes the role of planner and owner framing and formalising business re-

quirements. Company 'B' also intends to build up its EA/ITA from the perspective of the firm playing a role as designer and builder. While Companies A and B used EA/ITA frameworks to standardize development practices, Company C uses BRM to coordinate system development activities. In addition, a SR committee (called the SPEC Committee and specifying user requirements) operates as a governance mechanism in controlling IT resource issues. "System Development" specifications and "Maintenance & Operations" specifications are stored separately, while ITSM run-data is collected on a monthly basis.

IT Operation Phase

The operational phase in IT resource management involves the oversight of architectures, standards, IT services and overall infra-operations. In the case of Company A, most resources management decisions are delegated to the IT department as it engages in IT infra-operations. The company carries out service management through formalized processes and procedural frameworks (e.g., ITSM/ITIL). While acknowledging service requests for IT operations at a corporate level, the company nevertheless takes any IT-related operational decisions through RMs and the IT IRC. Even though the planning of optimal IT architectures and related activities is still at an initial stage, the IT planning team seems competent in managing current IT service operations and management.

In Company B, the IT planning staff in IT department selects and monitors outsourcing partners, while the technical staff takes charge of overall IT service operations and management (e.g., ITSM/ITIL). An IT Service Level Council (SLC) holds IT infrastructure strategy meetings, guiding outsourcing partners are guided through revisions of Service Level Agreement (SLA).

While both Company A and B outsource their operations to their family company, Company C coordinates its IT issues through a "Quality Improvement Committee" responsible for overall IT resource management. All companies review any related IT operational issues through their IT IRCs, with CIOs making final allocation decisions.

IT Investment Management

This decision area relates to firms' investment management systems, dealing with whole investment portfolios and system-related activities.

IT Planning Phase

Although Company A justifies their investment decisions using a formalized IT ROI methodology, the reliability of their methodology and performance indicators have yet to be validated and are not factored back into planning stages. However, Company C has systematically implemented an IT ROI methodology into their IT management system, though this is not fully automated with other system components. Firm business units define the KPIs for measuring IT ROI, with BRM measures of IT cost projected during pre-assessment sessions before plans are finally decided by the IT IRC (or by the Executive Steering Committee if budgets come in over a certain amount).

Similarly, Company B has also developed a comprehensive IT ROI methodology, as yet only partially implemented in practice. The firm's IT ROI indicators remain ambiguous and have not been empirically validated. At present, the firm undertakes preliminary ROI analysis on a partial basis only for reasons of economic feasibility and validity (e.g., most IT cost evaluation proceeds through qualitative analysis). In all companies, the IT planning team takes charge of related IT activity as coordinated for control purpose by both business and IT units.

IT Development Phase

Development activities occur during the IT project execution cycle and include such tasks as enterprises' pre-evaluation of their investment, project

management, and change management. The IT investment evaluation system of Company A relies on a portfolio method based on a classification of evaluation timing and types. Compared to a post-evaluation method, pre-evaluation is relatively simple depending on measurements taken from each business department. However, these measurements' credibility is low. In Company A, business and IT together take charge of investment proposals, carrying out detailed planning. Meanwhile, the IT IRC evaluates any proposition, reporting results to the senior executives through the central planning department. The planning department adjusts and finally decides the projects' budget. However, the company's CEO becomes involved in decision-making when budgets exceed a certain amount. As soon as projects' implementation phase gets underway after final approval, the firm sets up a steering committee composed of managers and directors from the IT department. This committee secures sponsorship for change management, largely through progress reports rather than backing for short-term decisions.

In Company B, new IT projects are proposed by either IT or current business units through a SRS. The initiating department conducts a pre-evaluation study of the cost/benefit of the project. The CIO and relevant IT team leader determine investment priorities according to projects' economic feasibility and fit with their strategic context. When project budgets exceed five thousand billion Korean won, the JC will decide on the investment with the CIO retaining ultimate authority over most investment decisions. Without establishing any separate organisational unit, IT teams manage projects and determine projects' human resource requirements. Although no separate control mechanism regulates the investment process, management participates in investment review. In Company A. all the projects undergo this investment review, and in Company B, only projects above a certain budget size are controlled in this way.

In Company B, projects are open to scrutiny in the sense that the management board exercises a passive checking over IT investment. Company C conducts a more detailed examination than Companies A and B, submitting proposals to analysis through defined KPIs at the IT planning stage. The company's governance mechanisms work in a similar way to Company A, where steering committees make decisions when IT budgets go over a certain amount.

IT Operational Phase

In operational stages, companies typically track the post-assessment of their implemented systems from an ROI perspective. In Companies A and C, IT planning teams assess IT ROI on the basis of a formalized methodology, reporting back to business units on an annual basis. Key IT ROI's KPIs measure how projects have improved ROI and determine wider business impact by cross-comparison with pre-assessment data.

Company B's IT planning team also takes responsibility for the postmanagement of all IT projects but is currently experiencing difficulties conducting this, since IT ROI's KPIs are not well leveraged by other parts of the organization.

IT Performance Management

This phase includes all activities planning for and managing an appropriate IT performance management methodology (e.g., IT BSC) for firms' IT organization.

IT Planning Phases

In Company A, a range of different measurement sets support IT related activities including IT KPIs, Business KPIs, and Service Level Agreement (SLA) performance indicators. However, research found that these indicators were not fully integrated with each other. This suboptimal situation may not improve overall IT performance,

possibly resulting in less effective performance improvements. The company has explicitly measured performance indicators from the viewpoint of both senior managers in business and IT units, but has yet to formulate governance mechanisms such as the creation of a single oversight body for IT planning. This leads to confusion in the definition and use of performance indicators amongst the firm's IT organizations.

In Companies B and C, the CIO and IT team leaders define KPIs, sharing these with the business as an organized part of management innovation activity. In this regard, the CIO and IT team leaders set an annual target for IT activities updated according to business unit objectives. This creates a tight strategic linkage between at least two parties, with the KPIs serving as a communication protocol supporting the improvement of business and IT performance.

Company C specifically sets CSFs and KPIs for its IT unit under the BSC system, measuring, monitoring, and directing these through its business unit (i.e., Performance Management Team), although it also lacks a formal governing mechanism (committees/council). These indicators are, however, mostly operational, showing levels of IT maintenance and IT service satisfaction.

IT Operational Phases

The IT planning team of Companies A and C is responsible for monitoring and evaluating IT performance, and for managing overall operational processes. These teams also conduct performance evaluations on IT systems and subsystems, communicating results to corresponding departments. Company B has implemented an IT BSC, focusing mainly on internal efficiency. In the absence of integrated systems of performance management, each company executes a performance evaluation limited to the operational level as measured by stated indicators. However, Company B relates their IT KPIs to wider corporate level business indicators, periodically monitoring IT performance. Systemic performance management is not in place, and no overarching organization exists controlling performance evaluation.

IT Risk Management

This decision area relates to firms' risk management, dealing with IT security and IT compliance activities.

IT Planning Phase

Risk management activities in the planning phase seek to identify and understand the risks that can occur throughout IT related processes. Planning identifies appropriate countermeasures, establishing policies, systems and management schemes. In both Companies A and B, independent IT risk management teams are formally in place taking responsibility for security planning, risk monitoring and correspondence system management. Current business departments do not participate in these security management systems or security architectures. Both companies have implemented and operate the IT security management system proper to the information protection management system of the Korea Ministry of Information and Technology; systems also meet international security standards. However, Company C has also established a control center called "Risk Management (RM)" center to coordinate any security and compliance issues raised by three different units: the Admin. Unit (managing risks connected with physical security), the CRM unit (managing the compliance of customer information with any external regulations), and the IT unit (managing any IT risks relating to applications and network security). All these units plan the firm's security policy jointly, reporting to the RM center as part of governance arrangements for security issues including IT risks.

IT Operational Phase

Activities in this phase entail the monitoring and evaluation of IT risks seeking to guarantee system security and business continuity over the IT operation process. The IT risk management team of Company A takes charge of this work, consulting about security-related issues through an IT security committee meeting monthly and quarterly. The firm runs a system security diagnosis process including an internal audit. In Company B, an IT Risk Management team sets up a security strategy, distributes a security check-list, and proposes security issues through the IT IRC under the coordination of the SRS. These security issues are mainly discussed with the IT Risk management team, with the CIO or IT security team finally formulating principles governing IT security. In respect of security, company 'C' operates two governing bodies: a standing IT security council and an IT security committee, which meets semiannually. The IT unit initials security principles, which are finalized in the RM center.

COMPARATIVE ANALYSIS OF THREE COMPANIES

Table 2 compares out three case companies in terms of their ITG related processes and activities based on previous sections. The horizontal axis lists five core decision areas of ITG and three phases of planning, while development and operation are listed on the vertical axis. For each phase, three critical management schemes are identified and compared: a decision-making mechanism (D/M); a coordination mechanism (Co/M); and a control mechanism (C/M). The D/M is concerned with the origin of IT related proposals (input: I) and the final locus of decision-making (decision: D). Through the comparative study of the three companies as shown in Table 2, we can draw certain implications. First, all companies manage IT related decisions and activities through an IT IRC. Companies have clearly defined roles for Input and Decision as shown on Table 2, with the locus of decision rights in reviewing and approving IT projects and services being significantly centralized to CIOs in all cases. Those coordination and control mechanisms that the companies have established are more frequently found in investment and resource management domains than elsewhere, raising the level of accountability and transparency level in both domains.

All the companies need to spell out the division of roles and responsibilities between business units and the IT department in IT decisions. Companies B and C run a "JC" and "Value Improvement Committees" respectively, are responsible for the strategic assessment of IT projects and for overseeing development through KPI measurement and subsequent action. However, for the core decision areas of ITG, centralized CIOs and IT departments (according to an IT monarchy in Weill's terminology) make major decisions themselves. Reporting upwards is limited on account of the limited legacy role played by the IT department in the company in the past, leading to a lack of coordination and communication between IT and business units in particular at the higher level of organizations. In this regard, it seems necessary for companies to enhance their ITG mechanisms to fully reflect the requirements and demands made by business at both board and operational decision levels. Effectively creating these mechanisms depends on improving the understanding of IT across the company, and progressively inducing participation from business side units aligning IT with their activities.

In Companies A and B, project suggestions, maintenance requests, and ordinary operation management pass up proposals for IT initiatives to higher levels. However, coordination channels connecting IT development and the operation of strategic alignments is relatively weak from a control perspective. In addition, the business or the board level rarely gets involved in IT performance management areas, with ITG proceeding according to an 'IT Monarchy'. Although Companies B and C use a BSC framework as part of a corporate performance measurement tool, their focus level is primarily operational, not strategic. The companies thus face a need to integrate their ITG with business areas not only in delivering requests, but in creating value through proactive coordination. Firms should aim to establish a formalized coordination mechanism between business and IT linking the entire corporation; these mechanisms should work on a continuous, not project-specific, basis. Although both companies claim to have implemented EA/ITA, these structures are controlled by strategic requirements, rather than integrated into day-to-day operational IT management. This partial implementation lowers the utility of such architectures.

From the perspective of IT control, firms need to put in place business alignment and control mechanisms to improve the transparency of IT investment management and IT risk management. While control mechanisms in other areas may simply be translated into internal IT controls by the IT IRC, IT investment controls have a control function in the form of the final decision on investment lying with the company boards (as supported by the advice of the CIO and IT team leaders; no separate organizational mechanism exists). All three companies are aware of the importance of compliance and security issues though companies act on these at different levels of ITG practices. Companies A and B are characterized by an IT monarchy decision-making structure dominantly operated by IT units, while Company C takes account of a much wider scope of IT risks considered together with other types of risks through the RM center.

Table 2. Comparing three cases using ITG framework

Phase			Strategic Alignment			IT Resource Mgmt.			IT Investment Mgmt.			IT Performance Mgmt.			IT Risk Mgmt.		
			'A'	'B'	'C'	'A'	'B'	'C'	'A'	'B'	'C'	'A'	'B'	'C'	'A'	'B'	'C'
IT Planning Phase	DM		I: Business IT; D: IT (CIO)	I: Business IT; D: IT (CIO)	I:IT; D: IT (CIO)	D: IT (CIO)	D: IT (CIO)	D: IT (CIO)	D: IT	I:IT; D: IT	I:IT; D: IT Business	D: IT	D: IT (CIO)	D: Business	D: IT	D: IT (CIO)	D: Business
	CoM		RM	Junior committee; KPI				Information Practices Council			Information Practices Council		KPI	KPI & Business.IT co-ordination			Information Security Council
	CM		IT Investment Review Committee	IT Investment Review Committee	Steering Committee	IT Investment Review Committee	IT Investment Review Committee		IT Investment Review Committee	IT Investment Review Committee	Value Improvement Committee				International/ Government Regulation	International/ Government Regulation	Information Security Committee
IT Development Phase	DM				I: Business IT; D: IT	I: Business IT; D: IT (CIO)	I: Business IT; D: IT (CIO)	IT (CIO)	I: Business IT; D: Business /CEO	I: Business IT; D: IT business	I: Business IT; D: IT/Business			D: IT (CIO)		N.A	D: IT (CIO)
	CoM		N.A			RM	SRS	RM	Steering Committee	SRS	IT BPM/Sys.; Value Improvement Committee		N.A		N.A		
	CM					IT Investment Review Committee	IT Investment Review Committee	Specification Meeting	Management Board	Junior Committee							
IT Operation Phase	DM		ITA; workshop; I: Business IT; D: Business / IT	ITA, IT service level council; I: Business IT; D: Business / IT	D: IT/CIO	I: Business IT; D: IT (CIO)	I: Business IT	I:IT (CIO); D: IT/CIO	I:IT; D: IT	I:IT; D: IT	IT (CIO)	I:IT; D:IT	I:IT; D: IT	D: IT (CIO)	I:IT; D: IT	I: Business IT; D: IT (CIO)	Information Security Council; D: Business (RM center)
	CoM		RM	RM	Information Practices Council								KPI		System security inspection	SRS	
	CM		IT investment review committee	IT investment review committee	Quality Improvement Committee											IT Investment Review Committee	

CONCLUSION

Our comparative case study conclusively found that the three companies make IT decisions independently of any governance mechanisms other than firms' IT Investment Review Committee. All three companies in our case need to design and implement more robust governance mechanisms in areas such as IT resource management (EA/ITA and IT Service Committee). Future discussion should focus on an optimal choice of organizational system, on coordination channels between business units and IT organization, and on control mechanisms serving objectives of transparency, efficiency, and accountability, promoting the optimization not just of IT, but of wider corporate performance.

The aim for companies will be to develop an ITG framework capable of integrating IT and business activities. In this respect, it would be desirable to see further studies treating specific indicators e.g. of IT performance, as well as case studies offering benchmarks or reference models of ITG. More detailed studies could also help corporations to implement plans to improve their actual ITG performance.

REFERENCES

ACADYDA (2002). European survey on the economy value of IT Edition 2002-2003.

Benbasat, I., Goldstain, D. K., & Mead, M. (1987). The case research strategy in studies of information systems. *MIS Quarterly, 11*(3), 369-386.

Bhattacharjya, J. & Chang, V. (2006). An exploration of the implementation and effectiveness of IT governance processes in institutions of higher education in Australia. In *Proceedings of the 2006 IT Governance International Conference*, Auckland, New Zealand.

Black, B., Jang, H., & Kim, W. (2003). Does corporate governance affect firms' market values? *Evidence from Korea, Stanford Law School Working Paper 237.* Stanford University.

Boynton, A. C., Zmud, R. W., & Jacobs, G. C. (1994). The influence of IT management practice on IT use in large organizations. *MIS Quarterly, 18*(3), 299-318.

Brown, A. E., & Grant, G. G. (2005). Framing the frameworks: A review of IT governance research. *Communications of the Association for Information Systems, 15*, 696-712.

Brown, C. V., & Magill, S. L. (1994). Alignment of the IS functions with the enterprise: Toward a model of antecedents. *MIS Quarterly, 18*(4), 371-403.

Brown, L. D., & Caylor, M. L. (2004). Corporate governance and firm performance. *Working Paper of Georgia State University.*

Bushman, R. M., & Smith, A. J. (2003). Transparency, financial accounting information, and corporate governance. *FRBNY Economic Policy Review (2003 April)*, 65-87.

Dahlberg, T., & Kivijärvi, H. (2006). An integrated framework for IT governance and the development and validation of an assessment instrument. In *Proceedings of the 39th Hawaii International Conference on System Sciences (HICSS)*, Hawaii: IEEE.

De Haes, S., & Van Grembergen, W. (2006). Information technology governance best practices in Belgian organizations. In *Proceedings of the 39th Hawaii International Conference on System Sciences (HICSS)*, Hawaii: IEEE.

Henderson, J. C., & Venkatraman, N. (1993). Strategic alignment: Leveraging information technology for transforming organizations. *IBM Systems Journal, 32*(1), 472-485.

IT Governance Institute (2000). COBIT : *Governance, control and audit for information and related technology.* IT Governance Institute. Retrieved May 11, 2008, from http://www.itgi.org

IT Governance Institute (2001). *IT governance executive summary.* IT Governance Institute. Retrieved May 11, 2008, from http://www.itgi.org

IT Governance Institute (2004). *IT governance global status report.* IT Governance Institute. Retrieved May 11, 2008, from http://www.itgi.org

IT Governance Institute (2006). *IT governance global status report - 2006.* IT Governance Institute. Retrieved May 11, 2008, from http://www.itgi.org

ITGI & PWC (2007). IT governance in practice: Insight from leading CIOs.

Jang, D. & Lee, J. (2005). A case study for the analysis of decision-making system of IT governance. In *Proceedings of the Korea Society of IT Services Conference*, Seoul, Korea.

Kose, J., & Senbet, L. (1998). Corporate governance and board effectiveness. *Journal of Banking and Finance, 22*, 371-403.

Lee, C., Lee, J., & Ahn, S. (2006). A comparative case study analysis of IT governance framework: Focused on the Korean service company. In *Proceedings of the 2006 IT Governance International Conference*, Auckland, New Zealand.

Letsoalo, K., Brown, I., & Njenga, K. N. (2006). An investigation of enablers and inhibitors of IT governance implementation: A case study of a South African enterprise. In *Proceedings of the 2006 IT Governance International Conference*, Auckland, New Zealand.

Lim, K., Lee, J., Rah, J., Yoon, S., & Lee, J. H. (2004). An empirical study on IT governance cognition and execution levels of Korean companies. *Entrue Journal of Information Technology, 13*(2), 111-123.

Loh, L., & Venkatraman, N. (1992). Diffusion of information technology outsourcing: Influence sources and the Kodak effect. *Information Systems Research, 3*(4), 334-359.

Luftman, J. (1996). *Competing in the information age: Practical applications of the strategic alignment model.* New York: Oxford University Press.

OECD (2004). OECD principles of corporate Governance, OECD.

Park, H., Jung, S., Lee, Y., & Jang, K. (2006). The effect of improving IT standard in IT governance. In *Proceedings of the International Conference on Computational Intelligence for Modeling Control and Automation(CIMCA06),* jointly with *International Conference on Intelligent Agents, Web Technologies and Internet Commerce(IAWTIC06)*, Sydney, Australia.

Park, J., Lee, J., & Lee, C. (2007). IT governance practices in telecommunication companies: A complex adaptive systems perspective. In *Proceedings of the International DSI Conference 2007*, Bangkok, Thailand.

Patel, N. V. (2003). An emerging strategy for e-business IT governance. In W. Van Grembergen (Ed.), *Strategies for Information Technology.* Hershey, PA: Idea Group Publishing.

Peterson, R., & Fairchild, A. M. (2003). Exploring the impact of electronic business readiness on leadership capabilities in information technology governance. In *Proceedings of the 39th Hawaii International Conference on System Sciences (HICSS)*, Hawaii: IEEE.

Peterson, R. (2004). Crafting information technology governance. *Information Systems Management, 21*(4), 7-23.

Posthumusa, S., & Solms, R. V. (2005). IT oversight: An important function of corporate governance. *Computer Fraud & Security, 2005*(6), 11-17.

Sambamurthy, V., & Zmud, R. W. (1999). Arrangements for information technology governance: A theory of multiple contingencies. *MIS Quarterly, 23*(2), 261-290.

Shleifer, A., & Vishny, W. (1997). A survey on corporate governance. *The Journal of Finance, 52*(2), 737-783.

Simonsson, M., & Johnson, P. (2006). *Defining IT governance–A consolidation of literature.* Working Paper of the Department of Industrial Information and Control Systems. Retrieved May 11, 2008, from www.ics.kth.se

Van Grembergen, W. (2003). Introduction to the minitrack: IT governance and its mechanisms. In *Proceedings of the 35th Hawaii International Conference on System Sciences(HICSS)*, Hawaii: IEEE.

Van Grembergen, W., & De Haes, S. (2005). Measuring and improving information technology governance through the balanced scorecard. *Information Systems Control Journal, 2*, 46-49.

Vishwanath, T., & Kaufmann, D. (1999). Toward transparency in finance and governance. *The World Bank Draft.*

Webb, P., Pollard, C., & Ridley, G. (2006). Attempting to define IT governance: Wisdom or folly? In *Proceedings of the 39th Hawaii International Conference on System Sciences(HICSS)*, Hawaii, IEEE.

Weill, P., & Vitale, M. (2002). What IT infrastructure capabilities are needed to implement e-business models? *MIS Quarterly, 1*(1), 17-34.

Weill, P., & Woodham, R. (2002). Don't just lead, govern: Implementing effective IT governance. *CISR Working Paper* (No. 326). Retrieved May 11, 2008, from http://dspace.mit.edu/bitstream/1721.1/1846/2/4237-02.pdf

Weill, P. (2004). Don't just lead, govern: How top-performing firms govern IT. *MIS Quarterly Executive, 3*(1), 1-17.

Weill, P., & Ross, J. W. (2004). *IT governance - How top performers manage IT decision rights for superior results.* Harvard Business School Press.

Vives, X. (Ed.) (2000). *Corporate governance: Theoretical & empirical perspectives.* Cambridge: Cambridge University Press.

Yin, R. K. (1984). Case study research: Design and methods. *Applied social research methods series* (Vol. 5). Sage Publication.

Chapter VIII
The Impact of ICT Governance within Australian Companies

Breanna O'Donohue
Deakin University, Australia

Graeme Pye
Deakin University, Australia

Matthew J. Warren
Deakin University, Australia

ABSTRACT

This chapter focuses upon the Australian Standard for the Corporate Governance of Information and Communication Technology (ICT) AS8015 (Standards Australia, 2005) and presents research findings that can be applied as recommendations to enhance the effective implementation of this Standard's principles within an organization. These recommendations relating to the principles outlined within the Standard concern such factors as, identifying and addressing issues surrounding the implementation of this Standard and the actions that could be undertaken to improve the effectiveness of ICT governance by sharply focusing upon the governance aspects of ICT within business, as opposed to the management aspect of ICT.

INTRODUCTION

This research investigates and identifies the organizational issues that surround the implementation of organizational governance of ICT, both within the business and in support of business strategies and goals, however before proceeding it is important to note that the terms "ICT governance" and "IT governance" are used interchangeably throughout this chapter, depending on the source being cited. Nevertheless, before investigating the issues that impact on organizational ICT governance, we must establish its genesis in relation to corporate governance and development as an associated governance discipline that is coming under greater focus due to recent public failures that have brought into sharp focus the issues of organizational governance and accountability.

Corporate governance is defined by the Organisation for Economic Cooperation and Development (OECD) as an activity which "involves a set of relationships between a company's management, its board, its shareholders and other stakeholders" (OECD, 2004), these recommendations were published in the OECD Principles of Corporate Governance (2004). These principles represent a common point of understanding between representative member countries and promote acceptable practices that assist business organizations to deliver transparent and informative reporting to shareholders and ensure boards of management are accountable for their actions (Witherell, 2004). The Australia Standard entitled *Good Governance Principles AS8000* (2003) is heavily based on the OECD principles of corporate governance and reflects the Australian perspective of corporate governance as concerned with conduct and relationships between company stakeholders (Standards Australia, 2003).

In relation to corporate governance, IT governance is a subset defined as "specifying the decision rights and accountability framework to encourage desirable behaviour in using IT" (Weill & Ross, 2004) and therefore, IT governance focuses on the governance of IT use within the particular organization. Van Grembergen (2004) further links IT governance to corporate governance by indicating that today's business and business strategies are now dependent to some extent on an underlaying IT infrastructure support. Therefore, corporate governance is responsible for setting high-level organizational strategies and controls, while IT governance provides the information and IT structure to facilitate strategic alignment and support of organizational goals. Furthermore, the linkage of IT governance and

corporate governance is more apparent because of the increasing dependence upon and utilisation of IT to support business operations, which can potentially expose and impinge adversely upon the critical functionality of the IT infrastructure supporting the business. This suggests that poor application of IT governance can affect corporate governance through loss of business, harm to corporate reputation and a weakening of competitive position (CPA, 2005).

This premise is supported by KPMG (2002) who found that IT failures accounted for 60% of all business interruptions in Australia, resulting in downtime, reduced income and loss of customers. There have also been a number of other cases in Australia and around the world where a lack of IT governance has resulted in significant financial losses. A further example is the widely reported situation at the National Australia Bank (NAB), here it found that employees were able to request changes to the IT systems that enabled them to erase records of their transactions and resulted in notable financial losses for the bank (Mair, 2004). In response to this and other failures of IT governance, a new Australian Standard within the AS8000 series, namely the Corporate Governance of ICT AS8015 (Standards Australia, 2005) was developed and released in early 2005. This standard consists of six principles applicable to the governance of ICT within a business organization and forms the initial reference point of this research.

This research seeks to investigate and identify corporate attitudes towards IT governance implementation within their organizations and also in comparison, the opinions of two industry professionals regarding their own professional experiences and attitudes towards the implementation of IT governance based on the Corporate Governance of ICT AS8015 (Standards Australia, 2005) standard. Initially, we will establish what IT or ICT governance specifically is and investigate some of the existing frameworks applicable to implementing a governance structure across an organization that takes into consideration IT, before progressing towards addressing IT governance in Australia and the Corporate Governance of ICT AS8015 (Standards Australia, 2005) standard itself. Then we will briefly outline the research questions and applied method of research, before providing a broad summation of our initial findings. With further elaboration regarding the specific recommendations that have arisen from our research concerning the implementation of IT governance and due diligence structures within Australian organizations, for which the findings may prove advantageous for those organizations considering future adoption of the Corporate Governance of ICT AS8015 (Standards Australia, 2005) standard.

BACKGROUND

Depending on the business situation and the perceived interpretations, there are various definitions of IT governance, each of which subtly encompasses different areas of the topic. For example, Van Grembergan (2004) states that "IT Governance is the organizational capacity exercised by the board, executive management and IT management to control the formulation and implementation of IT strategy and in this way ensure the fusion of business and IT." This definition highlights the role of the executive in ensuring governance of IT and the importance of ensuring alignment between business strategies set by the Board and the IT strategy itself.

Broadbent (2003) adopts a similar top-down focus for IT governance but proposes that good IT governance is the effective combination of three components: what decisions have to be made (leadership), who makes them (accountability) and how they are enacted (oversight). In this interpretation, the focus of accountability and decision making rights aligns closely to that of the Weill and Ross (2004) definition mentioned previously and is one of the more commonly adopted definitions within the literature.

The IT Governance Institute (ITGI) asserts that "IT governance is the responsibility of the Board of Directors and executive management and is an integral part of enterprise governance that consists of the leadership and organizational structures and processes that ensure that the organization's IT sustains and extends the organization's strategies and objectives" (ITGI, 2003). This definition includes the role of the Board and again the need for the alignment of IT aspirations with the organization's strategies and refers to leadership, organizational structures, and processes as a means of achieving this.

These views interpret IT governance differently, but commonality exists in the need to establish structure and processes that ensure appropriate leadership, accountability and oversight. We can now determine that IT governance leadership, relates to the setting of long term strategies for IT, and ensuring that goal alignment exists with those set by the organization that require frequent dialogue between the Board of Directors and the managers in the IT department (Alter, 2004). The accountability in IT governance, is the assigning of decision rights and creation of an accountability framework that encourages desirable behaviour in the use of the organization's IT (Weill & Ross, 2004), which includes definitions of organizational rules and regulations, who sets them and how compliance is monitored (ACS, 2005). Furthermore, IT governance can be concerned with the appraisal and critical review of major IT projects, technology architecture decisions (FedEx, 2005), the measurement metrics that quantify the performance of IT (Weill, 2003) as well as encompassing the management of technology-related business risks and determination of the financial value returned by enterprises' IT (ITGI, 2003).

Therefore, IT governance can be regarded as a business activity undertaken at high-level management that ensures: alignment of IT strategies with those of the business; ensures the responsible use of IT; clearly defines roles and accountabilities and continually monitors IT assets and projects to ensure they are performing effectively in support of the organization. However, the implementation of IT governance objectives and controls to address IT governance activities specifically, is not always immediately apparent, but there are a number of practical governance frameworks that can assist business organizations in the delivery of an effective governance structure that in-part incorporates IT governance.

CURRENT IT GOVERNANCE FRAMEWORKS

Factors such as the increased organizational controls implemented after the introduction of the Sarbanes Oxley (SOX) Act in the United States (U.S.) and the pressure on IT departments to demonstrate their contribution to the organization, are influencing directors to consider the value of a framework for the governance of IT. The use of a framework enforces a consistent approach throughout the organization and this delivers the ability to develop reports and apply measurements to gauge performance (Worthen, 2005).

The two primary IT governance frameworks are the American-based Control Objectives for Information Technology (COBIT) and the English-based Information Technology Infrastructure Library (ITIL). Both COBIT and ITIL are utilised extensively in the implementation of an IT governance framework within organizations but their individual focus remains broadly different. Generally, COBIT is utilized where there is a need for auditing functions, while the ITIL is better suited to operational process improvement (Alcyone Consulting, 2005).

COBIT

The Information Systems Audit and Control Association (ISACA) also established the IT Governance Institute (ITGI) to serve as a "think tank" *[sic]* for principles and concepts of IT

governance and instituted COBIT in 1998. This not-for-profit organization performed the original research on emergent IT governance issues and developed the COBIT framework that is globally recognised and adopted as a set of best practice and management guidelines for effective control of IT (Guldentops, 2004).

COBIT consists of several documents including an Executive Summary, Framework, Control Objectives, Audit Guidelines, Implementation Tool Set and Management Guidelines (ISACA, 2005). The main document is the Framework, which consists of thirty-four high level IT processes that come under 4 different control domains: planning and organization controls; acquisition and implementation controls; delivery and support controls and monitoring controls (Barnett, n.d.).

Each of these 34 organizational processes has a number of control objectives, with critical success factors that are required to successfully implement the process that incorporate specific numerical metrics that gauge improvements in quality and a maturity model to define the extent of business process automation. Altogether, these 34 processes can be further broken down into 318 specific control objectives for implementing the framework, including Key Goal Indicator and Key Performance Indicator measures as part of the continuous improvement cycle existing within the COBIT framework (Morency, 2005).

COBIT enables organizational wide implementation of IT governance through its strong top-down auditing and control perspective and has become particularly popular in the U.S. since the introduction of the SOX legislation, as its comprehensive framework now ensures SOX compliance-related regulations and legislations are adhered to within the organization (Symons, 2005).

Recently a new version of COBIT has been developed, COBIT 4.1 (ISACA, 2007), the new version of COBIT keeps the same structure of the earlier version. The new core content is divided according to the 34 IT processes. Each process is covered in four sections, combining to give a complete overview of how to control, manage and measure the process. The four sections for each process, in order, are (ISACA, 2007):

1. The high-level control objective for the process, which includes:
   - A process description summarizing the process objectives;
   - A high-level control objective represented in a waterfall summarizing process goals, metrics and practices;
   - The mapping of the process to the process domains, information criteria, IT resources and IT governance focus areas.
2. The detailed control objectives for the process;
3. Management guidelines: the process inputs and outputs, a RACI (Responsible, Accountable, Consulted and/or Informed) chart, goals and metrics;
4. The maturity model for the process.

The IT Governance areas have been expanded to cover the following areas (ISACA, 2007):

- *Strategic alignment* focuses on ensuring the linkage of business and IT plans, on defining, maintaining and validating the IT value proposition, and on aligning IT operations with enterprise operations;
- *Value delivery* is about executing the value proposition throughout the delivery cycle, ensuring that IT delivers the promised benefits against the strategy, concentrating on optimizing costs and proving the intrinsic value of IT;
- *Resource management* is about the optimal investment in, and the proper management of, critical IT resources: processes, people, applications, infrastructure and information. Key issues relate to the optimization of knowledge and infrastructure;

- *Risk management* requires risk awareness by senior corporate officers, a clear understanding of the enterprise's appetite for risk, transparency about the significant risks to the enterprise, and embedding of risk management responsibilities into the organization;
- *Performance measurement* tracks and monitors strategy implementation, project completion, resource usage, process performance and service delivery, using, for example, balanced scorecards that translate strategy into action to achieve goals measurable beyond conventional accounting.

However, with the updated version of COBIT it is still apparent that the governance practices are still directed towards maintaining and imposing governance from an organizational wide high-level perspective and less so on the lower level processes for delivering good governance practice.

ITIL

Conversely, the ITIL is a collection of best practices with an IT operational focus first developed by the British government some 20 years ago and has become the most widely used best practice reference for IT Service Management. Having long been preferred in Europe, ITIL is now gaining acceptance in the U.S. and other countries (ITIL, 2005), because ITIL delivers operational benefits to IT departments by enabling improved quality of service, reduced downtimes, swift resolution of problems and greater security (Worthen, 2005).

The ITIL framework consists of a series of eight books, each of which details a different aspect of the information framework required for implementation:

- Planning to Implement Service Management (Symons, 2005);
- The Business Perspective (Turbitt, 2005);

- Software Asset Management (Software Management Network, 2005);
- Service Support (Symons, 2005);
- Service Delivery (Mercury, 2005);
- Security Management (TSO, n.d.);
- ICT Infrastructure Management (OGC, 2005);
- Application Management (Symons, 2005).

ITIL is based upon the principles of service management and takes a bottom-up approach, while in comparison the COBIT focus is primarily a top-down, high-level focus on audit and control. As a result, these two frameworks tend to compliment each other with COBIT providing managerial processes and objectives that are applicable from the Board level perspective; whilst the ITIL delivers operational best practice that can be applied from the help desk level upwards in the implementation of IT governance within an organization (Symons, 2005).

In 2007 IITL was updated to reflect best practice within the industry. The main development was that V3 took a lifecycle approach to guidance, as opposed to organizing in accordance to IT delivery sectors. The ITIL V3 (ITIL Refreshed) framework consists of a series of five books in regards to implementation (ITIL, 2007):

- Service Strategy;
- Service Design;
- Service Transition;
- Service Operation;
- Continual Service Improvement.

While the ITIL framework is widely accepted from a European perspective to address IT governance issues, the Australian situation dictated that an alternative solution to addressing IT governance issues within business organizations should be managed with a different approach.

IT GOVERNANCE IN AUSTRALIA

The corporate failure of OneTel is an example where despite having spent large amounts of money on IT; good quality management information to support the business was not being produced. This highlights the fact that while IT can be functioning well on its own, a lack of goal alignment with the organizational strategic goals it is supporting is where problems can begin (Bushell, 2002). In response to this and similar events, together with the recent focus on IT governance, Australia became the first country in 2005 to formulate and publish a Standard addressing the governance of ICT to meet the concerns of ICT and business managers (ACS, 2005).

The Corporate Governance of ICT AS8015 (Standards Australia, 2005) standard is designed to be implemented in an organization of any size with the aim of providing guiding principles to Directors of such organizations to implement regarding the governance of their ICT. A "Director" could be an owner, board member, director, partner, senior executive, or similar depending on the titles of the relevant positions within an organization and its size (Standards Australia, 2005).

As described earlier in the chapter, ITIL and COBIT are two approaches that can be used to implement IT governance within organizations. The issues of such approaches is that they are generic and do not particularly suit the requirements of each individual country, the reason for developing ICT AS8015 is to target ICT governance with a uniquely Australian approach.

Principles of the Corporate Governance of ICT AS8015 Standard

This Australian Standard consists of six principles for promoting good corporate governance of ICT. The application of these principles is applicable to any organization regardless of size; however the implementation of them will differ slightly. The following list briefly outlines the six principles Standard (Standards Australia, 2005):

- Principle 1—Establish clearly understood responsibilities for ICT. The first principle addresses the need for Directors to clearly define the roles of people in their organization and ensure that they are responsible for their tasks as assigned.
- Principle 2—Plan ICT that best supports the organization. This principle relates to ensuring ICT plans are in line with the corporate plans, strategies and goals of the business.
- Principle 3—Acquire ICT validly. This principle relates to the acquisition of ICT components and ensuring that purchases will always provide value to the organization by following a defined process for each proposed acquisition.
- Principle 4—Ensure that ICT performs well, whenever required. This principle is concerned with the performance of ICT by ensuring user availability and that it supports the goals of the business.
- Principle 5—Ensure ICT conforms to formal rules. This principle addresses the issue of compliance with legislation, laws and industry standards as well as ensuring adherence to internal policies of the organization.
- Principle 6—Ensure ICT use respects human factors. The final principle addresses the issue of abiding by the needs of stakeholders within ICT process.

Lewis (2005) believes that this Standard will assist Directors in performing their responsibilities, through ensuring proper use of ICT, setting direction for IT specialists, allocating the resources needed for ICT, checking to see that ICT is providing what the organization requires, and providing leadership for the successful introduction of changes brought about by ICT. The Australian Computer Society (ACS) (2005) agreed, further emphasising that the Standard is to assist business directors with asking the appropriate governance questions of their respective IT departments, contractors and vendors to ensure adherence to the organization's governance values.

Therefore, in light of the introduction of the Australian Standard for the Corporate Governance of ICT (Standards Australia, 2005) this now presents a research opportunity to investigate the implementation of the ICT governance by Australian companies.

BASIC PRINCIPLES AND RECOMMENDATIONS

The aim of this research is to develop a number of recommendations that will assist Australian organizations with the implementation of the Australian Standard for the Corporate Governance of ICT AS8015 (Standards Australia, 2005), based on the responses to the following research questions:

- Which aspects of the AS8015 Standard do organizations find most difficult to implement?
- Which areas are being implemented at present?
- Which areas are being neglected?

In seeking answers to these questions the intention was to derive an understanding of the current situation and identify where improvements can assist with the implementation of the Corporate Governance of ICT AS8015 (Standards Australia, 2005) standard within business organizations. The findings from these supporting questions are used to further progress the investigation into the primary research question:

- How can organizations improve their implementation of ICT governance principles as recommended by Standards Australia?

In order to gather applicable research data, an attitudinal survey questionnaire and a set of targeted interviews would be the most appropriate approach to gather the information required to answer the research questions posed. The survey component of this research enabled the gathering of a wide range of views from various sized organizations throughout Australia, thus enabling conceptual generalisations to be drawn from the data collection in regard the ICT governance traits of the chosen organizations and facilitate the development of a broader characterisation of the adoption issues surrounding ICT governance, as situated within Australia.

The survey component consisted of two classes of organizational participants, namely SME's (Small to Medium Enterprises) and large organizations within Australia and from each of these two groups, 150 representatives were randomly chosen from the business directories within each class and forwarded the survey for completion. In return 37 responses were received equating to an overall survey response rate of 12.3% and of the 37 responses, only 10 identified themselves as SME's with the remaining 27 being from large organizations.

Following the survey a set of targeted interviews gathered more in-depth experiential information, allowing greater discussion and also enabling the ability to digress outside the interview structure to pursue subject perceptions more deeply. The interview subjects consisted of an IT governance software vendor representative and an IT professional body representative resulting in a total of 2 hours recorded interview material.

The interview research method chosen enabled that the anonymous information captured in the survey component could be utilised to enhance interview question content for deeper investigation during the interview process. This enabled a comparison of the various opinions of Australian organizations surveyed to those opinions of the interviewees from the IT governance software vendor and the IT professional body respectively.

OVERVIEW SUMMARY OF RESEARCH FINDINGS

The following summaries of the research findings give an overview of issues identified by the survey and the interview subjects in relation to the implementation of IT governance and indicates where commonality existed between the respondent data of the survey questionnaires and interviews.

The survey indicated that most organizations had basic processes in place that addressed each of the six principles of the Corporate Governance of ICT AS8015 (2005) standard. However, this did not necessarily mean that they have effective IT governance, as most of the answers given were from a management perspective rather than a governance perspective. Thus, highlighting some confusion as to whether the Standard is either addressing management as well as governance, or is too high level, vague and can therefore be misinterpreted. The IT professional body representative interviewee surmised that the difference between management and governance is the premise that it is the responsibility of governance to specify who the decision makers are, whilst it is management who actually take the decisions. The survey results indicated that some confusion between management and governance is common and that the contextual meaning of the terms is somewhat blurred. The IT governance software vendor interviewee indicated that this may be the result of the marketing campaigns for IT governance software tools, but also indicated in their interview that they do not necessarily see a difference between management and governance anyway.

However, as the majority of the survey questions were answered from a management perspective, the most informative IT governance question was the one which asked respondents, how they ensured that IT plans were in line with those of the organization? Whilst each respondent said that the business did have some kind of input into the process, less than half of the respondents explicitly stated that an IT representative met with the business to discuss IT planning.

Furthermore, the survey results also indicated a lack of interest or knowledge regarding IT governance from a SME perspective. There were few surveys returned from this demographic and those received, generally contained answers that either stated that such questions were irrelevant to them or that they did not have or need to have processes in place to address IT governance issues. This indicated that even though the Corporate Governance of ICT AS8015 (Standards Australia, 2005) standard is for organizations of all sizes, ICT governance was not applicable from a SME perspective. This finding was further supported by the IT professional body interviewee and the IT governance software vendor interviewee, who both mentioned that they believed IT governance, was much more important in larger organizations, because IT from the SME perspective was regarded less as a strategic asset and more as a cost burden to the business.

OUTCOME OF INTERVIEW FINDINGS AND COMPARISON

In summarising the interview findings, both interviewees identified similar barriers to the implementation of IT governance in larger organizations, with the main issue centring around that IT does not attract enough attention from senior management, which they thought was perhaps mostly due to their lack of education about IT. Therefore, without an understanding of how an investment in implementing IT governance can bring benefits to the organization, directors do not consider it a priority and will therefore invest time and funds elsewhere. The IT professional body interviewee also indicated that quite often there is no-one on the Board of Directors with sound IT expertise and therefore it becomes necessary to countenance IT advice to address the

board regularly. It can also be useful to bring in an external board member who can demonstrate the benefits of IT governance to the Board with examples from other organizations that indicate the benefits in language that they may understand and appreciate.

Another barrier identified was the apparent reliance of organizations on software and consultants to impose and implement IT governance for the organization, rather than in consultation with it. Both interviewees said that without initially changing the attitudes and culture within the organization and putting processes into place to support change, any plans developed by a consultant or software delivered would just sit on the shelf. These tools are part of the process, but cannot deliver the single answer to IT governance alone. The IT professional body interviewee said that software is very good at ensuring compliance, as it enables data tracking as proof of process adherence, but often lacks in the management performance area of IT governance. The software vendor interviewee believed that software could offer improvements in performance, but if attitudes and cultural changes were not forthcoming that encouraged people to embrace IT governance properly, then the underlying IT governance processes to which the software was tailored, would not work.

Responses to the survey and interviews indicated some problems with the Standard itself and highlighted the confusion often found between management and governance. The results of both the survey and interviews were further analysed for major findings and differences of opinion. These findings included the identification of a lack of knowledge surrounding IT governance, especially from a SME perspective. Another outcome was that getting the attention of the Board was a major barrier to championing IT governance, and that success depended on the changing of attitudes and culture within the organization, which consultants and software could not achieve alone.

While these summaries represent an overview of the research findings, deeper analysis of the survey and interview results presented two general recommendations that organizations can adopt to assist in promoting and establishing IT governance within an organization. Additionally, a number of relevant recommendations were identified that will assist an organization with the implementation of IT governance in concert with the Corporate Governance of ICT AS8015 (2005) standard.

IT Governance General Recommendations

The two general IT governance recommendations arising from this research study were that:

1. Organizations must regard IT as a strategic asset that is core to their business, to benefit commercially from the ICT Governance Standard principles;
2. When attempting to initiate cultural change in attitudes within the organization, this requires stakeholders' acceptance of governance principles and cannot be solely driven by consultants or software.

The intention of the general recommendations is to assist with the general implementation of IT governance within an organization and while they do not relate specifically to any of the Corporate Governance of ICT AS8015 (2005) standard principles, these recommendations can be used in conjunction with the Standard to improve and prepare the organization for the effective implementation of IT governance.

General Recommendation One

The survey responses revealed that in general terms SME businesses did not place a great focus on IT governance within their organizations and

therefore did not regard IT as a strategic asset. Whilst these organizations may benefit from the implementation of an IT governance framework or the Corporate Governance of ICT AS8015 (2005) standard, the cost of such a move may outweigh the benefit. SME's generally rely on IT for the day-to-day operations of the business rather than leveraging major organizational plans and competitive strategies. This is principally due to their lack of financial resources and expertise in this area and even for simple implementations of IT governance, the diversion of funds without a foreseeable return on investment is inappropriate as this money could be better utilised in core areas such as customer service or product development.

Conversely, in the majority of larger business organizations with a more complex IT architecture, there is often the budget, expertise and competitive pressure for IT to perform well and support organizational strategy as well as manage the day to day running of the business.

General Recommendation Two

IT governance can only work if it is embraced by all staff within the organization as attempting to instigate major changes within the organization will be met with resistance or ignored if people cannot see the benefits that the changes will bring. By involving stakeholders in the process of implementing an IT governance framework including people from different levels within the organization that are passionate, then people will to make decisions to ensure that the IT governance processes are strategically appropriate, supported and that everyone understands the value of governance for IT goal alignment with organizational goals. This ensures that IT governance is more likely to be successful when adopted in this manner rather than if new rules and processes are imposed upon staff by consultants or software products.

ICT Governance Specific Recommendations

After deeper analysis of the survey and interview results, several key points were identified that are listed as further specific recommendations that are designed to act as a companion to the standard principles to improve the effectiveness of their adoption and are discussed in further detail in relation to the six principles alluded to in the Corporate Governance of ICT AS8015 (Standards Australia, 2005) standard.

Principle 1—Establish Clearly Understood Responsibilities for ICT

Assigning decision rights accountabilities was identified by the IT professional body interviewee as one of the fundamental areas of IT governance and indicated that if this was followed through, then other areas such as goal alignment, compliance and performance would also fall into line.

Recommendation: Clearly Define the Areas where Decisions should be Made

Prior to delegation of decision rights, the areas where decisions are required must be identified with boundaries established. Weill and Ross (2004) clearly identify the following areas in which IT decisions must be made: IT Principles; IT Infrastructure Strategies; IT Architecture; Business Application Needs, and IT investment and Prioritisation. These decision domains are applicable in most organizations; some modifications may be made where appropriate, as different sized organizations have different levels of focus upon IT.

Recommendation: Discuss and Determine Who is Accountable for each Area of Decision Making

The research suggested that the best decisions about who should be accountable for each area were most effective when a group of the related stakeholders were able to hold passionate discussions raising any suggestions and develop a consensus decision that addresses the issues. Even though the ultimate decision lies with Directors, this consensus method was preferred, rather than having a delegated group of people dictate IT decisions, because the consensus decision management style drew on the knowledge and expertise of all decision area stakeholders as opposed to a few.

Recommendation: Implement an Exception Process

After the identification of decision areas and the assignment of accountabilities, an exception process will enable dispute resolution and enable decisions where the current processes do not suit a particular problem. Having an exception process enhances the refinement of IT governance, ensuring controlled flexibility and the opportunity to identify and address governance weaknesses and enhance the governance process.

Principle 2—Plan ICT to Best Support the Organization

The survey result analysis indicated that the large organizations surveyed claimed that the business had an influence over the decisions made regarding IT. Most indicated that business plans dictated IT plans and generally IT plans had to go through an approval process before implementation. Although many survey respondents said the business exerted control over IT, very few indicated from what knowledge base their decision-makers had taken their technical decisions, thus casting doubt on the apparent level of IT knowledge, expertise, and understanding.

Recommendation: Bring in External Board Members to Address Lack of IT Knowledge

The limited IT knowledge of some Board members or decision-makers can inhibit the adoption of IT governance, because they simply do not fully understand or comprehend the benefits that IT can offer their organization. Whilst IT representatives may have the opportunity to address the Board, they are unable to offer truly objective advice, as there is a perceived biased related to the IT departmental functions of their job. Seconding an external Board member or independent advisor with IT knowledge can address this issue in two ways. First the external person can bring advice, past experience and expertise to the business and offer examples of success that educate and inform the Board of Directors and secondly if there is no affiliation with the organization, they can offer truly independent advice without fear or favor.

Recommendation: Allow IT Representatives to Address the Board Regularly

Whilst the CIO does not necessarily require a seat on the Board of Directors, the Board still needs to know what their IT department is doing by ensuring that channels of communication are open, therefore a representative from the IT department of the organization should have a regular opportunity to update the board.

Principle 3—Acquire ICT Validly

The data analysis revealed that this principle identified as a management issue rather than as a governance issue. The respondent from the IT professional body believed that whilst assigning a party to make decisions about the procure-

ment process is management, ensuring directive adherence is governance and the specification of a process for acquisition and enforcement of this is the job of IT manager. This research did not offer any additional recommendations for the implementation of this principle.

Principle 4—Ensure that ICT Performs Well, whenever Required

Ensuring that IT performs well is a management issue rather than a governance issue. For example, it is not the job of the Board of Directors to ensure that there is sufficient data storage space on the system or to identify that technical capabilities are not performing or need upgrading. However, it is their job to ensure that the people who are accountable for these decisions are making valued decisions and following the governance checks to continue making good decisions so that IT can perform well whenever it is required.

Recommendation: Ensure that there are Tools that Provide Accurate Reporting on IT Performance

Whilst IT governance is an activity accompanied by changes in people and processes, measures must be in place to report and accurately appraise IT performance against the set performance indicators. Although directors are generally not interested in the lower level statistics, as it is the job of management to rectify these issues, being able to identify which areas are having problems enables them to see weaknesses in their decision-making processes and address these to improve performance. The large organizations surveyed indicated that they found ensuring performance to be the most difficult aspect of the Corporate Governance of ICT AS8015 (2005) standard, as there is no performance criteria stipulated. However, by having sufficient monitoring in place, the identification of problem areas becomes easier, thus enabling organizations to decide how to address these issues.

Principle 5—Ensure ICT Conforms with Formal Rules

According to the IT professional body interviewee, IT governance is about two things: performing and conforming. This principle of the Corporate Governance of ICT AS8015 (Standards Australia, 2005) standard deals with conforming, to internal business rules and external regulations. It is therefore essential that competent people are accountable for each area in the IT governance framework as this recommendation expands upon.

Recommendation: Ensure that Decisions Follow the Specified Framework to Ensure Accountability

Once a decision-making framework is in place, it is important that there is adherence to responsibly obligations and that careful consideration given to who are the most appropriate people to be accountable for each decision domain, failure to follow this may result in inexperienced people making poor decisions without having all the required knowledge. Additionally, enforcement of the decision-making processes within the organization can also reduce the risk of poor decisions by performing a regular governance audit on the process. This aims to highlight variation from the decision framework and allow directors to look at reasons for this, redress the issue and make possible amendments to the governance framework to overcome this problem.

Principle 6—Ensure ICT Use Respects Human Factors

The determination of appropriate recommendations related to this Corporate Governance of ICT AS8015 (Standards Australia, 2005) standard principle was not particularly forthcoming from the research conducted. However, as the interviewee from the IT professional body pointed out, this is a strange principle to have on an IT governance standard, as it is more like a core value most organizations that should apply to everything, not just IT.

The recommendations developed from this research have yet to be tested; this would form the basis of future research. In an organization considering implementing the Standard, two approaches are applicable here: an experimental or action research approach. Experimental research can be utilised to compare results between two organizations implementing the Corporate Governance of ICT AS8015 (Standards Australia, 2005) standard, one which has the recommendations from this research to utilize as a guide, and one which does not.

This kind of research could be useful to determine and measure the true value of the recommendations uncovered in this research. Utilising an action research approach would enable the refinement of these recommendations by having a researcher become involved in the implementation of the ICT governance Standard (Australian Standards, 2005) and following the effect of the recommendations drawn from this research. Any flaws discovered in the recommendations would be addressed through cyclical improvement until the IT governance structure is working effectively. Application of either of these approaches will determine the effectiveness of the recommendations developed in this research in a practical IT governance environment, but this element of the research still remains to be undertaken.

CONCLUSION

The major outcome of this research was a set of two general and seven specific principle recommendations to accompany the Corporate Governance of ICT AS8015 (Standards Australia, 2005) standard and improve its implementation. Originally it was planned that the recommendations would be developed for each of the six Corporate Governance of ICT AS8015 (Standards Australia, 2005) principles, however as this research progressed and greater understanding of the topic increased, it was realised that implementing certain recommendations would automatically result in improvement in the other principles being addressed.

The principles in the ICT Governance Standard (Australian Standards, 2005) have a high-level, top-down organizational focus and as the survey results indicated this can be easily misinterpreted. The recommendations developed in this study intentionally point an organization towards the important aspects of the topics that each of the governance principles addresses to ensure that the focus is on the governance of ICT rather than its operational management, to ensure maximum benefit.

REFERENCES

Alcyone Consulting (2005). *Getting in-control—Combining COBIT and ITIL for IT governance and process excellence.* Retrieved May 11, 2008, from http://www.technologyexecutivesclub.com/PDFs/ArticlePDFS/GettingInControl.pdf

Alter, A. E. (2004). *Richard Nolan: A committee of one's own.* Retrieved May 11, 2008, from http://www.cioinsight.com/print_article/0,1406,a=119427,00.asp

ACS (2005). ACS news. *Information Age, 15*(24).

Barnett, D. (n.d.). *Compliance framework and risk management for IT.* Retrieved May 11, 2008, from http://www.isaca.org/complianceframeworkv3

Broadbent, M. (2003). *The right combination.* Retrieved May 11, 2008, from http://www.cio.com.au/index.php/id;1043227491;fp;4;fpid;379170742

Bushell, S. (2002). *Lines of authority.* Retrieved May 11, 2008, from http://www.cio.com.au/index.php/id;1191641618;fp;4;fpid;9

CPA (2005). *No need to be savvy to practice IT governance.* Retrieved May 11, 2008, from http://www.cpaaustralia.com.au/cps/rde/xchg/SID-3F57FEDF-FAD610FA/cpa/hs.xsl/1019_16232_ENA_HTML.htm

FedEx (2005). *Committee charter, FedEx.* Retrieved May 11, 2008, from http://ir.fedex.com/governance/committeechar.cfm

Guldentops, E. (2004). *COBIT: Best practices in support of IT governance and regulatory Compliance.* Retrieved May 11, 2008, from http://www.disif.dk/information/COBIT_181104.pdf

ISACA (2005). *COBIT, ISACA.* Retrieved May 11, 2008, from http://www.isaca.org/COBIT

ISACA (2007). *COBIT 4.1. ISACA.* Retrieved May 11, 2008, from http://www.isaca.org/COBIT

ITGI (2003). *Board briefing on IT governance* (2nd ed.). Rolling Meadows, IL.

ITIL (2005). *What is ITIL?* Retrieved May 11, 2008, from http://www.itil.co.uk/faqs.htm#11

ITIL (2007). ITIL lifecycle publication suite (ITIL v3 - Complete Library). TSO, ISBN 10: 011331051X.

KPMG (2002). Delivering information 24x7. *Consumer Markets Newsletter,* (9).

Lewis, E. (2005). Australian world-first ICT governance standard. *The Global Standard, March,* 8-9.

Mair, P. (2004). *Psych up your culture.* Retrieved May 11, 2008, from http://www.cfoweb.com.au/freearticle.aspx?relId=9474

Mercury (2005). *Service delivery.* Retrieved May 11, 2008, from http://www.mercury.com/us/solutions/governance/itil/service-delivery/

Morency, J. (2005). *Best practice, practice, practice.* Retrieved May 11, 2008, from http://www.networkworld.com/research/2005/011005COBIT.html

OECD (2004). *OECD principles of corporate governance.* Retrieved May 11, 2008, from http://www.oecd.org/dataoecd/32/18/31557724.pdf

OGC (2005). ICT infrastructure management. Retrieved May 11, 2008, from http://www.ogc.gov.uk/sdtoolkit/deliveryteam/briefings/ITIL/itilchap7.html

Software Management Network (2005). *ITIL.* Retrieved May 11, 2008, from http://www.softwaremanagement.com/Publications/infra-structure.html

Standards Australia (2003). *Good governance principles, AS800-2003.* Sydney: Standards Australia International.

Standards Australia (2005). *Corporate governance of information and communication technology, AS8015-2005.* Sydney: Standards Australia International.

Symons (2005). *IT governance framework.* Retrieved May 11, 2008, from http://i.i.com.com/cnwk.1d/html/itp/Forr051103656300.pdf

TSO (n.d.). *Security management.* Retrieved May 11, 2008, http://itil.tso.co.uk/security_management.html

Turbitt (2005). *ITIL – The business perspective approach.* Retrieved May 11, 2008, from http://www.itsmwatch.com/itil/article.php/3530621

Van Grembergen, W. (2004). *Strategies for information technology governance.* Hershey, PA: Idea Group Publishing.

Weill, P. (2003). *Don't just lead, govern!* Retrieved May 11, 2008, from http://www.csbs.org/pr/presentations/2003/AMC2003_Weill_DontJustLead-Govern.pdf

Weill, P., & Ross, J. W. (2004). *IT governance.* Boston: Harvard Business School Press.

Witherell, B. (2004). *Corporate governance: Stronger principles for better market integrity.* Retrieved May 11, 2008, from http://www.oecdobserver.org/news/fullstory.php/aid/1231/Corporate_governance:_Stronger_principles_for_better_market_integrity.html

Worthen, B. (2005). *ITIL power.* Retrieved May 11, 2008, http://www.cio.com/archive/090105/itil_frameworks.html?page=1

Chapter IX
Improving ICT Governance:
A Radical Restructure Using
CobiT and ITIL

Mark Toleman
University of Southern Queensland, Australia

Aileen Cater-Steel
University of Southern Queensland, Australia

Brian Kissell
University of Southern Queensland, Australia

Rob Chown
University of Southern Queensland, Australia

Michael Thompson
University of Southern Queensland, Australia

ABSTRACT

Acting upon the recommendations of a review of information and communications technology (ICT) governance and services at USQ, a major restructure was effected merging ICT units previously scattered across the university. The new Division of ICT Services embodies both CobiT and ITIL principles. To ensure the radical change was managed professionally, a change manager was seconded to the project. The value and importance of this role was underestimated and in retrospect it was removed too early. With the new structure now in place, a single service desk has been implemented and service level agreements have been formulated. This chapter describes the new reporting structure of the Division of ICT Services, the internal structure, the goals of the Division and how they align with the USQ corporate goals. Care was taken to ensure that the new ICT structure was logical and conducive to operational effectiveness, efficiency and sound ICT governance. The new structure provides pathways and opportunities for career progression, reflects a client focus and provides role delineation and functional accountability.

INTRODUCTION

Recent corporate scandals such as HIH in Australia, and Enron and Worldcom in the United States have raised the importance of corporate governance and prompted governments to provide guidelines to reduce risks to shareholders, employees and consumers (Holloway, 2004). In the United States, the Sarbanes-Oxley Act 2002 introduced stringent corporate governance requirements. Organizations around the world are following the lead of the U.S. and focusing on corporate governance (Peterson, 2003). Organizations are establishing IT governance to ensure that IT is aligned with the objectives of the organization (Sledgianowski, Luftman & Reilly, 2006). Recently, poor IT governance was blamed for three failed Australian IT projects at OneTel, Sydney Water and RMIT (Avison, Gregor & Wilson, 2006). IT governance includes leadership, organizational structures, and processes to ensure that the organization's IT sustains and extends the organization's strategy (Sallé, 2004). A sustainable IT governance implementation framework is proposed by De Haes and Van Grembergen (2005) focusing on structures, processes and relational mechanisms where structures involve the existence of responsible functions such as IT executives and a diversity of IT committees. Processes refer to strategic decision making and monitoring using tools such as the IT balanced scorecard. The relational mechanisms include business/IT participation, strategic dialogue, shared learning, and proper communication.

The importance of having the correct organizational structure has been stressed by many researchers (for example Csaszar & Clemons, 2006). It is important to decide which form of structure is the most effective: centralised, federal, or decentralised (Peterson, 2003). Peterson claims the federal model offers the "best of both worlds" but can be difficult to implement as it "challenges managers in local business units to surrender control over certain business-specific

IT domains for the well-being of the enterprise" (Peterson, 2003, p. 47).

Sustainable ICT governance also relies on effective communication and knowledge sharing which can be achieved by a good participative collaborative relationship between business and the IT department (Van Grembergen, De Haes & Guldentops, 2003). Furthermore, it is vital to align the ICT strategies, investments and activities with the objectives of the organization (Luftman, 2004).

The aim of this chapter is to provide a detailed account of the changes brought about in a large organization to improve ICT governance. This chapter firstly provides background information related to the University of Southern Queensland (USQ) and its ICT resources, and the findings of a recent ICT review. The review resulted in major changes which are then described. The outcomes and results to date are then summarized. The final section identifies future directions and provides a conclusion focusing on the critical success factors of the restructure.

BACKGROUND

In 2006, USQ reported a total number of 25,900 student enrollments contributing to 12,249 equivalent full-time student load (EFTSL). Of these, 21,238 studied externally and 4,662 studied on-campus. All students have access to online study materials and learning management systems. Enterprise Resource Planning systems include the Peoplesoft modules for Student Administration, Human Resources and Finance. In addition to the main Toowoomba campus, the University operates integrated satellite campuses at Springfield (Brisbane) and Fraser Coast. The complex network infrastructure operates on a high-speed optic fibre backbone, servicing approximately 2600 PCs and 200 Macintosh staff and student laboratory computers from 250 servers, via 190 network devices.

An ICT Review Committee was established in May 2004 operating under broad terms of reference aimed at ensuring that the University's ICT governance and services meet the needs of staff, students and all stakeholders to a high standard, while at the same time being cost effective. The ICT Review Committee found a clear need for significant change to USQ's approach to ICT governance. An effective overarching ICT governance framework did not exist; decisions in ICT were not made strategically or linked with institutional strategy; effective planning and review processes were not in place; effective project and assets management were not practiced; the funding and procurement processes for ICT were seriously flawed; siloing, duplication, and general inefficiencies were clearly evident; and the relationship between some ICT staff in different sections of the University was strained.

Based on its extensive analysis, the ICT Review Committee made a large number of recommendations (53) aimed at establishing a sound ICT governance framework for USQ and reforming ICT services and practice. Many of the recommendations carried with them resource implications. As ICT expenditure represents at least ten percent of USQ's overall expenditure and ICT staffing costs represent around ten percent of USQ's total salary budget, the negative impact of USQ lacking an effective ICT governance framework, in terms of financial returns, operational efficiency and staff morale, is immense. The benefits of correcting this situation warranted the degree of change proposed.

Peterson defines IT Governance architecture as "the manner in which responsibilities and accountabilities for the IT portfolio are organised and integrated" (2003, p. 61). As shown in Figure 1, the ICT Strategy Committee is at the heart of USQ's ICT governance architecture, performing the role of steering committee. Previous research by Karimi, Bhattacherjee, Gupta, and Somers (2000) indicates that IT management capability is enhanced by steering committees. They found

that as well as giving visibility of IT initiatives, steering committees provide strategic direction, leadership and control of IT operations and management, resolve resource allocation decisions, and ensure top management support for IT activities.

USQ's ICT Strategy Committee is responsible for providing the strategic direction of information and communication technology (ICT) within the University, and ensuring the alignment of ICT and the University Strategic Plan. This committee coordinated and monitored the implementation of the recommendations of the ICT Review process, ensuring the establishment of good ICT strategic planning processes to secure alignment with the University's strategic directions. It regularly monitors the alignment of the ICT Strategic Plan with the University Strategic Plan and provides advice, on an annual basis, to the Vice-Chancellor on the funding for core ICT services to be allocated "off the top" of the University budget. The ICT Strategy Committee is chaired by the vice-chancellor, effectively the CEO of the organization. Raghunathan (1992) found that the CEO participation on the IT steering committee improves alignment with organizational plans, the perceived importance of IT, and its effectiveness. Other members of the ICT Strategy Committee include the most senior ranking executives of the University: chief information officer (CIO), deputy vice-chancellor (Scholarship), pro-vice-chancellor (learning and teaching), pro-vice-chancellor (planning and quality), pro-vice-chancellor (research), general manager university services, group manager finance and facilities, chief technology officer (CTO), a nominee from industry with ICT expertise.

The ICT Business Advisory Committee (also shown in Figure 1) reports to the USQ ICT Strategy Committee and is the delegated body, representative of the USQ Community, and tasked with considering and providing advice on the appropriateness of ICT architectures and the adoption of ICT technologies.

The degree of change being proposed had the potential to generate concern and opposition from certain members of staff and change management needed to be handled with sensitivity. Part of the malaise in ICT governance at USQ related to the development of a dysfunctional culture which had become deeply entrenched over many years. Changing this culture was to be assisted by carefully managed changes to structures and frameworks, as well as to processes and paradigms. Staff were reassured throughout the process that changes would be managed in ways that were inclusive, fair, and sensitive to their concerns and needs.

A commitment was made by the University that there would be no direct job losses or redundancies resulting from the change process. The timetable for change had to be appropriately paced; requiring sustained effort over a three-to-five-year period to be fully realized.

Key recommendations of the review included the creation of a common reporting structure for all core ICT staff through the establishment of a Division of ICT Services and the implementation of a formal ICT governance framework based around Control objectives for information and related Technology (CoBiT) and the Information Technology Infrastructure Library (ITIL). A

Figure 1. ICT governance structure at USQ

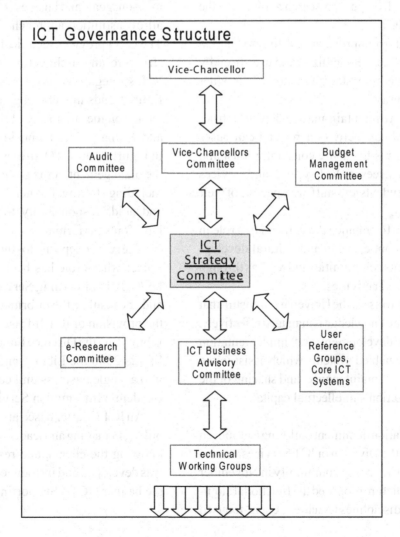

formal change management process based on the principles of inclusion, consultation and openness commenced in August 2005.

The USQ ICT Strategic Plan 2005 -2009 set the following key goals for ICT systems and services aligned to the USQ Strategic direction statement:

- **Goal 1:** To ensure ICT systems and services align with the University's strategic and operational directions.
- **Goal 2:** To integrate ICT, in a strategically planned, systematically integrated and institutionally comprehensive manner, into all aspects of the learning and teaching environment.
- **Goal 3:** To support research activity via the use of ICT.
- **Goal 4:** To improve access to information via flexible, personalized and user-friendly ICT systems for staff, students and the wider community.
- **Goal 5:** To maintain and develop infrastructure and connectivity across all campuses and centres to ensure constant, robust and efficient access to ICT systems and services for all students and staff, irrespective of their location.
- **Goal 6:** To enhance the University's role in the economic, social and cultural development of its communities and regions through ICT-based activities.
- **Goal 7:** To assist the University to ensure that corporate knowledge is managed effectively, via the development and implementation of ICT-enabled systems which assist in the collection, maintenance, and sharing of the organization's intellectual capital.

A consultation document outlining a proposed structure for the Division of ICT Services was released to the University community in November 2005. The structure proposed the functional alignment of ICT disciplines to achieve client-focused service delivery. This included establishment of virtual support teams and their alignment with ICT products and services, levels of cross-unit accountability and delegation (matrix management), establishment of service level agreements and the formalisation of existing project team environments within a formal project management framework. The proposed structure (Figure 2) was subsequently endorsed by the ICT Strategy Committee and the Vice-Chancellor's Committee in December 2005.

The chief technology officer (CTO) is responsible for providing leadership in developing and maintaining standardised ICT architecture and solutions for the University's ICT infrastructure, to support the achievement of the University's vision, mission, goals and business objectives through an all-of-institution approach to ICT provisioning. The CTO provides technical input on ICT infrastructure and architecture for the University's ICT strategic and operational plans, identifies future trends in technology and provides expert advice on the suitability of these technologies in addressing University business needs. As shown in Figure 2, the CTO also provides leadership of the management of the Division of ICT Services including staffing, financial and other resources, and holds responsibility for the quality of the Division's performance.

The CTO reports to the chief information officer whose role has been integrated with the DVC Global Learning Services role to converge and encapsulate the information focus relating to the provision of ICT Infrastructure and support, Library and the Distance Education Centre (DeC). In mid 2006 the Library and DeC were merged into a single business unit called the Division of Academic Information Services.

An ICT Charter based around four foundation pillars; managing and leadership, communication, knowing the clients, and resource management was developed and introduced in July 2006 under the banner "ICT - Supporting your success."

Figure 2. Management positions in division of ICT services organisational structure

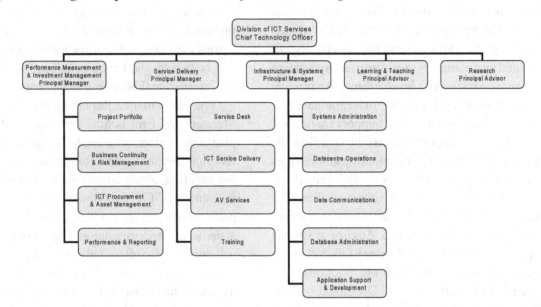

ACTIONS TAKEN

To implement the ICT charter, USQ adopted a federal ICT management model bringing about significant cultural and organizational change. Barriers and technology silos have been broken down; ICT service delivery harmonised; the ICT service and support paradigm has been changed to one recognising the value and personal contributions of staff; service management is proactive, not reactive, self assessing and constantly seeking opportunities for improvement; effective communication has been achieved, strengthening and maintaining partnerships. The end result is that client focus is the mantra and service delivery is aligned with business. This section details the actions taken to implement the new federal structure and the new measurement and management processes used.

Implementation of New Structure

An ICT Communications Advisory Group was established to enable effective communication of information about the change process to staff. The group included representation from faculties and organizational units identified in the ICT Review, along with trade union representatives. Separate meetings were held with trade union representatives and on-campus delegates from three trade unions. The chief technology officer (CTO), change manager and Human Resources were actively involved in ensuring all parties remained informed throughout the change process.

Four planning workshops were held to involve staff in the planning process. The workshops, attended by 116 staff, included the identification of values and attributes for the new Division, and the establishment of an outline of the functional service and system alignment required. A further two planning sessions were held with smaller groups of staff to progress development of the organizational structure for the Division.

A single University-wide service desk was established in May 2006 for ICT support adopting a highly visible Information Commons approach. The service desk provides the first line of staff and student help desk support (face-to-face, telephone, e-mail, and Web) for ICT related problems or queries. A number of staff from within the Division of ICT Services are now located in faculties and operational units across the Toowoomba, Fraser Coast and Springfield campuses with "dotted line" reporting to respective faculty and organizational unit managers to ensure user expectation is managed and service levels are met. An innovative approach sees third year undergraduate ICT students employed as "ICT Support Daemons" to assist ICT Support Officers in ensuring the operational capability of computing laboratories and student access computers is maintained.

To ensure stakeholder involvement from the academic community, the new Divisional structure includes two Principal Advisor positions reporting to the Chief Technology Officer. These are academic positions that are fractional and funded from within the ICT Divisional budget. The positions focus on research computing and the learning and teaching environment. These positions are filled on a fixed-term basis via secondments from within the University. Principal Advisors participate in Divisional planning exercises and assist the Chief Technology Officer to develop strategies for the effective deployment of ICT within the research, learning, and teaching environments at USQ.

The Information Systems Delivery Unit provides support for enterprise ICT systems and services. The structure of this Unit provides clear delineation of service delivery across ICT disciplines to improve the efficiency of service delivery and increase accountability. A matrix management model of service delivery is implemented, where virtual teams are assembled when and as required to enable effective functional service delivery based on the ICT disciplines required for the specific task.

Measurement

A capability maturity assessment using the CoBiT methodology was carried out in late 2005 and resulted in USQ assessing itself at level 1 or 2 on most criteria. Estimates were made using a "lowest common denominator" or "weakest link" approach. Various control objectives are almost at the next level and in many cases it will not require a great deal of effort to improve the maturity by one or two levels, hence equalling or bettering the international benchmark averages.

The Performance Reporting and Investment Management Unit is now providing a strategic planning, performance analysis and monitoring, risk management, audit compliance and reporting function, along with ensuring the return on investment of ICT is maximised through effective procurement processes and lifecycle management. A dedicated Performance and Reporting Analyst was appointed to effectively analyse, monitor and report against all aspects of operational performance of the Division. This includes operational and financial performance, compliance with service level agreements and establishing activity-based cost models and total cost of ownership for ICT functions, services and infrastructure. A project-based research function is also proposed within this area and this is expected to be filled by a postgraduate student or an academic.

The USQ staff performance planning and review system (BUILD) was implemented within the Division of ICT Services and commenced in March 2006 in concert with the appointment of staff to key management positions.

Three surveys were conducted during October and November 2005. A student ICT satisfaction online survey was conducted to give students an opportunity to rate their satisfaction with ICT services and provide an overall picture of ICT service provision and performance. This first survey will be used as a benchmark for future surveys to allow a process of continuous improvement in ICT at the university. In total, 953 responses were received, representing 8% of the student population of 12,000 EFTSU. A staff ICT Satisfaction Survey was also carried out during this period. 371 usable responses were received, representing 26.5 percent of staff FTE population of 1400. A self assessment Skills Review Survey was conducted with 135 surveys submitted by staff identified in the Review as having ICT responsibilities. This information was used to inform the change process and to identify professional development requirements.

In addition to the two academic advisor positions established within the Division of ICT Services, a student reference group will be established to provide advice to the chief technology officer. A focus group comprising undergraduate and postgraduate students with representation from on campus and off campus students (national and international) met during late 2006 providing student input into ICT planning and a direct feedback mechanism for user satisfaction. In 2007 the focus group will transition into a formal reference group to be established under the auspice of the Dean of Students.

Management Structure

The structure of the Division of ICT Services was designed to create an organizational hierarchy which establishes clear role delineation and functional accountability, while also providing pathways for individual career progression. The structure is based on the functional alignment of ICT disciplines to achieve client focused service delivery and in this regard there remain a number of operational practicalities to be considered. These include establishment of virtual support teams and their alignment with ICT products and services, levels of cross-unit accountability and delegation, documentation of processes, establishment of service level agreements and formalization of existing project team environments that will take a number of months to fully implement. Implementation of the proposed structure necessitated transitional arrangements including adopting a phased approach to the integration of ICT support staff located in faculties, sections, and in project roles.

Direct reporting relationships have been established for each position with the aim of a maximum of six direct operational ICT reporting relationships to each line management position (excluding secretarial and administrative roles). Where there are a large number of operational support staff within a functional business unit, teams have been established with Team Leaders or Senior Support positions.

The virtual team approach adopted within the proposed structure offers the capability to develop a number of common position descriptions for roles including analyst programmer and ICT support officer. This enables horizontal position portability across the structure and reduces the management workload associated with maintaining a large volume of individual position descriptions.

The ICT support function replaced the former desktop support model within ITS which segmented staff and student support environments. ICT Support Officers now provide a single resource pool of ICT staff to support the computing environment for staff and students. ICT support staff located within faculties and operational units can be backfilled and further supported when required from the central resource pool. ICT support officers are progressively rotated to ensure knowledge transfer of local environments. Responsibility for maintaining agreed service levels and coordination of service delivery is managed by dedicated ICT service delivery coordinators.

The former technical services team in the Distance and e-Learning Centre was an integral component to delivery of audio visual support services to lecture theatres, training and meeting rooms across USQ campuses. ICT support staff within information technology services (ITS) and at remote campuses carried out various aspects of these services and also supported the computing, networking and video conferencing capabilities within each environment. The new structure merged the technical services team into the Division of ICT Services, integrating and aligning service delivery functions within the Client Delivery Unit.

The Application Support and Development Unit operates as a virtual team of ICT support resources located across the Toowoomba, Springfield and Fraser Coast campuses, supporting core ICT applications across the University enterprise environment and participating in application development activities as members of formal project teams.

OUTCOMES AND RESULTS

By October 2006, all management positions within the division had been filled and the majority of staff had moved into their new roles. Service level agreements (SLAs) have been signed with the Faculties of Arts, Sciences, Engineering and Surveying, Business and the Division of Information and Academic Services.

Substantial progress had been achieved in a relatively short time frame:

- An executive management team comprising the principal managers and chief technology officer has been established and meets on a weekly basis. An ICT management team comprising line managers meets on a monthly basis.
- The positions of principal advisor learning and teaching and principal advisor research computing have been filled.
- The service desk has been colocated into a "One Stop Shop" with the Distance Education Centre, Switchboard and Customer Relationship Management Centre.
- Client service training has been carried out for staff within the service desk and an ICT client charter launched.
- An internal marketing campaign has been initiated to raise the profile of the division of ICT services and initiatives such as the inaugural Indigenous Intensive ICT workshop successfully facilitated.

- A formal ICT project management methodology has been developed and implemented, with the University using this as the basis for a whole of University project management methodology.
- ITIL Foundations training was completed by 97 ICT staff from across the University. 17 Senior Managers of the University attended a half day overview of the ITIL framework. An additional 29 staff who had ICT related jobs attended a one day overview of ITIL.
- The ICT Procurement and Asset management unit is in place and operational, assisting with the development and implementation of a new procurement model for USQ.
- The ICT governance framework has progressed to the point where User Reference Groups for core ICT systems are operational. Relationship managers are being identified within the division to function as the key liaison between faculties and departments as part of the implementation of SLAs. Figure 3 shows how the various ICT service delivery interfaces link.
- As shown in Figure 1, the ICT Business Advisory Committee has been established. Technical working groups are progressing a University e-mail solution, printing strategy, standard operating environment (SOE) for hardware and software, and video conferencing and Internet collaboration. Technology roadmaps are being developed for core ICT systems and services.
- The USQ ICT Strategic Plan has been updated for 2007 to 2011 and funding models implemented for infrastructure refresh programs and to meet recurrent expenditure associated with the nonsalary component of core ICT systems.

After the initial radical restructuring, the pace of change slowed. As at mid 2007, it is evident

Figure 3. ICT service delivery interface

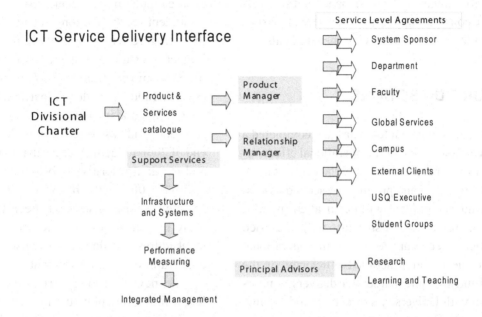

that the ICT changes are positioning the University on the right footing but progress is slower than anticipated. ICT is now more visible and accountable through the introduction of the new ICT governance processes and organizational structure; the continued adoption of the project management methodology to inform business about project benefits before committing resources; the linkage between client SLA agreements and relationship management, supported by improvements in regular reporting to various levels of management.

The ICT Strategy Committee is still coming to terms with its role and responsibilities. At the February meeting in 2007 it was agreed that the future focus would include:

1.   Ensuring alignment with USQ strategy;
2.   That ICT initiatives have business drivers;
3.   Maximizing the value of ICT investment;
4.   High level planning for ICT sustainability;
5.   Monitoring performance and audit compliance.

Core ICT System Sponsors will be assigned increased accountability for the operational management of their respective systems.

The recent release of the Val IT framework is a valuable resource to assist the work of the ICT Strategy Committee. Successful delivery of ICT services is being achieved by recognising the assignment of operational accountability and decision making within the ICT governance framework to ensure effective and efficient management. Business ownership and involvement in ICT decision-making is critical in determining ICT priorities. This process is being assisted by the formation of User Reference Groups responsible for each core ICT service advising the USQ ICT governance committees regarding priorities and funding allocations. For too long business groups have ignored their responsibilities and expected ICT to provide all of the answers and input.

The value and importance of the role and involvement of change management in major organizational changes before, during, and following the changes is critical and cannot be underestimated. For USQ, the removal of the change manager in April 2006 occurred too early with the last staff not completing their transition to the new division until January 1, 2007. Management and staff require constant support to ensure that all parties remain focussed on achieving the end goals.

FUTURE DIRECTIONS

The ICT management team has just completed a one-year assessment of the operational effectiveness of the structure to review the organization, recent initiatives and progress. A second assessment and realignment will occur at 24 months. A formal review of the structure will be carried out after three years to assess the operational effectiveness and functional efficiency of the model and to ensure that service delivery remains aligned with University's direction, and faculty, and operational unit requirements.

New service desk options and an ITIL-compliant service desk package are being investigated that are aligned to the aims and objectives of the new division of ICT services, and will enable ICT to address the ITIL components of incident management, integrated service level management, asset and configuration management, change management, and problem management. A products and services catalogue is in the process of being finalised. The products and services catalogue is the starting point for configuration management and the further development of service level agreements between the division and its clients. Service level agreements are being progressively developed with generic SLA templates for products and services, faculties and departments, campuses (Fraser Coast and Springfield), global services (voice and data networks, e-mail, etc.) and external clients.

In faculties and divisions where there is no existing ICT presence, a "Hot Desk" model is being negotiated. Desk space (full or part-time) is being established in client areas, with ICT support staff operating from the shared Hot Desk when working in the local environment to ensure regular presence and visibility. A number of student cadet positions are identified within the structure with one of these reserved for an indigenous student. It is proposed to commence the cadetship program in 2007 and to investigate creative funding models in partnership with the community and industry. Satisfaction surveys of staff and students were again undertaken at the end of 2006 to identify areas that have improved and to again prioritise efforts for improvement (DICTS, 2006a, 2006b). An evaluation and assessment of the surveys has been forwarded to the ICT governance committees to assist management address any deficiencies raised and identify opportunities for improvement.

The new divisional structure retained the ICT training function but moved this to a shared service model where University-wide training is coordinated through a virtual management environment and delivered by the respective faculty or organizational unit. ICT is working in partnership with the Learning and Teaching Support Unit, Human Resources, the Library, and other business units which offer staff training, to develop a single online training management environment that will act as the central training interface for staff, providing a single University training calendar, consistent course registration, certification and recording of completed training.

The COBIT maturity assessment was conducted in early 2007 against COBIT version 3. As well as providing a current benchmark for ICT, the assessment helped determine a target for an achievable and reasonable level of maturity. The ICT division plans to move to COBIT version 4 and implement Val IT for value management. A project plan and timeframe for achieving conversion of processes and supporting documentation to support compliance targets with the framework is being developed.

CONCLUSION

In summary, an extensive review of ICT at USQ identified significant areas for improvement across the whole range of ICT functions and personnel. Radical changes were required and have now been implemented. However, the transformation to a federal model of management of ICT has not been without some difficulties. Nevertheless, critical factors that contributed to progress with the implementation were commitment from the senior executive, organizational change management involving HR and trade unions, extensive communication about changes with ICT staff in USQ, governance guidance from COBIT and ITIL, and in particular, strong leadership from the CTO. The critical role of change management should not be underestimated. Evaluation of satisfaction with the change has begun and is now continuing. Anecdotal evidence suggests the perceptions will be positive both from within the ICT Division as well as the staff and students served.

REFERENCES

Avison, D. E., Gregor, S., & Wilson, D. (2006). Managerial IT unconsciousness. *Communications of the ACM, 49*(7), 89-93.

Csaszar, F., & Clemons, E. (2006). Governance of the IT function: Valuing agility and quality of training, cooperation and communications. In *Proceedings of the 39th Hawaii International Conference on System Sciences*, Hawaii.

De Haes, S., & Van Grembergen, W. (2005). IT governance structures, processes and relational mechanisms: Achieving IT/Business alignment in a major Belgian financial group. In *Proceedings of the 38th Hawaii International Conference on System Sciences*, Hawaii.

DICTS (2006a). *Staff satisfaction survey.* Retrieved May 11, 2008, from http://www.usq.edu.au/ict/staff/staffsvy/

DICTS (2006b). *Student satisfaction survey.* Retrieved May 11, 2008, from http://www.usq.edu.au/ict/students/studsvy/

Holloway, D. A. (2004). Corporate governance disasters and developments: Implications for university governing bodies. *Australian University Review, 46*(2), 23-30.

Karimi, J., Bhattacherjee, A., Gupta, Y. P., & Somers, T. M. (2000). The effect of MIS steering committees. *Journal of Management Information Systems, 17*(2), 207-239.

Luftman, J. N. (2004). *Managing the information technology resource: Leadership in the information age.* Upper Saddle River, NJ: Pearson Prentice Hall.

Peterson, R. (2003). Integration strategies and tactics for information technology governance. *Strategies for information technology governance* (pp. 37-80). Hershey, PA: Idea Group Publishing.

Raghunathan, T. S. (1992). Impact of CEO's participation on IS steering committees. *Journal of Management Information Systems, 8*(4), 83-96.

Sallé, M. (2004). IT service management and IT governance: Review, comparative analysis and their impact on utility computing (No. HPL-2004-98). Palo Alto: Hewlett-Packard Company.

Sledgianowski, D., Luftman, J. N., & Reilly, R. R. (2006). Development and validation of an instrument to measure maturity of IT business strategic alignment mechanisms. *Information Resources Management Journal, 19*(3), 18-33.

Van Grembergen, W., De Haes, S., & Guldentops, E. (2003). Structures, processes and relational mechanisms for IT governance. *Strategies for information technology governance* (pp. 14-36). Hershey, PA: Idea Group Publishing.

Section III
IT Governance:
Its Relationship to Business and Other Frameworks

Chapter XI
Managing IT Security Relationships within Enterprise Control Frameworks

Brian Cusack
AUT University, New Zealand

ABSTRACT

Security is a subprocess that affects all processes within an organization structure. The control frameworks of CobiT and ITIL provide a mapping of organizational roles from the capital interest at the highest level, through to the implementation level in an enterprise system. Both control frameworks provide varying capability for control at different levels in an organization and leave the problem of making control functional to the managerial layer. In this chapter the security process is mapped from two control frameworks at the strategic layer and the issue of effective management tactics discussed from the theoretical structures within the problem area. No attempt is made to transgress theory into practice.

INTRODUCTION

Security is a subprocess that impacts with different degrees on all processes within an organization structure. A security strategy is often described as defense in depth and conveys a metaphorical image of structured rigidity in the face of assessed risks. An effective business security strategy has elements of defense in depth theory but also other philosophical insights that include flexibility and rapid response. In the CobiT control framework security is defined as "Ensure Systems Security" (Delivery & Support (DS 5)) (ITGI, 2007a). The goal of security is to ensure systems security "to safe guard information against unauthorized use, disclosure or modification, damage or loss." In the ITIL control framework security is described as "Security Management" and has three distinct roles associated with the management (van Bon, 2004b). Its objective is to protect "the value of information in terms of confidentiality, integrity and availability". Both of these control frameworks acknowledge defense in depth and in the ITIL security management guidelines an additional discussion of flexibility is found: "While it is important to protect information assets with traditional stronghold / fortress approaches it has become equally important to have a skirmish capability when it comes to skirmish events. ... The organization must have the capability to rapidly put resources on the ground where trouble is before that trouble has a chance to spiral out of control" (van Bon, 2004a, pp. 181-183).

Protecting information strategically is consequently more than establishing defense in depth and related to strategic positioning and repositioning. Positioning occurs within the enterprise subsystem and in relation to the enterprise system as a whole. In the control frameworks of CobiT and ITIL careful specification of the security process is made and elaboration of the interrelation of the process to others. In CobiT the security process (defined as DS 5; see ITGI, 2007a; 2007b; 2007c) has three input processes, direct input to nine output processes, and influence on "other IT processes". Similarly in the ITIL control framework security management has relationships with eleven other management processes. The ITIL framework is more explicit as to the nature of the relationship and the consequence of the security process than is CobiT and the CobiT management guidelines. The importance of the security process is emphasized in both control frameworks in relation to the outcomes for the enterprise system. It would appear then that an understanding of process management for successful process outputs is more than the systematic control of one process and as it is acknowledged in the literature, security management has an enterprise wide (across all processes) mandate (Siponen, 2000). It is contended that the current elaboration of the enterprise wide management is lacking in specification for variation in process relationships, variation in impacts, and guidelines for flexible positioning. Analysis and clarification of variation can add knowledge to what is already

advocated in the control literature (ITGI, 2005a; Straub & Welke, 1998).

At the strategic level sufficient detail is provided for enterprise planning and goal and objective setting for protecting information. However at the tactical (managerial) level the specification of the relationships between different processes is inadequate to adequately plan for effective defense of the information system (Von Solms & Von Solms, 2005). For example in the CobiT framework, of the three inputs to the security process (PO9, AI6, DS1) (van Bon, 2004a) two are inward looking (within process) and one considerate of the external environment. Effective planning for flexible defenses at the tactical level would expect both PO9 and AI6 would also be considerate of both the internal and external process environments. PO9 adequately considers the external risk context by stating the goal to be, "Assess risks to support management decisions ... and responding to threats by increasing objectivity and identifying important decision factors" (van Bon, 2007). However, it would be expected that AI6 "Manage Changes" also had an outward consideration to define changing external factors and relationship weightings as well as the internal process concerns. The many-to-many relationship of security process to other processes has more variation and complexity than a good manager could be expected to control. The following sections define the problem area in greater detail and then consider possible scenarios where a manager may gain sufficient control that information protection may be assured.

CONTROL FRAMEWORKS

Control frameworks attempt to provide a one-stop-shop for business and systems managers. The differences between different control frameworks (for example, CobiT, ITIL, PRINCE2, PMBOK, and so on) are found in the evolutionary (historical) development, proprietry interests and also the perspective each takes. CobiT for example was developed specifically for audit and the top-down perspective of an organization, whereas PMBOK took the specialized perspective of project management, and ITIL the perspective of service management. Such differences are important and lead to an understanding that one size does not fit all. In practice, the effective organizational adoption of a control framework may be achieved by adopting and implementing the mutually supportive elements of different frameworks (Perry, 1991). For example ITIL has proven robust in the service management areas of IT but tends to lose traction at the higher levels of organization. To the contrary, CobiT effectively addresses the concerns of shareholders and executives in an organization but again is less effective in the middle and lower business organizational layers.

In the following subsections the control frameworks of ITIL and CobiT are reviewed to identify the controls for security process and the relationships between security process and the other business processes as advocated in the frameworks. The concept of defense-in-depth is also reviewed to critique the frameworks assumption regarding effective information systems protection. Defense in depth has been adopted as a sufficient strategy for protecting information systems and yet in many commercial occurrences it has been proven inadequate. The matters reviewed in these subsections introduce a problematic that has identifiable issues and problems for business managers who wish to control variation in information system risk.

Defense in Depth

Defense in depth is a strategy that requires the deployment of resources in a staggered network and over a regressive structure. It is a different strategy than the traditional "front line" defense. Defense in depth relies on the ability of a defender to delay and damage an attacker through successive engagements. In information security for example the defense in depth strategy deploys multiple techniques to help mitigate the risk of one component being compromised or circumvented (Forno & Baklarz, 1999). Hence, antivirus software may be found on servers, firewalls and workstations within the same environment. Multiple vendor software may also be deployed on different vectors within the same system to optimize defense. The "honey pot" tactic is also consistent with a defense in depth strategy. An attacker (i.e., a hacker) enters a protected construct that offers high risk information in a staged and progressively more demanding environment. The hacker is enticed to disclose a footprint, a path, and a description during the engagement so that identification may occur. Once identified further malicious entry may be shut down and beneficial entries maintained.

A well-planned information systems defence in-depth strategy is effective against an attacker who breaches a small number of control points across the information system. It is also effective if the organization can afford to compromise some information. The defence will deploy protection in mutually supportive control points and in appropriate roles so that a layered effect is created. Disclosure can then be forced from the attacker as successive layers are breached, extracting the highest price from an attacker. The strategy (see Hazlewood, 2006) provides three lines of defense. The first is is the people in the organisation who are to provide consistency across roles, policy performance, and awareness of requirements, so that a potential attacker may be stopped before breaching the first line of defense. In the case of a breach further layers are advocated behind the first line of defense to force disclosure from an attacker. For example notification and esclation trees can align mutually supportive control points and knowledge be built to accelerate disclosure. The second line of defense (a fall back position) is the information systems network. This includes the use of security components (such as VPN and so on), security software (such as firewalls, detection systems, and so on), and security frameworks (such as those to be discussed in the following sections). The third line of defense is the host (such as the routers, workstations, servers, and so on). This includes service controls, requirements audit, access controls, vulnerability detection and intervention, and configuration audit.

The disadvantages of defense in-depth strategy can be located at both the strategic and tactical layers. In the first instance it may be strategically unacceptable to allow the disclosure of any information of any type related to a brand. For example the leaking to the media of any information—wheather it is true or false, by a hacker could be detrimental to the brand. Hence a honey pot defense or other defense in-depth tactics may be unacceptable to the brand owners. A solid front line defense where the majority of protective resources are positioned at the points of entry may be a better defense in this case. Similarly at the tactical layer the required rigididy of the structural design that allows defense in depth to proceed may be unresponsive to learning (about the attacker strategy and tactics) and yeild unnecessary information in defense. Similarly rigidity in strategic design and defense in depth geometries may prevent better fit tactical solutions from being used.

CobiT Security Process

The CobiT security process is described in the process management domain of "Delivery and Support" as "Ensure Systems Security" (DS5). It has the goal to "protect all IT assets to minimize business impact of security vulnerabilities and incidents" (van Bon, 2007, p. 102), and in the CobiT Assurance Guide it has ten activities that are carried out in the security process. These are summarized in Table 1. The interrelation with other processes is discussed in subsection 2.4.

ITIL Security Process

The ITIL security process is described in the context of management and the safety of information. Security management is integrated into the organization from the service provider's perspective and the ISO 17799 standard (previously BS 7799, and to become the ISO / IEC 27000 series) provides guidance for the operationalization of the security process (van Bon, 2004b, p. 181). The security process has input from the customer and in the service level agreement (SLA) the levels of security services are defined. The security process has seven activities that are described in Table 2. Underpinning the activities is a plan-do-check-act

Table 1. CobiT security activity description

Activity	Description
1	Management of IT Security so that security actions are in line with business requirements.
2	Translate business risk and compliance into an overall IT security plan.
3	Identity management that assures that all users are uniquely identifiable.
4	User account management and review.
5	Security testing, surveillance and monitoring.
6	Incident management.
7	Protection of the security technology.
8	Key management so that secure usage is possible.
9	Malicious software prevention, detection, and correction.
10	Network security.

Table 2. ITIL security activity description

Activity	Description
1	SLA (security chapter) agreement between customer and provider.
2	Planning of SLAs, contract, operational level agreements (OLAs), and internal policies.
3	Implementation of security.
4	Evaluation of performance and audit.
5	Maintenance of cycle.
6	Control functions.
7	Reporting according to the SLA.

cycle adoption (similar to the CobiT adoption) and in the recently released up-date, a lifecycle. The interrelation with other processes is discussed in subsection 2.4.

Security Process Linkages

In each of the control frameworks discussed the security process has an interrelatedness to other processes in the enterprise system (see Table 3). Both frameworks specify the connections between the security process and the related processes but it is contended in the next section that the actual properties of the connections are underspecified. An ambiguity also enters the literature as the frameworks have been upgraded and refreshed over time. In CobiT version 3 for example, the security process has three inputs and 10 output linkages with other processes (including an undefined "other processes" option), whereas in version 4 it has 5 inputs and 5 output linkages. To add to the variation a number of the processes the security process connects with are different between the versions. In the case where a manager wishes to operationalize a control framework, connection is not a strong enough term on which to base tactical decisions (Baskerville, 1993). A manager would demand to know the linkage between processes so that the relationship may be specified in terms of control and operational audit. In addition further information is required to know the balance of interaction between all the process for best practice and performance. The ITIL description is also less specific regarding the interconnectedness and uses terms such as "normal way" and "consultation" to specify the relationships. The embedded assumption is that the security process is distinct but is to perform in a similar fashion to all other processes.

Table 3. Framework security process connections

Connection	ITIL	CobiT
Input	SLA security requirement; Policy documents; External requirements; Security incidents; and so on.	PO2; PO3; PO9; AI2; DS1.
Output	Reporting	PO9; DS7; DS8; AI6; ME1.

Note: ITIL defines the interaction of security process as the Management of: Customer relationship; Service level; Cost; Availability; Capacity; Continuity; Configuration; Release; Incident Response; Help Desk; Problem; and Change.

THE MANAGERIAL PROBLEM

Control frameworks communicate the interrelationship of different business and IT processes for a context that is dynamic and changing. The framework itself defines a preferred way of viewing the enterprise system and choices for organizing the knowledge base. The assertion that one framework adequately fits all contexts often over generalizes specific and important points within and between contexts, and is often the result of author preferences, brand allegiances, and mission blindness. The underlying structures and interests within enterprise systems give variations that are often unresponsive to general controls (Song & Thakor, 2006). Natural variation for example allows occurrences of non-control and equally the best planned system or structure is only effective within specified constraints. The management problem is hence the implementation of a control framework that minimizes variation around the control targets and yet allows sufficient natural variation to maximize cost efficiency. In the case of security the distribution of protection across all enterprise processes both horizontally and vertically has complexities that may trade against each other and one occurrence place a system out of control, for example the disassociation of brand and form (Davenport, Eccles & Prusak, 1992).

The management problem is the value of different choices a manager may make (Weill & Aral, 2006). The adoption of one control framework may enhance the operational performance on some objectives and still underperform, or not perform on others. The adoption of several control frameworks may increase complexity, ambiguity, and critical paths to successful performance outcomes. The issue that arises is the capability of management to make decisions of high value in a competitive and often over represented market place (Weill & Ross, 2004). The pitch of software sales and managerial consultancy often over-state the effects of any product or service leaving value deficits for which managerial capability must

compensate. In a similar sense the maturity of an organization has a direct influence on the value of a managerial decision. The higher the maturity rating the greater the number of controls in place and the higher the multiplier effect on good decisions (ITPI, 2006).

The basis of decision-making is a managerial assessment of beneficial effects that may be gained by choosing between a number of different control frameworks or a combination of several. The choice to implement a control framework must be based on the forecasted value that may be expected from the change. The performance of different control frameworks under different conditions, in varying circumstances (including scalability factors), and at different maturity levels all provide predictors from which an informed decision can be made. The trust that may be put in CobiT or ITIL to deliver high business values and to minimize costs can be assessed prior to implementation. The analysis of performance by context, the identification of conditions, and preconditions, and the identifications of limitations all provide preparation for expected outcomes (Castlewood & Sir, 2001). The extent of organizational change also has to be factored into calculations to compensate for shift during the implementation processes. One size does not fit all. Control frameworks attempt to generalize from a particular perspective in the enterprise system and even from developer experience (Davenport et. al, 1992). Both perspectives fail to capture the variation at the extremities of the advocated control framework scope. CobiT for example struggles to grasp the particular of process level control, as does ITIL at the boardroom level.

The identified problems are present to differing degrees and to different extents with relation to the security process in both control frameworks. It is insufficient to dismiss the concerns as problems a good manager can solve and expect robust protection of information assets (Avison, Gregor & Wilson, 2006). Further analysis of the problem can lead to a definition of the different influences different processes have into the security process, a definition of the different influences the security process exerts on other processes, and a summary of missing systems relationships not in the current control frameworks. Such analysis can lead to a better comprehension of the security process at the managerial (tactical) level and the elaboration of management guidelines that allow for flexible defense tactics that still retain the strength of defense in-depth strategies.

WORKING SOLUTIONS

The strengths and weaknesses identified previously, inherent in the adoption of control frameworks may be resolved into a range of pragmatic solutions. The manager is caught between the worlds of implementation particular and executive strategic generalizations. The managerial role is not only to provide controls that achieve performance targets but also to communicate outcomes into two very different worlds. The literature on project success is clear that success is defined and interpreted differently by different stakeholders (Campbell, Kay & Avison 2005; Young, 2005). Success at the implementation layer may not translate in to success at the executive layer and both groups choose to use different ways of communicating outcomes. The alignment of objectives is a managerial task. Attempts in the control framework literature to minimize variation between business and IT objectives have largely been unsuccessful from the enterprise perspective (Young, 2005). The variation of control variable measures at the implementation layer simply becomes too wide in the CobiT framework and the breakdown of communication of implementation outputs controlled by the ITIL framework at the executive layer obscures the business value of the control objectives.

A working solution is to take the strengths of the control frameworks CobiT and ITIL and to implement both control frameworks in the same

enterprise system. The objective is to identify where a framework minimizes the variation of business and IT objectives in relation to the enterprise wide benefits gained (Campbell, 2005; Perry, 1991). The mappings and published critiques to date (see for example Young, 2005; ITGI, 2005) suggest that commonalities exist between the frameworks and also differences. Young (2005) points out that no control framework has been successful on its own to solve the business benefits problem. The advocacy is hence for a selection of control objectives from both frameworks based on an effectiveness evaluation of where the framework performs well. The evaluation may be context specific so that one organization chooses a particular set of objectives that relate specifically to the enterprise requirements and another a different or similar set. Such an approach also raises the issue of competency of those in an enterprise system to act in the best interest of the enterprise and capability of the enterprise to intelligently build a working solution to the IT business alignment problem (Grembergen, et al., 2003).

The problematic of implementing two control frameworks is a possible solution for consistency in business value communication and enterprise wide process control. The effective implementation of control objectives is mediated by the managerial layer. In the IS triangle (Alter, 2002) the management layer in an enterprise system is singular and described as being "flat" or "minimal". Management in this sense is still the mediator between the executive layer (sometimes tagged as the "C's" layer) and implementation but the nature of mediation has changed. A manager is to communicate horizontally and vertically in two directions (compare with the industrial triangle) and to maintain control of the business processes (Crossman & Sorrenti, 1977). The communication role is to translate the different speak of implementers; mediate with control objectives, and to report performance outcomes to the executive layer. The tipping point is what performances are reported. The ITIL control framework outputs performance measures that are in keeping with the SLA's and the relevant service level standards. Such data is critical input to the managerial process. Similarly in the CobiT control framework, control objectives are delivered that are in keeping with the shareholder business performance interest. The performance measures are similar in expectation but often very different in atomic size. A CobiT control objective becomes more and more specific as it resolves into activities and metrics but never directly engages the specific particles in IT process control. CobiT remains general at the atomic level. ITIL may be critiqued to be similar but effective at the atomic level.

MANAGERIAL TACTICS

A holistic view of the enterprise system merges the system and its subsystems in an interactive dynamic that requires intelligent management tactics for effective strategy implementation (Nolan & McFarlan, 2005; Peploeski, 1998). The problem of difference within the enterprise system resolves into pragmatic solutions where differences become strengths and where appropriate communication and resource requirements are met by defining the required enterprise wide effect. The selection of control objectives is hence made by identifying the required effect and then by evaluating the performance of competing objectives from different control frameworks. The best performing objectives are selected and implemented. Others are rejected. Such strategy requires intelligent and experienced personnel to perform evaluation tasks and to maintain the effective systems operation. The discussion in the preceding section identified the business manager in the flat IS structure as the role to mediate and maintain control framework functionality.

Managerial tactics can be developed for enterprise wide control functionality. The role of business manager resolves into one of translation where the various communication modes,

process output reports, and structures intersect. A comprehensive view of the business processes and definitions are required to execute managerial strategy. The selection of performing control objectives is required to be viewed from the different perspectives in the enterprise system and then objectively judged against the business plan. Such activity can be seen in the context of theories in competition literature and the decision making process one that is multiperspectival. The choice of control objectives from different proprietary frameworks over rides the preferred theory of evidence constructed by the framework designers to justify the preferred position. The act of deconstruction in this context is tactical. The deconstructive act allows the evaluation of the control objective against other competitors and from evidence that may be found outside of the preferred proprietary theory of evidence. The selection and justification of preferred control objectives hence then forms its own new theory base and allows a construct that may be justified by performance for the particular enterprise system.

The concerns raised in section 2.4 regarding the specification of security process linkages to other processes within the enterprise system can now be addressed. In the CobiT control framework (version 3) the higher-level control objective "Ensure systems security" (DS5) was associated with three input controls and nine output controls and a general statement regarding influence on all other controls. In version 4 this was amended to 5 inputs, 5 outputs, and descriptive statements. In addition the "CobiT Management Guidelines" specify the use and application of the various tools. In brief the management guidelines address the information criteria, and the delivery of business value against the key goal and performance indicators (see ITGI, 2005a). Within the process the key output indicators that may guide a manager's use of the control framework are available. However, the relationship between controls and the relevant indicators is weak (the more recent Cobit 4.1 and IT Assurance Guide are explicit but still weak in this area). A similar analysis may be conducted on the ITIL security process and it may be argued that greater detail regarding management across processes in the context of IT service management is found. The ITIL control framework provides two levels for management. One that assures service support and the other assures service delivery. Security process is in the latter but has an influence on each of the former.

FUTURE DIRECTIONS

The management of IT security relationships is a complex activity that converges at the business manager's role. The obligation a business manager has to implement the business plan and to oversee the management of processes requires a developed tactic that considers the holistic implications of every activity. Security process has a part or an influence on every activity. Protecting information may occur within an adopted control framework, but the literature reviewed above suggests that any one-control framework lacks a comprehensive command of all the necessary elements of an enterprise wide control. It may also have irrelevant and debt relationships inherited from the developer or the proprietor. Similarly in the review of the defense in depth strategy, strategic and tactical limitations were identified with the adoption of a standard and often preferred security model. These concerns are not fully addressed in any control framework.

The advocacy for the enterprise-by-enterprise approach to adopting control objectives from different control frameworks provided a working solution for some of the problems and issues raised in the analysis. The potential for customizing a control framework from the best performing objectives in the specific enterprise entertains the possibility for responsible managerial action. One of the little discussed side effects of standardized control frameworks is the abdication of responsi-

bility for beneficial enterprise outcomes. Often the limits of the control framework are uncritically accepted and the performance measures considered the best from a constrained best practice. In theory responsibility can be passed up and down the IS triangle through plan-do-check-act cycles (the do step) but because of variation in processes, between processes and in the communication of outcomes errors can multiply. Personalization and customization may accentuate the appetite for risk but it also provides a counter balance in the corporate sense of ownership and personal sense of responsibility for beneficial outcomes. Customization (in the advocated tactic) also requires experienced and knowledgeable managers. The purchase and retention of such managers is a challenge for the organization as a whole and a future direction for revaluing the enterprise human resource. A further challenge is for the enterprise system to benchmark against capability maturity levels and to move upwardly through the capability maturity levels (CMI, CMMI, and so on).

A flexible defense of the enterprise information system requires many of the elements discussed above. As the ITIL literature pointed out, "While it is important to protect information assets with traditional stronghold / fortress approaches it has become equally important to have a skirmish capability when it comes to skirmish events. … The organization must have the capability to rapidly put resources on the ground where trouble is before that trouble has a chance to spiral out of control". However, the ensuing critique noted that one control framework does not fit all and the best effect may be gained by a tactical ploy of assessing and choosing control objectives from different control frameworks. This managerial tactic has potential for flexible yet robust information security whereby the hard structures of front line defense and defense in depth may be deployed in resource rich localized constructs. The uniqueness and complexity of such configurations also adds to the defense capability. Furthermore the potential to effectively target mobile resources to events and exceptions is heightened.

The future of secure protection is in the development and retention of business managerial capability. The simple adoption of standardized control frameworks opens an enterprise system to generic attacks and common faults. The enhancement of managerial knowledge also actuates the appetite for risk. The future is to reestablish managerial loyalty to brand and to see managers as lifetime partners in the enterprise system growth. Capability maturity measures provide benchmarks on which an enterprise system can audit progress and also to value the expected return from any decision. The research reviewed above asserts to a strong relationship between maturity and performance and assess the likely hood of security breach as being lower in enterprise systems that have higher maturity levels. In addition greater returns on investment are achieved using fewer resources when more control objectives are implemented (see ITGI, 2006 for the top 27 performing controls).

CONCLUSION

The premise that security is a sub process that affects all processes within an organization structure provides a foundation on which to critique the claims of any control framework. Such a critique is looking for best practice, best business architecture and strong information systems defense. An effective business security strategy has elements of defense in depth theory but also other philosophical insights that include flexibility and rapid response. A business manager may take strength in the fact that no one control framework has all the necessary elements for an effective business security strategy, but that the highest performing businesses have the most number of implemented control objectives and the highest measures on the capability maturity assessment.

REFERENCES

Alter, S. (2002). *Information Systems*. (4th ed.). New Jersey: Person.

Avison, D., Gregor, S., & Wilson, D. (2006). Managerial IT unconsciousness. *Communications of the ACM, 49*(7), 89-93.

Baskerville, R. (1993). Information systems security design methods: Implications for information systems development. *ACM Computing Surveys, 25*(4), 375-414.

Campbell, B., Kay, R., & Avison, D. (2005). Strategic alignment: A practitioner's perspective. *Journal of Enterprise Information Management, 18*(5/6), 653-661.

Castlewood, D. & Sir, M. (2001). Organizational development: A framework for successful information technology assimilation. *Organization Development Journal, 19*(1), 59-72.

Crossman, M., & Sorrenti, M. (1977). Making sense of improvisation. *Advances in Strategic Management, 14*, 155-180.

Davenport, T., Eccles, R., & Prusak, L. (1992). Information politics. *Sloan Management Review*, 53-65.

Forno, R., & Baklarz, R. (1999). *The art of information warfare*. New York: Universal Publishers.

Hazelwood (2006). *Defence in depth: An information assurance strategy for the enterprise*. Retrieved May 11, 2008, from http://www.sdsc.edu

ITGI (2005a). *Aligning CobiT ITIL ISO 17799 for business benefit*. Retrieved May 11, 2008, from http://www.isaca.org/

ITGI (2005b). *CobiT management guidelines*. Retrieved May 11, 2008, from http://www.isaca.org/

ITGI (2007a). *CobiT 4.1*. Retrieved May 11, 2008, from http://www.isaca.org/

ITGI (2007b). *IT governance implementation guide* (2nd ed.). Retrieved May 11, 2008, from http://www.isaca.org/

ITGI (2007c). *IT assurance guide*. Retrieved May 11, 2008, from http://www.isaca.org/

ITPI (2006). *IT controls performance study*. IT Process Institute. Retrieved May 11, 2008, from http://www.itpi.org/

Nolan, R. & McFarlan, F. (2005). Information technology and the board of directors. *Harvard Business Review, October*, 96-106.

Peploeski, K. (1998). The process of improvisation. *Organisational Science*, 9(5), 560-561.

Perry, L. (1991). Strategic improvisation: How to formulate and implement competitive strategies in concert. *Organizational Dynamics, 19*(4), 51-64.

Siponen, M. (2000). A conceptual foundation for organisational information security awareness. *Information Management and Computer Security Journal, 8*(1), 31-41.

Song, F. & Thakor, A. (2006). Information control, career concerns and corporate governance. *The Journal of Finance, 61*(4), 1845-1852.

Straub, D., & Welke, R. (1998). Coping with systems risk: Security planning models for management decision making. *MIS Quarterly, 22*(4), 441-464.

van Bon, J. (2004a). *IT governance a pocket guide based on CobiT*. Netherlands: Van Haren Publishing.

van Bon, J. (2004b). *IT service management, An introduction based on ITIL*. Netherlands: Van Haren Publishing.

van Bon, J. (2007). *IT service management, An introduction based on ITIL*. Netherlands: Van Haren Publishing.

Van Grenbergen, W., De Haes, S., & Guldentops, E. (2003). Structures, processes and relational mechanisms for IT governance. *Strategies for IT governance* (pp. 14-36). Hershey, PA: Idea Group Publishing.

Von Solms, B., & von Solms, R., (2005). From information security to business Security. *Computer and Security Journal*, 272-279.

Weill, P., & Aral, S. (2006). Generating premium returns on your IT investments. *MIT Sloan Management Review, 47*(2), 39-51.

Weill, P., & Ross, J. (2004). *IT governance – How top performers manage IT decision rights for superior results*. Boston: Harvard Business School Press.

Young, R. (2005). *Explaining senior management support through IT project governance*. Unpublished doctoral thesis, Macquarie University, Sydney.

Chapter XI
Unexplored Linkages between Corporate Governance and IT Governance:
An Evaluation and Call to Research

Michael A. Borth
The University of Tennessee, USA

Randy V. Bradley
The University of Tennessee, USA

ABSTRACT

This chapter discusses the overall importance of both corporate and IT governance, and demonstrates that IT governance is a very important subcomponent of corporate governance. The authors present a framework, based upon a framework previously presented by Weill and Ross (2004), which should facilitate a strong understanding of the different factors and mechanisms that impact firm governance. A number of interesting empirical results relating to these governance mechanisms are presented within the context of the framework. Finally, the chapter presents a number of examples that link corporate and IT governance. In presenting those linkages, the authors identify a number of areas that should provide fruitful avenues for researchers to explore IT governance as it relates to corporate governance, and vice versa.

INTRODUCTION

The attention given to the topic of corporate governance has increased substantially following a number of high-profile corporate accounting scandals which were uncovered between 2001 and 2002 at companies such as Enron, WorldCom, and Tyco. The discovery of significant management malfeasance at multiple large U.S. corporations shook the confidence of investors in U.S. markets:

the S&P 500 fell 16% in the first six months of 2002 while the tech-heavy NASDAQ fell 36% (Weill & Ross, 2004). There has been a good deal of academic research directed at identifying the effectiveness of corporate governance initiatives, much of which focuses on how corporate boards of directors (BODs) and audit committees carry out their duties to provide effective oversight of, and direction and control to, the organization. Corporate governance research in the accounting and finance literatures focuses on the governance mechanisms which can be instituted to ensure shareholder interest in financial assets.

Information technology (IT) has become an essential element for corporations as they carry out their day-to-day operations, a fact which is supported by corporate spending. IT expenditures exceed 50% of the total capital spending of many organizations (Weill & Ross, 2004). The development and application of good principles to govern the IT function and assets is therefore critical. Unfortunately, there is a surprising dearth of research focused on IT governance in the academic information systems (IS), accounting, or finance literatures. Much of the existing IS literature devoted to IT governance is focused on the rights and responsibilities for decisions related to IT activities (Sambamurthy & Zmud, 1999). A large gap therefore exists between the IT governance literature and corporate governance literature, which is primarily focused at the level of board oversight rather than at the operational level.

The objectives of this chapter are (1) to provide a framework which sheds light on the various factors and mechanisms which affect corporate governance and IT governance, (2) to discuss interesting empirical results relating to these governance mechanisms, and (3) to identify linkages between corporate and IT governance which we believe future academic research should explore further. The first section further reviews some of the governance collapses and accounting scandals which led to increased interest in corporate governance. In the second section, the

authors provide a review of the current treatment of topics related to corporate governance and IT governance within the accounting, finance, and IT literatures. Weill and Ross (2004) recognize the similarities between the application of good governance principles to financial assets and to IT assets, and present a framework to link corporate and IT governance. An expanded version of Weill and Ross's (2004) framework which considers additional external influences is provided. In the final section, the authors explore linkages between corporate governance and IT governance, and provides directions and recommendations for future research in the area of IT governance.

BACKGROUND ON THE INCREASING INTEREST IN GOVERNANCE

Researchers in accounting and finance have addressed topics related to the governance of corporations with increasing frequency for over 30 years, but the topic achieved a much broader following in the mainstream media as a wave of accounting scandals were uncovered in 2001 and 2002. The discovery of significant management malfeasance at multiple large U.S. corporations shook the confidence of investors in U.S. markets: the S&P 500 fell 16% in the first six months of 2002 while the tech-heavy NASDAQ fell 36% (Weill & Ross, 2004). The collapse of energy giant Enron in the fall of 2001 is perhaps the most infamous case of financial malfeasance in U.S. history, and the indictment of Enron's auditor, Andersen, led to the uncovering of a number of other high-profile fraud cases, when accounting problems were revealed at several former Andersen clients under the scrutiny of the companies' new auditors. The unprecedented number of high profile accounting scandals shook investor confidence and brought strong pressure to bear on the U.S. government. The government responded in July 2002 with the passage of the Sarbanes-Oxley Act of 2002

("SOX"), designed to enhance financial reporting standards for U.S. public companies.

The accounting scandals, the failure of Andersen, and the U.S. government's response with the passage of the SOX Act piqued public interest in the importance of strong corporate governance to the functionality of U.S. capital markets. Additionally, these events further propelled academic interest in corporate governance topics. There has been less academic interest in the application of governance mechanisms to the management of information technology assets, despite the increasing reliance on information technology for the achievement of firms' strategic goals. The next section explores and builds upon an existing framework which links corporate and IT governance, and reviews some academic topics of interest within the framework bounds.

A FRAMEWORK FOR GOVERNANCE AND LITERATURE REVIEW

Weill and Ross (2004) recognize the similarities between the application of good governance to financial assets and to IT assets, and present a framework to link corporate and IT governance. In their framework, ultimate responsibility for the establishment of strong governance and the protection of shareholders and other stakeholders (employees, customers, creditors) rests with the board of directors. The senior executive team acts as the board's agent in developing firm strategy and establishing a corporate culture which encourages desirable behaviors. It is through the clear articulation of the firm's strategy and behaviors consistent with the implementation of that strategy that senior executive teams may govern the use and management of six key assets: human assets, financial assets, physical assets, intellectual property assets, information and IT assets, and internal and external relationship assets.

While Weill & Ross's (2004) framework provides an excellent linkage between overall corporate governance and IT governance, it is important to recognize that corporate decision making is not shielded from influences external to the firm. Review of existing corporate governance research within accounting and finance literatures yields insight into a number of internal and external factors which impact the incentives and behaviors of the board of directors and management. The very need for effective corporate governance is largely described by Jensen and Meckling's (1976) agency theory of the firm, which describes a misalignment between the interests and incentives of firm managers and those of shareholders or creditors. The asymmetric nature of information regarding the firm's prospects exacerbates these problems in manager's dealings with providers of capital. A number of studies assert the existence of other factors which affect the incentives of board members and managers in ensuring that shareholder and creditor interests are protected. For example, a manager's consideration of potential future employment opportunities provides encouragement for a manager to use firm resources wisely, especially considering the asymmetric nature of information related to the firm (i.e., other potential employers, as firm outsiders, cannot gauge the individual performance of the manager and must therefore base their opinions of the managers performance on overall firm performance). The existence or absence of alternative future employment opportunities, and their effect on the firm's managers is described within the finance and accounting literatures as the labor market for managers. Other factors which may impact the efficacy of corporate governance measures include debt and equity capital markets, a labor market for directors, product markets, takeover markets, providers of services or information, laws and regulations, and political pressures. We expand upon Weill and Ross's (2004) framework to consider the implications of these additional factors on the strength of overall corporate governance, and review existing theoretical and empirical results related to all the factors relevant to the discussion of corporate governance. As literally thousands of academic articles have been written, the review does not intend to be exhaustive. Rather, the review is meant to give the reader a sense of the interesting interconnections between the factors within the framework by placing theoretical arguments and empirical results which have been especially interesting to the authors of this chapter within the framework.

INTERNAL GOVERNANCE MECHANISMS

Boards of Directors

The board of directors is arguably the most important factor in the establishment of stronger or weaker corporate governance. The board serves in a fiduciary capacity to the shareholders, and is therefore charged with monitoring the actions of management. Fama and Jensen (1983) argue that when the specific knowledge relevant to firm decisions is diffuse among many agents within an organization, it becomes most efficient to separate

Figure 1. Expanded corporate governance framework

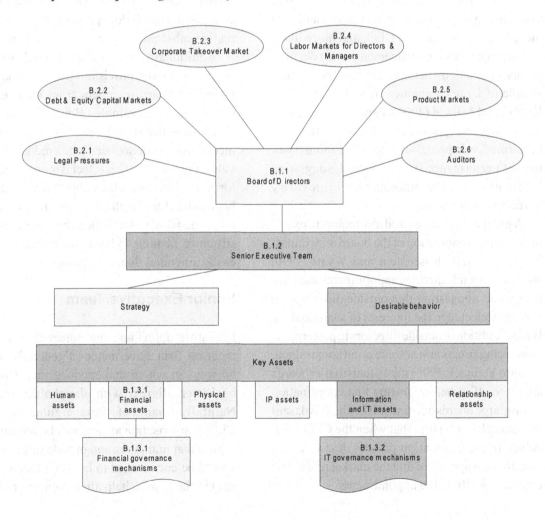

decision management from ownership, but that this separation results in agency problems that must be controlled by separating the decision-making functions of management from the decision-ratifying functions of a board of directors. Much of the literature which examines the effectiveness of the board in carrying out their oversight function focuses on an action which is predictable and observable: the replacement of poorly performing top management. Denis and Denis (1995) show evidence that although corporate boards are effective in replacing poorly performing CEO's, evidenced by the fact that operating performance does improve markedly under the guiding hand of the replacement manager, forced resignations are a rare event which are often accompanied by some form of corporate control activity (e.g., takeover attempts, or blockholder pressure). Parrino, Sias, and Starks (2003) find evidence that boards are more likely to replace the CEO, and more likely to appoint an outside replacement, when declines in institutional ownership are observed. In a sample of large companies from 1992 to 2005, Kaplan and Minton (2006) show that boards are more likely to replace CEOs not only when firm performance is poor, but also when industry or market performance is poor overall, suggesting both that boards are monitoring more aggressively in recent years.

A great deal of research also attempts to examine how the organization of the board may impact its effectiveness. Rosenstein and Wyatt (1990) show that outside director appointments increase firm value, suggesting that outside directors are generally elected in the interests of shareholders. But the addition of outside directors to perform the monitoring function is at some point constrained, because Yermack (1996) shows that smaller boards are more effective, suggesting that coordination among large boards becomes difficult. Shivdasani & Yermack (1999) find that when the CEO is involved in the nomination process, less effective directors are appointed and the market reacts less enthusiastically to the appointments.

Other research on board effectiveness examines the effect of outside pressures on board behavior. Harford (2003) shows that director incentives are misaligned with shareholder interests at the critical juncture when a takeover bid is entertained: directors are unlikely to be retained when a merger is approved, and the net financial impact is negative for outside directors. Del Guercio, Seery, and Woidtke (2006) show that boards targeted by just vote no campaigns become substantially more likely to dismiss a poorly performing CEO, presumably to protect reputational capital in the labor market for directors and avoid missing out on lucrative future directorships. Further, that when boards targeted by shareholder vote no campaigns respond in accordance with the concerns of shareholder activists, either by firing the CEO or adopting a concurrent shareholder proposal, the target firms realize subsequent operating improvements.

Additionally, interesting research exists on bylaw and charter provisions that firms may adopt to protect board members from these external pressures. For example, Bebchuk and Cohen (2005) show that staggered boards, an antitakeover mechanism, are associated with a reduction in firm value. Further, that this effect is more pronounced for those firms which established the staggered board structure in their corporate charter than for firms which established the staggered board structure in their bylaws, which may be more easily amended than the charter.

Senior Executive Team

Literature describing the influence of management on firm governance is generally focused on ways in which management incentives may be better aligned with shareholder interests. Naturally, many of these arguments involve CEO compensation arrangements. Jensen (1993) argues that managers and outside directors alike should be encouraged to hold significant ownership in the firm to help align their interests with those of the shareholders, suggesting that equity based compensation arrangement will encourage managers to maximize shareholder value. Demsetz and Lehn (1985), however, predict and find no linear relation between insider ownership and firm value. Subsequently, Morck, Shleifer, and Vishny (1988) show that there is a relation between firm value and inside equity ownership, but that it is nonlinear; they show that manager and shareholder interests appear to be aligned at high and low levels of ownership, but there exists a range between where management entrenchment is encouraged. There are also interesting research streams devoted to the appropriateness of CEO pay levels, as well as to management's incentives to manage earnings. For example, Kaplan and Minton (2006) show that while CEO pay may be rising in recent years, so too are CEO turnover rates; further, that since factors such as market and industry performance which are out of the control of the CEO are determinants of CEO turnover, the increasing pay may help offset decreases in job security. Leuz, Nanda, and Wysocki (2003) propose and find support for the argument that earnings management is more prevalent in countries with poor shareholder protections because controlling shareholders in these environments have greater private benefits of control that they desire to hide from minority shareholders by managing earnings.

Given that executive compensation strategies are generally tied to firm performance, the value inherent in strategic use of IT assets should be of great interest to senior executives. Dedrick, Gurbaxani, and Kraemer (2003) review over 50 empirical studies on the relationship between IT investment and productivity, and find that recent research shows significant and positive relations between IT investment and labor productivity at the firm level. Weill & Ross (2004) show the importance of effective IT governance to financial performance, finding that firms pursuing a specific business strategy with better than average IT governance exhibit ROAs over 20% higher than

firms with low IT governance pursuing the same strategy. Weill & Aral (2006) find that financial results are significantly impacted by a firm's level of IT savvy. Companies with high IT savvy earn higher net profits in years subsequent to investment, while companies with low IT savvy actually earn lower net profits. These topics, which support the financial import of a firm's decisions related to IT, will be addressed at greater length in a later section.

Recent studies also suggest a growing recognition among executives in the importance of IT-driven functions such as supply chain management activities to overall firm profitability. Ellram and Liu (2002) discuss a trend in results from a biennial study of compensation and financial accountability for Chief Purchasing Officers in manufacturing, general services and high tech sectors. The survey indicated that bonus or incentive payments for CPOs were increasingly tied to the firm's overall financial performance (from 57% in 1999 to 75% in 2001). At the same time, the CPO's compensation rewards were trending away from a more limited focus on the area long seen as supply chain management's primary area of fiscal contribution, cost reduction. These results suggest that, in top management's eyes, purchasing and supply management's focus "has shifted from providing functional efficiency (cost reduction) to contributing to the organization's overall financial effectiveness." Recognizing that supply chain managers still need to be able to better express the impact of their activities on overall firm financial performance, the authors present a mapping of procurement and supply management activities to elements of the financial statements and to financial performance ratio measures.

Key Asset Governance: Governance of Financial Assets

One of management's roles in setting corporate strategy is to determine and pursue an appropriate financing structure for the firm. Jensen and

Meckling (1976) develop an argument for the existence of an optimal capital structure using agency costs resulting from information asymmetry. Debt holders cannot be sure what managers will do with their money, so the debt holders will charge higher interest, which is the agency cost. Similarly, prospective new shareholders will force a higher issuance price to compensate for their concern that an original owner-manager will expropriate wealth the new shareholders. Agency costs of equity will decrease in leverage while agency costs of debt will increase in leverage; the authors argue that the agency costs associated with debt will be balanced against the agency costs associated with new equity to produce an interior solution. The optimal solution results in a firm value which is obviously less, however, than the value which could be realized in a world without information asymmetries between manager/owners and investors and the resultant agency costs. Demsetz and Lehn (1985) argue that corporate ownership structures do maximize firm value, in that shareholders will ultimately adopt the ownership pattern that maximizes expected return given the interplay of market forces affecting a particular business enterprise. The authors provide empirical support for their argument, predicting and finding no linear relation between ownership structure and firm value. Morck et al. (1988), however, show that there is a relation between firm value and inside equity ownership, but that it is nonlinear; they show that manager and shareholder interests appear to be aligned at high and low levels of ownership, but there exists a range where between which encourages management entrenchment. Jensen's (1986) free cash flow theory proposes that agency costs are more severe in firms with large free cash flows because investors worry that management will squander the excess cash, and argues that debt can be used to reduce these agency costs. By issuing debt and using the proceeds to buy back stock, management commits the firm to a steady stream of payments which serves to discipline

management decisions. Myers and Majluf (1984) show how information asymmetry affects a firm's issue-invest decisions and suggest explanations for some corporate financing choices "including the tendency to rely on internal sources of funds and to prefer debt to equity if external financing is required" as attempts by firms to avoid the underinvestment problem. Jung, Kim, and Stulz (1996) consider Myers and Majluf's "pecking-order" theory along with agency and timing models, and conclude that empirical results best support the agency model.

There is a good deal of international research with strong implications for capital structures around the world. Governance characteristics vary widely across countries. Thus, international research frequently offers opportunities to examine governance mechanisms in settings where the effects are likely to be especially pronounced. La Porta, Lopez-de-Silanes, Shleifer, and Vishny (1998) show that ownership concentration is inversely related to the level of investor protections offered within a country. Using a sample of East Asian firms, Claessens, Djankov, Fan, and Lang (2002) present evidence that firm value increases with cash flow rights consistent with positive incentive effects of ownership and decreases with separation of control rights from cash-flow rights, consistent with negative entrenchment effects, and that the entrenchment effects increase at higher levels of separation. Doidge, Karolyi, and Stulz (2004) argue that foreign firms choose to cross-list in the U.S. when they have valuable growth opportunities which are worth relinquishing the benefits of private control, and find support for the theory by showing that growth opportunities are valued more highly for firms that cross-list. Yeh and Woidtke (2005) show that Taiwanese firms are more likely to choose directors and supervisors who are affiliated with a controlling shareholder when there is a greater divergence between control and cash flow rights and that board affiliation and divergent ownership are more likely in family owned firms. Their findings suggest that a firm's board structure is a strong indicator of the strength or weakness of the firm's corporate governance when ownership is concentrated, shareholder protections are weak, and ownership structure is difficult to determine. Durnev & Kim (2005) show that a firm's ownership concentration affects the firm's choice of governance practice, especially in firms in weaker investor protection legal regimes.

Key Asset Governance: Governance of IT Assets

Discussion of asset management is restricted here to the management of IT assets for two reasons. One reason is that this chapter is primarily interested in exploring the relationship between corporate and IT governance. Another reason is that corporate governance topics in the finance and accounting literatures provide little attention to the management of assets. In fact, there is little research focused on the relationship between IT and corporate governance in the academic IS literature, a surprising result given the increasing reliance of many entities on IT for strategic and competitive advantages. As mentioned previously, much of the existing IS literature devoted to IT governance is focused on the rights and responsibilities for decisions related to IT activities (Sambamurthy & Zmud, 1999) and on the types of organizational governance structures.

There are three primary IT activities within an organization: (a) IT infrastructure management, which consists of the selection of hardware, software, and network architecture the organization will use and standards for procurement and deployment of IT assets; (b) IT use management, which consists of planning and prioritization decisions as well as the provision of everyday service; and (c) project management, which consists of the skills necessary to effectively manage the development of in-house solutions. The literature on IT governance focuses on the identification of the best organizational structure to facilitate decision

making for the aforementioned IT activities. The organizational structures, sometimes referred to as IT governance modes, are centralized, decentralized and federal (Sambamurthy & Zmud, 1999; Weill & Ross, 2004). The centralized mode calls for decision rights to be central to the corporate IT team, while the decentralized mode grants decision rights to divisional IT or line management. The federal mode is a hybrid, where the decision rights for some corporate IT activities are held by corporate IT and others by divisional IT or line management.

Karake (1992) examines the relations between IT structure and corporate control in a study of 72 large publicly-held firms. Karake shows that firms with higher levels of management ownership are more likely to exhibit a centralized IT structure, allowing management greater control over firm operations, while firms with more diffuse ownership structures exhibit more decentralized IT structures, consistent with increased conflicts among managers and shareholders. Sambamurthy and Zmud (1999) recognize that a number of factors interact to simultaneously impact the optimal locus of decision rights, and identify three scenarios of the interaction of multiple contingencies: reinforcing, conflicting and dominating. They hypothesize that organizations facing dominating or reinforcing contingencies are more likely to select either a centralized or decentralized IT structure, while those facing conflicting contingencies are more likely to select a federalized structure, supporting their hypotheses with case study data from a set of eight firms. Broadbent and Weill (1997) argue that successful firms create business driven IT infrastructure. To do so a firm must establish an understanding of the firm's strategic context, use this understanding to clearly articulate business and IT maxims, and then use the maxims to identify "specific IT infrastructure services that meet a firm's strategic context." Meyer (2004) identifies five fundamental organizational systems which guide employees in daily decision making: culture, structure, internal economy, methods and tools, and metrics are rewards. He argues that systemic governance practices may be implemented by overhauling one or more of the organizational systems as needed.

Several frameworks have been published to support managers in the implementation of better IT governance, including the Control Objectives for Information and Related Technology (COBIT) and the Information Technology Infrastructure Library (ITIL). COBIT is a framework developed by the Information Technology Governance Institute (ITGI) consisting of over 300 control objectives that are grouped into 34 processes which, in turn, are grouped into 4 domains (Campbell, 2005). The Information Technology Infrastructure Library (ITIL) is a series of documents which are used to help implement an efficient framework for IT service management (ITIL - IT Infrastructure Library, 2007). The ITIL documents were originally created by the United Kingdom's Office of Government Commerce.

Whereas academic literature provides direction with respect to the optimal organizational structure of the IT function within the organization, it largely fails to explore the responsibilities of various organizational roles (e.g., CIO, IT governance committee, BOD) in providing direction of and control over IT assets, or to explore the effectiveness of specific IT governance mechanisms or processes. A large gap therefore exists between the IT governance literature and corporate governance literature, which is primarily focused on relations between boards, managers, shareholders, and creditors and other external stakeholders.

Such a gap is particularly troubling given documented evidence of the importance of investment in IT and its relation to financial performance of organizations. Dedrick et al. (2003) reviewed over 50 empirical studies conducted between 1985 and 2002 that examine the relationship between IT investment and economic performance. Early work in the area found no relationship between IT

investment and productivity, but this lack of finding was primarily attributable to research design flaws such as inadequate data on IT investment, small sample sizes, or tests conducted in industries where output measurement is difficult (e.g., banking or insurance). The counterintuitive nature of these early finding, dubbed the "productivity paradox," encouraged additional research studies that used larger datasets and more refined research methods. This later research found significant and positive relations between IT investment and labor productivity at the firm level, and between IT investment and economic growth at the country level. The authors assert that the detection of a strong relationship which was not evident in earlier studies "may partly reflect the fact that the data was more recent, that levels of IT investment had increased, making it easier to distinguish its contributions, and that over time firms were learning to apply IT capital more productively" (Dedrick et al., 2003, p.7) Additionally, it may also "simply reflect better data sets and analytical tools that make it possible to isolate and measure the true impacts of IT investment" (Dedrick et al., 2003, p.7).

Delivering business value through information technology requires a great deal more than spending, however. Reviewing literature streams that assess the impact of IT on organizational performance, Melville, Kraemer, and Gurbaxani (2004) find that IT does add value, providing a wide-ranging set of benefits including flexibility, quality improvement, cost reduction, and productivity enhancement. The authors recognize that the mechanisms through which value is delivered are context-contingent and require "synergistic combinations of IT and other organizational resources, including workplace practices, change initiatives, organizational structure, and financial condition" (Melville, Kraemer, & Gurbaxani, 2004, p. 311). Kohli and Devaraj (2004) also recognize that the realization of value requires complementary investments and process changes, and present a framework to plan and implement an IT investment, ensure creation of the complementary resources needed to realize value, and adequately measure the actual outcomes.

Weill and Ross (2004) also recognize that the value of IT requires more than investment in IT. Rather, it requires that decisions related to IT be comprehensively integrated within the firm so that the firm has strong IT decision-making processes. They assert that effective IT governance identifies the decisions that must be made to ensure effective management and use of IT, determines who should make these decisions, and how the decisions will be made and monitored. Additionally, among a set of for-profit firms studied, Weill and Ross quantified the fact that good IT governance provides financial returns. More specifically, they found that firms "pursuing a specific strategy (for example, customer intimacy or operational excellence) with above-average IT governance performance... had ROAs more than 20 percent higher than the firms with poorer governance pursuing the same strategy" (Weill & Ross, 2004, p. 14)

Weill and Aral (2006) provide further evidence that obtaining bottom line results from IT requires more than investment in IT, even when the company uses IT portfolio management to regularly realign IT spending with strategic objectives. They study 147 U.S. companies over five years, and find that companies "with a mutually reinforcing set of practices and capabilities" that the authors term "IT savvy" earn a significant premium return on their investments in IT infrastructure. The authors find that for each dollar invested in IT infrastructure, firms with high (low) IT savvy have $247 higher ($909 lower) net profits in the year following the expenditure. The authors define IT savvy as referring to "the planned, ongoing use of a set of interlocking business practices and competencies that collectively derive superior value from IT investments" (Weill & Aral, 2006, p. 40).

EXTERNAL GOVERNANCE MECHANISMS

Legal Environment

Much of the literature on the legal environment depends on the perspective one takes. From a domestic perspective, some argue that U.S. laws will not, in and of themselves, constrain opportunistic behavior by managers and directors. Others who argue from an international perspective, however, define U.S. law tradition as it relates to shareholders as being among the most protective in the world.

Jensen (1993) argues that the political, regulatory, and legal environment in the U.S. is an "unwieldy" and "blunt" mechanism, which is reactionary in nature; the system is therefore too slow to provide effective management discipline and worse yet, often misguided in direction (for example, having rendered the market for corporate control ineffective). Examples of legislation, which may be misguided, are laws designed to restrict the operation of the takeover mechanism. Coles and Hoi (2003) examine the effect of boards' decisions as to whether to opt out of antitakeover protections afforded by Pennsylvania state law, and show evidence that both outside and inside directors who are in a majority presence on the board and therefore likely to meaningfully contribute to a decision as to whether to accept or reject the protection of the antitakeover provisions, are rewarded in the directorial labor markets for a decision to reject some or all of the provisions.

La Porta et al. (1998) examine the origins of legal systems around the world, and show that legal origins affect quality of shareholder and creditor rights across countries, and that ownership concentration is negatively related to the level of investor protection. The importance of investor protection is explored further in La Porta, Lopez-De-Silanes, Shleifer, and Vishny (1997), where the authors show that countries that protect shareholders have larger and more valuable stock markets and more frequent initial public offerings than countries that fail to protect shareholders, and countries that protect creditors have larger credit markets. In their review paper, La Porta, Lopez-de-Silanes, Shleifer, and Vishny (2000) argue that their legal approach is a better way to understand corporate governance and its reform than the conventional distinction between bank-centered and market-centered financial systems. Beck, Demirguc-Kunt, and Levine (2003) present an alternative argument, providing evidence that cross-country variability in financial intermediary and stock market development is more heavily influenced by whether European colonists found the locale more (less) hospitable and therefore set up institutions to protect property rights (extract resources).

Variation in shareholder protection is found to impact many management behavior and ownership structure in a number of ways. Leuz et al. (2003) show that earnings management is more prevalent in countries with poor shareholder protections, where controlling shareholders have greater private benefits of control that they desire to hide from minority shareholders by managing earnings. Kelley and Woidtke (2006) show that poor investor protection appears to attract foreign investment, and that U.S. multinationals appear to be motivated to invest in firms with weak investor protections due to comparative advantages arising from the ability to select better projects and better ability to raise debt and equity capital to take on these better projects.

There is evidence that firms may opt-in to more restrictive legal regimes, and thereby enhance their corporate governance. Doidge et al. (2004) show that there is a cross-listing premium for firms that cross-list in the U.S., and hypothesize the reason that only some firms cross-list is because the firms that do have valuable growth opportunities which are worth relinquishing the benefits of private control. They find support for the theory by showing that growth opportunities are valued more highly for firms that cross-list and that the valuation premium is especially pronounced for firms from countries with weak shareholder protections. Lel and Miller (2006) show that CEO turnover is more sensitive to performance at firms that crosslist on major U.S. exchanges, a result which suggests that firms can improve corporate governance by opting-in to a more restrictive legal environment.

Capital Markets

In addition to the effects of corporate governance on management decisions to raise capital in the external debt and equity markets, discussed in a previous section, governance quality can effect relations with influential shareholders subsequent to debt or equity issuances.

In the U.S., large portions of publicly traded companies are owned by large institutional shareholders. Through their large holdings, these investors have both the means and incentives to monitor the actions of management, but any relations they may have with management may impact institutional shareholders' incentives. For example, Brickley, Lease, and Smith (1988) show that outside blockholders that do not have business ties to management promote shareholder interests in voting against antitakeover amendments, while outside institutions that have existing or potential business with existing management may be subject to management influence when they cast their votes. Shivdisani (1993) strengthens this result, showing that the presence of blockholders that are not affiliated with management increases the likelihood of a takeover while higher managerial ownership decreases this risk, suggesting that unaffiliated blockholders and takeovers are complementary mechanisms for corporate control.

Differing incentives also play a large role in the likelihood of large institutional investors to engage in shareholder activist efforts to elicit desired changes from management or boards of directors. Karpoff, Malatesta, and Walkling (1996) show that while poorly performing firms are more likely to attract proposals from shareholder activists, the proposal have little effect on shareholder value or firm policies, and only persistent shareholder pressure prompts beneficial operating change. Using a private data set obtained from TIAA-CREF, Carleton, Nelson, and Weisbach (1998) show that institutional shareholders are in fact highly effective in affecting changes at target firms, a fact that had been understated in prior studies due to the private nature of negotiations between large institutional investors and target firms. Del Guercio and Hawkins (1999) recognize the heterogeneity among pension fund objectives and strategies, and show that not only are shareholder proposals effective in promoting change, but that pension fund activism is not inconsistent with value maximization and can therefore be considered an effective corporate governance mechanism. In treating private and public pension funds separately, Woidtke (2002) finds results consistent with arguments that performance-based compensation structures common among private pension fund administrators help to align their incentives with other shareholders, while public pension fund administrators appear to be motivated more by political and social influences which may lead them to take actions which hurt other shareholders.

Many smaller firms in the U.S. also raise capital through private equity, and the relationships between firms and private equity sources are unique in some ways from public equity issuances. Hertzel and Smith (1993) examine why private investors require and firms accept deep discounts on private equity placements, and why the market reacts positively to private equity placements, a reaction in stark contrast to the general negative reaction to public issuance. They find results consistent with the supposition that private equity placements are another answer to the Myers and Majluf (1984) underinvestment problem discussed in the previous section; discounts are attributed to information

costs incurred by the private investors (as well as compensation for forthcoming monitoring services), and the willingness of private investors to commit funds serves as a positive signal to the market regarding the firm's prospects. To further examine this issue, Hertzel, Lemmon, Linck, and Rees (2002) show that firms issuing private equity exhibit poor operating performance leading up to and earn poor stock market returns subsequent to the placement. Such evidence refutes the idea that the issuance is a positive signal to the market that the firm is undervalued (since the firm is shown to be overvalued), as well as hypotheses that suggest investors are overly optimistic upon issuance and subsequently underreact to negative information. By considering several heterogeneities (affiliated vs. unaffiliated investors, financially distressed vs. nondistressed firms, net returns to private investors vs. other shareholders), Krishnamurthy, Spindt, Subramaniam, and Woidtke (2005) show that private investors do earn abnormal returns, and while unaffiliated investors receive steeper discounts than affiliated investors (consistent with disparate information costs) both earn post-issuance returns on par with the market.

Takeover Market

Although the takeover market has been severely restricted since the early 1990's, the suggestion that the takeover market was an extremely effective tool in motivating corporate management to maximize firm value on behalf of the shareholders is a generally accepted notion within the finance literature. Very interesting theoretical work examines when the takeover market was and was not likely to be effective. Grossman and Hart (1980) argue that, due to the free-rider problem, the takeover bid mechanism is not an effective mechanism unless initial shareholders voluntary dilute their property rights by including in the corporate charter permissions for the raider to exclude minority shareholders from benefiting from improvements the raider makes. Jensen's (1986) free cash flow theory, discussed in the previous section, predicts that large firms with low growth prospects and substantial free cash flows will be desirable targets for takeover and that increased leverage will serve to force the firm to reorganize into a more efficient organization. Jensen (1993) argues that the market for corporate control, in fact, was until around 1990 *the most* efficient mechanism for early intervention to eliminate excess capacity and promote disciplined management behavior. Jensen explains, however, that the market for corporate control was shut down in the early 1990's "through court decisions, state antitakeover amendments, and regulatory restrictions on the availability of financing."

Labor Markets for Directors and Managers

Fama (1980) presented the "ex-post settling up" hypothesis, which argues that the only way the markets for managerial or directorial services have to evaluate talent is based on current *firm* performance, which will encourage these individuals to manage and monitor in a manner consistent with shareholder wealth maximization. According to Fama, the discipline imposed by managerial and directorial labor markets does a better job of resolving potential incentive problems resulting from the separation of ownership and control than does direct control of management by risk bearers or the threat of outside takeover. Fama and Jensen (1983) argue that outside directors have incentives to develop reputations as good corporate monitors of management decisions. Harford (2003) finds that directors at takeover targets often lose their board seat at the target, and that independent directors of poorly performing firms who act outside shareholder interests to block offers receive fewer outside directorships in the future while those who approve mergers are not subsequently penalized. Coles and Hoi (2003) examine the effect of boards' decisions as to whether to opt out of antitakeover protections

afforded by Pennsylvania state law, and show evidence that both internal and external labor markets for directors exist and function. Their results are strengthened by their finding that rewards only hold for inside or outside directors who are in a majority presence on the board (and therefore likely to meaningfully contribute to a decision as to whether to accept or reject the protection of the antitakeover provisions).

Product Markets

One obvious source of discipline for managers is the product market. If managers fail to guide the firm to produce products that are desired in the product markets, then the firm will fail. Kaplan and Minton (2006) show that boards are more likely to replace CEOs when industry or market performance is poor overall, suggesting that it is sometimes efficient to bring in a new CEO to respond to changing industry or market conditions. Product market discipline is not ideal, however. Jensen (1993) argues that product and factor markets can serve to correct overcapacity in the economy, but are not timely as corrective measures; they are the inevitable crises which result when no other disciplinary measure steps in first.

Auditors

Auditing studies tend primarily to rely upon one of two methodological approaches, archival and behavioral. Archival research in auditing tends to rely heavily on economic and financial theories which suggest that individuals are economically rational in their decision making such that the aggregation of individual decisions results in capital markets which are highly efficient. Behavioral research in auditing relies more heavily upon psychological and sociological theories which allow for the existence of biases which may result in individual decisions which are not always economically rational choices.

Behavioral research in auditing is primarily employed in the study of auditors' judgment and decision making (JDM). Nelson and Tan (2005) provide an excellent review of the JDM literature from 1980 through 2005, asserting that much of this literature may be classified into three broad tasks: (1) the audit task, (2) the auditor and his/her attributes, and (3) interaction between auditor and other stakeholders in task performance. These three features are integral features of the auditing setting, because auditors must perform a variety of tasks to form an overall opinion, personal attributes of the auditor influence the outcome, and auditors interact with other auditors and stakeholders of the firm. Most research activity on audit tasks relates to risk assessments, analytical procedures and evidence evaluation, auditors' decisions regarding whether to require clients to book proposed AJEs, and going concern judgments. Because auditing involves professional judgment, and as auditors approach an audit task they are subject to individual characteristics and cognitive limitations which leave them susceptible to judgmental biases, it is of both theoretical and practical interest to investigate the effects of attributes on auditor JDM. Research on the auditor and the auditor's attributes generally focuses on auditor knowledge and expertise, other individual characteristics, cognitive limitations, and decision aids designed to improve auditor performance. Much of the published research focuses on the JDM of individual auditors. Because auditors do not work in isolation, however, it is important to understand how the people auditors interact with influence their performance. Paper examining the auditors' relationships with other stakeholders generally focus on the interactions between auditors and other auditors, auditors and their clients, and auditors and other participants in the financial reporting process.

DeFond and Francis (2005) provide an examination of archival research in auditing, although it is primarily focused on the effects of the Sarbanes-Oxley Act of 2002. The authors note that the profession has come under intense scrutiny in the wake of the accounting scandals of the early millennium, that such criticism "essentially boils down to issues of audit quality, and audit quality in turn is affected by a number of basic economic institutions that define the basic nature of auditing practices." In the course of their arguments, the authors discuss empirical results related to several factors which impact audit quality, including the legal environment and characteristics of the audit engagement, the audit firm, and companies' audit committees. Literature which examines the effect of the legal environment on auditor incentives focuses on the auditor's civil liability and criminal enforcement. One of the more interesting streams of research which focus on engagement-specific characteristics examines the impact on audit quality of the auditor's fees for auditing and/or consulting, as large fees may economically bond the auditor to the client, thereby reducing the auditor's objectivity and independence. Other interesting streams related to the impairment of auditor independence relate to auditor tenure and to the "revolving door policy" in which "accounting firm alumni take positions at clients." A good deal of research investigates characteristics which may promote or curtail the effectiveness of the Audit Committee to whom the audit firm reports. Interesting work examines whether audit committee effectiveness is impacted by size, financial expertise, or the proportion of independent audit committee members. Additional interesting work examines whether or not larger accounting firms produce higher quality audits.

BRIDGING THE GAP BETWEEN CORPORATE AND IT GOVERNANCE RESEARCH

We view IT governance as an important subset of overall corporate governance, which is important to the overall health of a firm. Strong IT governance assures the board and other stakeholders that investments in IT will generate business value and that the firm's control risks related to IT will be minimized. This view is consistent with an excellent definition of IT governance provided by the IT Governance Institute's Board Briefing on IT Governance (Institute, 2003):

IT governance is the responsibility of the board of directors and executive management. It is an integral part of enterprise governance and consists of the leadership and organizational structures and processes that ensure that the organization's IT sustains and extends the organization's strategies and objectives.

Yet we show clearly in the second section that the governance of IT assets is largely overlooked in the corporate governance literature, in spite of the increasing importance of these assets to the achievement of strategic corporate objectives.

In our discussion of corporate governance mechanisms in the second section, we touch on several important linkages between corporate and IT governance which provide strong opportunities for fruitful research. We show a clear connection between executive and board incentives and the alignment of IT objectives and priorities with business objectives and priorities. We also show a strong linkage between financial asset governance and IT asset governance. Finally, we feel that research into the importance of IT controls in the financial statement audit is an important topic that is ripe for exploration.

We have discussed the increasing reliance on incentive based compensation structures in management contracts, such that achieving high levels of profitability is obviously a strong motivator for management action. To recognize the gains inherent in the proper governance and management of IT requires proper alignment of IT and business strategies. This is an essential requirement in securing high levels of return on investments ROI), specifically IT investments, and not necessarily in the traditional sense of the term ROI. Weill

and Aral (2006) provide one such measure of the appropriate alignment of business practices and competencies with their examination of the "IT savvy" of 147 U.S. companies based using survey instrument measures, but we encourage the development of additional methodologies to measure the degree of strength with which a company's IT objectives are aligned with corporate objectives. We also encourage research to identify the impact of other corporate governance factors on this alignment, such as board composition. For example, international studies could show whether this alignment becomes more or less important to firm value in alternate settings. Many countries around the world lack the strong regulatory oversight of the capital markets that is enjoyed by U.S. shareholders, and therefore exhibit more highly concentrated ownership. Does a stronger alignment between corporate and IT strategies encourage greater minority shareholding in those countries, thereby promoting greater economic development? Do firms which intend to subject themselves to more rigorous legal oversight by crosslisting on U.S. exchanges take action to align their corporate and IT strategies beforehand?

We also discussed the existence of a strong linkage between financial asset management and IT asset management. First, literature in finance suggests that management should undertake all positive NPV projects. Measurement of the value of investment in IT is particularly difficult, because the value of well planned and implemented IT projects is frequently realized throughout the organization in benefits which are tangible in some areas and intangible in others. The resistance with which the concept of IT value has been met, at least in practice, encourages continued research into the value of the planning and implementation of IT projects. We also call for additional research into the measurable benefits (inclusive of and beyond cost reduction) of IT in its complementary role to corporate functions (e.g., such as supply chain management, managing external relationships, interorganizational citizenship behavior). Several questions researchers can consider include, but are not limited to, the following:

- How do financial auditors become comfortable with the results of the systems review?
- How has this level of comfort with the results of the systems review changed when comparing the period immediately preceding SOX and the post-SOX era?
- What is the nature of the relationship between the strength of firms' ITGC and the results of their financial audits?
- What combination of the frameworks used for conducting financial audits and information systems audit tend to be better than others?
- How has the choice of internal control frameworks and IT control frameworks changed since the enactment SOX?
- What role does the quality and effectiveness of internal and IT controls play in decisions to enter into interorganizational partnerships (e.g., outsourcing specific functions, merging with other firms)?
- What is the nature of the linkage between the effective governance of IT assets and the CIO reporting structure in organizations where CEO and BOD Chairman is a joint position?
- What is the nature of the linkage between the effective governance of IT assets and the CIO reporting structure in organizations where CEO and BOD Chairman is not a joint position?
- What is the nature of the relationship between effective governance of financial assets and the CIO's presence at and participation in executive business meetings (including BOD meetings)?
- To what degree does the CIO's relationships with other members of a firms' governing body influence governance impact on firm performance?

- What's the relationship between a firm's reissuing of financial statements after SOX and the IT control framework(s) adopted by the organization?

Finally, we call for research into the role of IT controls in financial statement audits. Information systems, and their associated controls, tremendously affect a vast amount of the information reviewed by financial statement auditors in the conduct of their examination. If the system controls are weak and the information produced by various systems (e.g., ledger or subledger systems, asset management systems, revenue or inventory tracking systems) is not reliable, then examination of the information output from these systems is futile. The Big 4 and many other large accounting firms tend to separate, to some degree, their examination of the financial records and the examination of the underlying information systems. Since the reliability of the financial records depends on the information system's ability to produce information that is timely, accurate, and reliable, the audit firm's information systems auditors normally conduct their inspection prior to fieldwork for the financial audit. While this makes obvious sense, it is important to consider the strength of communication between the two teams. This is an area which is ripe for judgment and decision making (JDM) research in auditing. Furthermore, we encourage researchers to work towards the identification of a proxy for the strength of IT general controls (ITGC), IT controls which apply enterprise-wide as opposed to system-specific controls.

CHAPTER SUMMARY

This chapter has discussed the overall importance of both corporate and IT governance, and has demonstrated that IT governance is a very important subcomponent of corporate governance. We presented a framework, based on the framework previously presented by Weill and Ross (2004), which should facilitate a strong understanding of the different factors and mechanisms that impact firms' governance. Finally, we presented a number of examples that link corporate and IT governance. In presenting those linkages, we identified a number of areas that we believe provide fruitful avenues for researchers to explore IT governance as it relates to corporate governance, and vice versa.

REFERENCES

Bebchuk, L. A., & Cohen, A. (2005). The costs of entrenched boards. *Journal of Financial Economics, 78*(2), 409-433.

Beck, T., Demirguc-Kunt, A., & Levine, R. (2003). Law, endowments, and finance. *Journal of Financial Economics, 70*(2), 137-181.

Brickley, J. A., Lease, R. C., & Smith, C. W. (1988). Ownership structure and voting on antitakeover amendments. *Journal of Financial Economics, 20*, 267-291.

Broadbent, M., & Weill, P. (1997). Management by maxim: How business and IT managers can create IT infrastructures. *Sloan Management Review, 38*(3), 77-92.

Campbell, P. L. (2005). *A COBIT primer* (No. SAND2005-3455). Albuquerque, New Mexico: Sandia National Laboratories.

Carleton, W. T., Nelson, J. M., & Weisbach, M. S. (1998). The influence of institutions on corporate governance through private negotiations: Evidence from TIAA-CREF. *Journal of Finance, 53*(4), 1335-1362.

Claessens, S., Djankov, S., Fan, J. P. H., & Lang, L. H. P. (2002). Disentangling the incentive and entrenchment effects of large shareholdings. *Journal of Finance, 57*(6), 2741-2771.

Coles, J. L., & Hoi, C. K. (2003). New evidence on the market for directors: Board membership and Pennsylvania Senate Bill 1310. *Journal of Finance, 58*(1), 197-230.

Dedrick, J., Gurbaxani, V., & Kraemer, K. L. (2003). Information technology and economic performance: A critical review of the empirical evidence. *ACM Computing Surveys, 35*(1), 1-28.

DeFond, M. L., & Francis, J. R. (2005). Audit research after Sarbanes-Oxley. *Auditing, 24*, 5-30.

Del Guercio, D., & Hawkins, J. (1999). The motivation and impact of pension fund activism. *Journal of Financial Economics, 52*(3), 293-340.

Del Guercio, D., Seery, L. J., & Woidtke, T. (2006). Do board members pay attention when institutional investors "Just Vote No"? CEO and director turnover associated with shareholder activism. Retrieved May 13, 2008, from http://ssrn.com/abstract=575242

Demsetz, H., & Lehn, K. (1985). The structure of corporate ownership: Causes and consequences. *Journal of Political Economy, 93*(6), 1155-1177.

Denis, D. J., & Denis, D. K. (1995). Performance changes following top management dismissals. *Journal of Finance, 50*(4), 1029-1057.

Doidge, C., Karolyi, G. A., & Stulz, R. M. (2004). Why are foreign firms listed in the U.S. worth more? *Journal of Financial Economics, 71*(2), 205-238.

Durnev, A., & Kim, E. H. (2005). To steal or not to steal: Firm attributes, legal environment, and valuation. *Journal of Finance, 60*(3), 1461-1493.

Ellram, L. M., & Liu, B. (2002). The financial IMPACT of supply management. *Supply Chain Management Review, 6*(6), 30-37.

Fama, E. F. (1980). Agency problems and the theory of the firm. *Journal of Political Economy, 88*(2), 288-307.

Fama, E. F., & Jensen, M. C. (1983). Separation of ownership and control. *Journal of Law & Economics, 26*(2), 301-326.

Grossman, S. J., & Hart, O. D. (1980). Takeover bids, the free-rider problem, and the theory of the corporation. *Bell Journal of Economics, 11*(1), 42-64.

Harford, J. (2003). Takeover bids and target directors' incentives: The impact of a bid on directors' wealth and board seats. *Journal of Financial Economics, 69*(1), 51-83.

Hertzel, M., Lemmon, M., Linck, J. S., & Rees, L. (2002). Long-run performance following private placements of equity. *Journal of Finance, 57*(6), 2595-2617.

Hertzel, M., & Smith, R. L. (1993). Market discounts and shareholder gains for placing equity privately. *Journal of Finance, 48*(2), 459-485.

Institute, I. T. G. (2003). Board briefing on IT governance (2nd ed.) [Electronic Version]. Retrieved May 13, 2008, from http://www.itgi. org/Template_ITGI.cfm?Section=ITGI&Tem plate=/ContentManagement/ContentDisplay. cfm&ContentFileID=4667

ITIL - IT Infrastructure Library (2007). Retrieved May 13, 2008, from http://www.itil-officialsite. com/home/home.asp

Jensen, M. C. (1986). Agency costs of free cash flow, corporate finance, and takeovers. *American Economic Review, 76*(2), 323-329.

Jensen, M. C. (1993). The modern industrial revolution, exit, and the failure of internal control systems. *Journal of Finance, 48*(3), 831-880.

Jensen, M. C., & Meckling, W. H. (1976). Theory of the firm: Managerial behavior, agency costs and ownership structure. *Journal of Financial Economics, 3*(4), 305-360.

Jung, K., Kim, Y.-C., & Stulz, R. M. (1996). Timing, investment opportunities, managerial

discretion, and the security issue decision. *Journal of Financial Economics, 42*(2), 159-185.

Kaplan, S. N., & Minton, B. A. (2006). How has CEO turnover changed? Increasingly Performance Sensitive Boards and Increasingly Uneasy CEOs.

Karake, Z. A. (1992). An empirical investigation of information technology structure, control and corporate governance. *The Journal of Strategic Information Systems, 1*(5), 258-265.

Karpoff, J. M., Malatesta, P. H., & Walkling, R. A. (1996). Corporate governance and shareholder initiatives: Empirical evidence. *Journal of Financial Economics, 42*(3), 365-395.

Kelley, E., & Woidtke, T. (2006). Investor protection and real investment by U.S. multinationals. *Journal of Financial & Quantitative Analysis, 41*(3), 541-572.

Kohli, R., & Devaraj, S. (2004). Realizing the business value of information technology investments: An organizational process. *MIS Quarterly Executive, 3*(1), 53-68.

Krishnamurthy, S., Spindt, P., Subramaniam, V., & Woidtke, T. (2005). Does investor identity matter in equity issues? Evidence from private placements. *Journal of Financial Intermediation, 14*(2), 210-238.

La Porta, R., Lopez-de-Silanes, F., Shleifer, A., & Vishny, R. W. (1997). Legal determinants of external finance. *Journal of Finance, 52*(3), 1131-1150.

La Porta, R., Lopez-de-Silanes, F., Shleifer, A., & Vishny, R. W. (1998). Law and finance. *Journal of Political Economy, 106*(6), 1113-1155.

La Porta, R., Lopez-de-Silanes, F., Shleifer, A., & Vishny, R. (2000). Investor protection and corporate governance. *Journal of Financial Economics, 58*(1/2), 3-27.

Lel, U., & Miller, D. P. (2006). International cross-listing, firm performance and top management turnover: A test of the bonding hypothesis. *Working Papers—US Federal Reserve Board's International Finance Discussion Papers* (pp. 1-61).

Leuz, C., Nanda, D., & Wysocki, P. D. (2003). Earnings management and investor protection: an international comparison. *Journal of Financial Economics, 69*(3), 505-527.

Melville, N., Kraemer, K., & Gurbaxani, V. (2004). Review: Information technology and organizational performance: An integrative model of IT business vslur. *MIS Quarterly, 28*(2), 283-322.

Meyer, N. D. (2004). Systemic IS governance: An introduction. *Information Systems Management, 21*(4), 23-34.

Morck, R., Shleifer, A., & Vishny, R. W. (1988). Management ownership and market valuation: An empirical analysis. *Journal of Financial Economics, 20*(1/2), 293-315.

Myers, S. C., & Majluf, N. S. (1984). Corporate financing and investment decisions when firms have information that investors do not have. *Journal of Financial Economics, 13*(2), 187-221.

Nelson, M., & Tan, H.-T. (2005). Judgment and decision making research in auditing: A task, person, and interpersonal interaction perspective. *Auditing, 24*, 41-71.

Parrino, R., Sias, R. W., & Starks, L. T. (2003). Voting with their feet: Institutional ownership changes around forced CEO turnover. *Journal of Financial Economics, 68*(1), 3-46.

Rosenstein, S., & Wyatt, J. G. (1990). Outside directors, board independence, and shareholder wealth. *Journal of Financial Economics, 26*(2), 175-191.

Sambamurthy, V., & Zmud, R. W. (1999). Arrangements for information technology governance: A theory of multiple contingencies. *MIS Quarterly, 23*(2), 261-290.

Shivdasani, A. (1993). Board composition, ownership structure, and hostile takeovers. *Journal of Accounting & Economics, 16*(1-3), 167-198.

Shivdasani, A., & Yermack, D. (1999). CEO involvement in the selection of new board members: An empirical analysis. *Journal of Finance, 54*(5), 1829-1853.

Weill, P., & Aral, S. (2006). Generating premium returns on your IT investments. *MIT Sloan Management Review, 47*(2), 39-48.

Weill, P. & Ross, J. W. (2004). IT governance: How top performers manage IT decision rights for superior results (Hardcover). *Harvard Business School Press Books*.

Woidtke, T. (2002). Agents watching agents?: Evidence from pension fund ownership and firm value. *Journal of Financial Economics, 63*(1), 99-131.

Yeh, Y.-H., & Woidtke, T. (2005). Commitment or entrenchment?: Controlling shareholders and board composition. *Journal of Banking & Finance, 29*(7), 1857-1885.

Yermack, D. (1996). Higher market valuation of companies with a small board of directors. *Journal of Financial Economics, 40*(2), 185-211.

Chapter XII
I–Fit:
Optimizing the Fit between Business and IT

Alea Fairchild
Tilburg University, The Netherlands

Martin Smits
Tilburg University, The Netherlands

Piet Ribbers
Tilburg University, The Netherlands

Erik van Geel
KZA BV, The Netherlands

Geert Snijder
KZA BV, The Netherlands

ABSTRACT

This document summarizes the initial findings of the I-Fit research project that started in August 2006 as a joint activity of a regional ICT consultancy and a university research center. The main goal of the project is to help the consultants to improve alignment between business and IT in the client organizations. The I-Fit project takes the perspective of the business manager: how a business manager can influence and increase the value of the IT services that he receives. Based on the literature on strategic alignment and Information quality, we develop the I-Fit model. The model assumes causal relationships between IT governance, Strategic Alignment, Information Quality, and Business Performance in an organization.

INTRODUCTION TO I-FIT PROJECT AND ITS OBJECTIVES

The I-Fit research project is a joint effort between KZA and Tilburg University and aims to further develop the alignment model.

The objectives of the I-Fit project are: To predict the impact of the business environment on the IT function in an organization, and to identify and manage the factors that influence the Information services in an organization.

The starting point of both the I-Fit project (and this chapter) is the well-known Strategic Alignment Model (Parker, Benson, & Trainer, 1989; Henderson & Venkatraman, 1991). Strategic alignment, or "business-IT alignment," intends to support the integration of IT into business strategy. The classic "Strategic Alignment Model" distinguishes between the business domain (business strategy and business processes) and the technology domain (information strategy and IT processes, including systems development and maintenance) in an organization.

The I-Fit project focuses on three issues: identifying the key alignment processes, identifying performance indicators for alignment processes, and developing methods to improve alignment.

The deliverables of the I-Fit project include instruments or tools:

1. To provide insight for business managers in the IT consequences of decisions on Information services,
2. To support business managers to control Information services , based on alignment processes, and
3. To design strategies for the IT domain in order to maximize IT value added for the business, and (possibly) for benefits management.

This chapter summarizes the first three building blocks (Information Quality[1], alignment, and Business Performance (Figure 1)) for the creation

Figure 1. Building blocks for the I-Fit project

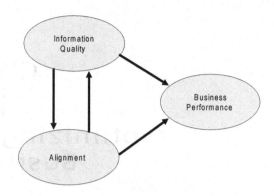

Note: The arrows indicate some possible relations between alignment, information quality and business performance

of these tools. We briefly discuss two case studies within the project, and conclude with a generic framework addressing the relations between IT governance, Alignment Processes, Information Quality, and Business Performance. We also discuss the next steps of this I-Fit project for interested readers.

LITERATURE REVIEW

Information Quality

Our work is based on Roest (1988), Van der Pijl (1994a, 1994b), and Vermeer (1999) and denotes a typical Dutch or European perspective on information management. In this perspective, the quality of information (coming from information systems) is the key issue to explain business success. The USA approach differs since it aims to explain business success not by focusing on information, but on information technology and information systems.

The well-accepted definition of information quality is "the degree to which information is fit for use" or "fitness for purpose" (Klobas, 1995). Therefore, information quality on the highest level can simply be determined by asking for user satisfaction. However, this does not provide insight into the origins of quality failures. To analyze the origins, information Quality can be determined in two distinct ways, also known as the teleological and the causal perspective (Van der Pijl, 1994a) (Figure 2 shows these two perspectives). In the I-Fit project we use these two perspectives to determine the quality of information.

Teleological Perspective

In the teleological perspective, information quality is the degree to which the information (data) that is delivered to the business fulfils the business needs. In the teleological model the quality of information is determined by the objective for which the information is intended to be used. Van der Pijl (1994a) argues that information depends on personal objectives that in their turn (partly) depend on organizational objectives. The importance of the teleological model is that it introduces organizational and business process objectives next to personal (e.g., user) objectives in the concept of information quality. From the te-

leological point of view the quality of information is seen as the degree to which it satisfies "stated or implicit needs," derived from the situation in which it is used.

Typical indicators for Information quality in the teleological perspective (Van der Pijl, 1994a) are: timeliness, accurateness, relevance, availability, and completeness[2]. Also, the flexibility of information (services) is important: how fast can Information services be changed in case of changes in the business needs? Note that, for instance, faster management reporting can relate to administrative requirements ("boekhoudkundige tijdigheid") and improved logistics of information processing.

Causal Perspective

Another perspective on Information quality is found in the causal model. In this perspective, Information quality is the degree to which the information that is delivered to the business is the result of a clear and correct chain of activities. These activities can be grouped in two phases:

Figure 2. Causal and teleological perspectives on quality of information

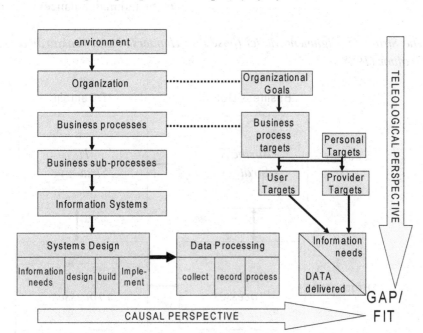

the information system development phase and the information system operation phase. The importance of the causal model of Information quality is that it is not possible to measure all aspects of the quality of information only from the information itself. The reliability of information also depends on the measures that are taken in the IS development and operational phase.

From the *causal perspective,* the quality of information is seen as the result of the quality of the processes in which it is produced. The first step in these processes is information analysis. During this stage the link between the organization's needs and the information systems is established. First the information policy is formulated and then the more detailed information needs are derived. The essence of the causal point of view in ex-post quality assessments is that not all aspects of the quality of information can be measured from that information itself. For some features it is necessary to look at one or more of the steps of the production process.

Typical indicators for Information quality from the causal perspective (Van der Pijl, 1994a) are "the information is provided according to the existing service level arrangements," "the infor-

mation creation process is accountable for and transparent," and "it is SOX compliant."

Interestingly, the variety of Information quality indicators from the two perspectives create the need for business managers to balance between timeliness, completeness, accurateness, and the flexibility of information services. Aiming for the maximum performance on all quality indicators leads to high costs for information services.

Strategic Alignment

Three concepts are important to determine the impact of IT on information quality (previous section) and Business Performance (final section). In this section we define alignment, fit, and IT governance.

Henderson and Venkatraman (1993) introduced "business-IT alignment," in short "alignment," intended to support the integration of IT into business strategy. They distinguish in their classic "Strategic Alignment Model" (Figure 3) between the business domain (consisting of "business strategy" and "business processes") and the technology domain (consisting of "IT strategy" and "IT processes," including systems development and maintenance) in an organization.

Figure 3. The Strategic Alignment Model (based on Henderson and Venkatraman (1993) and Parker, Benson & Trainor (1988))

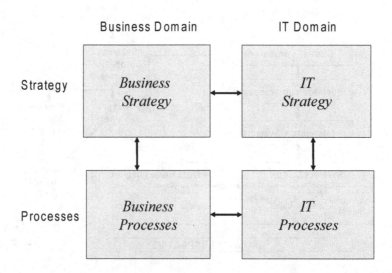

Since 1990, various changes have been proposed to the Strategic Alignment Model, refocusing IT strategy into Information Systems Strategy (Strategic Information Systems Planning) and Information Strategy, showing more focus on business relations.

Information strategy is a complex phenomenon. In many organizations and in much of the information systems (IS) literature different terminologies are used. We define information strategy as: "a complex of implicit or explicit goals, visions, guidelines and plans with respect to the supply and demand of formal information in an organization, sanctioned by management, intended in the long run to support the objectives of the organization and adjusted to the environment."

Operationally expressed, information strategy is an instrument to manage Information services and technology in an organization. A frequently used term, related to information strategy, is strategic information systems planning (SISP) (Earl, 1993; Galliers, 1991; King, 1988; Lederer & Sethi, 1988; Ward, Griffiths & Whitmore, 1990). SISP is defined as "the process of deciding the objectives for organizational computing and identifying potential computer applications which the organization should implement" (Lederer & Sethi, 1988). The two definitions look very similar, but a strict comparison shows that the SISP definition tends to focus on explicit objectives and on applications and technology. Our definition concentrates on the use and the importance of information in an organization, starting with the planning of information (in the end influencing IT, as well as influenced by IT). We preferred this definition as a starting point to investigate how contemporary organizations deal with their needs for information and the planning of IT.

Strategic alignment is pursued along two dimensions in Figure 3: strategic fit: the (vertical) fit between strategies (business and IT) and internal infrastructures and processes, and *functional integration*: the (horizontal) fit between the business and the technology domain) (Henderson & Venkatraman, 1993).

Alignment is an elusive concept (Chan, 2002). Definitions of alignment range from high level, broadly encompassing definitions such as:

The fit between an organization and its strategy, structure, processes, technology, and environment.

A more focussed definition is:

The convergent intention, shared understanding and coordinated procedures.

Well-received views are that IS alignment is:

the degree to which the IT mission, objectives, and plans support and are supported by the business mission, objectives and plans (Chan, 2002), and *alignment is not a state, but a journey – one that is not always predictable, rational, or tightly planned* (Ciborra, 1991; Sauer & Yetton, 1997).

Chan (2002) defines IS alignment as:

- **IS alignment:** The "bringing in line" of the IS function's strategy, structure, technology, and processes with those of the business unit, so that IS personnel and their business partners are working toward the same goals while using their respective competencies.
- **IS strategic alignment:** The subset of IS alignment that concerns IS strategy and Business Unit Strategy. This component includes both strategy and processes.
- **IS structural alignment:** The subset of IS alignment that concerns the formal structure of the IS function and the business unit structure.

In the remaining discussion on this topic in this chapter, we focus on two aspects of alignment: (1) alignment as a process consisting of driver, levers, and impact, aiming to improve fit and (2) alignment as the degree of strategic fit and functional integration. Additionally, IT governance is introduced as the control structure in an organization to realize effective alignment processes.

IT Governance Defined

IT governance is defined as the way in which IT in an organization is controlled and coordinated (Brown 1997; Sambamurthy & Zmud 1999). More precisely, IT governance is about the focus of IT decision-making authority (centralized vs. decentralized control) and the processes that are in place to communicate IT decisions (Peterson, 2002).

Effective IT Governance Leads to Successful Alignment Processes

Governance comes from "kybernan" (Greek) and is related to "cybernetics" (Wiener, 1948), meaning "to steer" and "keeping a ship on its course in the midst of unexpected changing circumstances" (Peterson, 2002). Governance can be regarded as "control" in a broad perspective, meaning that governance includes the total set of controlling activities that keep the system (ship, organization) on the right (chosen) course (Malone & Crowston, 1994). Governance is a purposeful intervention in order to achieve a desired output, and describes a subsystem of decision-making units for directing and coordinating operational subsystems.

The governance paradigm is based on a general systems approach of organizations (Ashby, 1956). Control is governance in a limited perspective, related to directing one subsystem.

Traditionally, three configurations have been distinguished for IT governance (Sambamurthy & Zmud, 1999). In each configuration, stakeholder constituencies take different lead roles and responsibilities for IT decision making:

- **Centralized:** In this configuration, corporate IT management has IT decision-making authority concerning infrastructure, applications, and development.
- **Decentralized:** In this configuration, division IT management and business-unit management have authority for infrastructure, applications, and development.
- **Federal:** In this configuration (a hybrid configuration of centralization and decentralization), corporate IT has authority over infrastructure, and division IT and business-units have authority over applications and development.

In general, it is argued that centralization provides greater efficiency and standardization, while decentralization improves business ownership and responsiveness (Brown 1997). Table 1 shows eight types of IT governance, varying from centralized to decentralized decision making.

Peterson (2001) indicated that as companies experience increased uncertainty and complexity, and adopt multifocused strategies, IT governance

Table 1. Hybrid configurations for IT governance

Configuration IT decisions	1 Low hybrid	2	3	4	5	6	7	8 High hybrid
Infrastructure	CIT	CIT	CIT	CIT	CIT	CIT	CIT	CIT
Applications	DIT	CIT	DIT	BM	CIT	BM	DIT	BM
Development	CIT	DIT	DIT	CIT	BM	DIT	BM	BM

CIT (Corporate IT Management), DIT (Division IT Management), BM (Business-unit Management)

Figure 4. IT governance design (Peterson, 2001)

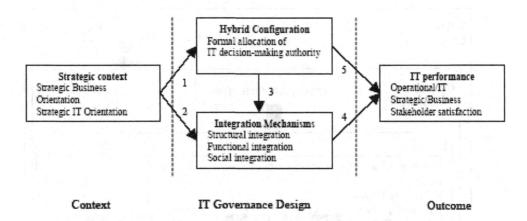

designs are more hybrid with increased coordination needs. Figure 4 shows how the strategic (business) context influences the type of governance design and the integration mechanisms for IT governance, ultimately influencing IT performance. Peterson showed that for organizations in a dynamic strategic context, the best IT governance structure is decentralized decision making, combined with rich integration mechanisms.

For I-Fit, it is shown later in this chapter that we have added two types of governance (information system (IS) and information (I)) to the classic IT governance definitions (e.g. the ISACA definition: "IT governance is the responsibility of executives and the board of directors, and consists of the leadership, organizational structures and processes that ensure that the enterprise's IT sustains and extends the organisation's strategies and objectives" (COBIT 4.0, www.itgi.org)).

Business Performance

Melville, Kraemer, and Gurbaxani (2004) reviewed the literature on IT and Organizational Performance and developed an integrative model of IT Business value (Figure 5). The term IT business value is commonly used to refer to the organizational performance impacts of IT, including productivity enhancement, profitability

improvement, cost reduction, competitive advantage, inventory reduction, and other measures of performance.

The core of the model shows the impact of IT and complementary organizational resources on business processes and business process performance. Mediating variables are trading partner resources, industry characteristics, and country characteristics. The term performance is used to denote both intermediate business process level measures (also indicated as first order effects) as well as organizational measures (indicated as higher level variables, such as market share).

The IT business value literature does not provide a convention regarding the incorporation of costs of system development and implementation.

ISSUES AND SOLUTIONS FOR I-FIT PROJECT

Addressing Information Quality

Issue: Linking Information Quality to Business Objectives

In both perspectives, the quality of information relates to the degree to which information supports

Figure 5. The IT business value model indicating the effect of IT resources on business processes, business process performance and organizational performance (Melville et al., 2004)

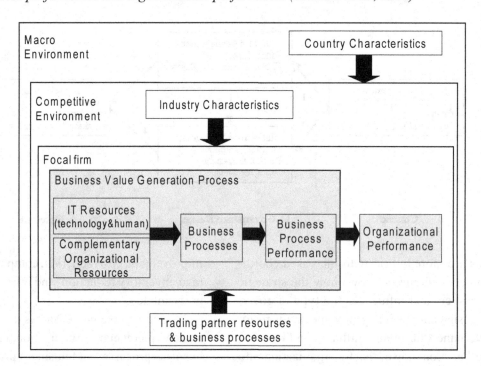

the goals (strategies, objectives) of the organization in which it is used. We outline these goal categories below (Van der Pijl, 1994b):

- **The organizational goals**. Almost every organization is characterized by the fact that its members come together to realize some kind of common goal. This common or organizational goal reflects the expectations, ambitions and aspirations of those who depend on the organization. At the level of the organization as a whole, organizational goals have to be translated into strategies that describe how these goals can be reached. Strategies arise in an interaction between structure, culture and goals of the organization. Traditionally we suppose that information has to support the organization's strategies. Recently we see, however, that information systems can also be used to shape, instead of support, organizational

strategies and that they make it possible to aim for new goals.

- **The business process goals**. The existing division of labour in the organization is the basis for translating organizational goals and strategies into targets for each business process, department and individual within the organization. The degree of detail to which these targets have to be described when studying the quality of information depends on the organizational level that is chosen as a starting point for the analysis. Some organizations have explicit mechanisms for adjusting organizational goals and business process targets for different processes and hierarchical levels, while others do not. In some organizations there even is no strictly hierarchical relationship between goals and targets at all levels (operations, managerial, and strategic).

- **The personal interests**. Each individual in the organization also has its own individual interests. Status, power, responsibility, prestige and money are well known examples of personal aims, which can be influenced by background, experience and knowledge. Since the information needs of a person in a certain function in the organization are influenced by both business process targets and personal interests, a judgement of the quality of information available to the individual has to take both elements into account.
- **The user's targets and the provider's targets**. Goals and targets can not only be subdivided according to levels in the organization but also into targets of those who are using information and targets of those who are providing others with information. A difference in position may lead to differences of opinion on the quality features and characteristics of the information received or provided.

Judging the *teleological aspects* of the quality of information in an organization means assessing the degree to which the information systems in the organization contribute to each of the goals and targets listed previously.

It is also possible to take only a subset of goals and targets into consideration. If we look at individual systems at the level of user's or provider's targets, we can study in detail which quality features and characteristics determine the contribution of systems to reaching the targets and how well the systems do so for each of these. If we look at the configuration of systems available to the organization as a whole, we take a much more global view. In that case we ask ourselves which functional contribution the systems make to the goals and targets of the organization without specifying detailed quality characteristics. Thus the detailed view of quality is replaced by a more global view in which quality of information in

the organization is understood as the degree of fit between the goals and targets of the organization and the information systems that support the organization.

The causal and the teleological point of view are combined in Figure 2. At the bottom of the figure we see the steps of the process that has to be studied in the causal approach. On the upper right-hand side of the figure the set of goals and targets are shown, to be considered in the teleological approach. The vertical lines indicate the correspondence between the different levels of goals and targets and the hierarchical levels of the organization depicted on the left-hand side.

Solution: Measuring Information Quality

We see two opportunities or tools to measure the quality of information.

The first tool is the INK Information Mirror (in Dutch "informatiespiegel"), published in "Perfect Information Services (in Dutch: Excellente Informatievoorziening. Luiten, www.ink.nl). The Information Mirror consists of 25 questions from both the causal and the teleological perspectives. Answering the questions on a four-point Likert scale leads to a total score indicating the quality of Information services . *Note that this tool aims to determine the quality of Information services and not –only- the quality of information that is the result of the services.*

The second tool is the method by Van der Pijl (1994b, pp. 119-124), adapted from Bedell (1985), and focusing on the teleological perspective. The method consists of 12 steps, starting with (1) describing the objectives of the organization, the process, and the individuals involved, and (2) describing the information systems in the organization. In the next step the information systems are related to the business processes and process objectives per process. Then the relative impact of each information system to each objective and process is estimated. By adding the scores for all information systems and business processes, the total value of all IS for the organization is calculated. *Note that this tool aims to determine the quality of (the functionality of) information systems, and not the quality of information!*

Addressing Strategic Alignment

Issue: Alignment as a Process: Driver, Lever, and Impact

Henderson and Venkatraman described four types of alignment. Two alignment types are driven by business needs: (1) *Strategic execution:* business strategy drives organizational infrastructure and processes, ultimately influencing IS infrastructure and processes, and (2) *Technology transformation*: business strategy drives IT strategy, ultimately influencing IT processes.

Two other alignment types are driven by IT opportunities: (3) *Competitive potential*: information strategy influences business strategy, ultimately influencing organizational infrastructure and processes, and (4) *Service level*: information strategy influences IT infrastructure and processes, ultimately influencing organizational infrastructure and processes.

Luftman (1996) found empirical evidence that alignment can be seen as a process with a typical sequence of activities. Each alignment process has three major components that form a complete pattern of strategic change: a driver, a lever, and an impact (see also Hsiao & Ormerod, 1998). In the first perspective the business strategy is the driver for business processes or information strategy (called "levers"), ultimately affecting the IT processes ("impact"). Analysis of driver-lever-impact sequences can be found in Smits and Huisman (2007) and Alt and Smits (2007).

Similar refinements of the original alignment model can be found in Hsiao and Ormerod (1998) and Sauer and Yetton (1994), who also analyzed the relationships and different patterns of influence (different sequences of drivers, levers, and impacts) between strategy, structure, technology, and management.

Chan (2002) and Sauer and Yetton (1994, 1997) acknowledge that alignment is not a state (a situation of equilibrium between the domains that an organization can reach), but a journey ('a continuous managerial effort, not always predictable, rational, or tightly planned').

This journey and process perspective on alignment is fully in accordance with our definitions of information quality and the gap between information services and information needs:

* Alignment is a process in an organization that aims to reduce the gaps between the business domain and the technology domain, and between strategies and processes, and, ultimately the gap between information needs and information services.

Solution: Alignment and Organizational Effectiveness

The IS literature has repeatedly outlined the fundamental importance of alignment for organizational effectiveness and several attempts have been made to define the alignment concept more precisely and to develop the strategic alignment model into more concrete managerial guidelines and tools (Chan, 2002). Based on a review of literature and practice, alignment is defined by Chan as a multidimensional phenomenon, and as "a superset of multiple, simultaneous component alignments that bring together an organization's structure, strategy, and culture at multiple levels (IT, business unit, and corporate) with all their inherent demands"

Cragg et al. (2002) aimed to focus on the relationship between alignment and organisational performance, based on the argument that strategic fit has performance implications. Generally spoken: the better the fit, the better the performance (Fry & Killing, 1989). More specifically, the study wished to focus on one aspect of IT alignment, that is, the alignment between business strategy and IT strategy (Henderson & Venkatraman, 1989). In the Cragg et al. (2000) study, IT alignment was viewed as the fit between business strategy and IT strategy, similar to Chan et al. (1997). Two approaches were modelled—fit as "matching" and fit as "moderation"[3] which both rely on the close correspondence between the nine IT strategy items and the nine business strategy items. Fit as matching was based on the difference between each of two pairs of related items. Fit as moderation was modelled as the interaction between each business strategy and the related IT strategy. Thus, a gap analysis is created as to the closeness of fit to purpose.

This concept of "alignment" or "fit" expresses an idea that the object of design, e.g. an organisation's structure or its information systems, must match its context in order to be effective (Iivari, 1992). Parsons (1983) was one of the first to argue that IT can affect a firm's ability to execute their business strategy. Since then, many others have emphasised the need to develop a fit between information technology strategies and business strategies (Chan et al., 1997; Galliers, 1991; Henderson & Venkatraman, 1993; Venkatraman, 1989).

Addressing Business Performance

Issue: Frameworks for Organizational, Process, and Network Performance

The Operations Research and Management Science disciplines have provided guidelines to measure Business Performance of individual companies as well as the performance of business networks and supply chains (SC). A well-known example is the Balanced Scorecard (Kaplan & Norton, 1992), distinguishing between performance in four domains: financial, customer, process, and innovation.

The Supply Chain Operations Reference model (SCOR) for supply chain process benchmarking and performance measurement within as well as across firms, is based on five distinct management processes: plan, source, make, deliver, and the return process (Supply Chain Council, 2005). The SCOR model shows that performance can be evaluated in many ways, for example, higher flexibility, customer orientation, customization, flexibility and better cost-effectiveness. Gunasekaran et al. (2004) use the SCOR perspective and conclude that supply chain performance refers to meeting the end customer requirements, including product availability, on-time delivery, and all the necessary inventory and capacity in the supply chain to deliver that performance in a responsive matter. So, performance can be regarded "good" when the performance objectives are achieved on all levels and as set by all managers and organizations involved. Obviously, matching all these objectives is not an easy task (Hausman, 2002).

Kleijnen and Smits (2003) investigated the metrics used by organizations to evaluate Business Performance in a SC. Starting point is the set of five classic SC performance metrics reported in SC literature and practice from a single company perspective: (1) Fill rate (the percentage of orders delivered "on time"; that is, no later than the delivery day requested by the customer); (2) Confirmed fill rate (the percentage of orders delivered no later than the day agreed between the customer and the supplier); (3) Response delay (the difference between the requested delivery day and the negotiated day); (4) Delay (actual delivery day minus confirmed delivery day); (5) Stock (total Work in Process (WIP)). Kleijnen and Smits (2003) conclude that organizations now often use multiple metrics (balanced scorecard) because a single measure does not suffice.

Recently, SCOR related frameworks have become available to evaluate multiple metrics across organizations in a supply chain to support supply chain integration:

- Lambert and Pohlen (2001) present a framework in which Customer Relationship Management and Supplier Relationship Management are the two processes that capture the overall performance of a SC. The two processes must be analyzed in every supplier-customer link in a multi-tiered network to provide the supply chain metrics.

- Gunasekaran et al. (2004) developed a framework for SC performance measurement distinguishing between twelve metric types based on three management levels or responsibilities (strategic, tactical, and operational) and –per level- the four major SC activities (Plan, Source, Make, Deliver). Gunasekaran lists 44 examples of different metrics, for instance, "supplier delivery performance" is a metric for "sourcing" at the "tactical level."

Fairchild, Ribbers, and Nooteboom (2004) distinguish seven success indicators for business networks. Four indicators relate to market context and three to market processes. Market context success indicators can be summarized as (1) a high number, high volume, high variability, and high frequency of the transactions, (2) low complexity, low specificity, and high value of the product, (3) convergence of stakeholder motives, and (4) the presence of government regulations. Market process success indicators can be summarized as (1) low learning costs and low entry barriers, (2) availability of multiple transaction mechanisms, (3) trust, based on neutrality of the market, partnership with domain experts, high quality of product- and trading partner information, security of information, and a local focus.

Solution: From Alignment to Performance

Chan et al. (1997) use a well-accepted model to link Business Strategic Orientation and IS Strategic Orientation to IS Strategic Alignment, Business Performance and IS Effectiveness.

Chan et al (1997) define IS Strategic Alignment as "the alignment between Business Unit Strategic Orientation and IS Strategic Orienta-

tion" and calculate IS Strategic Alignment as the degree to which a company employs the systems that supported the strategic orientation. Note that this is only part of the total alignment processes represented in the strategic alignment model.

Chan et al. (1997) examined whether the impact of IT on performance may not be a direct one, but intermediated by other factors, such as the alignment between Business Strategy and IT Strategy. They modified the well-known STROBE model (STRategic Orientation of Business Enterprises) of Venkatraman to include performance at the IS level as well as at the business unit level. The constructs are defined in Table 2.

I-FIT MODEL: COMBINED BUILDING BLOCKS

This document has summarized the three building blocks Information quality, Alignment, and Business Performance for the creation of tools:

- To provide insight for business managers in the IT consequences of decisions on information services,
- To support business managers to control I services, based on alignment processes, and
- To design strategies for the IT domain in order to maximize IT value added for the business, and (possibly) for benefits management.

Information Quality can be determined in two perspectives: the quality of the information that is provided to the business (the causal perspective) and the quality of the information that is needed by the business (the teleological perspective). The difference between the two quality indicators illustrates the "gap" showing a certain degree of (miss-) fit. We aim to qualify the gap by distinguishing between four types of information, following the balanced score card

Table 2. Dimensions to assess IS strategic alignment and business performance

Key Construct	Indicators	Key informants
STROBE (Strategic Orientation of Business Enterprises)(= Realized Business Strategy)	Company analysis, Company internal defensiveness, Company external defensiveness, Company futurity, Company proactiveness, Company Risk Aversion, Company Innovativeness	Chief Executive Officers
Business Performance[4]	Market Growth, Financial Performance, Product-Service Innovation, Company Reputation	Chief Financial Officers
IS Effectiveness (i.e., Current Value and Business Contribution of IS)	Satisfaction with IS staff and services; Satisfaction with the Information product; satisfaction with End User Knowledge and Involvement IS Contributions to Operational Efficiency, Managerial Effectiveness, Establishment of Market Linkages, Creation and Enhancement of Products and Services.	Vice Presidents of end-user, mission critical departments
STROEPS (Strategic Orientation of the Existing Portfolio of IS applications)(= Realized IS Strategy)	IS Supports for Aggressiveness, Analysis, Internal Defensiveness, External Defensiveness, Futurity, Proactiveness, Risk Aversion, Innovativeness	Executives familiar with the information systems used in the business unit (Chief Information Officers)
IS Strategic Alignment	This construct is calculated from the scores on STROBE and STROEPS	

perspectives: financial, process, customer, and innovation related information.

Strategic Alignment[5] in an organization can be determined by analyzing the alignment processes that occur in an organization (from driver, to lever, and impact) and to assess the IT governance structure and integration mechanisms in an organization aiming to manage alignment and to reduce the gap between information needs and Information services.

Business Process Performance in an organization can be determined by assessing performance at the business process level using balanced scorecard like performance indicators.

For the I-Fit project, based on the literature review in the previous sections, we propose the I-Fit model (Figure 6), to analyze alignment (the current situation IST) in an organization. Key hypothesis in Figure 6 is that "good alignment (effective driver-lever-impact processes and good IT governance) leads to good information quality (good fit between causal and teleological quality indicators), ultimately improving Business Performance."

Key questions for analysis of the current situation (IST) in an organization are:

- How is IT governance implemented in the organization?
- How do alignment processes exist in the organization?
- Are existing information systems aligned with the business strategy in the organization
- Do the Information services fit with the information needs in the organization?
- How mature is the IT and business organization? (similar to the concept of CMMi?)

Answering these questions means that there is a "FIT" between the four circles in Figure 6. If there is no "fit," a new situation should be designed (SOLL), by changing one or more circles. This design process would be a joint effort of consultants and the client organization: the effort can be considered successful if insight in the IST situation has increased, and if a shared basis for implementation of improvements has been accomplished.

Figure 6. The I-FIT model: A framework for tools to analyze alignment in an organization

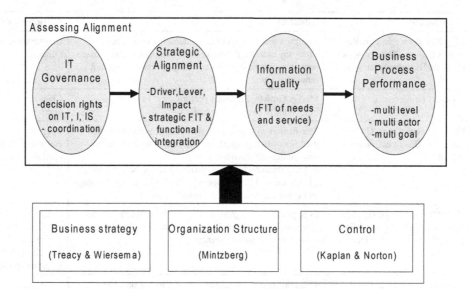

Cases to be Assessed in the I-Fit Project

The primary vertical focus of our initial cases is the financial industry in continental Europe. Both banks discussed here have their names withheld for privacy reasons.

Bank "A": Within Bank A"s IT and change organization, there are a significant number of improvement initiatives, which currently driven by business process improvement (BPI) metrics. These include not only process improvement, but also compliance. Both budget allocation and required cost cutting measures currently take place based on business process improvement (BPI) metrics. This is not a very transparent process for the client internally.

This bank's business model is transforming from a traditional insurance company towards an "issuance factory". The factory model is a shared service center for insurance companies. BPI is responsible for the transition. This means, in practice, that the regular business gets little attention from BPI.

In this context, we are introducing I-Fit to make things transparent and give insight in the consequences of the current state of alignment.

Bank "B": Bank "B" is a cooperation that has recently centralized the IT function ("Group ICT") and is now outsourcing portions of this organization. Within Bank "B", its international organization has its own IT function (IS&D). Nevertheless it also uses of "Group ICT" in some areas. Sometimes the international business contacts Group ICT directly; sometimes an internal intermediary handles the responsibility. Therefore, the consequences are:

- Miscommunication;
- No clear picture of who is responsible for what;
- Internal politics, along with;
- Internal bureaucracy.

We believe that the introduction of I-Fit will play a role in making the problem transparent, as well as give insight in the impact of certain problems.

CONCLUSION: FUTURE RESEARCH DIRECTION

The tools for I-Fit are in development between the two organizations. We propose to continue this research with:

- Further defining the tools for assessing fit, information quality, alignment, and business performance.
- Validating the tools by applying them in some business situations (case analysis).
- Assessment of the validity of the hypothesis in qualitative and quantitative research.

The next step for each of the building blocks is outlined below.

Next Steps to Determine Information Quality

The two tools that are available from theory do not completely match our needs. Therefore we aim to define a tool that helps us to define and determine the quality of the information that is provided (causal perspective) and confront this with the quality of the information that is needed (teleological perspective).

A possible approach to assess the quality of information as the gap between (or the fit of) information needs and Information services in an organization. Information needs are determined by surveying a set of business managers and grouping their information needs on the four dimensions of the balanced scorecard (financial information, information on business processes, information on customers, and information on business dynamics and innovation). Information services are determined by analyzing the information output in the (main) management reports. Comparison of the needs (in four balanced scorecard perspectives) and services (in the same perspectives) shows the gaps in financial, customer, process, and innovation perspectives.

We expect always to find a discrepancy (gap) between the information provided and the information needed, showing a certain degree of (miss-) fit. Key questions are:

- How much fit is there now?
- Is the gap acceptable?
- How dynamic are the business needs?
- Can fit remain when the business needs are changing?

One approach to determining the gap between information services and information needs in the current situation and the future situation is based on making an inventory of information needs and information services. We aim to distinguish between four types of information, following the balanced score card perspectives: financial, process, customer, and innovation related information.

Next Steps to Determine Alignment and Governance

In order to analyze alignment in an organization, we aim to select tools

- To assess the alignment processes that occur in an organization: describe examples of alignment (from driver, to lever and impact), and
- To assess the IT governance design and integration mechanisms (Peterson, 2001) in an organization, aiming to manage alignment processes and to reduce the gap between information needs and information services.

Instead of focusing on IT governance, we might prefer to develop tools for assessing IS governance, or maybe even better information governance because this might fit best our focus on Information quality.

In the previous sections we have addressed "IT governance," "alignment processes," and "information quality." In the next section we address "business performance."

Next Steps to Determine Business Performance

Summarizing, Business Performance should be measured by using multiple metrics per organization, and by using the same metrics on the supply chain level to avoid suboptimization. In practice, performance metrics vary across supply chains, across organizations in a supply chain, and depend on the strategic drivers for the actors involved. This implies that supply chain performance can be successful according to one actor and a failure when evaluated by others.

To be included in the tools to assess Business Performance are topics such as:

- Six Sigma
- How we address stakeholder perspective and types of metrics depends on the types of firms assessed and the industries they participate in.

REFERENCES

Alt, R. & Smits, M. T. (2007). Networkability of business networks. In H. Oesterle et al. (Eds), In *Proceedings of the European Conference on Information Systems* (pp. 119-130), St. Gallen.

Ashby, R. (1956). *An introduction to cybernetics*. London: Chapman & Hall.

Bedell, E. F. (1984). *Computer solution: Strategies for success in the information Age*. New York: McGraw-Hill, Inc.

Brown, C. V. (1997). Examining the emergence of hybrid IS governance solutions: Evidence from a single case site. *Information Systems Research, 8*(1), 69-95.

Chan et al. (1997). Business strategic orientation. *Information Systems Research, 8*(2), 125-150.

Chan, Y. E. (2002). Why haven't we mastered alignment? The importance of the informal organization structure. *MISQuarterly Executive, 1*(2), 97-112.

Ciborra, C. (1991). From thinking to tinkering: The grassroots of strategic information systems. In *Proceedings of the 12th International Conference of Information Systems* (pp. 283-291), New York.

Cragg, P. et al. (2000). IT alignment and organisational performance in small firms. In *Proceedings of ASPECIS*.

Davenport, T. H. & Prusak, L. (1997). *Information ecology: Mastering the information and knowledge environment*. New York: Oxford University Press.

Earl, M. J. (1993). Experiences in strategic information planning. *MIS Quarterly, 17*(1), 1-24.

Fairchild, A., Ribbers, P., & Nooteboom, A. (2004). A success factor model for electronic markets. *Business Process Management Journal, 10*(1), 63 – 79.

Fry, J. N. & Killing, J. P. (1989). *Strategic analysis and action* (2nd ed.). Scarborough, Ontario: Prentice-Hall Canada.

Galliers, R. D. (1991). Strategic information systems planning: Myths, reality and guidelines for successful implementation. *European Journal of Information Systems, 1*(1), 55-64.

Gunasekaran, A. et al. (2004). A framework for supply chain performance measurement. *Int. J. Production Economics, 87*, 333-347.

Hausman, W. H. (2002). Supply chain performance metrics. In C. Billington, T. Harrison, H. Lee, & J. Neale (Eds.), *The practice of supply chain management*. Boston: Kluwer.

Henderson, J. C. & Venkatraman, N. (1993). Strategic alignment: Leveraging information technology for transforming organizations. *IBM Systems Journal, 32*(1), 472-485.

Hsaio, R. & Ormerod, R. (1998). A new perspective on the dynamics of IT-enabled strategic change. *Information Systems Journal, 8*(1), 21–52.

Iivari, J. (1992). The organisational fit of information systems. *Journal of Information Systems, 2,* 3-29.

Kaplan, R. S. & Norton, D. P. (1992). The balanced scorecard: Measures that drive performance. *Harvard Business Review, 70,* 71–79.

King, W. R. (1988). How effective is your information systems planning? *Long Range Planning, 21*(3), 103-112.

Kleijnen J. & Smits, M. T. (2003). Performance metrics in supply chain management. *Journal of the Operatioal Research Society, 54,* 507-514.

Klobas, J. E. (1995). Beyond information quality: Fitness for purpose and electronic information resource use. *Journal of Information Science, 21*(2), 95-114.

Lambert, D. M. & Pohlen, T. L. (2001). Supply chain metrics. *The International Journal of Logistics Management, 12*(1), 1-19.

Lederer, A. L. & Sethi, V. (1988). The implementation of strategic information systems planning methodologies. *MIS Quarterly, 12*(3), 445-461.

Luftman, J. (1996). *Competing in the information age: Strategic alignment in practice.* New York: Oxford University Press.

Malone, T. W. & Crowston, K. C. (1994). The interdisciplinary study of coordination. *ACM Computing Surveys, 26*(1), 87-119.

Melville, Kraemer, & Gurbaxani (2004). IT and organizational performance: An integrative model of IT business value. *MISQ, 28,* 283-322.

Parker, M. M., Benson, R. J., & Traitor, H. E. (1988). *Information economics: Linking business performanance and information technology.* New Jersey: Prentice Hall Inc.

Parker, M., Trainer, H. E., & Benson, R. J. (1989). *Information strategy and economics.* Prentice Hall: NJ.

Parsons, G. L. (1983). Strategic information technology. In Somogyi & Galliers (Eds.), *The information systems as a strategic weapon.*

Peterson, R. (2001). Configurations and co-ordination for global information technology governance: Complex designs in a transnational European context. In *IEEE Proceedings of HICSS* (34).

Roest, W. F. (1988). *Grondslagen van het ontwikkelen van informatiesystemen,* Uitgeverij het glazen oog, Venlo-Vinkeveen, Nederland.

Sambamurthy, V. & Zmud, R. W. (1999). Arrangements for information technology governance: A theory of multiple contingencies. *MIS Quarterly, 23*(2), 261-291.

Sauer, C. & Yetton, P. W. (1997). *Steps to the future: Fresh thinking on the management of IT-based organizational transformation.* San Francisco: Jossey Bass.

Smits, M. T. & Huisman, W. (2007). Investing in networkability to improve supply chain performance. In R. Sprague, Jr. (Ed.), In *Proceedings of the Hawaiian International Conference on Systems Sciences.* Computer Society Press.

Smits, M. T. & Van der Poel (1996). The practice of information strategy in six information intensive organizations in the Netherlands. *Journal of Strategic IS, 5* 93-110.

Supply Chain Council (2005). Supply-chain operations reference-model. Overview of SCOR

Van der Pijl, G. J. (1994a). *Kwaliteit van informatie in theorie en praktijk,* Kluwer Bedrijfswetenschappen, Limpberg instituut, Amsterdam.

Van der Pijl, G. J. (1994b). Measuring the strategic dimensions of the quality of information. *Journal of Strategic Information Systems, 3*(3), 179-190.

Ward, J., Griffiths, P. & Whitmore, P. (1990). *Strategic planning for information systems*. John Wiley & Sons.

Wiener, N. (1948). *Cybernetics or control and communication in the animal and the machine*. Cambridge: MIT Press.

Venkatraman, N. (1989). The concept of fit in strategy research: Toward verbal and statistical correspondence. *Academy of Management Review, 14*(3), 423-444.

Vermeer, Bas H. P. J. (1999). Information logistics: A data integration method for solving data quality problems with article information in large interorganizational networks. In *Proceedings of Fourth Conference on Information Quality (IQ 1999)* (pp. 185-208).

ENDNOTES

[1] Note that we focus on (ex post) information for organizational or management control, that is, not for strategic control or operational control.

[2] See Chan et al. (1997) for balancing between information that is correct and 10% too late or 10% incomplete. See also the work of Davenport and Prusak (1997) on excess of information (information overload).

[3] For six perspectives of fit: see Venkatraman (1989): The concept of fit in strategy research: toward verbal and statistical correspondence. Academy of Management Review, 14(3), 423-444.

[4] Note that this construct differs from Business Process Performance, as defined by Davenport et al in the 1990s, and Hammer and Champy (see also Figure 4).

[5] Note that we might decide to focus on IS strategic alignment, thereby focusing on the left sections of the strategic alignment model.

Chapter XIII
Competence of Information Technology Professionals in Internet–Based Ventures

Tobias Kollmann
University of Duisburg-Essen, Germany

Matthias Häsel
University of Duisburg-Essen, Germany

ABSTRACT

This chapter articulates the knowledge and skills required by IT professionals in young Internet-based firms. Building on the general IT governance principle of aligning business and IT, it introduces an adequate competence model, outlines its dimensions, and suggests a framework for modeling the effects of factors internal and external to the firm on the value propositions of the different dimensions. The authors hope that a comprehensive understanding of the role of IT-related competence will assist founders not only in finding suitable partners, but also in aligning e-business strategy and information technology in Internet-based ventures.

INTRODUCTION

The growing relevance of information technology (IT) and, in particular, the proliferation of the Internet, has resulted in a new economic dimension that is characterized by new possibilities of creating value (Lumpkin & Dess, 2004). The so-called *Net Economy* inevitably facilitates various possibilities for developing innovative business concepts and realizing them by founding a new company (Kollmann, 2006; Kollmann & Häsel, 2006). In newly found ventures, founder competence represents a significant preceding indicator for success (Baum, Locke & Smith, 2001; Chandler & Jansen, 1992). Internet-based ventures are mostly established by heterogeneous teams of founders incorporating knowledge and skills from both the areas of business administration and information technology (Kollmann, 2006; Kollmann & Häsel, 2007). In particular, the founding team usually comprises at least one partner with a business background and one IT professional, as obtaining the required competence from external market participants is oftentimes unfeasible due to a lack of financial resources.

From an IT governance perspective, the choices regarding the acquisition, training and development of the individual competencies required to effectively manage and operate the IT infrastructure are of particular interest (Henderson & Venkatraman, 1999; Van Grembergen, De Haas & Guldentops, 2004). In fact, one important element of IT governance is the governance of human IT resources, that is, the knowledge and skills held by the IT employees of the firm (Gottschalk, 2006; Weill & Ross, 2004). Although the definitions of IT governance differ on some aspects, they are all focused on the link between business and IT (Van Grembergen et al., 2004). Within the Net Economy, IT governance is more complex than the traditional alignment of business and IT, as IT is integrated into business activity and thus the technological, managerial and organizational influences of e-business need to be understood (Patel, 2004). Accordingly, to explain successful venturing activities in the Net Economy, a comprehensive understanding of the various competencies involved is required. In practice, a deeper competence understanding could assist founders not only in finding suitable partners, but also in aligning e-business strategy and information technology.

From a researcher's perspective, the competence of IT professionals in Internet-based ventures is largely unexplored. Although entrepreneurship scholars have intensively explored the concept of competence among entrepreneurs and its various dimensions (Chandler & Jansen, 1992; Chandler & Hanks, 1994; Man, 2002), these competence concepts fail to describe the

various fields of professional knowledge required by IT professionals in Internet-based ventures. In a broader context, information systems (IS) literature has widely elaborated on IT/IS-related competence concepts, including the skills and knowledge required by IS professionals (Lee, Trauth & Farwell, 1995), the business competence of IT professionals (Bassellier & Benbasat, 2004), the IT competence of business managers (Bassellier, Benbasat & Reich, 2003), the competence of CIOs (Earl & Feeny, 1994) as well as the core IS capabilities on an organizational level (Feeny & Willcocks, 1998). However, studies such as these display on a more general approach of describing IT/IS-related competence and fail in capturing the particularities that IT professionals experience in Net Economy founding teams. In this regard, a number of authors point out that there is a lack of studies on the competencies that are required in e-business environments (Matlay, 2004; Sgobbi, 2002).

Similarly, questions of IT governance in the context of Internet-based ventures have not been answered yet (Peterson, 2004). In particular, despite the fact that Internet-based businesses are highly dependent on information technology, the value proposition of IT-related competencies remains unclear. While the strategic role of the CIO is widely recognized in IS literature (Henderson & Venkatraman, 1999; Sambamurthy, Bharadwaj & Grover, 2003), this is not the case for IT professionals engaged in co-founding Internet-based ventures. Human capital theory suggests that the potential value contribution of a partner depends on her competence to solve the tasks and problems that are connected with her job profile (Youndt, Snell, Dean, Jr. & Lepak, 1996). In this connection, a matter of particular interest is how business and IT people *actually* contribute to value creation and how they *perceive* the contribution of their distinct competencies, as in practice – despite the fact that both business and IT people contribute essential competence to the firm (Kollmann & Häsel, 2007) – an unequal distribution of shares can be observed in many Internet-based ventures. In this particular context, a missing awareness of critical competencies may lead to disturbances in venture performance if partners perceive their individual remuneration as inappropriate.

Despite its potential value for both academics and practitioners, a detailed framework for exploring the relevance of the various fields of IT-related knowledge that make up the competence of IT professionals in the Net Economy has not been developed up to now. Building on the general IT governance principle of aligning business and IT (Henderson & Venkatraman, 1999; Luftman & Brier, 1999), this chapter aims to establish the theoretical foundations required to fill this gap. Within this particular context, two research questions are addressed:

1. What are the areas of knowledge and skills that represent the required competence of IT professionals in Internet-based ventures?
2. What are the factors that determine the value of IT competence in the context of founding Internet-based businesses?

More specifically, this chapter articulates the concept of IT-related competence in Internet-based ventures, outlines its dimensions, and suggests a framework for modeling the effects of factors internal and external to the firm on the actual and perceived value propositions of the different dimensions.

BACKGROUND

In an Internet-based venture, the IT professional is usually responsible for implementing the Web platform and may take the role of the CIO at a later stage. In the classical sense, the CIO of a firm is responsible for the business and IT vision, the design of the IT architecture and the delivery of IT services (Earl & Feeny, 1994; Feeny &

Willcocks, 1998). However, in an Internet-based venture that generates revenue and profits through a Web-based platform independent from a physical value chain (Amit & Zott, 2001; Lumpkin & Dess, 2004; Weiber & Kollmann, 1998), the role of the CIO seems to be fairly different from its classical definition as IT-related issues of strategy are elevated from inward focused support functions to critical success factors (Bauer, 2001). Instead of designing the firm-wide IT infrastructure and delivering internal IT services, the CIO is mainly responsible for implementing, maintaining and enhancing the venture's Web platform, that is, the technological basis of the firm's value creation processes (Kollmann, 2006; Kollmann & Häsel, 2006). This unique position of IT professionals in Internet-based ventures suggests that their role demands a special set of knowledge and skills.

Basically, there are three alternatives to develop a competence construct (Lee et al., 1995). While a first approach is to empirically derive perceived competence dimensions, a second way is to define the dimensions *a priori* using an existing theory. A third alternative is to semantically classify a critical set of competencies utilizing existing studies that have identified and verified respective dimensions. The majority of studies use this third approach for reasons of validity and simplicity (Lee et al., 1995). It is not appropriate for exploring the competence of IT professionals in Internet-based ventures, as there are a number of contextual particularities such as scare financial resources, small entrepreneurial teams (Kollmann, 2006), the need for practical experience in developing Web-based systems (Murugesan, Deshpande, Hansen & Ginige, 2001), and the need for agility and proactiveness to cope with the fast-paced environment of the Net Economy (Bhandari, Bliemel, Harold & Hassanein, 2003; Highsmith, 2002; Sharma & Gupta, 2004). In order to avoid an intuitional and heuristic extension of existing models, a theoretical frame of reference is required to classify, adapt und extent the constitutive dimensions describing the competence of IT professionals in Internet-based ventures.

One may speak of competence only where there exists an agreement or fit between knowledge and a task (Von Krogh & Roos, 1995), that is, competence is based on knowledge, but manifests itself only in a specific context, enabling an individual to adequately solve new problems in unknown situations. Consequently, when developing competence models, a multidimensional perspective integrating the epistemological dimensions of theoretical knowledge and practical experience is required (Bassellier & Benbasat, 2004; Sgobbi, 2002). The majority of existing studies apply a taxonomy proposed by Polanyi (1967), distinguishing between *explicit* and *tacit* knowledge. While explicit knowledge may be verbalized, is uniquely communicable and may thus be taught, read and explained, tacit knowledge cannot be fully verbalized (Polanyi, 1967) and enables an individual to modify its actions as a result of the experience gathered in prior actions. Moreover, tacit knowledge covers cognitive aspects such as vision and business acumen (Nonaka, 1994).

Besides defining competence on an epistemological level, competence may also be defined on a functional or disciplinary level, differentiating between *professional* and *managerial* know-how (Sveiby & Lloyd, 1990). With respect to IT professionals, scholars agree that specialized IT knowledge must be accompanied by competencies that are not directly related to IT or computer science (Bassellier & Benbasat, 2004; Medlin, Dave & Vannoy, 2001; Tang, Koh & Lee, 2001). In particular, these non-IT competencies include conceptual knowledge on the potential problem solving areas and business knowledge, since the development of information systems always has to meet economic requirements (Bassellier & Benbasat, 2004).

Competence of IT professionals may thus be conceptualized as a dualism of IT and business knowledge. On an epistemological level, both areas apparently include both explicit and tacit knowledge. However, it may be argued that many problems that IT professionals are confronted with cannot be solved by the mere existence of functional or disciplinary (i.e., IT and business) knowledge. These *transdisciplinary* problems require knowledge on how to *integrate* disciplinary knowledge (Horlick-Jones & Sime, 2004). Transdisciplinary knowledge therefore enables IT professionals to combine their functional knowledge on instruments and methods, as it is required in the respective context, facilitating a "higher-order *thinking* about technical and managerial issues in a holistic manner" (Dalal, 1994, p. 26). The need for transdisciplinary competence is reflected in the 2003 curricula recommendation of the ACM, considering "technology-enabled business development" (Gorgone, Davis, Valacich, Topi, Feinstein & Longenecker, 2003, p. 13) as an intersection of the disciplinary fields that have been introduced in previous versions of the ACM recommendation (Couger, Davis, Dologite, Feinstein, Gorgone & Jenkins, 1995).

Besides the ACM recommendations, a number of researchers underline the interplay of specialized IT knowledge and general business knowledge. In an early study, Nelson (1991) explores the knowledge and abilities required by IT personnel. He identifies six dimensions of competence that describe both organizational and IT knowledge, but also highlights the transdisciplinary ability to sense the potential of IT in an organizational context. In a study surveying business managers, IT managers and IT consultants, Lee et al. (1995) find that IT professionals need to understand the business context and possess interpersonal and management knowledge/skills. Moreover, they need to possess technology management knowledge which is "concerned with where and how to deploy information technologies effectively and profitably for meeting strategic business objectives" (Lee et al., 1995, p. 323). Similarly, Fang, Lee, and Koh (2005) find that entry-level IS professionals need to possess both technically-oriented and business-oriented knowledge and skills, while the latter particularly includes knowledge and visions on how to use technology trends in a competitive environment.

In a survey of job advertisements for programmers, system analysts and IS managers Todd, McKeen, and Gallupe (1995) ascertain that all there job profiles require technical knowledge, systems knowledge and business knowledge. Similarly, Medlin et al. (2001) explore two technical and two non-technical skill sets among IS students, while Bailey and Stefaniak (2001) classify the skills of programmers as technical, soft and business concepts. The non-technical competence of IT professionals is investigated in detail by Bassellier & Benbasat (2004), who differentiate between organization-specific knowledge and interpersonal/management knowledge. The former includes knowledge of IT-business integration that enables IT professionals to understand synergies and interdependencies between IT and business activities. In line with this survey on the business competence of IT professionals, Bassellier, Reich, and Benbasat (2001) explore the IT competence of business managers, comprising five areas of explicit IT knowledge as well as tacit knowledge such as experience in IT projects and vision for the role of IT.

IT COMPETENCIES IN THE CONTEXT OF INTERNET-BASED VENTURES

The literature review in the preceding section reveals that the competence of IT professionals invariably covers a technical/methodical and a business/social dimension: "The perception exists that a successful IS professional blends technical knowledge with a sound understanding of the business while commanding effective interpersonal skills" (Todd et al., 1995, pp. 1-2). The literature review also highlights the importance of transdisciplinary knowledge that enables IT professionals to integrate the technical/methodical and business/social competence dimensions, that is, effectively applying specialized knowledge in a higher-order business context. However, the competence models described in the existing literature are not able to fully capture the role of IT professionals in Internet-based ventures, as young businesses in the Net Economy entail a multitude of contextual particularities. These particularities will be discussed in the following sections in order to derive a competence model for IT professionals in the Net Economy.

Contextual Particularities of Young Businesses in the Net Economy

In the last years, the platforms of Internet-based ventures have become complex software systems that should be referred to as *Web applications* rather than Websites (Ginige & Murugesan, 2001). In the Net Economy, Web applications implement the primary value creation activities of electronic businesses, forming the basis of electronic products and important interfaces to customers and cooperation partners (Kollmann, 2006; Kollmann & Häsel, 2007). It is especially the development of such interfaces that traditional IT governance has not had to deal with (Patel, 2004). Web applications in the context of the Net Economy are therefore considerably different from traditional enterprise applications, which have a supporting function with respect to value creation activities and are mostly used for internal purposes. Consequently, IT professionals are not required to act as an internal service provider (Farwell, Kuramoto, Lee, Trauth & Winslow, 1992), but take a central role in *product development*, requiring sound knowledge in the fundamental areas of computer science, such as databases, programming, computer graphics, analysis, and design as well as the management of software projects (Taylor, 2006). In contrast to traditional software projects, the development of Web applications for electronic businesses comprises a larger amount of standards, technologies and development tools, resulting in highly complex projects (Ginige & Murugesan, 2001; Taylor, England & Gresty, 2001). Moreover, unlike established technologies, Web technologies are characterized by a higher volatility (Reifer, 2002) that demands software developers to continuously upgrade their specialized IT knowledge (Sgobbi, 2002; Taylor et al., 2001).

Besides technological particularities, the development of electronic products entails several managerial issues that indirectly affect the competence requirements of IT professionals. Mostly, these issues result from the aforementioned technological volatility, as new technologies enable new business models as well as new forms of collaboration and competition (Bhandari et al., 2003). As the Web facilitates worldwide comparability, the implementation of new business models is associated with a substantial pressure of competition. Fierce competition also results from low chances of differentiation, a higher geographical reach of the single market participants, lower switching costs, lower entry barriers and new substitutive products (Porter, 2001). In particular, the turbulence of the Net Economy leads to the fact that electronic products are characterized by a very short time-to-market (Cash, Yoong & Huff, 2004). Consequently, the primary goal is not to produce high-quality products at a low cost, but rather launch high-quality products to the market as quickly as possible (Reifer, 2002). In many cases, there are radically new business models, which are as a result of interaction with customers, partners and competitors, not fully outlined until the cause of the development project or even after introducing the product to the market (Highsmith, 2002). As a result, electronic businesses need to gather practical experiences and market feedback as soon as possible in order to adapt their strategy. This is supported by empirical studies showing that product development processes in the Net Economy should focus "on getting an early (and by definition, incomplete) version of the product into customers' hands at first opportunity" (MacCormack, Verganti & Iansiti, 2001, p. 144).

In the light of continuously changing market requirements, flexibility and rapid response are the key to success in the Net Economy (Shi &

Daniels, 2003; Sharma & Gupta, 2004). Flexibility can be considered at three dimensions that include processes, products and people (Meso & Jain, 2006). On the *process* level, software development processes need to correspond to the fact that Web applications change and grow rapidly during their life cycle (Ginige & Murugesan 2001; Highsmith, 2002). Processes need to facilitate a continuous evolvement and maintenance of the electronic product, resulting in "perpetual beta" (O'Reilly, 2005) products that are released early and released often, treating users as co-developers. On the *product* level, flexibility is associated with the extensibility, scalability, maintainability, compatibility, interoperability, and security of the Web application. Only flexible system architectures can be adapted according to the volatile requirements in a timely and cost-effective manner (MacCormack et al., 2001; Shi & Daniels, 2003). On the *people* level, flexibility calls for IT professionals that understand the interdependencies between market and technology – and thus are able to anticipate upcoming requirements and transfer them into new products and functionalities. This requires intensified interpersonal skills, as informal planning and incremental development activities imply an effective interaction with interdisciplinary teams consisting of both business and IT people (Cash et al., 2004). In many Internet-based ventures, however, holding up flexibility may be impeded by a lack of financial resources (Kollmann, 2006) that precludes an enlargement of the team by hiring additional development expertise. Consequently, both development processes and application architectures heavily rely on the explicit and tacit knowledge of a small group of developers, or even on the individual development practices of a single IT professional (Ginige & Murugesan, 2001). In the context of IT governance, which focuses on transforming and positioning IT for meeting future business challenges (Peterson, 2004), the competence profile of the respective IT professional is thus critical with respect to enforcing fast and flexible processes, while at the same time developing flexible products of a high quality.

A Competence Model for IT Professionals in the Net Economy

Building on the various constructs identified in the IS literature as well as the previously discussed contextual particularities of Internet-based ventures, three competence dimensions may be derived, which include *IT competence*, *business competence* and *transdisciplinary competence*. According to their epistemological and functional/disciplinary characteristics, these dimensions may be further subdivided (see Figure 1). The resulting dimensions will be discussed in the following paragraphs.

IT competence: The aforementioned complexity and volatility of the knowledge required for Web application development renders an in-depth modelling of IT competence almost impossible. However, explicit IT knowledge may be roughly divided into two areas. One of these areas includes knowledge on available technologies that the IT professional may fall back on when implementing the electronic platform. *Technology knowledge*

should be rather broad than deep (Cash et al., 2004). Especially with respect to Web technologies, there exist a number of reusable standards and components that IT professionals need to be aware of (Bailey & Stefaniak, 2001). IT competence, though, must also cover knowledge on the formal methods and abstract concepts that the computer science discipline provides independently from concrete problems or technologies. This second area of IT competence, which should be referred to as *conceptual knowledge*, enables IT professionals to design flexible software architectures and implement high-quality electronic products. A taxonomy that differentiates between technology knowledge and conceptual knowledge is able to cover the explicit knowledge of the computer science discipline in an acceptable manner. However, it does not suffice to fully describe IT competence since tacit knowledge is not included. The missing tacit part of IT competence results from the practical use of Web technologies and computer science concepts. Practical experience, though, is always connected with the assimilation of further explicit knowledge, such as how to access external knowledge resources with the help of search engines (Bassellier et al., 2001; Taylor et al., 2001).

Figure 1. Competence model for IT professionals in Internet-based ventures

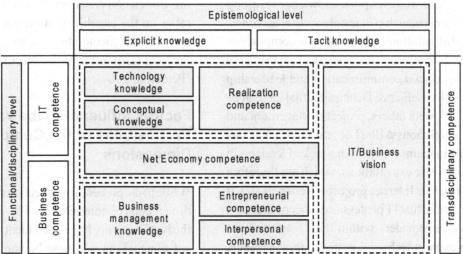

As a third subdimension, *realization competence* therefore enables IT professionals to apply their own explicit IT knowledge by enhancing it with both explicit and tacit experience components.

Business competence: Important enablers of alignment of business and IT are that IT people understand the business and demonstrate leadership (Luftman & Brier, 1999). Rather than being technical experts, they need to be business problem solvers (Venkatraman, 1999). Consequently, in order to actively participate in formulating strategy and processes of the venture as suggested by the basic principles of IT governance, IT professionals need a sound understanding of the business. Furthermore, business competence increases the intention of IT professionals to collaboratively work with their business partners (Bassellier & Benbasat, 2004). As IT professionals in Internet-based ventures need to implement entirely new business processes, they need to understand the respective operational use cases and have to be able to interpret managerial problems (Lee et al., 1995; Cash et al., 2004). Moreover, the software development processes themselves have to match economic requirements, which makes fundamental *business management knowledge* indispensable for IT professionals (Bassellier & Benbasat, 2004; Todd et al., 1995). This knowledge is related to the *entrepreneurial competence* which comprises the IT professional's experience in founding new businesses, as well as explicit knowledge resulting from entrepreneurship literature and/or teachings. As a third subdimension, business competence includes *interpersonal competence*, covering the abovementioned communication and leadership abilities (Bassellier & Benbasat, 2004), the ability to work with others, project management and customer relations skills (Lee et al., 1995). Various frictions in teams result from a lack of leadership and unrealistic expectations, which are therefore a major risk in Internet projects (Reifer, 2002). It is thus crucial that IT professionals become expert knowledge providers within their team and are able to explain technical issues to their partners (Cash et al., 2004).

Transdisciplinary competence: Alignment in e-business environments requires business visionaries that understand both the fundamental laws of the Net Economy and the technical foundations driving success in this arena (Bauer, 2001). As the IT professional is responsible for the technological aspects of the overall electronic product, a solid *Net Economy competence* is crucial. This competence dimension includes explicit knowledge on electronic value creation processes, electronic payment methods, legal aspects of electronic business as well as existing platforms and business models (Kollmann, 2006; Taylor et al., 2001). Moreover, Net Economy competence covers an experience component, i.e. tacit knowledge on operational problem-solving processes that cannot be classified as either IT- or business-related. From a strategic perspective, the IT professional needs to anticipate implications of external change and relate them to the venture's platform. This requires a holistic view on market and technology trends, and the own business and its Web application, incorporating both critical and creative thinking (Cash et al., 2004; Dalal, 1994; Fang et al., 2005; Tang et al., 2001;). The respective *IT-Business vision* is highly characterized by tacit knowledge and enables the IT professional to make intelligent decisions with respect to the product development processes and the architecture of the Web application. Modeling this dimension is reasonable since IT governance relies on the capability of *all* management team members to formulate strategy and understand the long-term interplay between business and IT (Peterson, 2004).

Factors Influencing the Value Propositions of the Competence Dimensions

While in the preceding subsections the constitutive dimensions of competence of IT professionals in the Net Economy have been identified, the different dimensions will now be analyzed in regard to their relevance. The following paragraphs will discuss potential factors that influence the value proposition of specific IT-related skills and knowledge areas in an Internet-based venture. Two kinds of influencing factors can be identified, including factors that have an effect on the *actual* value proposition of a competence dimension and factors that influence the *perception* of the value proposition by the partners. The perceived value proposition of a competence dimension results from the founder's interpretation of the actual value proposition of that competence, that is, a moderating effect of the respective factors can be constituted (Figure 2). In order to understand to what extent business and IT people contribute to value creation and how they perceive the contribution of each other's distinct competencies, both kinds of influencing factors need to be considered. In the following, supposable dependencies will be exemplarily discussed for each kind of influencing factor.

Factors influencing actual value propositions: Important factors influencing the actual relevance of the competence dimensions result from the characteristics of a venture's business model and its electronic products, as these characteristics directly affect the resource require-

ments of the software development process. On the one hand, this includes the complexity of the venture's platform, that is, the degree of difficulty in analysis, design and implementation of the software (Zhang, Windsor & Pavur, 2003). Complexity depends on functional requirements such as interactive elements and personalized content as well as non-functional requirements such as performance, availability, usability, security or maintainability (Bass, Clements & Kazman, 2003; Deshpande, Murugesan, Ginige, Hansen, Schwabe & Gaedke, 2002). Another important product characteristic is its degree of innovativeness, that is, the newness of the technology itself or in the newness of applications the technology offers to the customer. For instance, launching an E-Shop (Kollmann, 2006) can be expected to require low development efforts, because there exists a variety of ready-made Web applications for this business model. By contrast, newly found businesses with highly innovative platforms (such as *Google* with respect to their search technology) will initially focus on the perfection of their technology rather than on aspects of commercialization and generating revenues. In particular, technical problems at the beginning of business operations can be expected to give way

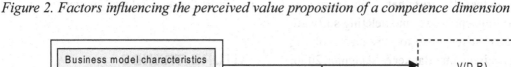

Figure 2. Factors influencing the perceived value proposition of a competence dimension

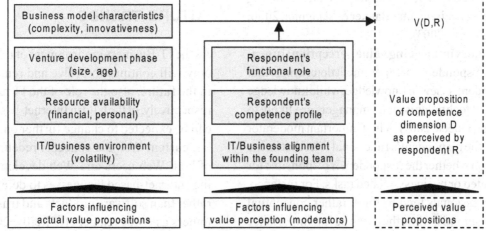

to environmental, commercial and competitive problems in later development phases (MacInnes, 2005). Consequently, a shift from IT competence to business and transdisciplinary competence can be postulated with the passing of time. Moreover, as resource availability and thus the number of IT personnel can be expected to increase during the growth of the young firm (Kollmann, 2006), a shift from operational to strategic tasks can be presumed (Sgobbi, 2002). While at an early stage, IT professionals need to posses entrepreneurial competence, an efficient programming style and sound technology knowledge, the later CIO is required to additionally possess business management knowledge and interpersonal competence in order to delegate operational development tasks to her IT staff. Similarly, the relevance of possessing conceptual IT knowledge and having an IT/Business vision can be expected to increase over time, as the focus moves from a short-term realization to a long-term intensification and diversification of the initial business idea (Kollmann, 2006). The aspect of changing requirements particularly applies to Web 2.0 platforms whose business models and Web applications are vague at the beginning, but evolve over time (Highsmith, 2002; O'Reilly, 2005). In this regard, another factor influencing the value propositions of IT-related competencies is the volatility of the IT/Business environment, as it necessitates software enhancement activities such as adding, changing, and deleting software functionality in response to new and evolving business requirements (Banker & Slaughter, 2000; Zhang et al., 2003).

Factors influencing value perception: In general, a respondent's temperament determines that respondent's view of knowledge, while knowledge views of technologists and managers are likely to diverge (Dueck, 2001). A first important moderator is thus the respondent's functional role, that is, the question whether the respondent is responsible for IT-related or business-related tasks. For instance, IT professionals tend to think rather conceptual than pragmatic, while they ascribe less importance to interpersonal relationships. Besides personality, views on knowledge depend on the respondent's knowledge itself, including practical experience in an area where the respective knowledge is required. It can be argued that value perception is distorted depending on the configuration of the respondent's competence profile, as social psychology suggests that individuals rate other people more positively the more similar they are to themselves (Byrne, 1971; Jackson, Brett, Sessa, Cooper, Julin & Peyronnin, 1991). In addition, business managers are often not aware of the multidimensionality of IT competence (Nakayama & Sutcliffe, 2003), while inexperienced IT professionals might underestimate the importance of their business competence. In contrast, shared domain knowledge between IT and business people positively affects a correct understanding of each other's contribution to the firm (Reich & Benbasat, 2000). Furthermore, shared domain knowledge positively affects the degree of IT/Business alignment within the founding team which "refers to the state in which business and IT executives understand and are committed to the business and IT mission, objectives, and plans" (Reich & Benbasat, 2000, p. 81). In this context, alignment itself can be expected to clarify the value perception of the competence dimensions critical to IT professionals. Misalignment, in contrast, is likely to distort the respondents' perceptions.

FUTURE TRENDS

As the IT/Business environment of the Net Economy will continue to evolve and remain volatile in the future, also the role of the IT professional, respectively, of the CIO in Internet-based ventures can be expected to change further on. In particular, current Web 2.0 concepts redefine the roles of both Web users and Web developers, requiring Internet-based businesses to deliver services rather than software products and trust their customers as co-developers (O'Reilly, 2005). Some of the resulting competency changes have been discussed in this chapter. However, the impact of Web 2.0 on the core competency requirements of Internet-based firms will further increase in the future. Furthermore, the prospective convergence of Web 2.0 and the Semantic Web (Wahlster & Dengel, 2006) will even more dramatically change the IT/Business environment of the Net Economy which will be characterized by intelligent search agents and semantic Web services in the future (Sheth, Verma & Gomadam, 2006). From an IT governance point of view, these changes will inevitably entail a need for IT professionals who understand the technology trends *and* the resulting managerial implications, as well as a well-aligned team of founders incorporating the wide range of skills and knowledge required for operating a business in the Net Economy.

The framework presented in this chapter sets up the theoretical foundations for understanding the IT-related competence requirements and competence perceptions within the founding teams of Internet-based ventures. With respect to future research activities, dependencies between factors influencing the actual value, factors influencing value perception and the perceived value of the individual competence dimensions need to be modelled and tested on an empirical basis.

CONCLUSION

Drawing upon the general IT governance principle of aligning business and IT, this chapter articulated the concept of IT-related competence in young firms of the Net Economy, outlined its dimensions and suggested a framework for modeling effects on the value propositions of the different dimensions as perceived by the partners. The proposed competence model comprises three dimensions, including IT competence, business (i.e., non-IT) competence, and transdisciplinary competence. According to their epistemological and functional/disciplinary characteristics, these dimensions have been subdivided in order to meet the contextual particularities of Net Economy ventures, resulting in eight subdimensions (technology knowledge, conceptual knowledge, realization competence, business management knowledge, entrepreneurial competence, interpersonal competence, Net Economy competence, and IT/Business vision). With respect to exploring the value propositions of these dimensions, two kinds of influencing factors have been identified: factors that have an effect on the actual value proposition of a competence dimension (such as business model, development phase, resource availability, and environmental dynamism), and factors that influence the perception of the value proposition by the partners (such as the respective partner's functional role and competence profile, and the degree of IT/Business alignment within the team). In order to understand to what extent business and IT people contribute to value creation and how they perceive the contribution of each other's distinct competencies, possible dependencies have exemplarily been illustrated for both kinds of influencing factors. Further exploring these dependencies and relating them to IT governance principles is crucial to comprehend the complex competence requirements of Internet-based ventures and the mutual understanding of the founders' value contributions within heterogeneous teams.

REFERENCES

Amit, R., & Zott, C. (2001). Value creation in e-business. *Strategic Management Journal, 22*(6/7), 493-520.

Bailey, J. L., & Stefaniak, G. (2001). Industry perceptions of the knowledge, skills, and abilities needed by computer programmers. In *Proceedings of the 2001 ACM SIGCPR conference on Computer personnel research* (pp. 93-98). New York: ACM Press.

Banker, R. D. & Slaughter, S. A. (2000). The moderating effects of structure on volatility and complexity in software enhancement. *Information Systems Research, 11*(3), 219-240.

Bass, L., Clements, P., & Kazman, R. (2003). *Software architecture in practice.* Boston, MA: Addison-Wesley.

Bassellier, G., & Benbasat, I. (2004). Business competence of information technology professionals: Conceptual development and influence on IT-business partnerships. *MIS Quarterly, 28*(4), 673-694.

Bassellier, G., Benbasat, I., & Reich, B. (2003). The influence of business managers' IT competence on championing IT. *Information Systems Research, 14*(4), 317-336.

Bassellier, G., Reich, B. H., & Benbasat, I. (2001). Information technology competence of business managers. *Journal of Management Information Systems, 17*(4), 159-182.

Bauer, C. (2001). Strategic alignment for electronic commerce. In R. Papp (Ed.), *Strategic information technology: Opportunities for competitive advantage* (pp. 258-272). Hershey, PA: Idea Group Publishing.

Baum, J. R., Locke, E. A., & Smith, K. G. (2001). A multidimensional model of venture growth. *Academy of Management Journal, 44*(2), 292-303.

Bhandari, G., Bliemel, M., Harold, A., & Hassanein, K. (2003). Flexibility in e-business strategies: A requirement for success. *Global Journal of Flexible Systems Management, 5*(2/3), 11-22.

Byrne, D. (1971). *The attraction paradigm.* New York: Academic Press.

Cash, E., Yoong, P., & Huff, S. (2004). The impact of e-commerce on the role of IS professionals. *The DATA BASE for Advances in Information Systems, 35*(3), 50-63.

Chandler, G. N., & Hanks, S. (1994). Founder competence, the environment, and venture performance. *Entrepreneurship Theory and Practice, 18*(3), 77-89.

Chandler, G. N., & Jansen, E. (1992). The founder's self-assesed competence and venture performance. *Journal of Business Venturing, 7*(3), 223-236.

Couger, J. D., Davis, G. B., Dologite, D. G., Feinstein, D. L., Gorgone, J. T., Jenkins, A. M., Kasper, G. M., Little, J. C., Longenecker, H. E. Jr., & Valacich, J. S. (1995). IS '95: guideline for undergraduate IS curriculum. *MIS Quarterly, 19*(3), 341-359.

Dalal, N. P. (1994). Higher-order thinking in MIS. *Journal of Computer Information Systems, 34*(4), 26-30.

Deshpande, Y., Murugesan, S., Ginige, A., Hansen, S., Schwabe, D., Gaedke, M., & White, B. (2002). Web engineering. *Journal of Web Engineering, 1*(1), 3-17.

Dueck, G. (2001). Views of knowledge are human views. *IBM Systems Journal, 40*(4), 885-888.

Earl, M. J., & Feeny, D. F. (1994). Is your CIO adding value? *Sloan Management Review, 35,* 11-20.

Fang, X., Lee, S., & Koh, S. (2005). Transition of knowledge/skills requirements for entry-level IS professionals: An exploratory study based on Recruiters' perception. *Journal of Computer Information Systems, Fall 2005,* 58-70.

Farwell, D., Kuramoto, L., Lee, D. M. S., Trauth, E., & Winslow, C. (1992). A new paradigm for MIS: Implications for IS professionals. *Information Systems Management, 9*(2), 7-14.

Feeny, D. F., & Willcocks, L. P. (1998). Core IS capabilities for exploiting information technology. *Sloan Management Review, 39,* 9-21.

Ginige, A., & Murugesan, A. (2001). Web engineering—An introduction. *IEEE Multimedia, 8*(1), 14-18.

Gorgone, J. T., Davis, G. B., Valacich, J. S., Topi, H., Feinstein, D. L., & Longenecker, H. E., Jr. (2003). IS 2002 model curriculum and guidelines for undergraduate degree programs in information systems. *Communications of the AIS, 2003*(11), 1-53.

Gottschalk, P. (2006). *E-business strategy, sourcing and governance.* Hershey, PA: Idea Group Publishing.

Henderson, J. C., & Venkatraman, N. (1999). Strategic alignment: Leveraging information technology for transforming organizations. *IBM Systems Journal, 38*(2/3), 472-484.

Highsmith, J. A. (2002). *Agile software development ecosystems.* Boston: Pearson Education.

Horlick-Jones, T., & Sime, J. (2004). Living on the border: Knowledge, risk and transdisciplinarity. *Futures, 36*(4), 441-456.

Jackson, S. F., Brett, J. F., Sessa, V. I., Cooper, D. M., Julin, J. A., Peyronnin, K. (1991). Some differences make a difference: Individual dissimilarity and group heterogeneity as correlates of recruitment, promotion, and turnover. *Journal of Applied Psychology, 76*(5), 675-689.

Kollmann, T. (2006). What is e-entrepreneurship? – Fundamentals of company founding in the net economy. *International Journal of Technology Management, 33*(4), 322-340.

Kollmann, T., & Häsel, M. (2006). *Cross-channel cooperation: The bundling of online and offline business models.* Wiesbaden: Deutscher Universitäts-Verlag.

Kollmann, T., & Häsel, M. (2007). Reverse auctions in the service sector: The case of LetsWorkIt. de. *International Journal of E-Business Research, 3*(3), 57-73.

Lee, D., Trauth, E., & Farwell, D. (1995). Critical skills and knowledge requirements of IS professionals: A joint academic/industry investigation. *MIS Quarterly, 19*(3), 313-340.

Luftman, J., & Brier, T. (1999). Achieving and sustaining business-IT alignment. *California Management Review, 42*(1), 109-122.

Lumpkin, G. T., & Dess, G. G. (2004). E-business strategies and internet business models: how the internet adds value. *Organizational Dynamics, 33*(2), 161-173.

MacCormack, A., Verganti, R., & Iansiti, M. (2001). Developing products on "Internet Time": The anatomy of a flexible development process. *Management Science, 47*(1), 133-150.

MacInnes, I. (2005). Dynamic business model framework for emerging technologies. *International Journal of Services Technology and Management, 6*(1), 3-19.

Man, T. W. Y., Lau, T., & Chan, K. F. (2002). The competitiveness of small and medium enterprises: A conceptualization with focus on entrepreneurial competencies. *Journal of Business Venturing, 17*(2), 123-142.

Matlay, H. (2004). E-entrepreneurship and small e-business development: Towards a comparative research agenda. *Journal of Small Business and Enterprise Development, 11*(3), 408-414.

Medlin, B. D., Dave, D. S., & Vannoy, S. A. (2001). Students' views of the importance of technical and non-technical skills for successful IT professionals. *Journal of Computer Information Systems, 42*(1), 65-69.

Meso, P., & Jain, R. (2006). Agile software development: Adaptive systems principles and best practices. *Information Systems Management, 23*(3).

Murugesan, S., Deshpande, Y., Hansen, S., & Ginige, A. (2001). Web engineering: A new discipline for development of web-based systems. In S. Murugesan & Y. Deshpande (Eds.), *Web engineering: Managing diversity and complexity of web application development* (pp. 3-13). Heidelberg: Springer.

Nakayama, M., & Sutcliffe, N. (2003). Skills, management of skills, and IT skills requirements. In M. Nakayama & N. Sutcliffe (Eds.), *Managing IT skills portfolios: Planning, acquisition and performance evaluation* (pp. 1-25). Hershey, PA: Idea Group Publishing.

Nelson, R. R. (1991). Educational needs as perceived by IS and end-user personnel: A survey of knowledge and skill requirements. *MIS Quaterly, 15*(4), 503-525.

Nonaka, I. (1994). A dynamic theory of organizational knowledge creation. *Organization Science, 5*(1), 14-37.

O'Reilly, T. (2005). *What is web 2.0: Design patterns and business models for the next generation of software.* Retrieved May 13, 2008, from http://www.oreillynet.com/pub/a/oreilly/tim/news/2005/09/30/what-is-web-20.html

Patel, N. V. (2004). An emerging strategy for e-business IT governance. In W. Van Grembergen (Ed.), *Strategies for information technology governance* (pp. 37-80). Hershey, PA: Idea Group Publishing.

Peterson, R. R. (2004). Integration strategies and tactics for information technology governance. In W. Van Grembergen (Ed.), *Strategies for information technology governance* (pp. 37-80). Hershey, PA: Idea Group Publishing.

Polanyi, M. (1967). *Tacit dimension.* London: Routledge & Kegan Paul.

Porter, M. E. (2001). Strategy and the internet. *Harvard Business Review, 79*(3), 62-78.

Reich, B. H., & Benbasat, I. (2000). Factors that influence the social dimension of alignment between business and information technology objectives. *MIS Quarterly, 24*(1), 81-113.

Reifer, D. (2002). Ten deadly risks in internet and intranet software development. *IEEE Software, 19*(2), 12-14.

Sambamurthy, V., Bharadwaj, A., & Grover, V. (2003). Shaping agility through digital options: Reconceptualizing the role of information technology in contemporary firms. *MIS Quarterly, 27*, 237-263.

Sgobbi, F. (2002). Web design skills and competencies: An empirical analysis. *Human Systems Management, 21*(1), 115-128.

Sharma, S. K., & Gupta, J. N. D. (2004). E-strategy model for creating flexible organizations. *Global Journal of Flexible Systems Management, 5*(2/3), 1-9.

Sheth, A., Verma, K., & Gomadam, K. (2006). Semantics to energize the full service spectrum. *Communications of the ACM, 49*(7), 55-61.

Shi, D., & Daniels, R. L. (2003). A survey of manufacturing flexibility: Implications for e-business flexibility. *IBM Systems Journal, 42*(3), 414-428.

Sveiby, K. E., & Lloyd, T. (1987). *Managing knowhow.* London: Bloomsbury Publishing.

Tang, H. L., Koh, S., & Lee, S. (2001). Educational gaps as perceived by IS educators: A survey of knowledge and skill requirements. *Journal of Computer Information Systems, 41*(2), 76-84.

Taylor, M. J., England, D., & Gresty, D. (2001). Knowledge for web site development. *Internet Research: Electronic Networking Applications and Policy, 11*(5), 451-461.

Taylor, T. (2006). Web competencies for IT students. In R. Brown (Ed.), In *Proceedings 7th*

International Conference on Information Technology Based Higher Education and Training (pp. 297-304). Sydney: University of Technology.

Todd, P. A., McKeen, J. D., & Gallupe, B. R. (1995). The evolution of IS job skills: A content analysis of IS job advertisements from 1970 to 1990. *MIS Quarterly, 19*(1), 1-17.

Van Grembergen, W., De Haas, S., & Guldentops, E. (2004). Structures, processes and relational mechanisms for IT governance. In W. Van Grembergen (Ed.), *Strategies for information technology governance* (pp. 1-35). Hershey, PA: Idea Group Publishing.

Venkatraman, N. (1999). *Valuing the IS contribution to the business.* Computer Sciences Corporation.

Von Krogh, G., & Roos, J. (1995). A perspective on knowledge, competence and strategy. *Personnel Review, 24*(3), 56-76.

Wahlster, W., & Dengel, A. (2006). *Web 3.0: Convergence of web 2.0 and the semantic web. Technology Radar Feature Paper Edition II/2006.* Deutsche Telekom Laboratories.

Weiber, R., & Kollmann, T. (1998). Competitive advantage in virtual markets—Perspectives of "Information-based marketing" in cyberspace. *European Journal of Marketing, 32*(7/8), 603-615.

Weill, P., & Ross, J.W. (2004). *IT governance.* Boston, MA: Harvard Business School Press.

Youndt, M. A., Snell, S. A., Dean, J. W., Jr., & Lepak, D. P. (1996). Human resource management, manufacturing strategy, and firm performance. *Academy of Management Journal, 39*(4), 836-866.

Zhang, X., Windsor, J., & Pavur, R. (2003). Determinants of software volatility: A field study. *Journal of Software Maintanance and Evolution: Research and Practice, 15*(3), 191-204.

Chapter XIV
The Role of Maturity Models in IT Governance:
A Comparison of the Major Models and Their Potential Benefits to the Enterprise

G. Philip Rogers
Analyst/Project Manager, USA

ABSTRACT

This chapter assesses what role maturity models can play in enterprise IT governance. Frameworks that are well known in the IT industry, such as the Capability Maturity Model, make it possible to assess maturity in key areas. The author describes additional maturity models that have no formal association with a comprehensive framework, the application of which represent significantly less overhead than the larger frameworks that include a maturity model component. The author seeks to present a broad perspective on maturity models that enterprises can use as a preliminary means of evaluating what tools are available to them. As such, this overview of maturity models is intended to facilitate the selection of a model that can bring about improved IT governance in one or more focus areas.

INTRODUCTION

Organizations have a number of tools and techniques at their disposal to facilitate governance of the enterprise, and one of their chief areas of focus continues to be how best to govern information technology (IT). Although the corporate scandals of recent years have invited greater scrutiny over enterprise business practices, it has been clear for quite some time that there is a need for greater oversight via corporate governance, and by extension, IT governance. During the mid-1980's, when the application of enterprise-wide IT to business problems was still a relatively new phenomenon, it was already becoming apparent to some industry leaders that there was a need for greater oversight over IT activities. As noted by McGovern, Ambler, Stevens, Linn, Sharan, and Jo (2004), one of the outcomes of that need for greater oversight was the development of the Capability Maturity Model (CMM) at Carnegie Mellon University's Software Engineering Institute (SEI) (2006). Since the introduction of the CMM, numerous variations of the original model have emerged, culminating with the merger of several of those models as the Capability Maturity Model Integration, or CMMI. Meanwhile, numerous other frameworks have emerged that include a capability maturity model component, as well as specialized maturity models that are not part of a formal framework. The purpose of this chapter is to introduce the most significant maturity models, to compare those models, and to assess the extent to which the various models can facilitate IT governance activities in the corporations of today and tomorrow.

Literature Review

Although a detailed treatment of corporate governance is beyond the scope of this chapter, a brief introduction to the topic is necessary to place IT governance within the larger governance context. Gottschalk (2006) suggests that it is necessary to consider three distinct views of the enterprise when preparing to assess and implement corporate governance and IT governance practices. According to what he calls the "resource-based view", differences in enterprise performance are directly attributable to differences in resources and capabilities, while the activity-based and value configuration-based views focus on enterprise performance in terms of measurement of resource flows within activities and measurement of business processes in terms of the creation of business value for customers, respectively. By way of contrast, Cingula (2006) diverges from

what he sees as the standard view of corporate governance where the focus is typically on financial regulations or decision making frameworks driven by legal considerations, instead changing the focus to the most important processes in the enterprise. Cingula goes on to suggest that some of the most important processes from a corporate governance perspective include strategic planning, financial reporting, controlling, and public relations processes.

Even if IT governance were not the focus of this volume, no discussion of corporate governance is complete without mention of IT governance. In a 2005 study completed by the United Kingdom Office of Government Commerce (OGC), the IT Governance Institute (ITGI), and the IT Service Management Forum (itSMF), the authors identify numerous business reasons for defining and following IT best practices. Examples of these business reasons include greater interest in and oversight over IT spending and return on investment, a growing body of regulatory and compliance instruments in industries such as finance, pharmaceuticals, and health care, and the need to exercise great care when selecting business partners such as those who specialize in service acquisition and outsourcing.

Because IT governance activities are typically broad in scope, it can be helpful to conceptualize the application of IT governance to an organization's day-to-day activities in terms of business processes. Betz (2007) describes what he considers the three most important process frameworks, which, in addition to the aforementioned CMMI, are the ITGI's Control Objectives for Information and related Technology (COBIT), and the OGC's Information Technology Infrastructure Library (ITIL), in particular, the two ITIL volumes that focus on IT Service Management (ITSM). What follows is an introduction to maturity models in general, followed by an overview of these three key maturity model frameworks.

Overview of Key Frameworks

The central concept behind a maturity model is the notion that it is possible to evaluate the maturity of various processes based on a hierarchical scale. Although numerous maturity models exist, a few of which have already been mentioned, and others that will be mentioned later in this chapter, what they have in common is the idea that it is possible to view organizational development as a continuum of stages (or levels) that organizations pass through as they go from process immaturity to process maturity. Despite minor differences in terminology, all models begin with a Level Zero (process nonexistent) or Level One (initial process), continuing on with Level Two (repeatable process), Level Three (defined process), Level Four (managed process), and Level Five (optimized process). De Haes and Van Grembergen (2004) thus see the value of a maturity model as a "tool [that] offers an easy-to-understand way to determine the 'as is' and 'to be' positions and enables the organization to benchmark itself against best practices and standard guidelines. In this way, gaps can be identified and specific actions can be defined to move toward the desired level of strategic alignment/governance maturity" (IT Alignment/Governance Maturity Models section, ¶ 1).

CMMI (and its predecessor models) focuses heavily on processes related to software development. Hass (2003) summarizes the distinction that the SEI makes between what CMMI calls capability and maturity levels. That is, the CMMI has six capability levels that can measure an organization's process improvement achievement relative to a generic goal and a set of practices associated with that goal. By way of contrast, for each of the five CMMI maturity levels, a predefined set of process areas and goals serves as a means of measuring organizational maturity. To use the SEI's own terminology (2006), capability levels are seen as a type of "continuous representation," in that process improvement is seen as a continuing

effort that should allow for working on different problems at different rates. For instance, applying capability levels can facilitate working on either a single problematic area associated with a particular process, or instead work could move forward on simultaneously improving several areas that might align well with an organization's strategic goals and objectives. With "staged representation," which is based on maturity levels, process improvement proceeds through one stage at a time, with the improvement that takes place at each level intended to provide a foundation for the stage that comes next.

With COBIT, the focus shifts to process control, that is, COBIT sees itself as a methodology that can enable organizations to manage IT governance processes, and in particular, to conduct audits. Lankhorst et al. (2006) characterize COBIT as a set of control objectives and management guidelines that organizations can apply to any of the 34 IT processes that the IT Governance Institute has identified. In addition to the control objectives, COBIT also features critical success factors, as well as a six-level maturity model that organizations can use to enable IT governance functions. As stated by the ITGI (2005) in its COBIT 4.0 documentation, determining what the desired state is for the maturity of any of the IT process areas depends primarily on the return on investment that a given enterprise seeks – that is, how decision makers manage and implement a particular capability in an IT environment is driven by cost-benefit considerations. In slight contrast to the capability and maturity levels that are central to the CMMI, in COBIT, there are three facets of maturity (capability, maturity, and control), all three of which need to be addressed in order to provide the requisite level of IT governance.

The OGC takes a different approach to assessing organizational maturity and performance. As Lankhorst points out, the key OGC objective in releasing a set of best practices that has grown to nine volumes was and is to develop and make known best practices for IT Service Management

(ITSM). Betz sees the origins of the OGC approach in the IBM "Yellow Books," and to Betz, the real focus of ITIL in general, and ITSM specifically, is "the concept of 'service,' a business-intelligible manifestation of the IT capability that represents value-adding functionality, from the business perspective" (Betz, 2007, pp. 38-39). Both Betz and Lankhorst observe that the Service Delivery and Service Support ITIL volumes are the most critical components of the larger library, such that service delivery includes processes such as service-level management, availability management, and financial management associated with the delivery of IT services, while service support includes processes such as problem management, incident management, configuration management, and release management. For the purposes of this

paper, arguably the most significant difference when comparing ITSM to CMMI and COBIT is that while the OGC does not include an integrated maturity model as a component of its ITSM (or ITIL, for that matter), both CMMI and COBIT provide formal mechanisms for measuring process maturity. Ultimately the selection of a maturity model requires a careful assessment of the models themselves and the organizational context to which they are to be applied.

To facilitate a very general comparison of the three frameworks, Table 1 shows selected processes from each framework. Because Betz and others have suggested that service delivery and service support are arguably the strongest areas of the ITIL framework, some of the ITIL process areas related to service delivery and ser-

Table 1. Comparison of selected ITIL, COBIT, and CMMI processes

ITIL Process	COBIT Process	CMMI Process
Establish service portfolio	DS1 Define and manage service levels	Organizational Process Definition (OPD)
Develop service plans	DS4 Ensure continuous service	Organizational Process Focus (OPF)
Manage service provision	AI1 Identify automated solutions	Organizational Process Performance (OPP)
Establish service reporting policy	P04 Define IT processes, organization, and relationships	Organizational Process Definition (OPD)
Create service management vision	DS1 Define and manage service levels DS2 Manage third-party services	Organizational Process Definition (OPD) Supplier Agreement Management (SAM)
Establish appropriate policies and standards	P06 Communicate management aims and direction	Organizational Process Definition (OPD)
Evaluate current organizational position – benchmarking/maturity assessment	M1 Monitor and evaluate IT performance	Measurement and Analysis (MA)
Report on delivery – progress monitoring and process improvements	M1 Monitor and evaluate IT performance	Measurement and Analysis (MA)
Review benefits and revise service improvement plans	DS1 Define and manage service levels	Measurement and Analysis (MA) Supplier Agreement Management (SAM)
Review underpinning contracts and OLAs	DS1 Define and manage service levels	Supplier Agreement Management (SAM)
Identify and record problems	DS10 Manage problems	Causal Analysis and Resolution (CAR)
Undertake configuration management planning	DS9 Manage the configuration	Configuration Management (CM)
Establish change approach, advisory board and procedures	AI6 Manage changes	Integrated Project Management (IPM)

vice support are shown in Table 1, with related process areas from COBIT and CMMI shown in the corresponding row. Note that all references are to ITIL Version 2, COBIT Version 4.0, and CMMI for Development Version 1.2.

BASELINE TAXONOMY OF MATURITY MODELS

By focusing on key processes, as Cingula suggests, and by identifying the most influential process frameworks (of which capability maturity models are a part), as Betz has done, it is possible to propose a baseline taxonomy for maturity models that can serve as an organizational scheme for a brief assessment of additional maturity models. Table 2 shows five categories that can serve as a metaphor for the maturity models that have been discussed, as well as maturity models associated with each of the five categories, some of which are briefly described below. Items shown in parentheses are models or frameworks with which the maturity model is associated, if the maturity model is not formally associated with a particular framework. It is important to emphasize that this is a very brief summary of some of the maturity models that exist—there are many others (most of which are described in the next section), and there are still more process frameworks for which no particular maturity model has been developed.

As previously mentioned, ITIL does not include a formal maturity model. That being the case, maturity models that are unique to IT service management have emerged. One of those is the IT Service Capability Maturity Model (IT Service CMM), which originated with two research projects that were sponsored by the Dutch Ministry of Economic Affairs, along with other Dutch government and research institutions. Much like ITIL's focus on the two pillars of service delivery and service support, Niessink, Clerc, Tijdink, and van Vliet (2005) have structured the IT Service CMM such that it focuses on what they call service level management and service process management, with service level agreements (SLAs) serving as a linkage between the two.

Although a description of Enterprise Architecture (EA) in general, and of EA frameworks in particular (such as The Open Group Architecture Framework [TOGAF]), are beyond the scope of this chapter, there are important reasons for EA to receive its share of corporate attention. Lankhorst maintains that one of the reasons for an organization's EA to be well understood and well documented is that doing so makes it easier for business and IT stakeholders to be in alignment. That is to say, when thinking of business strategy, it is vitally important to consider the type of IT infrastructure that can best support that strategy, and the converse is also true. It is based on this background understanding, then, that the value of employing a maturity model approach to EA could be a valuable practice in many corporations, and in 2003, the National Association of State Chief Information Officers (NASCIO) released their Enterprise Architecture Maturity Model for that purpose.

Table 2. Baseline maturity model taxonomy

	Maturity Model Categories				
	IT Governance	**Enterprise Architecture**	**Security**	**Design/ Development**	**Service Management**
Maturity Model Examples	COBIT	EAMM (CMMI/ TOGAF)	ISM3 (ISO9001:2000)	CMMI	IT Service CMM (ITIL/Software CMM)

A detailed discussion of Information Security issues, like a discussion about EA issues, is beyond the scope of this chapter. One of the things that is most notable about the Information Security arena is that given the great extent to which numerous sectors, such as government and finance, devote considerable resources to information protection, numerous regulations and guidelines exist that apply to this area. As such, the introduction of the Information Security Management Maturity Model (ISM3) (2007) to what is a complex area for organizations to manage serves as an additional IT governance resource. To briefly summarize, ISM3 consists of various processes, metrics, certification requirements, and an information security process model, all of which are intended to make it possible to apply ISO 9001 concepts in an information security context.

EXTENDED TAXONOMY OF MATURITY MODELS

In part because most of the maturity models in the previous section are a component of a larger process improvement framework, and as such require a significant amount of effort to apply to existing business processes, for the most part those models are adopted only in larger enterprise contexts. The maturity model concept has also proven to have considerable appeal as a construct for assessing the maturity of additional business processes. Because it is possible to develop a maturity model with no formal association with a larger process improvement framework, in recent years, many companies, organizations, and individuals have proposed maturity models of their own. Table 3 shows the initial set of maturity models from the previous section, referred to as "baseline maturity models," along with "extended maturity models" that have been proposed over the past ten years.

ISSUES, CONTROVERSIES, PROBLEMS

Perhaps the most significant challenge facing organizations, and likely one of the greatest frustrations of individuals external to an organization who happen to have either a personal interest in it (for example, how it performs on various social issues) or a vested interest in it (for example, how it performs financially), is that there are many who see the pursuit of corporate governance as an unnecessary diversion of resources away from activities that further the fundamental interests of the corporation. Davies (2006) suggests that much of the focus to date has been on the structure and processes of corporations. Instead, he would like to see greater focus on the strategic goals and objectives of corporations—and not only in areas such as risk management, but also in a broader strategic sense.

At a more tactical level, the adoption of process-centric approaches in the majority of organizational contexts typically meets with resistance, particularly when management does not take the time to clearly articulate the potential gains associated with the approach they have chosen to take. It is too often the case that what might seem like a very sound business decision at the most senior levels of management is lost on those who are directly impacted by initiatives such as business process improvement, because the key factors driving the decision are not necessarily communicated broadly across the enterprise.

A challenge that this paper illustrates particularly well is the potentially daunting variety of maturity models and process frameworks. Given this assortment of options, having a clear mandate from management on exactly what approach is to be used is especially important. In the absence of consistent and well-understood IT governance principles and practices, the IT practitioner typically follows whatever internal guidance might existence for the IT pratitioner's

Table 3. Extended maturity model taxonomy

	Maturity Model Categories						
	IT Governance/Program-Project-Portfolio Management	Data Architecture/Storage Management	Enterprise Architecture	Security/Security Architecture	Design/Development/Application Architecture	QA/Testing/Support	Service Management/Configuration Management
Baseline Maturity Models	COBIT EAMM			ISM3	CMMI		IT Service CMM
Extended Maturity Models	Knowledge Management Maturity Model	Database Administration Maturity Model	EA Assessment Framework	Capabilities Maturity Model for Security	Enterprise Service Orientation Maturity Model	Software Maintenance Maturity Model	CA Services Level Management Maturity Model
	Organizational Project Management Maturity Model (OPM3)	Information Lifecycle Management Maturity Model	Enterprise Architecture Management Maturity Framework (EAMMF)	Information Security Maturity Assessment (derived from COBIT)	Open Source Maturity Model	Testing Maturity Model (TMM)	Configuration Management Maturity Model
	Portfolio, Programme & Project Management Maturity Model (P3M3)	Information Maturity Model	Extended Enterprise Architecture Maturity Model	Security Maturity Model	Service Integration Maturity Model	The Testing Maturity Model (TMMi)	Tideway Configuration Management Maturity Levels
Extended Maturity Models (continued)	PRINCE2 Maturity Model	Meta Data Management Maturity Model			SOA Maturity Model *		
		Maturity Model for Data Integration			Usability Maturity Model		
					Web Services Maturity Model		

Note: Multiple instances of maturity models that include the term Service Oriented Architecture exist

team or business unit, which in practice often means that there are significant differences in practice across the enterprise, be it configuration management, release management, or any of the other activities described by the process frameworks and maturity models that have been mentioned in this chapter. In short, IT governance lacks a widely accepted, consistent set of practices and the means through which to leverage those

practices to achieve improved business results, as observed by Peterson (2004).

SOLUTIONS AND RECOMMENDATIONS

Arguably the greatest driver for the development and application of maturity models is the growing amount of corporate oversight, which has been a direct result of numerous factors, including corporate accounting scandals, greater scrutiny in highly regulated industries such as health care, pharmaceuticals, and finance, and growing demand for improved information protection and information security controls. It is clear, therefore, that the more regulated the enterprise, the easier it tends to be to make a business case for business process management and business process improvement, as well as putting in place various types of controls to facilitate corporate governance and IT governance.

Corporations, for their part, no matter what industry they are in, are most definitely influenced by public relations considerations. As more has become known to the public about corporate practices, and as voluntary codes of best practices have been introduced, not to mention formal legislation and statutory regulations, as Fasterling (2006) observes, corporations tend to gravitate toward practices that are receiving a great deal of attention, and therefore a set of practices gains greater authority merely because more corporations are willing to adopt it. In the UK, for example, Davies (2006) sees the Operating and Financial Report (OFR), a component of the proposed Companies Act, as a driver for greater focus on business performance as some organizations retool or refocus their governance efforts.

It is also important to distinguish between IT management and IT governance. Gottschalk argues that the proper role for IT management is in the areas of IT operations management and the effective delivery of IT services, while governance not only contributes to day-to-day performance and operations, as IT management does, IT governance must also play a transformational role so that IT can meet future business challenges.

The decision on whether to formally evaluate maturity in a particular business process area, and which maturity model is best suited to the purpose, should be based on a number of different considerations. Most importantly, anyone

contemplating an assessment of process maturity should identify a business problem that needs to be solved and formulate a set of clear, measurable goals that facilitate improvement in the desired area. Equally significant, an understanding of organizational cultural is critical, as is senior management support. For instance, in small- to –medium-sized organizations, it is unlikely that a process framework such as CMMI would be appropriate. Furthermore, it is difficult (and generally not advisable) to decouple a maturity model from the larger framework with which it is associated. In such situations, one of the maturity models that has no formal association with a larger framework might be a suitable alternative to help bring about improvement in the desired area.

FUTURE TRENDS

In 2005, the ITGI contracted with Price Waterhouse Coopers to conduct its second survey report based on its findings related to awareness and use of IT governance practices and frameworks (the first such survey report was in 2003). Given that ITGI was sponsoring the research, to some extent there was an effort to understand the use of COBIT in particular, but there was also a greater effort to determine how much awareness exists about other frameworks.

The findings of the IT Governance Global Status Report, which was published in 2006, are instructive. For instance, there are significant differences from one industry sector to another, such that in the financial and IT/telecom sectors, performance on IT governance in general was better than in sectors such as retail and manufacturing. Another important finding, and one that should come as little surprise to IT practitioners, is that it takes time to introduce solid IT governance practices, and that there is no such thing as a "one size fits all" approach (customization is always needed). What this means in real terms is that there has to be a lasting commitment from senior management to IT governance, because not only is it non-trivial to put IT governance practices in place, it requires ongoing assessment and communication to ensure that the governance measures are achieving the desired result.

In closing, there will continue to be a need for organizations of various sizes to assess their process maturity. Organizations that assess their business processes and take steps to improve those processes can realize significant benefits, regardless of which framework or methodology they choose to employ. As Betz (2007) points out, "Businesses are about activities, and optimizing these activities is a primary challenge… Framing IT activities in terms of business process leads to increased credibility with business stakeholders… Even if the business customer is unfamiliar with the particulars of IT process, the overall concepts of process improvement will resonate more successfully than any technical jargon" (p. 105).

REFERENECS

Betz, C. (2007). *Architecture and patterns for service management, resource planning, and governance: Making shoes for the cobbler's children.* San Francisco: Morgan Kaufmann.

Carnegie Mellon Software Engineering Institute [SEI] (2006, August). *CMMI for Development, Version 1.2. CMU/SEI-2006-TR-008. ESC-TR-2006-008.* Retrieved May 14, 2008, from http://www.sei.cmu.edu/pub/documents/06.reports/pdf/06tr008.pdf

Cingula, M. (2006). Corporate governance as a process-oriented approach to socially responsible organizations. In P. Ali & G. Gregoriou (Eds.), *International corporate governance after Sarbanes-Oxley* (pp. 65-94). Hoboken, NJ: John Wiley & Sons.

Davies, A. (2006). *Best practice in corporate governance: Building reputation and sustainable success.* Aldershot, Hampshire, England: Gower.

De Haes, S. & Van Grembergen, W. (2004). IT governance and its mechanisms. *Information Systems Control Journal, (1).* Retrieved May 14, 2008, from http://www.isaca.org/Template.cfm?Section=Home&CONTENTID=16700&TEMPLATE=/ContentManagement/ContentDisplay.cfm

Fasterling, B. (2006). Prospects and limits of corporate governance codes. In P. Ali & G. Gregoriou (Eds.), *International corporate governance after Sarbanes-Oxley* (pp. 467-84). Hoboken, NJ: John Wiley & Sons.

Gottschalk, P. (2006). *E-business strategy, sourcing and governance.* Hershey, PA: Idea Group.

Hass, A. M. J. (2003). *Configuration management principles and practice.* Boston: Addison-Wesley.

Information Security Management Maturity Model [ISM3] Consortium (2007). Retrieved May 14, 2008, from http://www.ism3.com/index.php?option=com_docman&Itemid=9

IT Governance Institute [ITGI] (2005). *COBIT 4.0: Control objectives, management guidelines, maturity models.* Retrieved May 14, 2008, from http://www.isaca.org/

IT Governance Institute [ITGI], Office of Government Commerce [OGC], & IT Service Management Forum [itSMF] (2005). *Aligning COBIT, ITIL, and ISO 17799 for business benefit: A management briefing from ITGI and OGC.* Retrieved May 14, 2008, from http://www.nysforum.org/documents/pdf/itil-6-6-06/AligningCOBITITIL.pdf

IT Governance Institute [ITGI] (2006). *IT governance global status report – 2006.* Retrieved May 14, 2008, from https://my.isaca.org/AMTemplate.cfm?Section=ITGI_Research_Publications&Template=/ContentManagement/ContentDisplay.cfm&ContentID=24224

Lankhorst, M. et al. (2005). *Enterprise architecture at work: Modelling, communication, and analysis*. Berlin: Springer.

McGovern, J., Ambler, S., Stevens, M., Linn, J., Sharan, V., & Jo, E. (2004). *A practical guide to enterprise architecture*. Upper Saddle River, New Jersey: Prentice Hall.

National Association of State Chief Information Officers [NASCIO] (2003). *Enterprise architecture maturity model*. Retrieved May 14, 2008, from http://www.nascio.org/publications/documents/NASCIO-EAMM.pdf

Niessink, F., Clerc, V., Tijdink, T., & van Vliet, H. (2005, January 28). *The IT service capability model*. Retrieved May 14, 2008, from http://www.itservicecmm.org/doc/itscmm-1.0rc1.pdf

Peterson, R. (2004). *Integration strategies and tactics for information technology governance*. In W. Grembergen (Ed.), *Strategies for information technology governance* (pp. 37-80). Hershey, PA: Idea Group Publishing.

United Kingdom Office of Government Commerce [OGC] (2000). *Service support*. Norwich, Norfolk, England: The Stationery Office.

United Kingdom Office of Government Commerce [OGC] (2001). *Service delivery*. Norwich, Norfolk, England: The Stationery Office.

APPENDIX: LIST OF EXTENDED MATURITY MODELS

IT Governance/Program-Project-Portfolio Management

Knowledge Management Maturity Model
http://www.kmmm.org/

Organizational Project Management Maturity Model (OPM3)
http://opm3online.pmi.org/

PRINCE2 Maturity Model
http://www.ogc.gov.uk/documents/PRINCE2_Maturity_Model_Version_1.pdf

Portfolio, Programme & Project Management Maturity Model (P3M3)
http://www.ogc.gov.uk/documents/p3m3.pdf

Data Architecture/Storage Management

Database Administration Maturity Model
http://orafaq.com/papers/dbamm.pdf

Meta Data Management Maturity Model
http://www.dmreview.com/article_sub.cfm?articleId=1038827

Maturity Model for Data Integration
http://blogs.msdn.com/nickmalik/archive/2007/08/14/a-maturity-model-for-data-integration.aspx

Information Lifecycle Management Maturity Model
http://www.sun.com/storagetek/white-papers/ILM_Maturity_Model.pdf

Information Maturity Model
http://mike2.openmethodology.org/index.php/Information_Maturity_Model

Enterprise Architecture

EA Assessment Framework
http://colab.cim3.net/forum/caf-forum/2005-12/pdfsttb7akoeS.pdf

Enterprise Architecture Management Maturity Framework (EAMMF)
http://www.gao.gov/new.items/d03584g.pdf

Extended Enterprise Architecture Maturity Model
http://www.enterprise-architecture.info/Images/E2AF/E2AMMv2.PDF

Security/Security Architecture

Capabilities Maturity Model for Security
http://all.net/MAP/CMM.html
Information Security Maturity Assessment (derived from COBIT)
http://www.auckland.ac.nz/security/InfomationSecurityMaturityAssessment.htm

Security Maturity Model
http://www.isaca.org/Template.cfm?Section=Home&CONTENTID=24174&TEMPLATE=/Content-Management/ContentDisplay.cfm

Design/Development/Application Architecture

Enterprise Service Orientation Maturity Model (ESOMM)
http://msdn2.microsoft.com/en-us/library/Bb245664.aspx

Open Source Maturity Model
http://www.navicasoft.com/pages/osmm.htm

SOA Maturity Model
http://www.sonicsoftware.com/solutions/service_oriented_architecture/soa_maturity_model/index.ssp

SOA Maturity Model
http://www.bptrends.com/publicationfiles/04-07-ART-The%20SOA%20MaturityModel-Inagantifinal.pdf

New Service Oriented Architecture Maturity Model (SOA MM)
http://www.omg.org/soa/Uploaded%20Docs/SOA/SOA_Maturity.pdf

Service Integration Maturity Model
http://www.ibm.com/developerworks/webservices/library/ws-soa-simm/

Usability Maturity Model
http://www.processforusability.co.uk/Usability_test/html/umm.html

Web Services Maturity Model
http://roadmap.cbdiforum.com/reports/maturity/maturity1.php

QA/Testing/Support

Software Maintenance Maturity Model
http://www.compaid.com/caiinternet/ezine/alainapril-maintenancemodel.pdf

Testing Maturity Model
http://www.asq.org/pub/sqp/past/vol1_issue4/burnstein.html

The Testing Maturity Model
http://www.tmmifoundation.org/downloads/resources/TestMaturityModel.TMMi.pdf

Service Management/Configuration Management

CA Services Level Management Maturity Model
http://ca.com/Files/ServicesBriefs/slm_services_brief.pdf

Configuration Management Maturity Model
http://erp4it.typepad.com/erp4it/2005/10/a_configuration.html

Tideway Configuration Management Maturity Levels
http://www.tideway.com/what_we_do/tideway_cmml

Chapter XV
Governance of Software Development:
The Transition to Agile Scenario

Yael Dubinsky
IBM Haifa Research Lab, Israel

Avi Yaeli
IBM Haifa Research Lab, Israel

Yishai Feldman
IBM Haifa Research Lab, Israel

Emmanuel Zarpas
IBM Haifa Research Lab, Israel

Gil Nechushtai
IBM Haifa Research Lab, Israel

ABSTRACT

Governance is the exercise of control and direction over a subject such as a society, an organization, processes, or artifacts, by using laws and policies that are defined, deployed, and executed. In this chapter we develop this definition into a formal conceptual model that can be applied to a variety of governance domains. At the heart of this model lies the concept of the governance solution and its life-cycle. The governance solution embodies the set of mechanisms—decision rights, policies, controls, and measurements—applied to a governance scope in order to achieve some governance goals. As part of the lifecycle, the effectiveness of the governance solution is measured, and corrections and alignments are made as necessary. We demonstrate how this model can be applied to multiple governance domains by providing examples from IT governance as well as software-development governance. We conclude by providing a detailed scenario in the software-development governance space, which looks at large software organizations undergoing transition to agile development methodology. We further demonstrate how the governance model is instantiated and evolved in the context of this scenario.

INTRODUCTION

The field of information technology (IT) governance has garnered an increased amount of attention in recent years. However, it is still struggling to provide a universally agreed-upon definition and a complete model for IT governance, along with the required tools and techniques.

The definitions of IT governance that can be found in the literature from Broadbent (1998), Chulani, Clay, Yaeli, Wegman, and Cantor (2006), Van Grembergen and De Haes (2004), Weill and Ross (2004), and Williams (2005) and they all share common ideas, such as the need to increase the value of IT to the organization while reducing risk. For example, *Weill and Ross (2004) focus on decision rights and define IT governance as* "specifying the decision rights and accountability framework to encourage desirable behavior in the use of IT" (p. 8). Van Grembergen and De Haes (2004) address the alignment of the IT organization with the business needs, and define IT governance as "the leadership and organizational structures, processes, and relational mechanisms that ensure that the organization's IT sustains and extends the organization's strategy and objectives" (p. 1).

Chulani et al. (2006) include both decision rights and the alignment with business needs: "Within IBM, a widely accepted definition for IT governance is:

- Governance that pertains to an organization's information technology activities and the way those activities support the goals of the business
- Decision making rights associated with IT as well as the mechanisms and policies used to measure and control the way IT decisions are made and carried out within the organization" (p. 10).

In recent years, several IT governance and control frameworks, such as CobiT[1], ITIL[2], ISO-17799[3] have been developed. These frameworks help business management, IT management, quality practitioners, and auditors understand what needs to be done; yet they are far from being complete. Dahlberg and Kivijärvi (2006) outline the limitations of CobiT as a process-centric framework and suggest a new framework that takes an integrated process and structural approach, and links into corporate governance.

Another limitation stems from the fact that CobiT is a high-level framework targeted at IT organizations that support a business unit or a business organization. CobiT considers software development activities only within the context of providing a supporting service in a value chain for another business unit, rather than as a central business activity in itself. Software development activities are briefly described in CobiT as part of the high-level control objective AI2, "Acquire and Maintain Application Software." CobiT thus lacks a description of governance mechanisms that are appropriate for organizations with a large focus on software development. To that end, organizations need to refer to other standards and frameworks that focus more on software development and control of software development activities.

This chapter is aimed at bridging the gap between high-level IT governance and software development governance. We first present a model for governance in general, and then use the model to describe IT and software development domain-specific governance. The model is built based on a review of the literature and a set of scenarios, as explained in the next section. We use the process of transition to agile software development (Beck & Andres, 2004; Dubinsky, Hazzan, Talby, & Keren, 2006; Highsmith, 2002) to demonstrate the domain-specific governance schemes.

The agile approach to software development has emerged over the last decade, becoming mainstream as more and more organizations adopt agile practices (Barnett, 2006). The approach is based on a manifesto[4] that emphasizes the individuals involved in the software development, collaboration with the customer, and the need to provide testable working software. Several principles and methods (Highsmith, 2002) are used by software teams in different capacities (Ambler, 2007). As agile software development becomes more common, software organizations are becoming more interested in governing the transition to an agile approach.

We present data from the first author's involvement in two software-development projects that were carried out at two different organizations that underwent the transition to agile. The first project was developed by the IT department of a financial organization. The second project was developed by the software group of an international product provider. The action research method (Lewin, 1948) is used in this field of transition to agile processes, where the researchers plan an action, execute it while collecting data, analyze the data and reflect on it, and then define the next action by refining their role. The data emerged from their participation in planning sessions, guiding retrospective processes, involvement in refining the process and product measures, and consulting to higher management on the adoption of agile methodologies into the work procedures.

GOVERNANCE MODEL

This section presents a model for governance. The purpose of the model is to uniformly represent the main concepts involved in a governing process and their interrelationships. The development of this model started with a literature review, and built upon existing work using a set of scenarios that relate to project management, software engineering, and development processes. The literature review included CobiT; Val IT[5]; ISO 17799; OCEG Foundation[6]; CMMI[7]; SWEBOK[8]; Weill and Ross (2004); and Abrams, von Känel, Mueller, Pfitzmann, and Ruschka-Taylor (2006). The set of scenarios is based on our field experience as well as experiences of other practitioners and

researchers with whom we collaborate. The model attempts to abstract the elements of governance found in the various references and domains. We therefore start with the dictionary definitions of the word governance rather than with one of the many domain governance definitions that exist in previous works.

We begin by examining the general meaning of governance and incrementally introduce elements of the model that stem from that basic definition. The model reflects our view of how governance and governance processes should be organized and may require modifications to describe some existing situations.

The word govern is defined[9] as "to exercise continuous sovereign authority over; especially to control and direct the making and administration of policy in" and also "to control, direct, or strongly influence the actions and conduct of." The first part of the definition implies that

- Governance is an ongoing process;
- There must exist an entity with legitimate rights to exercise authority over the things that are subject to governance;
- Governance is concerned with controlling the way policies and laws are established.

The second part of the definition suggests that the purpose of governance is to influence or affect the activities, state, or behavior of the subjects being governed. Hence, governance affects and regulates its subjects through the administration of policies.

Scoping Authority over Subjects

The definition of governance specifies that governance exercises legitimate authority over the subjects being administered. We need a way to describe the boundaries of the subjects and activities being governed, as well as the boundaries of the area of jurisdiction over which the governing entity will have legitimate authority.

Furthermore, we know that people are subject to multiple governing bodies, such as national and local governments, as well as the organizations where they work. It is therefore necessary to describe multiple authority hierarchies and the relationships across these levels.

A governance scope represents a set of entities and relationships that are subject to acts of governance. Governance scope is hierarchically decomposable so that it can capture the hierarchical nature of society and business organizations. However, in order to represent multiple overlapping hierarchies, a governance scope can belong to more than a single hierarchy. In principle, a scope can identify organizations, suborganizations, processes, activities, roles, and artifacts; it can then establish the boundaries over the entities that are governed. In the context of corporate governance, the scope would be the entire organization and its activities. In the case of IT governance, the scope would be the IT organization, processes, activities, roles, and resources. According to Cantor and Sanders (2007), it is often useful to express the scope of governance in terms of processes within organizations, since there are many existing standards that consistently decompose the entire activities of organizations into processes and activities. Examples of such standards include CobiT and ITIL.

A governing body, sometime referred to as the government, represents the set of roles that have the right to exercise authority over the governance scope. Within social and business organizations, it is common to find multiple governing bodies, each

of which focuses on different kinds of scopes and is concerned with different governance needs. It is therefore useful to think about the arrangement of governing bodies in hierarchies and to align them with the hierarchies of governance scopes. By doing so, we can express the delegation of legitimate authority between governing bodies across the organization hierarchy, and the fact that legislation enacted by one governing body needs to conform, or at least not conflict with, legislation done by another governing body higher in the governing hierarchy chain. For example, a local government cannot create laws that violate national and federal laws. Within business organizations, it is common to find a hierarchy of governing bodies based on an organizational structure. We also consider process owners as governing bodies who are given authority to exercise control and legislation within the scope of their processes. Figure 1 illustrates the hierarchical nature of governance scopes and the relationships between these and the governing bodies.

There is a large body of political science literature that talks about types of governments (e.g., democracy, monarchy), how they are established, and the accountability of the governors to their constituents. The current version of our model does not address those elements of political models of governments.

Goals of Governance

According to the second part of the definition, the purpose of governance is to influence the

Figure 1. Modeling governance scopes and governing bodies

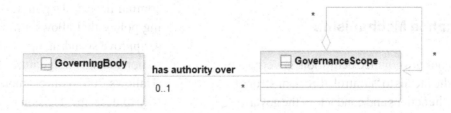

activities, state, or behavior of the subjects being governed. The need to influence the subjects in the first place often stems from external forces that place constraints or requirements on the activities within the governance scope. For example, state government regulations place constraints on organizations that do business within the jurisdiction of the state. Another example is the need to establish or update service delivery policies based on new security policies established by the larger organization. A final example is an IT organization that needs to control costs or improve performance based on business needs.

Hence, the context represents the overall situation and set of internal and external relationships in which a governance scope exists and in which its activities take place. The context sometimes acts as the driver or source of requirements for the act of governance.

A governance goal represents the desired state that the initiative or act of governance is trying to achieve within the governance scope. A goal needs to be measurable and provide a clear indication of how success and failure will be assessed. Governance goals are hierarchically decomposable, allowing the nesting of sub-goals. In this case, the success criteria of a high-level goal can be expressed as functions of the success criteria of the sub-goals. An example of a governance goal in business organizations is "ensuring that the organization performs effectively and efficiently against the requirements and imperatives coming from its context, and to ensure the delivery of the expected outcome." It is useful to express the governance goals in the terminology of the context; this enhances the communication between different stakeholders by providing a common vocabulary.

Governance Mechanisms

Based on our governance definition, governance requires the means to "control, direct, or strongly influence the actions and conduct" of the governed

subjects. A governance mechanism represents an abstraction of the possible mechanisms that can be used to regulate, influence, or control the actions and conduct of elements described within the governance scope in order to achieve some governance goal. There are many kinds of governance mechanisms that have been suggested and categorized by academia, industry standards, and vendors. Weill and Ross (2004) highlight three categories of mechanisms: decision-making structures, process alignment, and communication mechanisms. CobiT focuses on mechanisms to control processes, and identifies policies, procedures, practices, and organizational structures as means of control. IBM identifies two major groups of mechanisms that are established in the governance process (Chulani et al., 2006; Ericsson, 2007):

- **Static mechanisms:** Chains of responsibility, authority, and communication (decision rights);
- **Dynamic mechanisms:** Measurement, policy, standards, and control mechanisms.

All these definitions are compatible and cover more or less the same types of mechanisms, although the organization and focus are sometimes different. The following are several examples of these mechanisms and how they influence the governance scope:

- Decision rights mechanisms are the means through which an organization can establish, charter, and communicate the roles and responsibilities for particular management and decision-making processes. Typically, the decision rights are documented and communicated in a policy, such as a spending policy that allows a first-line manager to approve spending up to $3000 without a senior manager's signature. A RACI matrix (Hallows, 2001) is an example of a structured way to describe decision rights.

- Policies, procedures, guidelines, practices, and standards mechanisms all instruct the subjects under governance at varying level of formalism and strictness of the desired behavior or how to conduct their activities. Controls, measurements, and decision authority are often documented and communicated in policies and procedures.

- Control and measurement mechanisms provide the means for people with decision-making rights to control and monitor the activities for which they are responsible. Decision checkpoints, incentives, and policy assertions are examples of controls. For example, a project funding approval checkpoint is a control in the project funding process. An ROI measurement is a mechanism used to measure the return of investment in an asset. Another example is the measurement of estimated versus actual development time for software development tasks. Note that measurement has a dual role: it enables monitoring but also acts as an influencing mechanism that drives the behavior of the subjects.

The governance mechanism should provide a clear statement of its desired effect on the governance scope via one or more governance goals. Furthermore, governance mechanisms can be hierarchical, allowing governance goals to be met by a hierarchy of governance mechanisms. Figure 2 shows the part of the model that describes governance goals, scopes, and mechanisms. A governance mechanism affects a governance scope to realize a governance goal. In addition, a hierarchy of governance mechanisms can realize a hierarchy of governance goals.

Governance Points and Observables

In order for a governance mechanism to control and monitor an activity within the governance scope, it is necessary to identify the exact situation in the governance scope and the exact condition under which the governance mechanism should operate. This identification also serves as the specification for how to implement and deploy the governance mechanism. A governance point represents a specified location and situation within the governance scope to which a governance mechanism should be applied. For example, a policy that enables a first-line manager to approve vacations that do not exceed two consecutive weeks creates a governance point. This point is the set of situations in which first-line managers in the governance scope should decide upon vacation approvals.

From an operational perspective, it is useful to express governance points in the context of artifact lifecycles, where events, activities, and

Figure 2. Modeling governance scopes, mechanisms, and goals

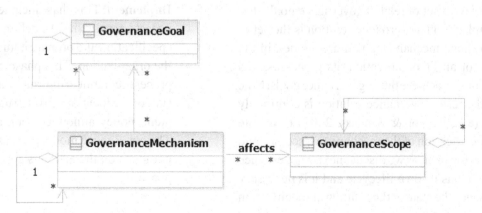

state transitions of the artifacts act as potential points to which governance mechanisms can be applied. This creates a common structure for the definition of governance points. It also supports the implementation and integration of the governance mechanism into the processes and software automation of the activities described in the governance scope.

A governance observable represents a metric, event, piece of information, or artifact metadata that can be observed by a governance mechanism at a governance point. This provides the means to characterize the behavior of the governance scope by identifying observable information that could be used to help achieve the governance goals. It also allows the identification of specific properties within the governance scope that are relevant to achieving a governance goal. For example, such properties may include an event or attribute that are used for calculating a metric.

Governance Solutions and the Governance Process

So far we have shown how governance mechanisms can be associated with governance scopes to achieve governance goals. Often, sets of mechanisms, scopes, and goals collectively have some significance from the perspective of an organization, process, or initiative. In such cases, it is useful to refer to them as a group. A governance solution represents the collection of governance mechanisms applied to a set of governance scopes to achieve a set of related governance goals. For example, an IT governance solution is the set of governance mechanisms that are applied in the scope of an IT organization, its processes, and activities, to achieve the IT governance goals. Note that the term governance solution is commonly used (e.g., Cantor & Sanders, 2007) to denote the specification of the mechanisms, scopes, and goals. However, as we discuss next, a governance solution has its own lifecycle and it is necessary to discuss the state of the solution at specification

time as well as at other phases of its lifecycle.

As presented in the definition, governance is an ongoing process. In fact, it is an iterative process through which the governance solution is established and evolved. In Figure 3, we present the lifecycle of that process and typical activities that are likely to take place in each phase of the lifecycle. Among different lifecycle views, such as the plan–do–study–act (PDSA) cycle (Tague, 2004), we have chosen to adapt the approach of Cantor and Sanders (2007) to governance lifecycle. This approach emphasizes the separation between activities to establish and evolve a governance solution, and those relating to the execution of the governance solution.

The governance process has four major phases:

1. **Assess:** The current governance solution is evaluated and new requirements for the governance solution are analyzed and planned. This includes measuring governance effectiveness metrics, assessing key performance indicators against previously defined governance goals, and planning how to address new governance needs arising from the context, such as new regulations.

2. **Define:** The governance solution is defined. The governance goals are captured and governance effectiveness measurements are defined. The scopes to bring under governance are determined and the governance mechanisms are specified.

3. **Implement:** This phase includes all the steps necessary to realize the defined governance specification and prepare it for execution by the organization. This phase could include process reengineering, automation and tool support, education, infrastructure deployment, policy announcement, and so forth. The governance model presented here does not focus on the artifacts generated in this phase.

4. **Execute:** The solution has already been deployed in the organization and management is expected to execute the governance solution. Managers and other specified roles are exercising their decision rights and playing a role in controlling and monitoring the scopes under their responsibility.

The governance lifecycle shows a clear separation between activities done to establish and evolve a governance solution and those that are done while executing a governance solution. This observation can be useful for understanding the relationships between the roles of governors and managers. It can be said that governors are responsible for establishing a governance solution while managers are responsible for executing the governance solution. Moreover, a governing body will sometimes assign decision rights to itself; in those cases, the governing body is also an actor in the execution of the governance solution. Similarly, some managers may sit in governing bodies; in those cases, they assume multiple roles of both governor and manager.

The governance solution can be viewed as having states that correspond to the governance process phases. It is interesting to note that there is always some version of a governance solution that is in the state of "executing" for any given scope. In each iteration of the lifecycle, the governance process can modify an executing governance solution by defining, implementing, and deploying a new version of that solution. Furthermore, some steps of the Assess phase of the governance lifecycle may also be running continuously by monitoring the executing governance solution.

A governance execution result represents the result of applying a governance mechanism at a particular time. It is a measurement that relates to the governance scope, but is used in the context of the governance assessment phase. Examples of such measurements might be compliance records/ status or governance performance indicators.

Figure 4 illustrates the model of the governance solution. A governance mechanism can be used to affect some behavior within a governance scope to realize some governance goal. The governance mechanism can be applied at specific governance

Figure 3. The governance lifecycle (adapted from Cantor & Sanders, 2007; used with permission)

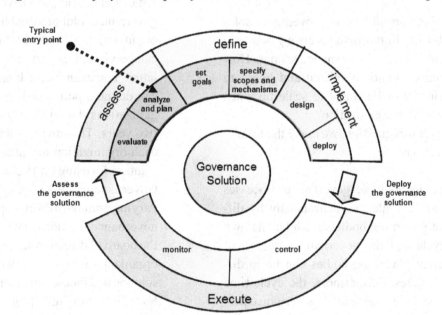

Figure 4. Modeling the governance solution

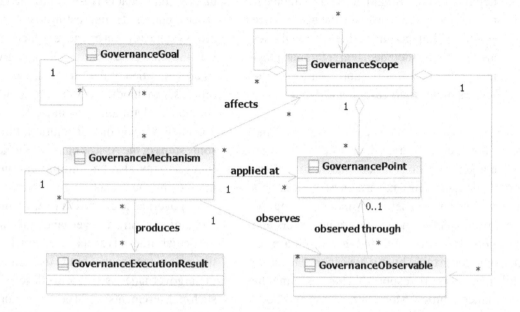

points within the governance scope to affect or observe some behavior within the scope. The result of applying the mechanisms is stored in a governance execution result that is produced by the mechanism.

Systems of Governance Solutions

We are seeing a proliferation of governance solutions established by multiple governing bodies to cover a wide range of governance scopes. How are governance solutions related and how can the solutions be orchestrated to scale up when governing a large organization?

To answer this question, we make the following observations:

- There are multiple governance processes that are executed asynchronously by different governing bodies. Each has its own lifecycle and the governance solution of different governing bodies can be in different states. Furthermore, the cycle time may not be the same in all governance pro-

cesses. Some processes may have a one-year cycle, while others have a quarterly cycle, depending on how adaptive and responsive the governance should be to the changing scope and context.

- Governance solutions have relationships. For example, governance decisions made by the large organization will have an effect on the governance solutions established for smaller organization scopes. In fact, the former can be viewed as part of the context of the latter. For example, a larger organization can define a policy stating that all sub-organizations should be ISO-certified within two years. This imposes a requirement for each organization to initiate a governance solution focusing on ISO certification.

- Governance solutions can be defined for varying granularities of scope. For example, governance solutions that are established by the board of directors and apply to an entire organization may coexist with a governance solution that focuses on development policies for a 30-person agile project.

To summarize, while the governance solution can autonomously execute for any given scope and goal, it can also link to other governance solutions either through the context or by establishing governance mechanisms that affect other governance solutions. These two characteristics ensure the scalability of the governance model.

TRANSITION TO AGILE SCENARIO: A GOVERNANCE PERSPECTIVE

In this section, we present some of the data that was gathered in two different organizations that underwent a transition to agile development. The first (denoted by A) is a financial organization using software developed by an agile team, which is part of the organization's IT department. The team actually works for another organization (denoted by Â) and is outsourced to organization A to develop and maintain its software products. The second organization (denoted by B) is a global company that manufactures devices with embedded software. Several distributed teams, one of which has started to use agile methods, develop the software. The data was gathered by observations in planning sessions and development activities, consultation to higher management, and by guiding the retrospective process of the agile team.

We use the governance concepts described in the previous section to present the case of software development governance and analyze the transition-to-agile processes in the two organizations.

Governance scope. In both organizations, the transition to agile development began with one project. The management of organization Â decided to improve the delivery time of software projects and selected the project in organization A as an experiment for the agile approach. The intention of the management of organization Â was to extend use of the agile approach to more of its software projects. Examining the governance scope in this case, we denote by GS_1 the scope that contains the project team and its activities. Figure 5 schematically shows GS_1 as an inner scope in the two different hierarchies of organizations A and Â. In organization A, GS_1 is part of the IT governance; in organization Â, GS_1 is part of the software development governance. The teammates are the employees of organization Â outsourced to A.

In organization B, the project team and its activities are defined as the governance scope, which is within the hierarchy of the software development governance in this organization. In this case, the project manager together with his team leaders learned about the agile approach and decided to start the transition in their jurisdiction. In parallel, they started the process of convincing their upper management that it was worthwhile. This was different from organization Â, where the direction of governance is top-down.

Governing body. The governing body in the case of GS_1 included governors from both orga-

Figure 5. Hierarchy of governance scopes in organizations A and Â

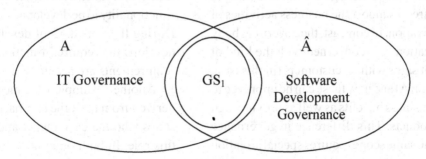

nizations A and Â. The governors from organization A were the CIO and the domain expert that served as the onsite customer. This expert was responsible for directing the team according to the release vision, giving them the requirements for each iteration, and prioritizing the requirements. The CIO and the domain expert could delegate authority to others in organization A, such as the people responsible for the infrastructure and those who tested the system as end users. The governors from organization Â continuously monitored this process in order to learn about its benefits and drawbacks. They worked together with the governors of organization A, who agreed to cooperate in implementing a new approach to software development.

In organization B, the project manager and team leaders served as the governing body. As part of the transition process, the role of methodologist was suggested. This person was in charge of maintaining and enhancing the methodology (Dubinsky & Hazzan, 2006). Although other roles that are concerned with the transition (e.g., tracker) were rotated among teammates, the person who performed this role did it consistently and continued to learn about agile methods. She also took upon herself to educate other teams in the organization about agile concepts. As a result, she naturally joined the governing body and is involved in every decision this body makes.

Governance goals. The governance goals of organization A are different from the governance goals of organization Â. Though they share the same scope, the context is different. The governing body of organization A is concerned with the needs of the IT users inside the organization and who use the software to support the business activities of this organization. In contrast, the governing body of organization Â is concerned with the kind of contracts it signs with its customers (in this case, organization A) and how these can be improved to increase business benefits as well as provide high quality products. This difference in governance goals on the same scope requires special attention

when dealing with the mechanisms that should be used in this compound solution.

In organization B, the governance goals were derived from previous experience of the governing body in running software projects in this and other organizations. The goals refer on the one hand to the professional aspects of software production and on the other hand to the way the project is viewed in the context of the organization. Hence, one goal is to improve the way software requirements are dealt with and to shorten the time-to-market. Another goal is to follow the software development process used in this organization and published in an internal handbook. The decision to implement the agile approach to cope with the first goal implied that the governing body should communicate to higher management the changes caused by the agile implementation, especially these that do not fit existing procedures. They would also need to reconcile the governance solutions used inside the team and in its relations with the rest of the organization.

Governance mechanisms. The adoption of an agile approach implied several governance mechanisms. The most conspicuous was the work procedure that required short development iterations. In both organizations A and B, a release contains about eight iterations of two weeks each. When uncertainty increased, usually towards the end of the release, the iterations were shortened to one week. An iteration of two weeks was composed of one day of presentations and planning, and nine days of development. During the day of presentations and planning, the team presents the artifacts of the previous iteration to the customer and, together with the customer, plans the functionality to be developed in the next iteration. During the nine days of development, the team develops the required functionality and no new requirements are accommodated.

Another example of a mechanism that was derived from the agile approach is the policy that states who the customer is and the definition of this role. In both organizations A and B, before the transition-to-agile process, the project manager played the role of the customer in setting the functionality developed by the team, along with the priorities and schedule. This behavior caused an on-going negotiation between the project manager and the real customer. The project manager generally refused to change requests that the real customer prioritized as important and continued to distribute work to the team as seemed necessary. The agile approach set the rules clearly: the customer is the one who provides the software requirements, decides what the team will develop in every iteration, and the priorities of these requirements. Of course, the customer can and should receive all the professional advice the team and the project manager can give. The customers should commit themselves to the process of development, be available during the iteration, particularly in the presentations where they gave feedback and in planning sessions where they reviewed the progress. The project manager should manage the development process and people so that a high quality software product will be developed.

The agile metrics are used in both organizations as the measurements of the process and product. Each team contains a tracker who is responsible for collecting the data required by the metrics and for communicating them at the end of the presentation of the iteration artifacts. The agile metrics can be used as governance observables. One measurement that was used by both teams is the calculation of estimated time of completed tasks versus the actual time that was invested to develop them. Next, we present governance observables that illustrate this measurement.

Governance points and observables as part of the governance lifecycle. The notions of governance scope, governing body, governance goals, and mechanisms are part of the Define and Implement phases of the governance lifecycle (see Figure 3). The governance points and observables exist in the Execute phase. The following are two kinds of governance mechanisms that are found in both organizations and that provide observables data:

- The measurement of estimated time of daily-completed tasks versus the actual time that was invested to develop them.
- The policy of conducting one-hour retrospectives at every iteration (Talby, Hazzan, Dubinsky & Keren, 2006).

These mechanisms belong to specific goals that are common in processes of transition to agile in general and were specifically set as goals also in our two cases.

- The first goal was to shorten delivery time. One of the mechanisms that serve this goal is measuring team velocity, which can be perceived as the amount of productive work units per iteration (Beck & Fowler, 2000). The agile approach recommends small releases of two to three months, each of which consists of short iterations of two to four weeks. Measuring team velocity per iteration enables ongoing visibility of the progress information as well as the ability to make decisions on how to continue.
- The second goal was to continuously improve the process by gradually adopting agile practices. One of the mechanisms that serve this goal is when teammates reflect on their activities (Hazzan, 2002; Kerth, 2001; Schön, 1983) after every iteration, before they start planning the next iteration. This is done as part of a retrospective process that enables individuals and teams to share ideas about the major issues that emerge in their software development environments, think about ways to improve, and make decisions to support these improvements.

The data on team velocity and retrospective processes can be presented as governance observables that emerged in the Execute phase and are used as part of the Assess phase of the governance lifecycle. We present these observables in the following sections. We note that there are further issues that are relevant to the transition to agile scenario, such as testing and quality assurance, simplicity as a concept, and the role scheme, which are not addressed here.

Team Velocity

The first governance observable is the graph of estimated time of completed tasks versus the actual time that was invested to develop them. One associated governance point occurs every development day when the tracker displays the graph during the stand-up-meeting that starts the team's workday. This is done in order to trace the team's daily progress. Another governance point that uses the same observable occurs every two weeks in the presentation of the iteration artifacts. This is done in order to trace the team's iteration progress. The daily progress is measured against the iteration commitment. The iteration progress is measured against the release commitment. We used this data to better understand the agile process. From the governance perspective, we can decide if this mechanism can assist us in the

Assess phase to follow up on the performance of the governance solution.

Each day, in each of the teams, the tracker added two new points to the graph. The "total estimated" point represented the cumulative estimations of all tasks that were completed by the previous day and the "total done" point represented the cumulative actual time devoted to those tasks. A completed task was counted when the developer in charge completed the coding, unit testing, and integration with the entire developed system.

Figure 6 shows the graphs of estimations versus actual time in the third iteration for the team in organization A. The third (linear) line provides the expected pace according to available time. As can be observed, there is a significant difference between the time that is available for development and the time that is actually used for development. This phenomenon also happened in the case of the team in organization B. There are several reasons that may cause this behavior. Firstly, only completed tasks are calculated. Although some teammates had invested time in other tasks, this time was not taken into consideration if the task was not complete before the end of the iteration. Secondly, there is often time invested in urgent tasks that come up, such as support service for end

Figure 6. Estimation vs. actual development time in iteration 3 (team A)

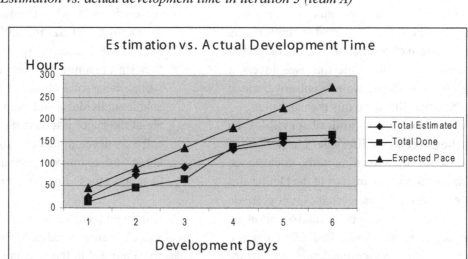

users who work with modules that are in production. Thirdly, some developers, whose time was taken into account, may have been absent.

Figure 7 shows the graphs of estimations versus actual time in the second (Figure 7a) and forth (Figure 7b) iterations of the team in organization B. The Expected Pace line is the ratio between the total working hours of all teammates in the iteration and the number of days in the iteration.

We observe that at the end of the second iteration (Figure 7a), the amount of time actually spent on completed tasks (159 hours) was 30%

less than the available time according to the expected pace (229 hours). This can be explained by the fact that tasks in progress that were not completed in this iteration were not counted. In the fourth iteration (Figure 7b), however, all tasks were completed. In such cases the total-expected point unites with the expected pace point since this was the amount of hours that was considered in the work planning.

We further observe that in both iterations, the distribution into tasks was reasonably good. Too many dependencies between tasks can delay their

Figure 7. Estimation vs. actual development time in iterations 2 and 4 (team B)

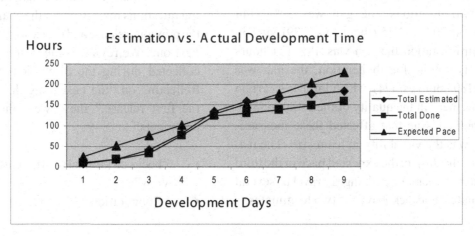

a) Iteration 2

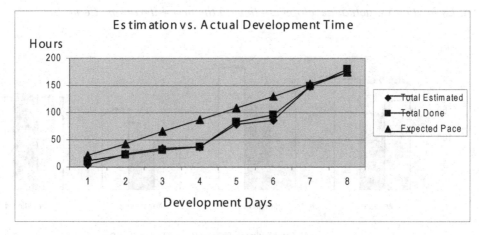

(b) Iteration 4

completion, causing a nearly flat total-done line until close to the end of the iteration and then a sudden increase when many tasks are completed together.

Figure 8 summarizes the estimation versus actual times and the expected pace for each of the first four iterations for this team. We observe that estimates are too high in the first three iterations: 14% in the first (167 hours estimate vs. 144 actual) and second iterations (184 hours estimate vs. 159 actual) and 20% in the third (92 hours estimate vs. 74 actual). In the fourth iteration, in contrast, estimates were low by 4% (174 hours estimate vs. 180 actual).

In the three first iterations, the total-done time was less than the expected pace. In the first two iterations, the gap was 30% (144 hours vs. 207 and 159 hours vs. 229), and in the third iteration the gap was 48% (74 hours vs. 144). In the fourth iteration, the gap was −4% (180 hours vs. 174), which implies a certain improvement in the quality of the estimations.

Another issue that affected these measurements was the variability in team size. The reasons for the drop in the expected pace in the third iteration are personnel changes, travel of several teammates, and sick leave for two teammates.

Retrospective Process

The second governance point that we present concerns the retrospective process that guides the software development process. The agile approach use reflection sessions and a retrospective process as an internal practice (Beck & Andres, 2004; Salo, 2005; Talby et al., 2006). The teams in organizations A and B adopted the practice of one-hour reflection between the presentation of the artifacts of the previous iteration and the planning of the next iteration (Talby et al., 2006).

A reflection session was conducted in organization A between the first two releases of the transition-to-agile process. Teammates filled out an anonymous individual questionnaire containing questions mainly about the characteristics of the previous release and the expectations from the next one. We review some of the data that was collected during the discussion that followed. Reflecting on "the best thing that happened in the first release," these were the teammates' comments:

- "Focus on the goal with the customer's global view"
- "Cooperation"

Figure 8. Estimation vs. actual development time in the first 4 iterations (team B)

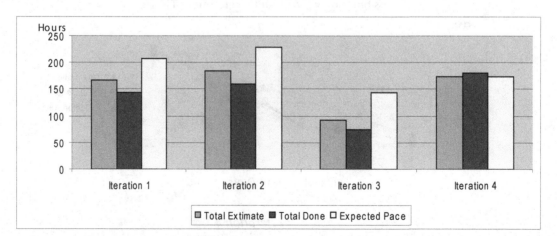

- "It takes less time to develop tasks compared with the previous method"
- "End to end [development] shortens processes and integration"
- "A platform to talk about problem was created, sit together and hear problems"
- "Good communication between team and customers, there is someone to approach with questions"
- "People started new things, like modules"
- "Setting priorities gives focus"

Reflecting on "what can be changed in the next release," teammates generated a list and then voted for the following as the most important:

- Improve the integration process
- Adopt the methodology into the QA process
- Perform better follow-up

One of the first reflection sessions in organization B was dedicated to the relationships between the team and the organization. Teammates filled out an anonymous individual questionnaire containing questions about the organization's goals and values, existing policies, and the way the team could contribute to the organization and vice versa. One of the questions asked them to rate their level of agreement with several statements on the organization's existing policy on software quality. Table 1 shows the teammates' answers; the number in each cell represents the number of people who gave that answer. Based on this and

similar data, we suggest that the reflection sessions can be considered as a governance mechanism that is activated in the Execute phase and feeds the Assess phase of the governance lifecycle.

In a broader perspective, the data that emerges from the retrospective process, together with other governance observables, can assist the governance follow-up in the Assess phase. During the Assess phase, a complete perspective on the governance solution lifecycle is gained. Specifically, we can follow up the transition-to-agile process and continuously steer it according to the governance information.

CONCLUSION AND FUTURE DIRECTIONS

Starting from a comprehensive definition of governance and its components, we presented a high-level governance model, which includes the main components and the relationships between them. To validate the model framework, we showed how to conceptually instantiate it for both IT governance and software development governance, in the context of transition-to-agile software development in large organizations.

We are now developing a governance lifecycle platform based on the model presented here. It should serve as a single point of administration for the governance of software development activities. The main parts of the governance solution platform are the governance module, the data module, the scheduler, and the user interface.

Table 1. Teammates reflection on the organizational policy on software quality (majority is marked with grey)

Statement	1 Strongly disagree	2	3	4	5 Strongly agree	No answer
I'm familiar with the policy		2	1	4	5	
I follow the policy in my project	1		6	3	2	
Most projects in the organization follow the policy		3	2	4		3

In brief, the governance module manages the governance lifecycle by supporting the governing body and relevant roles. The data module contains a data adapter that mediates between the application and the database. The database includes all the information from the different data sources available in software development environments:

- Software development artifacts such as code, test, specifications, models, and bug list
- Software management artifacts such as task plans and estimation graphs;
- Activity indicators that capture the state of the activities and tasks being performed; and
- Governance observables such as measures, policies, decision rights, and roles

The scheduler is responsible for scheduling tasks for governance mechanisms that are used within the governance solution. The user interface presents views appropriate to each of the different roles that are involved in the governance process.

In light of the development of the governance lifecycle platform, we suggest extending the development component of existing governance tools according to our model. This way, the model presented in this chapter can be used to augment existing IT governance models (e.g., CobiT and ITIL) to close the gap between the IT governance model and the governance of software development activities.

ACKNOWLEDGMENT

We would like to thank Clive Gee and Duncan Clark for their significant contribution to the UML model. We would like to thank Murray Cantor, Duncan Clark, Clive Gee, John Falkl, Steve Graham, Christine Draper, Greg Rader, and Calvin Powers for numerous discussions and ideas.

Orit Hazzan participated in consulting for one of the organizations. We would like to thank her for fruitful discussions.

REFERENCES

Abrams, C., von Känel, J., Mueller, S., Pfitzmann, B., & Ruschka-Taylor, S. (2006). Optimized enterprise risk management (Research Report RZ3657). IBM. Retrieved May 14, 2008, from http://domino. research.ibm.com/library/cyberdig.nsf/papers/ 0C4791FC96DEF130852571D0003F5F15/$File/ rz3657.pdf

Ambler, S. (2007). Agile adoption rate survey: March 2007. Retrieved May 14, 2008, from http:// www.ambysoft.com/surveys/agileMarch2007. htm

Barnett, L. (2006). And the agile survey says. Agile Journal March 6, 2006. Retrieved May 14, 2008, from http://www.agilejournal.com/articles/from-the-editor/and-the-agile-survey-says%85.html

Beck, K., & Andres, C. (2004). Extreme programming explained (2nd ed.). Boston, Massachusetts: Addison-Wesley.

Beck, K., & Fowler, M. (2000). Planning extreme programming. Boston, Massachusetts: Addison-Wesley.

Broadbent, M. (1998). Leading governance, business and IT processes: The organizational fabric of business and IT partnership. Findings Gartner Group, 31 December 1998, document #FIND-19981231-01.

Cantor, M., & Sanders, J. (2007). Operational IT governance. Retrieved May 14, 2008, from http://www.ibm.com/developerworks/rational/library/may07/cantor_sanders/index.html

Chulani, S., Clay, W., Yaeli, A., Wegman,, M. N., & Cantor, M. (2006). Understanding IT governance: Definitions, contexts, and concerns (Research Report RC24064). IBM. Retrieved May 14, 2008, from http://domino. research.ibm.com/library/cyberdig.nsf/papers/ 38905EEA124CDDFB852571FE00569CCE/ $File/rc24064.pdf

Dahlberg, T., & Kivijärvi, H. (2006). An integrated framework for IT governance and the development and validation of an assessment instrument. In Proceedings of the 39th Hawaii International Conference on Systems Sciences, Kauai, Hawaii.

Dubinsky, Y., & Hazzan, O. (2006). Using a role scheme to derive software project metrics. Journal of Systems Architecture, 52, 693–699.

Dubinsky, Y., Hazzan, O., Talby, D., & Keren, A. (2006). System analysis and design in a large-scale software project: the case of transition to agile development. In Proceedigns of the the Eigth International Conference on Enterprise Information Systems, Paphos, Cyprus.

Ericsson, M. (2007). The governance landscape: Steering and measuring development organizations to align with business strategy. Retrieved May 14, 2008, from http://www.ibm.com/developerworks/rational/library/feb07/ericsson/

Hallows, J. E. (2001). The project management office toolkit. Newton Square, Pennsylvania: Project Management Institute.

Hazzan, O. (2002). The reflective practitioner perspective in software engineering education. The Journal of Systems and Software, 63(3), 161-171.

Highsmith, J. (2002). Agile software development ecosystems. Boston: Addison-Wesley.

Kerth, N. L. (2001). Project retrospectives: A handbook for team reviews. New York: Dorset House Publishing Company.

Lewin, K. (1948). Resolving social conflicts; Selected papers on group dynamics. New York: Harper & Row.

Salo, O. (2005). Systematical validation of learning in agile software development environment. In Proceedings of the the Seventh International Workshop on Learning Software Organizations, Kaiserslautern, Germany.

Schön, D. A. (1983). The reflective practitioner. New York: Basic Books.

Tague, N. R. (2004). The quality toolbox (2nd ed.). Milwaukee, WI: ASQ Quality Press.

Talby, D., Hazzan, O., Dubinsky, Y., & Keren, A. (2006). Reflections on reflection in agile software development. In Proceedings of the Agile 2006 Conference, Minneapolis, Minnesota.

Van Grembergen, W., & De Haes, S. (2004). IT governance and its mechanisms. Information Systems Control Journal, 1. Retrieved May 14, 2008, from http://www.isaca.org/Template.cfm?Section=Home&Template=/ContentManagement/ContentDisplay.cfm&ContentID=16771

Weill, P., & Ross, J. W. (2004). *IT governance*. Watertown, MA: Harvard Business School Press.

Williams, P. A. (2005). *The buck stops here. IT Leadership, 1*. Retrieved May 14, 2008, from http://www.the-itleader.com/features/feature258/

ENDNOTES

[1]   Control Objectives for Information and related Technology (CobiT®); see http://www.itgi.org.

[2]   Details on ITIL® can be found at: http://www.itil.co.uk.

[3]   Information on ISO-17799 security controls can be found at: http://www.iso-17799.com,

[4]   The Agile Manifest at www.agilemanifesto.org.

[5]   Val-IT Governance Framework: www.isaca.org/valit.

6   Open Compliance & Ethics Group (OCEG) Foundation redbook: http://www.oceg.org/view/Foundation.

7   Capability Maturity Model Integration (CMMI): http://www.sei.cmu.edu/cmmi.

8   The Software Engineering Body of Knowledge (SWEBOK): http://www.swebok.org.

9   Merriam-Webster Online Dictionary definition at http://www.merriam-webster.com. Other dictionaries offer similar definitions.

Chapter XVI
The Governance Implications When it is Outsourced

Anne C. Rouse
Deakin University, Australia

ABSTRACT

This chapter considers the governance issues raised by the increasing use of external parties to supply IT resources (including packaged enterprise software). The chapter briefly reviews existing formal governance frameworks and their treatment of IT outsourcing, then introduces an analytical model for considering outsourcing benefits and risks. The chapter then goes on to highlight some strategic IT governance issues that become critical once a firm outsources a significant proportion of its IT services. The aim of the chapter is to alert decision makers to the fact that outsourcing IT incorporates residual risks even when widely recommended operational controls are implemented. It concludes that effective control processes are necessary, but not sufficient for good corporate governance and suggests that those responsible for corporate governance ensure that both operational and strategic governance issues are considered when IT is substantially outsourced.

INTRODUCTION

Despite ongoing debate about outsourcing's risks and benefits, more and more firms are choosing to outsource significant proportions of their information technology (IT) and information systems. Several general frameworks and principles have been proposed for governing outsourced IT arrangements and, more recently, formal IT governance frameworks have begun addressing issues associated with outsourced IT services. Yet, while these guidelines help address some of the inherent complexity of an outsourcing undertaking, in some ways they can obscure the need to think through the long-term IT governance implications of an IT outsourcing strategy.

This chapter explores the governance issues raised by the increasing use of external parties to supply IT resources (including packaged enterprise software) and argues that the reliance by firms on external vendors for IT services raises more fundamental governance issues than just operational control of vendors – effective control processes are necessary, but not sufficient for good governance. The chapter briefly reviews existing formal governance frameworks and their treatment of IT outsourcing, then introduces an analytical model for considering outsourcing benefits and risks. The chapter goes on to highlight some strategic IT governance issues that become critical once a firm outsources a substantial proportion of its IT services.

The basis of the chapter is a program of 10 years' study into IT outsourcing beginning with the author's PhD studies and extended by the work of Rouse and Corbitt (2001; 2003; 2007; see reference list). Studies by these authors have included a series of longitudinal IT outsourcing cases (in both the public and private sectors); a number of focus groups (with n=55 informants from vendors and purchasers of IT outsourcing), two case studies of business process outsourcing purchasers, and a survey of large IT outsourcing purchasers in both the pubic and private sectors (n=240).

BACKGROUND

The effective management, control, and alignment (with business needs) of IT resources have been a topic of interest to the information systems discipline for decades (e.g., see Earl, 1988). However, it is generally only since the 1990's (Loh & Venkatranam, 1992) that the term "IT Governance" has been used to describe this responsibility. Typically IT governance is seen as a subset of the corporate governance framework, which defines the institutional structures and processes for directing and controlling the firm in a way that encourages management to maximize the welfare of shareholders and other stakeholders

(Tirole, 2001; Weill & Ross, 2004). Governance is understood to encompass authority, accountability, stewardship, leadership, direction, control, and, importantly, management of corporate risks (ASX, 2003; Tirole, 2001).

IT Governance focuses particularly on getting value from the firm's substantial investments in information resources and systems, including their performance, efficiency, and value for money. IT Governance also focuses on identifying, reducing, and managing the significant risks that IT and information systems pose to a firm. IT Governance occurs at different levels within an organization and so is part strategy (enabling value by integrating risk consideration into strategic IT decision making) and part tactical/operational, where it is concerned with effective IT management and minimizing identified risks (including risk of compliance failure).

At the operational level, largely the responsibility of the CIO, governance is characterized by use of specific policies and procedures to improve IT performance, effectiveness and control. Operational IT governance is often reflected in application portfolio, infrastructure portfolio, project portfolio and sourcing portfolio policies and procedures. At a strategic level, governance is the concern of Board members and their delegates (e.g. Board subcommittees). Strategic governance addresses the context of specific IT governance processes and procedures, and the creation of an organizational environment where governance processes can be operated. Strategic governance thus needs to address interdependencies between the various actors, and the allocation of decision rights within the organization (Weill & Ross, 2004). Strategic level governance is also characterized by a substantially longer time frame than operational (or tactical) governance. Strategic governance affects operational governance largely indirectly, by the creation of context and clear goals, and by the allocation of specific responsibilities. Once these are defined at a strategic level, operational processes that might seem problematic can be more easily managed.

A central message of this chapter is that while IT outsourcing is addressed by some IT governance standards at an operational level, in view of the corporate risks associated with IT outsourcing IT governance also needs to be addressed at the strategic level.

The notion of corporate governance (and hence IT Governance) has received substantial attention over the last few years following highly publicised corporate collapses like those of Arthur Andersen, WorldCom, Enron, and Tyco; and, in Australia, HIH and One-Tel (Clarke, Dean & Oliver, 2003). These failures alerted shareholders, regulators, and governments that the risks of malfeasance and poor management were much higher than was generally recognized. Partly as a reaction to this recognition, legislation such as the 2002 US Sarbanes-Oxley Act; European and Australian data privacy laws, the international banking framework, Basel II; and, in Australia, the Australian Corporate Law Economic Reform Program (CLERP9) now impose tougher regulatory conditions on firms to ensure accountability and adequate management of corporate resources and risks. One consequence of these more stringent frameworks is that individual officers responsible for firm governance now have substantially higher obligations than previously, and they are seeking to acquit these obligations by instituting effective governance structures.

IT GOVERNANCE

Because of the nature of IT, and its pervasive impact in modern organizations, the governance challenges for IT are complex (Weill & Ross, 2004). Both the size of IT investments and the risks associated with corruption, theft, or loss of information resources, demand particular attention on the part of organizations.

These services are usually now supplied by a mix of internal and external providers, but governance responsibility cannot be delegated to an external vendor. The US Sarbanes-Oxley legisla-

tion (and related legislation elsewhere) requires that purchasing firms have demonstrable programs in place to manage the operations, systems and risks associated with any outsourced process or function. This obligation is particularly important in relation to outsourced IT functions, because information systems themselves serve to embody many of the firms' business control and governance processes. Under these new more stringent conditions, firms which have outsourced their information systems and IT are still responsible for protecting information resources, and for adequately controlling any outsourced arrangement (Coates, 2007).

When IT activities are outsourced, control of IT resources moves from internal, hierarchical structures and processes (including day to day supervision) to contract-based controls (Mylott, 1995). These controls rely largely on the formal specification of outcomes and standards to be achieved, supported by detailed performance monitoring and regular market testing or benchmarking. The control of IT activities in this way calls upon quite different skills, and demands a substantially higher level of discipline on the part of purchasing firms. The costs of these controls are high, and often unplanned when the initial positive "business case" for outsourcing IT services is developed. Furthermore, the formality of this form of control can introduce unexpected side effects (such as increased complexity and bureaucracy), which can sometimes impede line business activities.

There are many academic and trade publications outlining actions firms should take to effectively manage IT outsourcing, yet few of these recommendations have been subject to empirical test as to their practicality, and impacts. There is strong commonality amongst most of the recommendations for how firms should govern their outsourced arrangement, both in the wider literature, and, more recently, formal standards. However, in practical terms many common recommendations for successfully managing outsourcing, while plausible, are fundamentally unhelpful. Some common and apparently sensible recommendations are found in IT Governance guidelines, and many can be found in the trade literature to which corporate governance officers are exposed. While firms will not necessarily come to harm in following such recommendations, they may be left with a false sense of security that their outsourcing arrangements are consequently adequately managed and controlled.

The research underpinning this chapter suggests that many of the recommended processes for managing outsourcing are in real life difficult to do — such as choosing which IT services are "core" to a firm's business and which are not. Many others often have unintended consequences. An example of the latter—reported by Rouse (2002)—occurs when firms follow advice to keep outsourcing contracts short. While managing some risks, this also has the effects of increasing vendor's and purchaser's transaction costs, and in particular, of reducing a vendor's capacity to recoup its initial bidding costs. As a consequence, short outsourcing contracts often discourage good vendors from bidding. The true costs of short contracts to both vendor and client are substantially higher than might at first be recognized. Furthermore, because transaction costs and non-bids are not easy to discern, the higher costs may not be visible, particularly to the purchaser, for some time. Despite this, the notion that to have shorter contracts involves no trade offs, and is "good management practice" has taken root in the business community (Rouse, 2002). The unintended consequences of apparently sensible recommended practices form part of a significant set of risks associated with outsourcing that need to be considered as part of IT governance.

IT OUTSOURCING RISKS

Outsourcing involves potential benefits, and also risks. In their study of empirical (rather than theoretical risks) Rouse and Corbitt (2003)

categorized IT outsourcing risks into two types common risks (high probability but medium to low impact) and catastrophic risks (low probability, but high impact)– the latter, while very damaging, are hard to scope because they are rare, and often difficult to discern. Rouse and Corbitt found the incidence of common IT outsourcing risks (mostly related to unexpected costs, or failure to reap expected benefits) were much higher than the literature would suggest. Because they occur so rarely, and their consequences are often so difficult to observe, Rouse and Corbitt were unable to quantify the incidence of catastrophic risks, although in many cases if these risks eventuated, they would have far more fundamental effects on a firm's overall performance.

As an example of a potentially catastrophic risk, many of Rouse's (2002) informants suggested that a real, but downplayed outsourcing risk is the loss of intimate knowledge of the organization's business and the way the IT systems support this—highlighted by Earl (1996) and repeatedly mentioned in the academic and trade outsourcing literature. It is this organizational knowledge that enables firms to create innovative and strategic value from existing IT and information resources. While firms hope that they will still have access to this capability through their outsourcing vendor, they misunderstand the fundamental business of selling IT services (and in particular the risks to vendors of developing solutions that are "asset specific" to only one customer – see Fink, Edelman, Hatten & James, 2006). Vendor staff will rarely pursue an opportunity to use IT in novel ways to increase innovation in one particular customer firm, as they are rewarded for innovations that will appeal to (and be paid for by) a large number of customers. As a result, firms that outsource their IT usually lose the capacity to tailor innovative IT solutions to the firm's own particular needs and priorities. While this capacity might not be important to some firms, its loss generally has significant longer-term implications.

Another downplayed risk of outsourcing IT-related services is the theft or exposure of confidential customer records, a risk that recent events suggest is much less rare than vendors and consultants admit (Musaji, 2005). Theft of confidential records not only exposes officers of the firm to litigation or sanctions; it can have a substantial impact on customer trust, which is difficult to regain. After-the-fact remedies (such as litigation, or moving to an alternative vendor) will rarely address the losses, and will inevitably involve substantial costs and organizational resources. Firms that rely on contractual provisions to protect their customers' data often fail to recognize that if the data is held in foreign jurisdictions (an increasing practice), particularly if these are countries with high levels of corruption; legal contracts or threats to vendor reputation are likely to provide little protection.

One of the problems decision makers face is that there is limited existing research into the outcomes of outsourcing IT, and most claims for benefits (and low risks) for the strategy are based on theory or cases which are, necessarily, unrepresentative. What research into outcomes and risks of outsourcing that does exist suggests that while following sensible management practices will reduce some risks by encouraging firms to identify, scope, and plan for these, there will still remain a number of residual risks to the purchasing firm when IT services are outsourced (Rouse & Corbitt, 2007). The true costs of a firm's exposure to these residual, and often less concrete risks, can sometimes be substantially higher than recognized.

GOVERNANCE METHODS AND MODELS

A range of methodologies have been promulgated for ensuring IT governance, in addition to more general approaches such as those developed by researchers such as Weill and Ross (2004) and Willcocks and Feeny (1998). The Australian standard for corporate Governance of ICT (AS8015) provides a framework for strategic IT governance by firm Directors (Standards Australia, 2005).

Examples of formal methodologies aimed at the operational and tactical levels of governance include CoBIT (Lainhart, 2000) a set of standards and recommended activities developed by the American based IT Governance Institute (ITGI); and ITIL (the IT Infrastructure Library), developed by the UK Office of Government Commerce. These operational governance methodologies can be quite detailed, defining how the IT function should be organized and identifying key control processes. More recently—ITIL Version 3 (OGC, 2007) and ITGI's "Governance of [IT] Outsourcing" (ITGI, 2005)—these tactical guidelines have begun recognizing that IT is now sometimes outsourced, although they do not yet recognize that outsourced service delivery (including the use of packaged software, where the development has been outsourced) is becoming the dominant form of IT delivery in many firms.

Although most of these frameworks and methodologies include some recommended processes and actions to be taken when IT services are outsourced, at this stage these are largely concerned with tactical/operational governance. Consequently recommendations tend to miss many of the larger strategic governance issues introduced once a substantial part of the IT processes performed in a firm are sourced externally. Existing governance frameworks also tend to fail to recognize that many recommendations have downsides. For example, seemingly sensible control practices — such as renegotiating an outsourcing contract 12 to 14 months into the contract, as suggested by ITGI (2005)—are likely to be resisted by most vendors, unless the client has particular importance to the vendor. Other recommended processes (such as benchmarking vendor performance and costs) while desirable, may be impractical for all but basic commodity services. The ITGI (2005) has observed that most of approximately 200 firms it surveyed (around three quarters) failed to put in place what it saw as basic IT governance outsourcing controls. This is likely to be the case because many "good practices" have hidden downsides that are preventing their widespread adoption.

ASSESSING OUTSOURCING DECISIONS

Figure 1, adapted from that developed by Rouse and Corbitt (2007) and based partly on the analyses of Aubert, Patry, and Rivard (2005), can be used to more rigorously assess the net benefits of outsourcing. Figure 1 articulates the factors that lead to net benefits, and is based on determining residual risks after good management practices (as suggested by governance standards) have been introduced.

On the benefits side, benefits incorporate the production cost savings enabled by the arrangement, plus the verified financial impact of other benefits, often described as "strategic" (such as access to the latest technology which might lead to new business capabilities). As Rouse and Corbitt have suggested, production costs are easy to discern (though often overstated by vendors and other proponents of an outsourcing arrangement). The value of other strategic benefits is often much harder to discern, and again, often overstated by proponents, who fail to acknowledge that most "strategic" benefits from outsourcing (business flexibility, access to evolving technologies and skills, etc.) are rarely obtained unless specifically contracted for, usually at a substantial cost premium.

Figure 1 also illustrates that outsourcing benefits need to be discounted by the transaction costs associated with moving to an external, contract-based arrangement (c.f. Ang & Straub, 1998). Transaction costs include the costs of finding, choosing, and contracting with the vendor. These

are usually substantial, and are rarely taken into account in reports of outsourcing "savings" (Rouse & Corbitt, 2007). Sometimes market-search and contracting costs are treated as sunk costs (and so ignored), even though these costs tend to occur whenever a contract is renegotiated. Search and negotiation costs are magnified if the firm changes vendors or decides to reinsource (Whitten & Leidner, 2006) and in this case transition (switching) costs can be sizeable, sometimes to the extent of countering all the earlier production cost savings. Transaction costs also include the costs of monitoring and continually evaluating the vendor's performance, including regular benchmarking and market testing. Unfortunately, unless the IT services contracted for are generic, obtaining effective benchmarks is difficult and expensive, but without a check on vendor opportunism, almost certainly arrangements that are not market-tested will end up costing substantially more than market (or even in-house delivery) rates.

As shown in Figure 1, the expected benefits also need to be discounted by the increased risk exposure (Aubert et al., 2005) associated with outsourcing IT services. Risk exposure is a function of

Figure 1. Net benefits of outsourcing taking into account transaction and risk exposure costs

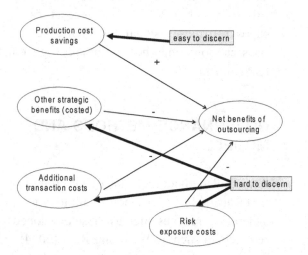

the costs incurred if a risk was to eventuate, multiplied by the likelihood of this happening. Risk exposure includes exposure costs for common risks (such as expected production cost savings being eaten up by changes to the contract, or the purchasing firm finding no alternative bidders at the end of a contract) as well as exposure to rarer, but potential major risks (such as theft or loss of critical records, or inability to adapt to changing business conditions because the knowledge of how to quickly redirect the firm's IT resources has been lost) which Rouse and Corbitt (2007) labelled "catastrophic" risks.

THE WIDER IT GOVERNANCE IMPLICATIONS OF OUTSOURCING

Existing IT Governance standards (e.g., COBIT, ITIL) tend to concentrate on established processes for controlling individual IT outsourcing arrangements (such as formal tendering and evaluation, elicitation and agreement of service level standards, budget/timeframe/functionality management and benchmarking of costs and performance). These are important to successful outsourcing, and should be treated by purchasers as minimal management expectations. They should also be budgeted for, because some controls (particularly related to articulating service levels and to benchmarking performance) are costly. However, the empirical studies conducted by the author have revealed that outsourcing IT services on a large scale raises several more strategic issues that at this stage are not fully addressed by these processes. These issues relate both to threats to the expected value of IT outsourcing, and longer-term strategic risks that are often ignored in the early days of outsourcing when purchasers and vendors alike are hoping their arrangements will be productive and satisfactory.

Outsourcing Outcomes Almost Always Involve Trade-Offs

While academic research has tended to talk about "IT outsourcing success" (Grover, Cheon & Teng, 1996) as a single concept, the empirical evidence indicates that firms tend to seek multiple, usually contradictory, benefits from outsourcing. Despite suggestions to the contrary (e.g., Seddon, Cullen & Willcocks, 2002), most firms seek substantial efficiencies (cost savings) from outsourcing, at the same time that they seek improved levels of service, more sophisticated IT and high quality strategic advice (Willcocks & Lacity, 1998). There are inherent tensions here because vendors cannot easily provide both, even though many appear to suggest this is possible in their precontract marketing. In addition, purchasing firms tend to expect to gain greater business flexibility from outsourced IT, particularly the flexibility to quickly increase and decrease demand for services, as well as to change requirements to accommodate new business conditions. However, while most outsourcing contracts allow for some changes to demand within a narrow range, large-scale changes in requirements (known as contract variations) are expensive for the vendor to service, and will normally attract a high financial penalty. The governance implications are that if firms are seeking cost savings, they should recognize that these normally come at the expense of customized service, and of, at least in the short term, business flexibility and adaptability.

Many Business Cases Supporting the Outsourcing Decision are Inadequate

Once an IT outsourcing arrangement has been entered into, it is usually difficult to reverse the decision, because the costs, organizational attention, and time needed to re-insource the service are substantial. In at least two of the cases studied by the author, the purchasers became aware that the vendor's prices were substantially higher than market rates, yet only one of these was able to address the problem by reinsourcing (at an expected transition cost of $3.5 million). The other was forced to remain with the existing vendor for several more years because of the absence of alternative bidders, and was able to sever the arrangement only by breaking up the contract amongst smaller vendors, at a substantial increase in transaction costs. Other cases studied by the author where the firm changed vendors were able to find at least one other bidder, but even if an alternative vendor is found, the additional transaction costs, and the costs of transition, are substantial for all but commodity IT services.

Given the high cost of unsatisfactory arrangements, it is critical that the initial business case (the financial analysis used to support the decision to outsource) be carefully scrutinized, as the costs of getting out of an arrangement (switching costs) are typically so high. Rouse and Corbitt (2003) reported several IT cases where the original outsourcing business case was subject to external audit. In three of the four audited firms, the auditor determined that expected cost savings (the increased "value" that the arrangements would supposedly bring) would never eventuate. Furthermore, because many millions of dollars had been spent in going to market (a transaction cost) the three outsourcing arrangements that had gone ahead had actually cost these firms substantially more than in-house delivery. Unfortunately for these firms, they too were unable to bring the services back in house and in one case the firm received only a single bidder (the incumbent) for the follow-on contract. Unsurprisingly, this new bid involved a substantial increase in costs. The other two firms were forced to break up their contracts amongst a number of smaller, and ultimately far more expensive, "best of breed" contracts.

Many business cases include overoptimistic assumptions about likely savings from outsourc-

ing IT. The evidence from a number of studies is that outsourcing IT onshore leads typically to only modest savings of between -22% (i.e., a loss) and 9-11%. These savings do not take into account ongoing management costs, switching costs, nor the initial transaction costs for locating, selecting, and negotiating with the vendor (see Rouse & Corbitt's (2007) meta analysis of reported savings). Possibly as a result, many firms are now seeking to outsource offshore in the belief that they will get better outcomes, though the evidence for sustainable long-term savings from offshoring is not yet available. Those charged with governing IT services need to treat projected savings sceptically, because the history of outsourcing is replete with examples of what Leslie Willcocks has described as "voodoo" economics (Willcocks & Graser, 2001, p. 187).

At a minimum an outsourcing business case needs to justify in detail the source of expected savings, particularly those associated with economies of scale, or future improvements in technology, because existing research suggests that only a minority of purchasers report obtaining such benefits (Rouse & Corbitt, 2003). The business case should also allow for transaction costs, including the costs associated with risk management practices recommended by governance models like COBIT and ITIL (such as early renegotiation of contracts, and ongoing benchmarking). These costs can be high, and once they and other transaction costs are included in the business case the attractiveness of the outsourced option is often substantially reduced. Another cost that should be incorporated into the business case is that for conducting an early evaluation of whether both the estimated benefits and levels of risks were accurate, and if they were not, what this implies. While such a review will be expensive, it may save firms millions of dollars in the longer term. Finally, costing models on which outsourcing decisions are made should be subject to detailed sensitivity analysis, as most are dependent on assumptions where values can vary considerably.

Anecdotal evidence obtained by the author is that this rarely occurs.

Many Purchaser Firms Underestimate the Impact of Loss of Knowledge and Expertise

Since the mid-1990's, academics have warned that one downside of outsourcing is the potential loss of knowledge and capabilities once IT staff leave the firm. Even if staff initially move to the vendor, skills and knowledge will not necessarily be available to the purchaser. However, the level of tacit knowledge held by staff is rarely apparent, and is often taken for granted until it is lost. Two important consequences occur with this loss of corporate knowledge and skill. The first is that the purchasing firm loses its source of strategic IT advice, as purchasers cannot rely on existing vendors to provide disinterested advice because of potential conflicts of interests and priorities. While advice can be purchased from alternative vendors, this is expensive and often unsatisfactory, as outsiders lack knowledge of both the firm's business and its IT environment. After substantial outsourcing, purchasers often find that they no longer provide an environment where the sophisticated skills required can be grown and rewarded, and where skilled staff can be retained. Second, a finding revealed by Rouse's (2002) focus groups and case studies is that an additional, and usually unexpected, increase in consulting fees tends to accompany outsourcing of IT. These costs are associated with the need to externally access capabilities like independent strategic IT advice.

Firms Must Identify, and Plan to Avoid "Vendor Lock In"

The issue of long-term dependence on vendors is one of the most intractable and difficult-to-evaluate downsides of outsourcing IT. The current industry-based solution – that firms manage their risks by contracting with multiple vendors – is not practical for many IT services, and results in much higher transaction costs (both those associated with contracting, and those associated with solving problems that fall "between vendors"). Other recommended solutions, such as to create a "risk-sharing" mutually interdependent relationship with vendor(s) are possible only for the handful of purchasers who have unique capabilities that the vendors themselves need. And while careful tendering and vendor evaluation processes are crucial for minimising the risks of dependence on an inadequate vendor, these practices do not negate the need to allow for the substantial switching costs that would be incurred if an arrangement proved unsatisfactory. Current empirical evidence suggests that unsatisfactory arrangements are a relatively frequent outcome (Kern & Willcocks, 2000; Rouse & Corbitt, 2003; Whitten & Leidner, 2006). Realistic switching costs should be estimated when initial outsourcing arrangements are entered into, and incorporated as "risk exposure" into the costing model, because once a sourcing arrangement is in place, without such a risk "reserve" of funds, options for the purchasing firm are limited. Given the widespread dependency of firms on IT-based business processes, IT outsourcing arrangement should be entered into as carefully and with as much preparation as a joint venture or takeover, because like those arrangements, the likelihood of failure is high, and the consequences substantial.

FUTURE TRENDS

Given the increasing adoption of IT outsourcing, as well as quasi-outsourcing in the form of packaged enterprise software and application service providers (ASPs), it is likely that formal IT governance frameworks will continue to be adapted to the purchaser-vendor delivery model. They will also begin to address the additional risks associated with offshore outsourcing. However, in future, IT governance frameworks will need to adapt to the fact that outsourcing IT usually involves residual risks that will not easily be managed by established control processes.

In future, it is hoped that IT governance frameworks will also begin to treat outsourcing in a more integrated way, reflecting the growing (and largely irreversible) dominance of the purchaser-vendor form of delivery. This is already happening, as indicated by the growing recognition of outsourcing in the most recent ITIL standards (OCG, 2007). In contrast to trade writers, many academic authors have adopted a more cautious view of outsourcing, and have warned that assumptions about outsourcing are often not supported by empirical data. Governance frameworks, in particular, will need to acknowledge that good control practices are expensive, and so reduce the cost-benefits of outsourcing arrangements. They should also acknowledge that many control practices have downsides as well as desirable consequences. However, it is unlikely that specific governance guidelines will be able to address the more intractable difficulties of outsourcing, and it is here that individual officers charged with firms' governance will need to become more informed, and to adopt a more critical view of the benefits and risks of outsourcing IT.

Future corporate governance committees will probably highlight to a much greater extent the need to avoid being locked into unsatisfactory arrangements, by providing for switching costs as an integral, and foreseeable, cost of outsourcing. However, governance officers will also need to address the issue of ensuring independent access to knowledgeable technical advice for planning IT investments and longer term IT strategy, and for specifying contract requirements. This too will add substantially to the transaction costs of outsourcing. It will also be up to governance officers within firms to ensure the firm does not heavily rely on a small number of vendors whose interests will only partly overlap those of their purchasers. Unless there is a large and competi-

tive market of vendors, firms risk having only one bidder in future, i.e. the incumbent, as many vendors are deterred from bidding against an incumbent vendor, whose risks are much lower because of prior experiences with the purchaser. Governance committees will also need to ensure higher quality business case development, and more critical analysis of underlying assumptions associated with outsourcing.

CONCLUSION

The last 15 years of research into IT outsourcing (including the author's own research) have resulted in several key principles that should inform IT governance when IT is outsourced.

The first is that most outsourcing arrangements are poorly thought through, and only superficially analysed. Many decisions to outsource rest on unexamined assumptions (for example, that the vendor can get economies of scale unavailable to the client, and will pass these on in the form of lower costs). The qualitative outsourcing research suggests that, overwhelmingly, unexamined estimates of benefits and cost savings are strongly overoptimistic. The nebulous nature of known risks of outsourcing (hidden costs, loss of innovative capacity, risk of vendor lock in, security threats to data and intellectual property) must compete with seemingly "hard" estimates of large financial benefits (which in real life may never be attained). Because to emphasise risks is often portrayed as negative, these known risks then get left out of the outsourcing business case, leading to further unrealistic inflation of expected benefits.

The second observation is that many "good outsourcing practices" (including governance practices) have substantial downsides, including, but not always restricted to, unforeseen costs. In a large number of the cases reported above, the transaction costs associated with good practice had invalidated the increased value supplied by the outsourcing arrangements. Because, once entered into, an IT outsourcing arrangement is difficult to reverse, purchaser firms do not have incentives to later institute expensive controls that may worsen a difficult purchaser-vendor relationship, and add to the costs of the arrangement, particularly if these controls may reveal a poor initial decision. So, unless these practices are allowed for in the costing model before the arrangement, they are not likely to be adopted.

The third observation is that many firms fail to think through where they will get independent strategic advice about their IT services once they have outsourced their skilled IT staff, and how this advice will be incorporated into the IT governance framework. The costs of seeking this service from an external consulting group are likely to be high (and should be factored in as a further transaction cost). Related issues are how external advisors unfamiliar with the firm's business, culture and processes will gain this familiarity so as to give valuable advice, and how these advisors will be integrated with the firm and its network of IT vendors.

The final observation is that recognizing, and costing the risk exposure of outsourcing arrangements is critical to effective IT governance, particularly when higher risk variations, such as business process outsourcing (BPO) and offshore outsourcing, are adopted. Firms should obviously attempt to reduce as many risks as possible, but need to recognize that, except for commodity services, even well managed IT outsourcing arrangements incorporate high levels of risk. As with other risky ventures, the risk exposure associated with both common and catastrophic risks should be calculated, and assumptions about risk exposure, benefits, and transaction costs tested through sensitivity analyses before any substantial IT outsourcing arrangement is entered into.

REFERENCES

Ang, S., & Straub, D. (1998). Production and transaction economies and IS outsourcing: A study of the US banking industry. *MIS Quarterly, 22*(4), 535-552.

ASX (Australian Stock Exchange) (2003). *Principles of good corporate governance and best practice recommendations.* Sydney: Australian Stock Exchange.

Aubert, B. A., Patry, M., & Rivard, S. (2005). A framework for information technology outsourcing risk management. *ACM SIGMIS Database, 36*(4), 9-28.

Clarke, F., Dean, G., & Oliver, K., (2003). *Corporate collapse: Accounting, regulatory and ethical failure.* Melbourne, Australia: Cambridge University Press.

Coates, J. C. (2007). The goals and promise of the Sarbanes–Oxley Act. *Journal of Economic Perspectives, 21*(1), 91-116.

Earl, M. J. (1988). *Information management: The strategic dimension.* Oxford: OUP.

Earl, M. J. (1996). The risks of outsourcing. *Sloan Management Review, 37*(3), 26-32.

Fink, R. C., Edelman, L. F., Hatten, K. J., & James, W. L. (2006). Transaction cost economics, resource dependence theory, and customer–supplier relationships. *Industrial and Corporate Change, 15*(3), 497-529.

Grover, V., Cheon, M. J., & Teng, J. T. C. (1996). The effect of service quality and partnership on the outsourcing of information systems functions. *Journal of Management Information Systems, 12*, 89-116.

ITGI (2005). *Governance of outsourcing.* Rolling Meadows, IL: IT Governance Institute.

Kern, T., & Willcocks, L. (2000). Exploring information technology outsourcing relationships: Theory and practice. *The Journal of Strategic Information Systems, 9*(4), 321-350.

Lainhart, J. W. (2000). CoBIT: A methodology for managing and controlling information and information technology risks and vulnerabilities. *Journal of Information Systems, 14*(1 Supp.), 21-25.

Loh, L., & Venkatraman, N. (1992). Diffusion of information technology outsourcing: Influence sources and the Kodak effect. *Information Systems Research, 3*, 334-358.

Musaji, Y. (2005). Sarbanes-Oxley and business process outsourcing risk. *Information Systems Control Journal, 5*. Retrieved May 14, 2008, from http://www.isaca.org

Mylott, T. R., III (1995). *Computer outsourcing: Managing the transfer of information systems.* Englewood Cliffs, NJ: Prentice Hall.

OGC (2007). *Information technology infrastructure library (ITIL): Version 3.* London: Office of Government Commerce.

Rouse, A. C. (2002). *Information technology outsourcing revisited: Success factors and risks.* Unpublished doctoral dissertation, University of Melbourne, Melbourne, Australia.

Rouse, A. C., & Corbitt, B. J. (2001). The Australian government's abandoned infrastructure outsourcing program: What can be learned? *Australian Journal of Information Systems, 10*(2), 81-90.

Rouse, A. C., & Corbitt, B. J. (2003). Revisiting IT outsourcing risks: Analysis of a survey of Australia's Top 1000 organizations. In *Proceedings of the 14th Australasian Conference on Information Systems 2003, Delivering IT and E-Business Value in Networked Environments* (pp. 1-11). School of Management Information Systems, Edith Cowan University, Perth, Western Australia

Rouse, A., C., & Corbitt, B. J. (2007). Understanding information systems outsourcing success and risks through the lens of cognitive biases. In *Proceedings of the 15th European Conference on Information Systems (ECIS)*, St. Gallen, Switzerland.

Seddon, P. B., Cullen, S., & Willcocks, L. P. (2002). *Does Domberger's theory of "the contracting organization" explain satisfaction with IT outsourcing?* International Conference on Information Systems (ICIS), Barcelona.

Standards Australia (2005). *AS8015-2005 corporate governance of information and communication technology.* Canberra: Standards Australia.

Tirole, J. (2001). Corporate governance. *Econometrica, 69*, 1-35.

Weill, P., & Ross, J. W. (2004). *IT governance: How top performers manage IT decision rights for superior results.* Boston: Harvard Business School Press.

Whitten, D., & Leidner, D. (2006). Bringing IT back: An analysis of the decision to backsource or switch vendors. *Decision Sciences, 37*(4), 605-621.

Willcocks, L. P., & Feeny, D. (1998). Core IS capabilities for exploiting information technology. *Sloan Management Review, 39*(3), 9-21.

Willcocks, L., & Graser, V. (2001). *Delivering IT and eBusiness value.* Oxford: Butterworth-Heinemann.

Willcocks, L. P., & Lacity, M. (1998). *Strategic sourcing of information systems: Perspectives and practices.* Chichester: Wiley.

Willcocks, L., Lacity, M., & Kern, T. (1999). Risk mitigation in IT outsourcing strategy revisited: Longitudinal case research at LISA. *Journal of Strategic Information Systems, 8*, 285-314.

Chapter XVII
IT Portfolio Management:
A Pragmatic Approach to Implement IT Governance

Muralidharan Ramakrishnan
Process Symphony, Australia

ABSTRACT

This chapter is intended primarily for managers who are preparing to implement portfolio management concepts in an organization and students of IT Project Management courses at the Masters level, who wish to understand the difference between Project and Portfolio Management. As IT Governance is gaining importance, the IT department should not be surprised if they are given a mandate from the senior management to implement a Governance framework. Portfolio Management principles are the foundations of building an effective governance. While there is literature available discussing portfolio management at the conceptual level, there is not enough available which translates these concepts into tactical implementation. This could be because implementation differs between organizations and there is no one size fits all solution. However, practitioners can benefit from discussing implementation approaches that can be tailored to suit individual needs. This chapter shows one of the many ways to implement a portfolio management framework.

INTRODUCTION

The chapter is divided into four sections.

The chapter commences with a hypothetical case study designed to illustrate that perceptions and personal preferences dominate IT Investment decisions. The case study highlights the need for structured decision making. This section also introduces IT Governance and portfolio management concepts.

The next section introduces a portfolio management life cycle consisting of three phases: *evaluation, monitoring,* and *benefits realization*. The section analyses the processes and techniques in each phase. This section provides guidance in the application of portfolio management concepts.

The third section consists of a real life case study; an application of one phase in the portfolio management life cycle, viz, *evaluation*, in a cross-government environment. The study analyses the "investment evaluation framework" proposed by the office of chief information officer (OCIO) in the Government of South Australia. The purpose is to show the application of a portfolio management framework in an organization and the associated challenges.

The final section summarizes the chapter and analyses the future trends in IT Portfolio Management.

IT PORTFOLIO MANAGEMENT CONCEPTS

Opening Case

Robert Malcolm felt the need to make an important decision for IT Governance meeting the following day. Three different departments were fighting for already stretched funds to initiate new projects into their departments. The operations manager, Julie, wanted to replace an ageing infrastructure; Raj, the marketing manager, was arguing a case for a new CRM system; and Darren wanted to enhance a functionality of the pay-roll system.

Robert knew he could not fund all the three projects. He could empathize with Julie, as he had been performing her role previously, before he was promoted to CIO. But he also knew that Raj would put a very convincing case, which could impress the CEO. Robert did not know much about the payroll system, so it is out-of-question for now, he thought. Well, not really, as the CFO might throw his weight behind Darren.

Robert wished he had a clear evaluation process to decide between these competing projects. He knew that if one of the on-going projects were

stopped, that would free up some additional money. But, in his organization, once a project was approved, there was no way it could be terminated mid way.

It was not that Robert was facing issues only with the new projects. He was having some issues from previous projects also. The organization had developed a Website that would increase the online revenue from one of their products. But by monitoring the Web statistics he realized that it did not attract enough visitors. He was aware that the organization had changed its strategy and gave higher priority to another product. However, Robert still incurred expenditure to maintain the Website. Terminating the Website had been on his *to do* list for the past six months, but he did not have time to execute the decision.

Robert knew what to do as a short term *fix*. He would play the political game and give his support to the CEO's favourite project. At the same time, he decided to explore the available process methodologies that would help him to solve the *real* problem.

Need for IT Governance

For many enterprises managing Information Technology (IT) has always been a challenge. It is critical to a business that the IT investments are managed effectively. Research shows that top-performing enterprises generate returns on their IT investments up to 40% greater than their competitors (Weill, 2004). IT Governance ensures that IT investments are prioritized and monitored throughout their life cycle.

Another driver for IT Governance in the wake of corporate scandals like Enron and Worldcom is the renewed interest in Corporate Governance. As IT cuts across all the organizational functions, Corporate Governance cannot be complete without IT Governance. The scandals also pushed regulators in the US to introduce the Sarbane-Oxely act requiring new levels of accountability and traceability (Maizlish & Handler, 2005)

The IT Governance Institute (ITGI) (IT Governance Institute, n.d.) is one of the organizations that promote Governance standards. The institute has developed *Control Objectives for Information and related Technology* (COBIT®) and Val IT™ framework. Val IT (Val IT, 2006, p. 10), states that *"there is an increasing demand from board and executive management for generally accepted guidelines for decision making and benefits realisation related to IT-enabled business investments"*. The need for transparency in IT investments is reflected in the following industry reports (Val IT, 2006, p. 10):

- *A 2002 Gartner publication claimed that 20 percent all expenditure on IT is wasted, representing on a global basis, annual value destruction of US $600 billion.*
- *A 2004 IBM survey of Fortune 1000 CIOs reported that, on average, 40 percent of all IT spending brought no return to their organisations.*
- *A 2004 Standish report found that only 29 percent of all IT projects succeeded while the remainder were either challenged or failed.*

In summary, we need IT Governance because:

- It is a critical component of Corporate Governance.
- Well managed IT investments create more business value.
- A lack of perceived transparency in IT investments by the senior management.

Defining IT Governance

COBIT® defines IT Governance as follows:

IT Governance is the responsibility of executives and the board of directors and consists of the leadership, organisational structures and processes that ensure that the enterprise's IT sustains and extends the organisation's strategies and objectives. (COBIT 4.1, 2007, p. 5)

Peter Weill (Weill, 2004, p. 8) defines IT Governance as "specifying the decision rights and accountability framework to encourage desirable behaviour in the use of IT."

Combining these definitions we can say that IT Governance is about structured decision making on IT Investments by the right people. Val IT expands the IT Investment decisions as "Four Ares" (Val IT, 2006, p. 9) as follows:

- *Are* we doing the right things?
- *Are* we doing them the right way?
- *Are* we getting them done well?
- *Are* we getting the benefits?

Figure 1 shows the "Four Ares" model proposed by Val IT™ (Val IT, 2006, p. 9).

How Do the Methodologies Fit?

The industry frameworks and best practices are mapped against the *Four Ares* in Table 1.

As we can see, many frameworks focus on the *delivery* aspect of IT, but very little on strategic alignment, architecture and value aspect of IT. It is because, as an evolving field, IT has been plagued with delivery issues. The industry methodologies and best practices tried to enforce a discipline in developing and implementing IT solutions. Now, the business stakeholders are asking the other *Four Ares* questions. We need a framework that addresses the entire life cycle of an IT investment. Portfolio Management is a concept that deals from choosing the right IT investment, monitoring the implementation and capturing the business benefits.

IT Portfolio Management: Concept

The concept of IT portfolio management is derived from the *financial portfolio investment model*. As shares are evaluated before investing, the IT

Figure 1 Val IT™ "Four Ares" Framework. Source: Val IT © 2006 IT Governance Institute. All rights reserved. Used with permission.

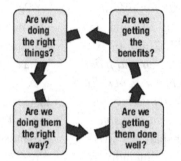

The **strategic** question. Is the investment:
- In line with our vision
- Consistent with our businesss principles
- Contributing to our strategic objectives
- Providing optimal value, at affordable cost, at an acceptable level of risk

The **architecture** question. Is the investment:
- In line with our architecture
- Consistent with our architectural principles
- Contributing to the population of our architecture
- In line with other initiatives

The **value** question. Do we have:
- A clear and shared understanding of the expected benefits
- Clear accountability for realising the benefits
- Relevant metrics
- An effective benefits realisation process

The **delivery** question. Do we have:
- Effective and disciplined management, delivery and change management processes
- Competent and available technical and business resouces to deliver:
  - The required capabilities
  - The organisational changes required to leverage the capabilities

Are we doing the right things?

Are we getting the benefits?

Are we doing them the right way?

Are we getting them done well?

portfolio management model proposes the evaluation of any IT investment before it is initiated. The high growth, risky shares (riskier IT projects), need to be balanced against low risk, low return (low risk maintenance IT projects). IT Portfolio management aims to provide a holistic view of IT Investment across the enterprise so that the management can take informed decisions.

In shares investment, share prices are monitored through out an investment. Decisions to hold, buy or sell are taken depending upon a share's performance. IT portfolio management is similar. IT Investments need to be monitored throughout their life cycle. Decisions to continue, modify or stop an investment need to be taken throughout its life cycle.

Portfolio Management: Definition

The Project Management Body of Knowledge defines project, program, and portfolio management as follows (PMBOK®, 2000):

Project management is the application of knowledge, skills, tools and techniques to project activities to meet project requirements.

A program is a group of related projects managed in a coordinated way to obtain benefits and control not available from managing them individually.

Portfolio is a collection of projects or programs and other work that are grouped together to facilitated effective management of that work to

Table 1. Industry frameworks alignment with Four Ares

Four Ares	Methodologies
Are we doing the right things?	Val IT
Are we doing them the right way?	The Open Group Architecture Framework (TOGAF), COBIT
Are we getting them done well?	COBIT, ITIL, CMMI, ISO/IEC 20000, Six Sigma, PRINCE2, PMBOK
Are we getting the benefits?	Val IT

meet strategic business objectives. The projects or programs in the portfolio may not necessarily be interdependent or directly related.

Val IT states: "The goal of portfolio management is to ensure that an organisation's overall portfolio of IT-enabled investments is aligned with and contributing optimal value to the organisations strategic objectives..." (2006, p. 14).

Portfolio management is strategic in nature. It is concerned more about doing the *right projects* than *executing the projects correctly*. In fact, Portfolio Management can terminate a project, which is being executed efficiently, if the project's benefits are no longer aligned with the strategic objectives of the organization.

Illustration of Portfolio Management

Portfolio Management enables senior management to better track the business benefits of a project, not only when the project was initiated but throughout its life cycle. For example, consider a company that specializes in building high-speed passenger catamarans. They have decided to build a new catamaran, in order to introduce a new service across a river.

The portfolio board has approved the construction of the catamaran, and project is progressing on time and, within budget. The project manager has announced that they have across a new technology which will make the catamaran operations cost effective. From the project management point of view, it will be a successful project.

During the portfolio management review, the senior management noted that the Government has sanctioned construction of a bridge across the river. If this bridge were constructed, it would reduce the catamaran traffic drastically. So the senior management decided no longer to invest in construction of the catamaran.

How many times has a *successful* IT project been terminated in your organization because the organization's strategic direction has changed?

PORTFOLIO MANAGEMENT LIFE CYCLE

This section deals with implementing a portfolio management framework in an organization. The portfolio management life cycle has three phases

1. Evaluation of IT Investments.
2. Monitoring the progress of IT investments.
3. Benefits realisation.

We will present a method to develop evaluation criteria for an IT Investment. It will be followed by a discussion on monitoring the progress of IT investments by establishing interface with project management structures. The benefits realisation process will be explained with an example.

Evaluation of IT Investments

It is very important for a business to have consistent evaluation while making decisions on IT investments. The evaluation criteria need to ensure that investment is aligned with strategic direction of the business and risks associated with the investments are clearly understood.

Developing an Evaluation Criteria

Developing evaluation criteria is the first step in IT Investment decision making. The evaluation should consider balancing the risks and rewards. There is no single way of developing the evaluation framework. We will explore one of the ways to develop a criterion.

In our approach, a business case will be *rewarded* if it is aligned with the strategic direction of the organization and it is financially sound. The reward score will be balanced against the risk score.

Overall Score = Reward Score / Risk Score

where

Reward Score = Strategic Direction Alignment * Financial Worth

such that

Overall Score = Strategic Direction * Financial Worth / Risk Score.

This evaluation scores can be used to create a portfolio view of all the IT Projects in an organization. The portfolio view will give an idea about the risk profile of the organization and potential improvement opportunities. Figure 3 illustrates a portfolio view based on risk and reward.

We will examine the individual scoring of each of the components that determine the overall score.

Strategic Alignment

Strategic alignment deals with an assessment of the degree of alignment that a proposal demonstrates against a business's strategic direction. An organization can have many business objectives that are aligned with the vision of the organization. When a new IT investment is proposed, it is important that stakeholders understand how the investment will impact on business objectives. Figure 2 illustrates the traceability between the IT Initiatives and the strategic vision of an organization.

It should be noted that one initiative could be aligned to more than one business objective. Also, it may be difficult for some objectives to demonstrate the alignment to strategic objectives. In Figure 2, IT Initiative-1 is aligned with business objectives 1 and 2. IT Initiatives 2 and 3 are aligned with business objective 3. IT Initiative 4 is not aligned with any of the business objectives.

Figure 2. Portfolio view based on risk and reward

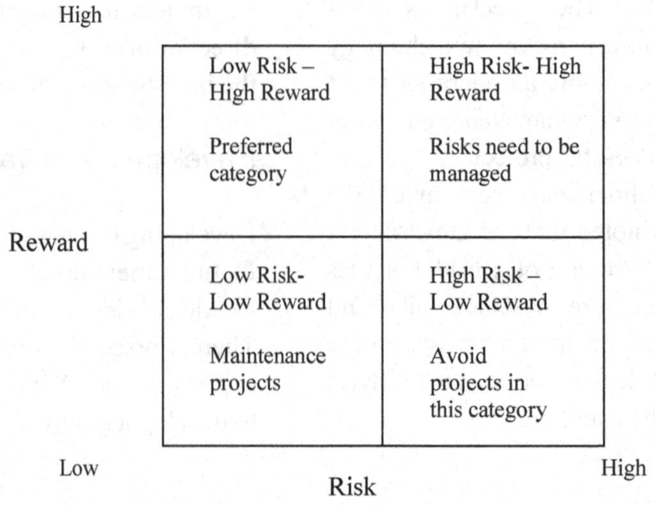

Figure 3. Strategic alignment

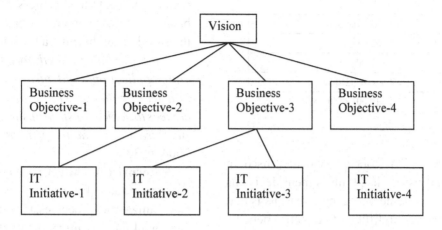

Similarly, business objective-4 does not have any IT initiatives that are supporting it.

It does not mean that an IT Initiative cannot be undertaken by the organization if it is not aligned with any of the business objectives. In a dynamic business environment, a decision can be taken to implement an initiative based on many other factors. However, portfolio management processes ensure that senior management is making informed decisions.

Table 2 shows a generic scoring guideline that scores a business case from 1 to 4 by evaluating the alignment against a business objective.

Financial Worth

The next step in determining a *reward* score is to evaluate an initiative from financial point of view. The Net Present Value (NPV) of an investment is a simple criterion for deciding whether or not to undertake an investment (Ross, 2002). NPV answers the question of how much cash an investor would need to have today as a substitute for making an investment. If the net present value is negative, taking on an investment today is not financially justified.

The NPV can be translated to a scoring range of 1 to 4. An example is shown in Table 3. Each organization needs to tailor how financial benefits translate to individual scores.

Table 2. Scoring guideline

High

Score	Interpretation
1	Business case addresses some components of a business objective
2	Business case address all the components of a business objective
3	Business initiative is applicable to a subsection of organization
4	Business initiative is applicable across the entire organization

Table 3. Financial worth scoring example

Score	NPV Value
1	Negative
2	< $5000
3	$5001 <$10000
4	$10,001 <$50,000

While the NPV concept is widely used in the financial world, in IT investment decisions it is rarely used. One of the main reasons is that practitioners find it difficult to quantity benefits in financial terms because most IT Initiatives are viewed as a technical challenge without analysing the problems from business/financial perspective.

Risks Assessment

One of the "Four Ares" is "Are we doing them the right way?" (Val IT, 2006, p. 9). This is an architecture question that ensures the proposed business investment is:

- In line with the organization's enterprise architecture.
- Consistent with the organization's architectural principle.
- Contributing to the population of the architecture.
- In line with other initiatives.

If a solution is not aligned with the architecture, then it is a risk to the business. For example, the business cost of maintenance can become high or the solution can become a security risk.

The IT Architecture is the organising logic for data, applications, and infrastructure, captured in a set of policies, relationships and technical choices to achieve desired business and technical standardisation and integration (Weill & Ross, 2004, p. 30).

Enterprise Architecture is the description of the current and/or future structure and behavior of an organization's processes, information systems, personnel and organizational subunits, aligned with the organization's core goals and strategic direction. (Enterprise Architecture-Wikipedia, n.d.). As the technology changes are faster than ever, if the standards are not set, technology integration and business process alignment will become a critical issue often affecting the operational costs.

If an organization does not have enterprise architecture defined, at least technical standards need to be documented and followed. For example, an organization can state that it will follow Microsoft platform for sales and support and UNIX platforms for technical development area. If a new business case is proposing to introduce a UNIX platform for a sales team, then the scoring for architecture risk will be high. The risk score will flag that the maintenance costs of a nonstandard technology will be high. This will enable the

Table 4. Architecture risk scoring example

Architecture Risk Score	Evaluation criteria
1	Fully aligned with the existing enterprise architecture
2	Alignment with most of the architecture; the nonalignment areas are not considered as a security threat
3	No alignment with existing standard, but a potential candidate for inclusion in the architecture library
4	No alignment with existing standards and not a candidate for inclusion in the architecture library

organization's governance to take an informed decision about the investment.

An example of architectural risk evaluation scoring is shown in Table 4.

Investment Evaluation: Summary

Investment prioritisation is one of the difficult processes to implement in portfolio management. It might require a cultural change in the organization if it is not used to formal decision making already. If the process is properly implemented, it will take away the political games and lobbying.

An investment evaluation assumes there is a Governance framework and decision making body responsible for IT investment decision making. The decision making body should be represented by the senior management and should have sufficient financial authority to take decision. The business should have commitment to make the formal decision making process happen.

ITIL® (Best Practice for Service Delivery, 2001, p. 59) states:

"Why does the IT organisation budget have be so large?"

"How much will it cost to implement and run this new system?"

..
These are examples of the questions asked inside and outside an IT organisation, often in emotive situations, such as project over-runs or during periods of loss of critical services. The answer is often: "We are doing the best we can with the money that we have"; but....is that true?

Is that true? This is an introspective question to the IT community. To answer it IT practitioners need to show the business that IT investments are aligned with the business direction and generate positive returns.

Monitoring the Progress of IT Investments

Once the IT Investment decisions are made, the implementations need to be managed as projects.

The progress monitoring can be built into the project management methodology. One of the widely used project methodology, Projects in Control Environments (PRINCE2), proposes that the projects need to be governed by a Project Board (Prince2.org.uk, 2007). The project board will review the business cases at regular intervals to ensure that the projects are still relevant to the strategic needs of the organization. *Figure 3* shows the project board structure hierarchy.

If an organization has already implemented a project board structure, similar to Prince2, it will be easier to implement an IT Investment monitoring process. However, it should be noted that Project Board cannot fulfil all the Portfolio Management monitoring requirements. There

Figure 4. Hierarchical project structure Source: Adapted from Managing Successful projects with Prince2 (1998, p. 18)

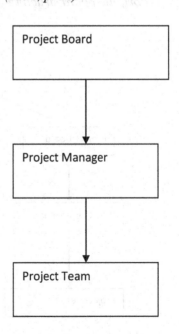

need to be a body at a higher level that oversees all the projects across the portfolio. Figure 4 shows a typical Portfolio Management board structure.

The role of the Portfolio Management board is to supervise the performance of the project board and advise the project, if there are any changes in the strategic direction of the organization. The Portfolio Management board need representation from the senior management of the organization. It should have the authority to terminate a project, if needed.

The Portfolio Management board should not duplicate the Project Board function. Prince2 (1998, pp. 22-23) defines the project board functions as follows:

- Provide overall direction and management of the project
- Accountable for the success of the project
- Approves all major plans and authorizes any deviations
- Authorizes the next stage of the project
- Ensures required resources are committed

The Portfolio board sits one step above the project board. The Portfolio board functions are:

- Receive progress reports from all the project boards
- Receive self assessment health-check reports from all the projects, through the boards
- Advise the project boards, if any changes in the strategic direction of the organization
- Advise the project boards, if any new projects are initiated in the organization
- Advise the project boards, if any changes in the budget allocation
- Advise the project boards, if any projects are terminated in the organization
- Advise any technology changes

Investment Monitoring: Summary

The investment monitoring process is built on the foundations of project management. The investment monitoring process oversees the project execution of an IT investment. The investment monitoring ensures that the approved IT project

Figure 5. Portfolio board structure

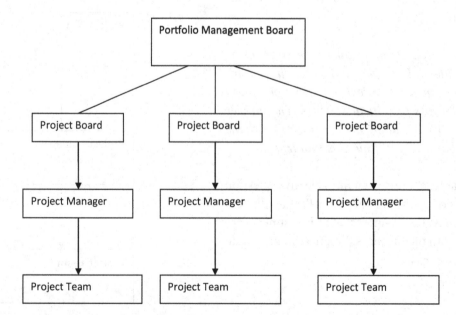

is aligned with business objectives throughout the implementation.

Ideally, the investment monitoring authority should be able to terminate an IT investment when it is no longer aligned with the business objectives. In order to deliver this mandate, it is important that the organization body responsible for investment monitoring has sufficient authority to terminate or change the scope of an investment.

Benefits Realization

Once the IT Initiative is delivered, it is important to monitor the benefits and compare with what had been promised in the initial business case. If this process, is omitted then business cases fall into the trap of over promising and under delivering. The organization will also gain knowledge on the reasons for not achieving the estimated benefits.

Like other portfolio management processes, there is no single way to implement the benefits monitoring. We will analyse a practical implementation of an Australian Government agency.

The New South Wales Government's Chief Information Office (http://www.gcio.nsw.gov.au/library/guidelines/769) proposes a Benefits realisation register (Appendix A) to track the benefits. The register contains the following:

- A description of the benefit to be achieved;
- The person responsible for realizing the benefit;
- A description of the current situation or performance measure of the business process;
- The current cost or performance measure of the business process;
- The target cost or performance measure of the business process after the planned change;
- The target date for the benefit to be realized;

- The trigger or event that will cause the benefit to be realized;
- The type of contribution to the business;
- The assessed value of the benefit or saving;
- Comments about the assessed value of the benefit or saving;
- State which strategic and corporate objectives and Results and Services Plan (RSP) outcomes are supported by the benefit;
- State how the benefit contributes to achieving strategic and corporate objectives and RSP outcomes;
- The value of the benefit realized and the date this is achieved.

Benefits Realization: Summary

Benefits realization ensures that the IT Investment delivers the benefit as stated in the business case. Some of the challenges in implementing the benefits monitoring process are:

- Lack of ownership of benefits realisation, as the IT project would have been completed before the realisation commences
- Difficulty in identifying the benefits
- Difficulty in isolating the benefits of a single project
- Political reasons that prevent one from admitting that the project did not achieve what was promised

CASE STUDY: SOUTH AUSTRALIAN IT INVESTMENT, PLANNING AND PORTFOLIO GOVERNANCE FRAMEWORKS

This is an independent case study prepared by the author. The views expressed in the case study do not represent the views of the Office of the Chief Information Officer or the South Australian Government.

When the new role of chief information officer (CIO) was created in the South Australian Government, the Government knew that it would be an uphill task for the CIO to bring the necessary culture change. Some of his priorities were to set a direction for IT investment prioritization and to improve and coordinate IT planning across government. The CIO would be responsible for streamlining the IT Investment decision-making process across the South Australian Government. This would be a challenging task, due to a number of factors, including a generally negative perception on IT's ability to deliver the required outcomes, the wide variety of existing agency and whole of Government processes, competing priorities for funding, diversity in IT investment needs, the Government's focus on transparency of decision making and audit comments.

The South Australian Government spends approximately $500 million on IT, or around 7 percent of the State's total budget per annum. Despite the significance of this expenditure across Government, IT planning is not as mature as planning for others functional areas, such as finance and HR. (ICT[1] Planning Framework, 2006, p. 4). So, it was not really a surprise when the South Australian Government's Auditor General Report in 2003, (Auditor Report, 2003) was quite critical on IT investment decision making and project execution. However, the Government of South Australia took this report seriously and decided to address these issues in a systematic way.

Creation of Office of CIO

The office of CIO (OCIO) was created to coordinate the whole of Government ICT planning and investment. The CIO reports directly to the minister for infrastructure.

The OCIO stipulates that the planning, execution and reporting of the ICT Projects are a business responsibility. The OCIO facilitates the coordination of ICT investment across agencies by publishing a suite of frameworks that set the minimum requirements to be complied with by all the South Australian Government agencies.

The OCIO Website (OCIO, n.d.) states the following key responsibilities:

ICT planning and investment

- Whole of Government strategic planning and prioritisation of ICT investment for business needs
- Guidance of strategic procurement process across Government
- Promotion of best practice ICT planning across agencies
- Use of ICT innovation to transform service delivery

Program Coordination

- Oversight of programs in alignment with across Government ICT strategy
- Oversight of the development and management of common ICT applications across Government, where appropriate
- Promotion of integrated service delivery and business integration initiatives across Government

Advice

- Provision of advice to the Minister for Infrastructure, Cabinet, Chief Executives and Senior Management on the value of ICT to business, the management of ICT investments and the effective use of ICT as a business tool
- Participation in a number of senior cross-government and cross-jurisdictional committees

ICT Portfolio Governance Life Cycle

The South Australian Government's ICT Governance framework (ICT Planning Framework,

2006) covers the entire life cycle of the ICT Investments. It has five distinct phases listed below:

- Strategic business and ICT planning
- Investment prioritisation and budgeting
- Projects and program portfolio management
- ICT operation and maintenance
- ICT asset renewal, replacement or retirement

Among these life cycle processes, we will examine "Investment Prioritisation and Budgeting" as an example of implementing the portfolio management framework discussed in chapter 3.

Investment Prioritisation and Budgeting

This is the first process area to be deployed by the OCIO as it was considered as a high priority need. The investment prioritisation is a key aspect of IT Governance on how the investment decisions are made. To effectively prioritize investments and ensure a balanced portfolio, each investment proposal needs to address a consistent set of criteria.

The OCIO's investment evaluation (ICT Investment Prioritisation Framework, 2005) includes assessing and considering the comparative weight of three dimensions in addition to cost:

- **Strategic alignment:** the degree of alignment that the business proposal demonstrates against an agency's strategies
- **Value:** the degree of business improvement that will be achieved
- **Risk Evaluation:** evaluation of business risks, delivery risks and benefits realisation risks

The introduction of business criteria for ICT investment evaluation provided a way for decision makers, who are largely not ICT experts, to understand the value proposition, contribution and scope of ICT proposals. Each of the dimensions has it's own practical challenges.

Strategic Alignment

All new South Australian Government ICT Initiatives should be aligned with the State strategic directions as set out in the SA Strategic Plan (SA Strategic Plan, n.d.) and with whole of Government policies and standards

For example, agencies need to demonstrate that their ICT initiatives are contributing to the specific targets for each of the six strategic objectives, outlined in South Australia's strategic plan:

- Growing prosperity
- Improving well being
- Attaining sustainability
- Fostering creativity
- Building communities
- Expanding opportunity

While value and risk are rated numerically, based on a preset evaluation scale, alignment with strategic direction is difficult to quantify. How does one determine the degree of strategic alignment for an IT infrastructure upgrade?

Initiatives are thus profiled into different categories, ranging from strategic to infrastructure. Each of these profiles will have different properties and strategic initiatives are expected to show a higher degree of strategic alignment than infrastructure or hardware replacement initiatives.

For example, an "ICT Infrastructure upgrade" business case that can not show a high degree of alignment with any of the strategic initiatives, will not be rejected, provided it meets all other criteria. In the end, the purpose of evaluation is not to "score" high ratings in all the three dimensions but to balance the risk and benefits of different investment types to create a balanced portfolio.

Value Assessment

The criteria for evaluating the business value of the proposal are (ICT Investment Prioritisation Framework, p. 9):

- Business improvement value
- Systems improvement value
- Organizational improvement value
- Other business benefits
- Financial value

Each of the criteria has detailed scoring guidelines so that there is consistency in the evaluation. For major business cases, the agencies need to complete Net Present Value (NPV) to demonstrate the financial worth of the ICT Initiative.

Risk Evaluation

The risks are assessed against the following criteria (ICT Investment Prioritisation Framework, p. 9):

- Business risk
- Benefits realisation risk
- Architectural alignment risk
- Project Management risk

Benefits realisation is one of the challenging areas to track as intended benefits need to be stated clearly before investment and measured after implementation of an initiative. Many businesses find it hard to quantify or express the business benefits of an IT initiative and to have measurement systems in place, to track the benefits once the project is completed.

Case Study: Summary

OCIO has made progress in the development and deployment of its IT portfolio governance frameworks. Experience from implementation and agency feedback will now be used to update the frameworks and progress towards future stages of maturity.

Some of the "lessons learnt" are:

- Do not force "alignment" to the evaluation criteria
- Make it clear that getting "high score' is not the purpose of evaluation
- Educate the business leaders in evaluation process; Show that the evaluation criteria, will guide decision making thought process
- Provide feedback to agencies, especially if the business case is rejected, clearly identifying the improvement opportunities

OCIO plays only a facilitator role in the deployment of the process. For example, the OCIO cannot create a "full portfolio" view across Government, as not all the investments go through the cabinet submission. In future, the agencies need to create their own ICT portfolio views and feed that information to the OCIO so that the "big picture" across south Australian government can be developed.

The main benefit of the Investment Evaluation framework is the transparency it provides across Government IT investments. Before implementation of the framework, there would have no visibility on the spending of the allocated IT budget by the agencies. The Investment Evaluation provides this visibility, which is a key step in achieving good Governance.

SUMMARY AND FUTURE TRENDS

We started the chapter with a hypothetical case study. If Robert had read the chapter he would have realized that, his organization lacked evaluation, monitoring and benefits realisation processes.

According to Garter (2007, p. 1), the project and portfolio management (PPM) has grown rapidly and morphed since mid-2006. It also states *"even as large enterprises seek expanded IT planning and control with PPM as a key enabler, PPM value has become apparent to organisations of all sizes... "*. It also warns that before choosing software for implementation, the organization should spend effort in changing roles, developing skills and implementing processes. The reports predict that integration of project portfolio, IT service and application life cycle management (ALM) into a coherent IT planning and Control (ITPC) offering is under way.

The industry methodologies also respond to the needs of the market. As pointed out in the introduction the IT Governance Institute has developed COBIT and Val IT methodologies that supports end-to-end IT investment lifecycle. Information Technology Infrastructure Library (ITIL) version 3 covers the entire life cycle of IT services, including service strategy, design, transition, operation and continual service improvement. According to the Office of Government Commerce (OGC) (OGC, n.d.), ITIL version 3, emphasizes Business and IT integration and Value Network Integration, which are essentially portfolio management concepts.

In summary we can conclude that the tools are maturing in portfolio management market space. Industry methodologies, processes are being developed that support portfolio management. However the real challenge is, people, especially senior decision makers, accepting the structured way of evaluating, monitoring, and realizing the benefits of an IT investment. If this acceptance does not happen, the portfolio management will be just another bureaucratic overhead.

REFERENCES

Auditor Report (2003). Retrieved May 15, 2008, from http://www.audit.sa.gov.au/02-03/itrep/summary.html

COBIT 4.1 (2007). *COBIT 4.1 excerpt: Executive summary and framework*. IT Governance Institute

Enterprise Architecture – Wikipedia (n.d.). Retrieved May 15, 2008, from http://en.wikipedia.org/wiki/Enterprise_Architecture

Gartner (2007). *Magic quadrant for IT project and portfolio management 2007, Gartner RAS core research note G00149082*, Matt Light, Daniel B, Stang

ICT Investment Prioritisation Framework (2005). *ICT investment prioritisation framework-Version 1.0*. Government of South Australia

ICT Planning Framework (2006). *SA government ICT planning framework*. Government of South Australia

IT Governance Institute (n.d.). Retrieved May 15, 2008 from http://www.itgi.org

ITIL® (2001). *Best practice for service delivery*. United Kingdom: Office of Government Commerce.

Luftman, J., Bullen, C., Liao, D., Nash, E., & Nuewmann, C. (2004). *Managing the information technology resource: Leadership in the information age*. Upper Saddle River, NJ: Pearson Education Inc.

NSW Government Chief Information Office Benefits Register (n.d.). Retrieved May 15, 2008 from http://www.gcio.nsw.gov.au/documents/Sample%20Benefits_register.pdf

Office of Government Commerce (n.d.). Retrieved May 15, 2008, from http://www.best-management-practice.com/Online-Bookshop/IT-Service-Management-ITIL/ITIL-Version-3/

OGC PRINCE2 (n.d.). Retrieved May 15, 2008 from http://www.ogc.gov.uk/methods_prince_2.asp

PRINCE2 (1998). *Managing successful projects with PRINCE2*. London: The Stationery Office.

SA Strategic Plan (n.d.). Retrieved May 15, 2008, from http://www.stateplan.sa.gov.au/

South Australia Office of CIO (n.d.). Retrieved May 15, 2008, from http://www.cio.sa.gov.au/

Val IT (2006). *Enterprise value: Governance of IT investments*. IT Governance Institute

Weill, P. & Ross, J. W. (2004). *IT governance: How top performers manage IT decision rights for superior results*. Boston: Harvard Business School Press.

ENDNOTE

[1]   **ICT:** information and communication technology; In this case study the abbreviations IT and ICT will be used interchangeably

APPENDIX: IT BENEFITS REGISTER

Description of the Benefit to be Achieved	Person Responsible for Realising the Benefit	Description of Current Situation/ Performance of the Business Process	Current Cost / Performance Measure of the Business Process	Target Cost / Performance Measure after the Planned Change	Target Date for the Benefit to be Realised	Triggers or events that will cause the Benefit to be Realised	Type of Contribution to the Business	Assessed Value of the Benefit or Saving	Comment about the Assessed Value	Strategic and Corporate Objectives and RSP outcomes Supported by this Benefit	Contribution of this Benefit to Achieving the Strategic and Corporate Objectives and RSP outcomes	Value of the Benefit Realised and Date Achieved
Example from a project to implement an intranet and internal E-mail system												
Reduce the amount of paper used to distribute information to staff.	Chief Information Officer	All information to staff is distributed in hard copy.	2,000 reams of paper per year are used to distribute information to staff at a total cost of $11,000.	All information to staff is distributed on the intranet and via e-mail.	June 2002	Intranet and e-mail systems deployed. All staff are trained in and have access to the intranet and e-mail systems. All information to staff is published on the intranet and distributed via e-mail.	Cost Reduction	$11,000 pa		Reduce administrative costs by 10% per year.	Value of benefit contributes a 0.01% p.a. reduction in administrative costs.	
Example from a project to implement an HR Employee Self Service (ESS) system												
Reduce the cost of processing sick leave forms.	Director, Corporate Services	Sick leave forms are generated and processed manually.	24,410 forms processed per year at a total cost of $317,860 ($13.00 per form).	ESS introduced to reduce processing costs to $0.73 per form.	January 2003	ESS System deployed. All staff are trained in and have access to the ESS system.	Cost Reduction Increased productivity	$300,000 pa	Remaining administrative cost relates to staff time to update their own leave records.	Reduce administrative costs by 10% per year.	Value of benefit contributes a 0.3% p.a. reduction in administrative costs.	
Example from a project to develop an Internet Website												
Satisfy an increasing demand for information without increasing costs	Chief Information Officer	Requests for information taken by phone are sent by mail. Requests are also made in person over the counter. Demand is increasing by 10% per year.	100 items of information are requested per day (26,000 per year) and cost $5 per item to satisfy or $130,000 per year.	2,600 items of information accessed via the website in first year.	June 2000	Website established and documents published. Availability of website is advertised via 'phone-hold' message, and branch signage.	Cost avoidance Increased productivity	$13,000 pa	Increased demand for information satisfied without increasing resources.	Reduce administrative costs by 10% per year.	Value of benefit avoids increases in administrative costs to satisfy increasing demand for information.	7,800 items of information accessed via the website in first year with $39,000 value of costs avoided. Benefit achieved June 2000.

Chapter XVIII
Applying Organizational Theories to Realize Adaptive IT Governance and Service Management

Andrew Dowse
Department of Defense, Australia

Edward Lewis
Australian Defence Force Academy, Australia

ABSTRACT

With the cost, complexity and risk associated with IT systems, the approach to IT governance and service management in many organizations is to centralize and standardize. Often executives pursue a generic approach to the management of information technology, without consideration of their organizational context. This chapter examines the adaptation of IT governance arrangements through the lens of organizational theory. It uses concepts from systems theory, differentiation, value chains and structural contingency theory to give an appreciation of the factors that influence how IT can best support an organization's business.

INTRODUCTION

The articulation of processes for the control of IT services in standards (such as AS 8015 and AS ISO/IEC 20000) over the past decade has established a common integrated framework for the management of IT assets and the efficient delivery of services, regardless of the sector in which the organization operates. Many organizations are adopting such standards in pursuit of potential improvements in the quality of an organization's information systems; however the prescription of these standards needs to be in the context of the organization: what works well in one environment may need to be modified in others.

As will be explained in this chapter, there is evidence that many implementations of IT governance and service management have focused internally on the IT function and have been driven by a rationalist approach to consolidating and standardising resources. While this may be a reasonable strategy in certain situations (when there are clear inefficiencies or barriers to interoperability in the way that the organization has managed IT), focusing only on consolidation can detract from the organization's effective use of technology. The adoption of IT governance and service management process frameworks in many organizations often occurs within a shift towards centralisation and a reduction in business-IT alignment (Dowse & Lewis, 2006).

The organizational science literature is relevant to the consideration of appropriate IT management arrangements, in the same way that an organization's structure can be modified to suit its environment. Applying environmental contexts to IT management arrangements in this way is

not new. Several noted researchers have applied contingency approaches to IT governance in assessing situations in which centralized, federal or decentralized modes may be preferred (Peterson, O'Callaghan & Ribbers, 2000; Peterson, Parker & Ribbers, 2002; Sambamurthy & Zmud, 1999).

The purpose of this chapter is to help business and information managers to adapt IT management arrangements to suit the organizational context by examining the issues associated with alignment of IT governance and service management, identifying contingencies and developing a framework. We will begin by examining the requirements for IT governance, then consider the organization as a system and look at competing needs for integration and differentiation within the organization. The emerging concept of information systems as a contributor of value will also be discussed before developing the framework.

THE RISE OF IT GOVERNANCE

Governance is concerned with the effective, efficient and acceptable use of an organization's

Figure 1. Model for IT governance (from AS 8015)

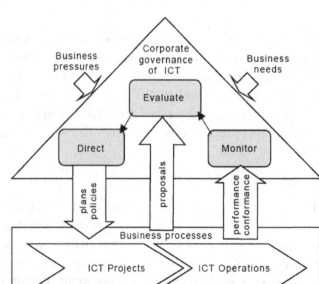

resources. Governance provides a means by which objectives, as well as the means of attaining those objectives and monitoring performance, are determined (OECD, 2004). The three key elements of governance are setting objectives and performance expectations, assigning those expectations to subordinates and ensuring they are being met (Carver, 2006). Whereas governance normally is associated with the apex of the organization (i.e., the activities of boards), there is no reason why this approach to systematic goal setting, delegation and control could not be applied throughout the hierarchy.

With the spate of corporate failures raising questions of executive management, the focus of the term *governance* has shifted to concern matters of corporate ethics, as evidenced in the Cadbury and Sarbanes-Oxley reports in the UK and US respectively. This common interpretation of governance thus relates to the accountability of the organizational executive to its owners or shareholders.

Similarly, whereas IT governance is concerned with the direction and control of current and future use of information technology (Standards Australia, 2005), it has come to be widely associated with ensuring accountability of investments in information technology to owners and shareholders. To some extent, efforts to implement IT governance mechanisms have suffered due to the definitional confusion (Keyes-Pearce, 2002; Webb, Pollard & Ridley, 2006). Critically, IT governance needs to be accountable not only to owners and shareholders, but to the business functions and users within the organization. Only then will IT governance be able to maximize business value through alignment of technology with business.

The Australian standard for IT governance (AS 8015) identifies six principles underlying the need for conformance and performance, as well as three main tasks for directors to govern IT (to evaluate, direct and monitor), as shown at Figure 1. A fourth task, implicit in this diagram, is the

need for the board to engage with stakeholders, including business units, to determine needs and pressures relevant to IT. Whereas the model suggests a singular cyclic process, it would be reasonable to suggest that a hierarchy of evaluate-direct-monitor processes may be employed, particularly in large, complex organizations. Standards Australia recognizes this hierarchy in its intended development of standards for the governance of business programs involving IT investment and for the operation of IT operations, including service management as a subset.

A common structure reflecting the hierarchy of governance and managerial decision-making is:

- **Strategic management:** Development of policies and longer term plans involving the whole enterprise and all of its objectives, including portfolio management (Thorpe, 2003);
- **Tactical management:** Development of processes and capabilities to meet the expectations for IT services, including programme management; and
- **Operations management:** Oversight of the provision of services and associated support.

Using the processes described by the UK Office of Government Commerce (OGC, 2004) provides a standardized framework for IT governance that involves a hierarchy of direction, development and delivery activities as shown at Figure 2. The delivery component comprises the function of IT service management, which is commonly implemented using the IT Infrastructure Library (ITIL). Figure 2 reflects the original ITIL structure in which service delivery processes establish the levels of service whilst service support processes maintain those levels (in the recently released version 3 of ITIL, these processes are restructured as a cycle of service design, transition and operation). Whilst the cyclic approach to service provision continues

Figure 2. Governance framework (adapted from OGC)

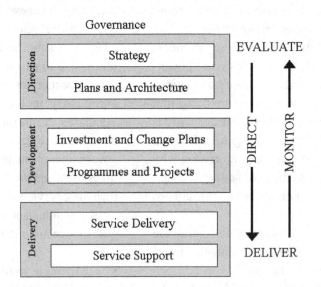

to be used in ITIL, the Australian standard (AS ISO/IEC 20000) presents an integrated framework comprising service delivery, relationship, control, release and resolution processes.

Notwithstanding the importance of the six principles described in AS 8015, we articulate four basic tenets to guide CIOs in constructing IT governance arrangements:

- IT governance is not a singular committee or activity but a **framework of mechanisms** to achieve objectives for conformance and performance of IT systems.
- In many organizations, IT governance is concerned with **establishing a balance** between competing requirements for specialisation and commonality (i.e., between the need for unique information capability and the need for common, interoperable capability).
- The essential requirement for IT governance is the conduct of planning and control to ensure **IT delivers value** by providing for the information needs of the organization.
- Optimal IT governance and service management arrangements are **determined by the organizational context**.

The following sections will consider these tenets in respect of applicable organizational theories, specifically systems theory, differentiation, value chains, and structural contingency theory.

THE ORGANIZATION AS A SYSTEM

Using systems theory elucidates how organizational components interact with each other and with their environment. Whilst an organization may be considered to be a "collection of components organized to achieve a common purpose", it is not a closed system and rarely is homogenous. A change in a component of the organization or in the environment in which it operates can affect the organization's performance. Interaction between the organization and its environment, as well as the levels of coupling and cohesion within the organization, determines its behaviour as a system. The variety of capabilities within the organization permits it to handle situations of uncertainty, dynamism and variety of its task environment (Ashby, 1976; Weick, 1969; Yolles, 2000). For some time, it has been realized that in such environments, the organization may be more effective by employing organic, rather than mechanistic, arrangements (Galbraith, 1973).

A simple, centralized approach to the IT governance framework at Figure 2, such as the use of a single IT governance committee with all IT services being controlled as a standardized infrastructure, would be considered to be mechanistic. Research into IT governance arrangements in Australian public sector organizations has shown that the use of mechanistic governance arrangements in diverse organizations has impacted upon the level of business satisfaction in IT and, to some extent, upon the performance of those organizations (Dowse & Lewis, 2006).

Weill and Ross (2004) identified 15 common IT governance mechanisms used for decision-making, alignment and communications. They include the use of committees covering executive management, information policies, technical architectures and investment, as well as the use of process teams and relationship managers to improve business-technology dynamics. Alignment processes include the tracking of projects and the use of resources, service level agreements, chargeback arrangements and performance measurement mechanisms, including measuring the value/utility/satisfaction of IT.

Communications mechanisms generally are means by which direction can be given (policies, announcements), but might also be important in receiving proposals or input to decisions. Broadbent and Kitzis (2005) noted that whilst the importance of governance mechanisms will vary, those that have the greatest impact in most situations are the use of business-IT relationship managers, the use of IT councils that are composed of business and IT executives, executive committees (with a business orientation) and IT leadership groups (with a technological orientation).

A key element of IT governance is the engagement between the IT function and the organization's business functions. At strategic-level governance, business units are involved in preparing proposals to the governing body. Business unit stakeholders are involved in tactical-level IT governance from the dual perspectives of being customers and contributing to the decision-making processes of steering committees or similar mechanisms.

The dynamics between the entities of the board, business and IT may be considered as a control system (Van Leeuwen, 2006). The business satisfaction with IT should be proportionate to the business value provided to the IT function (deLone & McLean, 2003). It should be reasonable also to assume that a purely economic approach to the control function would result in the provision of means through governance direction being inversely proportionate to the level of satisfaction. That is, a high level of satisfaction may indicate excess capacity and thus invite a reduction of IT resources, whereas a low level of satisfaction may indicate inadequate commitment to IT and invite an increase in the IT means. Conversely, if the board takes a value approach, IT governance would tend to be proportionate with business satisfaction (Van Leeuwen, 2006). As shown in Figure 3, in this approach, the IT governance control function rewards IT contribution to business value by tending to provide more means in pursuit of further value realisation. It would also tend to reduce the means if business perceives IT as not contributing value. Whether the board focuses on efficiencies or on business value depends upon whether the organization's business strategy is on the use of IT as a utility or as a transformational resource.

From a viable systems model viewpoint (Beer, 1981), it could be said that the activities of the board are but a reflection of the variety of interactions between the organization's operational (or "doing") elements and its environment. IT service management comprises the processes that guide interaction between the business and IT function at the tactical and operational levels of management. Expanding then upon the model at Figure 3, service management also may be considered to

Figure 3. IT governance as a control system (adapted from van Leeuwen)

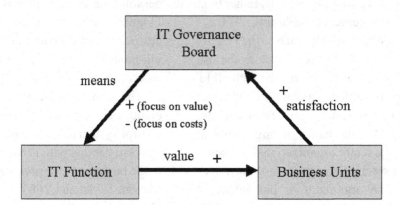

be a control system, in which the organization's business units assess the adequacy of IT services and seek to adjust levels accordingly. This relationship is shown at Figure 4.

INFRASTRUCTURE, INTEGRATION, AND ALIGNMENT

The promises of synergy across business units and efficiency in the management of information technology are leading many organizations to migrate their IT services to establish shared IT infrastructure (Broadbent, Weill & Neo, 1999). This migration confers Chief Information Officers with greater control over the quality of IT services, through standardization of capabilities and achievement of economies of scale. The introduction of corporate IT governance and service management arrangements complements the infrastructure approach.

The three objectives for greater investment in IT infrastructure are related to the three typical contingency factors featured in organizational

Figure 4. Service level management as a control system

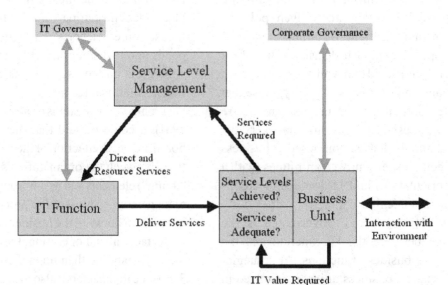

theory (size, interdependence, and uncertainty). Economies of centralisation are positively associated with an organization's size: the potential efficiencies gained from a shared infrastructure approach to an organization's information technology increases if rationalising a large number of systems of different departments. Cost reduction by standardization and centralisation corresponds with bureaucracy theory and the mechanistic organizational form, and represents the first stage of IT infrastructure maturity (Burn, 1997). The second reason, realizing synergy across business units, becomes more significant with increased interdependence across the organization as it attempts to increase the connectivity (reach) and functionality (range) of information sharing (Broadbent et al., 1999). Thirdly, achieving greater flexibility and responsiveness to the strategic context is more relevant in highly dynamic environments featuring task uncertainty. This is an interesting concept in that it could be seen as a departure from the law of requisite variety. That is, in the case of IT, less variety of technology might help an organization deal with greater variety of the environment. This contradiction may be explained in that reduced variety of organizational technology enables greater interactions between individuals and their

knowledge, the true source of internal variety. This interaction is the basis of an organization's ability to accommodate continuous change, which in a dynamic environment constitutes stability (Sauer & Yetton, 1994).

Broadbent and Weill elucidated the benefits of organizational IT in their various works on IT infrastructure. A diverse organization's technology may involve multiple levels of IT provision (local, corporate and contracted/public) as shown at Figure 5 (from Weill & Broadbent, 1998). In pursuing objectives associated with IT infrastructure, organizations have transitioned locally controlled technologies to corporate and even public infrastructure consistent with their context. Underinvesting in corporate IT infrastructure will limit the potential economies and synergies, with business units maintaining islands of automation and inadequate sharing of resources and information across specialisations (Weill, Subramani & Broadbent, 2002). Over-investing in IT infrastructure on the other hand may represent wasted resources. Moreover, over-investment coupled with a forced centralisation of IT (i.e., from local to corporate applications, support and control) may reduce the effectiveness of individual business units. Nevertheless, the trend in many

Figure 5. IT infrastructures (adapted from Weill & Broadbent)

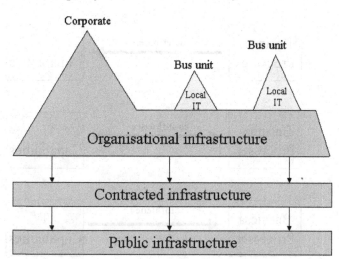

organizations is towards standardized, centrally managed infrastructure and away from locally managed IT.

The shift of control over IT to corporate management, whilst offering the benefits of integration discussed above, could be construed as a potential risk to the alignment between an organization's business and IT. Alignment is a measure of the fit of organizational capabilities, such as IT, with the strategic objectives of the organization (Thorp, 2003). Alignment between IT and the organization's business objectives is a key issue for information systems managers (Palvia & Palvia, 2003). This issue becomes more of a challenge if the organization operates in a dynamic environment.

In evolving his strategic alignment model, Venkatraman (1991) conceptualized that alignment necessitates strategic integration (between strategies and capabilities) and functional integration (between business and IT). Alignment also requires both the corporate strategy and technology to be in equilibrium with other aspects of the organization's capability such as structure, processes and individuals (Scott Morton, 1991). Many variations of Venkatraman's model have been developed in the literature, including Earl's

Organization Fit Framework (1996, 489-500), which introduces an information management domain to reflect the business utility of information; and Weill and Broadbent's (1998) alignment model, which simplifies alignment to a cyclic influence between strategic context, IT strategy and IT capability.

Sauer and Burn (1997) characterized alignment as a compromise between full business-IT integration and outsourcing. One view of alignment is that IT should make adjustments to fit the business. A contrasting view is that the business-IT relationship is more symmetrical and requires the business to make adjustments for IT (Burn, 1997). An even more divergent situation occurs when the IT organization provides a standardized service and expects all business to adjust accordingly. These three types of relationship are characterized as business dominant, symmetrical and IT dominant, as shown at Figure 6.

Most alignment models only focus on the strategic level, which is reasonable in a single business organization. However, in a multibusiness organization, a holistic approach to alignment does not account for the diversity of IT requirements across the organization. An important issue therefore is the relationship between a centralized IT

Figure 6. Business-IT relationships

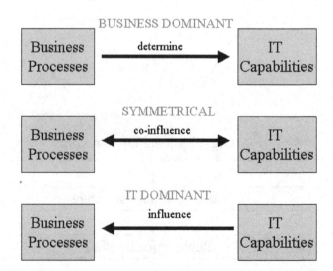

function and the potentially diverse requirements of the business units that it supports.

Lawrence and Lorsch (1967) defined an organization as "a system of interrelated behaviours of people who are performing a task that has been differentiated into several distinct subsystems, each subsystem performing a portion of the task, and the efforts of each being integrated to achieve effective performance of the system." A level of differentiation consistent with the organization's environment leads to improved performance and adaptiveness (Leavitt, 1978). Highly differentiated organizations typically have high cohesion within specialized units and loose coupling between units.

Lawrence and Lorsch (1986) defined integration as "the quality of the state of collaboration that exists among departments that are required to achieve unity of effort by the demands of the environment." Their research noted that differentiation and integration were often inversely related. That is, organizations whose subunits' culture had become highly diverse through associated specialisation did not coordinate with each other as much as less diverse organizations (that is, they are loosely coupled). However, they also found that organizations that matched high differentiation with high integration performed better than other organizations (Lawrence & Lorsch, 1986). Thus, in a diverse organization, performance will be dependent upon the effectiveness of both differentiation and integration. The greater the need for differentiation, the more integration that is required for effectiveness of the overall organization (Donaldson, 2001).

To borrow from Lawrence and Lorsch's work on complex organizations, IT is an integrating mechanism that facilitates lateral relations and balances the differentiation across specialized elements of the organization. The transition to centrally managed IT signals a fundamental shift in organizations from a differentiated, structural orientation to the integration of technology (Ribbers, Peterson & Parker, 2002). From a technol-

ogy perspective, efforts need to be directed at providing differentiation mechanisms to ensure alignment and effective performance of individual businesses in the organization.

The involvement of business units in IT governance mechanisms and the provision of business relationship and service level management processes within IT service management should all enable the differentiation required to support diverse business. Interestingly, a large proportion of organizations that have embarked upon an IT infrastructure approach have focused almost exclusively on consolidation and standardisation (Dowse & Lewis, 2006). This however is typical of the maturity model for IT management, in which organizations typically seek efficiencies before they turn their attention to providing value to the businesses they support. This sequential approach has its benefits, such as ensuring process quality and eliminating unnecessary legacies. However, it also creates a dip in business alignment as the organization strives for a controlled and efficient system, as shown at Figure 7.

The challenge here is that nearly 90% of organizations that have embarked upon a transformation of their IT processes remain at level 1 or 2 (Curtis, 2005). In these organizations, business alignment is minimal. The inability or reluctance of organizations to emerge out of the alignment dip could be attributed to a number of related factors. Rationalism may be a contributor, particularly with the richness of modern office and enterprise applications able to support a variety of businesses; this is exacerbated if the IT management does not have an appreciation of the unique information needs of the business or if interoperability and standardisation are seen as more important than differentiation. There also may exist a perception that IT management cannot differentiate services until the environment is standardized and all potential efficiencies are achieved. This point is made by Ross, Weill, and Robertson (2006), in their suggestion that Enterprise Architecture as strategy must go through a

Figure 7. The effect of process maturity on alignment (adapted from Curtis)

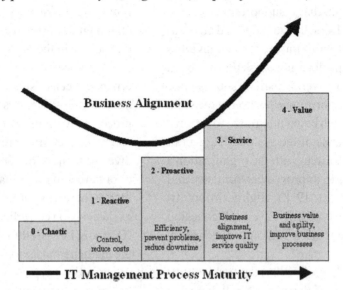

series of stages, from local/functional optimisation, through IT efficiency, process optimization, to strategic choices.

This strategy, however, can entrench the organization in mediocrity, as it may take years to migrate from legacy systems and the full realisation of economies will diminish the capacity of the IT function to differentiate services in the mature system. The employment of IT governance mechanisms as outlined earlier in this chapter (and articulated in Weill & Ross, 2004), including those that address operational alignment, will determine the ease of transition from the rationalist approach to the value-adding approach.

The problem with the provision of standardized infrastructure services in organizations that have diverse technology requirements is that IT may fail to provide the value and thus impact upon the effectiveness of the business. This situation leads us to the third tenet.

THE VALUE VIEWPOINT

The transition to the mature system will be enabled only when the IT function is viewed as a supply function that adds value to the organization's business. Porter (2004) developed the concept of the value chain, which describes the relationship between the activities that contribute to organizational products and services. Porter presented a typical value system as comprising primary activities (that provide a sequential end-to-end process to create the product from inbound logistics to service provision) and support activities (various enterprise-wide functions such as infrastructure, development, procurement and human resource support). The essence of the value chain approach is that the relationship between parts of the organization (as well as external suppliers) are seen in terms of supply and demand, with contributing services adding value to the overall process. Each activity combines purchased inputs, information, resources and technology to perform its function, and may be considered in terms of the value of its services and associated margin (value less collective costs; Porter, 2004).

If the organization provides a diverse range of services or products, then the IT function may need to support multiple value chains, as shown at Figure 8, and thus itself needs to be differentiated commensurate with the support required by the business units. If we consider the IS services to the organization to be $\Sigma_{i=1}^{n}$ IS(i), where n is the number of unique support relationships, then the IS-business relationship will become complex as n increases and as the nature of the support and variance of these relationships increase, especially if the feedback to the business is not coupled loosely. The nature of the support relates to the work associated with (and value contributed to) individual business units. The variance in IT support relationships with the organization's businesses represents the requirement for differentiated alignment. In a diverse organization, these differences need to be addressed not only at the strategic level, but also with the use of operational alignment mechanisms. Such mechanisms consider business requirements for variations from the standard architecture or from standard service provision.

Of course, the situation could be different in organizations where information is the primary business. Many banks and firms such as Sensis, in its production of paper and on-line directories, are "information factories". In such situations, information technology might be regarded as a primary rather than a support activity.

The more tightly and effectively the IT function integrates its services with the demands of each business unit, the more value it provides (OGC, 2004). Yet, in a highly differentiated organization, the more the IT function strives to align with the individual needs of business units, the more differentiated it too becomes. This differentiation may be achieved at the expense of the efficiency gains (and possibly also of potential synergies) of a more homogenous approach. Thus, the options facing organizational executives simplistically exist on a continuum between standardized infrastructure that reduces costs but might reduce the value of services and a differentiated architecture that retains the value of services but does not achieve potential efficiencies.

This corporate dilemma of costs versus value in IT service provision is exacerbated by three factors. Firstly, the creation of an integrated technological infrastructure not only produces efficiencies but also enables value through the synergies discussed previously. Secondly, in a diverse organization and when dealing with intangibles, it is difficult to determine the cost implication of increasingly differentiated relationships with business units or to compare that with the value that such differentiation delivers. Thirdly, it can be difficult to distinguish between the "needs" and the "wants" of business units. Business requirements for information system support may genuinely add value to services or may be a reflection of political desires for control and legacy usage of IT.

The value chain approach at Figure 8 also suggests that a prerequisite to determining alignment requirements is to understand the nature of the value that the business derives from IT. While there have been some research efforts to better comprehend IT business value through concepts such as the resource-based view (Melville, Kraemer & Gurbaxani, 2004), largely alignment is based upon subjective ideas of value.

Thus the question that immediately arises from the model is: How do we specify and measure the value of information services? The logical approach would be a top down development of organizational tasks, generating information requirements that necessitate information architecture functions such as collection, access, presentation, networking, knowledge management, security, interoperability and integration. Providing there is adequate predictability about the nature of the task, the requirements for information, particularly essential elements of information, can be defined to some extent and consequently measured. However, while the analytical rigour required of such an architectural approach has been applied in certain large-scale acquisitions of systems, there has been limited success in any organization in either defining information requirements in architectural terms or in measuring against those information requirements in the running system.

Figure 8. The IS value Chain view (adapted from OGC, 2004)

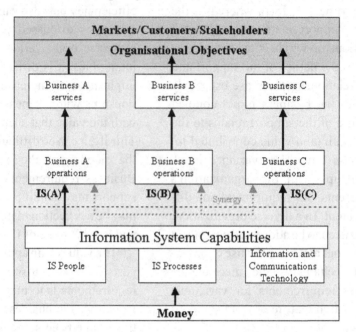

A typical problem with the architectural approach is that too often it takes a technology design viewpoint and disregards key competencies and information needs of the organization (Lewis & Munro, 2007; Sauer & Yetton, 1997). This can lead to the common situation in which greater investment in technology does not lead to noticeable value or competitive advantage, as strongly pointed out by Paul Strassmann (1997). Barney et al. (2001) suggest that a competitive advantage does not arise from the deployment of technology but in the translation of computing power into knowledge. Taking a resource-based view of the organization's information capabilities may assist in matching internal resources with the environmental demands on the organization. RBV theory considers a firm to be a collection of distributed resources, in which performance is determined by the blend of resources, including competencies and capabilities, residing in individuals and institutionalized through organizational learning (Sauer & Yetton, 1997). The market forces that make a resource valuable include scarcity, demand, and appropriability (Collis & Montgomery, 1995).

Above all, the resource-based view calls for consideration of information capabilities across the organization, not only in the specialist IT group, and targeted investments in technology through self-assessment and a close partnering between the business and IT groups (Bharadwaj, 2000).

Another approach to measuring value that is used in many organizations is the aggregation of the satisfaction of individual users as to the quality of information services. The use of surveys or IS success models (such as by deLone & McLean) by IT groups typically infer that individual attitudes reflect the level of success in the provision of information services. However, the needs of individuals do not always represent the needs of the organization and are a measure of perception rather than reality (Seddon, 1997). Thus, while surveys may be a useful indicator, they are not an accurate measure of the value of information services.

Finally, value may be measured by the specification of certain service levels from a technology perspective, such as the percentage of availability of systems or the time taken to resolve a problem.

Linking such service levels to the businesses of the organization, such as through a hierarchical cascade of business and IT scorecards (Van Grembergen, 2000), will provide some level of accountability and measurement of the value provided by information services. To truly measure the value of IT, this measurement would not only include performance metrics but some concept of cost attribution.

A CONTINGENCY MODEL

The contingency approach in general science is that the effect of one variable on another depends upon a third variable. There is no simply stated relationship between the first two variables without consideration of the third, moderating variable (Donaldson, 2001). In the contingency theory of organizations, the relationship is between characteristics of the organization (often organizational structure) and the performance of the organization, which is moderated by some context. The performance is usually referred to as effectiveness but could also relate to efficiency or acceptability. The context that moderates this relationship comprises contingency factors. The fit between the contingency factor and organizational structures determines performance. The challenge therefore is to distinguish the dominant contingency factors. In a dynamic environment, an organization must use controls to monitor those contingencies within its environment, as well as its performance, and then adapt its strategy and modify its structure accordingly.

Burns and Stalker (1961) identified that stable environmental conditions (thus leading to relative task certainty) suit a mechanistic form or organizational structure, featuring a traditional hierarchy, formal rules, vertical communications in line with lines of authority and structured decision-making. Conversely, they determined that more dynamic conditions (leading to task uncertainty) demand the use of an organic form of organization, with less rigidity, informal communication, more participation and innovation. Burns and Stalker examined the success of electronics firms during high dynamicism and found that firms with an organic structure thrived whilst those with mechanistic structures did not.

As mentioned in the introduction of this chapter, several researchers have applied contingency models to IT management arrangements; in fact, contingency theory was dominant in early information systems research (Weill & Olson, 1989). Sambamurthy, Zmud, and Byrd (1994) studied the moderating effect of environmental complexity/turbulence and level of consensus on the necessary comprehensiveness of IT planning. Subsequently Sambamurthy and Zmud (1999) examined the effect of multiple contingencies on IT governance arrangements, where factors interacted to amplify, dampen or override their influence. The contingency factors related to the nature of the organization (size, governance approach and geographic dispersion), economies of scope (diversification and exploitation of economies) and absorptive capacity (specifically, IT knowledge of line managers). Sambamurthy and Zmud determined that the federal mode of IT governance was appropriate in situations of conflicting contingencies, whereas cases of dominating or reinforcing contingencies indicated a suitability of centralized or decentralized governance.

The contingency factors used in IT management research vary from study to study and include one or combinations of strategy, structure, size, environment, technology, task and individuals (Weill & Olson, 1989). Swanson (1987) reviewed organizational theory and the IT literature to determine that characteristics of the organization's environment (heterogeneity, instability, assumptions), of tasks it undertakes (uncertainty, variety, complexity, equivocality) and of the organization itself (core technology, size and objectives) are all determinants of its utility and management of IT. Earl and colleagues developed perhaps the most complete contingency model, which considered the effect of organizational characteristics, perceived IT strategic impact, external IT environment, technology assimilation and heritage (Earl, 1996). However, of these factors, the authors established that only the structural characteristics of the organization influenced the IT management configuration that would maximize performance; that is, IT management arrangements should align with the key characteristics of the host organization (Earl, 1996).

With the emergence of IT governance for strategic control of organizational IT capability, the dominant consideration in determining arrangements for a particular organization is a balance of the respective benefits of centralization (organizational synergy and economy) vs. decentralization (responsiveness to business needs) (Peterson et al., 2000). Peterson (2004) characterized centralized IT governance as being associated with small sized organizations following a cost-focused business strategy, with a centralized business governance structure, environmental stability, low reliance on information and low business experience in managing IT. Decentralized IT governance is more likely to be associated with large, complex organizations with a innovation-focused strategy, decentralized business governance structure, environmental volatility, high reliance on information and high business experience in managing IT. In the typical case when these multiple factors are competing and there is friction between flexibility and efficiency, organizations tend to adopt a federal approach (Peterson, 2004). Typically in such an approach, IT governance decision making and service management are largely centralized but with substantial decentralized input (Weill & Ross, 2004).

In addition to Peterson's work, three other determinants for IT governance are supported by recent research into the performance of organizations employing different IT governance arrangements: **differentiation**, **interdependence** and **inertia** (Dowse & Lewis, 2006). Organiza-

tions with diversity of business (and consequent differentiation of IT needs) are more suited to a federal or decentralized approach, to facilitate greater influence by the business units. Those with low differentiation are able to achieve strategic alignment through a more centralized approach. Organizations with greater interdependence between business units present increased potential for synergy and standardization, thus are suited to a more centralized approach. Organizations that historically had a centralized IT function have less difficulty in implementing an infrastructure approach to IT management and tend to require less alignment mechanisms than those transitioning from a decentralized structure.

It would be useful here to drill down into what we mean by IT governance arrangements. Weill and Ross (2004) described how organizations might adopt a combination of governance approaches according to the type of decision (IT principles, architecture, infrastructure strategies, business applications and investment). They developed a decision rights framework based upon those types of decisions and accounting not only for responsibilities for the decisions, but for inputs from stakeholders (whether that be business input to an IT-dominant decision or IT input to a business-dominant decision).

Similarly, Dowse (2007) describes IT management arrangements flowing from governance in terms of seven attributes, consistent with the framework at Figure 2:

- Engagement between IT and business at the strategic (board) level;
- Level of standardisation of the architecture;
- Funding arrangements for the provision and accounting of IT capabilities;
- Use of service level management and business relationship processes so that IT adds value to the business;
- Performance management mechanisms to measure the quality of IT and serve the 'monitor' function of IT governance;

- Operational use of communications between the IT function and users; and
- The maturity of IT service management processes.

Typically, the contingent factors that tend to favour decentralisation will require greater engagement between IT and business, distributed IT decision-making, less standardisation of the architecture, more decentralized funding arrangements, more differentiated service levels, greater emphasis on performance management (especially tailored to business needs), increased use of communications and greater maturity of service management processes. That is, this engagement tightly couples IT and business. On the other hand, centralisation loosens the coupling between IT and business and so trades agility in response to business changes against predictability, reliability, and efficiency.

This contingent relationship is shown at Figure 9, in which the organizational characteristics moderate the value derived from the organization's IT management arrangements.

FUTURE TRENDS

The current trend for IT governance and service management is one of centralisation, standardisation and consolidation. This has been a necessary step in many organizations in which technology has previously evolved within "stovepipes" and thus potential synergies and economies could be realized. Organizations will increasingly turn to provision of specific value by the IT function to its supported businesses. This trend is reflected in the inclusion of the business relationship processes in the ITIL framework and related standards.

An interesting trend in IT governance might emerge from the business network concepts that followed on from the value chain work discussed earlier in this chapter. Value networks focus the relationship between two organizations or organizational elements on the edges of those elements, rather than through some centralized function. This approach is superior to administrative approaches (in which efficiencies are gained through centralisation) in situations in which the nature of the relationship (and associated value) is dynamic; this is consistent with the Galbraith (1973) concept of lateral relations and the viable

Figure 9. Contingency model of IT management

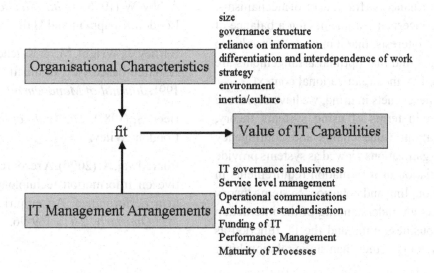

systems model view of an organization's adaptation to its environment. It also may ameliorate the situations of helplessness common within complex organizations, in which the business customers of an IT service are unable to influence that service.

The value network concept of distributing decision rights might seem on the surface to be inconsistent with the current trend of centralisation of IT related decision rights. However, the two approaches can coexist and even complement each other. IT governance mechanisms at the strategic level need to establish a common direction but ensure there is sufficient flexibility for localized adjustments to meet dynamic business needs. Such flexibility and ability to differentiate IT services (while still achieving overall synergies and economies) is at the heart of business relationship management, the implementation of which constitutes the key future trend.

CONCLUSION

This chapter has discussed the need for adaptation of IT governance and service management arrangements, and has applied various organizational theories for this purpose. We began by outlining the requirement for IT governance and identifying four basic tenets to guide adaptation: that IT governance is a framework of mechanisms, that it is concerned with achieving a balance of competing interests, that it must deliver value to the business and that optimal arrangements are determined by the organizational context.

With these tenets in mind, we have discussed adaptation in terms of using systems theory, differentiation, value chains and contingency theory. Organizations viewed as systems provide an appreciation of information requirements in terms of coupling and cohesion. Systems theory also fosters an understanding of the interaction between business units and the IT function as control systems, rather than static relationships.

The need for business-IT alignment is a critical consideration for CIOs and becomes all the more challenging when supporting a diverse range of businesses, each with their own needs. A rationalist approach to provision of IT infrastructure may reduce this alignment, thus it is important to achieve a balance of differentiation and integration to suit the strategic needs of the organization. It is also important that the IT function not lose sight of the need to provide value to the supported businesses, which itself requires a balance of cost and quality of varied services.

The optimal IT governance and service management arrangements, from strategic level committees to the development of IT capabilities to the operation of services, that maximize the value derived from IT will vary depending upon the organizational context. Such moderating factors include organizational size, corporate governance, reliance of information, the differentiation and interdependence of the task environment, business strategy, dynamicism and uncertainty of the environment and the organizational culture. These factors should be taken into consideration to establish effective, value-adding IT governance and service management arrangements.

REFERENCES

Ashby, W. (1956) *An introduction to cybernetics*. London: Chapman and Hall.

Barney, J., Wright, M., & Ketchen, D. (2001). The resource-based view of the firm: Ten years after 1991. *Journal of Management, 27*, 625-641.

Beer, S. (1981). *The brain of the Firm* (2nd ed.). London: Wiley.

Bharadwaj, A. (2000). A resource-based perspective on information technology capability and firm performance: An empirical investigation. *MIS Quarterly, 24*(1), 169-96.

Broadbent, M., & Kitzis, E. (2005). *The new CIO leader*. Boston: Harvard Business School Press.

Broadbent, M., Weill, P., & Neo, B. (1999). Strategic context and patterns of IT infrastructure capability. *Journal of Strategic Information Systems, 8*, 157-187.

Burn, J. (1997). *A professional balancing act: Walking the tightrope of strategic alignment*. In C. Sauer & P. Yetton (Eds.), *Steps to the future: Fresh thinking on the management of IT-based organizational transformation* (pp. 55-88). San Francisco: Jossey-Bass.

Burns, T., & Stalker, G. (1961). Mechanistic and organic systems. In f. Kast & J. Rosenzweig (Eds.), *Contingency views of organization and management* (pp. 74-80). Chicago: Science Research Associates.

Carver, J. (2006). *Boards that make a difference: A new design for leadership in nonprofit and public organizations* (3rd ed.). San Francisco: Jossey-Bass.

Collis, D., & Montgomery, C. (1995). Competing on resources: Strategy in the 1990s. *Harvard Business Review,* 118-128.

Curtis, D. (2005). The journey to IT service management starts with IT management process maturity. In *Proceedings of the Gartner ITXPO Symposium*, Sydney.

deLone, W., & McLean, E. (2003). The DeLone and McLean model of information systems success: A ten-year update. *Journal of management Information Systems, 19*(4), 9-30.

Donaldson, L. (2001). *The contingency theory of organizations*. Thousand Oaks: Sage Publications.

Dowse, A. (2007). *The diverse organisation: Operational considerations for managing organisational information resources*. Unpublished doctoral thesis, UNSW, Canberra.

Dowse, A., & Lewis, E. (2006). Whatever happened to alignment? In *Proceedings of the 2006 Information Technology Governance International Conference*, Auckland.

Earl, M. (1996). *Integrating IS and the organization: A framework of organizational fit*. In M. Earl (Ed.), *Information management: The organizational dimension* (pp. 485-502). Oxford: Oxford University Press.

Galbraith, J. (1973). *Designing complex organizations*. Reading, MA: Addison-Wesley.

Keyes-Pearce, S. (2002). Rethinking IT governance in the e-world. In *Proceedings of the Pacific-Asian Conference on Information Systems*, Tokyo.

Lawrence, P., & Lorsch, J. (1967). Differentiation and integration in complex organizations. *Administrative Science Quarterly, 12*(1), 1-47.

Lawrence P., & Lorsch, J. (1986). *Organization and environment: Managing differentiation and integration*. Boston: Harvard Business School.

Leavitt, H. (1978). *Managerial psychology* (4th ed.). Chicago: University of Chicago Press.

Lewis, E., & Munro, D. (2007). *Foundations of enterprise architecture*. Melbourne.

Melville, N., Kraemer, K., & Gurbaxani, V. (2004). Review: Information technology and organizational performance: An integrative model of IT business value. *MIS Quarterly, 28*(2), 283-322.

OECD (2004). *Principles of corporate governance*. Paris: Office of Economic Cooperation and Development Publications Service.

Office of Government Commerce (2004). *Business perspective: The IS view of delivering services to the business*. Norwich: The Stationery Office.

Palvia, P., & Palvia, S. (2003). Information systems plans in context: A global perspective. In R. Galliers & D. Leidner (Eds.), *Strategic information management* (pp. 151-180). Oxford: Butterworth-Heinemann.

Peterson, R. (2004). Integration strategies and tactics for information technology governance. In W. Van Grembergen (Ed.), *Strategies for information technology governance* (pp. 37-80). Hershey, PA: Idea Group Publishing.

Peterson, R., O'Callaghan, R., & Ribbers, P. (2000). IT governance by design: Investigating hybrid configurations and integration mechanisms. In *Proceedings of the 21st International Conference on Information Systems* (pp. 435-452), Brisbane.

Peterson, R., Parker, M., & Ribbers, P. (2002). Information technology governance processes under environmental dynamism: Investigating competing theories of decision making and knowledge sharing. In *Proceedings of the 23rd International Conference on Information Systems* (pp. 563-576).

Porter, M. (2004). *Competitive advantage: Creating and sustaining superior performance*. New York: Free Press, Simon and Schuster.

Ribbers, P., Peterson, R., & Parker, M. (2002). Designing information technology governance processes: Diagnosing contemporary practices and competing theories. In *Proceedings of 35th Annual Hawaii International Conference on System Sciences*.

Ross, J., Weill, P., & Robertson, D. (2006). *Enterprise architecture as strategy.*, Boston: Harvard Business School Press.

Sambamurthy, V., & Zmud, R. (1999). Arrangements for information technology governance: A theory of multiple contingencies. *MIS Quarterly, 23*(2), 261-278.

Sambamurthy, V., Zmud, R., & Byrd, T. (1994). The comprehensiveness of IT planning processes: A contingency approach. *Journal of Information Technology Management, 5*(1), 1-10.

Sauer, C., & Burn, J. (1997). The pathology of strategic alignment. In C. Sauer & P. Yetton (Eds.), *Steps to the future: Fresh thinking on the management of IT-based organizational transformation* (pp. 89-111). San Francisco: Jossey-Bass.

Sauer, C., & Yetton, P. (1994). The dynamics of fit and the fit of dynamics: Aligning IT in a dynamic organization. In *Proceedings of 15th International Conference on Information Systems* (pp. 41-50).

Scott Morton, M. (1991). *Introduction.* In M. Scott Morton (Ed.), *The corporation of the 1990s* (pp. 2-23). New York: Oxford University Press.

Seddon, P. (1997). A respecification and extension of the DeLone and McLean model of IS success. *Information Systems Research, 8*(3), 240-253.

Standards Australia (2005). *Corporate governance of information and communication technology, AS 8015-2005*. Sydney: Standards Australia.

Standards Australia (2007). AS ISO/IEC 20000.1 *Service management: Part 1 and 2*

Strassmann, P. (1997). *The squandered computer*. New Canaan: Information Economics Press.

Swanson, E. B. (1987). Information systems in organization theory: A review. In R. Boland & R. Hirschheim (Eds.), *Critical issues in information systems research* (pp. 181-204). Chichester: John Wiley and Sons.

Thorp, J. (2003). *The information paradox*. Toronto: McGraw Hill Ryerson.

Van Grembergen, W. (2000). *The balanced scorecard and IT governance*. Retrieved May 15, 2008, from www.itgi.org

Van Leeuwen, F. (2006). Balancing compliance, agility and risk. In *Proceedings of the Keynote Presentation to the IT Governance International Conference*, Auckland.

Venkatraman, N. (1991). IT-induced business reconfiguration. In M. Scott Morton (Ed.), *The corporation of the 1990s* (pp. 122-158). New York: Oxford University Press.

Webb, P., Pollard, C., & Ridley, G. (2006). Attempting to define IT governance: Wisdom or folly? In *Proceedings of the 39ᵗʰ Annual Hawaii International Conference on System Sciences.*

Weick, K. (1969). *The social psychology of organizing.*, Reading, MA: Addison-Wesley.

Weill, P., & Broadbent, M. (1998). *Leveraging the new infrastructure.* Boston: Harvard Business School Press.

Weill, P., & Olson, M. (1989). An assessment of the contingency theory of management information systems. *Journal of Management Information Systems, Summer, 6*(1), 59-85.

Weill, P., & Ross, J. (2004). *IT governance: How top performers manage IT decision rights for superior results.* Boston: Harvard Business School Press.

Weill, P., Subramani, M., & Broadbent, M. (2002). Building IT infrastructure for strategic agility. *MIT Sloan Management Review, Fall,* 57-65.

Yolles, M. (2000). Organisations, complexity and viable knowledge management. *Kybernetes, 29*(9/10), 1202-1222.

Section IV
IT Service Management Frameworks

Chapter XIX
Implementing IT Service Management:
Lessons Learned from a University IT Department

Jon Iden
Norwegian School of Economics and Business Administration, Norway

ABSTRACT

This chapter presents and analyzes a real life ITIL project, and it is based on a longitudinal case study. The purpose is to illustrate how the ITIL process reference model for some processes may be used almost as a blueprint, while ITIL for other processes may be profoundly adapted to suit the context and the needs of the implementer. Furthermore, the success factors and the impediments for successful implementation are discussed. As this case shows, although processes are being well defined and the ITIL project is being regarded by management as a success, employees may after all decide not to follow the adapted processes. The study finds that ITIL implementation will not be effective unless the organizational and cultural aspects of process change are being taken care of. This chapter will especially inform practitioners about how ITIL may be utilized and how an implementation project might be organized.

INTRODUCTION

The IT service management perspective is becoming more and more popular in the IT community. IT Service Management is an approach to operations that emphasizes IT services, customers, service levels agreements (SLAs) and best practice pro-cesses for handling the day-to-day activities in the IT department (OGC, 2005; Palmer, 2005). Several frameworks exist, such as Control Objectives for Information and related Technology (COBIT), Microsoft Operations Framework (MOF), IBM SMSL, HP ITSM, and IT Infrastructure Library (ITIL). Among them, ITIL seems to be especially well accepted. ITIL is primarily a collection of best practices implemented in the industry, and is administered by the UK Office of Government Commerce (OGC). It gives a detailed description of how to organize and handle central IT operations tasks such as incidents, problems, changes, configuration, availability, capacity and so on. ITIL is a process reference model, and views operations as a collection of processes. Process orientation means focusing on the cross-functional, organization-wide sets of activities that transform an input into an output that represents value for the customer, and does so by utilising a variety of organizational resources. Implementing ITIL means process change.

As a process reference model, ITIL seeks to capture characteristics common to many companies within the IT sector. A reference model may be defined as "an abstracted depiction of reality that serves as a standardized or suggestive conceptual basis for the design of enterprisSe specific models, usually within a like domain" (Taylor & Sedera, 2003, p.1). Misic and Zhao (2000) describe reference models as being "standard decomposition of a known problem domain" (p.484). Brocke and Thomas (2006) discuss the use of reference models and argue that a user will acknowledge a reference model when the effort needed for the construction of his own specific model is considerable reduced using the reference model. In addition, they argue, "the more specific a reference model is, the fewer the enterprises are for which it can be applied" (p. 681).

Although IT departments all over the world are improving their operations and processes based on the ITIL process reference model, there is, to date, little academic literature examining the characteristics of ITIL, how ITIL is implemented in industry, and the effects and the consequences of following such a process reference model. A notable exception is Aileen Cater-Steel and colleagues (Cater-Steel & Tan, 2005; Cater-Steel, Tan & Toleman, 2006a; Cater-Steel, Toleman & Tan, 2006b). Cater-Steel and Tan (2005) report

from a survey about the uptake of ITIL in the Australian IT community, that ITIL's service support processes Service Desk and Incident Management were at the most advanced stage of implementation. Further, survey respondents perceived "commitment from senior management," "champion to advocate and promote ITIL," and the "ability of staff to adopt to change" as the top three ranked factors for success. Noteworthy, 56% of respondents reported that ITIL had met or exceeded their expectations.

The purpose of this chapter is to present and analyze a real life ITIL project, through the lens of a case study approach, in order to provide insight into the nature, challenges and benefits of ITIL implementation. The chapter will especially focus on methodological- and project-related factors. In addition, exploring how a real-life industry implementation utilize the reference processes presented in the ITIL is a main goal.

Among the issues addressed in this research are:

- How are ITIL reference processes being adopted by the IT department?
- What are the success factors and the impediments for successful implementation?
- How is information technology being used to enable ITIL-processes?
- Does ITIL implementation affect organizational culture?

The research presented here has been organized as a longitudinal research project combining different research methods such as action research, interviews, surveys, and document studies.

BACKGROUND

This section gives a short introduction to *IT Service Management*, *ITIL* and *process change* for readers unfamiliar with these topics. Further, it presents the case organization and the reasons why an ITIL project was launched, and it includes an overview of the applied process change method and enabling technology.

IT Service Management and ITIL

IT Service Management is based on the idea that the IT department is a service organization, delivering IT services to the firm (OGC, 2005). Consequently, IT should focus on developing and delivering IT services that can fulfil business needs and requirements. The key concepts of IT Service Management are *service, quality* and *customers* (Palmer, 2005). An IT department should not focus just on running its technological infrastructure, but should pay attention to the IT services it provides. One definition of IT service is: "an integrated composite that consists of a number of components, such as management processes, hardware, software, facilities and people that provides a capability to satisfy a stated management need or objective" (Evans & Macfarlane, 2001). IT services support business processes, and enable businesses to reach their goals. Identifying and describing an IT service may be challenging for an IT department accustomed to managing technology. However, implementing IT Service Management requires that IT services are being defined and a service catalogue is being developed. A certain IT service must fulfil certain requirements and expectations of the customer. Therefore the quality of service must be agreed upon by the provider (the IT department) and the customer. The IT department and the customer must have a mutual understanding of what is expected from the service. Service hours, availability, performance, security, and customer support are key factors when service quality is negotiated and defined. The customer is a user representative, normally a business manager who is authorized to negotiate with IT on behalf of the business area. A customer is typically someone who is responsible for the cost of the service (OGC, 2001; OGC, 2005).

The IT Infrastructure Library (ITIL), first created in the late 1980's by the CCTA (a British government body) and now administrated by the Office of Government Commerce (OGC), is regarded as the *de facto* standard for IT Service Management. Version 2, published in 2000 and 2001, evolved into a collection of best practice processes meeting the operational demands related to the current state of technology and IT services. Version 3, published in 2007, brought the process framework further and includes a life-cycle approach for planning, designing, deploying, providing, and improving IT services. ITIL is designed to be usable by organizations of any size and structure. However, small IT departments may find ITIL's rich role-structure difficult to implement and manage. The International Standards Institute (ISO) and the British Standards Institute (BSI) have adopted standards based on the ITIL material, named ISO 20000 and BS 15000 respectively. These standards can be used by companies to demonstrate to customers and other stakeholders that their operations are in accordance with best industry practice.

ITIL has dedicated one book to the implementation of IT Service Management. It includes a general model for continuous service improvement organized around six phases: (1) what is the vision, (2) where are we now, (3) where do we want to be, (4) how do we get where we want to be, (5) how do we check that milestones have been reached, and (6) how do we keep the momentum going (Lloyd, Rudd & Littlewood, 2003)?

Process Change

It becomes more and more common for organizations within all industries to analyze and change their business and work processes (Hammer, 2007). The process perspective influences many different fields like organizational development, software development, e-business, quality systems, and management (Harmon, 2003). Different process change projects may have different levels of ambition. Some projects aim at radical change, as we find expressed in Business Process Reengineering (Hammer, 1990; Hammer & Champy, 1993), while others seek for more incremental change as expressed in Total Quality Management (Harrington, 1991; Oakland 2000). The purpose behind improving processes varies also. While some projects aim at improving process performance and the use of resources, others aim at improving process results and customer satisfaction. An array of available process change methodologies exists (Kettinger, Teng & Guha, 1997; Shen, Wall, Zaremba, Chen & Browne, 2004). The same is true for modelling techniques and tools (Aguilar-Savén, 2004). Although each methodology has its unique features, they all include a procedure where one first identifies the current situation (as is) and through analysis designs a new process to be implemented in the organization. Process change may affect workflows, roles, resources and rules, and may include both organizational and technological efforts (Harmon, 2003).

The IT Department

This case study has been carried out within an IT department at a European university. The university is the second largest university in its country, with nearly 20000 students and 4500 employees (faculty and administrative staff). The university has its own IT department providing IT services to university administration, faculty and students. The department is organized around three sections: *support, infrastructure and applications*, and employs between 80 and 90 people.

In the spring of 2003, an assessment presented by an external consulting firm concluded that the operational processes in the department were ad hoc and not very effective, leading to dissatisfied customers and users. A major potential for improvement was identified. During summer and autumn 2003, IT management had numerous meetings where they discussed how to approach these deficiencies. Among the different alterna-

tives discussed, management found IT Service Management and ITIL especially promising, and it was decided that operational processes should be improved according to the ITIL process reference model. As the external assessment had concluded that user support was an area for particular improvement, it was decided to start with implementing a Service Desk and an Incident Management process. This approach is in line with common industry practice as documented by Cater-Steel and Tan (2005). Later projects were launched for Change and Configuration Management.

The Process Change Method

The IT department did not possess beforehand any in depth competence or experience in process change or in ITIL. Therefore, a local consultant well familiar with both areas was engaged. A separate project was established for each of the processes. Each project organized its work according to a process change method provided by the consultant, consisting of the five phases presented in Table 1. For drawing workflow models (process modelling) a role-based modelling notation was used (Iden, 2005). This modeling notation emphasizes roles, activities and hand-offs between roles.

Enabling Technology

Before launching the projects on Service Desk and Incident Management, the software marked for IT Service Management and ITIL was analyzed, and contacts were made with other universities and academic institutions in order to identify a suitable and affordable standard software package with ITIL functionality. The technological culture in the IT department is strongly in favor of applying open source software and solutions where feasible. Instead of buying a complete and expensive ITIL software package, IT management decided to exploit the open source system *Issue-*

Table 1. Process change method applied

Phase:	Tasks:	Deliverables:
1. Establish	Appoint process owner, organize project group, train in ITIL and process change methodology, prepare mandate and plan.	Process owner, trained project group, project mandate, and plan.
2. Document	Document existing practice, including roles, resources, rules, and metrics. Model workflows. Identify weaknesses and areas for improvement.	"As is" description with workflow models.
3. Analyze and design	Analyze how best practice may be utilized and how existing practice can be improved. Understand the enabling potential of the technology. Define a new process with workflows, roles, resources, rules, and metrics. Define requirements for IT solutions. Make plan for implementation.	Process description with workflow models, requirements for IT solution, and implementation plan.
4. Implement	Implement organizational and technical arrangements and solutions. Provide training in new roles and IT solutions. Prepare solutions for measuring process.	New process implemented and solutions for managing the process in place.
5. Operate	Oversee that the new process reaches process goals. Continuously improve process according to shifting needs and requirements.	Metrics (quality, time, resources, customer satisfaction) for continuous improvement.

Tracker which is described as a user friendly issue tracking system written in PHP. An in-house Issue-Tracker developer was appointed. The IT department acknowledged that Issue-Tracker would not provide all the technical features necessary to implement a fully integrated ITIL solution, but decided to gain competence and experience through this simple system for eventually choosing a more comprehensive package later. Solutions for Incident and Change Management were implemented in Issue-Tracker.

BEST PRACTICE AND ACTUAL IMPLEMENTATION

ITIL is a collection of documented best practice processes for IT Service Management. However, ITIL is not presented as a blueprint that organizations can or should implement exactly as described. In fact, in many book-chapters, alternative approaches to the same task or problem

are presented, and it is often stated that "you have to decide for yourself". Design decisions must be taken according to each organization's individual needs and context. This section will present the process design decisions for Incident and Change Management taken by the project groups, and compare and discuss their choices according to ITIL reference processes as found in CTTA (2000) and OGC (2005). By applying workflow models, the design and comparison will focus on workflows, roles, rules, and resources.

Incident Management

ITIL presents Incident Management as a reactive task with the aim of reducing or eliminating the effects of actual or potential disturbances in an IT service (OGC, 2005). An incident is defined as "any event which is not part of the standard operation of a service and which causes, or may cause, an interruption to, or a reduction in the quality of that service" (OGC, 2005, p. 31). The basic principles are as follows. Users should contact the Service Desk when an incident occurs. All incidents should be registered in an IT-system and categorized and prioritised according to related service, impact, and urgency. If an incident cannot be resolved by first line support (Service Desk) within the agreed time, the incident should be escalated to personnel with more specialized skills. The objective of the Incident Management process is to return to normal service level as soon as possible, and not to try to find or solve the root cause that made the incident happen in the first place. The latter is the aim of Problem Management (OGC, 2005, p. 45). Thus, Incident Management has an interface to Problem Management; information about incidents should be forwarded to Problem Management for further investigation. It has also an interface to Change Management, for example when the resolution of an incident requires a change. ITIL distinguishes between an incident and a service request. A service request is a "request from a user for support, delivery, information, advice or documentation, not being a failure in the IT Infrastructure" (OGC, 2005, p. 32).

Although a major part of personnel resources was spent on handling and correcting failures, the IT department did not have a standard Incident Management process or a single point of contact for users when encountering failures. Developing a total solution for handling incidents involved three main activities: (1) designing and implementing a Service Desk, (2) designing and implementing an Incident Management process, and (3) building a technical solution for registering and tracking incidents in Issue-Tracker. The following discussion will focus on the design of the Incident Management process.

In phase 1 (Establish) a process manager and a project group were appointed and training provided. Proceeding to phase 2 (Document), the project group spent two days discussing the present practices of managing incidents and service requests, and an "as is" description report was prepared, focusing on user groups, channels (telephone, e-mail, personal), incident categories, volumes, service times and involved roles. Three workflow models were drawn, each documenting the practices of a major category of incidents. Weaknesses and areas for improvements were identified, for example:

- All IT personnel in the department receive incidents directly from users
- Few incidents are being registered
- Many incidents are directed to the wrong IT person or group
- Many incidents are not being followed up properly and incidents are sometimes lost
- Rules (e.g., priority) for handling incidents are not well defined

The discussions and the "as is" description gave the work group a systematic and common understanding of the present situation. Phase 3 (Analysis and design) was carried out by combining the understanding of three different perspectives: the current situation at the department, the ITIL description of best practice, and the functions and limitations of the selected software system. Based on this, a process for Incident Management was defined by the project group, and later implemented. The following is a presentation of the process design with a focus on workflow, roles, rules, and resources.

Workflow

ITIL illustrates the workflow of a normal incident by applying a general flowchart model. In order to compare the best practice workflow in ITIL with the one designed by the department, both workflows are modelled using the role-based notation. (See Figures 1 and 2.)

Roles, Rules, and Resources

The roles, rules and resources for Incident Management are summarized in Table 2.

Figure 1. Workflow model for incident management based on ITIL

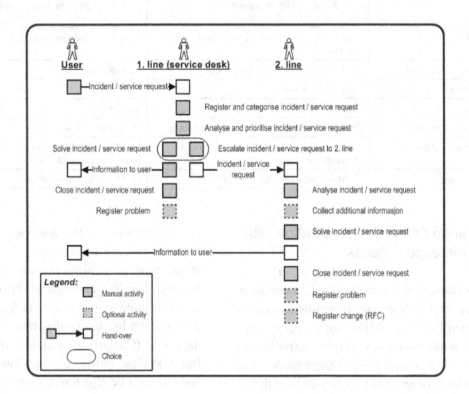

Figure 2. Workflow model for incident management designed by the IT Department

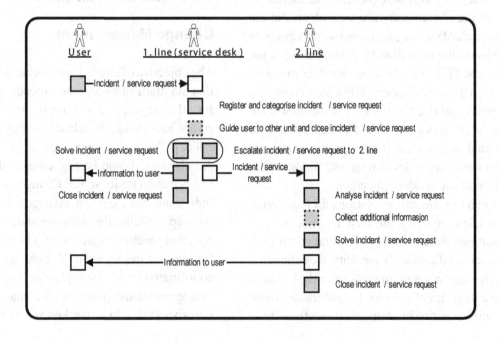

Table 2. Roles, rules and resources for incident management

	ITIL Best practice	IT Department implementation
Roles	User, 1.line (service desk), 2.line, 3.line, Incident manager	User, 1. line (service desk), 2.line, 3.line
Rules - categories	Incident, Major incident, Service requests	Incident, New order
Rules – urgency	High, medium, low	Not defined
Rules – impact	High, medium, low	Not defined
Rules - priority	Combination of values for urgency and priority	High, normal, low
Rules – status	New, accepted, planned, assigned, active, suspended, resolved, closed	New, work in progress, waiting on tech, waiting on client, closed
Resources	ITSM system, web-solution, CMDB, SLA	ITSM system, web-solution

Comparing Actual Implementation with ITIL Reference Process

The workflow models show that the IT department to a large extent followed the recommendations in ITIL when they designed their own process. They implemented a workflow with roles, activities and hand-offs in line with the reference model. The only major difference is that they did not define interfaces to problem management or change management. This can be explained by the fact that these two processes were non-existent at that time, and partly as a consequence of the shortcomings of the chosen software tool which did not have standard modules for these two processes. In addition to the roles directly participating in the workflow, ITIL introduces an incident manager role with a certain responsibility for driving the efficiency and effectiveness of the Incident Management process as a whole. The department did not establish this role explicitly, instead, a process owner was appointed with responsibilities similar to those of the incident manager.

When implementing solutions for registering an incident, most of the best practice recommendations were applied (rules and resources). However, for the sake of simplicity, they chose not to define urgency and impact explicitly, but used three categories of priority for separating those incidents requiring immediate actions from those less urgent. Since neither a service level management process nor individual SLAs were defined at the time of implementation, no connection between incident and agreed service level was set. The same was true for configuration items (CI). Only a limited configuration management data base (CMDB) existed, and therefore only free text descriptions of the related IT service and CI could be registered. As recommended by ITIL, for reducing the pressure on Service Desk personnel, a Web-solution enabling users registering incidents and service requests themselves was implemented in the system.

Change Management

The objective of change management is to ensure that standard methods and procedures are used for all changes, and to limit the introduction of errors and incidents related to changes (OGC, 2005, p. 75). The basic principles are as follows. All changes should be registered and requested beforehand (Request for Change – RFC). An individual role, change manager, is appointed the responsibility for assessing and approving (or rejecting) each change request. The development, testing and deployment of a change should be coordinated under the supervision of the change manager and the progress of a change through the process should be tracked and its status made visible through the forward schedule of changes (FSC). For high-risk changes and when higher authority is needed, a Change Advisory Board (CAB) with representatives from all major IT sections is involved.

The IT department did not have any formal or standard way of dealing with changes. There was no system where changes could be registered, and where information about completed and future changes could be made available to stakeholders. Five months after the implementation of an incident management process, the project for change management was launched, applying the same process change method as for incident management. First, the project group spent two days discussing present practices of managing changes and preparing an "as is" report that focused on change areas (network, client/server, database, Web etc.), change types, where the change process starts and ends, who are involved in handling changes, and how changes are being documented. Two workflow models were drawn, each documenting a major category of changes carried out, namely "upgrading of existing hardware and software," and "installing new components in the configuration." Weaknesses and areas for improvement were identified, for example:

- No formalized and standardized process for managing changes existed
- Changes are not being registered
- Responsibility and authority for changes are not defined
- Rules for handling changes are not well defined.

The "as is" report, as well as the discussions, gave the workgroup a thorough and common understanding of the present situation, and the group proceeded to the "analyse and design" phase. Combining the understanding of three different perspectives carried out analysis and design: the current situation, the ITIL description of best practice, and the functions and limitations

of the selected software system. Based on this a process for change management was designed. The following is a presentation of the process design with focus on workflow, roles, rules and resources.

Workflow

The ITIL change management process illustrates workflows for two types of changes: a normal change and an urgent change. General flowchart notation is applied. Here the focus is on normal changes. As for incident management and in order to compare the best practice workflow in ITIL with the one designed by the department, both workflows are modelled using the role-based notation. (See Figures 3 and 4).

Roles, Rules, and Resources

The roles, rules, and resources for change management are summarized in Table 3.

Comparing Actual Implementation with ITIL Reference Process

The two workflow models demonstrate that the IT department chose a different process design for change management than the one recommended by ITIL. First, rather than appointing a single change manager role, each section leader took on these responsibilities for changes within his or her section. As a consequence, RFCs are assessed and approved within department sections only and no role has the overall control of the total number of active changes. For standard changes, as the model implies, the change initiator is authorized to plan and implement a change after it has been registered. The project also decided not to define a special Change Advisory Board, but decided that "high risk changes" should be escalated to the IT director or be handled on regular IT management meetings when necessary. Further, they did not define unique roles for change developer and

Figure 3. Workflow model for change management based on ITIL

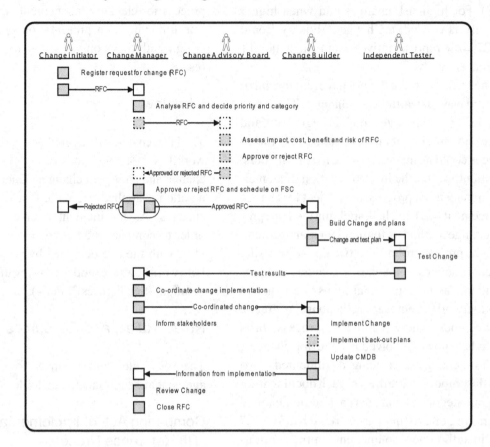

Table 3. Roles, rules and resources for change management

	ITIL Best practice	IT Department implementation
Roles	Change initiator, change manager, change advisory board, change developer, independent tester	Change initiator, section leader, IT director / IT management meeting
Rules - categories	Normal, standard, urgent	Normal, standard, urgent
Rules - risk	Low, medium, high	Low, medium, high
Rules – priority	Low, normal, high, highest	Low, normal, high, highest
Rules – impact	Minor, substantial, major	Not defined
Rules – status	Logged, assessed, rejected, accepted, sleeping, closed	Logged, assessed, rejected, in progress, closed
Resources	RFC, FSC, CMDB	RFC, FSC, CMDB

Figure 4. Workflow model for change management designed by the IT department

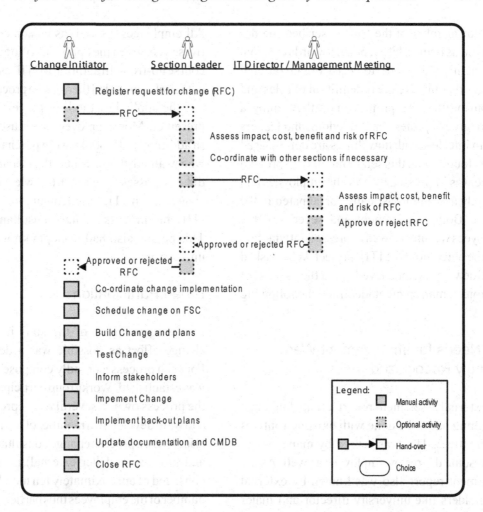

independent tester, but delegated the activities of these roles to the change initiator. As a result, a compact workflow with three roles compared to the five suggested by ITIL was designed. The main motivation for this process design was to minimize the introduction of new organizational roles.

When implementing solutions for registering a change, most of the best practice recommendations (rules and resources) were applied. However, as can be seen from Table 3, they chose not to define impact for each RFC. A comment must be made as to the use of a CMDB. Since only an incomplete CMDB existed, not every RFC could

be related to a configuration item. Further, sine few relations between configuration items were defined in the CMDB, the CMDB could not support the impact assessment activity to the degree that ITIL prefers.

LESSONS LEARNED

In this section, factors regarded by IT management as important for the successful implementation of ITIL's reference processes are presented, together with the results of an assessment after two years.

Success Factors

A senior member of the staff described the department as being a bit sceptical towards external consultants, and prone to resist organizational changes that involve the redefinition of roles and responsibilities. As professionals they enjoy a high degree of professional freedom, and leaders seldom interfere with how things are done. Based on this foundation, this senior member expressed that he was impressed by how the employees had willingly and enthusiastically participated in the project. Both management and several of the employees we interviewed expressed satisfaction with the outcome of the ITIL project. When asked to define what factors have lead to the success of the project, management identified the following factors.

The Needs for Improvement Were Strongly Recognized

The external assessment report left no doubt that something had to be done with existing routines and practices. This was sensed by management and to some degree by employees as well. As the assessment report also was known by external stakeholders like university director and major customers, there was an external pressure on the department "to do something." Without these external pressures, it is doubtful that the ITIL project had been launched at that time.

Openness

Having decided to run the ITIL effort, management prioritized to keep employees continuously informed during the project. General meetings were held, and the ITIL initiative was presented over the course of several internal seminars. In addition, presentations were held on open seminars where employees, customers and other stakeholders at the university were present. Employees, customer, and other stakeholders were well informed about the purpose, plans and results.

Training and Expertise

All employees, as well as customer representatives, were given the opportunity to attend an ITIL course up-front. In addition to ITIL essentials, this course also included theories on process thinking, and the applied method for process change was presented. Most employees made use of this offer. In addition, ITIL books were purchased for those who wanted them. Since the department itself did not possess practical knowledge in process change or in ITIL implementation, an external ITIL and process change consultant was hired. This person also had in-depth knowledge of the university.

Broad Participation

Involving as many of the staff in the process change effort as possible was a declared goal. For each process a broadly composed workgroup was established. Workgroup participants included the process owner, several role representatives, a software developer, a member of top management (vice CIO), a process change consultant (external), and a process modeller (external). Each workgroup consisted of approximately ten members. A large number of the employees thus participated actively in designing and implementing ITIL processes, resulting in local ownership.

A Standard but Flexible Methodology for Process Change

The process change effort was organized and supported by a comprehensive methodology provided by the external consultant. The methodology includes a method, a modelling notation and a modelling tool. The method consists of five distinct phases and templates for all deliverables, such as project mandate, "as is" description, process description, implementation plan, and requirement document. The methodology helped projects organize project activities and stay focused on present tasks.

Deliverables Were Produced Only at Group Meetings

One aspect that was frequently emphasized when the ITIL project was discussed and assessed was the fact that the process change method stated that all deliverables (documents and workflow models) should be produced at workshops only. Project members found it very advantageous that each workgroup member was involved in producing documents and models. No work on deliverables was done between meetings. The department found that this approach gave project members a unique sense of ownership of project results ("This is our achievement.") and made them more eager to implement the new designed process than is common with traditional consultant reports.

Short Timeline

The last success factor that was expressed was that projects had managed to keep a short timeline. The period from start-up to implementation was tight. The project for Service Desk and Incident Management had its first project meeting at the end of January, and made its implementation in April. The timeframe for the Change Management project was comparable, with start-up in late September and implementation in December. As a result, projects and line organization managed to stay focused, and project leaders managed to keep employees engaged.

An Assessment After Two Years

In autumn 2006, the organizational and technical implementations for the two ITIL processes were assessed. The assessments were carried out by interviewing process owners and stakeholders, reviewing process documentation and studying technical solutions. The existing state of each process was described and analyzed in relation to ITIL's reference processes. For each process,

improvements were identified, documented and presented for IT management.

Incident Management

The objective of introducing an incident management process was to improve the service level for user support, and to introduce a filter between the user and the individual IT professional in order to manage personnel resources better. From a management perspective, implementing an incident management process has been a success. Users now know who to contact when an incident occurs and response times are reduced. IT experts are protected from being interrupted by user calls, and it is easier to control personnel resources and delegate tasks. This change is also appreciated by the IT experts: "Earlier users contacted me directly. That could sometimes be very frustrating, so it's good for us that 1.line support now handles users while we can concentrate on our own tasks." However, the assessment revealed that many users are still contacting second- and third-line IT experts directly, bypassing first line, often leading to incidents not being registered.

The Service Desk and the Incident Management process are also appreciated by the users. From a gentle start with between 10 to 20 incidents reported per day, between 120 and 145 incidents are now received every day. A user satisfaction survey held two years after implementation shows more than 80% of the respondents reporting the standard service level as described in the department's Service Declaration as being satisfied "every time" or "nearly every time" they report an incident. However, compared to best practice solutions presented in ITIL in relation to system support there are still no direct interfaces between incidents, problems, releases and changes. Further, there is no support for relating an incident to a specific configuration item, only an optional free-text-field is provided.

Change Management

The objective of introducing a change management process was to track all changes and assess potential consequences of implementing a certain change. In the 22-month period from process implementation until this assessment, 2317 requests for change (RFC) have been registered: 60% standard, 36% normal, and 4% urgent. The high share of standard changes indicates that in the majority of cases (60%), IT experts implement changes without attaining approval from their superiors, and without having their changes being coordinated with other changes in the process. This is outside the fundamental perspective of ITIL. For standard changes the workflow is rather short. The change is registered and implemented, all within one role. Statistics show further that the spread between department sections and groups is uneven. While nearly 30% of all RCFs are being raised by the group responsible for servers (Unix and Windows), the network group on the other hand has only raised 3% of all RFCs during the same period. This difference cannot be explained by employee counts and responsibilities alone. In addition, only 50% of all employees have initiated changes. The process owner's comment on these variations was that some groups and individuals are implementing changes in the configuration without raising a request for change (RFC) even though this is mandatory. Departmental policies are not being followed by all. Another organizational finding is that very few RFCs are escalated to IT management meetings (Change Advisory Board). This can be seen as a consequence of the prevailing culture as described by a member of management; the IT professionals prefer managing the operation themselves without interference from senior management. A finding related to system use is that many changes are being registered (RFC) without explaining the reason why the change has to be implemented. No rules for documentation are defined, and as a consequence, many RFCs are not well documented.

Compared to best practice solutions presented in ITIL in relation to system support, there are no direct connections between incidents, problems, releases, and changes. Still, only a small part of all existing Configuration Items are defined in the CMDB, and few relations between Configuration Items are defined.

Cultural Change

Apart from providing training in ITIL and process thinking, the IT department did not focus explicitly on organizational culture as a factor for supporting or hindering change, or culture as an organizational attribute which they sought to preserve or deliberately alter accordingly. The ITIL initiative was first and foremost seen as changing organizational processes and practice. In ITIL, the authors acknowledge organizational culture and express that "implementing Service Management also affects the culture of the organization. In fact, culture is at the heart of the matter – a key issue – in implementing Service Management" (OGC, 2002, chapter 5.4.1).

A study of organizational culture and cultural change was included in our research. We utilized Cameron and Quins's (2006) "Opposing Values" framework and their organization culture assessment instrument (OCAI). According to Cameron and Quinn, every organization exists in a tension between four distinct organizational types: *clan*, which is typified as a friendly place to work; *adhocracy*, which is characterized as a dynamic, entrepreneurial, and creative workplace; *market*, which is a external- and result-oriented workplace; and *hierarchy*, which is characterized as a formalized and structured place where rules and policies govern what people do. Cameron and Quinn argue that organizations will have, to a varied degree, characteristics from all four types, and the OCAI instrument makes it possible to identify which organizational type an organization belongs to. We did two surveys, one focusing on the cultural status prior to the ITIL initiative, and one survey a year after the implementation of the Change Management process. We carefully selected respondents from the staff that had not been involved directly in the ITIL projects in order to avoid respondents being biased and ended up with 11 respondents participating in each survey. Although this is a small population, and the results must be interpreted bearing this in mind, our findings are interesting. By comparing the results of the first survey with those from the last, we found that the organizational culture in the IT department had moved slightly towards the market type and away from the hierarchy. The format of this chapter excludes us from discussing this in detail. However, we interpret this as a change that could be expected. First, IT Service Management holds a dominant perspective of external (customer and user) focus on IT services. The shift in culture may be a consequence of the ITIL training provided and process change efforts where ITIL best practice has been utilized. In addition, involving a large number of the employees in the Incident Management and Service Desk projects, raising the external focus of the department as a whole could be expected. The most interesting and attractive side of this finding is the fact that this change has not been deliberately stated as a goal by the IT department; the change has come as an implicit consequence of the ITIL project.

CONCLUSION

IT Service Management and IT Infrastructure Library have been recognized by industry as well suited instruments for leveraging the professional standards of IT operations. ITIL holds a process-oriented perspective and organizations implementing ITIL must commence a process change project. Despite the huge interest in ITSM and ITIL in industry, few academic texts are available analysing the practices and effects of undertaking these principles. Based on a longitudinal case study, this chapter provides insight into how IT

departments may approach an ITIL-based process change initiative and what affects such an initiative may have on organizational practices.

This study illustrates several aspects in relation to ITIL usage. First, the ITIL process reference model may for some processes be utilized almost as a blueprint and with good results. Incident Management is an example of this. The IT department has, apart from some more minor and technical details, implemented Incident Management more or less in accordance with the description found in ITIL. Second, the example of Change Management demonstrates how ITIL also is being profoundly adapted to suit the context and the needs of the implementer. The IT department chose to design and implement a workflow for handling changes that to a large extent is different from that of ITIL. Third, open source issue tracking software with modest standard ITIL-functionality may be utilized with good results, but may also hinder a full and integrated ITIL process solution. Developing computer screens with essential ITIL-functionality appeared to be a straightforward effort. However, the possibility of connecting the different processes and enabling CMDB support is limited. Fourth, the social side of process change and standardisation must be emphasized. As this case study illustrates, employees may decide not to follow the adopted processes. In the Incident Management case, users still continue contacting IT experts directly thus bypassing the Service Desk and the process. IT experts on their side find it difficult to reject such direct requests from users, and thus contribute to undermining the process. As the Change Management case exemplifies, some employees may not freely adapt themselves to the procedures and rules that a standard process implies. They are continuing to implement changes without registering RFCs and notifying others. For organizations with employees not used to formal workflows, roles and rules, standardizing work practices may be an enduring effort involving a considerable amount of management attention.

This research has provided more knowledge about a popular phenomenon in the IT community. However, more in-depth case studies are needed. The current findings are, of course, highly preliminary. They are based on one case study, and may thus not be generalisable to ITIL initiatives with different motivations and contexts. Further research is needed to replicate and expand on the current findings.

REFERENCES

Aguilar-Savén, R. S. (2004). Business process modelling: Review and framework. *International Journal of Production Economics, 90*(2), 129-149.

Brocke, J., & Thomas, O. (2006). Reference modeling for organizational change: Applying collaborative techniques for business engineering. In *Proceedings of the Twelfth Americas Conference on Information Systems*, Acapulco, Mexico.

Cameron, K. S., & Quinn, R. E. (2006). *Diagnosing and changing organizational culture: Based on the competing values framework.* San Francisco: Jossey-Bass.

Cater-Steel, A., & Tan, W-G. (2005). *Summary of responses to itSMF conference survey.* Retrieved May 15, 2008, from http://www.usq.edu.au/users/caterst/Summary%20respondents_20050930.pdf

Cater-Steel, A., Tan, W-G., & Toleman, M. (2006a). Challenge of adopting multiple process improvement frameworks. *ECIS - European Conference of Information Systems*, Göteborg, Sweden.

Cater-Steel, A., Toleman, M. & Tan, W-G. (2006b). Transforming IT service management – The ITIL impact. In *Proceedings of the 17th Australian Conference on Information Systems*, Adelaide, Australia.

CCTA - Central Computer and Telecommunications Agency (2000). *Service support.* London: The Stationary Office.

Evans, I., & Macfarlane, I. (2001). A dictionary of IT service management. *Terms, acronyms and abbreviations.* Reading, UK: itSMF Ltd.

Hammer, M. (1990). Reengineering work: Don't automate, obliterate. *Harvard Business Review*, July-August, 104-112.

Hammer, M., & Champy, J. (1993). *Reengineering the cooperation: A manifesto for business revolution.* New York: HarperCollins Publishers.

Hammer, M. (2007). The process audit. *Harvard Business Review*, April.

Harmon, P. (2003). *Business process change.* San Francisco: Morgan Kaufman Publishers.

Harrington, H. J. (1991). Business process improvement. *The breakthrough strategy for total quality, productivity, and competitiveness.* New York: McGraw-Hill Inc.

Iden, J. (2005). Prosessutvikling. Håndbok i modellering og analyse av prosesser (*Process change. Handbook in process modelling and analysis*). Trondheim, Norway: Tapir akademisk forlag. In Norwegian.

Kettinger, W. J., Teng, J. T. C., & Guha, S. (1997). Business process change: A study of methodologies, techniques, and tools. *Management Information Systems Quarterly, 21*(1), 55-80.

Lloyd, V., Rudd, C., & Littlewood, C. (2003). *Planning to implement service management.* Reading, UK: itSMF Ltd.

Misic, V. B., & Zhao, J. L. (2000). Evaluating the quality of reference models. In *Proceedings of the 19th International Conference on Conceptual Modeling*, Salt Lake City, Utah.

Oakland, J. (2000). Total quality management. *Text with cases.* Oxford, UK: Butterworth Heinemann.

OGC - Office of Government Commerce (2001). *Service delivery*. London: The Stationary Office.

OGC - Office of Government Commerce (2002). *Planning to implement service management* (CD version). London: The Stationary Office.

OGC - Office of Government Commerce (2005). *Introduction to ITIL*. London: The Stationary Office.

Palmer, R. (2005). *IT service management foundations: ITIL study guide*. Corinth, TX: Gulf Stream Press.

Shen, H., Wall, B., Zaremba, M., Chen, Y., & Browne, J. (2004). Integration of business modelling methods for enterprise information system analysis and user requirements gathering. *Computers in Industry, 54*, 307-323.

Taylor, C., & Sedera, W. (2003). Defining the quality business reference models. In Proceedings of the *14th Australian Conference on Information Systems*, Perth, Western Australia.

Chapter XX
A Model for IT Service Strategy

Neil McBride
De Montfort University, UK

ABSTRACT

This chapter describes a suggested model for developing a service strategy within IT services. It considers the context, the organization of IT services which might be appropriate for a service strategy. It discusses the content of an IT service strategy which it suggests should be presented as a portfolio of services. It reviews the process of developing the service strategy, suggesting a set of steps which may lead to the development of appropriate content within the right management structure. The example of hospital information systems is used to illustrate the strategic process. In order to set the scene for the strategic process, the state of information systems strategy research is discussed and set in the context of the developing service management research literature. The term service-centric is used and the difference between service-centric IT management and service-oriented architecture is clarified. A case is made for a migration from an IT strategy based primarily on the development of a portfolio of IT systems to a service-strategy based on the development of a portfolio of business services.

INTRODUCTION

In the last decade there has been a significant shift in many IT departments. IT departments increasingly recognize that IT within an organization is a service which, like other services within organizations, aims to deliver value to the organization through the way that it supports the activities of the business. This has led to an in-creasing emphasis on the delivery of IT operations as a service which not only involves the building and delivery of the software and hardware, but also the execution of a wide range of activities around the technology.

The influences that have led to the realignment of IT as a service are complex. Economies, particularly in the West, are changing from a goods base to a service base (Rai & Sambamurthy, 2006).

In terms of business models, many companies are repositioning themselves as service organizations. The technological products, which were previously the focus, become part of a larger service. The Volvo lorry is part of a logistics service and is seen in that context (Edvardsson, Gustafsson, Johnson & Sanden, 2000). A technological product is seen as a service waiting to happen. In addition to the manufactured goods being set in a service context, they are also surrounded by support services involving maintenance, replacement, and training.

In IT departments, the rise of outsourcing, the move from making software internally to buying it and the recasting of IT as a commodity has further aroused a service mindset. The service focus of these changes has particularly been around quality. In delivering services and IT products to clients, outsourcers had to work on the definition of what the service was that was being contracted by the client, how it could be measured and how it could be judged as being up to a mutually acceptable standard. Hence, outsourcing led not only to a focus on contracts, but to the development of service level agreements and to attention to the expectations and perceptions of the customer. It was not just the technology that mattered—its reliability, availability and security—but the customer-focused services around it. IT outsourcers were no longer judged by the number of bugs in their software and its usability, but by the empathy, adaptability, and competence of their staff. In IT, quality became a much more complex subject.

A third influence on IT departments has been ITIL which emerged in the 1980's as a UK government response to the need to increase the efficiency and effectiveness of IT in the public sector. ITIL was taken up by many companies during the 1990's and became the standard approach to running IT service operations. However, until the release of ITIL3 in 2007, the focus of ITIL was in service operations, and particularly in the support of information system applications.

Strategy was not effectively addressed. This recent recognition in ITIL of the importance of IT as a service function and of the need for a service strategy has been recognized for some time in industry in IS management, and expressed in a central concern for alignment: alignment of strategy, alignment of operations, and alignment of culture. In ITIL3, the Service Strategy text (Iqbal & Nieves, 2007) recognizes that the purpose of IT, like any service organization, is to provide value to the customer. The service must ensure that the customer can use her assets effectively to achieve business outcomes which are produced by business processes. This suggests a massive shift away from IT as technical support to IT as a service organization delivering business value to its customers.

However, even ITIL3 is weak on the processes by which a service strategy is developed. This chapter proposes a set of steps that may be undertaken in developing a service strategy and develops an IT governance approach that complements the organizational structures suggested in ITIL3. It also draws from the management literature to suggest service strategy techniques.

BACKGROUND

The development of the field of services marketing from the late 1980s onwards provided a new set of concepts which could be used in the academic development of IT as a service discipline. An initial focus of service marketing was around the intangible nature of services (Brown, Fisk & Bitner, 1994; Bitner & Brown, 2006). A definition of the characteristics of a service remains of great significance to IT practice because of the contrast that can be drawn with a manufactured product. Although it should be recognized that the definition of a "product" in marketing is wide ranging, since a product can involve a service as part of its makeup—financial products are a good example, for the IT practitioner, the idea that IT can be portrayed as service can come as somewhat of a shock. For the IT professional, whose interest and training has focused on the technology and its construction, the idea that the IT system is subservient to the information delivery service it provides to customers, may be difficult to take on board.

While the goods vs. service paradigm has more recently been questioned (Lovelock & Gummesson, 2004), a consideration of the concepts provides a strong marker for the types of changes in management and attitude needed in IT services. Services are indeed intangible (Lovelock, Vandermerwe & Lewis, 1996). They cannot be stored. Once a service is consumed – usually at a time and place where the producer and consumer are both present – it cannot be re-used, sold on or demonstrated. Unlike technical artifacts, the customer is an integral part of the service, must be present for the delivery of the services (excepting some electronic services) and takes part in service delivery.

Taking a service-centric view of IT means that the intangible and temporary characteristics of the service have wide-ranging consequences for the delivery of that service. The classification of services as service factories, service shops, mass services, and professional services according to the extent of customer involvement and the diversity of demand (Verma, 2000) has significant effects on IT delivery (Peppard, 2003; Rands, 1992). The extent of customer involvement can be managed and used as a basis for designing the service product.

The diffusion of service thought into the IT department has had significant effects on the management of quality. Service quality is itself ephemeral and difficult to measure. While the quality of the technical product, the IT hardware and software remains of importance, dimensions such as empathy, assurance and reliability come into play. Quality is much more a matter of customer expectation and perception, driven by the quality of service encounters and the

perceptions of moments of truth rather than the internal quality of IT technology as defined in quality manuals. The development and use of SERVQUAL (Berry & Parasuraman, 1991; Parasuraman, Zeithaml & Berry, 1988), has had some influence on IT services and has been well explored in the information systems academic literature (Kang & Bradley, 2002; Pitt, Berthon & Lane, 1998; Pitt, Watson & Kavan, 1995; Yoon & Suh, 2004). Furthermore, DeLone and McLean (2003) in their ten-year review of their information systems success model, describe the need for service quality, as measured by SERVQUAL, as an extension to the model.

SERVICE-CENTRIC IT MANAGEMENT AND SERVICE-ORIENTED ARCHITECTURE

The recognition of the service nature of IT has not only been a concern of IT managers and information systems academics, but has also come to the attention of computer scientists. Spohrer and Riecker (2006), in their introduction to a special service sciences issue of Communications of the ACM, discuss the rise of the service sector and its influence on IT services. In that same issue, Rust and Miu (2006) suggest that it is the rise of the service sector which is driving a computer revolution. In other words they are suggesting a link between IT and Industry cemented by the spread of service concepts.

However, for many IT professionals and computer scientists, "service-oriented" refers to an approach to software architecture in which software agents are loosely coupled to fulfill an application need. Here, customers, or rather customers' computers, request services from providers through a small set of well-defined, universally available interfaces. The service is then the unit of work offered by the service provider; and the customer can find out who can provide that service through a registry of services. The service-oriented architecture is used in the implementation of Web services (Barry, 2003). However, service-oriented architecture is about the design and management of dynamic technical architecture, not the management of people-oriented services.

Some confusion can be caused in IT circles by referring to the process of IT service management, which centres on the provision of service desks and the management of service operations, as service-oriented IT management. "Service-centric" may be a better term because it focuses on the service nature of the IT function. It is important to understand the need for a shift to a service mindset, which sets the technology – even service-oriented architecture – in the context of the people it serves.

The join between service-oriented architecture and service-centric IT management may be found in the glue of the service-level agreement which will define the nature of the service and the quality parameters of the service. Service-oriented architecture then provides a framework for delivering the technical components required as part of the service. IT service managers must then worry about the delivery of the service as a whole.

IT STRATEGY AND IT SERVICE STRATEGY

One field where the changes from techno-centric to service-centric should have a significant effect is in the field of strategic information systems planning. If we look at the academic literature, the underlying perception of strategic information systems planning has been that it is an exercise in defining a portfolio of information systems to be developed or procured which will contribute to the organization's competitive strategy (Earl, 1989; Elliot & Melhuish, 1995; Fidler & Rogerson, 1996; Hackney & Little 1999; Ward & Peppard, 2005).

The focus of such academic strategic exercises has moved away from competitive advantage towards a model using the resource-based view of the firm (Gordon, Lee & Lucas, 2005; Mata, Fuerst & Barney, 1995; Ward and Peppard, 2004). However, those models that are found in the literature take a techno-centric view of IT. Their concern is to identify a set of system requirements that can then become systems development or procurement projects. Their goal is to align the outputs, the strategy, and the development of IT with the whole business.

In organizations where information system planning occurs, the concern is with identifying projects that can be implemented (Earl, 1993). However, the view taken of projects may be more service-centric in industry. The role of the Chief Information Officer, ultimately responsible for information systems planning, may be more as a deliverer of cost-effective services. But there is a paradox here. This industrial shift from a focus on a technology portfolio to a focus on a service portfolio, with the accompanying development of a service-centric mindset, may be achieved at the cost of any role for IT management in driving business strategy (Teubner, 2007).

Indeed, there is a wide gap between academic discussion of strategic information systems planning and industrial practice. Industrial practice puts IT in a much more realistic context as a service provider, supporting the information and business processes of the organization.

Its role is then more behind the business than in front. IT strategic concerns differ significantly in academic studies as compared to business practice (Teubner, 2007).

Additionally to the academic-practitioner gap, there is a gap between the service-centric focus newly found in IT departments and the competitive, business strategy focus of the organization. An IT service department, following ITIL guidelines, may end up being less strategically focused than a techno-centric IT department.

But even in the context of a service-centric IT department, the services that are supplied are support services, in support of technical artifacts. The role of IT is again too limited. It is, in a sense, hiding behind the technology. Information Technology's service role is then in servicing business processes through the delivery and maintenance of technology. This is still the prevalent philosophy of ITIL v3 where the service disciplines of ITIL version 2 are maintained. The service involves support areas such as managing the availability of technology, managing incidents when technology fails, and providing contingency plans for dealing with any disasters occurring to technical capital.

Hence, even in a service-centric IT department, which is aware of the importance of services and pursuing ITIL best practice, the services offered are still techno-centric. It is still a case of services in the support of technology, rather than technology supporting services.

THE CASE FOR A SERVICE STRATEGY

Where organizations take a service-centric view of IT, adopt ITIL, and pursue ISO20000, they run the risk of focusing on the operations and neglecting strategy. The core of ITIL is about the efficient running of service processes, not the evolving of service portfolios to meet changing business needs. The focus remains on the smooth running of the technology.

Services designed within IT services are often support services for organizational customers, e.g. a service to support desktops, or a service to procure and support ERP. They are not business services. A business process or business unit may require a service from IT services. That service will involve infrastructure (system hardware, systems software, DBMS, networks) and applications. The business functionality and requirements will be decided, teams appointed, suppliers appointed and the service delivered. The model in ITIL3 Service Design (Lloyd & Rudd, 2007), still suggests focus on the IT systems to support the system. Requirements engineering is about the functional requirements; the design outputs are essentially the classic systems development outputs—forms, user interface, object model, use cases, and process models.

IT governance may be designed around the technology or around business groups (Sambamurthy & Zmud, 1999). Departments may be grouped around technical expertise—desktops, networking, Unix, for example, or by business grouping—sales, product development, marketing, manufacture, for example. However, IT governance is implemented, and however frequently it oscillates between different organizational structures, it can remain focused on the IT artifact.

What is required is an approach to IT service strategy and IT governance which puts the IT artifact back in place as only part of a business service or process. Such an approach should consider the whole service of which the IT artifact is only a part. It should involve the design of the whole service and the whole business process. The service-centric view should permeate the whole strategic process.

The following outlines a service-centric model for IT service strategy. The context is the IT governance model which structures the IT department around business services. The content is the output of the strategic exercise which is seen as a set of services to be designed, implemented and operated. The processes are a putative set of steps and modeling tools by which that output is obtained.

THE SERVICE STRATEGY MODEL

Context: Organizing IT around the Businesses Customer Facing Services

A service-centric model seeks to divide the IT infrastructure into service teams that support the services provided by the organization. Each team provides the information and system needs of a particular service element, business process or business function. A service-focused IT infrastructure then directs the attention of IT staff outwards to the organizations' services and customers and away from a notion of the primacy of the IT.

The service team may operate within a service unit. That service unit would be driven by defined service contracts and measurables. How the service is delivered would be up to the team. For example, the team would make decisions as to whether to meet the service need by tweaking an existing computer system, buying or building. Also the team would decide when to retire an existing computer system. The delivery of the service to the organizational service area or business unit should continue without the service customers needing to get involved with implementation of a new system and without them having to organize their activities according to an IT agenda. Thus the service team retains some autonomy concerning the delivery of the service. The IT service strategy then defines the nature of the service to be delivered, its scope and quality.

There are several key points to note in this model. Firstly, the focus of the service unit is on a business process. Whether that is loan processing, pharmaceutical sales, or patient administration, the process being supported is not an IT process. Secondly, the service unit team will need to be an integration of IT experts and business experts, all focused on the business needs. IT is subservient to, and only part of the business focus. Thirdly, it should be noted that the service is not just an in-frastructure service. Services such as application maintenance, information security, and document management and disaster recovery may be part of the service unit, but they are all subservient to the business process.

Take a hospital as an example. In a hospital, a separate IT department delivers the IT requirements of the whole hospital. The department may concentrate on the large IT developments as the expense of smaller services, departmental and specialty needs. In a service oriented IT organization, there is no visible IT department. Technical expertise is grouped around business structures. An outline service-based structure for a hospital may be envisaged as illustrated in Figure 1.

Here, service teams support bounded areas of hospital services and processes. IT is an important part of each service team, and may be the primary focus of effort, but each service team has service outcome goals to meet, not technology delivery goals. At the top level, these might be:

- **Patient administration:** Provision of integrated information flows to support the entire patient experience from outpatients, through inpatients stay and operations to discharge, including connections with primary care and other organizations.
- **Results:** The results services provides information support and information systems support for the requests for diagnostic procedures including pathology, x-ray and other procedures, and the delivery of the results of those procedures inside the hospital and to requestors outside the hospital.
- **Clinical governance:** Provision of information to enable effective clinical practice, including provision of systems and services to enable evidence-based medicine, the development of integrated care pathways and the development of information databases to enable effective clinical audit. Clinical governance at a primary care group level will also be supported where it interfaces with the hospital.

Figure 1. Service-centric IT management structure for a hospital trust

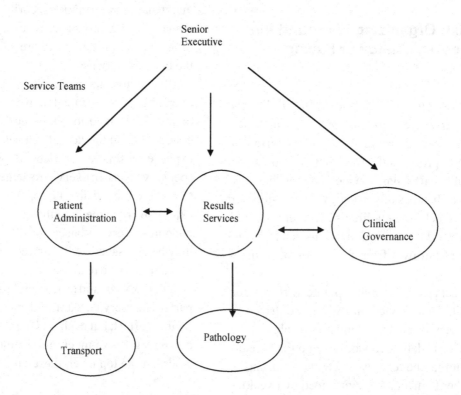

These service teams may interact with more departmentally based service teams in for example, transport and pathology. Smaller service teams supporting specialist service requirements within particular specialties (for example, intensive care and Magnetic Resonance Imaging) might be formed as subteams within the patient administration or clinical governance service teams. However, note that each service unit is defined in terms of the service it delivers to meet the needs of its customer base, not in terms of the technology it supports or provides. If we replace the development of information technology strategy, with its emphasis on boxes and their technical implementation, with the development of service strategy with its emphasis on the delivery of services which make business processes work, which achieve business outcomes, we are freed up in two ways. We can consider business processes and their delivery without being constrained or slowed down by considerations of IT implementa-

tion, and we can be freer with our consideration of IT requirements for a business process because the technology requirements have not been fixed in an IT strategy, but can be changed and adapted as required.

The effect of such an IT service structure may be to:

- Generate a service culture;
- Move the IT interface right next to the appropriate hospital services;
- Enable faster support for changes in services or processes;
- Generate greater understanding of the IT within the service area and
- Generate greater responsiveness from the technologists.

It should be noted that the skills set within the service teams would need to extend beyond the IT to the organizational services. A Patient

Administration Service team would need to understand the processes in outpatient clinics, medical records, ward-based services and theatre. Practitioners from these areas would be part of the team; defining services and working on the delivery of these services in concert with IT-Skilled staff who would quickly gain business and service understanding within the area. These teams may be managed by organizational service-centric staff. For example, clinical governance may be managed by a clinician.

While ideally the business and technical skills should be encapsulated within the service team, which is able to develop the service set and apply IT understanding to deliver it, we recognize that, in large organizations, economies of scale may demand that some of the IT elements are delivered by technical teams. For example, IT networking may be delivered by a networking team whose customers are the various service teams. Such technical elements may be outsourced.

However, an overall service philosophy can be used. In a service-centric IT infrastructure, business services are supported by IT services which draw on applications, training, and information resources to deliver a holistic service which meets the service needs for information and does not just focus on technology. This contrasts with a traditional model in which a computer application is built for the business and IT services support the computer application (Figure 2)

Content: IT Service Strategy as a Portfolio of Services

The content of an IT Service strategy focuses on the nature of the services to be delivered by the service teams within the IT management infrastructure and not on the computer systems and technology.

The content of the strategy will consist of a series of service definitions together with explanations of the philosophy behind each service and the strategy for service-delivery. At a greater level of detail, the IT service strategy would define the service level agreements and the level and type of service the internal customer might expect.

It may be appropriate for the strategy to define the resources required to deliver that service in terms of computer systems and applications, networking, staff training, IT staff and so on. The risk here is that the definition of the technology within what is a service strategy, moves the focus right back to the technology. However, it may be more effective to leave that level of implementation strategy to the service teams and restrict the IT service strategy to a definition of services, service content and SLA which the service teams will have to adhere to. Such a focus on services reduces the risk of the strategist's attention being deflected by the technology needs and hence the technology actually driving the service definitions.

The contents of an IT Service Strategy may include:

- Definition and description of business/customer services provided by the organization;
- Definition of the service teams and mapping of service teams to business services or business units;
- Description of mission and scope of each service team, including definition of strategy and philosophy behind the service;
- Definition of services provided by each team presented as a service catalogue;
- Description of service including a diagram of the service processes, delineating service team, activities, customer activities and the interaction between the two;
- Definition of one or more SLAs associated with that service;
- Constraints on service;
- Information provision associated with that service;
- Summary of resource requirements focused on enabling costing and pricing of the service;

Figure 2. Changing from IT application focus to information service focus

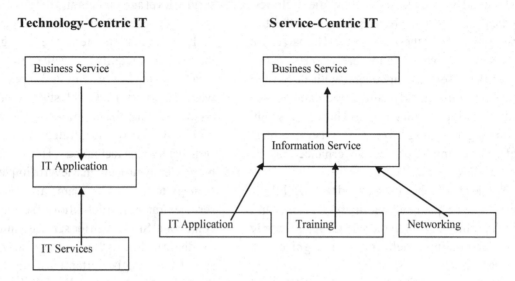

- Definition of quality measures associated with each service and description of process by which quality will be monitored, particularly including a definition of the outcomes expected from the service and the measures associated with those outcomes;
- Management policies associated with the service;
- Definition of any generic services which may be provided on behalf of the service teams, either centrally or outsourced. Examples may include installation and maintenance of physical IT infrastructure and servicing of PCs.

The IT service strategy provides a blueprint for the development of IT services within each service group. The level of detail for the definition of each service may vary. In some cases it may be appropriate for the service team to negotiate the SLAs with the business services it supports. Also, depending on the maturity of the service area, significant service innovation and design may be required.

Process: Developing an IT Service Strategy

The process of developing the service strategy may be tackled in a number of ways. A top-down/bottom-up approach may be considered, as has been used in Method/1 (Earl, 1989; Lederer & Gardiner, 1992). Alternatively, a more evolutionary approach may be considered. Regardless of the process model, a number of tasks must be tackled. Suggested tasks in the development of an IT Service Strategy follow:

Definition of business services. An understanding of what the organization does and the structure of its services must be gained since this will be required for mapping IT services and service teams to business services. If we take a purist service view, then where a company provides products we need to consider the customer service that the product is part of. This may generate ideas for new business services which will require IT services. The definition of services that are provided by the business should be split down enough to generate service support requests (i.e., definitions of what IT services are needed to make that service work or to underpin the service.).

The definition of business services will require a detailed understanding of the customer and her business processes. Iqbal and Nieves (2007) see this step as driven by a marketing exercise. Customer outcomes are analysed and a service catalogue defined to match them. Such an approach may be weighted toward type 3 services which are outsourced. Here the outsourcing company is trying to develop services – usually IT services—which will attract customers in a competitive market. In type 1, insourced IT services, an emphasis on the business processes of the host company may be more appropriate.

Definition of Service Teams. The analysis of the business's services will lead to the construction of a IT management structure consisting of a series of service teams which map to the business services.

Definition of service strategy. For each service team a service strategy should be developed. Competitive analysis and an analysis of organizational effectiveness may be carried out at this stage. While traditional management tools such as five forces and value chain can be used in determining the strategy (Botton & McManus, 1999), we would recommend the use of activity-system maps (Porter, 1996) An activity-system map enables the principle philosophy of the service and the activities which will be used to implement that philosophy to be defined (Edvardsson et al., 2000). Figure 3 illustrates an outline activity-system map for the clinical governance service team. Note that the strategy exercise is driven by the service needs of the business, taking a service view of both the organization and the information systems within it.

Definition of services. Exact service provision should be defined for each service team. Draft SLAs should be developed based on the business needs. Information needs should be explored and an initial set of services defined. Definition of services may also involve service innovation. It is in this step that technology innovation should be considered as a basis of new services. Services should be defined at a high level. Detailed service design may not take place until an understanding of current IT services is carried out and a gap analysis done.

Analysis of current IT services. Current IT in the organization may be product-oriented. The IT needs to be considered as a portfolio of services, so an understanding of how IT can currently be represented as services will be needed.

Gap analysis. Gaps between current IT services and the services required within the service teams will need to be analysed. The IT services will be mapped to the service teams. It is at this point that consideration of which IT service elements should be delegated to the service teams and which might be provided as a generic service may be considered. For example, while network administration may be offered as a centralized, generic service, all application development, application support, systems procurement, user training, and system evolution should be allocated to service teams. It should be a policy to minimize generic services since these can only be provided at a distance from the business services. We would suggest that the proliferation of generic IT services may only serve to widen the IT/ business service gap and reduce business effective and service focus.

IT business integration. Once the service gaps are understood plans can be developed for the integration of IT services and the business. How each service team is going to obtain its IT resources and take over appropriate applications should be considered.

Definition of SLAs. At this point there should be sufficient information and understanding of the services to generate detailed SLAs. These will involve negotiation between members or potential members of service teams and the business service areas.

Implementation. Detailed SLAs provide the core of the strategy. At this point a detailed IT service strategy can be written up and the focus moves to service team discussion of how the SLAs

Figure 3. Outline activity-system map for clinical governance service team

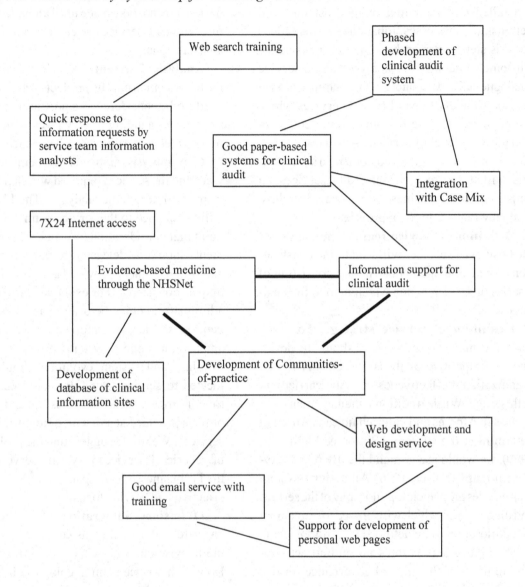

are to be fulfilled. Guidelines for implementation may form part of the written IT services strategy, but detailed implementation should, we suggest, be left to the service teams to encourage ownership and a close fit with the business services.

The IT service strategy development process needs to be conducted in a flexible manner. Since the strategy definition is a service in itself, the project team must contain a significant number of active representatives from the business service areas. Service innovation cannot be done without close involvement of internal customers. In plan-

ning the strategy development process, internal customer involvement must be defined.

CONCLUSION

It is widely recognized that there is a need for the integration of IT service elements with the business services. This process of alignment has become a major concern for IT departments. Alignment of IT services with the business it serves involves an engagement with the purpose and strategy of the business. The chief information officer cannot retreat into service support, while changing from a focus on the artifact and the technology to a focus on the service and the people. The strategic view must not become myopic. There must be continued effort to contribute strategically to the business.

Furthermore, the academic/practitioner gap must be bridged. Practitioners see strategy in terms of pursuing themes and investigating new technologies. Academics see strategy as using resources strategically to deliver competitive advantage. Both views are important and should be integrated.

While many writers have addressed the issue of IT services—for example, Applegate, Austin, and McFarlan (2003) see the managing of IT operations, the provision of reliable and secure IT services, and the management of diverse IT infrastructure as integral to corporate information strategy—the attention to service concepts is limited. There is a tendency to become techno-centric in both service strategy and service design.

At the core of this chapter is the idea that everything is a service. Even the most technical product is only of value when it is used in a service. The car is an element of a transport service. The computer is a part of an information service.

This chapter involves a call for a service first, technology second philosophy. Technology supports service. It is designed in the context of the service. Therefore at both a strategy and design level, the main concern of the IT service department should be in the developing of the service into which supporting technology is fitted.

Hence, the strategic exercise should be about the definition of services to be provided by the IT department. And those services should be business process services, centred on the services that the organization provides to its customers. Then the focus of IT is on its service catalogue, the list of what services it provides to its customers. This is of importance to its customers. For example, the service the customer gets in managing patient administration or the service the customer gets in managing materials planning is at the centre of the strategic exercise.

The information system tools used to deliver those services are of little interest to the customer, provided they support the service adequately. The technology used as platforms for those services—the relational database, the network system, the servers—and how the technology is implemented is not only of no interest to the customer but is more a positive hindrance to the customer's goals.

IT within organizations is becoming pervasive. The use of computers is a natural part of most business roles. The computer control of business environments, processes and activities is a given. But computers are not only becoming pervasive in organizations, they are disappearing. Eventually IT will become so embedded in the environment that the use of the technology will become as natural as breathing. In such an environment, technical issues are not a concern of the user who is only aware of a service, of the business processes that are being supported.

In such an environment, IT is seen by the customer as being responsible for the processes. The service is seen as business processes delivered to enable the internal customer to earn revenue for the business in some way. The technology behind those processes is invisible to the customer. It is a black box, a taken-for-granted. Issues concerning breakdowns of technology are invisible to the user: dealt with by IT without disturbing the customer. It is assumed that IT takes the best technical decisions concerning the technical support of processes and the provision of the invisible infrastructure, the invisible computers. There is no need for the customer to talk about the technology or even consider it. The customer comes to IT to talk about services, the request new services, to consider changes in existing services.

In terms of strategy, the IT department delivers those services; so the strategic exercise is about services. This chapter has provided one possible framework for developing that service strategy.

REFERENCES

Applegate, L. M., Austin, R .D., & McFarlan, F. W. (2003). *Corporate information strategy and management*. New York: McGraw-Hill.

Barry, D. K. (2003). *Web services and service-oriented architecture—The savvy manager's guide*. Morgan Kaufmann.

Berry, L. L., & Parasuraman, A. (1991). *Marketing services: Competing through quality*. New York: Free Press.

Bitner, M. J., & Brown, S. (2006). The evolution and discovery of service sciences in business schools. *Communications of the ACM, 49*(7), 73-78.

Botton, N., & McManus, N. (1999). *Competitive strategies for service organisations* Macmillan.

Brown, S. W., Fisk, R. P., & Bitner, M. J. (1994). The development and emergence of service marketing thought. *International Journal of Service Industry Management, 5*(1), 21-48.

De Lone, W., & McLean, E. (2003). The DeLone and McLean model of information systems success: A ten-year update. *Journal of Management Information Systems, 19*(4), 9-30.

Earl, M. J. (1989). *Management strategies for information technology*. Prentice Hall.

Earl, M. J. (1993). Experiences in strategic information systems planning. *MIS Quarterly, 17*(1), 1-24.

Edvardsson, B., Gustafsson, A., Johnson, M. D., & Sanden, B. (2000). *New service development and innovation in the new economy*. Studentlittereatur Sweden.

Elliot, S., & Melhuish, P. (1995). A methodology for the evaluation of IT for strategic implementation. *Journal of Information Technology, 10*, 87-100.

Fidler, C. & Rogerson, S. (1996). *Strategic management support systems*. Pitman.

Gordon, J. R. M., Lee, P-M., & Lucas, H. C. (2005). A resource-based view of competitive advantage at the Port of Singapore. *Journal of Strategic Information Systems, 14*, 69-86.

Hackney, R., & Little, S. (1999). Opportunistic strategy formulation for IS/IT planning. *European Journal of Information Systems, 8*, 119-126.

Iqbal, M. & Nieves, M. (2007). *ITIL service strategy*. Norwich: The Stationary Office.

Kang, H., & Bradley, G. (2002). Measuring the performance of IT services—An assessment of SERVQUAL. *International Journal of Accounting Information Systems, 3*(3), 151-164.

Lederer, A. L., & Gardiner, V. (1992). The process of strategic information planning. *Journal of Strategic Information Systems, 1*, 76-83.

Lloyd, V., & Rudd, C. (2007). *ITIL service design*. Norwich: The Stationary Office.

Lovelock, C., Vandermerwe, S., & Lewis, B. (1996). *Services marketing: A European perspective*. Essex: Prentice Hall.

Lovelock, C. F., & Gummesson, E. (2004). Whither services marketing? In search of a new paradigm and fresh perspectives. *Journal of Service Research, 7*(1), 20-41.

Mata, F. J., Fuerst, W., & Barney, J. B. (1995). Information technology and sustained competitive advantage: a resource-based view. *MIS Quarterly*, 487-505.

Parasuraman, A., Zeithaml, V. A., & Berry, L L. (1988). SERVQUAL: A multiple item scale for measuring consumer perceptions of service quality. *Journal of Retailing, 64*, 12-40.

Peppard, J. (2003). Managing IT as a portfolio of services. *European Management Journal, 21*(4), 467-483.

Peppard, J., & Ward, J. (2004). Beyond strategic information systems: Towards an IS capability. *Journal of Strategic Information Systems, 13,* 167-194.

Pitt, L. F., Watson, R. T., & Kavan, C. B. (1995). Service quality: A measure of information systems effectiveness. *MIS Quarterly,* 173-185.

Pitt L. F., Berthon, B., & Lane, N. (1998). Gaps within the IS department: Barriers to service quality. *Journal of Information Technology, 13,* 191-200.

Porter, M. (1996). What is strategy? *Harvard Business Review*, November, 61 - 78.

Rai, A. & Sambamurthy, V. (2006). Editorial notes—The growth of interest in services management: Opportunities for information systems scholars. *Information Systems Research, 17*(4), 327-331.

Rands, T. (1992). Information technology as a service operation. *Journal of Information Technology, 7,* 189-201.

Rust, R., & Miu, C. (2006). What academic research tells us about service. *Communications of the ACM, 49*(7), 49-54.

Sambamurthy, V., & Zmud, R. W. (1999). Arrangements for information technology governance: A theory of multiple contingencies. *MIS Quarterly, 23*(June), 261-290.

Sphorer, J., & Rieken, D. (2006). Introduction to special issue on service sciences *Communications of the ACM, 49*(7), 30-32.

Teubner, R. A. (2007). Strategic information systems planning: A case study from the financial services industry. *Journal of Strategic Information Systems, 16,* 105-125.

Verma, R. (2000). An empirical analysis of management challenges in service factories, service shops, mass services and professional services. *International Journal of Service Industry Management, 11*(1), 8-25.

Ward, J., & Peppard, J. (2005). *Strategic planning for information systems* Chichester: John Wiley.

Yoon, S., & Suh, H. (2004). Ensuring IT consulting, SERVQUAL and user satisfaction: A modified measuring tool. *Information Systems Frontiers, 6*(4), 341-351.

Chapter XXI
An Overview of Models and Standards of Processes in the SE, SwE, and IS Disciplines

Manuel Mora
Autonomous University of Aguascalientes, Mexico

Ovsei Gelman
Universidad Nacional Autónoma de México, Mexico

Rory O'Connor
Dublin City University, Ireland

Francisco Alvarez
Autonomous University of Aguascalientes, Mexico

Jorge Macías-Luévano
Autonomous University of Aguascalientes, Mexico

ABSTRACT

This chapter develops a descriptive-conceptual overview of the main models and standards of processes formulated in the systems engineering (SE), software engineering (SwE) and information systems (IS) disciplines. Given the myriad of models and standards reported, the convergence suggested for the SE and SwE models and standards and the increasing complexity of the modern information systems, we argue that these ones become relevant in the information systems discipline. Firstly, we report the rationale for having models and standards of processes in SE, SwE and IS. Secondly, we review their main characteristics. Thirdly, based on the identified aims and principles, we report and posit the concepts of process, system and service as conceptual building blocks for describing such models and standards. Finally, initial theoretical and practical implications for the information systems discipline of such models and standards are discussed, as well as recommendations for further research are suggested.

... in the current marketplace, there are maturity models, standards, methodologies, and guidelines that can help an organization improve the way it does business. However, most available improvement approaches focus on a specific part of the business and do not take a systemic approach to the problems that most organizations are facing (SEI, 2006, p. 3).

INTRODUCTION

The manufacturing of products and the provision of services in the modern world has increased process engineering (including manufacturing or provision) and process managerial complexity (Boehm & Lane, 2006). The engineering complexity has been raised because of the variety of design, manufacturing or provision process, machines and tools, materials and system-component designs, as well as for the high-quality, cost-efficiency relationships, and value expectations demanded from the competitive worldwide markets. The process managerial complexity has increased because of disparate business internal and external process must be coordinated. To meet the time to market, competitive prices, market sharing, distribution scope and environmental and ethical organizational objectives, among others financial and strategic organizational objectives contribute to increased organizational pressures and organizational complexity (Farr & Buede, 2003).

Such process engineering and/or managerial complexity is manifested in: (1) the critical failures of enterprises information systems implementa-

tions (CIO UK, 2007; Ewusi, 1997; Standish Group, 2003), (2) the unexpected appearance of large batches of defective products that have had a proved high-quality image for decades, and (3) the increasing of system downtimes and/or low efficiency and effectiveness in critical services such: electricity, nuclear plants, health services and governmental services (Bar-Yam, 2003).

Organizations with global and large-scale operations have fostered the exchange of the best organizational practices (Arnold & Lawson, 2004). The purpose is to improve business processes and avoid critical failures in the manufacturing of products and provision of services. Best practices have been documented (via a deep redesign, analysis, discussion, evaluation, authorization, and updating of organizational activities) through models and/or standards of process by international organizations for the disciplines of systems engineering (SE), software engineering (SwE) and information systems (IS). Some models and standards come from organizations with a global scope, like the International Organization for Standardization (ISO) but others limit their influences in some countries or regions, like the US-based Software Engineering Institute (SEI). Whilst both types of organizations can differ in their geographic scopes, both keep a similar efficacy purpose: to make available a set of generic process (technical, managerial, support and enterprise) that come from the best international practices to correct and improve their organizational process, with the expected outcome being improved quality, value and cost-efficiency issues with respect to the software products and services generated.

However, because of the myriad of models and standards reported in the three disciplines, the convergence suggested for SE and SwE engineering process, models and/or standards (Boehm 2000; Hecht, 1999; ISO, 2006c; ISO, in press; Sommerville, 1998; Thayer, 1997) and the increasing complexity of the modern information systems (Mora et al, 2008), we argue that these models and standards of processes become relevant in the Information Systems discipline. Then, in this chapter we develop a conceptual description (Glass, Armes & Vessey, 2004; Mora, 2004) of the main models and standards of processes formulated in the SE, SwE and IS disciplines with the general purpose to identify aims, purposes, characteristics, and core building-block concepts. Firstly, we report the rationale for having models and standards of processes in such disciplines. Secondly, we review their main characteristics. Thirdly, based in the identified aims and principles, we report and posit the concepts of *process*, *system* and *service* as the conceptual building-blocks for describing such models and standards. Finally, initial theoretical and practical implications for the Information Systems discipline of such models and standards are discussed, as well as recommendations for further research are suggested.

REVIEW ON MODELS AND STANDARDS OF PROCESSES

The Rationale of Models and Standards of Processes

Currently the global and large-scale organizations are faced with the challenge to meet the highest customer's expectations for their products and services, as well as to satisfy their own organizational financial and strategic objectives. To cope with such external and internal complexities, organizations have fostered the utilization (deployment and exchange) of best organizational practices. These global best practices have been documented via

models and standards of processes. According to Succi, Valerio, Vernazza, and Succi (1998, p. 140) *"standardization means that there is an explicit or implicit agreement to do certain things in a defined and uniform way"*.

Whilst the models are considered as *de facto* standards (not a legal mandatory use) and the standards as *de jure* (legal mandatory use when a country or business sector agrees use it), both help the organizations to improve the quality of their internal processes and to align them with international practices. In this way, the organizations foster an efficient and effective international exchange of goods and services. We consider that an insightful understanding of the models and standards concepts is required for their further analysis. The Table 1 (from several sources: Mora, Gelman, O'Connor, Alvarez & Macías, 2007a; Sheard & Lake, 1998; Tantara, 2001; Wright, 1998) shows the main conceptual attributes of the models and standards of process.

The main similarities between models and standards are the following: (1) both provide a map of generic processes from the best international practices; (2) both establish what-alike and must-be instructions rather than how-alike specific procedures, and (3) both do not impose a mandatory life-cycle but suggest a demonstrative one that is usually taken as a starting point. The implementers must complement such recommendations with detailed procedures and profiles of the deliverables. Regarding to the differences: (1) the models (at least the early reported[2]) have been focused on process improvement efforts (and consequently include a capability maturity level assessment such CMMI) while that the standards, on an overall complaint and not complaint general assessment (e.g., ISO, 1995), (2) models are used under an agreement between companies to legitimate their industrial acceptance (e.g., CMMI in the Americas) while that standards are used under a usually obligatory country-based agreement (e.g., ISO, 2003 in Europe and Australia), and (3) the models can be originated from any

Table 1. Models and standards of processes in SE and SwE

FEATURE	MODELS OF PROCESSES	STANDARDS[1] OF PROCESSES
General aim	To provide a set of best and generic management, engineering and organizational practices for performing high-quality processes (e.g., efficiency and effectiveness) related with SE, SwE and IT practices.	
Main purpose	- To improve processes -To measure the capability maturity level of organizational processes	- To define the processes - To measure compliance or not compliance of processes with the normative processes
	- To provide a generic map of processes	
Definition	*"A process model is a structured collection of practices that describe the characteristics of effective processes."* (SEI, 2006)	A set of the state-of-the-art practices and their related vocabulary that provides a model to be strictly followed and fulfilled by organizations in order to be certified in its utilization.
Origin	Any organization with resources (knowledge, time, money)	An industry-approval and/or nation-endorsed is required.
Mandatory utilization	No, but some of them are become in *de facto* standards	No, but these are merged with national or industry-based regulations or are directly adopted for being mandatory (*de jure*)
Life-cycle uniqueness	No, these are open to any life cycle (but usually suggest a generic one)	No, but lifecycle reported as example are taken as the best recommended
What vs How recommendations	Both have been designed to provide only what-alike recommendations on what must be done and produced (activities, tasks and deliverables) rather than on the detailed specifications on how doing these (specific procedures, techniques and profiles of deliverables). However, some could provide how-alike guidelines.	

organization while that the standards are strongly endorsed by nations.

It is worth noting that the first standards were product-oriented (Tripp, 1996) (design and final product attributes, tolerances, specifications) and could be objectively assessed through testing and evaluation of the devices using physical instruments. However, the standards for process convey additional difficulties for automatic assessment. Observations, records, interviews, analysis and questionnaires applied to core people in site are required. Furthermore, for the case of the software as a product/artifact, additional complications emerge. While that the standard ISO 9126:1991 offers an initial solution, their set of attributes still requires a final interpretation on how to measure them. Other sources of complexity are the time and the human resource performance variability in the certification of standards of processes.

It has been reported also the critical roles that are played by the information and communications technologies (ICT) and the systems of informa-

tion systems (SoIS) for supporting practically all business process in worldwide organizations (Mora, Gelman, Frank, Paradice, Cervantes & Forgionne, 2008). This assertion implies that for such organizations, the ICT infrastructure and the SoIS (and IS function), have become an essential resource and macroprocess (e.g., a system of systems of processes) for that the organization operates efficient and effectively. Relevant economic losses from ICT infrastructure downtimes or SoIS failures are present evidences of the high-dependability that worldwide organizations have on the correct availability, capacity, and reliability of such ICT resources and process.

Models and/or standards of processes for engineering and management of ICT and SoIS resources have been also developed. However, such development and deployment have increased the engineering and management complexity per se. To cope holistically with the technical and socio-organizational problems for their efficient and effective engineering and management, this chapter supports the premise[3] that an integrative and holistic approach based in an extended Systems Engineering philosophy and methods (Forsberg & Mooz, 1997; INCOSE, 2004; Sage, 1992, 2000; Sage & Amstrong, 2000) can provide the suitable conceptual lenses and methodological tools to study and cope with the increasing managerial, technical and organizational complexity of the engineering and management (E&M) of ICT and SoIS resources and processes. Overall expected contribution is to increase our understanding and control of such E&M processes.

This chapter then, is motivated by the reasons identified previously by authors (Mora et al., 2007a):

(i) the SE models and standards of processes have been ignored in IT&S or scarcely analyzed in SwE; (ii) the SwE literature has wrongly equaled the concept of software system with the concept of information systems when both constructs are ontologically different (Mora et al., 2003) and consequently relevant organizational issues have been ignored in SwE models and standards of processes; and (iii) the Systems Engineering field and the Systems Approach philosophy has proved to be very successful in large scale projects when it is correctly applied (Barker & Verma, 2003; Honour, 2002).

Furthermore, we have identified also (idem) core facts that become relevant the interaction of SE, SwE, and IT standards and models of processes for the IS discipline:

(i) the recognition that the scope and effects of software systems do not end with its completion but with its successful deployment of the whole (information) system (Boehm, 2000; Sommerville, 1998); (ii) the acceptance of the software engineering process involves also managerial, organizational, economic, sociopolitical, legal and behavioral issues (Fuggetta[4], 2000; Kellner, Curtis, deMarco, Kishida, Schulemberg & Tully,

1991); *(iii) the proposal of the integration of Systems Engineering (SE)[5] with Software Engineering[6] to enhance mutually their engineering and managerial process (Andriole & Freeman, 1993; Bate, 1998; Boehm, 2000, 2006; Deno & Feeney, 2002; Hecht, 1997; Hole, Verma, Jain, Vitale & Popick, 2005; Johnson, 1996; Johnson & Dindo, 1998; Nichols & Connaughton, 2005; Sommerville, 1998; Thayer, 1997, 2002); (iv) the identification that the Information Technology and Systems (IT&S) field, which traditionally has its focus in the management and evaluation of IT-intensive systems, is highly dependent of the engineering activities (Hevner, March, Park & Ram, 2004; Nunamaker, Chen & Purdin, 1991) conducted in SwE and SE, and despite this has generated its own set of models and standards of processes, their conceptual relation with SwE and SE models and standards has been few explored, and (v) the proposal to widen the scope of SE standards of processes to define business process architectures in organizations (Arnold & Lawson, 2004; Farr & Buede, 2003).*

History and Aims of the Main SE, SwE and IS Models of Standards of Processes

A generic aim of the SE, IS and SwE is the definition, development and deployment of large-scale cost-effective and trustworthy integrated systems, system of information systems or software-intensive systems respectively (Sage, 1992, 2000; Sage & Amstrong, 2000; Thayer, 1997). In pursuit of this aim, these disciplines have generated models and standards of processes to guide and control the engineering and managerial activities involved in the creation of such systems. The models and standards provide a set of processes for good (or best) SE, SwE and IS practices, but differs in some items exhibited in Table 1. The Table 2 (derived from Collin, 2004; Garcia, 1998; ISO, 2005; ITGI, 2000; Sheard & Lake, 1998; SEI, 2006; Tantara, 2001; Wright, 1998) shows the history of the main models and standards in SE, SwE, and IS.

Table 2. History of models and standards of processes in SE, SwE, and IT

YEAR	STD/ MOD	ORIGIN	SE	SwE	IS
1987, 2000	Std	TC 176/SC 2/WG 18		ISO 9001:2000 (Standard Base)	
1995, 2002, 2004	Std	JTC 1/ SC7		ISO/IEC 12207	
1999, 2002	Std	EIA	SECM (EIA-731)		
1996, 2002	Std	JTC 1/ SC7	ISO/IEC 15288		
2003, 2004, 2006	Std	JTC 1/ SC7	ISO/IEC 15504		
2004	Std			ISO/IEC 90003:2004	
1995, 2001, 2006	Mod	SEI	CMMI-DEV+IPPD 1.2 (SE,SW,HW)		CMMI-SVC[7] 1.2
1996, 2000, 2006	Std	ISACA			CobIT[8]
2005	Std	JTC 1/ SC7			ISO/IEC 20000[9]
2006	Std	JTC 1/ SC7	ISO/IEC 15289		

The main finding from Table 2 is the lack of models and standards of processes for IS area. Except for the ISO 20000 standard (published in 2006 but based in ITIL v.2.0 model from 1995) and the model CobIT, no significant model or standard of process has been posed[10]. SE and SwE disciplines have developed more standards in the last two decades but both face the challenge of integration toward single standards (e.g., ISO 15289, CMMI for SE and SwE). From the descriptions of the aims of the standards and models of processes in Table 3, we identify two core purposes: (1) the improvement/assessment of processes and (2) the definition/provision of processes.

Mora et al (2007a) report that such standards and models also exhibit a(n):

1. *... rationality to organize the managerial and engineering functions to define, develop and deploy products and services in a generic organization through a process approach;*

2. *... acknowledgement of the increasing inter-relationship between software, hardware and general IT-based products, services and/or systems, [that] has fostered the integration of SwE and SE standards and models to address the needs a whole product, service or system to be engineered;*

3. *... emergence of the service-oriented approach in the future (as the forthcoming CMMI-SVC, and the current ISO20000 standard)*

4. *... implicit need for an interdisciplinary body of knowledge and research related to the management and engineering of process from SE, SwE and IT&S disciplines including BPM;*

5. *... implicit utilization of the Systems Approach to establish the initial foundations such as concepts, principles and philosophy, for the design of standards.*

Table 3. Official description and status of models and standards of processes in SE, SwE and IT

STD/MOD	OFFICIAL DESCRIPTION OF THE STANDARD OR MODEL'S AIM	STATUS
ISO 9001:2000	*"Quality management systems – Requirements: ISO 9001:2000 specifies requirements for a quality management system where an organization needs to demonstrate its ability to consistently provide product that meets customer and applicable regulatory requirements, and aims to enhance customer satisfaction through the effective application of the system, including processes for continual improvement of the system and the assurance of conformity to customer and applicable regulatory requirements. All requirements of this International Standard are generic and are intended to be applicable to all organizations, regardless of type, size and product provided" (ISO, 2006a).*	Code ISO 90.92 (International Standard to be revised)
ISO/IEC 12207	*"Information technology – Software life cycle processes: Establishes a system for software life cycle processes with well-defined terminology. Contains processes, activities and tasks that are to be applied during the acquisition of a system that contains software, a stand-alone software product and software services" (ISO, 1995).*	Code ISO 90.92 (International Standard to be revised)
ISO/IEC 15504-1 to 5	*"Information technology – Process assessment: ... ISO/IEC 15504 (all parts) provides a framework for the assessment of processes. This framework can be used by organizations involved in planning, managing, monitoring, controlling and improving the acquisition, supply, development, operation, evolution and support of products and services" (ISO, 2003).*	Code ISO 60.60 (International Standard published)
ISO/IEC 90003	*"Software engineering -- Guidelines for the application of ISO 9001:2000 to computer software: ... ISO/IEC 90003:2004 provides guidance for organizations in the application of ISO 9001:2000 to the acquisition, supply, development, operation and maintenance of computer software and related support services ... identifies the issues which should be addressed and is independent of the technology, life cycle models, development processes, sequence of activities and organizational structure used by an organization" (ISO, 2004a).*	Code ISO 60.60 (International Standard published)
SECM (EIA/IS 731)	*System Engineering Capability Model: "... describes the essential systems engineering and management tasks that an organization must perform to ensure a successful systems engineering effort" (Minnich, 2002); "... (is) a method for assessing and improving the efficiency and effectiveness of systems engineering" (same core idea shared with SECAM former standard, INCOSE, 1996).*	(International Standard published)
ISO/IEC 15288	*"Systems engineering System life cycle processes: ... this standard encompasses the life cycle of man-made systems, spanning the conception of the ideas through to the retirement of the system. It provides the processes for acquiring and supplying system products and services that are configured from one or more of the following types of system components: hardware, software, and human interfaces. This framework also provides for the assessment and improvement of the project life cycle" (ISO, 2002; Magee, 2006).*	Code ISO 90.92 (International Standard to be revised)
ISO/IEC 15289	*"Systems and software engineering -- Content of systems and software life cycle process information products (Documentation): ... ISO/IEC 15289:2006 was developed to assist users of systems and software life cycle processes to manage information items (documents) ... may be applied to any of the activities and tasks of a project, system or software product, or service life cycle. It is not limited by the size, complexity or criticality of the project" (ISO, 2006c).*	Code ISO 60.60 (International Standard published)
CobIT	*"COBIT provides good practices for the management of IT processes in a manageable and logical structure, meeting the multiple needs of enterprise management by bridging the gaps between business risks, technical issues, control needs and performance measurement requirements" (ITGI, 2000).*	(International Model published)

continued on following page

Table 3. continued

ISO/IEC 20000	*"Information technology -- Service management: defines the requirements for a service provider to deliver managed services … promotes the adoption of an integrated process approach to effectively deliver managed services to meet business and customer requirements. For an organization to function effectively it has to identify and manage numerous linked activities. Coordinated integration and implementation of the service management processes provides the ongoing control, greater efficiency and opportunities for continual improvement" (ISO, 2005).*	Code ISO 60.60 (International Standard published)
CMMI-DEV	*"CMMI® (Capability Maturity Model® Integration) is a process improvement maturity model for the development of products and services. It consists of best practices that address development and maintenance activities that cover the product lifecycle from conception through delivery and maintenance. This latest iteration of the model as represented herein integrates bodies of knowledge that are essential for development and maintenance, but that have been addressed separately in the past, such as software engineering, systems engineering, hardware and design engineering, the engineering "-ilities," and acquisition. The prior designations of CMMI for systems engineering and software engineering (CMMI-SE/SW) are superseded by the title "CMMI for Development" to truly reflect the comprehensive integration of these bodies of knowledge and the application of the model within the organization. CMMI for Development (CMMI-DEV) provides a comprehensive integrated solution for development and maintenance activities applied to products and services" (SEI, 2006).*	(International Model published)

The aforementioned characteristics are based on the fact of the ISO 9000 family of standards (which deal with a generic industry-independent quality management system and an organizational encouragement toward a continuous process improvement) is identified as the main source for the SE, SwE, and IT standards and models of process. Table 3 shows the official self-description and status of these models and standards.

The Core Building-Block Concepts for Understanding Models and Standards of Processes: Process, Service and System

The ISO 9000 standard in its 2000-year version has established eight management principles where two of them (Principle 4 and 5) endorse the *process approach* and the *systems approach* as critical management paradigms respectively. Principle 4 establishes that an organization will be more likely to achieve the results expected efficiently, if the resources and activities are managed as

processes. In turn, the Principle 5 sets forth that an organization can identify, understand and manage more efficiently and effectively the *processes* if they conceptualized them as a *system*. Furthermore, the ISO 9001:2000 standard remarks that *"… concerns the way an organization goes about its work … concern processes not products—at least not directly"* (ISO, 2006b). However, this standard admits also that, *" … the way in which the organization manage its processes is obviously to affect its final (quality of) product"* (ibid).

This *process management premise* (e.g., *"the quality of a system is largely governed by the quality of the process used to develop and maintain it"*) has been largely used in quality management systems (Paulk, Chrissis, Weber & Perdue, 1987). With these insights, we posit that the concepts of *process*, *system* and *service* and their conceptual systemic interrelationships become critical to understanding the different standards and models under study. The relevance of the notion of *process* is self-evident. The notion of *service*, for SwE is becoming of critical relevance for the shifting from the object and component-based paradigm toward the Web service-computing paradigm. In SE and IS, the broad initiative on Service Science, Management and Engineering (SSME) (Chesbrough & Spohrer, 2006; Demirkan & Goul, 2006) justifies its relevance. The notion of *system* is justified by the ISO 9000:2000 principles.

In order to describe the relationships between *process, service* and *system* in the context of standards and models of process, we develop the Tables 4, 5 and 6 (updated from Mora et al., 2007a) to report the main definitions from such concepts.

Definitions in the Table 4 show that the concept of *process* is not unique. However several attributes are shared in the definitions: (1) an overall purpose (transform inputs in outputs), (2) activities interrelated, and (3) utilization of human and material resources, procedures and methods. Then, a *process* –based in all definitions-, can be defined as "an ordered set of processes (called sub-process) and/or activities that are performed by agents (either people and/or mechanisms) exercising roles and using procedures, tools and machines for its realization, to transform a set of inputs in a set of expected outputs" (extended from Mora et al., 2007a).

In the Table 5, the concept of *service* is implicitly used for most standards except by those focused on such an issue. Because the most important standards and models of processes for IS (ITIL, CobIT, ISO 20000) and for SwE/SE (CMMI-SVC) are now oriented toward services, a plausible generic definition of what is a *service* is fundamental. Similar to the notion of *process*, there is not unique definition but several attributes are also shared by the definitions: (1) intangible, (2) non-storable, (3) ongoing realization, and (4) people involved for the value appreciation attribute. Whilst the human beings can assess the value scale of nonliving artifacts, the automated processes (by using tools) can assess quality attributes (e.g., agreed physical specifications). Therefore, a *service* can be defined as "the intangible, non-storable and user value-appreciated ongoing outcome (but with a start and end time point) from a system of processes" and consequently a **product** can be defined as "the tangible, storable and quality-measured for instruments or users from a system of processes" (extensions from Mora et al., 2007a).

Table 4. Definitions of the concept of process

AREA	DEFINITION OF THE CONCEPT: PROCESS	SOURCE
Quality Management Systems	*"Set of interrelated or interacting activities, which transforms inputs into outputs. These activities require allocation of resources such as people and materials."*	ISO 9001:2000
SwE	*"The means by which people, procedures, methods, equipment, and tools are integrated to produce a desired end result."* A process can be also considered the *"glue that ties them"* in order to get a work done. (Based in CMMI-DEV (SEI, 2006)	CMM-SW, CMMI-DEV 1.2
SwE	*"... a (software development) process is a collaboration between abstract active entities called roles that perform operations called activities on concrete, tangible entities called artifacts."*	UPM (OMG, 2005)
BPM	*"A Process is an activity performed within a company or organization. In BPMN a Process is depicted as a graph of Flow Objects, which are a set of other activities and the controls that sequence them. The concept of process is intrinsically hierarchical. Processes may be defined at any level from enterprise-wide processes to processes performed by a single person. Low-level processes may be grouped together to achieve a common business goal."*	BPMN (OMG, 2006)
SE	*"A set of inter-related functions and their corresponding inputs and outputs, which are activated and deactivated by their control inputs."*	SysUML (2005)
IS	*"A connected series of actions, activities, changes, etc., performed by agents with the intent of satisfying a purpose or achieving a goal."*	ITIL (2004)

Table 5. Definitions of the concept of service

AREA	DEFINITION OF THE CONCEPT: SERVICE	SOURCE
Quality Management Systems	An explicit definition is not reported.	ISO 9001:2000
SwE	*"a service is a product that is intangible and non-storable."*	CMMI-DEV 1.2
SwE	*An explicit definition is not reported.*	UPM (OMG, 2005)
BPM	*An explicit definition is not reported.*	BPMN (OMG, 2006)
SE	*Missing concept. Instead of it, the concepts of: operation, function, activity and action are reported. In particular, the concept of operation is defined as "A feature which declares a service that can be performed by instances of the classifier of which they are instances."*	SysUML (2005)
IS	*"One or more IT systems which enable a business process."*	ITIL (2004)
SSME	*"Service can be defined as the application of competences for the benefit of another, meaning that service is a kind of action, performance, or promise that's exchanged for value between provider and client. Service is performed in close contact with a client; the more knowledge-intensive and customized the service, the more the service process depends critically on client participation and input, whether by providing labor, property, or information."*	Spohrer et al. (2007)

Hence, the main visible distinctions between *product* and *service* are: (1) its tangibility property that leads to the quality (e.g., the attributes expected in the product) vs. the value (e.g., the benefits to quality-prices rate perceived from a customers' perspective (e.g., human beings), and (2) the ongoing service experience (Teboul, 2007) vs. the time-discrete (includes also periods) utilization of products. An additional difficult to define the building blocks is the omission of the responsible entity that generates a *service*. The definitions proposed (because these appear in the standards) are the notions of *system* and *process*. Still, the difference between both concepts has not been still well reported.

For the aforementioned arguments and definitions showed in the Table 6, the construct *system* becomes a critical concept to link logically the *process* and *service/product* constructs. Hence, the utilization of a Systems Approach (Ackoff, 1971, 1973; Bertalanffy, 1972; Checkland, 2000) as well as the relevance of the correct conceptualization of what is a *system* can be considered fundamental notions to be untapped. Despite, it could be considered that the concept system is a well defined and understood construct, Gelman and Garcia (1989), Gelman et al. (2005), Mora, Gelman, Cervantes, Mejia, and Weitzenfeld (2003) and Mora, Gelman, Cano, Cervantes, and Forgionne (2006) studies on the formalization of the construct *system*, have proved the ambiguity, incompleteness and informality of main definitions reported in the context of SE and IS. Then, the concept of *system* used in these standards, despite can be considered practically illustrative and useful is theoretically incomplete from a systems science discipline. In Mora et al. (2007a) it is argued that "it has diminished the clarity on the critical role of the Systems Approach as the philosophical and practical source to establish the principles and methods of such standards and has increased consequently the complexity for a mutual understanding and integration. Whilst Process Approaches have been the corner stone for the development and utilization of standards and models of processes, we claim that the Systems Approach is in turn the corner stone that holds to the Process Approach."

Table 6. Definitions of the concept of system

AREA	DEFINITION OF THE CONCEPT: SYSTEM	SOURCE
Quality Management Systems	From the Principle 5 and other arguments reported in available documents, a system can be considered *as a network of interdependent processes connected for achieving expected products and services.*	ISO 9001:2000 (2000)
SwE	An explicit definition is not reported.	CMMI-DEV 1.2
SwE	An explicit definition is not reported.	UPM (2000)
BPM	An explicit definition is not reported.	BPMN (2006)
SE	*"An item, with structure, that exhibits observable properties and behaviors."*	SysUML (2005)
SE	*"An integrated set of elements that accomplish a defined objective. These elements include products (hardware, software, firmware), processes, people, information, techniques, facilities, services, and other support elements."*	INCOSE (2004)
IS	*"An integrated composite that consists of one or more of the processes, hardware, software, facilities and people, that provides a capability to satisfy a stated need or objective."*	ITIL (2004)
SSME	*"... a service system [is] a value-coproduction configuration of people, technology, other internal and external service systems, and shared information (such as language, processes, metrics, prices, policies, and laws). This recursive service system definition highlights the fact that service systems have internal structure (intraentity services) and external structure (interentity services) in which participants coproduce value directly or indirectly with other service systems."*	Spohrer et al. (2007)

However, from a practical worldview and with the purpose to propose a plausible relationship between the three concepts, a *system* as an abstract entity, can be defined as *"a whole into a wider system, with unique attributes co-generated by their parts, where the main attribute is its purpose, function or mission"*. Given that such a definition is open, a specific definition of a *system* abstraction in the context of organizations is required. In particular, the notion of ***organizational system*** is relevant for the context of standards and models of processes. In concordance with system foundations (Gelman & Garcia, 1989; Mora et al., 2006), this concept can be defined as: "a whole (the real physical system) into a wider system (the wider real physical system), with unique attributes co-generated by their parts (subsystems and process (that include the parts of every process has)), which the main attribute is its purpose, function or mission (to manufacturing a product or provision a service)". Such a notion is also congruent with the SSME's notion of **service system** (Spohrer et al., 2007).

As illustration, from a high practical worldview perspective, the following eleven conceptual relationships between the core building-block concepts can be posed[11].

- R1: a <S: system> is whole into a wider <SS: system>, with unique <A: attributes: a1,a2,...> co-produced by their (at least two) parts called <sB: subsystems>, where the main attribute is its purpose, function or mission <attribute: a*>.
- R2: a <sB: subsystem> is just a <S: system> that is part of a wider <SS: system>.
- R3: a <C: component> is a constituent of a <sB: subsystem> that is not decomposable in parts (from a modeling viewpoint) but with attributes.
- R4: an <O: organization> is a <S: system> composed of <OsS: organizational sub-systems>.
- R5: an <OsB: organizational sub-system> is a <S: system> composed of <OsB: organizational sub-systems> and/or <BP: business processes>.

- R6: a <BP: business process> is a <S: system> composed of <BsP: business sub-process> and/or <BA: business activities>.
- R7: a <BA: business activity> is a <C: component> with the <A: attributes: a-tasks, a-personnel, a-tools-infrastructure, a-methods-procedures and a-socio-political-mechanisms-structures>
- R8: a <Sv: service> is an intangible ongoing <BO: business outcome> of a <BP: business process> into an <OsB: organizational sub-system>
- R9: a <Pr: product> is a tangible and discrete <BO: business outcome> of a <BP: business process> into an <OsB: organizational sub-system>
- R10: a <BsP: business sub-process> is just a <BP: business process> that is into a <process>.
- R11: a <BO: business outcome> is a perceived output of a <BP: business process> with either <VoP: value-oriented people attributes: v1,v2, ...> or <QoM: quality-oriented machines attributes: q1,q2, ...>.

Hence, the manufacturing of *products* and the provision of *services* needs a *business process approach* where the *business process* can be conceptualized as a *system* (composed of *business subprocesses* and/or *business activities*) contained in an *organizational system* that affects to and it is affected by a wider system called the *suprasystem*. Initial but substantial theoretical and practical implications of such relationships are discussed in the final section.

INITIAL THEORETICAL AND PRACTICAL IMPLICATIONS FOR THE IS DISCIPLINE

This chapter is part of a research in progress and an extensive discussion of their contributions is out of the planned scope. However, initial results on the

how to apply such a set of conceptual relationships have been reported in Mora et al. (2007a, 2007b). From a theoretical viewpoint, however, we can argue that these conceptual findings contribute: (1) to identify the building-block concepts of the highest abstraction level to define and understand the rationale of standards and models of processes; (2) to establish a conceptual hierarchical set of initial relationships between such conceptual building-blocks that permits the development of a further formalization via an ontology; (3) to keep a theoretical congruence with the formal notions of what is a *system, subsystem* and *suprasystem*; and (4) to provide a parsimonious theoretical model of what is a *business organization, business process, business activity, service* and *product*.

From a practical viewpoint, this study contributes: (1) to help to practitioners to understand the conceptual relationships between *process, system* and the final outcomes of *services* and *products* using a domain vocabulary linked to formal systemic foundations; (2) to provide the foundation for the development of a computerized ontology for standards and models of processes that would permit automated knowledge-based inquires; and (3) to provide the foundations for the development of a framework/model to describe and compare the standards and models of processes from a top-bottom perspective according to the level of detail required by the modeler (Mora et al., 2007b).

CONCLUSION

In this chapter, we have developed a conceptual description of the main models and standards of processes formulated in the disciplines of SE, SwE and IS. Based in such descriptions, we have developed a conceptual analysis of the concepts of *process, system* and *service*. Such concepts have been identified as the core building blocks for describing models and standards of processes. Eleven semi-formal conceptual relationships between the building-blocks concepts have been also posed. The main theoretical contribution is the generation of a parsimonious model theoretically congruent with the Theory of Systems. The main practical contribution is the provision of a conceptual tool to describe and compare standards and models of processes. Two recommendations that emerge for further research are: (1) the refinement of the relationships to describe and compare standards and models of processes and (2) the development of a computerized ontology based in this theoretical model for permitting knowledge-based inquires on the digital description of standards and models of processes in SE, SwE and IT. These two research recommendations are part of the research goals of this study under progress.

ACKNOWLEDGMENT

This research is being developed with the financial support of the Autonomous University of Aguascalientes (www.uaa.mx) (Project PIINF-06-8) as well as from the Mexican National Council of Science and Technology (CONACYT, www.conacyt.mx) (Project P49135-Y).

REFERENCES

Ackoff, R. (1971). Towards a system of systems concepts. *Management Science, 17*(11), 661-671.

Ackoff, R. (1973). Science in the systems age: Beyond IE, OR and MS. *Operations Research, 21*(3), 661-671.

Andriole, S., & Freeman, P. (1993). Software the case systems engineering: For a new discipline. *Software Engineering Journal*, May, 165-179.

Arnold, S., & Lawson, H. W. (2004). Viewing systems from a business management perspective: the ISO/IEC 15288 standard. *Systems Engineering, 7*(3), 229-242.

Barker, B., & Verma, D. (2003). System engineering effectiveness: A complexity point paradigm for software intensive systems in the information technology sector. *Engineering Management Journal, 15*(3), 29-35.

Bar-Yam, Y. (2003). When systems engineering fails—Toward complex systems engineering. In *Proceedings of the 2003 International Conference on Systems, Man & Cybernetics* (pp. 2021-2028), Piscataway, NJ: IEEE Press.

Bate, R. (1998). Do systems engineering? Who, Me? *IEEE Software*, Jul-Aug, 65-66.

Bertalanffy, L. von (1972). The history and status of general systems theory. *Academy of Management Journal*, December, 407-426.

Boehm, B. (2000). Unifying software engineering and systems engineering. *Computer*, 114-116.

Boehm, B., & Lane, J. (2006). 21st century processes for acquiring 21st century software-intensive systems of systems. *Crosstalk: The Journal of Defense Software Engineering*, May, 1-9.

Checkland, P. (2000). Soft systems methodology: a 30-year retrospective. In P. Checkland (Ed.), *Systems thinking, systems practice*. Chichester: Wiley.

Chesbrough, C., & Spohrer, J. (2006). A research manifesto for services science. *Communications of the ACM, 49*(7), 35-40.

CIO UK Website. (2007). *Late IT projects equals lower profits*. Retrieved May 15, 2008, from http://www.cio.co.uk/concern/resources/news/index.cfm?articleid=1563

Collin, R. (2004). *An introductory overview of ITIL*. London: ITSMF.

Deno, P., & Feeney, A. B. (2002). Systems engineering foundations of software systems integration. In *Proceedings of the OOIS Workshops*.

Demirkan, H., & Goul, M. (2006). AMCIS 2006 panel: Towards the service oriented enterprise vision: Bridging industry and academics. *CAIS, 18*, 546-556.

Ewusi, K. (1997). Critical issues in abandoned information systems development projects. *Communication of the ACM, 40*(9), 74-80.

Farr, J., & Buede, D. (2003). Systems engineering and engineering management: Keys to the efficient development of products and services. *Engineering Management Journal, 15*(3), 3-9.

Forsberg, K., & Mooz, H. (1997). System engineering overview. In R. Thayer & M. Dorfman (Eds.), *Software requirements engineering* (pp. 44-72). Los Alamitos: IEEE Computer Society Press.

Fuggetta, A. (2000). Software process: A roadmap. In *Proceedings of the International Conference on Software Engineering*, Limerick, Ireland.

Garcia, S. (1998). Evolving improvement paradigms: Capability maturity models & ISO/IEC 15504 (PDTR). *Software Process Improvement and Practice, 3*(1), 1-11.

Gelman, O., & Garcia, J. (1989). Formulation and axiomatization of the concept of general system. *Outlet IMPOS (Mexican Institute of Planning and Systems Operation), 19*(92), 1-81.

Gelman, O., Mora, M., Forgionne, G., & F. Cervantes (2005). Information systems and systems theory. In M. Khosrow-Pour (Ed.), *Encyclopedia of information science and technology*, (Vol. 3, pp. 1491-1496). Hershey, PA: Idea Group.

Glass, R., Armes, V., & Vessey, I. (2004). An analysis of research in computing disciplines. *Communications of the ACM, 47*(6), 89-94.

Hecht, H. (1999). Systems engineering for software-intensive projects. In *Proceedings of the ASSET Conference*, Dallas, TX.

Hevner, A. R., March, S. T., Park, J., & Ram, S. (2004). Design science in information systems research. *MIS Quarterly, 28*(1), 75-105.

Hole, E., Verma, D., Jain, R., Vitale, V., & Popick, P. (2005). Development of the ibm.com interactive solution marketplace (ISM): A systems engineering case Study. *Systems Engineering, 8*(1), 78-92.

Honour, E. (2004). Understanding the value of systems engineering. In *Proceedings of the 2004 INCOSE Conference*, 1-16.

INCOSE (1996). *SECAM: Systems engineering capability assessment model* (version 1.5). INCOSE.

INCOSE (2004). *Systems engineering handbook*. INCOSE-TP-2003-016-02. INCOSE.

ISO (in press). *ISO/IEC NP 24748 Systems and software engineering—Life cycle management*. Geneva, Switzerland: ISO/IEC.

ISO (1995). *ISO/IEC 12207: Information technology—Software life cycle processes*. Geneva, Switzerland: ISO/IEC.

ISO (2002). *ISO/IEC 15288: Systems engineering—Systems life cycle processes*. Geneva, Switzerland: ISO/IEC.

ISO (2003). *ISO/IEC 15504-2: Information technology—Process assessment*. Geneva, Switzerland: ISO/IEC.

ISO (2004a). *ISO/IEC 90003:2004 software engineering—Guidelines for the application of ISO 9001:2000 to computer software*. Geneva, Switzerland: ISO/IEC.

ISO (2004b). *ISO/TMB Policy and principles statement global relevance of ISO technical work and publications*. TMB/SC/GR 2004-06-30. Geneva, Switzerland: ISO/IEC.

ISO (2005). *ISO/IEC 20000:2005 Information technology—Service management -- Part 1: Specification*. Geneva, Switzerland: ISO/IEC.

ISO (2006a). *Where ISO 9000 came from and who is behind it*. Retrieved May 15, 2008, from www.iso.org

ISO (2006b). *ISO 9000 and ISO 14000 in plain language*. Retrieved May 15, 2008, from www.iso.org

ISO (2006c). *ISO/IEC 15289: Systems and software engineering—Content of systems and software life cycle process information products (Documentation)*. Geneva, Switzerland: ISO/IEC.

ITGI (2000). *COBIT 3rd edition framework*. Illinois: IT Governance Institute..

Johnson, D. M. (1996). The systems engineer and the software crisis. *ACM SIGSOFT Software Engineering Notes, 1*(2), 64-73.

Johnson, K., & Dindo, J. (1998). Expanding the fcus of software process improvement to include systems engineering. *Crosstalk: The journal of defense software engineering*, 1-13.

Kellner, M., Curtis, B., deMarco, T., Kishida, K., Schulemberg, M., & Tully, C. (1991). Non-technological issues in software engineering. In *Proceedings of the 13th International Conference on Software Engineering*. Retrieved digital library at www.acm.org

Magee, S. (2006). *A successful software quality strategy using ISO/IEC 12207 & 15288*. Retrieved May 15, 2008, www.15288.com

Minnich, H. (2002). EIA IS 731 Compared to CMMI-SE/SW. *Systems engineering journal, 5*(1), 62-72.

Mora, M. (2004). *Manual of Conceptual Research* (Internal Tech. Rep. IS-2004-01). Autonomous University of Aguascalientes, Mexico.

Mora, M., Gelman, O., Cervantes, F., Mejia, M., & Weitzenfeld, A. (2003). A systemic approach for the formalization of the information system concept: Why information systems are systems? In Cano, J. (Ed.), *Critical reflections of information systems: Systemic approach* (pp. 1-29). Hershey, PA: Idea Group.

Mora, M., Gelman, O., Cano, J., Cervantes, F., & Forgionne, G. (2006). Theory of systems and information systems research frameworks. In *Proceedings of the 50th Annual Meeting of the International Society for the Systems Sciences*, Somona State Universiy, CA.

Mora, M., Gelman, O., O'Connor, R., Alvarez, F., & Macías, J. (2007a). On models and standards of processes in SE, SwE and IT&S disciplines: Toward a comparative framework using the systems approach. In K. Dhanda & R. Hackney (Eds), In *Proceedings of the ISOneWorld 2007 Conference Track in System Thinking/Systems Practice*, Las Vegas, Nevada.

Mora, M., Gelman, O., & Alvarez, F. (2007b). A systemic model for the description and comparison of models and standards of processes in the SE, SwE and IT disciplines. In *e-Proceedings, International Conference on Complex Systems 2007, NECSI*, Boston, MA.

Mora, M., Gelman, O., Frank, M., Paradice, D., Cervantes, F., & Forgionne, G. (2008). Toward an interdisciplinary engineering and management of complex IT-intensive organizational systems: A systems view. *The International Journal of Information Technologies and the Systems Approach, 1*(1), 1-24.

Nichols, R., & Connaughton, C. (2005). *Software process improvement journey: IBM Australia application management services* (A Report from the Winner of the 2004 Software Process Achievement Award). Technical Report CMU/SEI-2005-TR-002, ESC-TR-2005-002.

Nunamaker, J. F., Chen, M., & Purdin, T. D. (1991). System development in information system research. *Journal of Management Information Systems, 7*, 89-106.

OMG (2005). *Software process engineering management: The unified process model (UPM)*. Document ad/2000-05-05. Object Management Group

OMG (2006). *Business process modeling notation (BPMN) specification*. Document dtc/06-02-01. Object Management Group.

Paulk, M., Chrissis, M., Weber, C. & Perdue, J. (1987). *The capability maturity model for software, Version 2B*. SEI/CMU Presentation. Retrieved May 15, 2008, from a www.sei.cmu.edu

Sage, A. P. (1992). *Systems engineering*. New York: Wiley.

Sage, A. P. (2000). Systems engineering education. *IEEE TSMC-Part C, 30*(2), 164-174.

Sage, A. P., & Amstrong, J. (2000). *Introduction to systems engineering*. New York: Wiley.

Sheard, S., & Lake, J. (1998). *Systems engineering and models compared*. retrieved May 15, 2008, from www.software.org

SEI (2006). *CMMI for development, version 1.2: CMMI-DEV, V1.2. Software engineering institute*. CMU/SEI-2006-TR-008, ESC-TR-2006-008. retrieved May 15, 2008, from www.sei.edu

Sommerville, I. (1998). Systems engineering for software engineers. *Annals of Software Engineering, 6*, 111-129.

Spohrer, J., Maglio, P., Bailey, J., & Gruhl., D. (2007). Steps toward a science of service systems. *IEEE Computer*, January issue, 70-71.

Standish Group International (2003). *The extreme CHAOS report*. Retrieved May 15, 2008, from www.standish-group.com

Succi, G., Valerio, A., Vernazza, T., & Succi, G. (1998). Compatibility, standards and software production. *Standarview, 6*(4), 140-146.

Tantara (2001). *History and relationship of process standards/models*. Retrieved May 15, 2008, from www. tantara.ab.ca

Teboul, J. (2007). *Service is front stage: Positioning services for value advantage*. Paris: INSEAD.

Thayer, R. H. (1997). Software systems engineering: An engineering process. In R. Thayer & M. Dorfman (Eds.), *Software requirements engineering* (pp. 84-106). Los Alamitos: IEEE Computer Society Press.

Thayer, R. H. (2002). Software systems engineering: A tutorial. *IEEE Computer*, April, 68-73.

Tripp, L. (1996). International standards in system and software integrity. *Standardwiew, 4*(3), 146-150.

Wright, R. (1998). Process standards and capability models for engineering software-intensive systems. *Crosstalk*, October, 1-10.

ENDNOTES

[1] A standard is a " ... *document, established by consensus and approved by a recognized body, that provides, for common and repeated use, rules, guidelines or characteristics for activities or their results, aimed at the achievement of the optimum degree of order in a given context.*" (ISO, 2004b)

[2] Most recent standards have incorporated such improvement purpose (e.g., ISO 15504).

[3] The initial results from such a premise have been reported in Mora et al (2007a) and final findings will be reported in a further study.

[4] In particular, Fuggetta (2000, p. 28) points out that ".. rather, we (e.g., the software process community) must pay attention to the complex interrelation of a number of

organizational, cultural, technological and economic factors."

5   SE is an older discipline than SwE that copes with the definition, development/acquisition and deployment of large scale systems comprised of multiples components of people, facilities, hardware, software, mechanical, and so forth.

6   SwE is defined as the discipline to generate software components or systems on time, on budget and with the expected technical requirements achieved.

7   CMMI-SVC will be the constellation focused on the management and engineering of process for delivering services. It is planned be released in 2007. Other CMMI-ACQ constellation for acquisition process is also being developed for 2007.

8   In this chapter is analyzed the version 3.0 released in 2000. The new version 4.0 has been recently released ending 2006.

9   This standard is derived from the BS15000 standard. In turn, the later evolved from the ITIL V.2.0 (1995) Model. Because the ITIL V.3.0 was liberated during the ending of this study, this is not considered. Major change realized is a lifecycle approach to arrange the previous main six categories of processes.

10   Other IS standards (e.g., Computer standards) are oriented to computer sciences and these are not considered in this chapter. ICT security standards can be considered hybrid but are out of the scope of this research.

11   These definitions are based in Gelman & Garcia (1989), Mora et al. (2003), Gelman et al. (2005) and Mora et al. (2006, 2007b).

Chapter XXII
Perspectives of IT–Service Quality Management:
A Concept for Life Cycle Based Quality Management of IT–Services

Claus-Peter Praeg
University of Stuttgart, Germany

Dieter Spath
University of Stuttgart, Germany

ABSTRACT

This chapter introduces an IT-Service management framework for the use of quality management concepts in the context of the life cycle phases of IT-Services. It argues that IT-Service management, combined with quality management and a life cycle approach for IT-Services provides a new perspective for organizations to provide high quality IT-Services. Based on the IT-industrialisation and an increased customer orientation in the IT-Service management the aspect of quality becomes increasingly important. Therefore, the authors give an overview about existing concepts of IT-Service management, life cycle management and quality management for IT-Services. The aim is to support organizations in the effective use of quality management concepts depending on IT-Service life cycles.

INTRODUCTION

In context of IT-Governance there are numerous concepts and models that can enable organizations to be more effective and more efficient in using IT-Solutions. IT-Governance is supposed to help organizations to enhance their competitiveness by using Information Technology (IT). On the one hand a big issue in this discussion is the realization and evaluation of the business value due to the use of IT (Weill & Ross, 2004). On the other hand the constant change of business needs also demands a reliable and effective IT support for the business processes. Therefore IT-Governance and IT-Business alignment are key success factors for creating business value due to the use of IT-Services in an organization. In the wake of constantly changing business requirements the existing IT-Infrastructure and the IT-Services which support the business processes have to adapt as well. The developments in Information Technology and IT-Service management enable organizations to use IT-Solutions in a way which differs completely from earlier concepts. Therefore the management concepts for IT-Service management have to adjust to these new developments. In this situation the quality of the provided IT-Services becomes an important issue for IT-Service providers and service recipients. Hence quality management is one important aspect in the context of IT-Governance.

Experiences from the industrial sectors show that organizations are able to achieve strategic and operational targets concerning quality and customer satisfaction by using quality management approaches. In the context of IT-Quality management, IT-Governance defines the rules for the decision making process and competencies within an organization. It describes the framework for the IT-Strategy and defines the guidelines for the IT-Service management within an organiza-

tion. Based on the importance of service quality, as outlined above, this chapter focuses on the quality management of IT-Services in dependence on the life cycle phase of IT-Services.

In the current discussion about IT-Services and quality management has so far not provided a concept which integrates these two dimensions in a life cycle based concept for IT-service quality management. This chapter aims to close this gap and provide a model which enables organizations to map selected quality management methods with previously defined phases of an IT-Service life cycle. The goal is to present managers a practical approach for matching quality management methods with life cycle phases of IT-Services.

From a research point of view, relevant questions concern the possibilities of transferring quality management concepts from the industrial sector to IT-Service management. In the context of the developments for IT-Service management it is important how a holistic life cycle for IT-Services can be illustrated. The final research question in this chapter focuses on mapping the different life cycle phases of IT-services and quality management concepts. To answer these questions the chapter will follow the structure outlined below (see Figure 1). It illustrates the several aspects in the context of life cycle management and IT-Service quality management which shall

Figure 1. Structure of the chapter life cycle based IT-service management

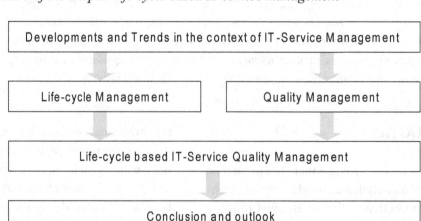

be merged into an integrated model of life cycle based IT-Service Quality Management.

Following Glass Ramesh, and Vessey (2004) the described solution promoted in this chapter is a conceptual analysis and an instrumental development based on a design science approach (Glass et al., 2004; Hevner, March, Park & Ram, 2004). In IT research science the design science creates and evaluates IT artifacts intended to solve organizational problems. In this context the organizational problem is the use of adequate quality management methods for IT-Service management within an organization. IT artifacts are generally defined as constructs (vocabulary and symbols), models (abstractions and representations), methods (algorithms and practices), and instantiations (implemented and prototype systems) (Hevner et al., 2004).

This chapter focuses on illustrating a model for the transfer and use of quality management methods depending on the life cycle phase of an IT-Service. One research hypothesis is that the transfer of engineering focused quality management methods to IT-Service management can support IT-Service providers and organizations to improve the quality of their IT-Services.

The first part of this chapter provides an overview of selected developments in IT-Service management and describes and the relation between the trends and their impact for IT-Service Quality Management. The following part introduces the life cycle concept for physical products and transfers this approach to a life cycle concept for IT-Services. The third part presents the basics of quality management, the total quality management concepts as well as several concepts in context of service quality. The fourth part integrates the life cycle concepts with quality management and presents a concept for a life cycle based IT-Service quality management approach. It also offers a brief overview of the theoretical basis of the concept. This combination of life cycle concepts and IT-Service quality aspects enables organizations to match selected quality management methods

with the different phases of the IT-Service life cycle and achieve increased service quality and customer satisfaction. The final part describes opportunities for further research and highlights challenges for the organizations in case of quality management for IT-Services.

DEVELOPMENTS IN IT-SERVICE MANAGEMENT

During the past years IT-Departments and IT-Service providers have been faced with new challenges. The main challenges are internal restructuring of the IT-Department, the importance of service orientation caused by increased market and customer orientation as well as the industrialisation in IT-Service management. As a result of the increasing focus on efficiency and performance, organizations recognize that the operation of IT is not their key competence. Hence the organizational structure of IT-Departments is changed from internal cost centres to market oriented service providers. Organizations have started to evaluate the added value and performance of their internal IT-Departments and benchmark them against market offers from external IT-Service providers. On the one hand, this follows in a changed position of the IT-Departments and IT-Service providers as well in a modified situation for managing IT-Services. On the other hand, this results in an increasing procurement of IT-Service via external markets for IT-Services (Kotabe & Murray, 2004).

To illustrate selected trends and developments in IT-Management this chapter shows the need for a new concept of IT-Service quality management. The goal is to emphasize important developments in IT-Service management and show their impact on the IT-Service quality management.

According to the situation mentioned before, there is an increased market and customer orientation in the IT-Management sector. The different departments in an organization become customers of the IT-Department or an external service provider. As a result, the relationship between the several departments and the IT-Provider is similar to a partnership with external customers. Both parties work together on basis of defined service levels under real market conditions.

Therefore, market and customer orientation makes new demands on IT-Departments and IT-Service providers. They are forced to define products and services which are provided for the customers. The definition of IT-Services, the "product" of the IT-Department, becomes a key challenge for the IT-Management (Zarnekow & Brenner, 2004). The development and customization of suitable service packages will be a future challenge for service providers in general (Spath, van Husen, Meyer & Elze, 2007). "IT-Products" are a combination of different IT-Services which support business processes (Uebernickel, Bravo-Sànchez, Zarnekow & Brenner, 2006). From a service providers' point of view, this product orientation implies that a portfolio of offered services has to be defined and regularly updated to the customers' demands. From a service recipient point of view, the IT-Service portfolio has to be actively managed and continuously adapted to the changing business requirements and the business processes.

The increased focus on business value and performance results puts an increasing pressure for IT-Service providers to improve their efficiency. In this context, the term "industrialisation" describes the transformation of productivity methods from the industry sector to IT-Service management.

There are four basic aspects concerning the IT-Industrialisation (Hochstein, Ebert, Ueber-nickel & Brenner, 2007): Firstly, automation and standardization, that is, IT-cost reduction due to standardisation of business processes and IT-Services. According to the standardisation of processes, there is also efficiency potential due to automation. The second aspect focuses on the modularisation of IT-Services. Comparable to the production industry the modularisation here enables the customizing of services to individual customer demands due to the use and combination of different standardized IT-Modules (Böhmann & Krcmar, 2003). Schnabel, Dold, Fröschle, Layer, Roll, and Skempes (2006) highlight the capability of customization of services to the stakeholder requirement as a key success factor especially for service companies. The third aspect of industrialisation focuses on the quality management and the implementation of continuous improvement processes within the providers' organization. Thanks to the use of quality management concepts, processes have to be improved, become more efficient and enable performance measurement (Hochstein et al., 2007). The fourth aspect is focussing on core competencies and fostering the outsourcing of processes and business fields which are not relevant for creating a unique selling proposition. According to this principle the depth of the value added chain in the organization will be reduced. Furthermore, this enables an organization to react faster on market developments and to provide high quality services for the market.

From a customers' point of view the focus on IT-Services highlights the increased meaning of the quality of IT-Services. Service quality is the output of different organizational processes and procedures which ensure a constant level of performance by systematically engineering IT-Services (Spath & Demuß, 2003). The quality parameters of IT-Services, like availability, reliability and functionality, instead of technical aspects of IT-Application and infrastructure should therefore be high priority (Zarnekow, Hochstein & Brenner, 2005). As a consequence of this increased service orientation and the supply of IT-Services through external providers, there is also a need for a systematic quality management by providers as well as service customers to ensure the availability and the quality of the IT-Services. Due to the increased meaning of IT-Services, the technical aspects became less important

Figure 2. IT-Service provider selection criteria's from customers' perspective

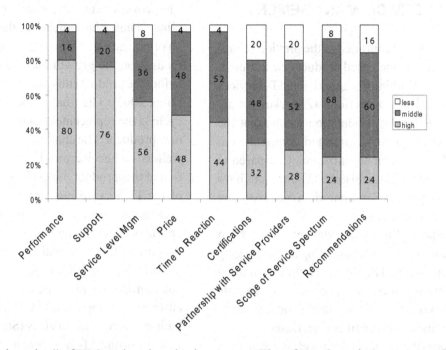

and. the "engineering" of IT-Services is pales in comparison to the perceived quality of the service provision. For IT-Departments and IT-Service providers this means an increased significance of quality management of offered IT-Services and customer services.

A survey form the IT-Service Management Forum (itSMF) in Germany, comprising 122 participating service providers and service recipients, highlights the importance of the offered service portfolio and the quality of the customer service (Praeg & Schnabel, 2006). This market survey proves that today, the most important criteria for customers in choosing an IT-Service Provider, is the performance of the IT-Service provider followed by the support and the performance of the service level management of an IT-Service provider (see Figure 2).

The results show that the price of the services is not the critical factor for organizations contracting a service provider. Customers focus on performance and quality of an IT-Service provider. The service quality depends strongly on the customer specific perception.

Therefore, the primary target of the IT-Service management is to align the offered service portfolio to the customer requirements and adjust the IT-Service portfolio to the customer demands regularly. To foster this management concept, the IT-Service providers must recognize that IT-Services have their own life cycle when used by the customers. The meaning of the IT-Services will change according to the change of the business processes which follow changed market situations. This concept of life cycle based management of IT-Services is not yet very common in existing IT-Management concepts. Most of the actual and instruments of IT-Management in practice are focused on separated phases (planning, development, operation) of IT-Management. But there is an important gap in the relation between the stages of the IT-Management phases. Therefore the following chapter gives an overview of different lifecycle concepts which can be adapted and used for the IT-Service management.

LIFE CYCLE BASED APPROACHES FOR IT-SERVICE MANAGEMENT

The developments outlined in the previous chapter illustrate the increased product orientation of IT-Services. Within an organization, IT-Services are managed like a portfolio (Zarnekow et al., 2004). This product orientation means that the IT-Services have to be managed comparable to physical assets in an organization. Compared to the life cycles of physical goods IT-Services have shown an equal development when they are being used in organizations.

Originally, life cycle concepts have been used in the context of engineering and managing physical products. The aim here is the distribution of existing resources in dependence of the life cycle phases and also the management of costs and benefits within the life cycle. Based on these experiences the concept of life cycle management was adapted for software and application development (Mercurio *et al.*, 1990). Regarding IT-Service management there are also different concepts which directly or indirectly consider life cycle phases. The subsequent paragraphs present selected concepts of life cycle based IT-Service management.

Life Cycle Model of Physical Products

In general, a life cycle characterizes the different stages of a product during its market appearance (Bullinger, 1994). The product life cycle management is the process of managing the entire life cycle of a product. For that reason the traditional life cycle concepts are described from a market perspective. For physical products the life cycle covers several phases, from conception, design, testing to manufacturing, market introduction and the disposal of products. In the first phase of the life cycle the products' requirements are defined based on customer and markets demands. In the following phase the detailed design, development

and also the testing of prototypes are center stage. This covers many engineering tasks and disciplines. These phases generate the highest costs for an organization. The subsequent life cycle phase focuses on the growth and the maturity period, before the product runs out of the market (Macharzina, 2003). The final phase of the product life cycle is the replacement of the product by other, new products. The challenge for organizations as well as IT-Service providers is the transformation of this product life cycle to the requirements of the IT-Service management. Thanks to life cycle management, organizations are able to get products faster on the market, provide improved support for their use, and manage end-of-life better. In today's highly competitive global markets, companies must meet the increasing demands of customers by rapidly and continually improving their products and services (Stark, 2004).

Concerning IT-Service management, the existing methods can be separated in public domain approaches and nonpublic domain approaches.

IT-Infrastructure Library (ITIL)

ITIL was developed at the end of the 1980's by the British Office of Government commerce (formerly Central Computer and Telecommunication Agency (CCTA)). ITIL is the de facto standard for IT-Service management and it is the most widely adopted approach for IT-Service management (Sallé, 2004). The ITIL framework is a collection of best practice processes for IT-Service management.

In the updated third version a life cycle based structure for IT-Service management was implemented. The different phases are Service Strategies, Service Design, Service Transition, Service Operation and continual Service Improvement (OGC, 2006). The Service Strategy defines the targets and the guidelines for the IT-Service management. The phases Service Design, Service Transition and Service Operation represent the implementation, operation and change of

IT-Service management within an organization. The continual service improvement supports the internal implementation of improvement programs and projects. One important issue of the ITIL version 3 is a glossary of standard terms and definitions, it emphasizes the integration between business and IT-aspects and should support the implementation of value added networks between IT-Service Providers and service recipients.

Control Objectives for Information and Related Technology (CobiT)

CobiT was developed from the Information Systems Audit and Control Association (ISACA) and is promoted by the IT-Government Institute. It is designed to be an IT-Government aid for the management in identifying and managing the risks and benefits associated with IT. CobiT creates the link between the business objectives of an entity and the specific IT and IT-Management tasks via statements about the control objectives (Sallé, 2004).

The CobiT-Framework covers a life cycle concept that is oriented on the use of IT within an organization and it is closely connected to the IT-Governance. The CobiT Framework identifies four domains which are covering 34 IT-processes. Furthermore, it defines 318 detailed control objectives and audit guidelines to assess the 34 IT-processes (Sallé, 2004).

The domains are Planning & Organization, Acquisition & Implementation, Delivery & Support and Monitoring. The domain Planning & Organization covers strategy as well as tactics and identifies ways on how IT can support the achievement of the business objectives most effectively. Acquisition & Implementation focuses on the identification, development or acquirement of suitable IT-solutions. The Delivery & Support domain is concerned with the actual delivery of required services. The Monitoring domain focuses on the assessment of quality and compliance with control requirements over time (Sallé, 2004).

Nonpublic Domain IT Service Management Methods

The HP IT Service Management Reference Model is a high level IT-process map, which provides a coherent representation of IT processes and a common language for defining IT process requirements and solutions. The model is structured around five groups: Business-IT alignment, Service design and management, Service delivery assurance, Service development and deployment and Service operations (Sallé, 2004).

The Microsoft Operations Framework provides technical guidance that supports organizations to achieve critical system reliability, availability, supportability, and manageability of IT solutions based on Microsoft products and technology. The process model is a functional model that operations teams perform to manage and maintain IT-Services. It is organized around four quadrants and twenty management functions the quadrants are changing, operating, supporting, and optimizing (Sallé, 2004).

The IBM System Management Solutions Lifecycle Framework provides a high level consulting road map. The four-phase process is similar to the former ITIL processes. The IBM approach considers the phases of process assessment, process improvement definition, analysis and design, and pilot deployment. Furthermore, there are extensions to provide an integrated and comprehensive solution (Sallé, 2004).

The Integrated Information Management Model

A life cycle concept focussing on information management is described by Zarnekow and Brenner (2003). The typical phases of the product life cycle, development, market introduction, growth, maturity and retention, can be adapted to a life cycle of IT-Systems which are defined as plan, built and run (Zarnekow & Brenner, 2004).

In their model of an integrated information management, they focus on IT-Products and describe the key processes and tasks of the life cycle from a service provider and a service recipient point of view (see Figure 3).

Traditionally, the IT-Management has a strong technology and project orientation. Conventional IT-Management focused on planning and developing IT-applications and maintaining IT-Infrastructures. Most of these tasks were organized in projects. Therefore, the management of the classical IT-life cycle is divided into three phases: Plan, Built and Run. Contrary to the traditional "plan, built and run" concept, Zarnekow and Brenner in their approach focus on the "source, make and delivery" processes (Zarnekow & Brenner, 2004). Accordingly, they regard the increased market orientation and the changed sourcing strategies of many organizations.

The sourcing process is the interface to the service provider and contains every task which is necessary for the procurement of IT-Products. The procured IT-Products are the basis for the "make"-process. This process describes all tasks which are necessary for the operation and maintenance of IT-solutions (Zarnekow & Brenner, 2004). The process is also responsible for managing the service portfolio, the development and the operation in the organization. The delivery process focuses on the customer relationship management. In this case, customers are all internal and/or external recipients of the IT-Services from the IT-Department. The delivery process comprises on the delivery of the IT-Services to support customers' business processes or other processes.

These concepts give a first impression that the benefits which accompany IT-Service in an organization will change during the different life cycle phases. For this reason it is necessary to have suitable and integrated management tools over the whole life cycle. Actually most of the life cycle concepts for IT issues are concentrate on the life cycle of software development projects (Zarnekow & Brenner, 2004). But the concept of Zarnekow and Brenner does not regard the entire life cycle. In this approach the life cycle ends with the operation phase and does not consider the replacement phase. The enhancement of the whole IT-Service life cycle is a real challenge for the IT-Management in organizations.

IT-Service Life Cycle Model

For the IT-Services there are different approaches which describe the life cycle of IT-Services in an organization. Praeg and Schnabel introduce an

Figure 3. Integrated IT-Management model (Source: Zarnekow & Brenner, 2004)

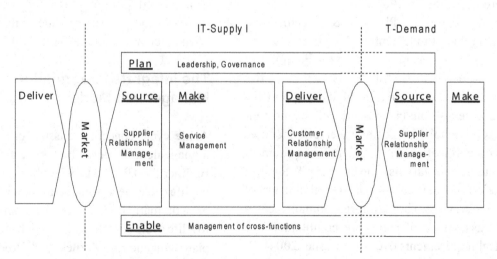

Figure 4. IT-service life cycle

Life-cycle phases	Requirement engineering phase	Sourcing and procurement phase	Design / test and orchestration phase	Operation/ Maintenance/ Support phase	Replacement phase
Processes	• Demand identification of stakeholders • Requirement analysis • Feasibility analysis • Concept development • Service modeling • Service concept • Resource planning • ...	• Development of Sourcing strategy • Sourcing Management • Evaluation of Service Provider • Procurement Process • Service Level Management • ...	• Service customization process • Technical feasibility management • Service orchestration • Testing • Deployment plans • Risk management • ...	• Managing relationships with service providers and stakeholders • IT-Service delivery Management • IT-Service support management • IT-Service Performance management • ...	• Replacement strategy • Change management • Risk management • ...

IT-Service life cycle model which describes five phases for the IT-Service management (Praeg & Schnabel, 2006). This model describes a complete service life cycle which considers the phases from the procurement until the replacement of the IT-Services. Other concepts do not consider this holistic view of an IT-Service life cycle. Contrary to the market perspective of a product life cycle this approach describes the IT-Service life cycle from an intraorganizational perspective.

As illustrated in Figure 4 this IT-Service life cycle model can be separated into five phases. The first phase, requirement engineering, considers all aspects which are necessary for the definition of requirements for IT-Services. In this phase it is necessary to know about the customer demands and consider the internal organizational structure, i.e. business processes as well as the existing IT-Infrastructure within the organization. As a result, during this phase the organization is able to document a description of the concrete service demands as well as a specification. With regard to the quality requirements in this phase it is necessary to ensure that the customer demands and expectations concerning the services are analyzed as detailed as possible. This is the foundation for the sourcing of IT-services from internal or external service providers.

The next step in the IT-Service life cycle covers the sourcing and procurement phase. After defining the service and customer requirements, potential service providers are identified and requested to submit an offer. Practical experience shows that the offers from different service providers differ in structure, wording, and complexity. Therefore, it is difficult to evaluate and compare the different offers with each other. Another common problem is the lack of suitable methods especially when it comes to finding and evaluating a suitable service provider. In this situation, the quality management must provide a suitable concept to evaluate the different offers as well as the service providers by providing a proofed set of quality indicators (Praeg & Schnabel, 2006).

During the design, test and orchestration phase a detailed description of the IT-service parameters is set up, the performance indicators have to be created and the measurement procedures have to be documented. The test must consider the quality in business process support, usability aspects as well as the interfaces to other IT-Services. Furthermore, the orchestration of the available IT-Services has to be tested and validated with regard to quality and performance. In this phase, the quality management has to provide test routines and configuration tests must ensure the availability and reliability of the IT-Support of the business processes. Additionally, it should start with the implementation of adequate structures, processes and methods for quality management.

The phase operation, maintenance and support cover all concepts which are relevant for a high quality service delivery. Most of the existing IT-Service management concepts focusing on this phase (Praeg & Schnabel, 2006). In this context existing IT-Service management and IT-risk management approaches can be used to support users in managing IT-services. With regard to the quality requirement for this phase, the quality management must ensure that the IT-support of the business processes is top-performing. Additionally, a continuous improvement process has to be implemented which ensures that the requirements for IT-Service quality management are met.

The final phase of the life cycle focuses on the replacement of IT-Services. Due to changed business requirements or technical developments the replacement of IT-Services could become necessary. In this phase, the demand made on quality management is to hold up the business processes and manage the possible risks caused by the replacement.

Conclusion for the Life Cycle Concepts

The benefits of a life cycle oriented management for the IT-Service management in organizations are obvious: It enables organizations to analyze new IT-Projects as well as the evaluation of the existing IT-Landscape. During the planning phase, it supports the management decision concerning the expected benefits from new IT-Services and it fosters the development of an organization-wide IT-Service portfolio management. For existing IT-Applications and services, the life cycle concept supports the economic evaluation of the possible detachment of IT-Solutions. Today, most of this decisions are made ad-hoc with neither an eco-

nomical foundation nor an institutional management process (Zarnekow & Brenner, 2004).

Recapitulatory, we can see that the different phases of the IT-Service life cycle define the requirements for the quality management. The previous chapter showed that the business value of IT-Services as well as the requirements according to quality management will change during the life cycle. Hence, adequate methods for the service management as well as the quality management are necessary for an organization.

OVERVIEW OF SELECTED QUALITY MANAGEMENT CONCEPTS FOR IT-SERVICES

The quality of services is a key success factor for service providers in the market competition. Therefore it is important for the service providers to find a suitable quality management concept for managing the quality of services. Regarding the IT-Service life cycle there is no possibility for a "one-size-fits-all" quality management. An IT-Service provider has to adapt different quality management methods and match them with the different phases of the IT-Service life cycle. This chapter gives an overview about selected quality management concepts which are relevant in the context of IT-Service management. As illustrated in Figure 5, the structure of this chapter starts with a definition of quality and quality management. Based on this, quality management is introduced and selected approaches for service quality are described. The final part describes concepts and requirements for IT-Service quality management.

Quality and Quality Management

In general, the International Standard ISO 8402 defines "quality" as the total characteristic of a product or service concerning their suitability to fulfil predefined requirements (ISO 8402). Based

Figure 5. From quality management to IT-service quality management

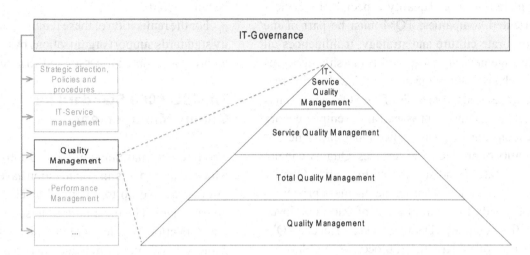

on this definition there are two perspectives for the interpretation of the term "quality":

Firstly, quality can be described as the "degree to which a set of inherent characteristics fulfils requirements" (ISO 9000). This approach focuses on hard facts and objective criteria of products or services (product based view). Secondly, quality can be interpreted from a customers' point of view. In this case, quality is perceived by the customer conception (user-based). Contrary to the product based view, this approach focuses on the subjective perception of a service product by the customer. The customer individually evaluates the quality of a product or service with regard to his personal values. Hence, the challenge for companies is the fulfilment of a great number of heterogeneous customer demands (Bruhn, 2004).

The term "quality management" was intensively discussed in theory and in practice. Based on these discussions quality management can be described by the integration of all parts of the management which enable the internal and external analysis, planning, organization, operation and controlling of all quality relevant aspects in service offering by a service company (Bruhn, 2004). Quality management is the coordinated management task for governing an organization in terms of quality. Therefore quality management

defines quality policies, quality targets, quality controlling and continuous quality improvement within an organization. To achieve these goals, quality management focuses on human resources within an organization and also considers business processes and the technological infrastructure. Based on this concept, quality of services and products is the result of a commitment from the employees to quality standards (Kamiske & Umbreit, 2001). Therefore, quality cannot only be defined and managed within an organization – first and foremost it has to be exemplified though the performance of all involved parties and employees. Besides this human aspect, quality management has to ensure that the existing processes and infrastructure enable the engineering of products and services with predefined quality levels. The management of quality also takes into account the use of different concepts and methods for achieving the quality goals in an organization. In the following paragraph selected concepts for quality management are introduced.

Total Quality Management (TQM)

The Total Quality Management approach is the foundation for an integrated quality management concept in an organization. But TQM is more than a quality management concept. Due to the high importance of quality, especially in service-oriented companies, TQM must be part of the corporate culture and strategy. It influences all management activities and leadership concepts which are used in the organization. For this reason, the conceptual basis of the TQM approach is that the management as well as the employees are responsible for the insurance and improvement of quality of products and services. Quality can not be "created" and supervised by audits. Quality must be implemented in the business processes and needs the commitment of each employee in the company (Deming, 1982). Hence, TQM focuses on all structures, processes, regulations, instructions, and measures which are relevant for ensuring and continuously improving the produced quality of products and services in all departments of an organization under participation of all employees to achieve the highest possible level of satisfaction of customer demands. The basis of this management concept is the conviction that quality is the most important key success factor for companies.

Translated into the context of service providers the TQM concept can be focused on three parts (Bruhn, 2004; Wonigeit, 1994):

- **Total:** The integration of all persons, which are involved in the service development and operation
- **Quality:** The consequent concentration on the quality demands of internal and external customers concerning all activities and processes in the service company
- **Management:** The responsibility of the management for a systematic identification with the quality culture and goals as well as continuos quality improvement.

According to the requirements of IT-Service quality management this means that customer demands, organizational structure, organizational and business processes, employee commitment as well as a quality focused corporate culture must be considered.

For the realisation of these requirements quality standards support organizations by the implementing adequate processes and structures.

The ISO 9000 Standard for Quality Management

The International Standards ISO 9000ff. define which requirements an organization have to fulfil in order to live up to a defined level of quality management. The most important standards out this collection are the ISO 9000 (describes fundamentals of quality management systems and specifies the terminology of quality management), 9001 (specifies requirements for quality management) and 9004 (provides guidelines that consider both the effectiveness and efficiency of quality management systems) (ISO 9000). The ISO 9000 standards interpret quality management as a leadership task for the continuous improvement of the organizational processes to meet customer requirements and expectation and generate customer satisfaction.

The standards promote the adoption of a process approach when developing, implementing, and improving the effectiveness of a quality management system (ISO 9001). According to the ISO 9001 "… this process orientation emphasizes the importance of:

- Understanding and meeting requirements
- The need to consider processes in terms of added value
- Obtaining results of process performance and effectiveness
- Continual improvement of process based on objective measurements."

The standard ISO 9004 suggests the implementation of quality management principles in order to lead organizations towards improved performance. According to ISO 9004 these principles are: customer focus, leadership, involvement of people, process approach, system approach to management, continual improvement, factual approach to decision making, mutually beneficial supplier relationship (ISO 9004).

Usually the ISO 9000 standards are oriented on conventional production organizations. They are focussing on distributed production processes and procedures which are typical for the production sector. Nevertheless, service organizations also recognized the advantages of a quality management system based on the ISO 9000 standards.

All the concepts and quality perspectives described above are originally developed from a traditional industrial oriented understanding of quality and quality management. Because of the focus on services in general and IT-Services in particular, it cannot focus on the customer demands but must also consider further requirements such as the competition and the general situation of the company.

Service Quality Concepts

During the last couple of years, service quality has become of great interest to researches as well as practitioners and managers. One reason is the strong impact of service quality to business performance, cost reduction, customer satisfaction, customer loyalty and profitability (Seth, Deshmukh & Vrat, 2005). Conceptual models of service quality enable organizations to identify quality problems and thus help managing a quality improvement program and support the improvement of efficiency and performance.

According to Bruhn (2004) service quality is defined "as the capability of a service provider, to provide primary intangible and customer oriented service on a predefined performance level corresponding with the customer expectations." Based on this definition service quality represents a defined performance level of service.

For a systematic development and implementation of service quality management, certain requirements must be fulfilled. There are several criteria which help to evaluate the quality of services (Figure 7).

Figure 6. ISO 9000 process based quality management model (Source: ISO 9000)

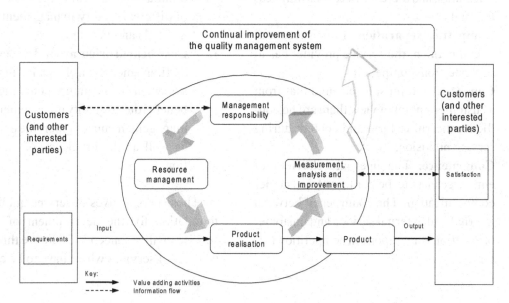

Figure 7. Service quality principles (Source: Bruhn, 2004)

As illustrated in Figure 7, there are ten principles describing service quality management (Bruhn, 2004):

- **Customer orientation:** For successful service management the perceived quality of service by the customers is a key success factor.
- **Consequence:** Everyone within the organization has to align with the customer orientation and there is a need for awareness for quality.
- **Competitor separation:** To be successful in competition, the service provider has to separate from competitors.
- **Consistence:** It must be ensured that from a customer's point of view there are no conflicts concerning form and content during service provision.
- **Congruence:** The internal behaviour of employees has to be conform to customer communication. The congruency between internal and external service and customer orientation is an important competition factor.

- **Coordination:** Every task in the organization has to be aligned to the quality goals.
- **Communication:** The internal and external communication of the organization must be aligned with the quality requirements.
- **Completeness:** The quality management system has to take up a holistic view on quality in the organization.
- **Continuity:** The implementation of an integrated quality management needs medium and long-term experience in the use of different quality management concepts, methods and instruments.
- **Cost-benefit orientation:** The development and implementation of a quality management system must take into account the costs and benefits due to quality management. Quality management must support the performance as well as the efficiency of an organization.

These perspectives of service quality are the foundation for the development of numerous service quality concepts. There are three characteristics of services which have to be considered when managing service quality: the intangibility of services, the uno-actu principle (concurrent providing and consuming of services) and the integration of external factors (Haller, 2002).

During the last years, numerous models have been developed for managing service quality. One common goal of all these models is to operationalize service quality in order to be able to measure and manage service quality (Bruhn, 2004). An overview of selected concepts of service quality management is documented in Seth et al. (2005). Due to space restrictions, only the models of Grönroos and Parasuraman are highlighted in the following paragraphs.

The model from Grönroos defines the perceived quality as the difference between the customer expectations and their experiences according to the service (Grönroos, 1984). For an organization this means that it has to match the expected service and the perceived service to each other so that customer satisfaction will be accomplished. A high service quality is achieved if the perceived quality is higher than the expected quality level. Grönroos identified three components of service quality: technical quality, functional quality and image. The technical quality is the quality of what customers actually receives as a result of the interaction with the service provider, the importance and the evaluation of the service quality (Seth et al., 2005). Functional quality focuses on how the customer gets the technical outcome and emphasizes the subjective perception. In addition to these two dimensions the image of an organization also influences the customer perception of the service quality. The image of an organization can enforce or weaken the perception of the technical and functional quality (Bruhn, 2004).

The GAP Model of Parasuraman et al. (1985) argues that service quality is a result of the differences between expectations and performance of the service (Parasuraman, Zeithamel & Berry, 1985). In their model Parasuraman et al. describe how consumer evaluate service quality. The basis of their model is the interaction between consumers and service providers and possible gaps in this relationship. The authors identified five possible gaps (Seth et al., 2005):

- **GAP 1:** Difference between consumers' expectations and the management perceptions of those consumer expectations.
- **GAP 2:** Differences between management's perceptions of consumer's expectations and service quality specifications.
- **GAP 3:** Difference between service quality specifications and service actually delivered.
- **GAP 4:** Difference between service delivery and the communication to consumers about service delivery.
- **GAP 5:** Difference between consumer's expectation and perceived service. This gap depends on direction and size of the four gaps mentioned before, associated with the delivery of service quality on the providers' side.

The performance expectations and the performance level are defined from a customer's point of view. Service quality has a strong focus on the customer demands and the customer perception of quality. For service providers this means that they have to match requirement according to expected services and perceived services to achieve customer satisfaction (Seth et al., 2005). For the measurement of the service quality a combination between the product-based view and the user-based view is helpful.

As a result of their exploratory research Parasuraman et al. identified ten quality dimensions which are relevant for the evaluation of the perceived service quality from customers' point of view. Based on this results they refined the SERVQUAL model for measuring customers' perception of service quality (Parasuraman, Zeithamel, & Berry, 1988; Seth et al., 2005).

The SERVQUAL approach covers five dimensions which are used to measure service quality: reliability, responsiveness, tangibles, assurance and empathy.

Based on the developments in the IT-Service area which are described in the previous chapters, the IT-Service management has to adapt to the demands of IT-Services. In the past there are no international agreed standards which are focusing on the quality management of IT-Services. With the implementation of the International Standard 20000 this situation has changed.

The ISO 20000 Standard for IT-Service Quality Management

The ISO 20000 Standard suite provides a basis for a measurable quality standard for IT-Service management. It is the further development of the former British Standard (BS) 15000. Therefore the original orientation of the ISO 20000 standard was derived from the BS 15000. On the basis of the ISO 20000 standard organizations can be audited and certified to proof the compliance with this international standard. Furthermore the ISO 20000 fosters the implementation of an integrated process approach for the IT-Service

management within an organization. The standard covers all aspects which are relevant to implement an optimal service management. Hereby the standard especially focuses on the service providers perspectives. ISO 20000 consists of two parts. The first part promotes the adoption of an integrated process approach to effectively deliver managed services to meet the business and customer requirements (ISO 20000). The second part is a code of practice and describes the best practices for service management within the scope of the first part.

The goal of the standard focuses on the provision of a common reference standard for all organizations which provides services to internal and/or external customers. Due to the great importance of the communication between service provider and service recipients one of the main targets of the standard is the definition of a common glossary for the service providers and their customers.

To ensure the provision of a defined quality of the IT-Services the ISO 20000 Standard specifies and describes the necessary processes which an organization has to implement to provide quality proofed IT-Services. For that reason the ISO 20000 Standard describes a set of management

Figure 8. Structure of the ISO 20000 model for IT-service management (Source: ISO 20000)

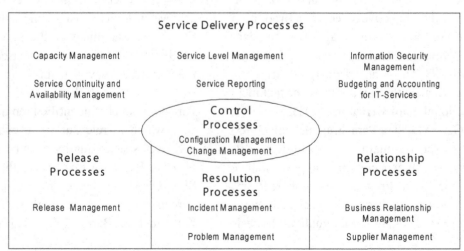

processes ("Objectives and Controls") which are oriented on the ITIL-processes and expand this process model (see Figure 8).

The ISO 20000 enables organizations to implement standardized processes for IT-Service management and supports the improvement of the IT-Service quality management.

Conclusions for Quality Management Concepts

This chapter showed the basic concepts of quality management and service quality management. It was shown that the implementation of a quality management system in an organization is complex and is a strategically issue. Furthermore the overview showed that there are numerous quality management methods which can be used for organizational quality management. As a finding of the description of the different quality management methods it can be shown that from a management perspective quality management has to support the organizational goals in case of value, quality and reliability. At a high level primary management goals can be a high level of customer satisfaction, the organizational and business process performance, aligned IT-Services and –products, contracting the right IT-providers and achieve employee satisfaction. Based on these management goals, factors for quality management can be derived to manage the achievement of these goals. In this case quality management has to consider the following factors: customer demands, organizational structures and processes, IT-Services, service provider performance and employees. A challenge for organizations is to find the most relevant and suitable methods according to the life cycle phase. This mapping between quality management methods and the IT-Service life cycle phases is described in the following chapter.

MODEL FOR A LIFE CYCLE BASED IT-SERVICE QUALITY MANAGEMENT

The previous chapters illustrate basic concepts for IT-Service quality management and give an overview about life cycle concepts for IT-Service management. For the model which will be described in the following paragraphs the life cycle model from Praeg & Schnabel (2006) is the basis, because it is the only approach which describes a complete life cycle for IT-Services. With regard to the industrial sector it is common to use different quality management concepts on different parts of the organizational added value chain (Malorny & Kassebohm, 1994).

Due to the great number of quality methods and instruments and the limited space of this book we can only show the principle and make a suggestion about possible criteria for the matching between the life cycle phases and the quality management methods. The organizational implementation of this approach must regard the individual situation and competencies of the organization.

The mapping process between the IT-Service life cycle phases and the quality management methods is described in two steps. The first step covers the mapping between quality factors, derived from the methods in the previous chapter and the different life cycle phases. The reason is that each phase set different focuses for quality management. On this basis the second step in the mapping process is focussing on the association between quality management methods and the different life cycle phases. Each quality management method concentrates on the support and the fulfilment of one or more quality factors. Therefore for each life cycle phase different quality management methods can be used to support the quality factors. As illustrated in the following paragraphs there is no strict one-to-one mapping between a life cycle phase and a quality management method. Due to the different situations and competencies in organizations a regit one-to-one mapping makes no sense. The intention here is to sensitize organizations and IT-Managers to think about using suitable quality methods in dependence of the situation according to the expected goals of the IT-Service management instead of focusing on one quality management method for IT-Service management. In the following paragraphs the process of mapping is illustrated.

Mapping of Quality Factors

To match different quality management methods with IT-Service life cycle phases the life cycle approach described here suggests a two-step procedure. In the first step organizations have to think about the quality factors which are aligned with the strategic goals. The quality factors are the targets for organizational management. These are the outcomes from the use of quality management methods. The quality management methods are focusing on input variables which have an influence on the later outcome. Therefore it is necessary to implement an PDCA cycle (plan-do-check-act) (Deming, 1982) to measure how the different input variables influences the outcome in case of quality and in case of the achievement of the quality factors. Based on the results of

Chapter 4 the following factors for managing quality within organizations and according to IT-Service are relevant for the life cycle based quality management approach:

- Customer demands,
- Organizational structure and business processes,
- Product and services,
- Employees
- Performance of service provider

As previously described the relevance of these quality factors depends on the life cycle phase and will change from one phase to another. For example in the development phase of the services, the consideration of the customer demands is more important than the focus on service providers because the goal of this phase is the documentation on the requirements for the service based on customer requirements and demands. Therefore a quality management method which focuses on considering customer requirements is better matched with the goals of this phase than a method which focuses on organizational structures or business processes. Based on this fact Table 1 show the relation and relevance of the quality factors for each life cycle phase of the IT-Services.

Table 1. Life cycle phases and quality factors

Quality focus \ Life-cycle phase	Requirement engineering	Sourcing and procurement	Design / test and orchestration	Operation / Maintenance / Support	Replacement
Customer demands	•		•	•	
Organisational structure and business processes			•	•	•
IT-Services and -products	•	•	•	•	•
Employees			•	•	•
Service provider performance		•		•	

The markers highlight the quality factors with the highest priority in each life cycle phase. By example in the sourcing phase quality aspects regarding to the IT-Services and IT-Service providers (internal and/or) external have a higher priority in this phase than aspects according to customer demands. Due to this evaluation Table 1 highlights the focal points according to quality issues in each life cycle phase.

Mapping of Quality Management Methods

In the second step of the life cycle based quality management procedure, selected quality management methods are mapped with the life cycle phases based on the focus of the quality criteria. Due to the scope of the quality management methods it does not make sense to restrict one quality method exactly to one life cycle phase. Based on the connections between different phases the use of the quality methods may vary.

As shown in Figure 9 the quality concepts described in the previous chapter do not depend on a life cycle phase. They are defining the framework for the quality management. The quality management methods are mapped with the life cycle phases of IT-Services.

As illustrated in Figure 9 it is necessary to map one or more adequate quality management methods to the different life cycle phases. The quality factors help to select the suitable methods due to prioritize the importance of the items.

Quality Management Methods for the Life Cycle Phase 1

From a quality management point of view it is necessary to focus on the customer demands in the first phase of the IT-Service life cycle. As seen in Chapter 0 quality of service is defined by the customer requirements. Therefore it is required to find an adequate quality management method which focuses on the customer demands and requirements. But on the other hand the other quality items must also be considered in this phase but with a minor priority. As a result in this phase a quality management method is needed, which focuses on customer requirements and also consider business processes, products and services with a minor priority.

Figure 9. Life cycle phases and quality management methods

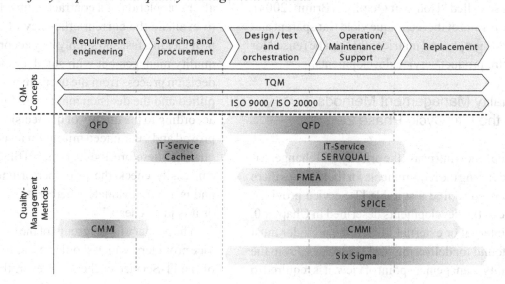

In this case the Quality Function Deployment (QFD) is a suitable method. Quality Function Deployment is a method which focuses on the planning phase of quality management. QFD supports the transformation of customer needs into engineering characteristics (and appropriate test methods) of a product or service, prioritizing each product/service characteristic while simultaneously setting development targets for product or service development. QFD can strongly help an organization focus on the critical characteristics of a new or existing product or service from the separate viewpoints of the customer market segments, company, or technology-development needs.

The QFD method covers a six-step process. The first step focuses on the identification of relevant customer groups. In a second step the customer demands and requirements are documented and evaluated. The third step focuses on the derivation of necessary performance and quality indicators, followed by the definition of target values for each goal in the fourth step. In step five possible negative or positive correlations between the different performance and quality indicators must be analyzed. The final step focuses on internal or external customers evaluates the provided services and compares them with the services from competitors. The results of this process are documented in a so called "House of Quality" (Bruhn, 2004). The results of the technique yield transparent and visible graphs and matrices that can be reused for future product/service developments.

Quality Management Methods for the Life Cycle Phase 2

In the following phase the priority will change. After defining the requirements for the services there is a need to find a suitable IT-Service provider. Due to the developments described in Chapter 0, an internal or external IT-Service provider must be found for delivering the IT-Services. From the quality management point of view, it is required to evaluate the IT-Service provider prior signing the provider contract. In this phase a suitable quality management method must focus on the evaluation of the quality of an IT-Service provider and should also consider aspects of business processes and the delivered services. In this case organizations could use the IT-Service Cachet (Praeg & Schnabel, 2006).

The IT-Service cachet is developed by a consortium of IT Service Management Forum (itSMF, Chapter Germany) together with well-known IT-Service providers and the participation of the Fraunhofer Institute for Industrial Engineering and other research institutions. The Cachet supports organizations in evaluating IT-Service provider from a customer point of view. The cachet is developed to audit service providers concerning the quality of their offers and IT-Services from a customers' point of view in the IT-Service procurement process (Praeg & Schnabel, 2006). To define a quality management approach for service some characteristics of service have to be considered. It must be taken into account that services are intangible and their quality is only measured with difficulties. The second aspect refers to the uncertainty in the procurement process, which exists from the customer point of view to minimize the possible consequences of an erroneous decision as far as possible. Even after completion of a contract it must be possible to evaluate the current efficiency of the service provider in a fast and simply way according to the quality management with suitable features. The decision process from the user site would be simplified and the decision maker will be supported according to the quality of his decision through a proved and guaranteed minimum level of service quality. Therefore, the customer of the IT services can easily check the price-performance payoff and is able to evaluate whether it is a good offer or it is just "cheap."

The primary target groups of the cachet are service providers, which should be audited by means of the IT-Service cachet. However, the cachet is

Figure 10. Structure of the IT-Service Cachet

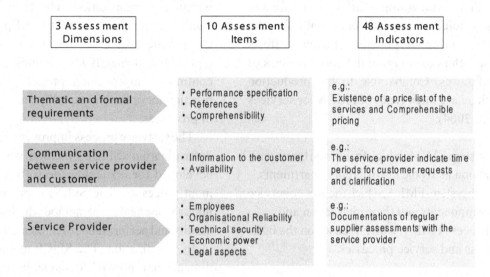

also helpful for the service recipients evaluating the service offers from the providers.

The evaluation catalog for the IT-Service cachet contains 48 assessment criteria to evaluate the quality of the IT-Service offers. The cachet measures the different quality dimensions with the level of fulfilment of quality indicators. These indicators for the service offers can be separated into ten dimensions.

The first part describes the "thematic and formal requirements of the offers," the second part focuses on the "Communication between service provider and Customer" and the third part concentrates on the characteristics of the "Service Provider." For each part several assessment items are developed which are measured due to assessment indicators. For each assessment indicator, there is a detailed description on how to measure, document and evaluate the criteria and there are defined levels of fulfilment (Praeg & Schnabel, 2006).

Quality Management Methods for the Life Cycle Phase 3

The third phase of the defined IT-Service life cycle describes the development, orchestration and testing of the IT-Services. Hence the quality items organizational structure and business processes as well as the services have a high priority in this phase. Therefore adequate quality management methods must regard these aspects. In the area of the software development there are some quality management methods which can be used for this phase. But it has to be mentioned that these methods have to customize to the requirements of IT-Service management.

In this phase suitable quality management methods are the Failure Mode and Effects Analysis (FMEA), Capability Maturity Model, software process improvement capability determination (SPICE) and the ISO 15504.

From a service provider's point of view the avoidance of failures is a central aspect for the quality management. Especially due to the concurrent providing and consumption of services an improvement of the delivered service is not possible. For this reason the Failure Mode and Effects Analysis (FMEA) is a method, which enables organization previously analyzes and evaluates potential problems and risks before they are realized. Therefore the FMEA method provides a risk assessment technique for systematically identifying potential failures in a system or a process. Failure modes mean the way, or modes, in which something might fail. Failures are any errors or defects, especially ones that affect the customer, and can be potential or actual. Effects analysis refers to studying the consequences of those failures. Comparable to the production area, there are three types of FMEA for services (Bruhn, 2004):

- System FMEA, which focuses on the organization as whole or different departments,
- Subsystem-FMEA, which focuses on service components and their interaction and
- Process FMEA, which focuses on the business and service processes.

The process of the FMEA covers the steps of failure description, risk assessment, generating suitable measures and the evaluation of the achieved results. The FMEA method supports organizations in controlling and managing the quality of IT-Services during various phases of the product life cycle.

The Capability Maturity Model Integration (CMMI) is a process improvement approach that provides organizations with the essential elements of effective processes. For the quality management CMMI can be used to improve the management maturity as well as the quality of services. According to a five level scale the processes of service providing can be systematically analyzed and the management quality improved. Originally CMMI was developed by the Software Engineering Institute from Carnegie Mellon University in 1987. This method is focused on the structured and systematically improvement of software engineering processes. During the past years CMMI was adapted to several other business areas. The CMMI model describes five levels of process maturity. On the first level (initial) there are processes defined. On the second level (repeatable) several tasks for a process management are implemented and processes can be managed with repeatable levels of performance. In the third level

(defined) processes are defined and documented within the organization. The level four (managed) focuses on the quality and performance measurement of the existing processes. Level five (optimized) demands for the implementation of continuous improvement programs in the organization for optimizing quality and performance of processes.

The software process improvement capability determination (SPICE) method was originally developed for managing the software development processes. The SPICE approach is also a maturity management method which supports the quality and performance of implemented services in an organization. The SPICE method is a two dimensional approach for managing development processes. The first dimension consists of the processes that are actually assessed (the process dimension which is grouped into five categories). The second dimension consists of the capability scale that is used to evaluate the process capability (the capability dimension). The same capability scale is used across all processes (El Emam & Birk, 2000). The ISO/IEC 15504 is an international standard on software process assessment. It defines a number of software engineering processes, and a scale for measuring their capability. In ISO/IEC 15504, there are 5 levels of capability that can be rated, from Level 1 to Level 5. The rating scheme consists of a 4-point achievement scale for each attribute. The four points are designated as F, L, P, N for Fully Achieved, Largely Achieved, Partially Achieved, and Not Achieved (El Emam & Birk, 2000).

Quality Management Methods for the Life Cycle Phase 4

In the fourth phase of the life cycle the operation, maintenance and the support of the used IT-Services must be managed in the organization. Most of the established IT-Service management concepts are focussing on this phase of the life cycle (Praeg & Schnabel, 2006). From the quality management point of view it is necessary to focus on the business processes and the organizational structure which is responsible for the Service providing. Additional to this the quality of the service provider is also from high interest as well as the service itself. Therefore suitable quality management methods must consider these aspects in a proper way.

In this phase possible quality management methods are Six Sigma and IT-Service SERVQUAL.

Six Sigma is a quality management concept which focuses on the improvement of business processes in organization. It is a statistically based quality improvement program which should organization help to improve business processes by reducing costs resulting from poor quality (Hensley & Dobie, 2005). It should also support improving the levels of efficiency and effectiveness in processes (Hensley & Dobie, 2005). These processes improvement should result in an improved customer satisfaction with the firm's products and services and an increased firm's profitability (Antony & Banuelas, 2001).

The most common used tool in the six-sigma concept is the DMAIC cycle (define, measure, analyze, improve, control).

- During the definition part the processes for improvement are identified and the identified problems as well as the targeted goals are documented.
- In the measurement part the focus is on the measurement of the current process and collect relevant data for benchmarking and also determination how good the process meets the customer expectations is made.
- The analyze-part concentrates on the verification of relationships and causality of the quality factors. It determines what the relationship is and attempts to ensure that all factors have been considered.
- The improvement part optimizes and improves the process based upon the analysis

using techniques like Design of Experiments.
- The part control ensures that any variances are corrected before they result in defects. Set up pilot runs to establish process capability, transition to production and thereafter continuously measure the process and institute control mechanisms.

Six Sigma was originally used in manufacturing environments but there are also transformations to the service sector. Especially financial service companies started to use Six Sigma to improve the customer satisfaction (Hensley & Dobie, 2005).

The traditional SERVQUAL is an instrument for analysing functional performance of service units. It is an instrument for assessing customer perceptions of service quality (Hochstein, 2004; Parasuraman et al., 1985). Characteristic for the SERVQUAL approach is that the different quality dimensions are measured with indicators. Quality is defined as the gap between the real value and a target-value. SERVQUAL is a multi-attributive measurement procedure, which uses five dimensions to define service performance quality. Parasuraman et al. (1985) developed this multiple-item approach consisting of five quality dimensions:

"Tangibles" describe the convenience of the material environment in which the service is rendered. Facilities, premises, technical equipment, phenotype of the staff etc., are part of it. "Reliability" is the trustworthiness of the supplier that indicates the ability to deliver the promised performance reliably and exactly. "Responsiveness" concerns the availability of the support, that the customer at the demands of the service (open-mindedness). "Assurance" refers to the safety of the performance claims on credibility of the supplier according to of competence, politeness and trustworthiness. "Empathy" concerns the ability of the service provider to cater to individual customer needs and the readiness to satisfy them (Hochstein, 2004; Parasuraman et al., 1985).

Figure 11. SERVQUAL dimensions

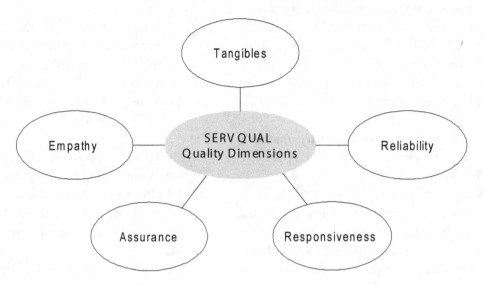

Therefore, the service performance quality arises from the difference between customer expectations and the customer perception. According to Donabedian, the five dimensions used in the SERVQUAL approach can be assigned to the dimensions of the process-, potential- and outcome- quality (Donabedian, 1980). While "Reliability" can be corresponded with the result quality and assigned to "Tangibles" and "Assurance" of the potential quality, analogies exist between "Responsiveness" and "Empathy" to the process quality (Praeg & Schnabel, 2006).

According to the special requirements Hochstein customized the SERVQUAL approach with regard to IT-Service management (Hochstein, 2004). In this approach IT-SERVQUAL is proposed due to adjusting elements for the traditional concepts and institutionalized to a service specific approach.

Quality Management Methods for the Life Cycle Phase 5

The final phase of the life cycle describes the detachment of the IT-Services which are no longer used in the organization. Most of the life cycle management concepts do not mention this phase but it is important to manage the detachment of IT-Services. Due to the connections and interfaces between different Services or due to a new release of an implemented serviced there is a need for the detachment of "old IT-Services" and it is also a great challenge for the organization to ensure the operation of the business processes. Therefore the suitable quality management methods have to consider aspects of change and risk management as well as the operational business process in the organization. In this phase the quality management methods previously described can also be used in this phase.

Conclusion for Life Cycle Based IT-Service Quality Management

This chapter shows the changing relevance of different quality aspects during the IT-Service life cycle phases. As a result organizations should use different quality management methods regarding to their individual situation. The described framework gives an example how organizations can map quality management methods with the changing requirements of the different life cycle phases to establish an effective and efficient IT-Service Quality Management. A great challenge from customer and providers point of view is the evaluation in which life cycle phase the different IT-Services are used. A further challenge will also be the organizational implementation of an adequate set of suitable quality management methods and instruments in the organization. Therefore the skills and capabilities for the selected quality management methods must be developed and systematically managed. It is obvious that the implementation of this model is a strategic decision in the organization and it needs time to realize and establish this concept in the organizational management processes.

CONCLUSION AND OUTLOOK

This chapter showed that IT-Service quality management is an important issue for implementing and managing IT-Governance. Due to the dynamic developments in IT-Service management and the increasing focus on IT-Services, market orientation and use of external service providers as well as the quality management of services becomes more important for organizations. But not only on the customer side, there is a growing importance for this issue. The management of IT-Service quality becomes also a key success factor for internal and external service providers. In future, the satisfaction of changing customer demands will be a great challenge for them.

As a result of the industrialisation of IT in organizations, the services of IT-Providers will be more and more separated into individual IT-products which have several life cycle phases. Hence, the IT-Service quality management must consider the requirements of the different life cycle phases. The use of quality management methods have to be adapted to the demands of the life cycle phase and the business requirements.

This chapter illustrated a general life cycle concept of IT-Services and highlighted requirements according to the quality management and quality methods. Based upon this approach, a model for

a life cycle based IT-Service quality management was developed. According to the traditional use case, the industry sector, the use of existing quality management methods must align with the requirements of the different life cycle phases. In the context of IT-Service quality management this perspective has not been adopted yet. In the past, there were a lot of discussions concerning the translation of approaches for service quality into the special demands of IT-Services, but the dynamics of IT-Service management were not considered.

For future developments there is a strong demand for the transformation of experiences from industrial quality management to IT-Service management. With regard to the production industry, the implementation of quality gates helps to ensure the quality from external providers. For IT-Services this concept must customized to the special demands of the organization and the services.

Due to the increased meaning of IT-Services and the importance of service quality as a key success factor, this topic has great potential and offers ample possibilities for future research. As seen in this chapter, quality management is a Top-Management issue for organizations. Consequently, there is a need for implementing suitable quality management concepts and research has to provide adequate evaluation concepts for improving quality management in dependence of the individual life cycle. Furthermore, there is a need for the organization implementation of the life cycle based IT-Service quality management. Especially the training of employees and the development of a quality focused culture within the organization represent great challenges for the management. A further challenge is the implementation and adaptation of existing infrastructures in an organization to manage the requirements which are tied to increased service orientation. An additional challenge is to establish trust between the service provider and the service recipient. Such confidence between the parties supports service perception and as a result service quality management.

Quality management is a continuous process, which will never stops and creates potential for future competitive advantages of service providers. Thus, the perspectives of IT-Managers and the focus of IT-Governance should expand to life cycle aspects of IT-Service quality management, because the quality of IT-Services is the key success factor for creating competitive advantages in the IT-Service market.

REFERENCES

Antony, J., & Banuelas, R. (2001). A strategy for survival. *Manufacturing Engineer, 80*(3), 119-121.

Böhmann, T., & Krcmar, H. (2003). Modulare Servicearchitekturen. In H.-J. Bullinger & A.-W. Scheer (Eds.), *Service Engineering - Entwicklung und Gestaltung innovativer Dienstleistungen.* Berlin.

Bruhn, M. (2004). *Qualitätsmanagement für Dienstleistungen: Grundlagen, Konzepte, Methoden* (5. ed.). Berlin [u.a.]: Springer.

Bullinger, H.-J. (1994). *Einführung in das Technologiemanagement: Modelle, Methoden, Praxisbeispiele.* Stuttgart: Teubner.

Deming, W. E. (1982). *Quality, productivity, and competitive position.* Cambridge, Mass.

Donabedian, A. (1980). *Explorations in quality, assessment and monitoring—The definition of quality and approaches to its assessment.* Ann Arbour.

El Emam, K., & Birk, A. (2000). Validating the ISO/IEC 15504 measure of software requirements analysis process capability. *Software Engineering, IEEE Transactions, 26*(6), 541.

Glass, R. L., Ramesh, V., & Vessey, I. (2004). An analysis of research in computing disciplines. *Communications of the acm, 47*(6), 89-94.

Grönroos, C. (1984). A service quality model and its marketing implications. *European Journal of Marketing, 18*(4), 36-44.

Haller, S. (2002). *Dienstleistungsmanagement* (2. ed.). Wiesbaden.

Hensley, R. L., & Dobie, K. (2005). Assessing readiness for six sigma in a service setting. *Managing Service Quality, 15*(1).

Hevner, A. R., March, S. T., Park, J., & Ram, S. (2004). Design science in information systems research. *MIS Quarterly, 28*(1), 75-105.

Hochstein, A. (2004). Managing IT service quality as perceived by the customer. In *Proceedings of the ITS 15th Biennial Conference*, Berlin.

Hochstein, A., Ebert, N., Uebernickel, F., & Brenner, W. (2007). Die neuen Wertschöpfungsketten. *Computerwoche, 16*, 32.

Kamiske, G., & Umbreit, G. (2001). *Qualitätsmanagement.* München, Wien: Carl Hanser Verlag.

Kotabe, M., & Murray, J. Y. (2004). Global procurement of service activities by service firms. *International Marketing Review, 21*(6), 615-633.

Macharzina, K. (2003). *Unternehmensführung das internationale Managementwissen Konzepte - Methoden - Praxis* (4., grundlegend überarb. Aufl. ed.). Wiesbaden: Gabler.

Malorny, C., & Kassebohm, K. (1994). *Brennpunkt TQM.* Stuttgart [u.a.]: Schäffer-Poeschel.

Mercurio, V. J., Meyers, B. F., Nisbet, A. M., & Radin, G. (1990). AD/Cycle strategy and architecture. *IBM Systems Journal, 29*(2), 170-188.

OGC (2006). *ITIL refresh: Scope and development plan.* Retrieved May 15, 2008, from www.itil.org

Parasuraman, A., Zeithamel, V., & Berry, K. L. (1985). A conceptual model of service quality an its implications for future research. *Journal of Marketing,* 41-50.

Parasuraman, A., Zeithamel, V. A., & Berry, K. L. (1988). SERVQUAL: A multiple item scale for measuring consumer perception of service quality. *Journal of Retailing, 64*(1), 12-37.

Praeg, C.-P., & Schnabel, U. (2006). IT-service Cachet—Managing IT-service performance and IT-service quality. In *Proceedings of the 39th Annual Hawaiian International Conference on System Sciences (HICSS)* (Vol. 2, pp. 10). Hawaii.

Sallé, M. (2004). *IT service management and IT governance: Review, comparative analysis and their impact on utillity computing* (No. HPL-2004-98). HP Laboratories Palo Alto: Trusted System Laboratory.

Schnabel, U., Dold, D., Fröschle, H.-P., Layer, B., Roll, U., & Skempes, A. (2006). *Das wertorientierte Management des intellektuellen Kapitals (ICM).* Stuttgart: Fraunhofer IRB Verlag.

Seth, N., Deshmukh, S. G., & Vrat, P. (2005). Service quality models: A review. *International Journal of Quality & Reliability Management, 22*(9).

Spath, D., & Demuß, L. (2003). Entwicklung hybrider Produkte—Gestaltung materieller und immaterieller Leistungsbündel. In H.-J. Bullinger & A.-W. Scheer (Eds.), *Service Engineering*: Springer.

Spath, D., van Husen, C., Meyer, K., & Elze, R. (2007). Integrated development of software and service—The challenge of IT-enabled service Products. In D. Spath & K.-P. Fähnrich (Eds.), *Advances in service innovations.* Berlin: Springer.

Stark, J. (2004). Product lifecycle management. *Paradigm for 21st century product realisation: 21st century paradigm for product realisation.* London: Springer.

Uebernickel, F., Bravo-Sànchez, C., Zarnekow, R., & Brenner, W. (2006). *Eine Vorgehensmethodik zum IT-Produktengineering.* Paper presented at the Multikonferenz für Wirtschaftsinformatik 2006, Berlin.

Weill, P., & Ross, J. W. (2004). *IT governance how top performers manage IT decision rights for superior results.* Boston: Harvard Business School.

Wonigeit, J. (1994). *Total quality management.* Wiesbaden.

Zarnekow, R., & Brenner, W. (2004). Integriertes informationsmanagement: Vom Plan, Built and Run zum Source, Make, Deliver. In R. Zarnekow, W. Brenner & H. H. Grohmann (Eds.), *Informationsmanagement Konzepte und Strategien für die Praxis* (pp. 289). Heidelberg: dpunkt.verlag.

Zarnekow, R., Brenner, W., & Grohmann, H. H. (2004). *Informationsmanagement Konzepte und Strategien für die Praxis.* Heidelberg: dpunkt.verlag.

Zarnekow, R., Hochstein, A., & Brenner, W. (2005). *Serviceorientiertes IT-Management ITIL-Best-Practices und -Fallstudien.* Berlin: Springer.

Chapter XXIII
Measuring Return on Investment from Implementing ITIL:
A Review of the Literature

Chee Ing Tiong
HD Digital Solutions, Australia

Aileen Cater-Steel
University of Southern Queensland, Australia

Wui-Gee Tan
University of Southern Queensland, Australia

ABSTRACT

This study reviews literature related to financial metrics that organizations could use in measuring the return on investment from their adoption of the IT Infrastructure Library (ITIL) framework. ITIL outlines an extensive set of best practices for IT service management in organizations but as yet there is limited academic research on measuring the return on investment from ITIL adoption. This review considers appropriate metrics which service managers could use to build a business case for ITIL adoption, or ongoing ITIL projects.

INTRODUCTION

The Information Technology Infrastructure Library (ITIL) framework outlines an extensive set of best practices for IT service management in organizations but as yet there is limited academic research on measuring the return on investment from ITIL adoption. After all, business organizations are most interested in the financial return that investment in ITIL could bring to their organization.

This literature review is organized in five sections. The first section describes the literature review method. The second section provides a brief description of the ITIL framework. The third section discusses the importance of measuring return on investment in ITIL. The fourth section discusses some of the available measurement metrics for IT investment that could be adapted to this study. The fifth section discusses a proposed measurement model and metrics for measuring investment return on ITIL service management.

LITERATURE REVIEW METHOD

This systematic literature review was conducted in four phases. The first phase involved the identification of relevant keywords for this study. The initial keywords were identified through ITIL literature and more keywords were added as more literature was reviewed. The second phase involved searching in online academic libraries for documents that contains the keywords. Four online academic libraries were used in this study: ACM Digital library, EBSCOHost, Emerald Insight and IEEEXplore. The focus of the review was on publications during the time period from 2000 to 2006 although some prior studies were also included. The third phase saw the classification of the literature according to keywords. A single research article may appear in more than one keyword category. Appendix A contains a summary of the research articles and keywords. The fourth phase comprised a systematic analysis of the literature based on the keywords. The analysis extracts the research objective, research method and measurement variables, and is summarized in Appendix B.

ITIL SERVICE MANAGEMENT FRAMEWORK

The purpose of ITIL as a framework of best practice is to facilitate the delivery of high quality information technology services. ITIL outlines an extensive set of management procedures that are intended to support businesses in achieving both quality and value for money in IT operations. ITIL is built around a process-model based view of controlling and managing operations. ITIL version 2 contains a subsection entitled IT service management and the subsection is further divided into service support and service delivery.

ITIL makes a distinction between *users* and *customers*: customers are the people in an organization who commission and fund the IT services whereas users are those who use the services on a day-to-day basis. Service support defines six processes that ensure *users* have sufficient access to support business function (OGC, 2002b):

1. **Configuration management:** Provides a logical model of the infrastructure by identifying, controlling, maintaining and verifying the versions of all components.
2. **Change management:** Responsible for ensuring changes are evaluated, approved, controlled, tracked and implemented safely without side effects to the quality of the service itself.
3. **Release management:** Undertakes the planning, design, building, configuration and testing of hardware and software to create a set of release components for a live environment.
4. **Incident management:** Restores normal service operation as quickly as possible and minimizes the adverse impact on business operation.
5. **Problem management:** Reduces both the number and severity of incidents and problems within business to proactively prevent recurrence of incidents and problems.
6. **Service desk:** Receipt and resolution of service requests, technical guidance, communication, etc. The central contact point between users and IT staff.

Service delivery defines what services the ICT provider is required to provide to the *customer*. Service delivery consists of five processes (OGC, 2002a):

1. **Service level management:** Planning, co-ordinating, drafting, agreeing, monitoring and reporting on service level agreements (SLAs).
2. **Financial management:** Budgeting, accounting and charging for IT services.
3. **Capacity management:** Timely and cost effective provisioning of IT resources to meet the expanding business needs from IT.
4. **Continuity management:** Managing an organization's ability to continue to provide a pre-determined and agreed level of IT services to support the minimum business requirements following an interruption to the business.
5. **Availability management:** Planning, implementation and management of IT services to meet the agreed availability requirement of the business.

There is a need to understand the processes involved in ITIL service management before any attempt to measure the costs and benefits of implementing ITIL. It is also important to remember that ITIL is only an IT management standard and its implementation would vary in different organizations.

WHY MEASURE RETURN ON INVESTMENT FOR ITIL IMPLEMENTATION?

Many organizations are becoming increasingly aware of the importance of metrics: "Measurements are the key. If you cannot measure it, you cannot control it. It you cannot control it, you cannot manage it. If you cannot manage it, you cannot improve it" (Harrington, 1991). Management costs money and ITIL is a standard that assists in guiding the management of IT services in organization. Costs associated with implementing ITIL can be substantial and include hardware, software, training, IT consultants, and internal IT staff labour. However, cost savings can be achieved from successful ITIL implementation through improved IT productivity and reliability leading to improved business productivity. Barua, Konana, Whinston, and Yin (2004) commented that technology creates new business processes from the old processes and new processes could potentially lead to improved informational and coordination capabilities, and such capabilities lower costs and improve services that affect revenues.

According to Lubbe and Remenyi (1999), IT investment opportunities are generated by strategic IS planning or "flashes of commercial insight" (p.149). The latter leads to intuitive-informal assessment. Time is also another important consideration in investment evaluation. Repenning and Sterman (2001) recognize the time delay working on improving process prior to capability being enhanced and the fact that capability is eroded over time, leaving a gap between desired performance and actual performance.

Prior to implementing any process improvement initiative, processes should be measured and if possible assigned a monetary value. Dibbern, Goles, Hirschheim, and Jayatilaka (2004) suggest that return on IS investment should be improved by generating new revenue and profit, and offsetting cost. Investment is made up of costs and expenses. Costs and expenses must be determined before return on investment can be measured.

IT investment evaluation is often difficult (Seddon, Graeser & Willcocks, 2002). There are many variables to consider especially tangible and intangible costs and benefits. There is a need to first determine what costs can be measured in relation to implementing ITIL, and then determine the benefits that could be used to calculate the return on investment.

Currently, there are few studies that are specific on financially measuring ITIL service management in organizations. Therefore, some of the measurement metrics and measurement variables are adapted from IT investment evaluation studies and IT project evaluation studies.

REVIEW OF AVAILABLE MEASUREMENT METHODS

A study to understand the return on investment concept in the IT context was conducted by Dehning and Richardson (2002). They developed a model to guide future research in the area. Their study provides a comprehensive analysis of literature from the year 1993 to 2002. They classified the measurements into accounting measurements and market measurements. Accounting measurements are metrics such as return on investment (ROI), return on sales (ROS), return on assets (ROA), return on equity (ROE), and so forth. Market measurements are metrics on stock market returns, such as Tobin's q (market value/asset value), shareholder value etc. Stock market return is one of the main measurement variables. They also describe IT investment in three classes: differences in the amount of money spent on IT, type of IT purchased, and how IT is managed. Business performances are measured in terms of gross margin, inventory turnover, customer service, quality, efficiencies, and other cost, profit margins and turnover ratio. It is possible to adapt the model to reflect direct and indirect effects of ITIL on business processes, which affects the organization performance. This study is further extended by Lim, Richardson, and Roberts (2004).

A meta-analysis approach was taken by Lim, Richardson, and Roberts (2004) to investigate IT value to determine whether it is possible to detect payoffs from investment in IT. Meta-analysis examines the results of existing studies to extract patterns or relatively consistent relations and causalities that conduct general principles and synthesize the results of past years of research. The study concluded that financial market measurements moderate the relationship between IT investment and firm performance. The findings indicate that financial market measurements are strong moderators of IT payoff.

A case study of three firms was conducted by Kohli and Hoadley (2006) to examine two measurements: organizational level and process level measurements. Their objective was to identify the effects of IT enabled business process redesign (BPR) projects. Organizational level measurements are customer value, efficiency and profitability. Process oriented measurements are labour costs, cycle time, efficiency, administrative expenses, responsiveness, resource usage, reporting, throughput, effectiveness. ITIL implementation could be treated as a BPR exercise and measurements in this study could be applied.

Lei and Rawles (2003) proposed the use of total cost of ownership (TCO) and real option analysis in evaluating IT investment. Total cost of ownership identifies, quantifies and aims to reduce the overall ownership cost of hard and soft costs. They indicate three main classes of TCO costs – acquisition cost, control costs and operation costs. Acquisition costs consist of the hardware and software costs. Control costs consist of centralisation and standardisation costs. Operation costs consist of support, evaluation, installation, upgrade, training, downtime, audit, and documentation costs. Real option analysis considers the options to defer, expand, contract, abandon, switch use, or alter a capital investment.

In evaluating IT projects, Bardhan, Bagchi, and Sougstad (2004) also used real option analysis to determine the value of an option to exchange risky development costs for risky revenue. They estimated project costs, benefits, variances of project return, and the time to option expiration date. Project costs are treated as one-time costs and ongoing investment. The project benefit is treated as the difference in cash flow over a certain period. It is possible to adapt this study by representing the measurement process in the ITIL framework in a project approach, which has its own associated costs, benefits and evaluation period.

Ballantine and Stray (1999) examined the way organizations evaluate information systems and other capital investments. They divided the metrics into cost analysis and risk analysis in this study. The metrics for cost analysis are payback, cost benefit analysis, return on investment, net present value, internal rate of return, return on management, and profitability index. The risk analysis metrics include sensitivity analysis, raising required rate of return, brainstorming, shortening payback period, scenario planning, tree diagrams, beta analysis, Delphi method, utility method, and Monte Carlo simulation.

Based on an insurance company, List and Machaczek (2004) conducted a study on measuring business process performance. Their study facilitated the use of a data warehouse in measuring the performance of the insurance company. They believed that current performance measurement system do not measure business processes systematically. Their study began with an understanding of the insurance business processes and proposed a measurement model for the processes. Six key measurement variables were extracted from their study: working time, waiting time, cycle time, number of instances, number of revisions and number of complaints. Their study concluded that incorporating a process perspective into a data warehouse represents a step towards sound and integrated performance measurement, which in turn represents a prerequisite to improve business processes on a continuous basis and achieving long term organizational goals. Their study also demonstrated some similarities with the study by Seddon, Graeser, and Willcocks (2002).

The views of 80 IT managers about their IT evaluation approaches and the benefits provided by the IT infrastructure were reported by Seddon, Graeser and Willcocks (2002). This study concluded that IT firms do not conduct rigorous evaluations of all their IT investments. They also commented on a balanced scorecard approach with six perspectives when measuring IT effectiveness:

1. **Corporate financial perspective:** Profit per employee
2. **System project perspective:** Time, quality, cost
3. **Business process perspective:** Purchase invoice per employee
4. **Customer perspective:** On-time delivery
5. **Innovation/learning perspective:** Rate of cost reduction for IT services
6. **Technical perspective:** Development efficiency, capacity utilisation

Three steps in financial evaluation are illustrated by Anandarajan and Wen (1999). Step 1 determines tangible and intangible benefits. Step 2 determines cost of technology and process. Step 3 determines the net present value and risk. Some of the benefits included expected value of faster response time, expected value of increased flexibility, and expected value of higher quality. Customer turnover also causes changes in revenue generation. Cost is divided into development cost and operation cost. They also conducted a sensitivity analysis to measure the possible changes in the benefits and revenue. Their study could be coordinated with Chaya and Mitra's (1996) study in identifying operation costs.

After identifying operating expenses and operating margins, Chaya and Mitra (1996) concluded that firms with higher IT investment have lower operating costs and higher operating margins (operating margin is net sales minus operating costs). Their study used IT budget as a percentage of sales. Therefore, it is possible to substitute net sales with another value in measuring ITIL-based service management.

A study by Giaglis, Paul, and O'Keefe (1999) sought to investigate the potential of integrating different simulation models to facilitate concurrent engineering of business processes and information technology and to support the process of investment evaluation. They divided cost and benefits into quantitative costs and benefits, and qualitative costs and benefits. Quantitative costs consist of costs or direct savings that could be expressed in monetary terms and CBA/ROI analysis. Qualitative costs cannot be easily expressed in quantitative terms and thus cannot be incorporated in traditional investment evaluation theories. Among the extracted costs are communication costs, migration costs, training costs, operation costs, coordination costs, delivery costs, staffing costs, and response time.

The study by Oh, Kim, and Richardson (2006) examined the moderating effect of context on the market reaction to IT investment announcement. Context could include external factors that can be measured to evaluate performance of ITIL implementation. Some of the measurement variables include cumulative abnormal return, market-to-book ratio, variability in daily stock return, asset specificity, firm size, and industry.

Finally, Moura, Sauve, Jornada, and Radziuk (2006) proposed the use of financial loss functions to estimate the impact that IT Service Level Agreements (SLAs) have on business performance. This study has the highest relevance to ITIL evaluation. This study described the SLA as a core instrument in ITIL. The study took a balanced scorecard approach dividing business processes into four classes: customer, financial, learning and innovations, and internal operations. The financial loss function they propose consists of the total overall (potential) business loss in the four classes of processes due to SLA violation over an evaluation period.

PROPOSED MEASUREMENT MODEL

Based on the literature review, a model is proposed to evaluate the possibility of applying the extracted metrics in evaluation of ITIL-based service management. Figure 1 illustrates the proposed model. In Figure 1, CAR refers to the cumulative abnormal return, and MBR is the market to book ratio.

A list of examples of cost and time variables related to service support and service delivery processes is provided in Table 1. This list could be used by managers to calculate useful metrics. The Financial Management process in ITIL provides advice on metrics that report on costs. Metrics are also used to systematically measure and improve IT performance. Many organizations determine the maturity level of their IT service management processes to select appropriate metrics.

ITIL metrics are designed to measure obtained benefits (tangible and intangible) to justify the adoption of the ITIL framework. Examples of tangible benefits include cost reduction/avoidance and improved productivity of users and IT staff. Intangible benefits are important but more difficult to measure and include in a business case, for example, ITIL may help management to spot danger in time to correct problems before downtime is experienced, may improve morale in an organization, may stimulate healthy competition between process owners, and most importantly, help align IT with business goals.

CONCLUSION

In conclusion, the return on investment from implementing ITIL could be measured when the associated cost and time in the business processes are identified. It also depends on the measurement approach. Managers could treat the measurement process as a project and gather measurement data within a period, or apply a simulation model to

Figure 1. Proposed model to evaluate ITIL investment

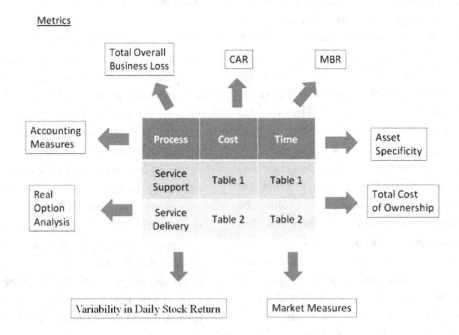

Table 1. ITIL service support and delivery metrics (adapted from Brooks, 2006)

ITIL Process		Examples of ITIL Metrics	
		Cost	Time
Service Support	Configuration Management	Number of licenses not used Cost associated with breaches in SLAs caused by accurate CMDB	Duration that the CMDB has been consistently up-to-date
	Change Management	Cost to recover failed changes Cost incurred by outage during changes	Time to complete change
	Release Management	Cost of release Cost of meeting urgent releases Cost of conducting end-user training sessions for new releases	Time to complete investigation of reported bugs Service time lost due to release activity
	Incident Management	Savings from incidents resolved right first time	Call time with no escalation Mean time to resolve incident
	Problem Management	Cost associated with user downtime Cost to overcome missed target resolution time	Time to close a problem
	Service Desk	Cost of meeting SLAs that require changes Cost of SLA breaches caused by 3rd party support contracts	Duration of calls Time spent calling back customer for more information or to give a solution

continued on following page

Table 1. continued

Service Delivery	Service Level Management	Service Delivery costs Cost associated with SLA breaches caused by third party support contracts	Elapsed time to follow up and resolve issues
	Financial Management	Actual costs against budgeted costs Software license fees vs. available licenses Percentage of unaccounted total IT costs	Staff time spent on costing activities
	Capacity Management	Cost arising from SLA breaches due to poor service performance	On-line response time
	Continuity Management	Cost to rectify wrong entries in crisis control team directory Cost of changes that have caused major issues	Delay in IT service continuity plan completion/update
	Availability Management	Cost to repair per incident	Downtime due to unavailability of service Response time per incident

generate the necessary measurement data related to ITIL service management processes. It is also important to decide which perspective the manager wishes to take to measure the return on investment in ITIL implementation.

This review of the literature has provided many candidate metrics of varying complexity. Care needs to be taken to ensure that the effort involved in collecting and analysing the metrics is in itself cost effective. The review has not included reference to the recently approved international standard ISO/IEC 20000, or the updated version of ITIL. Prior to adopting ITIL, organizations need to carefully consider which version of ITIL is most appropriate for their requirements.

REFERENCES

Alshawi, S., Irani, Z., & Baldwin, L. (2003). Benchmarking information technology investment and benefits extraction. *Benchmarking: An International Journal, 10*(4).

Amico, M., Pasek, Z., Asl, F., & Perrone, G. (2003). Simulation methodology for collateralized debt and real options: A new methodology to evaluate the real options of investment using binomial trees and monte carlo simulation. In *Proceedings of the 35th Winter Conference on Simulation: Driving Innovation*, New Orleans, Louisiana.

Anandarajan, A. & Wen, J. (1999). Evaluation of information technology investment. *Management Decision, 37*(4).

Au, Y. A. & Kauffman, R. J. (2003). Information technology investment and adoption: a rational expectations perspective.In *Proceedings of the 36th Hawaii International Conference on System Sciences.*

Ballantine, J. A. & Stray, S. (1999). Information systems and other capital investments: evaluation practices compared. *Logistics Information Management, 12*(1/2).

Bardhan, I., Bagchi, S., & Sougstad, R. (2004). A real options approach for prioritization of a portfolio of information technology projects: A case study of a utility company. In *Proceedings of the 37th Hawaii International Conference on System Sciences.*

Barua, A., Konana, P., Whinston, A. B., & Yin, F. (2004). An empirical investigation of net-enabled business value. *MIS Quarterly, 28*(4), 585-620.

Brooks, P. (2006). *Metrics for IT service management* (1st ed.). Zaltbommel, Netherlands: Van Haren.

Cavusoglu, H., Mishra, B., & Raghunathan, S. (2004). A model for evaluating IT security investments. *Communications of the ACM, 47*(7), 87-92.

Chandrasekaran, N. & Ensing, G. (2004). ODC: A global IT services delivery model. *Communications of the ACM, 47*(5), 47-49.

Chaya, A. & Mitra, S. (1996). Exploring the relationships between IT investments and organizational performance: preliminary empirical evidence. In *Proceedings of the 29th Annual Hawaii International Conference on System Sciences*.

Chen, L., Sheng, O., Goreham, D., & Watanabe, J. (2005). A real option analysis approach to evaluating digital government investment. In *Proceedings of the National Conference on Digital Government Research*, Atlanta, Georgia.

Chikofsky, E. & Rubin, H. A. (1999). Using metrics to justify investment in IT. *IT Professional, 1*(2), 75-77.

Chowdhary, P., Bhaskaran, K., Caswell, N. S., Chang, H., Chao, T., Chen, S. K., et al. (2006). Model driven development for business performance management. *IBM Systems Journal, 45*(3), 587-605.

Craighead, C. & Shaw, N. (2003). E-commerce value creation and destruction: A resource-based, supply chain perspective. *SIGMIS Database, 34*(2), 39-49.

Cronk, M. C. & Fitzgerald, E. P. (1999). Understanding IS business value: Derivation of dimensions. *Logistics Information Management, 12*(1/2).

Dehning, B. & Richardson, V. J. (2002). Returns on investments in information technology: A

research Synthesis. *Journal of Information Systems, 16*(1), 7-30.

Dehning, B., Richardson, V. J., & Stratopoulos, T. (2003). Reviewing event studies in MIS: An application of the firm value. In *Proceedings of the 36th Hawaii International Conference on System Sciences*.

Dibbern, J., Goles, T., Hirschheim, R., & Jayatilaka, B. (2004). Information systems outsourcing: a survey and analysis of the literature. *SIGMIS Database, 35*(4), 6-102.

Dixon, K. (2004). *Ken Dixon's ITIL Overview.*

Fairchild, A. M. (2002). Knowledge management metrics via a balanced scorecard methodology. In *Proceedings of the 35th Hawaii International Conference on System Sciences*.

Fitsilis, P. (2006). Practices and problems in managing electronic services using SLAs. *Information Management & Computer Security, 14*(2).

Giaglis, G., Paul, R., & Keefe, R. (1999). Research note: Integrating business and network simulation models for IT investment evaluation. *Logistics Information Management, 12*(1/2).

Goh, K. H. & Kauffman, R. J. (2005). Towards a theory of value latency for IT investments. In *Proceedings of the 38th Hawaii International Conference on System Sciences*.

Hanemann, A., Sailer, M., & Schmitz, D. (2004). Assured service quality by improved fault management. In *Proceedings of the 2nd International Conference on Service Oriented Computing*, New York, NY.

Harrington, J. (1991). *Business process improvement - The breakthrough strategy for total quality, productivity and competitiveness*. New York: McGraw-Hill.

Hassan, S. Z. & Saeed, K. A. (1999). A framework for determining IT effectiveness: An empirical approach. In *Proceedings of the 32nd Hawaii International Conference on System Sciences*.

Katchabaw, M., Lutfiyya, H., & Bauer, M. (1998). Driving resource management with application-level quality of service specifications. In *Proceedings of the First International Conference on Information and Computation Economies*, Charleston, South Carolina.

Kohli, R. & Hoadley, E. (2006). Towards developing a framework for measuring organizational impact of IT-enabled BPR: Case studies of three firms. *SIGMIS Database, 37*(1), 40-58.

Kraemer, K. L., Dedrick, J., & Yamashiro, S. (2000). Refining and extending the business model with information technology: Dell Computer Corporation. *Information Society, 16*(1), 5-21.

Lamberton, D. (1998). Information economics: Research strategies. *International Journal of Social Economics, 25*(2/3/4).

Lee, I. (2004). Evaluating business process-integrated information technology investment. *Business Process Management Journal, 10*(2).

Lee, S.-H., Thomas, S. R., Macken, C. L., Chapman, R. E., Tucker, R. L., & Kim, I. (2005). Economic Value of Combined Best Practice Use. *Journal of Management in Engineering, 21*(3), 118-124.

Lei, K. & Rawles, P. (2003). Strategic decisions on technology selections for facilitating a network/systems laboratory using real options \& total cost of ownership theories. In *Proceedings of the 4th Conference on Information Technology Curriculum*, Lafayette, Indiana.

Lim, G., Lee, H., & Kim, T. (2005). Formulating business strategies from a stakeholder perspective: Korean healthcare IT business cases. *International Journal of Information Technology & Decision Making, 4*(4), 541-566.

Goh, K. H. & Kauffman, R. J. (2005). Towards a theory of value latency for IT investments. In *Proceedings of the 38th Hawaii International Conference on System Sciences*.

List, B. & Machaczek, K. (2004). Towards a corporate performance measurement system. In *Proceedings of the ACM Symposium on Applied Computing*, Nicosia, Cyprus.

Lu, J. & Zhang, G. (2003). Cost benefit factor analysis in e-services. *International Journal of Service Industry Management, 14*(5).

Lubbe, S. & Remenyi, D. (1999). Management of information technology evaluation - the development of a managerial thesis. *Logistics Information Management, 12*(1/2).

Malhotra, Y. & Galletta, D. F. (2004). Building Systems that Users Want to Use. *Communications of the ACM, 47*(12), 89-94.

Mandeville, T. (1998). An information economics perspective on innovation. *International Journal of Social Economics, 25*(2/3/4).

Martinsons, M. G., & Martinsons, V. (2002). Re-thinking the Value of IT, Again. *Communications of the ACM, 45*(7), 25-26.

Mayo, D. D., Dalton, W. J., & Callaghan, M. J. (2003). Strategy simulations: steering strategic decisions at London underground: Evaluating management options with system dynamics. In *Proceedings of the 35th Winter Simulation Conference: Driving Innovation*, New Orleans, Louisiana.

Menachemi, N., Burkhardt, J., Richard, S., Darrell, B., & Robert, G. B. (2006). Hospital information technology and positive financial performance: A different approach to finding an ROI. *Journal of Healthcare Management, 51*(1), 40-58.

Moura, A., Sauve, J., Jornada, J., & Radziuk, E. (2006). A quantitative approach to IT investment allocation to improve business results. In *Proceedings of the Seventh IEEE International Workshop on Policies for Distributed Systems and Networks (POLICY'06)*.

OGC (2002a). *IT infrastructure library- Service delivery*. London: Stationery Office.

OGC (2002b). *IT infrastructure library- Service Support*. London: Stationery Office.

Oh, W., Kim, J. W., & Richardson, V. J. (2006). The moderating effect of context on the market reaction to IT investments. *Journal of Information Systems, 20*(1), 19-44.

Presley, A. (2006). ERP investment analysis using the strategic alignment model. *Management Research News, 29*(5).

Reed, K. (2006). EQUITY and the problem of return on IT investment. *Software, IEEE, 23*(1), 114-115.

Repenning, N. P. & Sterman, J. D. (2001). Nobody ever gets credit for fixing problems that never happened: creating and sustaining process improvement. *California Management Review, 43*(4), 64-88.

Seddon, P., Graeser, V., & Willcocks, L. (2002). Measuring organizational IS effectiveness: An overview and update of senior management perspectives. *SIGMIS Database, 33*(2), 11-28.

Senn, J. A. & Gefen, D. (1998). How managers assess the business value returned from information technology spending. *In Proceedings of the 31st Annual Hawaii International Conference on System Sciences*.

Serafeimidis, V. & Smithson, S. (1999). Rethinking the approaches to information systems investment evaluation. *Logistics Information Management, 12*(1/2).

Sherer, S. A., Ray, M. R., & Chowdhury, N. M. (2002). Assessing information technology investments with an integrative process framework. *In Proceedings of the 35th Hawaii International Conference on System Sciences*.

Stevenson, B. & Romney, G. (2004). Teaching security best practices by architecting and administering an IT security lab. In *Proceedings of the 5th conference on Information Technology Education*, Salt Lake City, UT.

Sundaresan, S. & Zuopeng, Z. (2004). Facilitating knowledge transfer in organizations through incentive alignment and IT investment. In *Proceedings of the 37th Hawaii International Conference on System Sciences*.

Tan, J., Wen, J., & Awad, N. (2005). Health care and services delivery systems as complex adaptive systems. *Communications of the ACM, 48*(5), 36-44.

Tillquist, J. & Rodgers, W. (2005). Using asset specificity and asset scope to measure the value of IT. *Communications of the ACM, 48*(1), 75-80.

Tonge, R., Larsen, P., & Roberts, M. (2000). Information systems investment within high-growth medium-sized enterprises. *Management Decision, 38*(7).

Wagenaar, R. (2006). Governance of shared service centers in public administration: dilemmas and trade-offs. *In Proceedings of the 8th International Conference on Electronic Commerce: The New E-Commerce: Innovations for Conquering Current Barriers, Obstacles and Limitations to Conducting Successful Business on the Internet*. Fredericton, New Brunswick, Canada.

Walker, R. H., Craig-Lees, M., Hecker, R., & Francis, H. (2002). Technology-enabled service delivery: An investigation of reasons affecting customer adoption and rejection. *International Journal of Service Industry Management, 13*(1).

Wilson, A. (2000). The use of performance information in the management of service delivery. *Marketing Intelligence & Planning, 18*(3).

Yao, C. & Joe, Z. (2004). Measuring Information Technology's Indirect Impact on Firm Performance. *Information Technology & Management, 5*(1/2), 9-22.

APPENDIX A. RESEARCH ARTICLES BY KEYWORD AND ONLINE LIBRARY

Keywords	Source Library			
	ACM Digital Library	EBSCOHost	Emerald Insights	IEEEXplore
ITIL	(Hanemann, Sailer, & Schmitz, 2004) (Stevenson & Romney, 2004)			(Moura, Sauve, Jornada, & Radziuk, 2006)
Service Level Management	(Hanemann, Sailer, & Schmitz, 2004; Katchabaw, Lutfiyya, & Bauer, 1998) (Dibbern, Goles, Hirschheim, & Jayati-laka, 2004) (Wagenaar, 2006)		(Fitsilis, 2006)	(Moura, Sauve, Jornada, & Radziuk, 2006)
Service Delivery	(Tan, Wen, & Awad, 2005) (Mayo, Dalton, & Callaghan, 2003)	(Kraemer, Dedrick, & Yamashiro, 2000) (Chandrasekaran & Ensing, 2004)	(Fitsilis, 2006) (Wilson, 2000) (Walker, Craig-Lees, Hecker, & Francis, 2002)	(Moura, Sauve, Jornada, & Radziuk, 2006)
Service Support	(Mayo, Dalton, & Callaghan, 2003)		(Fitsilis, 2006) (Wilson, 2000) (Walker, Craig-Lees, Hecker, & Francis, 2002)	(Moura, Sauve, Jornada, & Radziuk, 2006)
Service Management	(Tan, Wen, & Awad, 2005)		(Wilson, 2000) (Walker, Craig-Lees, Hecker, & Francis, 2002)	(Moura, Sauve, Jornada, & Radziuk, 2006)
Business Case	(Dibbern, Goles, Hirschheim, & Jayati-laka, 2004) (Wagenaar, 2006)	(Kraemer, Dedrick, & Yamashiro, 2000) (Barua, Konana, Whinston, & Yin, 2004) (G. Lim, Lee, & Kim, 2005)	(Presley, 2006)	(Sherer, Ray, & Chowd-hury, 2002)
Performance Measurement	(List & Machaczek, 2004)	(Menachemi, Burkhardt, Richard, Darrell, & Robert, 2006) (Bruce Dehning & Rich-ardson, 2002) (Kraemer, Dedrick, & Yamashiro, 2000) (Chowdhary et al., 2006) (Barua, Konana, Whinston, & Yin, 2004) (S.-H. Lee et al., 2005) (Malhotra & Galletta, 2004) (Martinsons & Martinsons, 2002) (Yao & Joe, 2004) (G. Lim, Lee, & Kim, 2005)	(Anandarajan & Wen, 1999) (I. Lee, 2004) (Lubbe & Remenyi, 1999) (Ballantine & Stray, 1999) (Cronk & Fitzgerald, 1999)	(Hassan & Saeed, 1999) (Sherer, Ray, & Chowd-hury, 2002) (Goh & Kauffman, 2005) (Chaya & Mitra, 1996) (Au & Kauffman, 2003) (B. Dehning, Richard-son, & Stratopoulos, 2003) (J. Lim, Richardson, & Roberts, 2004) (Reed, 2006)
Best Practices Frameworks	(Stevenson & Romney, 2004) (Wagenaar, 2006)	(Kraemer, Dedrick, & Yamashiro, 2000) (Chowdhary et al., 2006)	(Giaglis, Paul, & Keefe, 1999) (Alshawi, Irani, & Bald-win, 2003)	(Fairchild, 2002)

continued on following page

Appendix A. continued

Keywords	Source Library			
	ACM Digital Library	EBSCOHost	Emerald Insights	IEEEXplore
IT Benchmarking	(Seddon, Graeser, & Willcocks, 2002)	(S.-H. Lee et al., 2005) (Yao & Joe, 2004)	(Lubbe & Remenyi, 1999) (Alshawi, Irani, & Baldwin, 2003)	(Hassan & Saeed, 1999) (Goh & Kauffman, 2005) (Au & Kauffman, 2003) (B. Dehning, Richardson, & Stratopoulos, 2003)
IT Value	(Tillquist & Rodgers, 2005) (Kohli & Hoadley, 2006) (Craighead & Shaw, 2003)	(Cavusoglu, Mishra, & Raghunathan, 2004) (Kraemer, Dedrick, & Yamashiro, 2000) (Barua, Konana, Whinston, & Yin, 2004) (S.-H. Lee et al., 2005) (Martinsons & Martinsons, 2002)	(Anandarajan & Wen, 1999) (Serafeimidis & Smithson, 1999) (I. Lee, 2004) (Ballantine & Stray, 1999) (Alshawi, Irani, & Baldwin, 2003) (Presley, 2006) (Cronk & Fitzgerald, 1999)	(Hassan & Saeed, 1999) (Chikofsky & Rubin, 1999) (Sherer, Ray, & Chowdhury, 2002) (Goh & Kauffman, 2005) (Chaya & Mitra, 1996) (Senn & Gefen, 1998) (B. Dehning, Richardson, & Stratopoulos, 2003) (J. Lim, Richardson, & Roberts, 2004)
Return on Investment	(Lei & Rawles, 2003)	(Cavusoglu, Mishra, & Raghunathan, 2004) (Menachemi, Burkhardt, Richard, Darrell, & Robert, 2006) (Bruce Dehning & Richardson, 2002)	(Giaglis, Paul, & Keefe, 1999) (Anandarajan & Wen, 1999) (Serafeimidis & Smithson, 1999) (Ballantine & Stray, 1999) (Presley, 2006)	(Sherer, Ray, & Chowdhury, 2002) (Fairchild, 2002) (Goh & Kauffman, 2005) (Chaya & Mitra, 1996) (Au & Kauffman, 2003) (Bardhan, Bagchi, & Sougstad, 2004) (J. Lim, Richardson, & Roberts, 2004) (Sundaresan & Zuopeng, 2004) (Reed, 2006)
IT Investment Evaluation	(Chen, Sheng, Goreham, & Watanabe, 2005) (Lei & Rawles, 2003) (Amico, Pasek, Asl, & Perrone, 2003) (Seddon, Graeser, & Willcocks, 2002)	(Cavusoglu, Mishra, & Raghunathan, 2004) (Menachemi, Burkhardt, Richard, Darrell, & Robert, 2006) (Bruce Dehning & Richardson, 2002)	(Giaglis, Paul, & Keefe, 1999) (Anandarajan & Wen, 1999) (Serafeimidis & Smithson, 1999) (I. Lee, 2004) (Lubbe & Remenyi, 1999) (Ballantine & Stray, 1999) (Tonge, Larsen, & Roberts, 2000) (Alshawi, Irani, & Baldwin, 2003) (Presley, 2006)	(Hassan & Saeed, 1999) (Chikofsky & Rubin, 1999) (Sherer, Ray, & Chowdhury, 2002) (Fairchild, 2002) (Goh & Kauffman, 2005) (Chaya & Mitra, 1996) (Senn & Gefen, 1998) (Au & Kauffman, 2003) (J. Lim, Richardson, & Roberts, 2004) (Sundaresan & Zuopeng, 2004) (Reed, 2006) (Moura, Sauve, Jornada, & Radziuk, 2006)

continued on following page

Appendix A. continued

Keywords	Source Library			
	ACM Digital Library	EBSCOHost	Emerald Insights	IEEEXplore
Cost Benefit Analysis	(Lei & Rawles, 2003) (Seddon, Graeser, & Willcocks, 2002)	(Bruce Dehning & Richardson, 2002)	(Anandarajan & Wen, 1999) (Alshawi, Irani, & Baldwin, 2003) (Lu & Zhang, 2003)	(Goh & Kauffman, 2005) (Senn & Gefen, 1998) (Bardhan, Bagchi, & Sougstad, 2004)
Return on Management	(Lei & Rawles, 2003) (Seddon, Graeser, & Willcocks, 2002)		(Anandarajan & Wen, 1999) (Ballantine & Stray, 1999)	(Fairchild, 2002) (Senn & Gefen, 1998) (Bardhan, Bagchi, & Sougstad, 2004) (J. Lim, Richardson, & Roberts, 2004)
Information Economics	(Lei & Rawles, 2003) (Seddon, Graeser, & Willcocks, 2002)	(Bruce Dehning & Richardson, 2002)	(Tonge, Larsen, & Roberts, 2000) (Alshawi, Irani, & Baldwin, 2003) (Mandeville, 1998) (Lamberton, 1998)	(Sherer, Ray, & Chowdhury, 2002) (Goh & Kauffman, 2005)

APPENDIX B. SUMMARY OF KEY RESEARCH ARTICLES

Literature	Research Objective	Research Method	Extracted Measurement
(Kohli & Hoadley, 2006)	Examine organizational level measures and process level measures that were used to identify the effects of IT enabled business process redesign projects.	Case study of three firms.	Organizational level measurements Process level measurements
(Oh, Kim, & Richardson, 2006)	Examines moderating effects of firm and IT characteristics on the market reaction to IT investment announcement.	Event studies of IT investment announcement.	Cumulative abnormal return (CAR) Market to Book Ratio (MBR) Variability in Daily Stock Return Asset Specificity
(Moura, Sauve, Jornada, & Radziuk, 2006)	Proposes using financial loss functions to estimate the impact that IT Service Level Agreement (SLA) have on business performance.	Case study of a company	Total Accumulated (Potential) Business Loss due to SLA violation in Customer, Learning and Innovation, Internal Operations, and Financial loss over an evaluation period.
(Bardhan, Bagchi, & Sougstad, 2004)	Provides a methodology to use real options analysis to value and prioritize a portfolio of IT initiatives in a real world setting	Case study of 31 IT investment project in an organization.	Project costs Project benefits Variance of Return Time to option expiration date
(J. Lim, Richardson, & Roberts, 2004)	Use meta-analysis to summarize and synthesize the pattern of relatively consistent relations from empirical studies of IT investment returns during the last decade.	Literature reviews	Accounting Measures (Return on Investment, Return on Sales, Return on Equity, Return on Assets) Market Measures (Market Shares, Tobin's Q)

continued on following page

Appendix B. continued

Literature	Research Objective	Research Method	Extracted Measurement
(List & Machaczek, 2004)	Illustrate how a data warehouse can be used to facilitate a corporate performance measurement system by the integration of business process performance information into a traditional data warehouse that generally represents only the functional organization.	Feasibility study of a large insurance company in Europe.	Working Time Waiting Time Cycle Time Number of Instances Number of revisions Number of Complaints
(Lei & Rawles, 2003)	Investigate different combinations of enabling technologies and approaches.	Computer benchmarking Survey and observations	Total Costs of Ownership (Acquisition costs, control costs, operation costs) Real Option Analysis
(Bruce Dehning & Richardson, 2002)	Understand the return on investment in IT Develop a model to guide future research in evaluation of information technology investment	Literature reviews	Accounting Measures (Return on Investment, Return on Sales, Return on Equity, Return on Assets) Market Measures (Market Shares, Tobin's Q)
(Seddon, Graeser, & Willcocks, 2002)	Report views of 80 IT managers about IT evaluation approaches, and the benefits that IT provides for their organizations.	Survey analysis.	Profit per employee Time quality costs Purchase invoice per employee Rate of cost reduction On-time delivery Development efficiency Capacity utilisation.
(Anandarajan & Wen, 1999)	Show how traditional methods using the concepts of net present value can be used to quantify both tangible and intangible benefits and costs.	Case study	Expected value of faster response time Expected value of increased flexibility Expected value of higher quality Customer turnover Sensitivity Analysis Development Cost Operation Cost
(Ballantine & Stray, 1999)	Address the extent to which evaluation depends of organizational factors Examine the way organizations evaluate IT and other capital investment.	Study of two survey data sets.	Payback Cost Benefit Analysis Return on Investment Net Present Value Internal Rate of Return Return on management Profitability Index
(Giaglis, Paul, & Keefe, 1999)	Investigate the potential of integrating different simulation models to facilitate concurrent engineering of business processes and IT, and to support the process of investment evaluation	Case study	Communication costs Migration costs Training costs Operation costs Coordination costs Delivery costs Staffing costs Response time
(Chaya & Mitra, 1996)	Reports some preliminary results of an on-going research effort to better understand the relationship between firms IT investment and its financial performance.	Secondary data (IT and financial data) analysis on 609 large US companies	Operating expenses Operating margin

Chapter XXIV
Integrated Product Life Cycle Management for Software:
CMMI[1], SPICE, and ISO/IEC 20000

Dirk Malzahn
OrgaTech GmbH, Germany

ABSTRACT

This chapter describes how models for software development and service delivery can be integrated into a common approach to reach an integrated product life cycle for software. The models covered by this chapter are the capability maturity model integration (CMMI), SPICE (software process improvement and capability determination, ISO 15504) and ISO 20000 (service management). Whilst the CMMI constellation approach delivers an integration perspective defined in three models (development, acquisition and services), SPICE and ISO 20000 need additional alignment to be usable in an integrated approach.

INTRODUCTION

The focus of the market for IT solutions has changed. Whilst many companies and organizations followed the latest "hype" several years ago, they now trust in reliable and sustainable solutions.

To ensure this, standardization of quality evaluation becomes more and more important. For supplier selection, make-or-buy decisions and outsourcing strategies, a powerful set of procedures, that can help to assess the capability of internal and external software processes, is required. These procedures have to be based on best practices and must be widely accepted.

On this basis, standards offer the best possibilities: they are usually defined by a wide group of experts, which all contribute their experiences and best practices. Standards are either sponsored by an industry or by national bodies—therefore making these standards de facto mandatory for an industry, nation, or combination of both enforces the acceptance. If a significant group uses a standard, market dynamics have an additional impact. Official certificates, levels, and so forth can be and are used for marketing activities.

In the field of software related standards, lots of different standards have been defined for special topics, but one standard is still missing: a standard that covers a software product from the very beginning—the first idea—up to the very end—the retirement of the software.

On the one hand powerful standards, for example the capability maturity model integration (CMMI) or SPICE (ISO 15504), have been defined for software development. On the other hand, standards for service delivery, for example ITIL or ISO 20000, have been well established; but there is still a wall between the worlds of software development and service delivery. Even though some standards – like SPICE – take a look over the wall, an integrated approach has not been delivered yet.

The need for this integration is obvious. A customer is not interested in having some quality for development and some other quality for service delivery—the customer needs one quality approach that covers the full life cycle of a software product.

BACKGROUND

The Wall Between Software Development and Service Delivery

When IT systems are planned, the focus of the planning is mostly restricted to software development. Topics like operation environment or data management are discussed, but the strategy usually ends with the delivery of the software product.

On the other hand, service-delivering organizations mostly just provide "services" and are not really interested in the software development process.

This behavior leads to multiple difficulties and inefficiencies:

- Software developers and service people do not understand each other. They work in different worlds and have their own "language" and processes.
- The efficiency and effectiveness of service delivery highly depends on the architecture of and assumptions for the software, therefore the service organization has to be integrated early into the software development.
- Service level agreements can be optimized, when both sides reach a common understanding. The development of service level agreements is often based on the "what we need" position of both sides and not on the "what will be best for the customer" position.
- Problem Management is not transparent to the customer. The customer is not interested whether he has a service problem or a software problem—the customer wants a quick and reliable solution. If the software side does not understand the service side, problems often become ping-pong balls.
- Software usually lives longer than the original developer intends. Systems often have to be enhanced just to fulfil the requirements of a new service platform. If this is not taken into account when the software is developed, the effort for updating software may become enormous. Sometimes software has to be retired, just because it is not executable on the new platform!
- New approaches like service oriented architectures (SOA) demand the high integration of software and service elements. Future trends will rather lead to small combined software/service environments than to big software solutions operated by massive computer environments.

Just to ensure that I am not misunderstood: software developing and service delivering organizations will still deliver and operate solutions with high quality—but the will not do it in the most efficient and effective way. Organizations and companies aiming for the delivery of sustainable and reliable solutions have to ensure, that the solutions are not only developed in the best way but will meet the requirements of the future efficiently, effectively and still with high quality.

Standards for Software Development and Service Delivery

Regarding software development, two standard are widely accepted all over the world: the Capability Maturity Model Integration, published by the Software Engineering Institute (SEI) at the Carnegie Mellon University, and SPICE (Software Process Improvement and Capability Determination), which is published as ISO standard 15504. Both standards define a process framework based on best practices and provide an assessment model to evaluate process capability.

A process reference model (PRM) and a process assessment model (PAM) usually characterize a process framework. The PRM defines processes that have shown evidence to support high quality for the defined domain – in our case software development. The PAM builds the basis for collecting evidence that the PRM is adhered to and to evaluate the capability of the processes defined in the PRM.

In the world of service delivery, ITIL (IT Infrastructure Library) is the most acknowledged standard. To make ITIL assessable, the ISO 20000 standard was developed.

But as it was said before, none of these standards cover the complete software life cycle. This gap is seen by the SEI and discussed by relevant contributors to the ISO standards. In this article two approaches for this integration are discussed—one based on the CMMI and the other based on the connection of SPICE and ISO 20000.

CMMI INTEGRATION PERSPECTIVE

CMMI is one of the best-established process frameworks for software development. Starting with the publication of Watts Humphreys book "Managing the Software Process" in 1989, the CMM and its successor—the CMMI—nearly became a synonym for process improvement in the software world.

Nevertheless, until 2006, the CMMI was restricted on software and systems development. Since then a new initiative has been started to further develop the CMMI in the direction of acquisition and service processes. If one is talking about "CMMI" mostly the CMMI-DEV (for Development) is meant. This is the classical CMMI stream that covers service development. Other ideas concerning the usage and benefits of the CMMI for organizations that only acquire software, lead to the CMMI-ACQ (for Acquisition), which was published in November 2007. In 2006 and 2007 a CMMI for Services (CMM-SVC) has been developed to close the gap between software development and service delivery. The CMMI-SVC awaits publication in 2008.

CMMI Basics

Independent from the different CMMIs each of these models follows the same structure as shown in Figure 1.

In each CMMI a set of process areas is defined. For each process area the purpose is described, some introductory notes are given and other process areas which have a relation to this process area are listed. To satisfy the process area, goals must be fulfilled. Each process area has specific goals which are unique for this process area. Additional generic goals are defined, which are common for all process areas. For each goal a set of practices is defined, which are considered important for reaching the goal. For each practice subpractices, typical work products and elaborations are defined.

Figure 1. CMMI structure

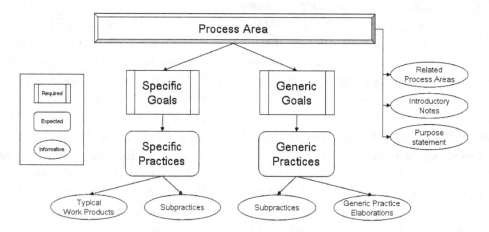

From an evaluation perspective, only the goals are required. To reach a so-called "level" an organization has to fulfil the goals of the processes for this level. Nevertheless it is expected, that the defined practices are also fulfilled.

Process Capability vs. Organization Maturity

Talking about the CMMI always means talking about "level". But before the different levels can be explored, the different representations have to be discussed. CMMI knows two different representations, staged and continuous. In the staged representation each process area is assigned to a specified maturity level. To reach a maturity level, all specific goals of the assigned processes and a subset of generic goals have to be fulfilled.

In the continuous representation, each process area is evaluated separately by fulfilling generic goals for this process area. Based on the set of generic goals that are fulfilled, the capability of the process area is measured.

In both representations, the generic goals have high importance. In total 5 generic goals are defined:

- **GG1:** The process supports and enables achievement of the specific goals of the process area by transforming identifiable input work products to produce identifiable output work products[2].
- **GG2:** The process is institutionalized as a managed process.
- **GG3:** The process is institutionalized as a defined process.
- **GG4:** The process is institutionalized as a quantitatively managed process.
- **GG5:** The process is institutionalized as an optimizing process.

In the staged representation 5 levels are defined. The lowest level is level 1, which means that the processes of the organization are still overwhelmingly chaotic. Goals for process maturity start with the definition of maturity level 2. For this level the specific goals of the assigned process areas and generic goal 2 have to be satisfied. For maturity level 3 the specific goals of the process areas assigned to level 2, the specific goals of the process areas assigned to level 3 and the generic goals 2 and 3 have to be satisfied. For level 4 and 5 specific goals of other process areas are added, but even for these higher levels, only generic goal 2 and 3 have to be satisfied.

Figure 2. CMMI constellation approach

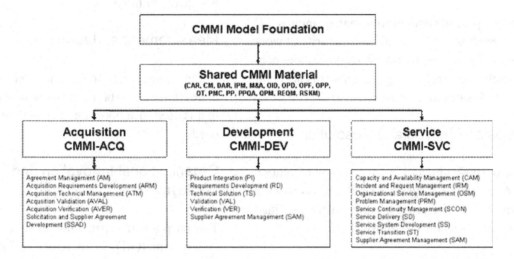

In the continuous representation, 6 levels are defined, starting with level 0 and ending with level 5. Remembering, that a capability level is evaluated for each process area, the level is given by the fulfilment of the generic goals. On level 0 no generic goal is satisfied. On level 1, GG1 has to be satisfied, on level 2 GG1 and GG2 have to be satisfied and so on.

As this article is focused on the integration of activities and not mainly on evaluation issues, we will restrict the following chapters to the parts specific to certain process areas. For more information on the generic parts and evaluation procedures the CMMI itself should be used (Software Engineering Institute, 2006a).

The Constellation Approach

As said before, there is not the "one" CMMI. The idea of the current CMMI version is to have different constellations which share some process areas that are common for all constellations and have additional process areas that are unique for the constellation.

Currently, three constellations are published or planned to be published in 2007:

- **CMMI-DEV:** For development (June 2006) (Software Engineering Institute, 2006-1)
- **CMMI-ACQ:** For acquisition (November 2007) (Software Engineering Institute, 2007)
- **CMMI-SCV:** For services (2008, initial draft September 2006) (Software Engineering Institute, 2006b)

These constellations only differ in the number and content of process areas. All other contents of the CMMI, for example generic elements, level definitions, typographical conventions, build the model's foundation and are identical for all constellations.

In a first overview the constellation approach can be structured as shown in Figure 2.

The purposes of all process areas are explained in the next chapter.

Shared Process Areas

Causal Analysis and Resolution

The purpose of causal analysis and resolution (CAR) is to identify causes of defects and other problems and take action to prevent them from occurring in the future.

Configuration Management

The purpose of configuration management (CM) is to establish and maintain the integrity of work products using configuration identification, configuration control, configuration status accounting, and configuration audits.

Decision Analysis and Resolution

The purpose of decision analysis and resolution (DAR) is to analyze possible decisions using a formal evaluation process that evaluates identified alternatives against established criteria.

The IPPD Addition (Integrated Product and Process Development)

Before describing the next process area, a new term has to be defined: the "IPPD addition". In CMMI, "additions" are used to include material that may be of interest to particular users. The IPPD group of additions covers an IPPD approach that includes practices that help organizations achieve the timely collaboration of relevant stakeholders throughout the life of the product to satisfy customers' needs, expectations, and requirements (Department of Defense, 1996). If you apply the CMMI, you are free to add the IPPD addition or not.

Integrated Project Management + IPPD

The purpose of integrated project management (IPM) is to establish and manage the project and the involvement of the relevant stakeholders according to an integrated and defined process that is tailored from the organization's set of standard processes.

IPPD Addition: For IPPD, integrated project management +IPPD also cover the establishment of a shared vision for the project and the estab-

lishment of integrated teams that will carry out objectives of the project.

Measurement and Analysis

The purpose of measurement and analysis (MA) is to develop and sustain a measurement capability that is used to support management information needs.

Organizational Innovation and Deployment

The purpose of organizational innovation and deployment (OID) is to select and deploy incremental and innovative improvements that measurably improve the organization's processes and technologies. The improvements support the organization's quality and process-performance objectives as derived from the organization's business objectives.

Organizational Process Definition + IPPD

The purpose of organizational process definition (OPD) is to establish and maintain a usable set of organizational process assets and work environment standards.

IPPD Addition: For IPPD, organizational process definition +IPPD also cover the establishment of organizational rules and guidelines that enable conducting work using integrated teams.

Organizational Process Focus

The purpose of organizational process focus (OPF) is to plan, implement, and deploy organizational process improvements based on a thorough understanding of the current strengths and weaknesses of the organization's processes and process assets.

Organizational Process Performance

The purpose of organizational process performance (OPP) is to establish and maintain a quantitative understanding of the performance of the organization's set of standard processes in support of quality and process-performance objectives, and to provide the process-performance data, baselines, and models to quantitatively manage the organization's projects.

Organizational Training

The purpose of organizational training (OT) is to develop the skills and knowledge of people so they can perform their roles effectively and efficiently.

Project Monitoring and Control

The purpose of project monitoring and control (PMC) is to provide an understanding of the project's progress so that appropriate corrective actions can be taken when the project's performance deviates significantly from the plan.

Project Planning

The purpose of project planning (PP) is to establish and maintain plans that define project activities.

Process and Product Quality Assurance

The purpose of process and product quality assurance (PPQA) is to provide staff and management with objective insight into processes and associated work products.

Quantitative Project Management

The purpose of quantitative project management (QPM) is to quantitatively manage the project's

defined process to achieve the project's established quality and process-performance objectives.

Requirements Management

The purpose of requirements management (REQM) is to manage the requirements of the project's products and product components and to identify inconsistencies between those requirements and the project's plans and work products.

Risk Management

The purpose of risk management (RSKM) is to identify potential problems before they occur so that risk-handling activities can be planned and invoked as needed across the life of the product or project to mitigate adverse impacts on achieving objectives.

Acquisition Process Areas

Solicitation and Supplier Agreement Development

The purpose of solicitation and supplier agreement development (SSAM) is to prepare a solicitation package and to select one or more suppliers for delivering the product or service and establish and maintain the supplier agreement.

Acquisitions Management

The purpose of agreement management (AM) is to ensure that the supplier and the acquirer perform according to the terms of the supplier agreement

Acquisition Requirements Development

The purpose of the acquisition requirements development (ARD) is to produce and analyze customer and contractual requirements.

Acquisition Technical Management

The purpose of the acquisition technical management (ATM) is to evaluate the supplier's technical solution and to manage selected interfaces of that solution.

Acquisition Validation

The purpose of the acquisition validation (AVAL) is to demonstrate that an acquired product or service fulfils its intended use when placed in its intended environment.

Acquisition Verification

The purpose of acquisition verification (AVER) is to ensure that selected work products meet their specified requirements.

Development Process Areas

Product Integration

The purpose of product integration (PI) is to assemble the product from the product components, ensure that the product, as integrated, functions properly, and deliver the product.

Requirements Development

The purpose of requirements development (RD) is to produce and analyze customer, product, and product component requirements.

Supplier Agreement Management

The purpose of supplier agreement management (SAM) is to manage the acquisition of products from suppliers.

Technical Solution

The purpose of technical solution (TS) is to design, develop, and implement solutions to requirements. Solutions, designs, and implementations encompass products, product components, and product-related lifecycle processes either singly or in combination as appropriate.

Validation

The purpose of validation (VAL) is to demonstrate that a product or product component fulfils its intended use when placed in its intended environment.

Verification

The purpose of verification (VER) is to ensure that selected work products meet their specified requirements.

Service Process Areas

As mentioned before, the CMMI-SVC has not been published yet. Nevertheless, it is available as initial draft (Software Engineering Institute, 2006b) and was already widely discussed on several conferences (Hollenbach & Buteau, 2006).

Capacity and Availability Management

The purpose of capacity and availability management (CAM) is to plan and monitor the effective provision of resources to support service requirements.

Incident and Request Management

The purpose of the incident and request management (IRM) process area is to ensure the timely resolution of requests for service and incidents that occur during service delivery.

Organizational Service Management*

The purpose of the organizational service management (OSM) process area is to establish and maintain standard services that ensure the satisfaction of the organization's customer base.

Problem Management

The purpose of the problem management (PRM) process area is to prevent incidents from recurring by identifying and addressing underlying causes of incidents.

Service Continuity*

The purpose of the service continuity (SCON) is to establish and maintain contingency plans for continuity of agreed services during and following any significant disruption of normal operations.

Service Delivery

The purpose of the service delivery (SD) process area is to deliver services in accordance with service agreements.

Service System Development*

The purpose of the service system development (SSD) process area is to analyze, design, develop, integrate, and test service systems to satisfy existing or anticipated service agreements.

Service Transition

The purpose of the service transition (ST) process area is to deploy new or significantly changed service systems while managing their effect on ongoing service delivery.

Supplier Agreement Management

The purpose of supplier agreement management (SAM) is to manage the acquisition of products from suppliers.

The process areas marked with an asterisk (*) are additions (like IPPD in the CMMI for Development) and therefore optional.

CMMI Process Categories

In order to develop a better understanding for the dependencies between the process areas, the CMMI-DEV defines 4 categories which are applied to the other constellations below, and collect process areas with a similar focus. Therefore, 3 categories are identical for all constellations. These are

- Process management
- Project management
- Support

The fourth category is focussed on the field of application of the constellation and is labelled

- Acquisition (in CMMI-ACQ)
- Engineering (in CMMI-DEV)
- Service Establishment and Delivery (in CMMI-SVC)

Based on this categorization the complete set of CMMI process areas can be categorized as follows.

For shared process areas see Table 1; for CMMI-ACQ see Table 2; for CMMI-DEV see Table 3; for CMMI-SVC see Table 4.

Constellation Based Maturity Levels

As described before, each process area is assigned to a defined maturity level. Whilst on level 4 and

5 only shared process areas are assigned, the assignment on level 2 and 3 is dependent on the constellation (see Table 5).

The shared processes assigned to level 4 are

- Organizational process performance
- Quantitative project management

The shared processes assigned to level 5 are

- Causal Analysis and Resolution
- Organizational Innovation and Deployment

Table 1. Shared process areas

	Process Management	Project Management	Support	Acquisition / Engineering / Service Establishment and Delivery
Shared process areas	Organizational Innovation and Deployment, Organizational Process Definition +IPPD, Organizational Process Focus, Organizational Process Performance, Organizational Training	Project Monitoring and Control, Project Planning, Quantitative Project Management, Risk Management	Causal Analysis and Resolution, Configuration Management, Decision Analysis and Resolution, Measurement and Analysis, Process and Product Quality Assurance	Requirements Management

Table 2. CMMI-ACQ process areas

	Process Management	Project Management	Support	Acquisition / Engineering / Service Establishment and Delivery
CMMI-ACQ				Solicitation and Supplier Agreement Development, Agreement Management, Acquisition Requirements Development, Acquisition Technical Management, Acquisition Validation, Acquisition Verification

Table 3. CMMI-DEV process areas

	ProcessManagement	Project Management	Support	Acquisition / Engineering / Service Establishment and Delivery
CMMI-DEV		Supplier Agreement Management		Product Integration, Requirements Development, Technical Solution, Validation, Verification

Table 4. CMMI-SVC process areas

	Process Management	Project Management	Support	Acquisition / Engineering / Service Establishment and Delivery
CMMI-SVC	Organizational Service Management	Supplier Agreement Management, Capacity and Availability Management	Problem Management	Incident and Request Management, Service Continuity, Service Delivery, Service System Development, Service Transition

A CMMI Based, Integrated Product Life Cycle

Even though the CMMI provides 3 different constellations, these constellations can be used to define 2 different integrated product life cycles:

- Organizations which provide service delivery for acquired software products should use the process areas of the CMMI-ACQ in combination with the process areas of the CMMI-SVC.
- Organizations which develop software and provide service delivery should use the pro-

cess areas of the CMMI-DEV in combination with the process areas of the CMMI-SVC.

Even the combination of all three constellations is thinkable, when a service delivering organization partially acquires and partially develops the software.

SPICE / ISO 20000 INTEGRATION PERSPECTIVE

Besides the CMMI world, another possibility for an integrated product life cycle is the combina-

Table 5. Maturity level 2 and 3 for CMMI constellations

	Maturity Level 2	Maturity Level 3
Shared process areas	Requirements Management, Project Planning, Project Monitoring and Control, Measurement and Analysis, Process and Product Quality Assurance, Configuration Management	Decision Analysis and Resolution, Integrated Project Management +IPPD, Organizational Process Definition +IPPD, Organizational Process Focus, Organizational Training, Project Management
CMMI-ACQ	Solicitation and Supplier Agreement Development, Agreement Management, Acquisition Requirements Development	Acquisition Technical Management Acquisition Validation, Acquisition Verification
CMMI-DEV	Supplier Agreement Management	Product Integration, Requirements Development, Technical Solution, Validation, Verification
CMMI-SVC	Supplier Agreement Management, Incident and Request Management	Capacity and Availability Management, Service Continuity Service Delivery, Service System Development, Service Transition, Organizational Service Management, Problem Management

tion of two ISO standards: the ISO 15504—better known as SPICE—and the ISO 20000.

SPICE Basics

The ISO 15504 (SPICE) is structured in 5 parts. Part 1 defines the basic concept and the vocabulary. In part 2 rules for performing an assessment are defined, and in part 3 guidance for the assess-ment is given. Part 4 gives additional guidance on the use for process improvement and capability determination.

The interesting part under the integration per-spective is part 5. This part defines an exemplar process assessment model.

Whilst the capability determination is widely similar to the approach of the CMMI continuous representation, the process model is different from the CMMI.

SPICE defines 3 categories. These categories are structured in groups and each group has several processes (ISO/IEC, 2006). The categories with their groups are:

- Primary life cycle processes
  - Acquisition process group (ACQ)
  - Supply process group (SPL)
  - Engineering process group (ENG)
  - Operation process group (OPE)
- Organizational life cycle processes
  - Management process group (MAN)
  - Process improvement process group (PIM)
  - Resource and infrastructure process group (RIN)
  - Reuse process group (REU)
- Supporting life cycle processes
  - Supporting process group (SUP)

Comparing the SPICE categories with the CMMI constellations, strong connections can be identified between the process groups of the primary life cycle processes and the CMMI constellations. The acquisition process group and supply process group have the same focus as the CMMI-ACQ as well as the engineering process group and the CMMI-DEV. Only the CMMI-SVC does not have a counterpart in SPICE. The operation processes group and some processes of the supporting process group address service related topics, but a common approach is not delivered.

To better understand the content of the SPICE process groups each group with its processes should be further described—as defined in SPICE (ISO/IEC, 2006):

Primary Life Cycle Processes

The primary life cycle processes consist of processes that serve primary parties during the life cycle of software. A primary party is one that initiates or performs the development, operation, or maintenance of software products. These primary parties are the acquirer, the supplier, the developer, the operator, and the maintainer of software products.

- The acquisition process group (ACQ) consists of processes performed by the customer, in order to acquire a product and/or a service. The processes of this group are:
  - ACQ.1: Acquisition preparation
  - ACQ.2: Supplier selection
  - ACQ.3: Contract agreement
  - ACQ.4: Supplier monitoring
  - ACQ.5: Customer acceptance
- The supply process group (SPL) consists of processes performed by the supplier in order to propose and deliver a product and/or a service. The processes of this group are:
  - SPL.1: Supplier tendering
  - SPL.2: Product release
  - SPL.3: Product acceptance support
- The engineering process group (ENG) consists of processes that directly elicit and manage the customer's requirements, specify, implement, and/or maintain the software product and it's relation to the system. The processes of this group are:
  - ENG.1: Requirements elicitation
  - ENG.2: System requirements analysis
  - ENG.3: System architectural design
  - ENG.4: Software requirements analysis
  - ENG.5: Software design
  - ENG.6: Software construction
  - ENG.7: Software integration
  - ENG.8: Software testing
  - ENG.9: System integration
  - ENG.10: System testing
  - ENG.11: Software installation
  - ENG.12: Software and system maintenance
- The operation process group (OPE) consists of processes performed in order to provide for the correct operation and use of the soft-

ware product and/or service. The processes of this group are:
- ∘ OPE.1: Operational use
- ∘ OPE.2: Customer support

Organizational Life Cycle Processes

The organizational life cycle processes consist of processes employed by an organization to establish and implement an underlying structure made up of associated life cycle processes and personnel and continuously improve the structure and processes. They are typically employed outside the realm of specific projects and contracts; however, lessons from such projects and contracts contribute to the improvement of the organization.

- The management process group (MAN) consists of processes that contain practices that may be used by anyone who manages any type of project or process within a software life cycle. The processes of this group are:
  - ∘ MAN.1: Organizational alignment
  - ∘ MAN.2: Organizational management
  - ∘ MAN.3: Project management
  - ∘ MAN.4: Quality management
  - ∘ MAN.5: Risk management
  - ∘ MAN.6: Measurement
- The process improvement process group (PIM) consists of processes performed in order to define, deploy, assess and improve the processes performed in the organizational unit. The processes of this group are:
  - ∘ PIM.1: Process establishment
  - ∘ PIM.2: Process assessment
  - ∘ PIM.3: Process improvement
- The resource and infrastructure process group (RIN) consists of processes performed in order to provide adequate human resources and necessary infrastructure as required by any other process performed by the organizational unit. The processes of this group are:
  - ∘ RIN.1: Human resource management
  - ∘ RIN.2: Training
  - ∘ RIN.3: Knowledge management
  - ∘ RIN.4: Infrastructure
- The reuse process group (REU) consists of processes performed in order to systematically exploit reuse opportunities in the organization's reuse programmes. The processes of this group are:
  - ∘ REU.1: Asset management
  - ∘ REU.2: Reuse program management
  - ∘ REU.3: Domain engineering

Supporting Life Cycle Processes

The supporting life cycle processes consist of processes that support another process as an integral part with a distinct purpose and contribute to the success and quality of the software project. A supporting process is employed and executed, as needed, by another process. The processes of this group are:

- ∘ SUP.1: Quality assurance
- ∘ SUP.2: Verification
- ∘ SUP.3: Validation
- ∘ SUP.4: Joint review
- ∘ SUP.5: Audit
- ∘ SUP.6: Product evaluation
- ∘ SUP.7: Documentation
- ∘ SUP.8: Configuration management
- ∘ SUP.9: Problem resolution management
- ∘ SUP.10: Change request management

Each SPICE process has a well-defined structure. After the process ID (e.g., SUP.10) and the process name (e.g., change request management), the purpose of the process is described. Then the process outcomes are defined. These process outcomes—plus process attributes—have to be achieved to reach a capability level in SPICE. Afterwards base practices for each process are defined and work products of the process are listed.

Table 6. CMMI and SPICE process structure

CMMI	SPICE
Acronym	Process ID
Process Name	Process Name
Purpose Statement	Process Purpose
Specific Goals	Process Outcomes
Specific Practices	Base Practices
Generic Goals	Process Attributes
Typical Work Products	Work Products

Comparing the structure of a CMMI process area and a SPICE process, there are lots of similarities (see Table 6).

All in all, SPICE has 48 processes that mainly cover software development and have only small focus on service delivery. For this part, the ISO 20000 seems more applicable.

ISO 20000 Basics

ISO 20000—Service Management covers the classical service delivery processes. Regarding the scope of ISO 20000, this standard represents "an industry consensus on quality standards for IT service management processes. These service management processes deliver the best possible service to meet a customer's business needs within agreed resource levels" (ISO/IEC, 2005b).

ISO 20000 defines 13 processes in 5 process groups.

Regarding each process group,

- The objective of the service delivery process group is to define, agree, record and manage levels of service, and consists of the processes
  ◦ Capacity management
  ◦ Service continuity and availability management
  ◦ Service level management
  ◦ Service reporting
  ◦ Information security management
  ◦ Budgeting and accounting for IT services
- The objective of the relationship process group is to describe the related aspects of supplier management and business relationship management, and consists of the processes
  ◦ Business relationship management
  ◦ Supplier management
- The objectives of the resolution process group are to restore agreed service and minimize disruption to the business, and consists of the processes
  ◦ Incident management
  ◦ Problem management
- The objective of the control process group is to define and control the components of service and infrastructure, and consists of the processes
  ◦ Configuration management
  ◦ Change management
- The objective of the release process group is to deliver, distribute and track changes, and consists of the process
  ◦ Release management

Figure 3. ISO 20000 processes

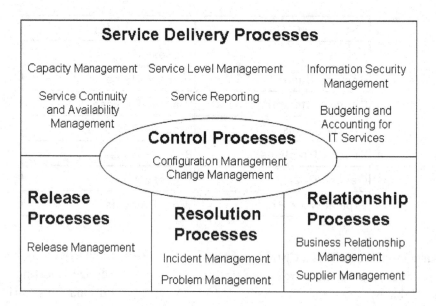

Those who know ITIL may have found lots of similarities in the process names and structure of ISO 20000. The ISO 20000 is well aligned with ITIL. Whilst ITIL is a collection of best practices, ISO 20000 defines specifications to support a service provider in delivering high quality services. The other way round, ITIL best practices help to achieve the quality of service management as defined by ISO 20000. It has to be recognized that ISO 20000 and ITIL are developed in strong connection, often impacted by the same persons.

Interfaces Between SPICE and ISO 20000

Trying to integrate SPICE and ISO 20000 it has to be taken into account, that both standards cover similar or identical elements in some processes. If an integrated product life cycle should be defined, these interfaces have to be harmonized.

First of all, the operational process group of SPICE has to be analyzed. This process group consists of two processes, operational use (OPE.1) and customer support (OPE.2).

The operational use process has the purpose to ensure the correct and efficient operation of the product for the duration of its intended usage and in its installed environment. Topics like operational risks, operational testing, criteria for operational use and the monitoring of the operational use are covered by this process.

The customer support process has the purpose of establishing and maintaining an acceptable level of service. Topics of this process are establishing of product support, performance monitoring and customer satisfaction.

Even though these processes address service aspects, they only deliver a high level overview. Nevertheless these topics address similar elements as the ISO 20000 processes service level management and business relationship management.

Other service delivery related processes can be found in the group of the supporting life cycle processes. The processes in focus are:

- SUP.8: Configuration management
- SUP.9: Problem resolution management
- SUP.10: Change request management

With configuration management the integrity of work products is established and maintained and these work products are made available to parties concerned. The problem resolution management process focuses on identification, analysis, management and controlling of discovered problems, while change request management ensures that change requests are managed, tracked and controlled.

Some other useful information for service delivery can be found in the process related to supplier management (acquisition / supply process groups).

Integration of SPICE and ISO 20000

To reach a fully integrated product life cycle, two requirements have to be satisfied:

- A set of processes has to be defined, which covers all stages of the life cycle—a so called process reference model (PRM)
- A model to evaluate the process capability has to be defined and must be applicable to all processes—a so called process assessment model (PAM)

Both requirements are satisfied by the CMMI constellations: the PAM is defined in the model foundation which is mandatory for all constellations and the PRM is given by the defined process areas.

For the SPICE and ISO 20000 integration, this is not that easy. On the one hand SPICE and ISO 20000 address identical topics in different processes, on the other hand, only SPICE has an assessment model. A way to solve this problem was defined in early 2007 (Malzahn, 2007) and should be described in the following chapters.

A Combined PRM for SPICE and ISO 20000

As described before, double definitions in SPICE and ISO 20000 have to be eliminated and all processes need to have an identical structure. Therefore in a first step, the ISO 20000 processes have to be restructured into the SPICE process

Figure 4. Integrated Product Life Cycle based on SPICE and ISO 20000

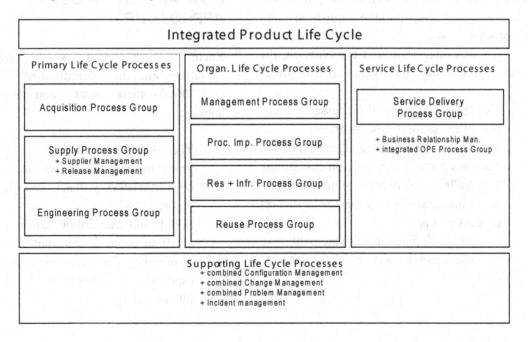

structure. In a second step, processes with a similar focus must be aligned.

For the first step, the ISO 20000 process groups and processes become process groups and processes of the combined model. For each ISO 20000 process the defined objective becomes the process purpose. For the rest of the text it has to be decided, which text passage becomes an outcome, a base practice, or a work product.

In the second step, all processes with a similar focus have to be aligned. Concerning SPICE and ISO 20000 it is proposed to

- Integrate the SPICE OPE process group into the service level management, service reporting and business relationship management processes of ISO 20000,
- Combine configuration management
- Combine problem resolution management and problem management,
- Combine change request management and change management.

Other possibilities for further alignment are e.g., given by the combination of the ISO 20000 release management process and the SPICE product release process, and by integrating the relationship processes into the acquisition / supply process group.

After this integration and combination, the process groups may be restructured as follows:

- The ISO 20000 control processes become part of the support process group,
- The ISO 20000 release management process becomes part of the Supply process group,
- ISO 20000 problem management and incident management become part of the support process group,
- Business relationship management may become part of the service delivery process group.

In the very end, a combined PRM for SPICE and ISO 20000 may consist of the SPICE process categories and a new service life cycle category with the following amendments:

A Combined PAM for ISO 20000 and SPICE

The definition of a process assessment model for the integration of SPICE and ISO 20000 is easy to define—it is the approach defined for SPICE. Regarding ISO 20000, no measurement framework is defined. The requirements concerning measurement are given in part one of the ISO 20000 as follows:

"The service provider shall apply suitable methods for monitoring and, where applicable, measurement of the service management processes" (ISO/IEC, 2005a). Therefore no inconsistencies in the measurement and rating can occur. The SPICE definitions are applicable because each ISO 20000 process was restructured in the PRM and therefore all contextual and structural requirements are satisfied.

COMPARISON OF BOTH APPROACHES

Regarding both approaches—the CMMI constellations and the integration of SPICE and ISO 20000—there are pros and cons for each approach:

- The CMMI constellations are highly integrated by using the same model foundation, but CMMI-SVC will not see the light of day before 2008
- SPICE and ISO 20000 require additional effort to be integrated, but both are ISO standards and therefore widely accepted— especially if legal matters have to be taken into account.

Other impacts may be the region or industry of the organization. The CMMI is very strong in the United States; SPICE is heavily used in Europe. Most defence industry companies are interested in CMMI, whilst major parts of the automotive industry prefer SPICE.

FUTURE TRENDS

This article covers two possible integration approaches. Nowadays more and more approaches see the light of day. Especially the integration of ITIL and CMMI or SPICE is widely discussed (Barafort, Di Renzo, Lejeune, Prime & Simon, 2005; Foegen & Graumann, 2007). Nevertheless ITIL is a best practice collection and not a measurement framework and therefore we still see some problems in the ITIL integration.

Hopefully the CMMI-SVC proves that it is a powerful tool for this intended integration and maybe at some point in time the ISO will find a way to publish an assessment model that covers the complete product life cycle for software.

Another promising approach will be the Enterprise SPICE initiative. The goal of this initiative is to "integrate and harmonize existing standards […] to provide a single process reference model and process assessment model that addresses broad enterprise processes. Enterprise SPICE will provide an efficient and effective mechanism for assessing and improving processes deployed across an enterprise" (SPICE User Group, 2007).

Using Integrated Models

Defining an integration approach is only a short part on the way to software development and service delivery integration. Even though it builds the indispensable basis, integration only works, if it is accepted by organizations, teams, and people. To reach this, some simple rules of the thumb should be followed:

- Integrate the working level of development and service delivery at least in the review of an integrated model – preferably in the development. If the working level understands the need for integration and is part of the integration process, the integrated model is better accepted.
- Provide translation between the development, service delivery and integration approach. Only if software development and service delivery people reach a common understanding, an integrated approach can be established.
- Provide training on the approach. Training must not be focused on "we combine standard A with standard B" but on "we define an approach for the complete life cycle". There is no longer "their work" and "our work" but a common responsibility from first idea to retirement.

If and only if the need for integration is understood and accepted by people on working level, integration can be established – otherwise there will still be two worlds with all their differences and borders.

CONCLUSION

The decision, which approach may deliver the best benefit, must be taken by the organization itself. But one thing is inevitable: if the capability of the processes of an organization is not evaluated against accepted standards and for the complete life cycle, the organization keeps the back door open for chaotic elements in their process suite and therefore has an open door for abusing strategies, processes, and procedures.

REFERENCES

Barafort, B., Di Renzo, B., Lejeune, V., Prime, S., & Simon, J. M. (2005). ITIL based service management measurement and ISO/IEC 15504 process assessment: A win-win opportunity. In *Proceedings of the SPICE 2005 Conference*, Klagenfurt, Austria.

Department of Defence (1996). *Guide to integrated product and process development (Version 1.0).* Washington, DC: Office of the Under Secretary of Defense (Acquisition and Technology).

Foegen, M., & Graumann, S. (2007, June). CITIL: ITIL integrated into CMMI. In *Proceedings of the 12th annual European SEPG Conference*, Amsterdam, Netherlands.

Hollenbach, R., & Buteau, B. (2006, November). CMMI for services, introducing the CMMI for service constellation. In *Proceedings of the CMMI Technology Conference*, Denver CO.

Humphrey, W. (1989). *Managing the software process*. Boston, MA: Addison-Wesley.

ISO/IEC (2005a). *ISO/IEC 20000-1Information technology—Service management—Part 1: specification*, ISO/IEC.

ISO/IEC (2005b). *ISO/IEC 20000-2- Information technology – Service management – Part 2: Code of practice*, ISO/IEC.

ISO/IEC (2006). *ISO/IEC 15504-5 -Information technology—Process assessment—Part 5: An exemplar process assessment Model*, ISO/IEC.

Malzahn, D. (2007, May). *A service extension for SPICE?* In Proceedings of the SPICE 2007 Conference. Seoul, South Korea.

Software Engineering Institute (2007). *CMMI for acquisition, Version 1.2.* Pittsburgh, PA.

Software Engineering Institute (2006a). *CMMI for development, Version 1.2.* Pittsburgh, PA.

Software Engineering Institute (2006b): *CMMI for services* (Initial Draft). Pittsburgh, PA.

SPICE User Group (2007). *Enterprise SPICE introduction*. Retrieved May 15, 2008, from http://www.enterprisespice.com/web/Introduction.html

ENDNOTES

1. CMMI is a registered trademark of the Software Engineering Institute, Carnegie Melon University.
2. This explains why the continuous representation only requires to satisfy generic goals. GG1 specifies, that the specific goals have to be achieved.

Compilation of References

Abrams, C., von Känel, J., Mueller, S., Pfitzmann, B., & Ruschka-Taylor, S. (2006). Optimized enterprise risk management (Research Report RZ3657). IBM. Retrieved May 14, 2008, from http://domino.research.ibm.com/library/cyberdig.nsf/papers/0C4791FC96DEF130852571D0003F5F15/$File/rz3657.pdf

ACADYDA (2002). European survey on the economy value of IT Edition 2002-2003.

Ackoff, R. (1971). Towards a system of systems concepts. *Management Science, 17*(11), 661-671.

Ackoff, R. (1973). Science in the systems age: Beyond IE, OR and MS. *Operations Research, 21*(3), 661-671.

Ackoff, R. L. (1967). Management misinformation systems. *Management Science, 14*(4), 147–156.

ACS (2005). ACS news. *Information Age, 15*(24).

Aguilar-Savén, R. S. (2004). Business process modelling: Review and framework. *International Journal of Production Economics, 90*(2), 129-149.

Ahn, J., Yang, J., & Han, S. (2006). A study on recognition and implementation of IT governance in Korean public institutions. In B. Cusack (Ed.), In *Proceedings of the 2006 IT Governance International Conference* (pp.107-120), Auckland, New Zealand.

Alcyone Consulting (2005). *Getting in-control—Combining COBIT and ITIL for IT governance and process excellence*. Retrieved May 11, 2008, from http://www.technologyexecutivesclub.com/PDFs/ArticlePDFS/GettingInControl.pdf

Alshawi, S., Irani, Z., & Baldwin, L. (2003). Benchmarking information technology investment and benefits extraction. *Benchmarking: An International Journal, 10*(4).

Alt, R. & Smits, M. T. (2007). Networkability of business networks. In H. Oesterle et al. (Eds), In *Proceedings of the European Conference on Information Systems* (pp. 119-130), St. Gallen.

Alter, A. E. (2004). *Richard Nolan: A committee of one's own*. Retrieved May 11, 2008, from http://www.cioinsight.com/print_article/0,1406,a=119427,00.asp

Alter, S. (2002). *Information Systems*. (4th ed.). New Jersey: Person.

Ambler, S. (2007). Agile adoption rate survey: March 2007. Retrieved May 14, 2008, from http://www.ambysoft.com/surveys/agileMarch2007.htm

Amico, M., Pasek, Z., Asl, F., & Perrone, G. (2003). Simulation methodology for collateralized debt and real options: A new methodology to evaluate the real options of investment using binomial trees and monte carlo simulation. In *Proceedings of the 35th Winter Conference on Simulation: Driving Innovation*, New Orleans, Louisiana.

Amit, R., & Zott, C. (2001). Value creation in e-business. *Strategic Management Journal, 22*(6/7), 493-520.

Anandarajan, A. & Wen, J. (1999). Evaluation of information technology investment. *Management Decision, 37*(4).

ANAO (2004). Auditing in an evolving environment (A focus on auditing standards and framework). In *Proceedings of the Institute of Certified Public Accountants and CPA Australia, CPA forum*. Retrieved May 11, 2008, from www.anao.gov.au/uploads/documents/Auditing_in_an_Evolving_Environment.pdf

Andriole, S., & Freeman, P. (1993). Software the case systems engineering: For a new discipline. *Software Engineering Journal*, May, 165-179.

Ang, S., & Straub, D. (1998). Production and transaction economies and IS outsourcing: A study of the US banking industry. *MIS Quarterly, 22*(4), 535-552.

Anthes, G. H. (2004). Model mania. *Computerworld, 38*(10), 41–45.

Antony, J., & Banuelas, R. (2001). A strategy for survival. *Manufacturing Engineer, 80*(3), 119-121.

Applegate, L. M., Austin, R .D., & McFarlan, F. W. (2003). *Corporate information strategy and management.* New York: McGraw-Hill.

Arnold, S., & Lawson, H. W. (2004). Viewing systems from a business management perspective: the ISO/IEC 15288 standard. *Systems Engineering, 7*(3), 229-242.

AS (2005). *Corporate governance of information and communication technology, AS 8015 - 2005.* Sydney: Standards Australia.

AS 8015-2005 (2005). *Australian standard: Corporate governance of information and communication technology.* Standards Australia: Sydney, Australia.

Ashby, R. (1956). *An introduction to cybernetics.* London: Chapman & Hall.

Ashby, W. (1956) *An introduction to cybernetics.* London: Chapman and Hall.

Ask, U., Bjornsson, H., Johansson, M., Magnusson, J., & Nilsson, A. (2007). IT governance in the light of paradox: A social systems theory perspective. In *Proceedings of the 40th Hawaii International Conference on System Sciences,* Hawaii.

ASX (2003). *Principles of good corporate governance and best practice recommendations.* Retrieved May 10, 2008, from http://www.asx.com.au/about/pdf/ASXRecommendations.pdf

ASX (Australian Stock Exchange) (2003). *Principles of good corporate governance and best practice recommendations.* Sydney: Australian Stock Exchange.

Ataya, G. (2003). Risk-aware decision making for new IT investments. *Information Systems Control Journal, 2,* 12-14.

Au, Y. A. & Kauffman, R. J. (2003). Information technology investment and adoption: a rational expectations perspective. In *Proceedings of the 36th Hawaii International Conference on System Sciences.*

Aubert, B. A., Patry, M., & Rivard, S. (2005). A framework for information technology outsourcing risk management. *ACM SIGMIS Database, 36*(4), 9-28.

Auditor Report (2003). Retrieved May 15, 2008, from http://www.audit.sa.gov.au/02-03/itrep/summary.html

Avison, D. E. & Fitzgerald, G. (2003). *Information systems development: Methodologies, techniques and tools* (3rd ed.). Maidenhead: McGraw-Hill.

Avison, D. E., Gregor, S., & Wilson, D. (2006). Managerial IT unconsciousness. *Communications of the ACM, 49*(7), 89-93.

Avison, D. E., Wilson, D., & Hunt, S. (2003, May). An IT failure and a company failure: A case study in telecommunications. *Paper presented at the 8th Congress of Association for Information Management,* Grenoble, France.

Avison, D., Jones, J., Powell, P., & Wilson, D. (2004). Using and validating the strategic alignment model. *Journal of Strategic Information Systems, 13*(3), 223-246.

Bacon, C. (1992). The use of decision criteria in selecting information systems/technology investments. *MIS Quarterly, 16*(3), 335 – 342.

Bahli, B. & Rivard, S. (2005). Validating measures of information technology outsourcing risk factors. *Omega, 33*(doi:10.1016/jomega.2004.04.003), 175-187.

Bailey, J. L., & Stefaniak, G. (2001). Industry perceptions of the knowledge, skills, and abilities needed by computer programmers. In *Proceedings of the 2001 ACM SIGCPR conference on Computer personnel research* (pp. 93-98). New York: ACM Press.

Ballantine, J. & Stray, S. (1998). Financial appraisal and the IS/IT investment decision-making process. *Journal of Information Technology, 13*(3), 3 – 14.

Ballantine, J. A. & Stray, S. (1999). Information systems and other capital investments: evaluation practices compared. *Logistics Information Management, 12*(1/2).

Banker, R. D. & Slaughter, S. A. (2000). The moderating effects of structure on volatility and complexity in software enhancement. *Information Systems Research, 11*(3), 219-240.

Barafort, B., Di Renzo, B., Lejeune, V., Prime, S., & Simon, J. M. (2005). ITIL based service management measurement and ISO/IEC 15504 process assessment: A win-win opportunity. In *Proceedings of the SPICE 2005 Conference,* Klagenfurt, Austria.

Bardhan, I., Bagchi, S., & Sougstad, R. (2004). A real options approach for prioritization of a portfolio of information technology projects: A case study of a utility company. In *Proceedings of the 37th Hawaii International Conference on System Sciences.*

Barker, B., & Verma, D. (2003). System engineering effectiveness: A complexity point paradigm for software intensive systems in the information technology sector. *Engineering Management Journal, 15*(3), 29-35.

Barnett, D. (n.d.). *Compliance framework and risk management for IT.* Retrieved May 11, 2008, from http://www.isaca.org/complianceframeworkv3

Barnett, L. (2006). And the agile survey says. Agile Journal March 6, 2006. Retrieved May 14, 2008, from http://www.agilejournal.com/articles/from-the-editor/and-the-agile-survey-says%85.html

Barney, J., Wright, M., & Ketchen, D. (2001). The resource-based view of the firm: Ten years after 1991. *Journal of Management, 27,* 625-641.

Barry, D. K. (2003). *Web services and service-oriented architecture—The savvy manager's guide.* Morgan Kaufmann.

Barua, A., Konana, P., Whinston, A. B., & Yin, F. (2004). An empirical investigation of net-enabled business value. *MIS Quarterly, 28*(4), 585-620.

Bar-Yam, Y. (2003). When systems engineering fails—Toward complex systems engineering. In *Proceedings of the 2003 International Conference on Systems, Man & Cybernetics* (pp. 2021- 2028), Piscataway, NJ: IEEE Press.

Baskerville, R. (1993). Information systems security design methods: Implications for information systems development. *ACM Computing Surveys, 25*(4), 375-414.

Bass, L., Clements, P., & Kazman, R. (2003). *Software architecture in practice.* Boston, MA: Addison-Wesley.

Bassellier, G., & Benbasat, I. (2004). Business competence of information technology professionals: Conceptual development and influence on IT-business partnerships. *MIS Quarterly, 28*(4), 673-694.

Bassellier, G., Benbasat, I., & Reich, B. (2003). The influence of business managers' IT competence on championing IT. *Information Systems Research, 14*(4), 317-336.

Bassellier, G., Reich, B. H., & Benbasat, I. (2001). Information technology competence of business managers. *Journal of Management Information Systems, 17*(4), 159-182.

Bate, R. (1998). Do systems engineering? Who, Me? *IEEE Software*, Jul-Aug, 65-66.

Bauer, C. (2001). Strategic alignment for electronic commerce. In R. Papp (Ed.), *Strategic information technology: Opportunities for competitive advantage* (pp. 258-272). Hershey, PA: Idea Group Publishing.

Baum, J. R., Locke, E. A., & Smith, K. G. (2001). A multidimensional model of venture growth. *Academy of Management Journal, 44*(2), 292-303.

Beath, C. M. (1991). Supporting the information technology champion. *MIS Quarterly, 15*(3), 355 – 372.

Bebchuk, L. A., & Cohen, A. (2005). The costs of entrenched boards. *Journal of Financial Economics, 78*(2), 409-433.

Becht, M., Bolton, P., & Röell, A. (2002). *Corporate governance and control.* ECGI - Finance Working Paper No. 02/2002. Retrieved May 1, 2008, from http://ssrn.com/abstract =343461

Beck, K., & Andres, C. (2004). Extreme programming explained (2nd ed.). Boston, Massachusetts: Addison-Wesley.

Beck, K., & Fowler, M. (2000). Planning extreme programming. Boston, Massachusetts: Addison-Wesley.

Beck, T., Demirguc-Kunt, A., & Levine, R. (2003). Law, endowments, and finance. *Journal of Financial Economics, 70*(2), 137-181.

Bedell, E. F. (1984). *Computer solution: Strategies for success in the information Age.* New York: McGraw-Hill, Inc.

Beer, S. (1981). *The brain of the Firm* (2nd ed.). London: Wiley.

Benbasat, I., Goldstain, D. K., & Mead, M. (1987). The case research strategy in studies of information systems. *MIS Quarterly, 11*(3), 369-386.

Benbasat, I., Goldstein, D., & Mead, M. (1987). The case research strategy in studies of information systems. *MIS Quarterly, 11*(3), 368-386.

Benvenuto, N. A. & Brand, D. (2005). Outsourcing - A risk management perspective. *Information Systems Control Journal, 5,* 35.

Bergeron, F., Raymond, L., & Rivard, S. (2004). Ideal patterns of strategic alignment and business performance. *Information & Management, 41,* 1003-1020.

Berry, L. L., & Parasuraman, A. (1991). *Marketing services: Competing through quality.* New York: Free Press.

Bertalanffy, L. von (1972). The history and status of general systems theory. *Academy of Management Journal,* December, 407-426.

Betz, C. (2007). *Architecture and patterns for service management, resource planning, and governance: Making shoes for the cobbler's children.* San Francisco: Morgan Kaufmann.

Bhandari, G., Bliemel, M., Harold, A., & Hassanein, K. (2003). Flexibility in e-business strategies: A requirement for success. *Global Journal of Flexible Systems Management, 5*(2/3), 11-22.

Bharadwaj, A. (2000). A resource-based perspective on information technology capability and firm performance: An empirical investigation. *MIS Quarterly, 24*(1), 169-96.

Bhattacharjya, J. & Chang, V. (2006). An exploration of the implementation and effectiveness of IT governance processes in institutions of higher education in Australia. In B. Cusack (Ed.), In *Proceedings of the 2006 IT Governance International Conference* (pp. 153-164), Auckland, New Zealand.

Bhattacharjya, J. & Chang, V. (2006). An exploration of the implementation and effectiveness of IT governance processes in institutions of higher education in Australia. In *Proceedings of the 2006 IT Governance International Conference*, Auckland, New Zealand.

Bitner, M. J., & Brown, S. (2006). The evolution and discovery of service sciences in business schools. *Communications of the ACM, 49*(7), 73-78.

Black, B., Jang, H., & Kim, W. (2003). Does corporate governance affect firms' market values? *Evidence from Korea, Stanford Law School Working Paper 237.* Stanford University.

Blythe, J. (2005). *Management challenges of technology; Speech to Wharton Global Alumni Forum: The Wharton School.* Retrieved May 8, 2008, from http://knowledge.wharton.upenn.edu/index.cfm?fa=viewfeature&id=1228

Bodnar, G. H. (2006). What's new in CobiT 4.0. *Internal Auditing, 21*(4), 37-44.

Boehm, B. (2000). Unifying software engineering and systems engineering. *Computer,* 114-116.

Boehm, B., & Lane, J. (2006). 21st century processes for acquiring 21st century software-intensive systems of systems. *Crosstalk: The Journal of Defense Software Engineering,* May, 1-9.

Böhmann, T., & Krcmar, H. (2003). Modulare Servicearchitekturen. In H.-J. Bullinger & A.-W. Scheer (Eds.), *Service Engineering - Entwicklung und Gestaltung innovativer Dienstleistungen.* Berlin.

Botton, N., & McManus, N. (1999). *Competitive strategies for service organisations* Macmillan.

Bowen, P. L., Cheung, M. Y. D., & Rohde, F. H. (2007). Enhancing IT governance practices: A model and case study of an organization's efforts. *International Journal of Accounting Information Systems, 8*(3), 191-221.

Boynton, A. C., Jacobs, G. C., & Zmud, R. W. (1992). Whose responsibility is IT management? *Sloan Management Review, 33*(4), 32 – 38.

Boynton, A. C., Zmud, R. W., & Jacobs, G. C. (1994). The influence of IT management practice on IT use in large organizations. *MIS Quarterly, 18*(3), 299-318.

Brickley, J. A., Lease, R. C., & Smith, C. W. (1988). Ownership structure and voting on antitakeover amendments. *Journal of Financial Economics, 20,* 267-291.

Brigham, E. & Houston, J. (2004). *Fundamentals of financial management* (10th ed.). London: Harcourt/Thomson.

Broadbent, M. & Weill, P. (1993). Improving business and information strategy alignment: Learning from the banking industry. *IBM Systems Journal, 32*(1), 162.

Broadbent, M. & Weill, P. (1997). Management by Maxim: How business and IT managers can create IT infrastructures. *Sloan Management Review, 38*(3), 77.

Broadbent, M. (1998). Leading governance, business and IT processes: The organizational fabric of business and IT partnership. Findings Gartner Group, 31 December 1998, document #FIND-19981231-01.

Broadbent, M. (2003). *The right combination.* Retrieved May 11, 2008, from http://www.cio.com.au/index.php/id;1043227491;fp;4;fpid;379170742

Broadbent, M. (2003a). Keys to effective security. *CIO, 11*(7).

Broadbent, M. (2003b). The right combination. *CIO Canada, 11*(4), 13-14.

Broadbent, M. (2003c). Understanding IT governance. *CIO Canada, 11*(4).

Broadbent, M., & Kitzis, E. (2005). *The new CIO leader.* Boston: Harvard Business School Press.

Broadbent, M., & Weill, P. (1997). Management by maxim: How business and IT managers can create IT infrastructures. *Sloan Management Review, 38*(3), 77-92.

Broadbent, M., Kitzis, E., & Hunter, R. (2004). Armed against risk. *Optimize, 44.*

Broadbent, M., Weill, P., & Neo, B. (1999). Strategic context and patterns of IT infrastructure capability. *Journal of Strategic Information Systems, 8*, 157-187.

Brocke, J., & Thomas, O. (2006). Reference modeling for organizational change: Applying collaborative techniques for business engineering. In *Proceedings of the Twelfth Americas Conference on Information Systems*, Acapulco, Mexico.

Brooks, P. (2006). *Metrics for IT service management* (1st ed.). Zaltbommel, Netherlands: Van Haren.

Brown, A. E. & Grant, G. G. (2005). Framing the frameworks: A review of IT governance research. *Communications of the Association for Information Systems, 15*, 696-712.

Brown, C. V. & Magill, S. L. (1994). Alignment of the IS function with the enterprise: Toward a model of antecedents. *MIS Quarterly, 18*(4), 371 – 403.

Brown, C. V. (1997). Examining the emergence of hybrid IS governance solutions: Evidence from a single case site. *Information Systems Research, 8*(1), 69-94.

Brown, C. V., & Magill, S. L. (1994). Alignment of the IS functions with the enterprise: Toward a model of antecedents. *MIS Quarterly, 18*(4), 371-403.

Brown, L. D., & Caylor, M. L. (2004). Corporate governance and firm performance. *Working Paper of Georgia State University*.

Brown, S. W., Fisk, R. P., & Bitner, M. J. (1994). The development and emergence of service marketing thought. *International Journal of Service Industry Management, 5*(1), 21-48.

Brown, W., & Nasuti, F. (2005). What ERP systems can tell us about Sarbanes-Oxley. *Information Management & Computer Security, 13*(4), 311.

Bruce, K. (1998). Can you align IT with business strategy? *Strategy and Leadership, 26*(5), 16-21.

Bruhn, M. (2004). *Qualitätsmanagement für Dienstleistungen: Grundlagen, Konzepte, Methoden* (5. ed.). Berlin [u.a.]: Springer.

Brynjolfsson, E. (1993). The productivity paradox of information technology. *Communications of the ACM, 36*(12), 66-77.

Buckby, S. (2008). *Board review of IT governance in Australian universities*. Unpublished doctoral dissertation, Queensland University of Technology, Australia.

Bullinger, H.-J. (1994). *Einführung in das Technologiemanagement: Modelle, Methoden, Praxisbeispiele*. Stuttgart: Teubner.

Burn, J. (1997). *A professional balancing act: Walking the tightrope of strategic alignment*. In C. Sauer & P. Yetton (Eds.), *Steps to the future: Fresh thinking on the management of IT-based organizational transformation* (pp. 55-88). San Francisco: Jossey-Bass.

Burn, J. M. & Szeto, C. (1999). A comparison of the views of business and IT management on success factors for strategic alignment. *Information & Management, 37*, 197-216.

Burns, T., & Stalker, G. (1961). Mechanistic and organic systems. In F. Kast & J. Rosenzweig (Eds.), *Contingency views of organization and management* (pp. 74-80). Chicago: Science Research Associates.

Bushell, S. (2002). *Lines of authority*. Retrieved May 11, 2008, from http://www.cio.com.au/index.php/id;11 91641618;fp;4;fpid;9

Bushell, S. (2007). When egos dare. *CIO, June*, 37-44.

Bushman, R. M., & Smith, A. J. (2003). Transparency, financial accounting information, and corporate governance. *FRBNY Economic Policy Review (2003 April)*, 65-87.

Butler, M. (2004). Cover story: IT governance - Who is the godfather of governance? *Information Economics Journal*, 7-9.

Byrne, D. (1971). *The attraction paradigm*. New York: Academic Press.

Cameron, K. S., & Quinn, R. E. (2006). *Diagnosing and changing organizational culture: Based on the competing values framework*. San Francisco: Jossey-Bass.

Campbell, B., Kay, R., & Avison, D. (2005). Strategic alignment: A practitioner's perspective. *Journal of Enterprise Information Management, 18*(5/6), 653-661.

Campbell, P. L. (2005). *A COBIT primer* (No. SAND2005-3455). Albuquerque, New Mexico: Sandia National Laboratories.

Cantor, M., & Sanders, J. (2007). Operational IT governance. Retrieved May 14, 2008, from http://www.ibm.com/developerworks/rational/library/may07/cantor_sanders/index.html

Carleton, W. T., Nelson, J. M., & Weisbach, M. S. (1998). The influence of institutions on corporate governance through private negotiations: Evidence from TIAA-CREF. *Journal of Finance, 53*(4), 1335-1362.

Carnegie Mellon Software Engineering Institute [SEI] (2006, August). *CMMI for Development, Version 1.2. CMU/SEI-2006-TR-008. ESC-TR-2006-008.* Retrieved May 14, 2008, from http://www.sei.cmu.edu/pub/documents/06.reports/pdf/06tr008.pdf

Carver, J. (2006). *Boards that make a difference: A new design for leadership in nonprofit and public organizations* (3rd ed.). San Francisco: Jossey-Bass.

Cash, E., Yoong, P., & Huff, S. (2004). The impact of e-commerce on the role of IS professionals. *The DATA BASE for Advances in Information Systems, 35*(3), 50-63.

Castlewood, D. & Sir, M. (2001). Organizational development: A framework for successful information technology assimilation. *Organization Development Journal, 19*(1), 59-72.

Cater-Steel, A. & Tan, W. (2005). Implementation of IT infrastructure library in Australia: Progress and success factors. In *Proceedings of the IT Governance International Conference*, Auckland.

Cater-Steel, A., & Tan, W-G. (2005). *Summary of responses to itSMF conference survey.* Retrieved May 15, 2008, from http://www.usq.edu.au/users/caterst/Summary%20respondents_20050930.pdf

Cater-Steel, A., Mark Toleman, B. K., & Chown, R. (2006). ICT governance - Radical restructure. In B. Cusack (Ed.), In *Proceedings of the 2006 IT Governance International Conference* (pp. 87-96), Auckland, New Zealand.

Cater-Steel, A., Tan, W-G., & Toleman, M. (2006). Challenge of adopting multiple process improvement frameworks. *ECIS - European Conference of Information Systems*, Göteborg, Sweden.

Cater-Steel, A., Toleman, M. & Tan, W-G. (2006). Transforming IT service management – The ITIL impact. In *Proceedings of the 17ᵗʰ Australian Conference on Information Systems*, Adelaide, Australia.

Cavusoglu, H., Mishra, B., & Raghunathan, S. (2004). A model for evaluating IT security investments. *Communications of the ACM, 47*(7), 87-92.

CCTA - Central Computer and Telecommunications Agency (2000). *Service support.* London: The Stationary Office.

Chan et al. (1997). Business strategic orientation. *Information Systems Research, 8*(2), 125-150.

Chan, Y. E. (2000). IT value: The great divide between qualitative and quantitative and individual and organizational measures. *Journal of Management Information Systems, 16*(4), 225.

Chan, Y. E. (2002). Why haven't we mastered alignment? The importance of the informal organization structure. *MIS Quarterly Executive, 1*(2), 97-112.

Chandler, G. N., & Hanks, S. (1994). Founder competence, the environment, and venture performance. *Entrepreneurship Theory and Practice, 18*(3), 77-89.

Chandler, G. N., & Jansen, E. (1992). The founder's self-assesed competence and venture performance. *Journal of Business Venturing, 7*(3), 223-236.

Chandrasekaran, N. & Ensing, G. (2004). ODC: A global IT services delivery model. *Communications of the ACM, 47*(5), 47-49.

Chapin, D. A. & Akridge, S. (2005). How can security be measured? *Information Systems Control Journal, 2*, 43.

Chatfield, A. T. & Wanninayaka, P. (2006). IT governance silo in the firm: An analysis of governance research literature. In B. Cusack (Ed.), In *Proceedings of the 2006 IT Governance International Conference* (pp. 121-130), Auckland, New Zealand.

Chaya, A. & Mitra, S. (1996). Exploring the relationships between IT investments and organizational performance: preliminary empirical evidence. In *Proceedings of the 29th Annual Hawaii International Conference on System Sciences*.

Checkland, P. (2000). Soft systems methodology: a 30-year retrospective. In P. Checkland (Ed.), *Systems thinking, systems practice*. Chichester: Wiley.

Chen, L., Sheng, O., Goreham, D., & Watanabe, J. (2005). A real option analysis approach to evaluating digital government investment. In *Proceedings of the National Conference on Digital Government Research*, Atlanta, Georgia.

Chesbrough, C., & Spohrer, J. (2006). A research manifesto for services science. *Communications of the ACM, 49*(7), 35-40.

Chickowski, E. (2004). Taking models of IT governance – Is it time to evaluate your decision-making process? *Processor, 26*(15). Retrieved May 10, 2008, from http://www.processor.com/editorial/article.asp

Chikofsky, E. & Rubin, H. A. (1999). Using metrics to justify investment in IT. *IT Professional, 1*(2), 75-77.

Chin, P. O., Brown, G. A., & Hu, Q. (2004). The impacts of mergers & acquisitions on IT governance structures:

A case study. *Journal of Global Information Management, 12*(4), 50-74.

Chowdhary, P., Bhaskaran, K., Caswell, N. S., Chang, H., Chao, T., Chen, S. K., et al. (2006). Model driven development for business performance management. *IBM Systems Journal, 45*(3), 587-605.

Chulani, S., Clay, W., Yaeli, A., Wegman,, M. N., & Cantor, M. (2006). Understanding IT governance: Definitions, contexts, and concerns (Research Report RC24064). IBM. Retrieved May 14, 2008, from http://domino.research.ibm.com/library/cyberdig.nsf/papers/38905EEA124CDDFB852571FE00569CCE/$File/rc24064.pdf

Ciborra, C. (1991). From thinking to tinkering: The grassroots of strategic information systems. In *Proceedings of the 12th International Conference of Information Systems* (pp. 283-291), New York.

Cilli, C. (2003). IT governance: Why a guideline? *Information Systems Control, 3*. Retrieved May 8, 2008, from http://www.isaca.org/Template.cfm?Section=Home&Template=/ContentManagement/ContentDisplay.cfm&ContentID=15933

Cingula, M. (2006). Corporate governance as a process-oriented approach to socially responsible organizations. In P. Ali & G. Gregoriou (Eds.), *International corporate governance after Sarbanes-Oxley* (pp. 65-94). Hoboken, NJ: John Wiley & Sons.

CIO UK Website. (2007). *Late IT projects equals lower profits*. Retrieved May 15, 2008, from http://www.cio.co.uk/concern/resources/news/index.cfm?articleid=1563

Claessens, S., Djankov, S., Fan, J. P. H., & Lang, L. H. P. (2002). Disentangling the incentive and entrenchment effects of large shareholdings. *Journal of Finance, 57*(6), 2741-2771.

Clarke, F., Dean, G., & Oliver, K., (2003). *Corporate collapse: Accounting, regulatory and ethical failure*. Melbourne, Australia: Cambridge University Press.

Coates, J. C. (2007). The goals and promise of the Sarbanes–Oxley Act. *Journal of Economic Perspectives, 21*(1), 91-116.

COBIT 4.1 (2007). *COBIT 4.1 excerpt: Executive summary and framework*. IT Governance Institute

Cole, A. (1995). Runaway projects—Cause and effects. *Software World, 26*(3), 3 – 5.

Coles, J. L., & Hoi, C. K. (2003). New evidence on the market for directors: Board membership and Pennsylvania Senate Bill 1310. *Journal of Finance, 58*(1), 197-230.

Collin, R. (2004). *An introductory overview of ITIL*. London: ITSMF.

Collis, D., & Montgomery, C. (1995). Competing on resources: Strategy in the 1990s. *Harvard Business Review*, 118-128.

Committee of Sponsoring Organizations of the Treadway Commission (COSO) (2004). *Enterprise risk management - Integrated framework*. Retrieved April 29, 2008, from http://www.coso.org/publications.htm

Cooper, D. R. & Schindler, P. S. (2002). *Business research methods* (8th ed.). McGraw-Hill/Irwin.

Couger, J. D., Davis, G. B., Dologite, D. G., Feinstein, D. L., Gorgone, J. T., Jenkins, A. M., Kasper, G. M., Little, J. C., Longenecker, H. E. Jr., & Valacich, J. S. (1995). IS '95: guideline for undergraduate IS curriculum. *MIS Quarterly, 19*(3), 341-359.

Coughlan, J., Lycett, M., & Macredie, R. D. (2005). Understanding the business-IT relationship. *International Journal of Information Management, 25*(4), 303-319.

CPA (2005). *No need to be savvy to practice IT governance*. Retrieved May 11, 2008, from http://www.cpaaustralia.com.au/cps/rde/xchg/SID-3F57FEDF-FAD610FA/cpa/hs.xsl/1019_16232_ENA_HTML.htm

Cragg, P. et al. (2000). IT alignment and organisational performance in small firms. In *Proceedings of ASPECIS*.

Craighead, C. & Shaw, N. (2003). E-commerce value creation and destruction: A resource-based, supply chain perspective. *SIGMIS Database, 34*(2), 39-49.

Cronk, M. C. & Fitzgerald, E. P. (1999). Understanding IS business value: Derivation of dimensions. *Logistics Information Management, 12*(1/2).

Crossman, M., & Sorrenti, M. (1977). Making sense of improvisation. *Advances in Strategic Management, 14*, 155-180.

Croteau, A.-M. & Bergeron, F. (2001). An information technology trilogy: Business strategy, technological deployment and organizational performance. *Journal of Strategic Information Systems, 10*, 77-99.

Csaszar, F. & Clemons, E. (2006). Governance of the IT function: Valuing agility and quality of training, cooperation and communications. In *Proceedings of* the *39th Hawaii International Conference on System Sciences*, Hawaii.

Cumps, B., Viaene, S., Dedene, G., & Vandenbulcke, J. (2006). An empirical study on business/ICT alignment in European organizations. *Paper presented at the 39th Hawaii International Conference on System Sciences*, Hawaii.

Cumps, B., Viaene, S., Dedene, G., & Vandenbulcke, J. (2006). An empirical study on business/ICT alignment in European organisations. In *Proceedings of the 39th Hawaii International Conference on System Sciences*, Hawaii.

Curtis, D. (2005). The journey to IT service management starts with IT management process maturity. In *Proceedings of the Gartner ITXPO Symposium*, Sydney.

D'Souza, D. & Mukherjee, D. (2004). Overcoming the challenges of aligning IT with business. *The Executive's Journal*, Winter, 23-31.

Dahlberg, T. & Kivijärvi, H. (2006). An integrated framework for IT governance and the development and validation of an assessment instrument. In *Proceedings of the 39th Hawaii International Conference on System Sciences*, Hawaii.

Dahlberg, T. & Kivijarvi, H. (2006). An integrated framework of IT governance and the development and validation of an assessment instrument. *Paper presented at the 39th Hawaii International Conference on System Sciences*, Hawaii.

Dahlberg, T. & Lahdelma, P. (2007). IT governance maturity and IT outsourcing degree: An exploratory study. In *Proceedings of the 40th Hawaii International Conference on System Sciences*, Hawaii.

Dahlberg, T., & Kivijärvi, H. (2006). An integrated framework for IT governance and the development and validation of an assessment instrument. In *Proceedings of the 39th Hawaii International Conference on System Sciences(HICSS)*, Hawaii: IEEE.

Dalal, N. P. (1994). Higher-order thinking in MIS. *Journal of Computer Information Systems, 34*(4), 26-30.

Damianides, M. (2005). Sarbanes-Oxley and IT governance: New guidance on IT control and compliance. *Information Systems Management*, 77-85.

Davenport, T. H. & Prusak, L. (1997). *Information ecology: Mastering the information and knowledge environment*. New York: Oxford University Press.

Davenport, T., Eccles, R., & Prusak, L. (1992). Information politics. *Sloan Management Review*, 53-65.

Davern, M. J. & Kauffman, R. J. (2000). Discovering potential and realizing value from information technology investments. *Journal of Management Information Systems, 16*(4), 121.

Davies, A. (2006). *Best practice in corporate governance: Building reputation and sustainable success*. Aldershot, Hampshire, England: Gower.

De Haes, S. & Van Grembergen, W. (2004). IT governance and its mechanisms. *Information Systems Control Journal, 1*, 27.

De Haes, S. & Van Grembergen, W. (2004). IT governance and its mechanisms. *Information Systems Control Journal, (1)*. Retrieved May 14, 2008, from http://www.isaca.org/Template.cfm?Section=Home&CONTENTID=16700&TEMPLATE=/ContentManagement/ContentDisplay.cfm

De Haes, S. & Van Grembergen, W. (2005). IT governance structures, processes and relational mechanisms: Achieving IT/business alignment in a major Belgian financial group. *Paper presented at the 38th International Conference on Systems Sciences*, Hawaii.

De Haes, S. & Van Grembergen, W. (2006). Information technology governance best practices in Belgian organizations. *Paper presented at the 39th Hawaii International Conferences on System Sciences*, Hawaii.

De Haes, S., & Van Grembergen, W. (2004). IT governance and its mechanisms. *Information Systems Control Journal, 1*.

De Haes, S., & Van Grembergen, W. (2006). Information technology governance best practices in Belgian organizations. In *Proceedings of the 39th Hawaii International Conference on System Sciences(HICSS)*, Hawaii: IEEE.

De Lone, W., & McLean, E. (2003). The DeLone and McLean model of information systems success: A ten-year update. *Journal of Management Information Systems, 19*(4), 9-30.

Dearden, J. (1987). The withering away of the IS organisation. *Sloan Management Review, 28*(4), 87 – 91.

Debreceny, R. S. (2006). Re-engineering IT internal controls: Applying capability maturity models to the evaluation of IT controls. In *Proceedings of the 39th Hawaii International Conference on System Sciences*, Hawaii.

Dedrick, J., Gurbaxani, V., & Kraemer, K. L. (2003). Information technology and economic performance: A critical review of the empirical evidence. *ACM Computing Surveys, 35*(1), 1-28.

Dedrick, J., Gurbaxani, V., & Kraemer, K. L. (2003). Information technology and economic performance: A critical review of the empirical evidence. *ACM Computing Surveys, 35*(1), 1-28.

DeFond, M. L., & Francis, J. R. (2005). Audit research after Sarbanes-Oxley. *Auditing, 24*, 5-30.

Dehning, B. & Richardson, V. J. (2002). Returns on investments in information technology: A research Synthesis. *Journal of Information Systems, 16*(1), 7-30.

Dehning, B., Richardson, V. J., & Stratopoulos, T. (2003). Reviewing event studies in MIS: An application of the firm value. In *Proceedings of the 36th Hawaii International Conference on System Sciences.*

Dekkers, T. (2004). IT governance requires quantitative (Project) management. *IWSM/MetriKon.* Retrieved May 1, 2008, from http://www.sogeti.nl/images /ACFf-tCN2J_tcm6-1776.pdf

Del Guercio, D., & Hawkins, J. (1999). The motivation and impact of pension fund activism. *Journal of Financial Economics, 52*(3), 293-340.

Del Guercio, D., Seery, L. J., & Woidtke, T. (2006). Do board members pay attention when institutional investors "Just Vote No"? CEO and director turnover associated with shareholder activism. Retrieved May 13, 2008, from http://ssrn.com/abstract=575242

deLone, W., & McLean, E. (2003). The DeLone and McLean model of information systems success: A ten-year update. *Journal of management Information Systems, 19*(4), 9-30.

Deming, W. E. (1982). *Quality, productivity, and competitive position.* Cambridge, Mass.

Demirkan, H., & Goul, M. (2006). AMCIS 2006 panel: Towards the service oriented enterprise vision: Bridging industry and academics. *CAIS, 18*, 546-556.

Demsetz, H., & Lehn, K. (1985). The structure of corporate ownership: Causes and consequences. *Journal of Political Economy, 93*(6), 1155-1177.

Denis, D. J., & Denis, D. K. (1995). Performance changes following top management dismissals. *Journal of Finance, 50*(4), 1029-1057.

Deno, P., & Feeney, A. B. (2002). Systems engineering foundations of software systems integration. In *Proceedings of the OOIS Workshops.*

Department of Defence (1996). *Guide to integrated product and process development (Version 1.0).* Washington, DC: Office of the Under Secretary of Defense (Acquisition and Technology).

Deshpande, Y., Murugesan, S., Ginige, A., Hansen, S., Schwabe, D., Gaedke, M., & White, B. (2002). Web engineering. *Journal of Web Engineering, 1*(1), 3-17.

Dibbern, J., Goles, T., Hirschheim, R., & Jayatilaka, B. (2004). Information systems outsourcing: a survey and analysis of the literature. *SIGMIS Database, 35*(4), 6-102.

Dibbern, J., Goles, T., Hirschheim, R., & Jayatilaka, B. (2004). Information systems outsourcing: A survey and analysis of the literature. *ACM SIGMIS Database, 35*(4), 6-102.

DICTS (2006). *Staff satisfaction survey.* Retrieved May 11, 2008, from http://www.usq.edu.au/ict/staff/staffsvy/

DICTS (2006). *Student satisfaction survey.* Retrieved May 11, 2008, from http://www.usq.edu.au/ict/students/studsvy/

Dixon, K. (2004). *Ken Dixon's ITIL Overview.*

DoD C4ISR Architecture Working Group (1997). *C4ISR architecture framework* (Version 2). Retrieved May 11, 2008, from http://www.fas.org/irp/program/core/fw.pdf

Doidge, C., Karolyi, G. A., & Stulz, R. M. (2004). Why are foreign firms listed in the U.S. worth more? *Journal of Financial Economics, 71*(2), 205-238.

Doll, W. J., Deng, X., & Scazzero, J. A. (2003). A process for post-implementation IT benchmarking. *Information and Management, 41*(2), 199 – 212.

Donabedian, A. (1980). *Explorations in quality, assessment and monitoring—The definition of quality and approaches to its assessment.* Ann Arbour.

Donaldson, L. (2001). *The contingency theory of organizations.* Thousand Oaks: Sage Publications.

Doughty, K. (2000). *The myth or reality of information technology steering committees.* Retrieved April 29, 2008, from www.isaca.org/art3a.htm

Dowse, A. & Lewis, E. (2006). Whatever happened to alignment? In B. Cusack (Ed.), In *Proceedings of the 2006 IT Governance International Conference* (pp. 49-57), Auckland, New Zealand.

Dowse, A. (2007). *The diverse organisation: Operational considerations for managing organisational information resources*. Unpublished doctoral thesis, UNSW, Canberra.

Dowse, A., & Lewis, E. (2006). Whatever happened to alignment? In *Proceedings of the 2006 Information Technology Governance International Conference*, Auckland.

Du, S., Keil, M., Lars, M., Shen, Y., & Tiwana, A. (2006). The role of perceived control, attention-shaping, and expertise in IT project risk assessment. *Paper presented at the 39th Hawaii International Conference on System Sciences*, Hawaii.

Dubie, D. (2005). Taking on IT service management. *Network World, 2*(23), 8.

Dubinsky, Y., & Hazzan, O. (2006). Using a role scheme to derive software project metrics. Journal of Systems Architecture, 52, 693–699.

Dubinsky, Y., Hazzan, O., Talby, D., & Keren, A. (2006). System analysis and design in a large-scale software project: the case of transition to agile development. In Proceedigns of the the Eigth International Conference on Enterprise Information Systems, Paphos, Cyprus.

Dueck, G. (2001). Views of knowledge are human views. *IBM Systems Journal, 40*(4), 885-888.

Duffy, J. (2003). *IT governance and business value part 1: IT governance – An issue of critical influence*. Retrieved May 10, 2008, from http://www.networkworld.com/research/ reports/IDC27291.html

Durnev, A., & Kim, E. H. (2005). To steal or not to steal: Firm attributes, legal environment, and valuation. *Journal of Finance, 60*(3), 1461-1493.

Earl, M. (1996). *Integrating IS and the organization: A framework of organizational fit*. In M. Earl (Ed.), *Information management: The organizational dimension* (pp. 485-502). Oxford: Oxford University Press.

Earl, M. J. (1988). *Information management: The strategic dimension*. Oxford: OUP.

Earl, M. J. (1989). *Management srategies for information technology*. Hemel Hempstead: Prentice-Hall.

Earl, M. J. (1993). Experiences in strategic information systems planning. *MIS Quarterly, 17*(1), 1-24.

Earl, M. J. (1996). The risks of outsourcing. *Sloan Management Review, 37*(3), 26-32.

Earl, M. J., & Feeny, D. F. (1994). Is your CIO adding value? *Sloan Management Review, 35*, 11-20.

Eclipse (2007). *Eclipse process framework*. Retrieved May 11, 2008, from http://www.eclipse.org/epf

Edvardsson, B., Gustafsson, A., Johnson, M. D., & Sanden, B. (2000). *New service development and innovation in the new economy*. Studentlittereatur Sweden.

El Emam, K., & Birk, A. (2000). Validating the ISO/IEC 15504 measure of software requirements analysis process capability. *Software Engineering, IEEE Transactions, 26*(6), 541.

Elliot, S., & Melhuish, P. (1995). A methodology for the evaluation of IT for strategic implementation. *Journal of Information Technology, 10*, 87-100.

Ellram, L. M., & Liu, B. (2002). The financial IMPACT of supply management. *Supply Chain Management Review, 6*(6), 30-37.

Enterprise Architecture – Wikipedia (n.d.). Retrieved May 15, 2008, from http://en.wikipedia.org/wiki/Enterprise_Architecture

EQuest (2004). *The Australian IT project landscape*. Sydney: EQuest Consulting and iGATE Global Solutions. Retrieved May 8, 2008, from http://www.eqc.com.au/EQuest%20iGate%20Project%20Management%20Survey%20May%202004.pdf

Erickson, T. J., Magee, J. F., Roussel, P. A., & Saad, K. N. (1990). Managing technology as a business strategy. *Sloan Management Review, 31*(3), 73.

Ericsson, M. (2007). The governance landscape: Steering and measuring development organizations to align with business strategy. Retrieved May 14, 2008, from http://www.ibm.com/developerworks/rational/library/feb07/ericsson/

EUROSAI (undated). *EUROSAI institutional information* Webpage. Retrieved May 11, 2008, from http://www.eurosai.org/Ingles/info_inst.htm

EUROSAI IT Working Group (undated). *IT self assessment flyer*. Retrieved May 11, 2008, from http://www.eurosai-it.org/9282000/d/flyer_it.pdf

Evans, I., & Macfarlane, I. (2001). A dictionary of IT service management. *Terms, acronyms and abbreviations*. Reading, UK: itSMF Ltd.

Ewusi, K. (1997). Critical issues in abandoned information systems development projects. *Communication of the ACM, 40*(9), 74-80.

Ezingeard, J.-N., Irani, Z., & Race, P. (1999). Assessing the value and cost implications of manufacturing information and data systems: An empirical study. *European Journal of Information systems, 7*(4), 252 – 260.

Fairchild, A. M. (2002). Knowledge management metrics via a balanced scorecard methodology. In *Proceedings of the 35th Hawaii International Conference on System Sciences.*

Fairchild, A. M. (2004). Information technology outsourcing (ITO) governance: An examination of the outsourcing management maturity model. In *Proceedings of the 37th Hawaii International Conference on System Sciences*, Hawaii.

Fairchild, A., Ribbers, P., & Nooteboom, A. (2004). A success factor model for electronic markets. *Business Process Management Journal, 10*(1), 63–79.

Fama, E. & Jensen, M. (1983). Separation of ownership and control. *Journal of Law and Economics, 26*, 301–325.

Fama, E. F. (1980). Agency problems and the theory of the firm. *Journal of Political Economy, 88*(2), 288-307.

Fama, E. F., & Jensen, M. C. (1983). Separation of ownership and control. *Journal of Law & Economics, 26*(2), 301-326.

Fang, X., Lee, S., & Koh, S. (2005). Transition of knowledge/skills requirements for entry-level IS professionals: An exploratory study based on Recruiters' perception. *Journal of Computer Information Systems, Fall 2005*, 58-70.

Farr, J., & Buede, D. (2003). Systems engineering and engineering management: Keys to the efficient development of products and services. *Engineering Management Journal, 15*(3), 3-9.

Farwell, D., Kuramoto, L., Lee, D. M. S., Trauth, E., & Winslow, C. (1992). A new paradigm for MIS: Implications for IS professionals. *Information Systems Management, 9*(2), 7-14.

Fasterling, B. (2006). Prospects and limits of corporate governance codes. In P. Ali & G. Gregoriou (Eds.), *International corporate governance after Sarbanes-Oxley* (pp. 467-84). Hoboken, NJ: John Wiley & Sons.

Federal Office of Management and Budget (2007). *Federal enterprise architecture framework.* Retrieved May 11, 2008, from http://www.whitehouse.gov/omb/egov/a-2-EAModelsNEW2.html

FedEx (2005). *Committee charter, FedEx.* Retrieved May 11, 2008, from http://ir.fedex.com/governance/committeechar.cfm

Feeny, D. F., & Willcocks, L. P. (1998). Core IS capabilities for exploiting information technology. *Sloan Management Review, 39*, 9-21.

Fidler, C. & Rogerson, S. (1996). *Strategic management support systems.* Pitman.

Fink, R. C., Edelman, L. F., Hatten, K. J., & James, W. L. (2006). Transaction cost economics, resource dependence theory, and customer–supplier relationships. *Industrial and Corporate Change, 15*(3), 497-529.

Fitsilis, P. (2006). Practices and problems in managing electronic services using SLAs. *Information Management & Computer Security, 14*(2).

Foegen, M., & Graumann, S. (2007, June). CITIL: ITIL integrated into CMMI. In *Proceedings of the 12th annual European SEPG Conference*, Amsterdam, Netherlands.

Forno, R., & Baklarz, R. (1999). *The art of information warfare.* New York: Universal Publishers.

Forsberg, K., & Mooz, H. (1997). System engineering overview. In R. Thayer & M. Dorfman (Eds.), *Software requirements engineering* (pp. 44-72). Los Alamitos: IEEE Computer Society Press.

Fry, J. N. & Killing, J. P. (1989). *Strategic analysis and action* (2nd ed.). Scarborough, Ontario: Prentice-Hall Canada.

Fuggetta, A. (2000). Software process: A roadmap. In *Proceedings of the International Conference on Software Engineering*, Limerick, Ireland.

Galbraith, J. (1973). *Designing complex organizations.* Reading, MA: Addison-Wesley.

Galliers, R. D. (1991). Strategic information systems planning: Myths, reality and guidelines for successful implementation. *European Journal of Information Systems, 1*(1), 55-64.

Galliers, R. D. W. (1987). Information systems planning in the UK and Australia - A comparison of current practice. *Oxford Surveys in IT, 4*, 223–255.

Garcia, S. (1998). Evolving improvement paradigms: Capability maturity models & ISO/IEC 15504 (PDTR). *Software Process Improvement and Practice, 3*(1), 1-11.

Gartner (2007). *Magic quadrant for IT project and portfolio management 2007, Gartner RAS core research note G00149082*, Matt Light, Daniel B, Stang

Gellings, C. (2007). Outsourcing relationships: The contract as IT governance tool. In *Proceedings of the 40th Hawaii International Conference on System Sciences*, Hawaii.

Gelman, O., & Garcia, J. (1989). Formulation and axiomatization of the concept of general system. *Outlet IMPOS (Mexican Institute of Planning and Systems Operation), 19*(92), 1-81.

Gelman, O., Mora, M., Forgionne, G., & F. Cervantes (2005). Information systems and systems theory. In M. Khosrow-Pour (Ed.), *Encyclopedia of information science and technology*, (Vol. 3, pp. 1491-1496). Hershey, PA: Idea Group.

Gerber, M. & Von Solms, R. (2005). Management of risk in the information age. *Computers & Security, 24*(1), 16-30.

Gerke, L. B., & Ridley, G. (2006). Towards an abbreviated CobiT framework for use in an Australian state public sector. In S. Spencer & A. Jenkins (Eds.), In *Proceedings of the 17th Australasian Conference on Information Systems*, Adelaide: Australasian Association for Information Systems.

Getter, J. R. (2007). Enterprise architecture and IT governance: A risk-based approach. In *Proceedings of the 40th Hawaii International Conference on System Sciences*, Hawaii.

Gewald, H. & Helbig, K. (2006). A goverance model for managing outsourcing partnerships. *Paper presented at the 39th Hawaii International Conference on System Sciences*, Hawaii.

Giaglis, G., Paul, R., & Keefe, R. (1999). Research note: Integrating business and network simulation models for IT investment evaluation. *Logistics Information Management, 12*(1/2).

Ginige, A., & Murugesan, A. (2001). Web engineering—An introduction. *IEEE Multimedia, 8*(1), 14-18.

Glass, R. L., Ramesh, V., & Vessey, I. (2004). An analysis of research in computing disciplines. *Communications of the acm, 47*(6), 89-94.

Glass, R., Armes, V., & Vessey, I. (2004). An analysis of research in computing disciplines. *Communications of the ACM, 47*(6), 89-94.

Goh, K. H. & Kauffman, R. J. (2005). Towards a theory of value latency for IT investments. In *Proceedings of the 38th Hawaii International Conference on System Sciences.*

Gold, R. S. (2002). Enabling the strategy-focused IT organization. *Information Systems Control Journal, 4*, 21.

Gold, R. S. (2003). Building the IT organization balanced scorecard. *Information Systems Control Journal, 5*, 46.

Gonzalez, R., Gasco, J., & Llopis, J. (2006). Information system outsourcing: A literature analysis. *Information & Management, 43*(7), 821-834.

Gordon, J. R. M., Lee, P-M., & Lucas, H. C. (2005). A resource-based view of competitive advantage at the Port of Singapore. *Journal of Strategic Information Systems, 14*, 69-86.

Gorgone, J. T., Davis, G. B., Valacich, J. S., Topi, H., Feinstein, D. L., & Longenecker, H. E., Jr. (2003). IS 2002 model curriculum and guidelines for undergraduate degree programs in information systems. *Communications of the AIS, 2003*(11), 1-53.

Gottschalk, P. (2006). *E-business strategy, sourcing and governance*. Hershey, PA: Idea Group Publishing.

Green, P. & Ali, S. (2006). Effective information technology governance mechanisms in public sectors: An australian case. In *Proceedings of the 10th Pacific Asia Conference on Information Systems* (pp. 1070-1089), Kuala Lumpur, Malaysia.

Gregor, S., Fernandez, W., Holtham, D., Martin, M., Stern, S., Vitale, M., et al. (2005). *Achieving value from ICT: Key management strategies*. Canberra: Department of Communications, Information Technology and the Arts, ICT Research Study.

Grembergen, W. V. & Haes, S. D. (2005). Measuring and improving information technology governance through the balanced scorecard. *Information Systems Control Journal, 2*.

Grembergen, W. V. (Ed.) (2004). *Strategies for information technology governance*. Hershey, PA: Idea Group Publishing Inc.

Grembergen, W. V., Haes, S. D., & Brempt, H. V. (2007). Prioritising and linking business and IT goals in the financial sector. In *Proceedings of the 40th Hawaii International Conference on System Sciences*, Hawaii.

Grönroos, C. (1984). A service quality model and its marketing implications. *European Journal of Marketing, 18*(4), 36-44.

Grossman, S. J., & Hart, O. D. (1980). Takeover bids, the free-rider problem, and the theory of the corporation. *Bell Journal of Economics, 11*(1), 42-64.

Grover, V., Cheon, M. J., & Teng, J. T. C. (1996). The effect of service quality and partnership on the outsourcing of information systems functions. *Journal of Management Information Systems, 12*, 89-116.

Guldentops, E. (2003). Maturity measurement - First the purpose, then the method. *Information Systems Control Journal, 4*, 15.

Guldentops, E. (2004). *COBIT: Best practices in support of IT governance and regulatory Compliance*. Retrieved May 11, 2008, from http://www.disif.dk/information/COBIT_181104.pdf

Guldentops, E., van Grembergen, W., & de Haes, S., (2002). Control and governance maturity survey: Establishing a reference benchmark and a self-assessment tool. *Information Systems Control Journal*, 6. Retrieved May 11, 2008, from http://www.isaca.org/Template.cfm?Section=Archives&CONTENTID=16122&TEMPLATE=/ContentManagement/ContentDisplay.cfm

Guldentops, E., Van Grembergen, W., & Haes, S. (2002). Control and maturity survey: Establishing a reference benchmark and a self-assessment tool. *Information Systems Control Journal, 6*, 32-35.

Gunasekaran, A. et al. (2004). A framework for supply chain performance measurement. *Int. J. Production Economics, 87*, 333-347.

Gunasekaran, A., Love, P. E. D., Rahimi, F., & Miele, R. (2001). A model for investment justification in information technology projects. *International Journal of Information Management, 21*, 349 – 364.

Hackney, R., & Little, S. (1999). Opportunistic strategy formulation for IS/IT planning. *European Journal of Information Systems, 8*, 119-126.

Hadden, L. B., DeZoort, F. T., & Hermanson, D. (2003). IT risk oversight: The role of audit committees, internal auditors and external auditors. *Internal Auditing, 18*(6).

Haes, S. D. & Grembergen, W. V. (2005). IT governance structures, processes and relational mechanisms: Achieving IT/business alignment in a major Belgian financial group. In *Proceedings of the 38th Hawaii International Conference on System Sciences*, Hawaii.

Haes, S. D. & Grembergen, W. V. (2006). Information technology governance best practices in Belgian organisations. In *Proceedings of the 39th Hawaii International Conference on System Sciences*, Hawaii.

Haller, S. (2002). *Dienstleistungsmanagement* (2. ed.). Wiesbaden.

Hallows, J. E. (2001). The project management office toolkit. Newton Square, Pennsylvania: Project Management Institute.

Hamaker, S. (2000). Your IT applications inventory is all in your head - An observation related to IT governance tools. *Information Systems Control Journal, 5*, 21.

Hammer, M. (1990). Reengineering work: Don't automate, obliterate. *Harvard Business Review*, July-August, 104-112.

Hammer, M. (2007). The process audit. *Harvard Business Review*, April.

Hammer, M., & Champy, J. (1993). *Reengineering the cooperation: A manifesto for business revolution*. New York: HarperCollins Publishers.

Hanemann, A., Sailer, M., & Schmitz, D. (2004). Assured service quality by improved fault management. In *Proceedings of the 2nd International Conference on Service Oriented Computing*, New York, NY.

Hardy, G. & Guldentops, E. (2005). CobiT 4.0: The new face of CobiT. *Information Systems Control Journal, 6*.

Hardy, G. (2006). Using IT governance and COBIT to deliver value with IT and respond to legal regulatory and compliance challenges. *Information Security Technical Report, 11*(1), 55-61.

Harford, J. (2003). Takeover bids and target directors' incentives: The impact of a bid on directors' wealth and board seats. *Journal of Financial Economics, 69*(1), 51-83.

Harmon, P. (2003). *Business process change*. San Francisco: Morgan Kaufman Publishers.

Harrington, H. J. (1991). Business process improvement. *The breakthrough strategy for total quality, productivity, and competitiveness*. New York: McGraw-Hill Inc.

Harrington, J. (1991). *Business process improvement - The breakthrough strategy for total quality, productivity and competitiveness*. New York: McGraw-Hill.

Hass, A. M. J. (2003). *Configuration management principles and practice*. Boston: Addison-Wesley.

Hassan, S. Z. & Saeed, K. A. (1999). A framework for determining IT effectiveness: An empirical approach. In *Proceedings of the 32nd Hawaii International Conference on System Sciences*.

Hausman, W. H. (2002). Supply chain performance metrics. In C. Billington, T. Harrison, H. Lee, & J. Neale (Eds.), *The practice of supply chain management*. Boston: Kluwer.

Hazelwood (2006). *Defence in depth: An information assurance strategy for the enterprise*. Retrieved May 11, 2008, from http://www.sdsc.edu

Hazzan, O. (2002). The reflective practitioner perspective in software engineering education. The Journal of Systems and Software, 63(3), 161-171.

Hecht, H. (1999). Systems engineering for software-intensive projects. In *Proceedings of the ASSET Conference*, Dallas, TX.

Hegel, J. & Brown, J. S. Your next IT strategy. *Harvard Business Review, 9*(79), 105 – 113.

Heier, H., Borgman, H. P., & Maistry, M. G. (2007). Examining the relationship between IT governance software and business value of IT: Evidence from four case studies. *Paper presented at the 40th Hawaii International Conference on System Sciences*, Hawaii.

Henderson, J. C. & Sifinos, J. G. (1988). The value of strategic IS planning: Understanding consistency, validity, and IS markets. *MIS Quarterly, 12*(2), 187-200.

Henderson, J. C. & Thomas, J. B. (1992). Aligning business and information technology domains: Strategic planning in hospitals. *Hospital & Health Services Administration, 37*(1), 71.

Henderson, J. C. & Venkatraman, N. (1991). Understanding strategic alignment. *Business Quarterly, 55*(3), 72.

Henderson, J. C. & Venkatraman, N. (1992). Strategic alignment: A model for organizational transformation through information technology. In T. A. Kochan & M. Useem (Eds.), *Transforming organizations*. Oxford: Oxford University Press.

Henderson, J. C. & Venkatraman, N. (1993). Strategic alignment: Leveraging information technology for transforming organizations. *IBM Systems Journal, 32*(1), 472-485.

Henderson, J. C. & Venkatraman, N. (1999). Strategic alignment: Leveraging information technology for transforming organizations. *IBM Systems Journal, 38*(2/3), 472-484.

Henderson, J. C. (1990). Plugging into strategic partnerships: The critical IS connection. *Sloan Management Review, 31*(3), 7.

Henderson, J. C., & Venkatraman, N. (1993). Strategic alignment: Leveraging information technology for transforming organizations. *IBM Systems Journal, 32*(1), 472-485.

Henderson, J. C., & Venkatraman, N. (1999). Strategic alignment: Leveraging information technology for transforming organizations. *IBM Systems Journal, 38*(2/3), 472-484.

Henderson, J. C., Rockart, J. F., & Sifonis, J. G. (1987). Integrating management support systems into strategic information systems planning. *Journal of Management Information Systems, 4*(1), 5-24.

Henry, R. M., Kirsch, L. J., & Sambamurthy, V. (2003). The role of knowledge in information technology project governance. In S. T. March, A. Massey & J. I. DeGross (Eds.), In *Proceedings of the 24th International Conference on Information Systems* (pp. 751-758), Seattle, Washington.

Hensley, R. L., & Dobie, K. (2005). Assessing readiness for six sigma in a service setting. *Managing Service Quality, 15*(1).

Hertzel, M., & Smith, R. L. (1993). Market discounts and shareholder gains for placing equity privately. *Journal of Finance, 48*(2), 459-485.

Hertzel, M., Lemmon, M., Linck, J. S., & Rees, L. (2002). Long-run performance following private placements of equity. *Journal of Finance, 57*(6), 2595-2617.

Hevner, A. R., March, S. T., Park, J., & Ram, S. (2004). Design science in information systems research. *MIS Quarterly, 28*(1), 75-105.

Hevner, A. R., March, S. T., Park, J., & Ram, S. (2004). Design science in information systems research. *MIS Quarterly, 28*(1), 75-105.

Higher Education IT Consultative Forum (2000). *The way forward – Higher education action plan for the information economy department of education science and training*. Retrieved May 10, 2008, from http://www.backingaustralias future.gov.au/ fact_sheets.htm

Highsmith, J. (2002). Agile software development ecosystems. Boston: Addison-Wesley.

Highsmith, J. A. (2002). *Agile software development ecosystems*. Boston: Pearson Education.

Hinz, D. J. & Malinowski, J. (2006). Assessing the risks of IT infrastructure - A personal network perspective. *Paper presented at the 39th Hawaii International Conference on System Sciences*, Hawaii.

Hirschheim, R. & Sabherwal, R. (2001). Detour in the path toward strategic information systems alignment. *California Management Review, 44,* 1(87-108).

Hirschheim, R., Klein, H. K., & Lyytinen, K. (1995). *Information systems development and data modelling – Conceptual and philosophical foundations.* Cambridge: Cambridge University Press.

Hoappa, J. M. & Wiander, T. J. (2006). Implementation experiences of the information security management system - Case study. In B. Cusack (Ed.), In *Proceedings of the 2006 IT Governance International Conference* (pp. 79-85), Auckland, New Zealand.

Hochstein, A. (2004). Managing IT service quality as perceived by the customer. In *Proceedings of the ITS 15th Biennial Conference*, Berlin.

Hochstein, A., Ebert, N., Uebernickel, F., & Brenner, W. (2007). Die neuen Wertschöpfungsketten. *Computerwoche, 16,* 32.

Hodgkinson, S. T. (1996). The role of the corporate IT function in the federal IT organization. In M. J. Earl (Ed.), *Information management: The organizational dimension.* Oxford: Oxford University Press.

Hoffman, T. (2004, May 17). IT oversight gets attention at board level. *Computerworld*

Hoffmann, F. G.-M. & Weill, P. (2004). *Banknorth: Designing IT governance for a growth-oriented business environment.* Cambridge: Center for Information Research, Sloan School of Management.

Hogg, R. (2002). Keynote address. *Paper presented at the CIO 2002*, Sydney. Retrieved May 8, 2008, from http://www.acs.org.au/news/050302.htm.

Hole, E., Verma, D., Jain, R., Vitale, V., & Popick, P. (2005). Development of the ibm.com interactive solution marketplace (ISM): A systems engineering case Study. *Systems Engineering, 8*(1), 78-92.

Hollenbach, R., & Buteau, B. (2006, November). CMMI for services, introducing the CMMI for service constellation. In *Proceedings of the CMMI Technology Conference*, Denver CO.

Holloway, D. A. (2004). Corporate governance disasters and developments: Implications for university governing bodies. *Australian University Review, 46*(2), 23-30.

Honour, E. (2004). Understanding the value of systems engineering. In *Proceedings of the 2004 INCOSE Conference*, 1-16.

Hoogeveen, D. & Oppelland, H. J. (2002). A socio political model of the relationship between IT investments and business performance. In *Proceedings of the 35th Hawaii International Conference on System Sciences*, Hawaii.

Horlick-Jones, T., & Sime, J. (2004). Living on the border: Knowledge, risk and transdisciplinarity. *Futures, 36*(4), 441-456.

Hsaio, R. & Ormerod, R. (1998). A new perspective on the dynamics of IT-enabled strategic change. *Information Systems Journal, 8*(1), 21–52.

Huang, R., Zmud, R. W., & Price, R. L. (2006). Evaluating the effects of IT governance structures in small and medium-sized enterprises. In *Proceedings of the 12th Americas Conference on Information Systems*, Acapulco, México.

Huff, S. L., Maher, M. P., & Munro, M. C. (2004). What boards don't do - but must do - about information technology. *Ivey Business Journal On-Line* (September/October), 1 - 4. Retrieved May 8, 2008, from http://www.iveybusinessjournal.com/view_article.asp?intArticle_ID=511

Humphrey, W. (1989). *Managing the software process.* Boston, MA: Addison-Wesley.

Hussain, S. J. & Siddiqui, M. S. (2005). Quantified model of COBIT for corporate IT governance. In *Proceedings of the 1st International Conference on Information and Communication Technologies (ICICT)* (pp. 158-163), Karachi, Pakistan.

Hyde, A. (2002). Defining IT project success and failure. In B. Runciman (Ed.), *BCS review 2002.* Swindon: British Computer Society.

ICT Investment Prioritisation Framework (2005). *ICT investment prioritisation framework-Version 1.0.* Government of South Australia

ICT Planning Framework (2006). *SA government ICT planning framework.* Government of South Australia

Iden, J. (2005). Prosessutvikling. Håndbok i modellering og analyse av prosesser (*Process change. Handbook in process modelling and analysis*). Trondheim, Norway: Tapir akademisk forlag. In Norwegian.

IEAD (Institute for Enterprise Architecture Developments) (2004). *Extended enterprise architecture framework.* Retrieved May 11, 2008, from http://www.enterprise-architecture.info

IEEE Standard 1003.0-1995 (1995). *IEEE guide to the POSIX open system environment.* Retrieved May 11, 2008, from http://standards.ieee.org/reading/ieee/std_public/description/posix/1003.0-1995_desc.html

IEEE Standard 1471-2000 (2000). *IEEE recommended practice for architectural description of software-intensive systems*. Retrieved May 11, 2008, from http://standards.ieee.org/reading/ieee/std_public/description/se/1471-2000_desc.html

Iivari, J. (1992). The organisational fit of information systems. *Journal of Information Systems, 2*, 3-29.

INCOSE (1996). *SECAM: Systems engineering capability assessment model* (version 1.5). INCOSE.

INCOSE (2004). *Systems engineering handbook*. INCOSE-TP-2003-016-02. INCOSE.

Information Security Management Maturity Model [ISM3] Consortium (2007). Retrieved May 14, 2008, from http://www.ism3.com/index.php?option=com_docman&Itemid=9

Information Systems and Control Foundation. (2000). *CobiT* (3rd ed.). USA: Information Systems Control Foundation.

Institute, I. T. G. (2003). Board briefing on IT governance (2nd ed.) [Electronic Version]. Retrieved May 13, 2008, from http://www.itgi.org/Template_ITGI.cfm?Section=ITGI&Template=/ContentManagement/ContentDisplay.cfm&ContentFileID=4667

International Organization for Standardization (ISO) & International Electrotechnical Commission (IEC). (2004a). *ISO/IEC 12207 - Software lifecycle processes Amd 2*. Retrieved April 29, 2008, from www.iso.org

International Organization for Standardization (ISO) & International Electrotechnical Commission (IEC). (2004b*). ISO 15504-4:2004 - Process assessment - Part 4: Guidance on use for process improvement and process capability determination*. Retrieved April 28, 2008, from www.iso.org

International Organization for Standardization (ISO) & International Electrotechnical Commission (IEC) (2005a). *ISO/IEC 27001 information technology - Security techniques- Information security management systems requirements*. Retrieved April 29, 2008, from www.iso.org

International Organization for Standardization (ISO) & International Electrotechnical Commission (IEC) (2005b). *ISO/IEC 27002 standard - Information technology – Security techniques - Code of practice for information security management*. Retrieved April 29, 2008, from www.iso.org

Iqbal, M. & Nieves, M. (2007). *ITIL service strategy*. Norwich: The Stationary Office.

ISACA (2005). *COBIT, ISACA*. Retrieved May 11, 2008, from http://www.isaca.org/COBIT

ISACA (2007). *COBIT 4.1. ISACA*. Retrieved May 11, 2008, from http://www.isaca.org/COBIT

ISO (1995). *ISO/IEC 12207: Information technology—Software life cycle processes*. Geneva, Switzerland: ISO/IEC.

ISO (2000). *Standards of 2000*. Retrieved May 10, 2008, from http://www.iso.org

ISO (2002). *ISO/IEC 15288: Systems engineering—Systems life cycle processes*. Geneva, Switzerland: ISO/IEC.

ISO (2003). *ISO/IEC 15504-2: Information technology—Process assessment*. Geneva, Switzerland: ISO/IEC.

ISO (2004). *ISO/IEC 90003:2004 software engineering—Guidelines for the application of ISO 9001:2000 to computer software*. Geneva, Switzerland: ISO/IEC.

ISO (2004). *ISO/TMB Policy and principles statement global relevance of ISO technical work and publications*. TMB/SC/GR 2004-06-30. Geneva, Switzerland: ISO/IEC.

ISO (2005). *ISO/IEC 20000:2005 Information technology—Service management—Part 1: Specification*. Geneva, Switzerland: ISO/IEC.

ISO (2005). *ISO/IEC 20000 benchmarks provision of IT service management*. Retrieved May 10, 2008, from http://www.iso.org

ISO (2005). *ISO/IEC 27001 - Information technology - Security techniques - Information security management systems - Requirements*. Geneva: International Standards Organisation

ISO (2005). *ISO/IEC 17799 Information technology—Code of practice for information security management*. Geneva: International Standards Organisation. Retrieved May 8, 2008, from http://www.iso.org/iso/en/StandardsQueryFormHandler.StandardsQueryFormHandler?scope=CATALOGUE&sortOrder=ISO&committee=ALL&isoDocType=ALL&title=true&keyword=17799

ISO (2005). *ISO/IEC 27001 international information security standard published*. Retrieved May 10, 2008, from http://www.iso.org

ISO (2006). *Where ISO 9000 came from and who is behind it*. Retrieved May 15, 2008, from www.iso.org

ISO (2006). *ISO 9000 and ISO 14000 in plain language.* Retrieved May 15, 2008, from www.iso.org

ISO (2006). *ISO/IEC 15289: Systems and software engineering—Content of systems and software life cycle process information products (Documentation).* Geneva, Switzerland: ISO/IEC.

ISO (2007). *Draft international standard ISO/IEC DIS 29382 corporate governance of information and communication technology.* Retrieved May 10, 2008, from http://www.iso.org

ISO (in press). *ISO/IEC NP 24748 Systems and software engineering—Life cycle management.* Geneva, Switzerland: ISO/IEC.

ISO/IEC (2005). *ISO/IEC 20000-1Information technology—Service management—Part 1: specification,* ISO/IEC.

ISO/IEC (2005). *ISO/IEC 20000-2- Information technology – Service management – Part 2: Code of practice,* ISO/IEC.

ISO/IEC (2006). *ISO/IEC 15504-5 - Information technology—Process assessment—Part 5: An exemplar process assessment Model,* ISO/IEC.

IT Governance Institute (2000). COBIT : *Governance, control and audit for information and related technology.* IT Governance Institute. Retrieved May 11, 2008, from http://www.itgi.org

IT Governance Institute (2001). *IT governance executive summary.* IT Governance Institute. Retrieved May 11, 2008, from http://www.itgi.org

IT Governance Institute (2004). *IT governance global status report.* IT Governance Institute. Retrieved May 11, 2008, from http://www.itgi.org

IT Governance Institute (2006). *IT governance global status report - 2006.* IT Governance Institute. Retrieved May 11, 2008, from http://www.itgi.org

IT Governance Institute (ITGI) (2000). IT governance roundtable - Sponsored by the IT governance institute. *Information Systems Control Journal, 4,* 27-28.

IT Governance Institute (ITGI) (2001). *Board briefing on IT governance.* Retrieved April 29, 2008, from www.itgi.org

IT Governance Institute (ITGI) (2003). *Board briefing on IT governance* (2nd ed.) Retrieved April 29, 2008, from www.itgi.org

IT Governance Institute (ITGI) (2004). *IT governance status report.* Retrieved April 29, 2008, from www.itgi.org

IT Governance Institute (ITGI) (2005). *CobiT 4.0.* Rolling Meadows, IL: IT Governance Institute.

IT Governance Institute (ITGI) (2005). *Governance of outsourcing.* Retrieved April 29, 2008, from www.itgi.org

IT Governance Institute (ITGI) (2005). *Information risks: Whose business are they?* Retrieved April 29, 2008, from www.itgi.org

IT Governance Institute (ITGI) (2005). *Information security governance - Top action for security managers.* Retrieved April 29, 2008, from www.itgi.org

IT Governance Institute (ITGI) (2005). *IT alignment: Who is in charge?* Retrieved April 29, 2008,, from www.itgi.org

IT Governance Institute (ITGI) (2005). *Measuring and demonstrating the value of IT.* Retrieved April 29, 2008, from www.itgi.org

IT Governance Institute (ITGI) (2005). *Optimising value creation from IT investments.* Retrieved April 29, 2008, from www.itgi.org

IT Governance Institute (ITGI) (2006). *Enterprise value: Governance of IT investments, The Val IT framework.* Retrieved April 29, 2008, from www.itgi.org

IT Governance Institute (ITGI) (2006). *Information security governance: Guidance for boards of directors and executive management.* Retrieved April 29, 2008, from www.itgi.org

IT Governance Institute (ITGI) (2006). *IT governance global status report 2006.* Retrieved April 29, 2008, from www.itgi.org

IT Governance Institute (ITGI) (2007). *CobiT 4.1.* Rolling Meadows, IL: IT Governance Institute.

IT Governance Institute (n.d.). Retrieved May 15, 2008 from http://www.itgi.org

IT Governance Institute [ITGI] (2005). *COBIT 4.0: Control objectives, management guidelines, maturity models.* Retrieved May 14, 2008, from http://www.isaca.org/

IT Governance Institute [ITGI] (2006). *IT governance global status report – 2006.* Retrieved May 14, 2008, from https://my.isaca.org/AMTemplate.cfm?Section=ITGI_Research_Publications&Template=/ContentManagement/ContentDisplay.cfm&ContentID=24224

IT Governance Institute [ITGI], Office of Government Commerce [OGC], & IT Service Management Forum [itSMF] (2005). *Aligning COBIT, ITIL, and ISO 17799 for business benefit: A management briefing from ITGI and OGC*. Retrieved May 14, 2008, from http://www.nysforum.org/documents/pdf/itil-6-6-06/AligningCO-BITITIL.pdf

IT Governance Ltd. (2006). *BS 7799-3:2006 – Risk management guidelines*. Retrieved May 10, 2008 from http://www.itgovernance.co.uk

IT Leader (2006). Time for CIOs to get on board. *IT leader*. Retrieved May 8, 2008, from http://www.the-itleader.com/features/feature434/

IT Service Management (ITSM) (2007). *Overview of ITSM*. Retrieved April 29, 2008, from www.itsm.info/ITSM.htm

ITGI & PWC (2007). IT governance in practice: Insight from leading CIOs.

ITGI (2000). *CoBiT 3rd edition - Executive summary*. IT Governance Institute, USA.

ITGI (2000). CoBiT 3rd edition management guidelines. Retrieved May 11, 2008, from http://www.isaca.org/Template.cfm?Section=Obtain_COBIT

ITGI (2000). *CoBiT 3rd edition audit guidelines*. Retrieved May 11, 2008, from http://www.isaca.org/Template.cfm?Section=Obtain_COBIT

ITGI (2000). *CoBiT 3rd edition control objectives*. Retrieved May 11, 2008, from http://www.isaca.org/Template.cfm?Section=Obtain_COBIT

ITGI (2002). *CoBIT: Control objectives for information and related technology* (3rd Ed.). Rolling Meadow, IL: IT Governance Institute. Retrieved May 8, 2008, from http://www.isaca.org/AMTemplate.cfm?Section=Downloads&Template=/MembersOnly.cfm&ContentID=15988

ITGI (2003). *Board briefing on IT governance* (2nd ed.). IT Governance Institute. Retrieved May 1, 2008, from http://www.isaca.org/Content/ContentGroups/ITGI3/Resources1 /Board_Briefing_on_IT_Governance/26904_Board_Briefing_final.pdf

ITGI (2003). *Board briefing on IT governance*. Retrieved May 10, 2005, from http://www.itgi.org

ITGI (2004). *IT governance global status report*. Retrieved May 10, 2008, from http://www.isaca.org

ITGI (2005). *CoBiT 4.0 – Control objectives, management guidelines, maturity models*. Retrieved May 10, 2008 from http://www.itgi.org

ITGI (2005). *COBIT 4.0*. IT Governance Institute. Retrieved May 1, 2008, from http://www.itgi.org/template_ITGI.cfm?template=/ContentManagement/ContentDisplay.cfm&ContentID=27263

ITGI (2005). *Governance of outsourcing*. Rolling Meadows, IL: IT Governance Institute.

ITGI (2005). *Aligning CobiT ITIL ISO 17799 for business benefit*. Retrieved May 11, 2008, from http://www.isaca.org/

ITGI (2005). *CobiT management guidelines*. Retrieved May 11, 2008, from http://www.isaca.org/

ITGI (2006). *IT governance global status Report – 2006*. IT Governance Institute. Retrieved May 1, 2008, from http://www.itgi.org/template_ITGI.cfm?template=/Content Management/ContentDisplay.cfm&ContentID=24226

ITGI (2007). *CoBiT 4.1 executive summary*. Retrieved May 11, 2008, from http://www.isaca.org/AMTemplate.cfm?Section=Downloads&Template=/ContentManagement/ContentDisplay.cfm&ContentID=34172

ITGI (2007). *CobiT 4.1*. Retrieved May 11, 2008, from http://www.isaca.org/

ITGI (2007). *CoBiT 4.1: Framework control objectives, management guidelines, maturity models*. Retrieved May 11, 2008, from http://isaca.org/Content/Navigation-Mengu/Members_and_Leaders/COBIT6/Obtain_CO-BIT/Obtain_COBIT.htm

ITGI (2007). *IT governance implementation guide* (2nd ed.). Retrieved May 11, 2008, from http://www.isaca.org/

ITGI (2007). *IT assurance guide*. Retrieved May 11, 2008, from http://www.isaca.org/

ITIL - IT Infrastructure Library (2007). Retrieved May 13, 2008, from http://www.itil-officialsite.com/home/home.asp

ITIL (2005). *What is ITIL?* Retrieved May 11, 2008, from http://www.itil.co.uk/faqs.htm#11

ITIL (2007). *Information technology infrastructure library*. Retrieved May 11, 2008, from http://www.itil.org.uk

ITIL (2007). ITIL lifecycle publication suite (ITIL v3 - Complete Library). TSO, ISBN 10: 011331051X.

ITIL (2007). *What is ITIL*. Retrieved May 10, 2008, from http://www.itil-officialsite.com/AboutITIL/WhatisITIL.asp

ITIL (2007). *Service management – ITIL ® (IT Infrastructure Library) Version 3*. Retrieved May 10, 2008, from http://www.best-management-practice.com/ officialsite.asp?FO=1245494

ITIL® (2001). *Best practice for service delivery*. United Kingdom: Office of Government Commerce.

ITPI (2006). *IT controls performance study*. IT Process Institute. Retrieved May 11, 2008, from http://www.itpi.org/

Jackson, S. F., Brett, J. F., Sessa, V. I., Cooper, D. M., Julin, J. A., Peyronnin, K. (1991). Some differences make a difference: Individual dissimilarity and group heterogeneity as correlates of recruitment, promotion, and turnover. *Journal of Applied Psychology, 76*(5), 675-689.

Janssen, M. & Joha, A. (2006). Governance of shared services in public administration. In *Proceedings of the 12th Americas Conference on Information Systems*, Acapulco, México.

Jensen, M. C. (1986). Agency costs of free cash flow, corporate finance, and takeovers. *American Economic Review, 76*(2), 323-329.

Jensen, M. C. (1993). The modern industrial revolution, exit, and the failure of internal control systems. *Journal of Finance, 48*(3), 831-880.

Jensen, M. C., & Meckling, W. H. (1976). Theory of the firm: Managerial behavior, agency costs and ownership structure. *Journal of Financial Economics, 3*(4), 305-360.

Jeong, S. R., Kang, J., & Lee, B. G. (2007). The conceptual definition and the measurement development for IT governance. *Journal of Korea Information Processing Society, 14-D*(2), 225-234.

Jogani, A. (2006). Governance of mobile technology in enterprises. *Information Systems Control Journal, 4*, 25-27.

Johannessen, R. (2004). Risk-based sampling Using Cobit. *intoIT The INTOSAI IT Journal, 19*. Retrieved May 11, 2008, from http://www.nao.org.uk/intosai/edp/intoit_articles/19_09_COBIT.pdf

Johnson, D. M. (1996). The systems engineer and the software crisis. *ACM SIGSOFT Software Engineering Notes, 1*(2), 64-73.

Johnson, K., & Dindo, J. (1998). Expanding the fcus of software process improvement to include systems engineering. *Crosstalk: The journal of defense software engineering*, 1-13.

Johnstone, D., Huff, S. L., & Hope, B. (2006). IT projects: Conflict, governance and systems thinking. *Paper presented at the 39th Hawaii International Conference on System Sciences*, Hawaii

Johnstone, D., Huff, S., & Hope, B. (2006). IT projects: Conflict, governance and systems thinking. *Paper presented at the 39th Hawaii International Conference on System Sciences*, Hawaii.

Johnstone, D., Huff, S., & Hope, B. (2006). IT projects: Conflict, governance, and systems thinking. In *Proceedings of the 39th Hawaii International Conference on System Sciences*, Hawaii.

Jordan, E. & Musson, D. J. (2003, June 9 - 11). The board view of electronic business risk. *Paper presented at the 16th Bled eCommerce Conference*, Bled, Slovenia

Jordan, E. & Silcock, L. (2005). *Beating IT risks*. Milton, Qld: Wiley.

Jung, K., Kim, Y.-C., & Stulz, R. M. (1996). Timing, investment opportunities, managerial discretion, and the security issue decision. *Journal of Financial Economics, 42*(2), 159-185.

Kamiske, G., & Umbreit, G. (2001). *Qualitätsmanagement*. München, Wien: Carl Hanser Verlag.

Kang, H., & Bradley, G. (2002). Measuring the performance of IT services—An assessment of SERVQUAL. *International Journal of Accounting Information Systems, 3*(3), 151-164.

Kaplan, R. & Norton, D. (1992). The balanced scorecard-measures that drive performance. *Harvard Business Review*, January-February, 71-79.

Kaplan, R. B. & Norton, D. P. (1992). The balanced scorecard - Measures that drive performance. *Harvard Business Review, 70*(1, Jan/Feb), 71 – 79.

Kaplan, R. B. & Norton, D. P. (1993). Putting the balanced scorecard to work. *Harvard Business Review, 71*(5), 134 – 142.

Kaplan, R. B. & Norton, D. P. (1996). Using the balanced scorecard as a strategic management system. *Harvard Business Review, 74*(1), 75 – 85.

Kaplan, R. S. & Norton, D. P. (1992). The balanced scorecard: Measures that drive performance. *Harvard Business Review, 70*, 71–79.

Kaplan, S. N., & Minton, B. A. (2006). How has CEO turnover changed? Increasingly Performance Sensitive Boards and Increasingly Uneasy CEOs.

Karake, Z. A. (1992). An empirical investigation of information technology structure, control and corporate governance. *Journal of Strategic Information Systems, 1*(5), 258-265.

Karimi, J., Bhattacherjee, A., Gupta, Y. P., & Somers, T. M. (2000). The effect of MIS steering committees. *Journal of Management Information Systems, 17*(2), 207-239.

Karpoff, J. M., Malatesta, P. H., & Walkling, R. A. (1996). Corporate governance and shareholder initiatives: Empirical evidence. *Journal of Financial Economics, 42*(3), 365-395.

Katchabaw, M., Lutfiyya, H., & Bauer, M. (1998). Driving resource management with application-level quality of service specifications. In *Proceedings of the First International Conference on Information and Computation Economies*, Charleston, South Carolina.

Kearns, G. S. & Lederer, A. L. (2003). A resource-based view of strategic IT alignment: How knowledge sharing ceates competitive advantage. *Decision Sciences, 34*(1), 1-27.

Keider, S. P. (1984). Why information systems development projects fail. *Journal of Information Systems Management, 1*(3), 33 – 38.

Kelley, E., & Woidtke, T. (2006). Investor protection and real investment by U.S. multinationals. *Journal of Financial & Quantitative Analysis, 41*(3), 541-572.

Kellner, M., Curtis, B., deMarco, T., Kishida, K., Schulemberg, M., & Tully, C. (1991). Non-technological issues in software engineering. In *Proceedings of the 13th International Conference on Software Engineering*. Retrieved digital library at www.acm.org

Kern, T., & Willcocks, L. (2000). Exploring information technology outsourcing relationships: Theory and practice. *The Journal of Strategic Information Systems, 9*(4), 321-350.

Kerth, N. L. (2001). Project retrospectives: A handbook for team reviews. New York: Dorset House Publishing Company.

Kettinger, W. J., Teng, J. T. C., & Guha, S. (1997). Business process change: A study of methodologies, techniques, and tools. *Management Information Systems Quarterly, 21*(1), 55-80.

Keyes-Pearce, S. (2002). Rethinking IT governance in the e-world. In *Proceedings of the Pacific-Asian Conference on Information Systems*, Tokyo.

Keyes-Pearce, S. V. (2002). Rethinking the importance of IT governance in the e-world. In *Proceedings of the 6th Pacific Asia Conference on Information Systems* (pp. 256-272), Tokyo, Japan.

Kim, S. M. (2003). *Information technology and governance: Substitution and complementary.* University of Illinois at Urbana-Champaign, Illinois.

King, J. L. (1983). Centralised versus decentralised computing: Organisational considerations and management options. *Computing Surveys, 15*(4), 320–349.

King, W. R. (1988). How effective is your information systems planning? *Long Range Planning, 21*(3), 103-112.

Kleijnen J. & Smits, M. T. (2003). Performance metrics in supply chain management. *Journal of the Operatioal Research Society, 54*, 507-514.

Kliem, R. (2004). Managing the risks of offshore IT development projects. *Information Systems Management, 21*(3), 22.

Klobas, J. E. (1995). Beyond information quality: Fitness for purpose and electronic information resource use. *Journal of Information Science, 21*(2), 95-114.

Kohli, R. & Devaraj, S. (2004). Realizing the business value of information technology investments: An organizational process. *MIS Quarterly Executive, 3*(1), 53-68.

Kohli, R. & Hoadley, E. (2006). Towards developing a framework for measuring organizational impact of IT-enabled BPR: Case studies of three firms. *SIGMIS Database, 37*(1), 40-58.

Kollmann, T. (2006). What is e-entrepreneurship? – Fundamentals of company founding in the net economy. *International Journal of Technology Management, 33*(4), 322-340.

Kollmann, T., & Häsel, M. (2006). *Cross-channel cooperation: The bundling of online and offline business models.* Wiesbaden: Deutscher Universitäts-Verlag.

Kollmann, T., & Häsel, M. (2007). Reverse auctions in the service sector: The case of LetsWorkIt.de. *International Journal of E-Business Research, 3*(3), 57-73.

Korac-Kakabadse, N. & Kakabadse, A. (2001). IS/IT governance: Need for an integrated model. *Corporate Governance, 1*(4), 9-11.

Kose, J., & Senbet, L. (1998). Corporate governance and board effectiveness. *Journal of Banking and Finance, 22*, 371-403.

Kotabe, M., & Murray, J. Y. (2004). Global procurement of service activities by service firms. *International Marketing Review, 21*(6), 615-633.

KPMG (1997). *What went wrong? Unsuccessful information technology projects.* San Francisco: KPMG. Retrieved May 8, 2008, from www.audit.kpmg.ca/vl/surveys/it_wrong.htm

KPMG (2002). Delivering information 24x7. *Consumer Markets Newsletter,* (9).

KPMG (2004). *Creating stakeholder value in the information age: The case for information systems governance.* Sydney: KPMG.

KPMG (2005). *Strategic risk management survey.* Sydney: KPMG. Retrieved May 8, 2008, from http://www.kpmg.com.au/Portals/0/ias_whitepaper-str-risk-mgt-survey200502_071441.pdf

KPMG (2005). *Global IT project management survey.* Sydney: KPMG. Retrieved May 8, 2008, from http://www.kpmg.com.au/Portals/0/irmprm-global-it-pm-survey2005.pdf

Kraemer, K. L., Dedrick, J., & Yamashiro, S. (2000). Refining and extending the business model with information technology: Dell Computer Corporation. *Information Society, 16*(1), 5-21.

Krishnamurthy, S., Spindt, P., Subramaniam, V., & Woidtke, T. (2005). Does investor identity matter in equity issues? Evidence from private placements. *Journal of Financial Intermediation, 14*(2), 210-238.

Kruchten, P. (2003). *The rational unified process: An introduction* (3rd ed.). Massachusetts: Addison Wesley.

Kumar, K. (1990). Post implementation evaluation of computer-based information systems: Current practice. *Communications of the ACM, 33*(2), 203 – 212.

Kwon, D. & Watts, S. (2006). IT valuation in turbulent times. *Journal of Strategic Information Systems, 15,* 327-354.

La Porta, R., Lopez-de-Silanes, F., Shleifer, A., & Vishny, R. (2000). Investor protection and corporate governance. *Journal of Financial Economics, 58*(1/2), 3-27.

La Porta, R., Lopez-de-Silanes, F., Shleifer, A., & Vishny, R. W. (1997). Legal determinants of external finance. *Journal of Finance, 52*(3), 1131-1150.

La Porta, R., Lopez-de-Silanes, F., Shleifer, A., & Vishny, R. W. (1998). Law and finance. *Journal of Political Economy, 106*(6), 1113-1155.

Lainhart, J. W. (2000). CoBIT: A methodology for managing and controlling information and information technology risks and vulnerabilities. *Journal of Information Systems, 14*(1 Supp.), 21-25.

Lambert, D. M. & Pohlen, T. L. (2001). Supply chain metrics. *The International Journal of Logistics Management, 12*(1), 1-19.

Lamberton, D. (1998). Information economics: Research strategies. *International Journal of Social Economics, 25*(2/3/4).

Lambeth, J. (2007). Using CobiT as a tool to lead enterprise IT organizations. *Information Systems Control Journal, 1*(28-29).

Lankhorst, M. et al. (2005). *Enterprise architecture at work: Modelling, communication, and analysis.* Berlin: Springer.

Lawrence P., & Lorsch, J. (1986). *Organization and environment: Managing differentiation and integration.* Boston: Harvard Business School.

Lawrence, P., & Lorsch, J. (1967). Differentiation and integration in complex organizations. *Administrative Science Quarterly, 12*(1), 1-47.

Leavitt, H. (1978). *Managerial psychology* (4th ed.). Chicago: University of Chicago Press.

Lederer, A. L. & Sethi, V. (1988). The implementation of strategic information systems planning methodologies. *MIS Quarterly, 12*(3), 445-461.

Lederer, A. L. & Sethi, V. (1996). Key prescriptions for strategic information systems planning. *Journal of Management Information Systems, 13*(1), 35 – 62.

Lederer, A. L., & Gardiner, V. (1992). The process of strategic information planning. *Journal of Strategic Information Systems, 1,* 76-83.

Lee, B. & Menon, N. M. (2000). Information technology value through different normative lenses. *Journal of Management Information Systems, 16*(4), 99.

Lee, C., Lee, J., & Ahn, S. (2006). A comparative case study analysis of IT governance framework: Focused on the Korean service company. In *Proceedings of the 2006 IT Governance International Conference*, Auckland, New Zealand.

Lee, D., Trauth, E., & Farwell, D. (1995). Critical skills and knowledge requirements of IS professionals: A joint academic/industry investigation. *MIS Quarterly, 19*(3), 313-340.

Lee, I. (2004). Evaluating business process-integrated information technology investment. *Business Process Management Journal, 10*(2).

Lee, S.-H., Thomas, S. R., Macken, C. L., Chapman, R. E., Tucker, R. L., & Kim, I. (2005). Economic Value of Combined Best Practice Use. *Journal of Management in Engineering, 21*(3), 118-124.

Legrenzi, C. (2003). The second edition of the European survey on the economic value of information technology: Inventory of practices concerning IT governance. *Information Systems Control Journal, 3*, 50.

Lei, K. & Rawles, P. (2003). Strategic decisions on technology selections for facilitating a network/systems laboratory using real options \& total cost of ownership theories. In *Proceedings of the 4th Conference on Information Technology Curriculum*, Lafayette, Indiana.

Leih, M. (2007). Regulatory impact on IT governance: A multiple case study on the Sarbanes-Oxley Act. In *Proceedings of the 13th Americas Conference on Information Systems*, Keystone, Colorado.

Lel, U., & Miller, D. P. (2006). International cross-listing, firm performance and top management turnover: A test of the bonding hypothesis. *Working Papers—US Federal Reserve Board's International Finance Discussion Papers* (pp. 1-61).

Letsoalo, K., Brown, I., & Njenga, K. N. (2006). An investigation of enablers and inhibitors of IT governance implementation: A case study of a South African enterprise. In B. Cusack (Ed.), In *Proceedings of the 2006 IT Governance International Conference* (pp.27-35), Auckland, New Zealand.

Letsoalo, K., Brown, I., & Njenga, K. N. (2006). An investigation of enablers and inhibitors of IT governance implementation: A case study of a South African enterprise. In *Proceedings of the 2006 IT Governance International Conference*, Auckland, New Zealand.

Leuz, C., Nanda, D., & Wysocki, P. D. (2003). Earnings management and investor protection: an international comparison. *Journal of Financial Economics, 69*(3), 505-527.

Levine, R. (2004). Risk management systems: Understanding the need. *Information Systems Management, 21*(2), 31.

Lewin, K. (1948). Resolving social conflicts; Selected papers on group dynamics. New York: Harper & Row.

Lewis, E. (2005). Australian world-first ICT governance standard. *The Global Standard, March*, 8-9.

Lewis, E., & Munro, D. (2007). *Foundations of enterprise architecture*. Melbourne.

Liew, K. (2006). Challenges of compliance – The CoBiT bridge. *Computerworld, 12*(15). Retrieved May 10, 2008, from http://www.computerworld.com.sg

Lim, G., Lee, H., & Kim, T. (2005). Formulating business strategies from a stakeholder perspective: Korean healthcare IT business cases. *International Journal of Information Technology & Decision Making, 4*(4), 541-566.

Lim, K., Lee, J., Rah, J., Yoon, S., & Lee, J. H. (2004). An empirical study on IT governance cognition and execution levels of Korean companies. *Entrue Journal of Information Technology, 13*(2), 111-123.

Lin, C. & Pervan, G. (2001). IS/IT investment evaluation and benefits realisation issues in a government organization. *Paper presented at the The Twelfth Australasian Conference on Information Systems*, Coffs Harbour.

List, B. & Machaczek, K. (2004). Towards a corporate performance measurement system. In *Proceedings of the ACM Symposium on Applied Computing*, Nicosia, Cyprus.

Liu, Q., & Ridley, G. (2005). IT control in the Australian public sector: An international comparison. In D. Bartmann, F. Rajola, J. Kallinikos, D. Avison, R. Winter, P. Ein-Dor, Becker, Jr, F. Bodendorf, C. Weinhardt (Eds.), In Proceedings of 13th European Conference on Information Systems, Regensburg: ECIS Standing Committee.

Lloyd, V., & Rudd, C. (2007). *ITIL service design*. Norwich: The Stationary Office.

Lloyd, V., Rudd, C., & Littlewood, C. (2003). *Planning to implement service management*. Reading, UK: itSMF Ltd.

Loh, L., & Venkatraman, N. (1992). Diffusion of information technology outsourcing: Influence sources and the Kodak effect. *Information Systems Research, 3*(4), 334-359.

Lovelock, C. F., & Gummesson, E. (2004). Whither services marketing? In search of a new paradigm and fresh perspectives. *Journal of Service Research, 7*(1), 20-41.

Lovelock, C., Vandermerwe, S., & Lewis, B. (1996). *Services marketing: A European perspective*. Essex: Prentice Hall.

Lu, J. & Zhang, G. (2003). Cost benefit factor analysis in e-services. *International Journal of Service Industry Management, 14*(5).

Lubbe, S. & Remenyi, D. (1999). Management of information technology evaluation—The development of a managerial thesis. *Logistics Information Management, 12*(1/2).

Luftman, J. (1996). *Competing in the information age: Strategic alignment in practice.* New York: Oxford University Press.

Luftman, J. (2005). Key issues for IT executives 2004. *MIS Quarterly Executive, 4*(9), 269-285.

Luftman, J. N. & Brier, T. (1999). Achieving and sustaining business-IT alignment. *California Management Review, 42*(1), 109-121.

Luftman, J. N. (2000). Addressing business-IT alignment maturity. *Communications of the Association for Information Systems, 4*(14), 1-50.

Luftman, J. N. (2003). Assessing IT/business alignment. *Information Systems Management*, Fall, 9-15.

Luftman, J. N. (2003). *Competing in the information age: Align in the sand.* Oxford: Oxford University Press.

Luftman, J. N. (2004). *Managing the information technology resource: Leadership in the information age.* Upper Saddle River, NJ: Pearson Prentice Hall.

Luftman, J. N., Lewis, P. R., & Oldach, S. H. (1993). Transforming the enterprise: The alignment of business and information technology strategies. *IBM Systems Journal, 32*(1), 198.

Luftman, J. N., Lewis, P. R., & Oldach, S. H. (1993). Transforming the enterprise: The alignment of business and information technology strategies. *IBM Systems Journal, 32*(1), 198 – 221.

Luftman, J. N., Papp, R., & Brier, T. (1999). Enablers and inhibitors of business-IT alignment. *Communications of the Association for Information Systems, 1*, 1-32.

Luftman, J., & Brier, T. (1999). Achieving and sustaining business-IT alignment. *California Management Review, 42*(1), 109-122.

Luftman, J., Bullen, C., Liao, D., Nash, E., & Nuewmann, C. (2004). *Managing the information technology resource: Leadership in the information age.* Upper Saddle River, NJ: Pearson Education Inc.

Luftman, J., Kempaiah, R., & Nash, E. (2006). Key issues for IT executives 2005. *MIS Quarterly Executive, 4*(2), 81-99.

Lumpkin, G. T., & Dess, G. G. (2004). E-business strategies and internet business models: how the internet adds value. *Organizational Dynamics, 33*(2), 161-173.

Lyytinen, K. & Hirschheim, R. (1987). Information system failures - A survey and classification of the empirical literature. *Oxford Surveys in Information Technology*, (4), 257–309.

MacCormack, A., Verganti, R., & Iansiti, M. (2001). Developing products on "Internet Time": The anatomy of a flexible development process. *Management Science, 47*(1), 133-150.

Macharzina, K. (2003). *Unternehmensführung das internationale Managementwissen Konzepte - Methoden - Praxis* (4., grundlegend überarb. Aufl. ed.). Wiesbaden: Gabler.

MacInnes, I. (2005). Dynamic business model framework for emerging technologies. *International Journal of Services Technology and Management, 6*(1), 3-19.

Maes, R. (1999). *A generic framework for information management.* Retrieved April 29, 2008, from http://primavera.fee.uva.nl/html/working_papers.cfm

Maes, R., Rijsenbrij, D., Truijens, O., & Goedvolk, H. (2000). *Redefining business-IT alignment through a unified framework.* PrimaVera Working Paper Series - University of Amsterdam.

Magee, S. (2006). *A successful software quality strategy using ISO/IEC 12207 & 15288.* Retrieved May 15, 2008, www.15288.com

Mähring, M. (2002). *IT project governance: A process-oriented study of organisational control and executive involvement.* SSE/EFI Working Paper Series in Business Administration, No 2002:15. Retrieved May 1, 2008, from http://swoba.hhs.se /hastba /papers/hastba2002_015.pdf

Mähring, M. (2006). The role of the board of directors in IT governance: A review and agenda for research. In *Proceedings of the 12th Americas Conference on Information Systems*, Acapulco, México.

Mair, P. (2004). *Psych up your culture.* Retrieved May 11, 2008, from http://www.cfoweb.com.au/freearticle.aspx?relId=9474

Malhotra, Y. & Galletta, D. F. (2004). Building Systems that Users Want to Use. *Communications of the ACM, 47*(12), 89-94.

Malone, T. W. & Crowston, K. C. (1994). The interdisciplinary study of coordination. *ACM Computing Surveys, 26*(1), 87-119.

Malorny, C., & Kassebohm, K. (1994). *Brennpunkt TQM.* Stuttgart [u.a.]: Schäffer-Poeschel.

Malzahn, D. (2007, May). *A service extension for SPICE?* In Proceedings of the SPICE 2007 Conference. Seoul, South Korea.

Man, T. W. Y., Lau, T., & Chan, K. F. (2002). The competitiveness of small and medium enterprises: A conceptualization with focus on entrepreneurial competencies. *Journal of Business Venturing, 17*(2), 123-142.

Mandeville, T. (1998). An information economics perspective on innovation. *International Journal of Social Economics, 25*(2/3/4).

Markus, M. L. (2000). Toward an integrative theory of risk control. In R. Baskerville, J. Stage & J. I. DeGross (Eds.), *Social perspectives on information technology* (pp. 167 - 178). Boston: Kluwer Academic Publishers.

Martin, N., Gregor, S., & Hart, D. (2005). The social dimension of business and IS/IT alignment: Case studies of six public-sector organizations. *Australian Accounting Review, 15*(3), 28-38.

Martino, C. L. (1983). *Information systems planning to meet business objectives: A survey of practices.* New York: North Holland.

Martinsons, M. G., & Martinsons, V. (2002). Rethinking the Value of IT, Again. *Communications of the ACM, 45*(7), 25-26.

Mata, F. J., Fuerst, W., & Barney, J. B. (1995). Information technology and sustained competitive advantage: a resource-based view. *MIS Quarterly,* 487-505.

Matlay, H. (2004). E-entrepreneurship and small e-business development: Towards a comparative research agenda. *Journal of Small Business and Enterprise Development, 11*(3), 408-414.

Mayo, D. D., Dalton, W. J., & Callaghan, M. J. (2003). Strategy simulations: steering strategic decisions at London underground: Evaluating management options with system dynamics. In *Proceedings of the 35th Winter Simulation Conference: Driving Innovation,* New Orleans, Louisiana.

McGovern, J., Ambler, S., Stevens, M., Linn, J., Sharan, V., & Jo, E. (2004). *A practical guide to enterprise architecture.* Upper Saddle River, New Jersey: Prentice Hall.

McKenney, J. L., Copeland, D. G., & Mason, R. O. (1995). *Waves of change: Business evolution through information technology.* Boston: Harvard Business School Press.

Medlin, B. D., Dave, D. S., & Vannoy, S. A. (2001). Students' views of the importance of technical and non-technical skills for successful IT professionals. *Journal of Computer Information Systems , 42*(1), 65-69.

Melville, N., Kraemer, K. L., & Gurbaxani, V. (2004). Review: Information technology and organizational performance: An integrative model of IT business value. *MIS Quarterly, 28*(2), 283-322.

Menachemi, N., Burkhardt, J., Richard, S., Darrell, B., & Robert, G. B. (2006). Hospital information technology and positive financial performance: A different approach to finding an ROI. *Journal of Healthcare Management, 51*(1), 40-58.

Mendez, M. A. (2005). *The state of IT governance in Europe: Business technographics Europe.* Retrieved May 10, 2008, from http://www.forrester.com/Research/Document/Excerpt/0,7211,37201,00.html

Mercurio, V. J., Meyers, B. F., Nisbet, A. M., & Radin, G. (1990). AD/Cycle strategy and architecture. *IBM Systems Journal, 29*(2), 170-188.

Mercury (2005). *Service delivery.* Retrieved May 11, 2008, from http://www.mercury.com/us/solutions/governance/itil/service-delivery/

Meredith, J. R. & Mantel, S. J. (1995). *Project management: A managerial approach.* Chichester: John Wiley.

Meso, P., & Jain, R. (2006). Agile software development: Adaptive systems principles and best practices. *Information Systems Management, 23*(3).

Meyer, N. D. (2004). Systemic IS governance: An introduction. *Information Systems Management, 21*(4), 23-34.

Milis, K. & Mercken, R. (2004). The use of balanced scorecard for the evaluation of Information and communication technology projects. *International Journal of Project Management, 22*(2), 87 – 97.

Minnich, H. (2002). EIA IS 731 Compared to CMMI-SE/SW. *Systems engineering journal, 5*(1), 62-72.

Misic, V. B., & Zhao, J. L. (2000). Evaluating the quality of reference models. In *Proceedings of the 19th International Conference on Conceptual Modeling,* Salt Lake City, Utah.

Mora, M. (2004). *Manual of Conceptual Research* (Internal Tech. Rep. IS-2004-01). Autonomous University of Aguascalientes, Mexico.

Mora, M., Gelman, O., & Alvarez, F. (2007b). A systemic model for the description and comparison of models and standards of processes in the SE, SwE and IT disciplines. In *e-Proceedings, International Conference on Complex Systems 2007, NECSI*, Boston, MA.

Mora, M., Gelman, O., Cano, J., Cervantes, F., & Forgionne, G. (2006). Theory of systems and information systems research frameworks. In *Proceedings of the 50th Annual Meeting of the International Society for the Systems Sciences*, Somona State Universiy, CA.

Mora, M., Gelman, O., Cervantes, F., Mejia, M., & Weitzenfeld, A. (2003). A systemic approach for the formalization of the information system concept: Why information systems are systems? In Cano, J. (Ed.), *Critical reflections of information systems: Systemic approach* (pp. 1-29). Hershey, PA: Idea Group.

Mora, M., Gelman, O., Frank, M., Paradice, D., Cervantes, F., & Forgionne, G. (2008). Toward an interdisciplinary engineering and management of complex IT-intensive organizational systems: A systems view. *The International Journal of Information Technologies and the Systems Approach, 1*(1), 1-24.

Mora, M., Gelman, O., O'Connor, R., Alvarez, F., & Macías, J. (2007a). On models and standards of processes in SE, SwE and IT&S disciplines: Toward a comparative framework using the systems approach. In K. Dhanda & R. Hackney (Eds), In *Proceedings of the ISOneWorld 2007 Conference Track in System Thinking/Systems Practice*, Las Vegas, Nevada.

Morck, R., Shleifer, A., & Vishny, R. W. (1988). Management ownership and market valuation: An empirical analysis. *Journal of Financial Economics, 20*(1/2), 293-315.

Morency, J. (2005). *Best practice, practice, practice.* Retrieved May 11, 2008, from http://www.networkworld.com/research/2005/011005COBIT.html

Moura, A., Sauve, J., Jornada, J., & Radziuk, E. (2006). A quantitative approach to IT investment allocation to improve business results. In *Proceedings of the Seventh IEEE International Workshop on Policies for Distributed Systems and Networks (POLICY'06)*.

Mukherji, A. (2001). The evolution of information systems: Their impact on organizations and structures. *Management Decision, 40*(5/6), 497-507.

Murphy, P. (2004). *Forrester report: Application portfolio management tools*. Retrieved May 11, 2008, from http://www.forrester.com/Research/Document/Excerpt/0,7211,34229,00.html

Murray, J. P. (2004). Judging IT department performance. *Information Systems Management*, Spring.

Murugesan, S., Deshpande, Y., Hansen, S., & Ginige, A. (2001). Web engineering: A new discipline for development of web-based systems. In S. Murugesan & Y. Deshpande (Eds.), *Web engineering: Managing diversity and complexity of web application development* (pp. 3-13). Heidelberg: Springer.

Musaji, Y. (2005). Sarbanes-Oxley and business process outsourcing risk. *Information Systems Control Journal, 5*. Retrieved May 14, 2008, from http://www.isaca.org

Myers, S. C., & Majluf, N. S. (1984). Corporate financing and investment decisions when firms have information that investors do not have. *Journal of Financial Economics, 13*(2), 187-221.

Mylott, T. R., III (1995). *Computer outsourcing: Managing the transfer of information systems*. Englewood Cliffs, NJ: Prentice Hall.

Na, J., Lee, J., Lee, J., & Lim, G. (2005). A study of CIO's perception and execution level of ITG in Korean companies. In *Proceedings of the Korea Society of Management Information Systems Conference*, Seoul, Korea.

Nakayama, M., & Sutcliffe, N. (2003). Skills, management of skills, and IT skills requirements. In M. Nakayama & N. Sutcliffe (Eds.), *Managing IT skills portfolios: Planning, acquisition and performance evaluation* (pp. 1-25). Hershey, PA: Idea Group Publishing.

Nalbone, J., Vizdos, M., & Ambler, S. (2005). *The enterprise unified process: Extending the rational unified process*. New Jersey: Prentice Hall PTR.

National Association of State Chief Information Officers [NASCIO] (2003). *Enterprise architecture maturity model*. Retrieved May 14, 2008, from http://www.nascio.org/publications/documents/NASCIO-EAMM.pdf

Nelson, B. (2002). *Higher education at the crossroads–An overview paper*. Retrieved May 10, 2008, from http://www.backingaustraliasfuture.gov.au/fact_sheets.htm

Nelson, M., & Tan, H.-T. (2005). Judgment and decision making research in auditing: A task, person, and interpersonal interaction perspective. *Auditing, 24*, 41-71.

Nelson, R. R. (1991). Educational needs as perceived by IS and end-user personnel: A survey of knowledge and skill requirements. *MIS Quaterly, 15*(4), 503-525.

Nelson, R. R. (2005). Project retrospectives: Evaluating success, failure and everything in between. *MIS Quarterly Executive, 4*(3). Retrieved May 8, 2008, from http://www.misqe.org/jsp/showpaper.jsp?ob1=67&ob2=92&ob3=false

Nevo, S., Wade, M. R., & Cook, W. D. (2007). An examination of the trade-off between internal and external IT capabilities. *Journal of Strategic Information Systems, (16)1,* 5–23.

Nichols, R., & Connaughton, C. (2005). *Software process improvement journey: IBM Australia application management services* (A Report from the Winner of the 2004 Software Process Achievement Award). Technical Report CMU/SEI-2005-TR-002, ESC-TR-2005-002.

Niessink, F., Clerc, V., Tijdink, T., & van Vliet, H. (2005, January 28). *The IT service capability model.* Retrieved May 14, 2008, from http://www.itservicecmm.org/doc/itscmm-1.0rc1.pdf

Njenga, K. N. & Brown, I. (2006). On improvisation: Framework for the soft approach to managing security risk in South African. In B. Cusack (Ed.), In *Proceedings of the 2006 IT Governance International Conference* (pp. 97-106), Auckland, New Zealand.

NOIE (2003). *Productivity and organisational transformation: Optimising investment in ICT.* Canberra: National Office of the Information Economy. Retrieved May 8, 2008, from http://www2.dcita.gov.au/ie/publications/2003/03/ovum_report

Nolan, R. & McFarlan, F. W. (2005). Information technology and the board of directors. *Harvard Business Review, 83*(10), 96-106.

Nolan, R. L. & McFarlan, F. W. (2005). Information technology and the board of directors. *Harvard Business Review, 83*(10), 96–106.

Nolan, R. L. (1982). Managing information systems by committee. *Harvard Business Review, 60*(4), 72–79.

Nonaka, I. (1994). A dynamic theory of organizational knowledge creation. *Organization Science, 5*(1), 14-37.

NSW Government Chief Information Office Benefits Register (n.d.). Retrieved May 15, 2008 from http://www.gcio.nsw.gov.au/documents/Sample%20Benefits_register.pdf

Nunamaker, J. F., Chen, M., & Purdin, T. D. (1991). System development in information system research. *Journal of Management Information Systems, 7,* 89-106.

O'Connor, A. D. (1993). Successful strategic information systems planning. *Journal of Information Systems, 3*(2), 71 – 83.

O'Reilly, T. (2005). *What is web 2.0: Design patterns and business models for the next generation of software.* Retrieved May 13, 2008, from http://www.oreillynet.com/pub/a/oreilly/tim/news/2005/09/30/what-is-web-20.html

Oakland, J. (2000). Total quality management. *Text with cases.* Oxford, UK: Butterworth Heinemann.

OECD (2004). *OECD principles of corporate governance.* Retrieved May 11, 2008, from http://www.oecd.org/dataoecd/32/18/31557724.pdf

Office of Government Commerce (2004). *Business perspective: The IS view of delivering services to the business.* Norwich: The Stationery Office.

Office of Government Commerce (n.d.). Retrieved May 15, 2008, from http://www.best-management-practice.com/Online-Bookshop/IT-Service-Management-ITIL/ITIL-Version-3/

OGC - Office of Government Commerce (2001). *Service delivery.* London: The Stationary Office.

OGC - Office of Government Commerce (2002). *Planning to implement service management* (CD version). London: The Stationary Office.

OGC - Office of Government Commerce (2005). *Introduction to ITIL.* London: The Stationary Office.

OGC (2002). *IT infrastructure library- Service delivery.* London: Stationery Office.

OGC (2002). *IT infrastructure library- Service Support.* London: Stationery Office.

OGC (2004). ITIL publications. Retrieved May 8, 2008, from http://www.ogc.gov.uk/index.asp?docid=1000364

OGC (2005). ICT infrastructure management. Retrieved May 11, 2008, from http://www.ogc.gov.uk/sdtoolkit/deliveryteam/briefings/ITIL/itilchap7.html

OGC (2006). *ITIL refresh: Scope and development plan.* Retrieved May 15, 2008, from www.itil.org

OGC (2007). *Information technology infrastructure library (ITIL): Version 3.* London: Office of Government Commerce.

OGC PRINCE2 (n.d.). Retrieved May 15, 2008 from http://www.ogc.gov.uk/methods_prince_2.asp

Oh, W., Kim, J. W., & Richardson, V. J. (2006). The moderating effect of context on the market reaction to IT investments. *Journal of Information Systems, 20*(1), 19-44.

Olsen, M. H. & Chervany, N. L. (1980). The relationship between organisational characteristics and the structure of the information services function. *MIS Quarterly, 4*(2), 57–68.

OMG (2006). *Business process modeling notation (BPMN) specification.* Document dtc/06-02-01. Object Management Group.

OMG (2005). *Software process engineering management: The unified process model (UPM).* Document ad/2000-05-05. Object Management Group

OMG (Object Management Group) (2007). *Model driven architecture.* Retrieved May 11, 2008, from http://www.omg.org/mda

OpenUP (2007). OpenUP/Basic development process. Retrieved May 11, 2008, from http://www.eclipse.org/epf/openup_component/openup_vision.php

Palmer, R. (2005). *IT service management foundations: ITIL study guide.* Corinth, TX: Gulf Stream Press.

Palvia, P., & Palvia, S. (2003). Information systems plans in context: A global perspective. In R. Galliers & D. Leidner (Eds.), *Strategic information management* (pp. 151-180). Oxford: Butterworth-Heinemann.

Papp, R. (1999). Business-IT alignment: Productivity paradox payoff? *Industrial Management & Data Systems, 99*(8), 367.

Parasuraman, A., Zeithamel, V. A., & Berry, K. L. (1988). SERVQUAL: A multiple item scale for measuring consumer perception of service quality. *Journal of Retailing, 64*(1), 12-37.

Parasuraman, A., Zeithamel, V., & Berry, K. L. (1985). A conceptual model of service quality an its implications for future research. *Journal of Marketing,* 41-50.

Parasuraman, A., Zeithaml, V. A., & Berry, L L. (1988). SERVQUAL: A multiple item scale for measuring consumer perceptions of service quality. *Journal of Retailing, 64,* 12-40.

Pareek, M. (2006). Living with risk. *Information Systems Control Journal, 6,* 35-38.

Park, H., Jung, S., Lee, Y., & Jang, K. (2006). The effect of improving IT standard in IT governance. In *Proceedings of the International Conference on Computational Intelligence for Modeling Control and Automation(CIMCA06),* jointly with *International Conference on Intelligent Agents, Web Technologies and Internet Commerce(IAWTIC06),* Sydney, Australia.

Park, J., Lee, J., & Lee, C. (2007). IT governance practices in telecommunication companies: A complex

adaptive systems perspective. In *Proceedings of the International DSI Conference 2007,* Bangkok, Thailand.

Parker, M. M. & Benson, R. J. W. (1988). *Information economics: Linking business performance to information technology.* Englewood Cliffs, NJ: Prentice Hall.

Parker, M. M., Benson, R. J., & Traitor, H. E. (1988). *Information economics: Linking business performance and information technology.* New Jersey: Prentice Hall Inc.

Parker, M., Trainer, H. E., & Benson, R. J. (1989). *Information strategy and economics.* Prentice Hall: NJ.

Parr, A., Shanks, G., & Darke, P. (1999). The identification of necessary factors for successful implementation of ERP systems. In N. Ojelanki, L. Introna, M. D. Myers & J. I. DeGross (Eds.), In *Proceedings of IFIP Working Group 8.2 Conference on New Information Technologies in Organizational Processes: Field Studies and Theoretical Reflections on the Future of Work.* Boston: Kluwer Academic Publishers.

Parrino, R., Sias, R. W., & Starks, L. T. (2003). Voting with their feet: Institutional ownership changes around forced CEO turnover. *Journal of Financial Economics, 68*(1), 3-46.

Parsons, G. L. (1983). Strategic information technology. In Somogyi & Galliers (Eds.), *The information systems as a strategic weapon.*

Patel, N. V. (2003). An emerging strategy for e-business IT governance. In W. Van Grembergen (Ed.), *Strategies for Information Technology.* Hershey, PA: Idea Group Publishing.

Patel, N. V. (2004). An emerging strategy for e-business IT governance. In W. Van Grembergen (Ed.), *Strategies for information technology governance* (pp. 37-80). Hershey, PA: Idea Group Publishing.

Paulk, M., Chrissis, M., Weber, C. & Perdue, J. (1987). *The capability maturity model for software, Version 2B.* SEI/CMU Presentation. Retrieved May 15, 2008, from a www.sei.cmu.edu

Peak, D. & Guynes, C. S. (2003). Improving information quality through IT alignment planning: A case study. *Information Systems Management,* Fall, 22-28.

Pederiva, A. (2003). The CobiT maturity model in a vendor evaluation case. *Information Systems Control Journal, 3,* 26.

Peploeski, K. (1998). The process of improvisation. *Organisational Science, 9*(5), 560-561.

Peppard, J. (2003). Managing IT as a portfolio of services. *European Management Journal, 21*(4), 467-483.

Peppard, J. (2005). The application of the viable systems model to information technology governance. In D. Avison, D. Galletta & J. I. DeGross (Eds.), In *Proceedings of the 26th International Conference on Information Systems* (pp. 45-58), Las Vegas, Nevada.

Peppard, J., & Ward, J. (2004). Beyond strategic information systems: Towards an IS capability. *Journal of Strategic Information Systems, 13*, 167-194.

Peppard, J., Edwards, C., & Lambert, R. (1999). *A governance framework for information management in the global enterprise.* School of Management Working Papers;9/99. Retrieved May 1, 2008, from https://dspace.lib.cranfield.ac.uk/bitstream/1826 /459/2/SWP0999.pdf

Perry, L. (1991). Strategic improvisation: How to formulate and implement competitive strategies in concert. *Organizational Dynamics, 19*(4), 51-64.

Peterson, R. (2001). Configurations and coordination for global information technology governance: Complex designs in a transnational European context. *Paper presented at the 34th International Conference on Systems Sciences*, Hawaii.

Peterson, R. (2001). Configurations and coordination for global information technology governance: Complex designs in a transnational European context. In *IEEE Proceedings of HICSS* (34).

Peterson, R. (2003). Integration strategies and tactics for information technology governance. In W. Van Grembergen (Ed.), *Strategies for information technology governance* (pp. 37-80). Hershey, PA: Idea Group Publishing.

Peterson, R. (2004). Integration strategies and tactics for information technology governance. In W. Van Grembergen (Ed.), *Strategies for information technology governance* (pp. 37-80). Hershey, PA: Idea Group Publishing.

Peterson, R. (2004). *Integration strategies and tactics for information technology governance.* In W. Grembergen (Ed.), *Strategies for information technology governance* (pp. 37-80). Hershey, PA: Idea Group Publishing.

Peterson, R. K. (2004). Crafting information technology governance. *Information Systems Management,* (Fall), 7 - 22. Retrieved May 8, 2008, from http://www.itknowledgebase.net/dynamic_data/3619_2288_governance.pdf

Peterson, R. K., Parker, M. M., & Ribbers, P. M. A. (2002, December 15 - 18). Information technology governance processes under environmental dynamism: Investigating competing theories of decision making and knowledge sharing. *Paper presented at the 23rd Annual International Conference on Information Systems*, Barcelona

Peterson, R. R. & Fairchild, A. M. (2003). Exploring the impact of electronic business readiness on leadership capabilities in information technology governance. In *Proceedings of the 36th Hawaii International Conference on System Sciences*, Hawaii.

Peterson, R. R. (2004). Configurations and coordination for global information technology governance designs in a transnational European context. In *Proceedings of the 34th Hawaii International Conference on System Sciences*, Hawaii.

Peterson, R. R. (2004). Integration strategies and tactics for information technology governance. In W. Van Grembergen (Ed.), *Strategies for information technology governance* (pp. 37-80). Hershey, PA: Idea Group Publishing.

Peterson, R. R., O'Callaghan, R., & Ribbers, P. M. A. (2000). Information technology governance by design: Investigating hybrid configurations and integration mechanisms. *Paper presented at the International Conference of Information Systems*, Brisbane, Queensland, Australia.

Peterson, R. R., Parket M. M., & Ribbers, P. M. A. (2002). Information technology governance processes under environmental dynamism: Investigating competing theories of decision making and knowledge sharing. In L. Applegate, R. Galliers & J. I. DeGross (Eds.), In *Proceedings of the 26th International Conference on Information Systems* (pp. 563-576), Barcelona, Spain.

Peterson, R., & Fairchild, A. M. (2003). Exploring the impact of electronic business readiness on leadership capabilities in information technology governance. In *Proceedings of the 39th Hawaii International Conference on System Sciences (HICSS)*, Hawaii: IEEE.

Peterson, R., O'Callaghan, R., & Ribbers, P. (2000). IT governance by design: Investigating hybrid configurations and integration mechanisms. In *Proceedings of the 21ˢᵗ International Conference on Information Systems* (pp. 435-452), Brisbane.

Peterson, R., Parker, M., & Ribbers, P. (2002). Information technology governance processes under environmental dynamism: Investigating competing theories of decision making and knowledge sharing. In *Proceedings of the 23ʳᵈ International Conference on Information Systems* (pp. 563-576).

Pironti, J. P. (2006). Information security governance: Motivations, benefits and outcomes. *Information Systems Control Journal, 4*, 45-48.

Pitt L. F., Berthon, B., & Lane, N. (1998). Gaps within the IS department: Barriers to service quality. *Journal of Information Technology, 13*, 191-200.

Pitt, L. F., Watson, R. T., & Kavan, C. B. (1995). Service quality: A measure of information systems effectiveness. *MIS Quarterly,* 173-185.

Polanyi, M. (1967). *Tacit dimension.* London: Routledge & Kegan Paul.

Porter, M. (1996). What is strategy? *Harvard Business Review*, November, 61 - 78.

Porter, M. (2004). *Competitive advantage: Creating and sustaining superior performance.* New York: Free Press, Simon and Schuster.

Porter, M. E. (2001). Strategy and the internet. *Harvard Business Review, 79*(3), 62-78.

Posthumusa, S., & Solms, R. V. (2005). IT oversight: An important function of corporate governance. *Computer Fraud & Security, 2005*(6), 11-17.

Powell, A. & Yager, S. E. (2004). Exploring reputation differences in information systems groups. *Journal of Information Technology Cases and Applications, 6*(2), 5-26.

Praeg, C.-P., & Schnabel, U. (2006). IT-service Cachet—Managing IT-service performance and IT-service quality. In *Proceedings of the 39th Annual Hawaiian International Conference on System Sciences (HICSS)* (Vol. 2, pp. 10). Hawaii.

Presley, A. (2006). ERP investment analysis using the strategic alignment model. *Management Research News, 29*(5).

PRINCE2 (1998). *Managing successful projects with PRINCE2.* London: The Stationery Office.

Purdue University (1989). *The Purdue enterprise reference architecture.* Retrieved May 11, 2008, from http://pera.net

Putman, J. R. (2001). *Architecting with RM-ODP.* New Jersey: Prentice Hall PTR.

PwC (2004). *IT governance global status report.* Rolling Meadows: IT Governance Institute.

PwC (2006). *IT governance survey.* Rolling Meadows: IT Governance Institute.

Radcliffe, R. C. (1982). *Investment: Concepts, analysis, strategy.* Glenview, IL: Scott, Foreman and Co.

Raghunathan, T. S. (1992). Impact of CEO's participation on IS steering committees. *Journal of Management Information Systems, 8*(4), 83-96.

Rai, A. & Sambamurthy, V. (2006). Editorial notes—The growth of interest in services management: Opportunities for information systems scholars. *Information Systems Research, 17*(4), 327-331.

Rands, T. (1992). Information technology as a service operation. *Journal of Information Technology, 7*, 189-201.

Rau, K. G. (2004a). The CIO dashboard performance management program: Measuring and managing the value of IT. *The Executive's Journal*, Winter.

Rau, K. G. (2004b). Effective governance of IT: Design objectives, roles, and relationships. *Information Systems Management, 21*(4), 35.

Reed, K. (2006). EQUITY and the problem of return on IT investment. *Software, IEEE, 23*(1), 114-115.

Reich, B. H. & Benbasat, I. (2000). Factors that influence the social dimension of alignment between business and information technology objectives. *MIS Quarterly, 24*(1), 81-113.

Reich, B. H., & Benbasat, I. (2000). Factors that influence the social dimension of alignment between business and information technology objectives. *MIS Quarterly, 24*(1), 81-113.

Reifer, D. (2002). Ten deadly risks in internet and intranet software development. *IEEE Software, 19*(2), 12-14.

Remenyi, D., Sherwood-Smith, M., & White, T. (1997). *Achieving maximum value from information systems: A process approach.* Chichester: John Wiley & Sons.

Renkema, T. J. W. (1998). The four P's revisited: Business value assessment of the infrastructure impact of IT investments. *Journal of Information Technology, 13*(3), 181 – 190.

Repenning, N. P. & Sterman, J. D. (2001). Nobody ever gets credit for fixing problems that never happened: creating and sustaining process improvement. *California Management Review, 43*(4), 64-88.

Ribbers, P. M. A., Peterson, R. R., & Parker, M. M. (2002). Designing information technology governance processes: Diagnosing contemporary practices and competing theories. *Paper presented at the 35th International Conference on Systems Sciences*, Hawaii.

Ribbers, P. M. A., Peterson, R. R., & Parker, M. M. (2002). Designing information technology governance processes: Diagnosing contemporary practices and competing theories. *Paper presented at the Proceedings of the 35th Hawaii International Conference on System Sciences - 2002*, Hawaii. Retrieved May 8, 2008, from http://csdl.computer.org/comp/proceedings/hicss/2002/1435/08/14350241b.pdf

Ribbers, P. M. A., Peterson, R. R., & Parker, M. M. (2002). Designing information technology governance processes: Diagnosing contemporary practices and competing theories. In *Proceedings of the 35th Hawaii International Conference on System Sciences*, Hawaii.

Ribbers, P., Peterson, R., & Parker, M. (2002). Designing information technology governance processes: Diagnosing contemporary practices and competing theories. In *Proceedings of 35th Annual Hawaii International Conference on System Sciences*.

Ridley, G., Young, J., & Carroll, P. (2004). COBIT and its utilization: A framework from the literature. In R. H. Sprague, Jr. (Ed.), In *Proceedings of the 37th Hawaii International Conference on System Science (HICSS)*, Los Alamitos: IEEE Computer Society.

Robinson, N. (2007). The many faces of IT governance: Crafting an IT governance architecture. *Information Systems Control Journal, 1*, 14-16.

Rockart, J. F. & De Long, D. W. (1988). *Executive support systems: The emergence of top management computer use*. Homewood, IL: Dow Jones-Irwin.

Roest, W. F. (1988). *Grondslagen van het ontwikkelen van informatiesystemen*, Uitgeverij het glazen oog, Venlo-Vinkeveen, Nederland.

Rosenstein, S., & Wyatt, J. G. (1990). Outside directors, board independence, and shareholder wealth. *Journal of Financial Economics, 26*(2), 175-191.

Ross, J., Weill, P., & Robertson, D. (2006). *Enterprise architecture as strategy.*, Boston: Harvard Business School Press.

Ross, S. J. (2006). IS security matters: Converging need, diverging response. *Information Systems Control Journal, 2*, 8-9.

Rouse, A. C. (2002). *Information technology outsourcing revisited: Success factors and risks.* Unpublished doctoral dissertation, University of Melbourne, Melbourne, Australia.

Rouse, A. C., & Corbitt, B. J. (2001). The Australian government's abandoned infrastructure outsourcing program: What can be learned? *Australian Journal of Information Systems, 10*(2), 81-90.

Rouse, A. C., & Corbitt, B. J. (2003). Revisiting IT outsourcing risks: Analysis of a survey of Australia's Top 1000 organizations. In *Proceedings of the 14th Australasian Conference on Information Systems 2003, Delivering IT and E-Business Value in Networked Environments* (pp. 1-11). School of Management Information Systems, Edith Cowan University, Perth, Western Australia

Rouse, A., C., & Corbitt, B. J. (2007). Understanding information systems outsourcing success and risks through the lens of cognitive biases. In *Proceedings of the 15th European Conference on Information Systems (ECIS)*, St. Gallen, Switzerland.

Rust, R., & Miu, C. (2006). What academic research tells us about service. *Communications of the ACM, 49*(7), 49-54.

Ryan, S. D. & Harrison, D. A. (2000). Considering social subsystem costs and benefits in information technology investment decisions: A view from the field on anticipated payoffs. *Journal of Management Information Systems, 16*(4), 11.

SA Strategic Plan (n.d.). Retrieved May 15, 2008, from http://www.stateplan.sa.gov.au/

Sääksjärvi, M. (2006). Success of IS outsourcing as a predictor of IS effectiveness: Does IT governance matter? In R. Hirschheim, A. Heinzl & J. Dibbern (Eds.), *Information systems outsourcing, enduring themes, new perspectives and global challenges* (2nd ed.) (pp. 283-302), Springer, Berlin Heidelberg.

Sage, A. P. (1992). *Systems engineering*. New York: Wiley.

Sage, A. P. (2000). Systems engineering education. *IEEE TSMC-Part C, 30*(2), 164-174.

Sage, A. P., & Amstrong, J. (2000). *Introduction to systems engineering.* New York: Wiley.

Sallé, M. (2004). IT service management and IT governance: Review, comparative analysis and their impact on utility computing. *HP Labs* (Tech. Rep. HPL-2004-98). Retrieved May 7, 2008, from http://www.hpl.hp.com/techreports/2004/HPL-2004-98.pdf

Salo, O. (2005). Systematical validation of learning in agile software development environment. In Proceedings of the the Seventh International Workshop on Learning Software Organizations, Kaiserslautern, Germany.

Sambamurthy, V. & Zmud, R. W. (1999). Arrangements for information technology governance: A theory of multiple contingencies. *MIS Quarterly, 23*(2), 261-290.

Sambamurthy, V. & Zmud, R. W. (1999). Arrangements for information technology governance: A theory of multiple contingencies. *MIS Quarterly, 23*(2), 261-290.

Sambamurthy, V., & Zmud, R. W. (1999). Arrangements for information technology governance: A theory of multiple contingencies. *MIS Quarterly, 23*(2), 261-290.

Sambamurthy, V., Bharadwaj, A., & Grover, V. (2003). Shaping agility through digital options: Reconceptualizing the role of information technology in contemporary firms. *MIS Quarterly, 27*, 237-263.

Sambamurthy, V., Venkatraman, S., & DeSanctis, G. (1993). The design of information technology planning systems for varying organizational contexts. *European Journal of Information Systems, 2*(1), 23-35.

Sambamurthy, V., Zmud, R., & Byrd, T. (1994). The comprehensiveness of IT planning processes: A contingency approach. *Journal of Information Technology Management, 5*(1), 1-10.

SAS Ltd. (2004). *Operational risk management in the financial services industry.* April 30, 2008, from http://www.sas.com/industry/banking/oprisk/index.html

Sauer, C. & Yetton, P. W. (1997). *Steps to the future: Fresh thinking on the management of IT-based organizational transformation.* San Francisco: Jossey Bass.

Sauer, C. (1993). *Why information systems fail: A case study approach.* Henley-on-Thames: Waller.

Sauer, C., & Burn, J. (1997). The pathology of strategic alignment. In C. Sauer & P. Yetton (Eds.), *Steps to the future: Fresh thinking on the management of IT-based organizational transformation* (pp. 89-111). San Francisco: Jossey-Bass.

Sauer, C., & Yetton, P. (1994). The dynamics of fit and the fit of dynamics: Aligning IT in a dynamic organization. In *Proceedings of 15th International Conference on Information Systems* (pp. 41-50).

Saull, R. (2000). The IT Balanced Scorecard- A Roadmap to Effective Governance of a Shared Services IT Organization. *Information Systems Control Journal, 2*, 31-38.

Schnabel, U., Dold, D., Fröschle, H.-P., Layer, B., Roll, U., & Skempes, A. (2006). *Das wertorientierte Management des intellektuellen Kapitals (ICM).* Stuttgart: Fraunhofer IRB Verlag.

Schön, D. A. (1983). The reflective practitioner. New York: Basic Books.

Schwalbe, K. (2002). *Information technology project management* (2nd ed.). Boston: Course Technology.

Schwarz, A. & Hirschheim, R. (2003). An extended platform logic perspective of IT governance: managing perceptions and activities of IT. *The Journal of Strategic Information Systems, 12*(2), 129-166.

Schwarz, A. & Hirschheim, R. (2003). An extended platform logic perspective of IT governance: Managing perceptions and activities of IT. *Journal of Strategic Information Systems, 12*(2), 129-166.

Scott Morton, M. (1991). *Introduction.* In M. Scott Morton (Ed.), *The corporation of the 1990s* (pp. 2-23). New York: Oxford University Press.

Seddon, P. (1997). A respecification and extension of the DeLone and McLean model of IS success. *Information Systems Research, 8*(3), 240-253.

Seddon, P. B., Cullen, S., & Willcocks, L. P. (2002). *Does Domberger's theory of "the contracting organization" explain satisfaction with IT outsourcing?* International Conference on Information Systems (ICIS), Barcelona.

Seddon, P. B., Graeser, V., & Willcocks, L. P. (2002). Measuring organizational IS effectiveness: An overview and update of senior management perspective. *The Data Base for Advances in Information Systems, 33*(2), 11 – 28.

Seddon, P., Graeser, V., & Willcocks, L. (2002). Measuring organizational IS effectiveness: An overview and update of senior management perspectives. *SIGMIS Database, 33*(2), 11-28.

SEI (2006). *CMMI for development, version 1.2: CMMI-DEV, V1.2. Software engineering institute. CMU/SEI-2006-TR-008, ESC-TR-2006-008.* retrieved May 15, 2008, from www.sei.edu

Senn, J. A. & Gefen, D. (1998). How managers assess the business value returned from information technology spending. *In Proceedings of the 31st Annual Hawaii International Conference on System Sciences.*

Serafeimidis, V. & Smithson, S. (1999). Rethinking the approaches to information systems investment evaluation. *Logistics Information Management, 12*(1/2).

Serafeimidis, V. & Smithson, S. (2000). Information systems evaluation in practice: A case study of organizational change. *Journal of Information Technology, 15*(2), 93–105.

Seth, N., Deshmukh, S. G., & Vrat, P. (2005). Service quality models: A review. *International Journal of Quality & Reliability Management, 22*(9).

Sgobbi, F. (2002). Web design skills and competencies: An empirical analysis. *Human Systems Management, 21*(1), 115-128.

Shan, T .C., & Hua, W. W. (2006). Solution architecture of n-tier applications. In *Proceedings of 3rd IEEE International Conference on Services Computing* (pp. 349-356), California: IEEE Computer Society.

Sharma, S. K., & Gupta, J. N. D. (2004). E-strategy model for creating flexible organizations. *Global Journal of Flexible Systems Management, 5*(2/3), 1-9.

Sheard, S., & Lake, J. (1998). *Systems engineering and models compared.* retrieved May 15, 2008, from www.software.org

Shen, H., Wall, B., Zaremba, M., Chen, Y., & Browne, J. (2004). Integration of business modelling methods for enterprise information system analysis and user requirements gathering. *Computers in Industry, 54*, 307-323.

Sherer, S. A. (2004). IS project selection: The role of strategic vision and IT governance. *Paper presented at the 37th Hawaii International Conference on System Sciences*, Hawaii.

Sherer, S. A. (2004). IS project selection: The role of strategic vision and IT governance. In *Proceedings of the 37th Hawaii International Conference on System Sciences*, Hawaii.

Sherer, S. A., Ray, M. R., & Chowdhury, N. M. (2002). Assessing information technology investments with an integrative process framework. *In Proceedings of the 35th Hawaii International Conference on System Sciences.*

Sheth, A., Verma, K., & Gomadam, K. (2006). Semantics to energize the full service spectrum. *Communications of the ACM, 49*(7), 55-61.

Shi, D., & Daniels, R. L. (2003). A survey of manufacturing flexibility: Implications for e-business flexibility. *IBM Systems Journal, 42*(3), 414-428.

Shivdasani, A. (1993). Board composition, ownership structure, and hostile takeovers. *Journal of Accounting & Economics, 16*(1-3), 167-198.

Shivdasani, A., & Yermack, D. (1999). CEO involvement in the selection of new board members: An empirical analysis. *Journal of Finance, 54*(5), 1829-1853.

Shleifer, A. & Vishny, R. W. (1997). A survey of corporate governance. *The Journal of Finance, 52*(2), 737-783.

Silvius, A. J. G. (2007). Business and IT alignment in theory and practice. *Paper presented at the 40th Hawaii International Conference on System Sciences*, Hawaii.

Simonsson, M., & Johnson, P. (2006). *Defining IT governance–A consolidation of literature.* Working Paper of the Department of Industrial Information and Control Systems. Retrieved May 11, 2008, from www.ics.kth.se

Simonsson, M., Johnson, P., & Wijkström, H. (2007). Model-based IT governance maturity assessments with Cobit. In H. Österle, J. Schelp & R. Winter, R. (Eds.), In *Proceedings of the 15th European Conference on Information Systems* (pp. 1276-1287), University of St. Gallen, St. Gallen, Swiss.

Siponen, M. (2000). A conceptual foundation for organisational information security awareness. *Information Management and Computer Security Journal, 8*(1), 31-41.

Sircar, S., Turnbow, J. L., & Bordoloi, B. (2000). A framework for assessing the relationship between information technolgy investments and firm performance. *Journal of Management Information Systems, 16*(4), 69.

Sledgianowski, D. & Luftman, J. (2005). IT-business strategic alignment maturity- A case study. *Journal of Cases of Information Technology, 7*(2), 102.

Sledgianowski, D., Luftman, J. N., & Reilly, R. R. (2006). Development and validation of an instrument to measure maturity of IT business strategic alignment mechanisms. *Information Resources Management Journal, 19*(3), 18-33.

Smaczny, T. (2001). Is an alignment between business and information technology the appropriate paradigm to manage IT in today's organizations? *Management Decisions, 39*(10), 797-802.

Smits, M. T. & Huisman, W. (2007). Investing in networkability to improve supply chain performance. In R. Sprague, Jr. (Ed.), In *Proceedings of the Hawaiian International Conference on Systems Sciences*. Computer Society Press.

Smits, M. T. & Van der Poel (1996). The practice of information strategy in six information intensive organizations in the Netherlands. *Journal of Strategic IS, 5* 93-110.

Software Engineering Institute (2006). *CMMI for development, Version 1.2.* Pittsburgh, PA.

Software Engineering Institute (2006): *CMMI for services* (Initial Draft). Pittsburgh, PA.

Software Engineering Institute (2007). *CMMI for acquisition, Version 1.2.* Pittsburgh, PA.

Software Engineering Institute (2007). *What is CMMI?* Retrieved April 30, 2008, from www.sei.cmu.edu/cmmi/general/index.html

Software Engineering Institute (SEI) at CMU (2007). *Scenario-based architecture analysis method.* Retrieved on May 11, 2008, from http://www.sei.cmu.edu/architecture/scenario_paper

Software Management Network (2005). *ITIL.* Retrieved May 11, 2008, from http://www.softwaremanagement.com/Publications/infrastructure.html

Soh, C. & Markus, M. L. (1995). How IT creates business value: A process theory synthesis: A process theory synthesis. In G. Ariav, C. Beath, J. I. DeGross, R. Hoyer & C. F. Kemerer (Eds.), In *Proceedings of the 16th International Conference on Information Systems* (pp. 29-41), Amsterdam, The Netherlands.

Sohal, A. S. & Fitzpatrick, P. (2002). IT governance and management in large Australian organisations. *International Journal of Production Economics, 75*(1), 97-112.

Sohal, A. S. & Ng, L. (1998). The role and impact of information technology in Australian business. *Journal of Information Technology, 13*(3), 201 – 217.

Sommerville, I. (1998). Systems engineering for software engineers. *Annals of Software Engineering, 6,* 111-129.

Sommerville, I. (2004). *Software engineering* (7th ed.). Harlow: Pearson Education.

Song, F. & Thakor, A. (2006). Information control, career concerns and corporate governance. *The Journal of Finance, 61*(4), 1845-1852.

South Australia Office of CIO (n.d.). Retrieved May 15, 2008, from http://www.cio.sa.gov.au/

SOX (2002) Sarbanes-Oxley Act (Public Company Accounting Reform and Investor Protection Act of 2002), No. 107-204, 116 Stat. 745 C.F.R.

Spafford, G. (2003). *The benefits of standard IT governance frameworks.* Datamation Internet Website. Retrieved May 11, 2008, from http://itmanagement.earthweb.com/netsys/article.php/2195051

Spafford, G. (2003, April 22). The benefits of standard IT governance frameworks. *Datamation on-line.*

Spath, D., & Demuß, L. (2003). Entwicklung hybrider Produkte—Gestaltung materieller und immaterieller Leistungsbündel. In H.-J. Bullinger & A.-W. Scheer (Eds.), *Service Engineering*: Springer.

Spath, D., van Husen, C., Meyer, K., & Elze, R. (2007). Integrated development of software and service—The challenge of IT-enabled service Products. In D. Spath & K.-P. Fähnrich (Eds.), *Advances in service innovations.* Berlin: Springer.

Sphorer, J., & Rieken, D. (2006). Introduction to special issue on service sciences *Communications of the ACM, 49*(7), 30-32.

SPICE User Group (2007). *Enterprise SPICE introduction.* Retrieved May 15, 2008, from http://www.enterprisespice.com/web/Introduction.html

Spohrer, J., Maglio, P., Bailey, J., & Gruhl., D. (2007). Steps toward a science of service systems. *IEEE Computer,* January issue, 70-71.

Standards Australia & Standards New Zealand (2004). *Risk management AS/NZS 4360:2004:* Standards Australia/Standards New Zealand.

Standards Australia (2003). *Good governance principles, AS800-2003.* Sydney: Standards Australia International.

Standards Australia (2005). *AS 8015-2005: Corporate governance of information and communication technology.* Retrieved May 10, 2008, from http://www.standards.com.au

Standards Australia (2005). *AS8015-2005 corporate governance of information and communication technology.* Canberra: Standards Australia.

Standards Australia (2005). *Corporate governance of information and communication technology, AS8015-2005.* Sydney: Standards Australia International.

Standards Australia (2007). AS ISO/IEC 20000.1 *Service management: Part 1 and 2*

Standards Australia (2007). *AS ISO/IEC 20000.1-2007 information technology – Service management – Part 1: Specification.* Retrieved May 10, 2008, from http://www.standards.com.au

Standards Australia (2007). *AS ISO/IEC 20000.2-2007 information technology – Service management – Part 2: Code of practice.* Retrieved May 10, 2208, from http://www.standards.com.au

Standish (2003). *CHAOS Chronicles v3.0.* West Yarmouth, MA: The Standish Group International, Inc.

Standish Group (2007). The Standish group chaos report 2006. Retrieved May 11, 2007, from http://www.standishgroup.com

Standish Group International (2003). *The extreme CHAOS report*. Retrieved May 15, 2008, from www.standish-group.com

Stark, J. (2004). Product lifecycle management. *Paradigm for 21st century product realisation: 21st century paradigm for product realisation*. London: Springer.

Stevenson, B. & Romney, G. (2004). Teaching security best practices by architecting and administering an IT security lab. In *Proceedings of the 5th conference on Information Technology Education*, Salt Lake City, UT.

Stewart, A. (2004). On risk: Perception and direction. *Computers & Security, 23*(5), 362-370.

Strassman, P. A. (1990). *The business value of computers*. New Canaan, CT: The Information Economics Press.

Strassmann, P. (1997). *The squandered computer*. New Canaan: Information Economics Press.

Straub, D., & Welke, R. (1998). Coping with systems risk: Security planning models for management decision making. *MIS Quarterly, 22*(4), 441-464.

Strnadl, C. F. (2006). Aligning business and IT: The process-driven architecture model. *Information Systems Management, 23*(4), 67-77.

Succi, G., Valerio, A., Vernazza, T., & Succi, G. (1998). Compatibility, standards and software production. *Standarview, 6*(4), 140-146.

Sundaresan, S. & Zuopeng, Z. (2004). Facilitating knowledge transfer in organizations through incentive alignment and IT investment. In *Proceedings of the 37th Hawaii International Conference on System Sciences*.

Supply Chain Council (2005). Supply-chain operations reference-model. Overview of SCOR

Sveiby, K. E., & Lloyd, T. (1987). *Managing knowhow*. London: Bloomsbury Publishing.

Swanson, E. B. (1987). Information systems in organization theory: A review. In R. Boland & R. Hirschheim (Eds.), *Critical issues in information systems research* (pp. 181-204). Chichester: John Wiley and Sons.

Symons (2005). *IT governance framework*. Retrieved May 11, 2008, from http://i.i.com.com/cnwk.1d/html/itp/Forr051103656300.pdf

Symons, C. (2005). *IT governance survey results: More work to be done*. Retrieved May 10, 2008, from http://www.forrester.com/Research/Document/Excerpt/0,7211,36804,00.html

Symons, C. (2006). *COBIT 4.0 is a strong governance platform*. Retrieved http://www.forrester.com/Research/Document/Excerpt/0,7211,39122,00.html

Tague, N. R. (2004). The quality toolbox (2nd ed.). Milwaukee, WI: ASQ Quality Press.

Talby, D., Hazzan, O., Dubinsky, Y., & Keren, A. (2006). Reflections on reflection in agile software development. In Proceedings of the Agile 2006 Conference, Minneapolis, Minnesota.

Tallon, P. P. (2007). Does IT pay to focus? An analysis of IT business value under single and multi-focused business strategies. *Journal of Strategic Information Systems, 16*(3), 278-300.

Tallon, P. P., Kraemer, K. L., & Gurbaxani, V. (2000). Executives' perceptions of the business value of information technology: A process-oriented approach. *Journal of Management Information Systems, 16*(4), 145.

Tan, J., Wen, J., & Awad, N. (2005). Health care and services delivery systems as complex adaptive systems. *Communications of the ACM, 48*(5), 36-44.

Tang, H. L., Koh, S., & Lee, S. (2001). Educational gaps as perceived by IS educators: A survey of knowledge and skill requirements. *Journal of Computer Information Systems, 41*(2), 76-84.

Tanriverdi, H. (2006). Performance effect of information technology synergies in multibusiness firms. *MIS Quarterly, 30*(1), 57-77.

Tantara (2001). *History and relationship of process standards/models*. Retrieved May 15, 2008, from www.tantara.ab.ca

TAO (2004). Tasmanian Audit Office Webpage. *Who we are and what we do*. Retrieved May 12, 2008, from http://www.audit.tas.gov.au/aboutus/whowhat.html

Tavakolian, H. (1989). Linking the information technology structure with organisational competitive strategy: A survey. *MIS Quarterly, 13*(3), 309 – 317.

Taylor, C., & Sedera, W. (2003). Defining the quality business reference models. In Proceedings of the *14th Australian Conference on Information Systems*, Perth, Western Australia.

Taylor, M. J., England, D., & Gresty, D. (2001). Knowledge for web site development. *Internet Research: Electronic Networking Applications and Policy, 11*(5), 451-461.

Taylor, T. (2006). Web competencies for IT students. In R. Brown (Ed.), In *Proceedings 7th International Conference on Information Technology Based Higher Education and Training* (pp. 297-304). Sydney: University of Technology.

Teboul, J. (2007). *Service is front stage: Positioning services for value advantage.* Paris: INSEAD.

Teubner, R. A. (2007). Strategic information systems planning: A case study from the financial services industry. *Journal of Strategic Information Systems, 16,* 105-125.

Thatcher, M. E. & Pingry, D. E. (2007). Modeling the IT value paradox. *Communications of the ACM, 50*(8), 41-45.

Thayer, R. H. (1997). Software systems engineering: An engineering process. In R. Thayer & M. Dorfman (Eds.), *Software requirements engineering* (pp. 84-106). Los Alamitos: IEEE Computer Society Press.

Thayer, R. H. (2002). Software systems engineering: A tutorial. *IEEE Computer,* April, 68-73.

The Open Group (2007). *The open group architecture framework.* Retrieved May 11, 2008, from http://www.opengroup.org/togaf

Thorp, J. (2003). *The information paradox.* Toronto: McGraw Hill Ryerson.

Thorp, J. (2006). Value management-responding to the challenge of value. *Information Systems Control Journal, 5,* 21-22.

Tillquist, J. & Rodgers, W. (2005). Using asset specificity and asset scope to measure the value of IT. *Communications of the ACM, 48*(1), 75-80.

Tirole, J. (2001). Corporate governance. *Econometrica, 69,* 1-35.

Todd, P. A., McKeen, J. D., & Gallupe, B. R. (1995). The evolution of IS job skills: A content analysis of IS job advertisements from 1970 to 1990. *MIS Quarterly, 19*(1), 1-17.

Tonge, R., Larsen, P., & Roberts, M. (2000). Information systems investment within high-growth medium-sized enterprises. *Management Decision, 38*(7).

Treasury Department CIO Council (2000). *Treasury enterprise architecture framework* (Version 1). Retrieved May 11, 2008, from http://www.eaframeworks.com/TEAF/teaf.doc

Tricker, R. I. (1984). *Corporate governance: Practices, procedures and powers in British companies and their boards of directors.* Aldershot: Gower.

Tripp, L. (1996). International standards in system and software integrity. *Standardwiew, 4*(3), 146-150.

Trites, G. (2003). Director responsibility for IT governance. *Paper presented at the University of Waterloo IS Assurance Symposium,* University of Waterloo Canada.

TSO (n.d.). *Security management.* Retrieved May 11, 2008, http://itil.tso.co.uk/security_management.html

Turbitt (2005). *ITIL – The business perspective approach.* Retrieved May 11, 2008, from http://www.itsmwatch.com/itil/article.php/3530621

Tyler, R. (2000). Implementing CobiT in New South Wales Health. *Information Systems Control Journal, 3,* 30-32.

Uebernickel, F., Bravo-Sànchez, C., Zarnekow, R., & Brenner, W. (2006). *Eine Vorgehensmethodik zum IT-Produktengineering.* Paper presented at the Multikonferenz für Wirtschaftsinformatik 2006, Berlin.

United Kingdom Office of Government Commerce & IT Service Management Forum (2005). *The information technology infrastructure library (ITIL) - Version 3.* Retrieved April 30, 2008, from www.itil.uk.com, www.itsm.info/ITIL.htm

United Kingdom Office of Government Commerce [OGC] (2000). *Service support.* Norwich, Norfolk, England: The Stationery Office.

Val IT (2006). *Enterprise value: Governance of IT investments.* IT Governance Institute

van Akkeren, J. & Cavaye, A. L. M. (1999). Factors affecting entry-level internet technology adoption by small business in Australia – Evidence from three cases. *Journal of Systems and Information Technology, 3*(2), 33-48.

van Bon, J. (2004). *IT governance a pocket guide based on CobiT.* Netherlands: Van Haren Publishing.

van Bon, J. (2004). *IT service management, An introduction based on ITIL.* Netherlands: Van Haren Publishing.

van Bon, J. (2007). *IT service management, An introduction based on ITIL.* Netherlands: Van Haren Publishing.

Van den Berghe, L. A. A. & Baelden, T. (2005). The monitoring role of the board: One approach does not fit all. *Corporate Governance, 13*(5), 680–690.

Van den Heijden, H. (2001). Measuring IT core capabilities for electronic commerce. *Journal of Information Technology, 16*(1), 13–22.

Van der Pijl, G. J. (1994). *Kwaliteit van informatie in theorie en praktijk*, Kluwer Bedrijfswetenschappen, Limpberg instituut, Amsterdam.

Van der Pijl, G. J. (1994). Measuring the strategic dimensions of the quality of information. *Journal of Strategic Information Systems, 3*(3), 179-190.

Van Der Zee, J. T. M. & De Jong, B. (1999). Alignment is not enough: Integrating business and information technology management with the balanced business scorecard. *Journal of Management Information Systems, 16*(2), 137-156.

Van Grembergen, W. & Amelinckx, L. (2002). Measuring and managing e-business projects through the balanced scorecard. *Paper presented at the 35th Hawaii International Conference on System Sciences*, Hawaii.

Van Grembergen, W. & De Haes, S. (2005). CobiT's management guidelines revisited: The KGIs/KPIs cascade. *Information Systems Control Journal, 6*, 54.

Van Grembergen, W. & De Haes, S. (2005). *IT governance and its mechanisms.* Retrieved April 30, 2008, from www.uam.be

Van Grembergen, W. & De Haes, S. (2005). Measuring and improving IT governance through the balanced scorecard. *Information Systems Control Journal, 2*, 35.

Van Grembergen, W. & Van Bruggen, R. (1997). Measuring and improving corporate information technology through the balanced scorecard technique. *Paper presented at the Fourth European Conference on the Evaluation of Information Technology*, Delft, (pp.163-171).

Van Grembergen, W. (2000). The balanced scorecard and IT governance. *Information Systems Control Journal, 2*, 40-43.

Van Grembergen, W. (2000). *The balanced scorecard and IT governance.* Retrieved May 15, 2008, from www. itgi.org

Van Grembergen, W. (2002). Introduction to the minitrack on IT Governance and its Mechanisms. *Paper presented at the The 35th Hawaii International Conference on System Sciences (HICSS)*, Hawaii.

Van Grembergen, W. (2003). Introduction to the mini-track: IT governance and its mechanisms. In *Proceedings of the 35th Hawaii International Conference on System Sciences(HICSS)*, Hawaii: IEEE.

Van Grembergen, W. (2004). *Strategies for information technology governance.* Hershey, PA: Idea Group Publishing.

Van Grembergen, W., & De Haes, S. (2004). IT governance and its mechanisms. Information Systems Control Journal, 1. Retrieved May 14, 2008, from http://www.isaca.org/Template.cfm?Section=Home&Template=/Content-Management/ContentDisplay.cfm&ContentID=16771

Van Grembergen, W., & De Haes, S. (2005). Measuring and improving information technology governance through the balanced scorecard. *Information Systems Control Journal, 2*, 46-49.

Van Grembergen, W., De Haas, S., & Guldentops, E. (2004). Structures, processes and relational mechanisms for IT governance. In W. Van Grembergen (Ed.), *Strategies for information technology governance* (pp. 1-35). Hershey, PA: Idea Group Publishing.

Van Grembergen, W., De Haes, S., & Amelinckx, I. (2003). Using CobiT and the balanced scorecard as instruments for service level management. *Information Systems Control Journal, 4*, 56.

Van Grembergen, W., De Haes, S., & Guldentops, E. (2003). Structures, processes and relational mechanisms for IT governance. *Strategies for information technology governance* (pp. 14-36). Hershey, PA: Idea Group Publishing.

Van Grembergen, W., De Haes, S., & Moons, J. (2005). Linking business goals to IT goals and CobiT processes. *Information Systems Control Journal, 4*, 18-22.

Van Grembergen, W., De Haes, S., & Van Brempt, H. (2007). Prioritising and linking business and IT goals in the financial sector. *Paper presented at the 40th Hawaii International Conference on System Sciences*, Hawaii.

Van Grembergen, W., Saull, R., & De Haes, S. (2003). Linking the IT balanced scorecard to the business objectives at a major Canadian financial group. *Journal of Information Technology Cases and Applications, 5*(1), 23-45.

Van Grenbergen, W., De Haes, S., & Guldentops, E. (2003). Structures, processes and relational mechanisms for IT governance. *Strategies for IT governance* (pp. 14-36). Hershey, PA: Idea Group Publishing.

Van Leeuwen, F. (2006). Balancing compliance, agility and risk. In *Proceedings of the Keynote Presentation to the IT Governance International Conference*, Auckland.

Van Lier, J. & Dohmen, T. (2007). Benefits management and strategic alignment in an IT outsourcing context. *Paper presented at the 40th Hawaii International Conference on System Sciences*, Hawaii.

Venkatraman, N. (1989). The concept of fit in strategy research: Toward verbal and statistical correspondence. *Academy of Management Review, 14*(3), 423-444.

Venkatraman, N. (1991). IT-induced business reconfiguration. In M. Scott Morton (Ed.), *The corporation of the 1990s* (pp. 122-158). New York: Oxford University Press.

Venkatraman, N. (1999). *Valuing the IS contribution to the business.* Computer Sciences Corporation.

Verma, R. (2000). An empirical analysis of management challenges in service factories, service shops, mass services and professional services. *International Journal of Service Industry Management, 11*(1), 8-25.

Vermeer, Bas H. P. J. (1999). Information logistics: A data integration method for solving data quality problems with article information in large interorganizational networks. In *Proceedings of Fourth Conference on Information Quality (IQ 1999)* (pp. 185-208).

Violino, B. (2005). IT frameworks demystified. *Network World, 22*(7), S18- 20.

Violino, B. (2006). Sorting the standards. *Computerworld, 40*(16), 46- 47.

Vishwanath, T., & Kaufmann, D. (1999). Toward transparency in finance and governance. *The World Bank Draft.*

Vives, X. (Ed.) (2000). *Corporate governance: Theoretical & empirical perspectives.* Cambridge: Cambridge University Press.

Von Krogh, G., & Roos, J. (1995). A perspective on knowledge, competence and strategy. *Personnel Review, 24*(3), 56-76.

Von Solms, B. & Von Solms, R. (2004). The 10 deadly sins of information security management. *Computers & Security, 23*(5), 371-376.

Von Solms, B., & von Solms, R., (2005). From information security to business Security. *Computer and Security Journal,* 272-279.

Von Solms, S. H. (2005). Information security governance - Compliance management vs. operational management. *Computers & Security, 24*(6), 443-447.

Wagenaar, R. (2006). Governance of shared service centers in public administration: dilemmas and trade-offs. *In Proceedings of the 8th International Conference on Electronic Commerce: The New E-Commerce: Innovations for Conquering Current Barriers, Obstacles and Limitations to Conducting Successful Business on the Internet.* Fredericton, New Brunswick, Canada.

Wagner, E. L. & Newell, S. (2004). Best for whom?: The tension between "Best practice" ERP packages and diverse epistemic cultures in a university context. *Journal of Strategic Information Systems, 13*(4), 305 – 328.

Wagner, H. -T. (2006). Managing the impact of IT on firm success: The link between the resource-based view and the IT infrastructure library. In *Proceedings of the 39th Hawaii International Conference on System Sciences*, Hawaii.

Wagner, H.-T., Beimborn, D., Franke, J., & Weitzel, T. (2006). IT business alignment and IT usage in operational processes: A retail banking case. *Paper presented at the 39th Hawaii International Conference on System Sciences*, Hawaii.

Wahlster, W., & Dengel, A. (2006). *Web 3.0: Convergence of web 2.0 and the semantic web. Technology Radar Feature Paper Edition II/2006.* Deutsche Telekom Laboratories.

Walker, R. H., Craig-Lees, M., Hecker, R., & Francis, H. (2002). Technology-enabled service delivery: An investigation of reasons affecting customer adoption and rejection. *International Journal of Service Industry Management, 13*(1).

Ward, J. & Peppard, J. (2002). *Strategic planning for information systems.* Chichester: John Wiley & Sons Ltd.

\Ward, J., & Peppard, J. (2005). *Strategic planning for information systems* Chichester: John Wiley.

Ward, J., De Hertogh, S., & Viaene, S. (2007). Managing benefits from IS/IT investments: An empirical investigation into current practice. *Paper presented at the 40th Hawaii International Conference on System Sciences*, Hawaii.

Ward, J., Griffiths, P. & Whitmore, P. (1990). *Strategic planning for information systems.* John Wiley & Sons.

Warland, C., & Ridley, G. (2005). Awareness of IT control frameworks in an Australian state government:

A qualitative case study. In R. H. Sprague, Jr. (Ed.), In *Proceedings of the 38ᵗʰ Hawaii International Conference on System Science (HICSS)*, Los Alamitos: IEEE Computer Society.

Webb, P., Pollard, C., & Ridley, G. (2006). Attempting to define IT governance: Wisdom or folly? In *Proceedings of the 39ᵗʰ Annual Hawaii International Conference on System Sciences*.

\Webb, P., Pollard, C., & Ridley, G. (2006). Attempting to define IT governance: Wisdom or folly? In *Proceedings of the 39th Hawaii International Conference on System Sciences*, Hawaii.

\Webster, J. & Watson, R. T. (2002). Analyzing the past to prepare for the future: Writing a literature review. *MIS Quarterly, 26*(2), xiii-xxiii.

Weiber, R., & Kollmann, T. (1998). Competitive advantage in virtual markets—Perspectives of "Information-based marketing" in cyberspace. *European Journal of Marketing, 32*(7/8), 603-615.

Weick, K. (1969). *The social psychology of organizing.*, Reading, MA: Addison-Wesley.

Weill, P. & Broadbent, M. (1998). *Leveraging the new infrastructure: How market leaders capitalize on information technology.* Boston: Harvard Business School Press.

Weill, P. & Broadbent, M. (2003). *Creating effective IT governance, A Gartner EXP premier research report.* Stamford, CT: Gartner.

Weill, P. & Olson, M. (1989). Managing investment in information technology. *MIS Quarterly, 13*(1), 2–17.

Weill, P. & Ross, J. W. (2004). *IT governance: How top performers manage IT decision rights for superior results.* Boston: Harvard Business School Press.

Weill, P. & Ross, J. W. (2005). A matrixed approach to designing IT governance. *Sloan Management Review, 46*(2), 26-34.

Weill, P. & Woodham, R. (2002). *Don't just lead, govern: Implementing effective IT governance* (Working Paper No. 4237-02). Boston: MIT Sloan School of Management. Retrieved May 8, 2008, from http://papers.ssrn.com/sol3/Delivery.cfm/SSRN_ID317319_code020724590.pdf?abstractid=317319&mirid=1

Weill, P. & Woodham, R. (2002). Don't just lead, govern: Implementing effective IT governance. *CISR working paper* (No. 326). Retrieved May 7, 2008, from http://dspace.mit.edu/bitstream/1721.1/1846/2/4237-02.pdf

Weill, P. (2003). *Don't just lead, govern!* Retrieved May 11, 2008, from http://www.csbs.org/pr/presentations/2003/AMC2003_Weill_DontJustLead-Govern.pdf

Weill, P. (2004). Don't just lead, govern: How top-performing firms govern IT. *MIS Quarterly Executive, 3*(1), 1-17.

Weill, P., & Aral, S. (2006). Generating premium returns on your IT investments. *MIT Sloan Management Review, 47*(2), 39-48.

Weill, P., & Aral, S. (2006). Generating premium returns on your IT investments. *MIT Sloan Management Review, 47*(2), 39-51.

Weill, P., & Broadbent, M. (1998). *Leveraging the new infrastructure.* Boston: Harvard Business School Press.

Weill, P., & Olson, M. (1989). An assessment of the contingency theory of management information systems. *Journal of Management Information Systems, Summer, 6*(1), 59-85.

Weill, P., & Ross, J. (2004). *IT governance: How top performers manage IT decision rights for superior results.* Boston: Harvard Business School Press.

Weill, P., & Ross, J. (2005). A matrixed approach to designing IT governance. *MIT Sloan Management Review, 46*(2), 26-34.

Weill, P., & Ross, J. W. (2004). *IT governance how top performers manage IT decision rights for superior results.* Boston: Harvard Business School.

Weill, P., & Ross, J. W. (2004). *IT governance.* Boston: Harvard Business School Press.

Weill, P., & Ross, J. W. (2004). *IT governance: How top performers manage IT decision rights for superior results.* Boston: Harvard Business School Press.

Weill, P., & Ross, J.W. (2004). *IT governance.* Boston, MA: Harvard Business School Press.

Weill, P., & Vitale, M. (2002). What IT infrastructure capabilities are needed to implement e-business models? *MIS Quarterly, 1*(1), 17-34.

Weill, P., & Woodham, R. (2002). Don't just lead, govern: Implementing effective IT governance. *CISR Working Paper* (No. 326). Retrieved May 11, 2008, from http://dspace.mit.edu/bitstream/1721.1/1846/2/4237-02.pdf

Weill, P., Subramani, M., & Broadbent, M. (2002). Building IT infrastructure for strategic agility. *MIT Sloan Management Review, Fall*, 57-65.

Whittaker, B. (1999). What went wrong? Unsuccessful information technology projects. *Information Management and Computer Security, 7*(1), 23–29.

Whitten, D., & Leidner, D. (2006). Bringing IT back: An analysis of the decision to backsource or switch vendors. *Decision Sciences, 37*(4), 605-621.

Wiederkehr, B. J. (2000). Group wide implementation of CobiT framework. *Information Systems Control Journal, 5*, 27-29.

Wiederkehr, B. J. (2003). IT security awareness program. *Information Systems Control Journal, 3*, 30-32.

Wiegers, K. (1998). Know your enemy: Software risk management. *Software Development*, October. Retrieved May 8, 2008, from http://www.processimpact.com/articles/risk_mgmt.html

Wiener, N. (1948). *Cybernetics or control and communication in the animal and the machine*. Cambridge: MIT Press.

Willcocks, L. & Griffiths, C. (1994). Predicting risk of failure in large-scale information technology projects. *Technological Forecasting and Social Change*, (47), 205 – 228.

Willcocks, L. P., & Feeny, D. (1998). Core IS capabilities for exploiting information technology. *Sloan Management Review, 39*(3), 9-21.

Willcocks, L. P., & Lacity, M. (1998). *Strategic sourcing of information systems: Perspectives and practices*. Chichester: Wiley.

Willcocks, L., & Graser, V. (2001). *Delivering IT and eBusiness value*. Oxford: Butterworth-Heinemann.

Willcocks, L., Feeny, D., & Olson, N. (2006). Implementing core IS capabilities: Feeny-Willcocks IT governance and management framework revisited. *European Management Journal, 24*(1), 28-37.

Willcocks, L., Lacity, M., & Kern, T. (1999). Risk mitigation in IT outsourcing strategy revisited: Longitudinal case research at LISA. *Journal of Strategic Information Systems, 8*, 285-314.

Willcoxson, L. & Chatham, R. (2006). Testing the accuracy of the IT stereotype: Profiling IT managers' personality and behavioural characteristics. *Information & Management, 43*, 697-705.

Williams, P. A. (2005). *The buck stops here. IT Leadership, 1*. Retrieved May 14, 2008, from http://www.the-itleader.com/features/feature258/

Wilson, A. (2000). The use of performance information in the management of service delivery. *Marketing Intelligence & Planning, 18*(3).

Wilson, T. D. (1989). The implementation of information systems strategies in UK companies: Aims and barriers to success. *International Journal of Information Management, 9*, 245–258.

Witherell, B. (2004). *Corporate governance: Stronger principles for better market integrity*. Retrieved May 11, 2008, from http://www.oecdobserver.org/news/fullstory.php/aid/1231/Corporate_governance:_Stronger_principles_for_better_market_integrity.html

Woidtke, T. (2002). Agents watching agents?: Evidence from pension fund ownership and firm value. *Journal of Financial Economics, 63*(1), 99-131.

Wonigeit, J. (1994). *Total quality management*. Wiesbaden.

Worthen, B. (2005). *ITIL power*. Retrieved May 11, 2008, http://www.cio.com/archive/090105/itil_frameworks.html?page=1

Wright, R. (1998). Process standards and capability models for engineering software-intensive systems. *Crosstalk*, October, 1-10.

Wu, Y. (2006). Controlling adverse selection in information security budgeting: An IT governance approach. In *Proceedings of the 12th Americas Conference on Information Systems*, Acapulco, México.

Yao, C. & Joe, Z. (2004). Measuring Information Technology's Indirect Impact on Firm Performance. *Information Technology & Management, 5*(1/2), 9-22.

Yeh, Y.-H., & Woidtke, T. (2005). Commitment or entrenchment?: Controlling shareholders and board composition. *Journal of Banking & Finance, 29*(7), 1857-1885.

Yermack, D. (1996). Higher market valuation of companies with a small board of directors. *Journal of Financial Economics, 40*(2), 185-211.

Yin, R. K. (1984). Case study research: Design and methods. *Applied social research methods series* (Vol. 5). Sage Publication.

Yolles, M. (2000). Organisations, complexity and viable knowledge management. *Kybernetes, 29*(9/10), 1202-1222.

Yoon, S., & Suh, H. (2004). Ensuring IT consulting, SERVQUAL and user satisfaction: A modified measuring tool. *Information Systems Frontiers, 6*(4), 341-351.

Youndt, M. A., Snell, S. A., Dean, J. W., Jr., & Lepak, D. P. (1996). Human resource management, manufacturing strategy, and firm performance. *Academy of Management Journal, 39*(4), 836-866.

Young, R. (2005). *Explaining senior management support through IT project governance.* Unpublished doctoral thesis, Macquarie University, Sydney.

Young, R. C. & Jordan, E. (2002). IT governance and risk management: An integrated multistakeholder framework. *Paper presented at the Asia Pacific Decision Sciences Institute*, Bangkok, Thialand.

Young, R. C. & Jordan, E. (2003). Passion & IT governance. In *Proceedings of the 7th Pacific Asia Conference on Information Systems* (pp. 941-955), Adelaide, Australia.

Young, R. C. (2006). What is the ROI for IT project governance? Establishing a benchmark. In B. Cusack (Ed.), In *Proceedings of the 2006 IT Governance International Conference* (pp. 59-68), Auckland, New Zealand.

Zachman, J. A. (1987). A framework for information systems architecture. *IBM Systems Journal, 26*(3), 276-295.

Zarnekow, R., & Brenner, W. (2004). Integriertes informationsmanagement: Vom Plan, Built and Run zum Source, Make, Deliver. In R. Zarnekow, W. Brenner & H. H. Grohmann (Eds.), *Informationsmanagement Konzepte und Strategien für die Praxis* (pp. 289). Heidelberg: dpunkt.verlag.

Zarnekow, R., Brenner, W., & Grohmann, H. H. (2004). *Informationsmanagement Konzepte und Strategien für die Praxis*. Heidelberg: dpunkt.verlag.

Zarnekow, R., Hochstein, A., & Brenner, W. (2005). *Serviceorientiertes IT-Management ITIL-Best-Practices und -Fallstudien*. Berlin: Springer.

Zhang, X., Windsor, J., & Pavur, R. (2003). Determinants of software volatility: A field study. *Journal of Software Maintanance and Evolution: Research and Practice, 15*(3), 191-204.

About the Contributors

Aileen Cater-Steel is a senior lecturer in Information Systems at USQ. Her current research interests include IT governance, IT service management and software process improvement. She has also published research related to software engineering standards, organisational and national culture, and electronic commerce. Aileen's PhD thesis was awarded the ACPHIS medal in 2005. Prior to her academic appointment, Aileen worked in private and government organisations where her career progressed from programmer, systems analyst and project manager, to IT manager.

* * *

Francisco Alvarez-Rodríguez is an associate professor of Software Engineering and the Dean of the Basic Sciences Center in the Autonomous University of Aguascalientes. He holds a BA in informatics (1994) and a MA (1997) from the Autonomous University of Aguascalientes and a EdD degree from the Education Institute of Tamaulipas, México and he is Ph(c) from the National Autonomous University of Mexico. He has published research papers in several international conferences in the topics of software engineering and e-learning process. His research interests are software engineering lifecycles for small and medium sized enterprises and software engineering process for e-learning.

Peter Best is head of the School of Accounting, Economics & Finance at the University of Southern Queensland. He has held positions at University of Queensland, Newcastle University, Adelaide University, Flinders University and Queensland University of Technology. He has qualifications in accounting, operations research and information technology. His PhD examined the feasibility of machine-independent audit trail analysis in large computer systems. His teaching, research and consulting experience includes electronic business intelligence and data mining (SAS), enterprise systems (SAP R/3), IT governance processes and measurement, information systems security (SAP R/3), computer assisted audit techniques (SAS, ACL), knowledge based systems, fraud detection, anti-money laundering, and audit trail analysis.

Jyotirmoyee Bhattacharjya is a full-time PhD candidate in business information systems at the Faculty of Economics and Business at The University of Sydney. Her research interests include, IT governance, strategic information systems planning, e-business strategy and design science. Her work has been published in a number of peer-reviewed international conferences and journals. She has an M.Com. in Information Systems Management from Curtin University of Technology, Australia and an MA in Astronomy from Boston University, USA.

Michael Borth is a second year doctoral student with research interests in auditing and corporate governance. His teaching interests are in auditing and financial accounting. Michael received a BS in Accounting (1999) from Auburn University and a Master of Accountancy (2002) degree from the University of Tennessee. Prior to entering the doctoral program at the University of Tennessee, Michael worked as an auditing professional for PricewaterhouseCoopers and for the U.S Department of Energy's Office of Inspector General.

Randy V. Bradley is an assistant professor in the Department of Accounting and Information Management at The University of Tennessee, Knoxville. He holds a BS in computer engineering, an MS in MIS, and a PhD in Management of Information Technology and Innovation, all from Auburn University. His research has appeared or is forthcoming in the Journal of Management Information Systems, Decision Sciences Journal of Innovative Education, Communications of the Association for Information Systems, the Journal of Computer Information Systems, International Journal of Networking and Virtual Organisations, and the Encyclopedia of Multimedia Technology and Networking. His research interests include the strategic value of enterprise architecture, diffusion of information technology in the healthcare domain, strategic information systems planning, and innovative technologies that facilitate improvement of students' teaming and dynamic decision-making skills.

Sherrena Buckby is a lecturer in the School of Accountancy, Faculty of Business at Queensland Univerisity of Techology. She has held previous positions in professional accounting firms and mining companies. Sherrena's teaching and research focuses on computerised accounting systems, electronic business, business intelligence and data mining, IT governance processes, IT fraud detection, corporate governance and audit committee operations. Sherrena is currently undertaking a PhD focusing on the role of governing bodies in university IT governance processes.

Rob Chown is the manager, Project Portfolio within the Division of Information and Communication Technology Services (ICT) at the University of Southern Queensland (USQ). In this role he manages the operation of the ICT project portfolio function and provides leadership and management for the effective and efficient facilitation of ICT project planning and project portfolio management across the University. Rob is a champion for the introduction and implementation of CobIT and ITIL within the University. He previously managed the IT quality management system which gained ISO 9000 accreditation in 1996, a "first" for an Australian University IT department.

Vanessa Chang is currently head of School of Information Systems at Curtin Business School at Curtin University of Technology, Perth, Australia. She received her BS in management information systems from Indiana State University, Terre Haute, Indiana; and her MS and PhD from Curtin University of Technology, Perth, Australia. Her research interests are in the area of global information technology management, IT governance, strategic IS/IT planning, e-learning in SMEs, and digital business ecosystems. Her work has been published at a number of refereed journals, book chapters, and international conferences. She is actively involved as technical and organizing chairs at several international conferences.

Brian Cusack is the director of the Center for Information Systems Research (CRISM) Security at AUT University. He supervises post-graduate research and research programs in Information Systems Research, Information Systems Security, and Information Systems Governance and Control. He actively participates in the negotiation of ISO / IEC standards, is a frequent speaker at international conferences, guest lecturer, and industry facilitator of IT control best practice.

Andrew Dowse has served in the Royal Australian Air Force since 1981 as an electronic engineer. He has a BE (RMIT), MSc (UNSW), GradDip Legal Studies (QUT) and a PhD (UNSW). Andrew currently is the Director of Enabling Capability at Air Force Headquarters in Canberra, Australia.

Yael Dubinsky is a visiting member of the human-computer interaction research group at the Department of Computer and Systems Science at La Sapienza, Rome, and has been the instructor of project-based courses in the Department of Computer Science at the Technion, Israel's Institute of Technology, for over ten years. She is also affiliated with the Software and Services group in IBM's Haifa Research Lab. Her research interests involve topics in software engineering and information systems. Yael has significant experience guiding agile implementation processes in industry and academia. She has presented her work (since 2002) and cofacilitated tutorials (since 2005) in Agile and XP conferences. Her book on Agile Software Engineering, coauthored with Orit Hazzan, will be published by Springer in 2008.

Alea Fairchild is a senior researcher in information management in the Faculty of Economics and Business Administration at Tilburg University. Her research interests focus on value networks, interoperability and the use of technology for strategic planning. Her field of interest also includes open systems theory and the use of system theory and transaction cost economics in ICT, particularly in financial services and in SMEs.

Yishai Feldman has joined IBM's Haifa Research Lab in 2006, after many years in academia. He is interested in the creation of intelligent tools, mainly for software development. His previous research includes tools for program understanding and transformation, contract-based software development, and video editing. Several of these tools were successful commercially. He has published on various topics, including automated theorem-proving, static analysis of programs, design by contract, software engineering, and agile methodologies. At IBM he leads a group developing program analysis tools for legacy software.

Erik van Geel is a principal consultant with KZA, based in Baarn, The Netherlands.

Lynne Gerke is working towards her PhD at the School of Accounting and Corporate Governance within the Hobart campus of the University of Tasmania. She is currently researching in the field of public sector information technology audit methodology and building on an undergraduate degree in Commerce (majoring in accounting) and honours research in Information Systems. This is her second publication documenting her first academic research project.

Ovsei Gelman-Muravchik is a senior researcher at the Center of Applied Sciences and Technology Development (CCADET) of the National Autonomous University of Mexico (UNAM). He holds a BS, MS, and PhD in physics and mathematics from the University of Tbilisi, Georgia. In the last 35 years he has contributed to the advance of the Systems Science discipline and Interdisciplinary Research through the publication of approximately 250 research papers in books, national and international journals and conference proceedings, as well as by the participation as an advisor in the Engineering Graduate Program at UNAM and by the consulting for governmental and private organizations.

Matthias Häsel holds a degree in computer science and a Master's degree in multimedia management. After his graduation at the University of Applied Sciences, Osnabrück, Germany in 2004, he started his postgraduate studies at the University of Kiel, having a main focus on e-business and being awarded the title "Student of the Year" with his graduation in 2005. Since then, he has been a research associate at the chair of e-business and e-entrepreneurship at the University of Duisburg-Essen, Germany.

Winnie Hua is a principal consultant in CTS Inc. She has more than 15-year project and consulting experience on a broad range of leading-edge technologies. She holds a MS in computer science. As a solution architect/lead, she has led lifecycle design and development of large-scale eCommerce systems on diverse platforms using a variety of cutting-edge technologies and unified/agile methodologies. She has initiated/participated in advanced research on various emerging web technologies. She is a member of numerous professional associations, a regular speaker in conferences/seminars, and also a cofounder of Charlotte Architecture and Technology Symposium (CATS).

Jon Iden has a PhD (1995) and an MS (1990) in information science, both from the University of Bergen, Norway. He is currently the associate professor in Information Systems at the Department of Strategy and Management at the Norwegian School of Economics and Business Administration (NHH), Norway. His main areas of interest are currently Business Process Management, Process Modelling and IT Service Management. Jon Iden has wide industry experience.

Brian Kissell is the chief technology officer of the University of Southern Queensland and responsible for providing leadership in developing and maintaining standardised information and communication technology architecture and infrastructure solutions to support the achievement of the University's Vision, Mission, Goals, and Business Objectives. Prior to joining the University of Southern Queensland Brian held roles including chief information officer for the Queensland Studies Authority, director of IT Services at Macquarie University and successfully ran his own telecommunications consultancy. Brian has developed organisational policy in relation to the implementation and operation of a diverse range of information systems and telecommunication networks and has significant experience in strategic planning, change management, budget formulation, business and workforce planning, implementation of quality systems, and developing and implementing governance frameworks in both government and private sectors.

Tobias Kollmann received his PhD in 1997 with a thesis on the acceptance of innovative telecommunication and multimedia systems. Since 1996 his special interests include e-business, e-commerce and, in particular, the phenomenon of virtual marketplaces. He also was a founder of autoscout24, the largest used car electronic trading platform in Europe. In 2001, he followed a call to the University of Kiel, Germany, where he held a professorship for e-business. Since 2005, he has been holding the chair of e-business and e-entrepreneurship at the University of Duisburg-Essen, Germany.

Changjin Lee is a PhD student at the Graduate School of Information, Yonsei University, Seoul, Korea. He earned his BS/MS in computer science from Chonnam National University, Korea. He works for Korea Exchange as a senior manager of Stock Trading System Team, Stock Market Division. His research interests include IT governance, IT outsourcing, information privacy and security.

Ja Young Lee received her BS from Sungkyunkwan University and MS from the Graduate School of Information, Yonsei University, Seoul, Korea. She works for SK C&C Co., Ltd. as a system engineer. Her research interests include IT governance, IT outsourcing, IT ROI.

Junghoon Lee is an assistant professor at the Graduate School of Information, Yonsei University, Seoul, Korea. He received his BE/MS in electronic engineering/information systems engineering and MS in information systems from University of Manchester and London School of Economics respectively. He obtained his PhD from Manufacturing Engineering and Management from Institute for Manufacturing, University of Cambridge, U.K. His current research interests include IT governance, IT performance measurements, IT outsourcing, information systems control and audit, He has published papers in *International Journal of Production Research*, *Information Systems Review*, and *Journal of the Korea Society of IT Services*.

Jungwoo Lee is currently an associate professor of Information Systems in Graduate School of Information at Yonsei University in Korea. He received his PhD in computer information systems from Georgia State University in 1998. His research interest is focused around systems analysis and design but spans over related issues such as IS/IT competence, e-governance, e-business and e-government. He has published articles in *Information & Management*, *Information Systems Journal*, *Government Information Quarterly*, *Journal of Computer Information Systems*, and numerous conference proceedings. He is serving as the associate dean and the faculty editor for Yonsei Chunchu.

Edward Lewis is a senior lecturer at the ADFA campus of UNSW, where he teaches IT governance and systems planning to undergraduate and postgraduate students. He consults on and carries out research into tools and techniques for systems planning. Ed chairs the IT-030 committee that prepares ICT management and governance standards for Standards Australia, and convenes the Study Group for Joint Technical Committee 1 of the International Organization for Standardization (ISO). He received his BS and PhD from the University of Newcastle.

Jorge Eduardo Macías-Luévano is an associate professor of Information Systems in the Autonomous University of Aguascalientes (UAA), México, since 1986. MSc. Macías holds a BS in computer systems engineering (1985) from Monterrey Tech (ITESM) and a MSc in information systems (1997) from the Autonomous University of Aguascalientes (UAA). He has worked as information systems consultant for many organizations in México from 1986, and is the coordinator of the IS/IT MS program at UAA since 2000.

Dirk Malzahn is a principal consultant and quality management head of OrgaTech, a consulting company that provides process optimization and quality management services. Dirk studied mathematics and computer science at Bochum University, Germany. During 1991-2001 he worked for the electrical steel group of Thyssen Krupp in both technical and managerial positions. Dirk teaches Software Quality Management at the Dortmund University of Applied Science and the Technical Academy of Esslingen. He has published several articles and books on quality management in Germany.

Neil McBride is a principal lecturer in information systems in the School of Computing at De Montfort University, Leicester, United Kingdom, where he teaches IT Service Management and the Social Context of ICT. He is researching the implementation of ITIL3, IT service education and new models for developing computer systems. He is responsible for the development of a new BS in information and communication technology which takes a service-centric view of ICT. He has most recently published in *Information Technology and People* and the *International Journal of Information Management*.

Manuel Mora-Tavarez is an associate professor of Information Systems in the Autonomous **University** of Aguascalientes (UAA), Mexico, since 1994. Mora holds a BS in computer systems engineering (1984) and a MS in artificial intelligence (1989) from Monterrey Tech (ITESM), and an EngD in systems engineering (2003) from the National Autonomous University of Mexico (UNAM). He has published around 30 research papers in international top conferences, books and/or journals. His main research interest is the development of a common management and engineering body of knowledge for software engineering, systems engineering and information systems underpinned in the Systems Approach.

David Musson spent his working life in the computer industry, with positions in design, development, support, sales and marketing of computer systems. He has a PhD from Macquarie University in Sydney, Australia and is a fellow of the British Computer Society and a Chartered Information Technology Professional. He lives in Sydney.

Gil Nechushtai joined IBM as a research staff member in 2000. Through 2006 he led several research activities in the area of event processing, including complex event processing and temporal awareness. Gil specialized in developing event-driven applications, mainly for the financial services sector. Late in 2006, he joined a research activity in the area of application portfolio management, and played a technical role in driving the tools strategy and the methodology for Portfolio Management. Recently, he was appointed as the manager of the Governance and Portfolio Management group in IBM's Haifa Research Lab.

Rory O'Connor is a senior lecturer in Software Engineering at Dublin City University and a senior researcher with Lero, The Irish Software Engineering Research Centre. He has previously held research positions at both the National Centre for Software Engineering and the Centre for Teaching Computing, and has also worked as a software engineer and consultant for several European technology organizations. His research interests are centered on the processes whereby software intensive systems are designed, implemented, and managed.

Breanna O'Donohue completed her final honours year project based upon the impact of ICT Governance. Since graduating Breanna has worked for a large Australian bank dealing with issues relating to Corporate and ICT Governance.

Claus-Peter Praeg is project manager and member of academic staff at the Institute of Human Factors and Technology Management (IAT) at the University of Stuttgart and at the Fraunhofer Institute of Industrial Engineering (IAO) since August 2000. He is responsible for research and consulting projects in the business fields of IT-service performance management, business performance management and IT-industrialisation. Praeg is author and coauthor of several market studies and refereed articles in the areas of IT-service management and business performance management.

Graeme Pye is a lecturer of Information Systems at Deakin University. Graeme is currently undertaking a PhD in the area of Information Security. His PhD is concerned with modelling critical infrastructure using Petri Nets.

Murali Ramakrishnan is an experienced IT consultant based at Adelaide, Australia. Murali specializes in project management and process improvement methodologies. In his career, Murali has successfully led projects in electronic design automation, telecommunication, financial services, manufacturing, government and utilities sectors. Murali is a project management professional (PMP) and a Six Sigma Black Belt. He has a MS in software systems, and an MBA from the University of South Australia. He is an executive committee member of IT Service Management Forum (ITSMF), South Australian Chapter and the Coordinator of Special Interest Group in IT Service Management, in association with the Australian Computer Society (ACS). Murali is an amateur flute player and gives performances in Indian classical music.

Pieter M. Ribbers is professor of Information Management at Tilburg University, School of Economics and Business Administration, The Netherlands, where he chairs the TIAS Postgraduate School of Information Management and the Department of Information Management. His interests span management of information technology (in particular questions related to alignment and information economics), inter-organizational systems (in particular electronic commerce), and the strategic and organizational consequences of the use of Information Technology.

Gail Ridley works as an academic in Hobart, Australia, at the School of Accounting & Corporate Governance, within the Faculty of Business at the University of Tasmania. Most of Gail's publications have examined research methods, information technology (IT) governance and IT control. She was an early academic to see the potential of the Control Objectives for Information and related Technology (COBIT) framework for helping organisations to use IT to achieve their business goals. Having been "COBITised" some years ago, much of Gail's more recent research interests have had a link to COBIT. The IT control and COBIT journey has been a fascinating one, providing her with research settings that have ranged from IT audit in government audit offices to counter-terrorism in the Department of Defence.

G. Philip Rogers is one of a very select number of people in the world who hold the Certified business analysis professional (CBAP), project management professional (PMP), and Six Sigma Green Belt credentials. Currently a senior systems analyst/project manager for a leading financial services company, he has over twenty years of experience in people, program, and project management, business analysis, systems analysis, and technical communications. Past employers include Cisco Systems, Intel Corporation, and the U.S. Air Force. Readers are encouraged to contact him at g.philip.rogers@gmail. com with any questions or comments.

Anne Rouse is associate professor in Business and IT Strategy at the Deakin Business School in Melbourne. The School is part of Deakin University, one of Australia's largest universities. Rouse's doctoral research involved an industry sponsored Australian Research Council grant to study IT outsourcing risks and benefits, at a time when the strategy was causing substantial controversy. Her dissertation was awarded the 2003 ACPHIS medal for the best Australasian information systems PhD thesis. Rouse has over fifteen years' experience in industry working as a management consultant and project manager. She is also a licensed organizational psychologist. Rouse has published widely in Australia and Europe on outsourcing strategy and is a co-author of the Australian Government's Guide to ICT Sourcing Practice (with Boston Consulting Group and Consulting Insights).

Tony Shan is a renowned expert working in the computing field for 20+ years with extensive experience on architecture engineering, technology strategies, and system designs in a number of multimillion dollar IT projects in a broad range of industries. Having been involved in Web technologies since the earliest Html, Java and .Net versions, he has, as an enterprise/solutions/chief architect, directed the lifecycle design and development of large-scale award-winning distributed systems on diverse platforms using a variety of cutting-edge technologies and unified/agile methodologies. He has initiated advanced research on emerging computing technologies, resulting in an invention patent and many unified methodologies and platform models as well as dozens of publications.

Martin Smits is an associate professor of Information Systems and Management at the School of Economics and Business Administration of Tilburg University. He has published more than 100 articles in journals and conference proceedings such as the Journal of Strategic Information Systems, the International Journal of Electronic Markets, the journal Group Decision and Negotiation, the Journal of the Operational Research Society, and the European Conference of Information Systems.

Geert Snijder is a senior quality consultant with KZA, based in Baarn, The Netherlands.

Dieter Spath is director of the Fraunhofer Institute of Industrial Engineering (IAO) and professor at the Institute for Human Factors and Technology Management (IAT) at the University of Stuttgart. Before he was managing director for KASTO-enterprises and professor at the Institute for Machine Tools and Production Science and dean of the faculty of Mechanical Engineering at the University of Karlsruhe (TH). Dieter Spath is board member at acatech, the Council for Technical Sciences of the Union of German Academies of Sciences and Humanities, fellow at the International Institution for Production Engineering Research (CIRP), secretary general of the International Foundation of Production Research (IFPR) and member of the European Academy for Industrial Management (EAIM).

Jenny Stewart is a professor in the Griffith Business School, Griffith University. She has held previous positions at Queensland University of Technology, the University of Queensland, Nanyang Technological University (Singapore), Lincoln University (New Zealand) and the University of Adelaide. Jenny's main research interests are in corporate governance and auditing. She has published extensively in international refereed journals and is editor-in-chief of the *International Journal of Auditing*.

Wui-Gee Tan's IT career spans over 30 years. He spent the first half with multinational corporations in various IT roles and the second, in the academia, involved in teaching, consulting and researching IT. He started his career as a systems analyst and later as a project manager and IT auditor before moving to a systems development management role. Prior to joining USQ in 2004 Wui-Gee was a program director at the National University of Singapore. Wui-Gee received his doctorate from the Queensland University of Technology and he is a certified member of the Project Management Institute. He has foundation certificates in ITIL, ISO/IEC 20000 and CobiT.

Michael Thompson has been employed at the University of Southern Queensland (USQ) since 1977 and has worked in various computing roles dating back to 1986. He currently holds the position of principal manager—performance measurement and investment measurement within the Division of ICT Services. Michael's extensive experience covers microcomputing support, help desk and service desk, training, microcomputing hardware and software vendor relationships and agreements, IT quality assurance and control processes, and project management. During this time, he has had the opportunity to play an active role in the origins and development of microcomputing at USQ, and at the same time he has also played an active role in fostering and developing young people into professional IT staff. Michael is a USQ graduate with an MBA in information systems and BBus majoring in computing and operations management.

Chee Ing Tiong is an IT consultant in Melbourne. He specialises in System Analysis and Design especially in redesigning business processes. He recently completed an MIT degree at USQ focussing on investigating factors that influence healthcare professional's decision in adopting wireless technology in healthcare environment. His interests are business process reengineering, system analysis and design, network design, IT service management, and e-commerce applications.

Mark Toleman is professor and head of School of Information Systems at the University of Southern Queensland. His research interests are wide and include IT service management, IT governance, systems development methodologies, research-practitioner nexus, novice developers, and information systems education. He has published over 100 articles in books, refereed journals, and refereed conference proceedings.

Matthew Warren is a professor in the School of Information System, Deakin University, Australia. He has a PhD in information security management from Plymouth University, UK and worked on several large European Union research projects concerning security. Professor Warren has gained international recognition for his scholarly work in the areas of information security, risk analysis, eBusiness, information warfare and critical infrastructure protection.

Avi Yaeli joined IBM's Haifa Research Lab in 1998 as a Research Staff Member. His current research focus is on models, processes, and tools for governance in IT and software development organizations. He currently leads a research project in the area of governance tooling and infrastructure. Prior to that, he served a technical strategy role in IBM's research center in New York. Previously, Avi held a senior technical lead responsibility for the Software Asset Management group in the Haifa Research Lab and was involved in leading several research activities in the area of program analysis including applications for change impact analysis, application migration, and code search.

Emmanuel Zarpas joined IBM in 2000 as a Research Staff Member after three years as a program manager in Thales Group. Through 2006 he led several research activities in the area of formal verification, including verification of a game processor security unit, bounded model checking and the satisfiability problem, and verification of business continuity solutions and policies. In 2007 he joined the Application Portfolio Management team and has been working on IT Governance and on valuation, forecasting, and optimization of IT portfolios.

Index